Conservation
for the Twenty-first Century

Conservation
for the Twenty-first Century

Edited by

DAVID WESTERN
MARY C. PEARL

Wildlife Conservation International
New York Zoological Society

WILDLIFE
CONSERVATION
INTERNATIONAL
NYZS·1895

New York   Oxford
Oxford University Press
1989

Oxford University Press

Oxford   New York   Toronto
Delhi   Bombay   Calcutta   Madras   Karachi
Petaling Jaya   Singapore   Hong Kong   Tokyo
Nairobi   Dar es Salaam   Cape Town
Melbourne   Auckland

and associated companies in
Berlin   Ibadan

Library of Congress Cataloging-in-Publication Data
Conservation for the twenty-first century /
edited by David Western, Mary C. Pearl.   p.   cm.
Selected papers from a conference held in New York, Oct. 19–22,
1986.   Bibliography: p.
Includes index.   ISBN 0–19–505474–1
1. Nature conservation. I. Western, David.
II. Pearl, Mary C.   QH75.C663 1989
333.9572—dc19   88–18773   CIP

9 8 7 6 5 4 3 2 1
Printed in the United States of America
on acid-free paper

Fairfield Osborn

by WILLIAM CONWAY

Fairfield Osborn was born in 1887 and died in 1969. He was a tall, thin man with penetrating eyes and a wonderful nose. His father was Henry Fairfield Osborn, a distinguished paleontologist, who became president of both the New York Zoological Society and the American Museum of Natural History. Fair graduated from Princeton in 1909, took further courses at Trinity College, Cambridge, and, thus prepared, spent the next several years working in the San Francisco freight yards and laying track in Nevada. Among other things, he became a delightfully competent singer of cowboy songs. In 1914 he married Marjorie Lamond, raised three daughters, and became an investment banker on Wall Street. His tie with the Zoological Society began in 1922 and lasted until his retirement in 1968, the last twenty-eight years as president. It was a happy time, and it was my good fortune to work with Fair for nearly thirteen years.

I suspect that most readers are familiar with Osborn's pioneering environmental writings, especially *Our Plundered Planet,* which was published in 1948. In the introduction to that volume he wrote:

There is beauty in the sound of the words "good earth." They suggest a picture of the elements and forces of nature working in harmony. The imagination of men through all ages has been fired by the concept of an "earth-symphony." Today we know the concept of poets and philosophers in earlier times is reality. Nature may be a thing of beauty and is indeed a symphony, but above and below and within its own immutable essences, its distances, its apparent quietness and changelessness it is an active, purposeful, coordinated machine. Each part is dependent upon another, all are related to the movement of the whole. Forests, grasslands, soils, water, animal life—without one of these the earth will die—will become dead as the moon. Parts of the earth, once living and productive, have thus died at the hand of man. Others are now dying. If we cause more to die, nature will compensate for this in her own way, inexorably, as already she has begun to do.

Fair observed in the same book that the 1948 world population was over two billion, and that the rate of increase was a frightening 1 percent. He predicted that by the year 2000 the earth's population could increase by as much as half a billion more and could well be over three billion in the year 2048—a cautionary note for the predictions contained in the present collection of essays.

Fairfield Osborn dedicated *Our Plundered Planet* simply "To All Who Care About Tomorrow." It is a fitting directive for this volume.

Foreword

Message from His Holiness the Dalai Lama

The beginning of the twenty-first century is only a few years away, and such a landmark in time provides a good focus for review of life's values and directions.

A year, a century, or a millennium ends, another begins. The cycle continues. For much life on earth, however, cycles are coming to an end, not just because of natural selection, but as a result of human destruction, born out of ignorance, greed, and lack of respect for other forms of life.

Science and technology alone cannot solve the problems of environmental destruction. After all, they are only a means to an end, a tool in our hand.

It is up to us to determine our goals and to use these powerful tools for the good of all. How the instruments of science are employed depends on human attitudes.

If we wish to find any lasting solutions to our problems, we must act at the root cause. The only cure for present world problems, including that of the natural environment, is for people to replace ignorance with knowledge, greed with generosity, and lack of respect for life with humanitarian values.

World peace and protection of nature are related, interdependent goals. Both are possible if people are committed to humanitarian values—respect and love, compassion and tolerance for all forms of life.

The theme for World Environment Day in June 1986 was "Peace and the Environment." As experts met in October to discuss the subject "Conservation 2100," they were reminded that the world has many calendars. In Thailand, for example, it was the Buddhist Era 2529, while for the Tibetans it was the Royal Year of 2113.

Each variation enriches life. If we are to preserve the world's cultural and natural treasures, we must respect diversity which does not divide us, and we must look ahead intelligently and behave ethically.

Preface

Conservation for the Twenty-first Century brings together voices from around the world with two broad objectives in mind: to look at the diversity of approaches unified by a common interest in conserving nature; and to review the future prospects for wildlife and habitat with a view to identifying those approaches and techniques required to secure their place through the twenty-first century. Authors include managers, planners, researchers, philosophers, media representatives, aid donors, national and international non-governmental organizations, government servants and private citizens from the developing and developed world, all of whom have in one way or another had some influence on conservation. The book is organized around four themes to give focus and continuity to the varied points of view:

• Tomorrow's World. The changes in human activity most likely to affect wildlife in the 21st century.

• Conservation Biology. The biological basis of conserving nature and predicting the consequences of human action on species and ecosystems.

• Conservation Management. Management approaches, tools and techniques for conserving wildlife.

• Conservation Realities. The measures required to gain support for wildlife conservation.

In addition, controversial and pivotal topics have been incorporated into a Conservation Agenda (chap. 33). The Agenda identifies areas in need of action now if conservation is to meet the formidable challenges of coming decades.

While concerned with natural resources and the environment generally, the book centers on wildlife because of its great vulnerability to human impact and the urgency of securing its place in our world before many more species are lost forever. The intended audience for *Conservation for the Twenty-first Century* is the inquisitive and concerned individual, whether directly or indirectly involved in conservation, who has an interest in the future of our natural world. To that end, we have for the most part chosen authors who span a wide spectrum of conservation endeavours, who can draw on personal experience, yet are willing to make broad generalizations. We have maintained the integrity of their varied voices and styles of presentation.

Conservation for the Twenty-first Century, though a small sample of the breadth of modern conservation and the challenges it faces, shows the value of bringing diverse views together for a common purpose. Insofar as any consensus was intended or reached, it is that collective foresight and collaborative action can change the seemingly gloomy outlook for wildlife and its habitat.

D.W.
M.P.

Overview

Humanity is killing off wildlife and eradicating habitats at an alarming rate. Every year 200,000 km² of tropical forest are destroyed or impoverished, 100,000 km² of rangeland are desertified, and hundreds, if not thousands, of species are exterminated. By the turn of the century mushrooming human activity could wipe out a staggering 15 to 25% of all species. While the figures and the impact of such extinctions are debatable, the more pervasive impact to our planet is not. Those same forces of extinction also degrade 150,000 km² of cropland, erode 75 billion tons of top soil, pour millions of tons of toxic waste and pollutants into the oceans and freshwater, and belch enough carbon, nitrogen and sulfur into the atmosphere to raise global temperatures and acidify rainfall. The very quality of our lives is at stake.

The twentieth century may prove as significant for our ability to change the state of our plant—its soils, waters, atmosphere, climate, habitats and wildlife—as for its technological advancement. Fortunately, the public, media, governments and scientists are awakening to the losses and risks and the need to take evasive action. *Environment, ecology, conservation, planet earth, global stewardship* and *sustainable development* are a few of the many household words expressing a common awareness and growing concern for the state of our world. But, concern must lead to understanding, and understanding to action. The question is, what sort of action? However well motivated, action without insight will not be enough to avert an avalanche of extinctions and tremendous environmental destruction.

A knee-jerk response to the extinction crisis is to rush out to save any and all species that capture our attention and fire-up public indignation—usually concerning the big and lovable creatures. The conservation firefights are exhilarating. The spectacular successes, like saving the mountain gorilla from poachers and returning the Arabian oryx to its desert home, give the illusion of success. The lengthening list of endangered and threatened animals—3117 according to IUCN's 1986 scorecard—says otherwise. Worse yet, many Third World nations have tired of being harangued by an indignant industrialized world with all too many wildlife skeletons of its own in museum closets. Even within the developed world, the clash between preservation and development, the snail-darter wars, has increasingly pitted conservationists against each other to the detriment of wildlife by weakening public support and government funding.

Disparate conservation voices can be either healthy or destructive depending on the circumstances. On a positive note, differences of opinion signify a diversity of views. People the world over value nature for reasons as diverse as their cultures, religions and economies. For some, nature means a supply of renewable resources; for others, recreation, spiritual solace, beauty, inspiration, education, adventure or safety in a hostile world. Conservation is no longer the strident pro-nature anti-development voice of bygone years. In the process of broadening its appeal by embracing the many traditional and modern reasons for protecting our natural environment, conservation has matured and gained universal recognition. The landmark 1972 Stockholm Conference on the Environment, which led to the establishment of the United Nations Environmental Program, gave political legitimacy to conservation, most obviously with the launching in 1980 of the World Conservation Strategy. The strategy stresses conservation as the basis of sustainable development, rather than an antagonist of human progress.

On the negative side, such healthy diversity of opinion can become crippling divisiveness when conservation factions battle each other, rather than the forces of extinction and ecological deterioration. Species such as the California condor are victims of the emotional maelstroms whipped up when conservation views clash destructively.

Conservation for the Twenty-first Century brings together a diversity of views to focus on the common goal of how to conserve nature in the twenty-first century. It is based on the conference "Conservation 2100," held in New York at the Caspary Auditorium of the Rockefeller University October 20–23, 1986. The conference was convened by Wildlife Conservation International, a division of the New York Zoological Society and co-hosted by The Rockefeller University under the auspices of The Fairfield Osborn Memorial Fund. While meetings are no substitute for action, the stage had been reached where it was time to take stock of the overwhelming forces arrayed against nature, consider the future outlook, and figure out how conservation can respond. A number of conferences and publications have recently considered the future of our environment and tools for conserving nature and natural resources. For example, *The Global 2000 Report to the President* (1980), *The Resourceful Earth* (1984) and *The Global Possible* (1985) look at the state of our earth and its future; *Sustaining Tomorrow: A Strategy for World Conservation and Development* (1984) and *Sustainable Development of the Biosphere* (1986) consider strategies for conserving resources; *The United States Strategy on the Conservation of Biological Diversity* (1985) and the *National Forum on Biodiversity* (held in 1986) review the outlook for biodiversity and ways to preserve it; *National Parks, Conservation and Development* (1984), *Proceedings of the Workshop on Genetic Management of Captive Populations* (1986), *Conservation Biology* (1986) and a number of others look at specific strategies and techniques for conserving wildlife and habitat.

This book brings together a broad range of voices, each of which has contributed practically, philosophically, scientifically, financially or politically to conservation. It looks at the diversity of ideas and approaches to conservation to identify the lacunae in our knowledge and management practices that must be filled in order to save wildlife in the decades ahead. Each approach has something to offer, but each alone is too specialized for the complexity of modern conservation and the multiplicity of responses it demands. We need to create an awareness among practitioners of the value of a broader, longer view, a realization that single remedy conservation could, through ignorance and mismanagement, exterminate as many species as habitat fragmentation and poaching.

The wildlife focus reflects the special concerns of the sponsoring institution, New York Zoological Society, and the great sensitivity and vulnerability of wildlife to human impact. Top soil can regenerate, waters reform and air cleanse itself when human abuses cease, but "when the last individual of a race of living things breathes no more, another heaven and another earth must pass before such a one can be again," as William Beebe so poignantly put it. Wildlife is our earthly scientific frontier, one far more intriguing than the cosmos, and a facet of our world outside human control. The challenge is to keep it that way, in contrast to all other resources we use, value and conserve out of self-interest.

Conserving wildlife, which recognizes neither ownership nor boundaries, calls for good science, first-rate technology, excellent management, and a broad constituency willing to make some concessions to save it. The challenge is daunting. Even if we could predict the course and intensity of human activity, which we can't, even if we knew our biology well enough to predict species losses, which we don't, and even if we had the technology and skills to do so, it would not be enough.

Why? Because to save nature we need financing, public support, and above all, the integrated management skills which even the most sophisticated high-tech farming systems lack. And farm production systems are studies in simplicity compared to the natural systems we must preserve, repair, and reconstruct. That is a tall order, far beyond our existing abilities. But now is the time to look ahead, coordinate and plan, before our options are further narrowed, before ignorance and small-mindedness become the biggest threats to wildlife.

In addressing the challenges facing conservation, we focus on four broad topics: Tomorrow's World—what we can forecast about the future pressures and opportunities confronting wildlife; Conservation Biology—how wildlife can benefit from scientific knowledge; Conservation Management—what techniques and strategies will preserve wildlife; and Conservation Realities—how wildlife conservation must take account of a larger world of human interests. I will touch briefly on some of the main points highlighted in this book.

TOMORROW'S WORLD

The twenty-first century will be as different from today's world as ours is from the nineteenth century, and perhaps far more so, given the accelerating pace of change in lifestyle and technology. Where in the nineteenth century it took months to ferry a letter half way round the world, in the twenty-first century entire libraries will be transmitted instantly on a beam of light. If today's world is Marshall McLuhan's global village, tomorrow's will shrink to a global household.

Barring calamities, we can from historical trends guess a few other things about the twenty-first century. Population will be far higher, more aggregated and more mobile. Fewer people will produce more goods and spend less time and money procuring food. Everyone will be literate. What we cannot forecast is the rate and extent of those changes, and the impact of new technologies and cultural ideas. Without that foresight, we are future blind.

Is there any point then in speculating on the fate of wildlife when our descendants may not share our concerns for wildlife, given their superior power to create other, more fantastic worlds? I think so, for if we have one unique commodity to hand on, it is our natural world. Our descendants will be technologically superior to us and better placed to solve environmental problems. Knowing that progress has heightened our own appreciation of wilderness, should we grant our descendants the means to advance technologically, yet deny them the chance to celebrate nature?

The conservationist tends to anti-development in the belief that if wildlife is victim of humanity, further development is abhorrent. That view is too simple and ultimately futile, for if humanity is the sole threat to wildlife, it is also its only hope. The challenge is not to shun humanity, but to make conservation *and* development the twin criteria of human progress.

That means understanding more than the raw statistics of population growth. It means gauging how populations will be redistributed in the process of growth, where the conservation pressures and opportunities will arise. It means looking at the sociology of wealth and poverty, at the consequences of better education, more recreation, improved communications and easier travel, and how it can benefit wildlife. It means looking ahead to see how innovations in energy production, water and soil conservation, agricultural technology, and genetic engineering can improve the quality of our environment. And, above all, it means learning to live off nature's dividends, rather than its capital. We need no longer be the starving victims of mindless growth and lagging production in the Malthusian sense. If imbued with foresight and concerns about the quality of life, we are in a position to plan our options rather than wallow in despair.

Wildlife is one of those options. Our survival does not depend on it; few urbanites ever confront nature. But for many of us now, and I suspect many more in the future, our sense of well-being and freedom is rooted in the natural world. Its future hinges on our outlook, policies, political systems, economies and so on. For example, a large portion of the developed world's agricultural lands will go out of commission if $150 billion in subsidies is diverted to more productive use. That might bode well for American wilderness, yet such is the intricacy of global economies and environment that, as a result, much of Africa would face starvation, and wildlife, an old drought remedy, would suffer.

This is where the neat projections falter. Who can say whether a new political or military regime will impede or advance progress, or whether society will choose the security of more weapons over a cleaner environment? Uncertainty in human affairs is as much a hazard for the environment as it is for people.

We can only proceed by aiming for the possible, mapping out the areas of special concern, noting where the clash of human and wildlife interests are avoidable or reparable, and figuring out what it will take to improve the prospects for nature.

CONSERVATION BIOLOGY

The next hundred years could decide nature's future as no other evolutionary event has done. It will decide how much, and what kind of nature survives.

What species, processes and ecosystems are vulnerable? Are there common ecological and behavioral traits that distinguish threatened and tolerant life forms and processes? Does this imply new evolutionary selection pressures, or simply a narrowing of old ones? Can we save the vulnerable species by active intervention? If so, how will management change them?

Will there be any place for them in the new nature, or will they be dependent on human welfare? How will the changing selection pressures affect genomes, population structure, life history and behavioral traits?

These are a few of the questions biologists must address. The answers depend as much on sound judgment about the future as on scientific insight into the structure of nature and its sensitivity to human perturbations. Both are indispensable tools in predicting the magnitude of extinctions, for example.

Going beyond species to ecosystems, do we know enough to even hazard a guess at what factors are vital to diversity? Is diversity, rather than say, ecological integrity, the right thing to be concerned about, given our future potential to enrich ecosystems? And how do we deal with perturbation, which judiciously practiced, could boost diversity? Is it unrealistic to think we can maintain ecosystems as they are when we can tailor them to fit in better with our future world? As heretical as that may seem, it is the norm for Europe. Will it be any different for the third world and, if so, would it be a major tragedy? The most curious of naturalists, Charles Darwin, after five years circumnavigating the earth investigating its natural history, was moved to comment that "the picturesque beauty of many parts of Europe far exceeds anything we have beheld." Ecosystems, no less landscapes, can be created as well as destroyed by humanity.

If we can't save all nature, should our priorities be sample ecosystems, or sample species, or some combination? Can biologists agree on priorities, and are they the right people to set them?

CONSERVATION MANAGEMENT

Regardless of whether we wish to protect nature as it is, reconstitute it, correct imbalances, or merely keep options open, will we have the ability to plan such complex exercises, and the techniques to implement them?

Techniques vary from saving nature by banishing humanity, to saving species by removing them from nature. Are existing techniques adequate? What others might we need? What others can we conceive that will help in species preservation?

Genetic mapping, protein assembly, cryobiology; how might these affect species conservation, or genome diversity? And what of reproductive manipulations, whether cross-fostering or ex-utero technology. Is it conceivable that we could replenishment heterozygosity in cheetah, for example, by genetic implants? If so, is that desirable, and under what circumstances?

What role can zoos, zoo-parks and waste and rehabilitated lands play? Should we consider *de novo* or experimental ecosystems as a way of diversifying nature and learning how it operates?

What are the prospects for national parks? How can we buffer them from humanity? How can ex-situ practices help preserve in-situ options, and what role can areas outside parks play in conservation?

Non-park areas have great wildlife potential. Cultural landscapes, interstices between heavily used land, unused and unusable landscapes, old areas out of commission, areas where wildlife is compatible with human exploitation, or complements it, are just a few of the possibilities.

CONSERVATION REALITIES

So what if we have the foresight, knowledge and techniques to conserve most of nature? Whether we act, and how, depends on factors such as policies, education, socioeconomics, recreational interests and planning capabilities, which vary from one society to another, and are likely to continue doing so in the future. How do cultural values affect our perceptions of nature? Is a universal conservation ethic possible or desirable, or is it a cultural attitude palmed off by one society on another? Finally, how can we ensure that our sense of what is best for nature is not merely what is best for society?

How do we plan conservation, and who does the planning? What legal and protective provisions can and should we make to give teeth to that effort? This question can only be resolved by individual nations according to their political systems, which implies accepting a pluralistic approach to conservation.

Given national sovereignty over wildlife and the diversity of cultures and economies, how meaningful are international conservation strategies and legislative agreements? The success of CITES (The Convention on International Trade in Endangered Species) in stemming the trade in crocodilians and spotted cats on the one hand but failing to halt rhino poaching on the other, hints at a complex answer. Why the successes in some cases, and failures in others? Though national sovereignty of wildlife is not in question, time is often so short and resources so few that a massive "means transfer" from developed to developing countries is called for, whether it involves surveys, technology, management or finance. How can the developed world help poorer nations conserve wildlife? Non-government organizations, bi-lateral and multilateral aid, the media and industry can each contribute something, but how can they do so on terms acceptable to developing nations, without adopting a "copy us" or finger-wagging superciliousness so reviled in the third world? The track record is mixed. The press, for example, highlights habitat destruction and species extinctions, but seldom the conservation successes, or how the poor suffer from wildlife.

The time has come to explore new collaborative ventures to protect the last of our natural world.

A CONSERVATION AGENDA

A book of this nature usually ends with a series of resolutions, a state-of-the-art synthesis, or dire warnings about the future. We have shunned exhortation and synthesis in the belief that the diverse nature and rapid evolution of modern conservation, no less than the problems it addresses, eludes simple characterization and has few easy solutions. Instead we have asked the participants to identify the gaps in our knowledge and the weaknesses in our management practices that must be filled and strengthened if we are to anticipate conservation problems and successfully resolve them. Asking conservationists to think about distant problems when they are unable to deal with the present crisis may seem unrealistic, even a touch masochistic, but it is warranted. If we don't build long-range thinking and planning into conservation, other human interests, such as urban or agricultural development, will divide up our future world to the exclusion of nature. And, by spelling out the lacunae, we set the goals for a new generation hoping to tackle the unresolved and explore the unknown.

In the Conservation Agenda, we have drawn together the significant lacunae that emerged during the conference. Given early attention, they should help prepare us to preserve earth's biological wealth in the twenty-first century.

D.W.

Acknowledgments

For help in planning and implementing the conference "Conservation 2100: A Fairfield Osborn Symposium," the proceedings of which comprise this volume, the editors wish to thank H.R.H. Prince Bernhard of the Netherlands, William Conway, Joshua Lederberg, William Lowrance, Archie Carr III, George Schaller, Martha Schwartz, David Hales, April Oja, Sandee Walsh, Geoffrey Mellor, Matthew Hatchwell, Luanne Brauer, Catherine Belden, Noreen Skinner, Sharon Kramer, Augusta Nix, and the Buddhist Perception of Nature project. Glenn Close graciously delivered the Dalai Lama's message at the conference. The conference could not have taken place without the support of the Fairfield Osborn Lecture Fund, The New York Zoological Society, The Rockefeller University, and the Reed Foundation. Some publication costs were borne by Allied-Signal Inc. We also wish to thank William Curtis, Henry Krawitz, and Oxford University Press for help with the publication of the proceedings of the conference.

In addition, David Western wishes to thank the following people for their ideas and encouragement in conceptualizing the conference: Bill Conway, George Schaller, Arturo Tarak, James Ssemakula, Nick Georgiadis, Shirley Strum, Norman Myers—and above all Mary Pearl, whose insight, drive, and coordination in planning and running the conference made the latter a reality. Regarding chapters 2, 16, and 33, and the introductions to parts I, II, III, he wishes to thank his wife, Shirley Strum, who thoughtfully reviewed and critiqued each of his papers and continually gave him great encouragement, and Mary Pearl, who provided helpful comments on the introductions to parts II and III.

For contributions of time, advice, and other forms of help, Mary Pearl wishes to thank William Conway, Jared Diamond, Tom Foose, Don Goddard, Eugene Gould, Eugene Hargrove, Lawrence Heaney, Steve Johnson, Don Melnick, Norman Myers, Justina Ray, George Schaller, Martha Schwartz, Bruce Wilcox, and Edward Wolf. She would like to acknowledge David Western's generosity in sharing his vision of wildlife conservation so freely and giving her the opportunity to participate in the preparation of the conference and the proceedings. For helpful comments in the preparation of the introduction to part IV and chapters 29 and 33, she wishes to thank Buff Bohlen, Alexander Goncharenko, Robert Goodland, Eugene Hargrove, Paul Hughes, Stephen Krasner, Molly Kux, Don Melnick, Jerry Moles, and David Western.

In addition, the following authors wish to express individual acknowledgments:

Ian Atkinson (chap. 7: Introduced Animals and Extinctions). Attendance at the "Conservation 2100" conference in New York City was made possible through the financial support of Wildlife Conservation International and the New York Zoological Society. I am grateful to Don V. Merton, Susan M. Timmins, and Drs. Phil Cowan, Warwick Harris, Rod Hay, and Phil Moors for discussion and critical comment of earlier drafts of the chapter. I thank Carolyn Powell for preparing the diagrams and Tessa Roach for typing the manuscript.

David Woodruff (chap. 8: The Problems of Conserving Genes and Species). My research has been supported by the National Science Foundation, Wildlife Conservation International, and the Academic Senate of the University of California at San Diego. I thank Kurt Benirschke, Warren Brockelman, the late Sheldon Campbell, Michael Gilpin, Adina

Merenlender, Mary Pearl, Oliver Ryder, Alan Templeton, Bob Vrijenhoek, David Western, and Edward Wilson for helpful discussions.

Robert Vrijenhoek (chap. 9: Population Genetics and Conservation). I would like to thank G. K. Meffe, M. E. Douglas, J. E. Brooks, and C. Sakowski for their collaboration in studies of Sonoran topminnows; D. Baldwin and J. Graham for their critiques of the manuscript; and P. Morin for his help in preparing the graphics. I am most grateful for continued support by the National Science Foundation whose grants have made the long-term field and laboratory studies of topminnows possible (current grant: BSR 8500661).

Sam McNaughton (chap. 11: Ecosystems and Conservation in the Twenty-first Century). Preparation of this chapter was facilitated by NSF grant BSR 8505862.

Brian Walker (chap. 12: Diversity and Stability in Ecosystem Conservation). I thank Roger Bradbury and Graeme Caughley for permission to use their work, and Immanuel Noy-Meir for a stimulating discussion on the topic of stability.

Jeffrey McNeely (chap. 15: Protected Areas and Human Ecology). This paper was prepared in my personal capacity and should not be taken to represent the official views of IUCN or any of its member organizations. I benefited greatly from discussions with Kenton Miller, Jared Diamond, Mike Soulé, Paul Wachtel, and David Hales. Several colleagues at IUCN—including George Frame, Pat Dugan, Mark Halle, Taghi Farvar, Danny Elder, Jeff Sayer, Jim Thorsell, and Simon Stuart—read the paper and made helpful comments. My thanks goes to them for their help.

Larry Harris and John Eisenberg (chap. 17: Enhanced Linkages: Necessary Steps for Success in Conservation of Faunal Diversity). Neither this paper nor our articulation of the ideas in it would have been possible without the patient help and counsel of our colleagues. Kathleen Deagan provided guidance and insight to the Columbian contact and Spanish resource literature; and Stuart Marks, Gerald Murray, Kathleen Deagan, and Brenda Siegler Eisenberg have helped shape our views about anthropological aspects of conservation. S. David Webb has given freely of his paleontological data and insights, and Charles Woods has provided the opportunity to study and participate in the Haiti National Parks enterprise. We are grateful for this help.

William Conway (chap. 19: The Prospects for Sustaining Species and Their Evolution). I thank Tom Foose, Oliver Ryder, and Dan Wharton for helpful comments on an earlier draft of this paper.

Arturo Tarak (chap. 26: A National Perspective). Different people and institutions have helped me in the development of the ideas expressed herein. In particular I want to thank the New York Zoological Society for its lengthy support. Dr. William G. Conway has had particular influence in stimulating this kind of analysis, though he has none of the responsibilities for my mistakes. I also want to thank the following for useful comments for this paper: Mary Pearl, Michael Christie, Marcelo Canevari, Pedro Tarak, and my wife, Mane Sarafian. Finally I want to thank A. Avedissian for his invaluable help with the word processor.

Michael Soulé (chap. 32: Conservation Biology in the Twenty-first Century: Summary and Outlook). I am very grateful to Dr. Patricia Romans for her excellent critique and many suggestions for improving the manuscript.

Contents

Contributors

Ian Atkinson
Botany Division Regional Station
c/o N. Z. Soil Bureau
DSIR Private Bag
Lower Hutt
New Zealand

Michael J. Bean
Environmental Defense Fund
1616 P Street NW, Suite 150
Washington, DC 20036

William G. Conway
New York Zoological Society
Bronx Zoological Park
Bronx, NY 10460

Lester Crystal
MacNeil/Lehrer Newshour
356 West 58th Street
New York, NY 10019

Jared Diamond
University of California at Los Angeles
53-238 Center for Health Sciences
Los Angeles, CA 90024

David Ehrenfeld
Department of Horticulture and Forestry
Cook College
Rutgers University
New Brunswick, NJ 08903

John F. Eisenberg
Florida State Museum
University of Florida
Gainesville, FL 32611

Bryn H. Green
Department of Environmental Studies
Wye College (University of London)
Near Ashford, Kent TN25 5AH
England

David Hales
Commission of Radioactive Waste Authority
Department of Management and Budget
Hollister Building
108 West Allegan Street, Suite 554
Lansing, MI 48909

Eugene C. Hargrove
Department of Philosophy
The University of Georgia
Athens, GA 30602

Larry D. Harris
School of Forest Resources and Conservation
118 Newins-Ziegler Hall
Gainesville, FL 32611

James A. Lee
World Bank
1818 H Street NW, Room D-1018
Washington, DC 20433

S. J. McNaughton
Department of Botany, Syracuse University
514 Bioresearch Laboratory
130 College Place
Syracuse, NY 13210

Jeffrey A. McNeely
IUCN
Av. du Mont-Blanc
CH-1196 Gland
Switzerland

Norman Myers
Upper Meadow, Old Road
Headington
Oxford OX 38SZ
England

Bryan G. Norton
Division of Humanities
New College of the University of South
    Florida
5700 North Tamiami Trail
Sarasota, FL 34243-2197

Reuben J. Olembo
United Nations Environment Program
P.O. Box 30552
Nairobi
Kenya

Perez Olindo
Wildlife Conservation and Management
    Department
P.O. Box 45464
Nairobi
Kenya

Storrs L. Olson
Division of Birds
National Museum of Natural History
Washington, DC 20560

Mary C. Pearl
Wildlife Conservation International
New York Zoological Society
Bronx Zoological Park
Bronx, NY 10460

Stuart L. Pimm
Graduate Program in Ecology
University of Tennessee
Knoxville, TN 37996

Holmes Rolston III
Department of Philosophy
Colorado State University
Fort Collins, CO 80523

Michael E. Soulé
School for Natural Resources
Dana Building
University of Michigan
Ann Arbor, MI 48109

Mark R. Stanley Price
African Wildlife Foundation
P.O. Box 48177
Nairobi
Kenya

Arturo Tarak
Casilla de Correo 1182
8400 S.C. de Bariloche
Río Negro
Argentina

Alvaro F. Ugalde
Fundación de Parques Nacionales
Aptdo. 236 COD 1002
San José
Costa Rica

Tarzie Vittachi
UNICEF
United Nations
New York, NY 10017

Robert C. Vrijenhoek
Center for Applied Genetics
Cook College
Rutgers University
New Brunswick, NJ 08903

Brian Walker
CSIRO
PO Box 84
Lyneham Act 2602
Australia

David Western
Wildlife Conservation International
P.O. Box 62844
Nairobi
Kenya

Edward O. Wilson
Peabody Museum
Harvard University
Cambridge, MA 02138

David S. Woodruff
Department of Biology, C-106
University of California, San Diego
La Jolla, CA 92093

Abbreviations

AAZPA	American Association of Zoological Parks and Aquariums
ACM	Andean Common Market
AI	Artificial Insemination
CIDIE	Committee on International Development Institutions on the Environment
CITES	Convention on International Trade in Endangered Species
CNPPA	Commission on National Parks and Protected Areas
ESB	Ex Situ Care and Biotechnology
FAO	Food and Agriculture Organization (UN)
GEMS	Global Environmental Monitoring System (UNEP)
GNP	Gross National Product
IUDZG	International Union of Directors of Zoological Gardens
ISIS	International Species Inventory System
IUCN	International Union for the Conservation of Nature and Natural Resources
KREMU	Kenya's Rangeland Ecological Monitoring Unit
LDC	Less Developed Country
MDB	Multilateral Development Bank
MNC	Multinational Corporation
mtDNA	Mitochondrial deoxyribonucleic acid
MVP	Minimum Viable Population
nDNA	Nuclear deoxyribonucleic acid
NGO	Nongovernmental Organization (private charity)
NIC	Newly Industrialized Country
NPS	National Park Service (U.S.)
NRC	National Research Council
OPEC	Organization of Petroleum Exporting Countries
PETC	Proposed Endangered or Threatened Category
PVA	Population Vulnerability Analysis
SDI	Species Defense Initiative
SSC	Species Survival Commission
SSP	Species Survival Plan
UNEP	United Nations Environmental Program
UNESCO	United Nations Educational and Scientific Organization
USAID	United States Agency for International Development
USFWS	United States Fish and Wildlife Service

Conservation
for the Twenty-first Century

1

Conservation: The Next Hundred Years

EDWARD O. WILSON

The tide of the earth's population is rising, the reservoir of the earth's living resources is falling. . . . There is only one solution: Man must recognize the necessity of cooperating with nature. He must temper his demands and use and conserve the natural living resources of this earth in a manner that alone can provide for the continuation of his civilization. The final answer is to be found only through comprehension of the enduring processes of nature. The time for defiance is at an end.

Fairfield Osborn's closing declaration in *Our Plundered Planet* (1948) could have been written this morning. Its relevance after forty years serves as a reminder that accelerating technology guided by material acquisitiveness has brought no remedies, that a generation of new scientific research has only focused the problem into a sharper, more frightening image. The pace of population growth and environmental destruction has continued with no visible pause, having become a case study in the principle of unintended results wherein mass effects float up from vast numbers of seemingly innocent individual decisions.

What is needed is a fuller sense of what we possess, and stand to lose, by the innocent slippage. It can be said that every country has three forms of wealth: material, cultural, and biological. The first two are the basis of almost all our economic and political life. The third, composed of the fauna and flora and the uses put to natural diversity, is far more potent for long-term human welfare than generally appreciated, and it is declining irreversibly through the accel-

erating extinction of species and genetic strains. Furthermore, the problem is distinctively international in scope. By far the greatest variety of life occurs in the developing countries, especially in the tropics, and it is there also that population growth, environmental degradation, and species extinction have reached crisis levels.

The scope of the problem can be briefly summarized as follows: The rate of population growth has begun to slow on every continent except Africa, where it remains as rapid as ever. But even with a modest amount of global amelioration, most demographers still project a doubling of the standing population, from the present five billion to at least ten billion, before it finally levels off around the middle of the 2100s. Most of the growth is destined to be concentrated in just a few regions, principally the Indian subcontinent, the Middle East, Africa, and Latin America. So disproportionate is this distribution that the projected growth for North America, all of Europe, and the Soviet Union is less than the additions expected in either

Bangladesh or Nigeria. The World Bank has estimated that Nigeria, now home to ninety-one million people, will add 527 million, more than the current population of the entire continent. Few believe that it can support this number and escape appalling misery.

Well over two billion people have already been added in the developing countries since 1932, more than the entire world population of that time. This spurt of growth is entirely unprecedented in the history of the world, and it has already led to a great deal of poverty and failed hopes. According to The World Bank, of the 2.5 billion people now living in the tropics, one billion live in a condition of absolute poverty. This means that the family head is unable to count on being able to provide food, shelter, and clothing for himself and his family from one day to the next. Furthermore, according to the World Health Organization, one of four persons in the tropics is malnourished. These are the people who are exerting the greatest pressure on the most species-rich habitats, with predictably devastating results. They are abetted by large-scale, poorly planned development projects initiated by governments and corporations. In light of these facts, the linkage between population growth, economic welfare, and the preservation of the earth's biological wealth becomes obvious.

THE AMOUNT OF BIOLOGICAL DIVERSITY

How great is the earth's biological wealth? Since Carolus Linnaeus began the binomial system of nomenclature in 1753 (*Musca domestica, Panthera tigris, Homo sapiens,* and so forth), between 1.5 and 1.6 million species of all kinds of organisms have been described. Approximately 750,000 are insects, 57,000 are vertebrates, and 250,000 are plants (i.e., vascular plants and bryophytes). The remainder consist of a complex array of invertebrates, fungi, algae, and microorganisms. Most systematists agree that this picture is still very incomplete except in a few well-studied groups such as the vertebrates and flowering plants. If insects are included, constituting the most species-rich of all major groups, I believe that the absolute number is likely to exceed five million.

Recent intensive collections in the canopy of

the Peruvian Amazon rain forest have moved the plausible upper limit much higher. Previously unknown insects proved to be so numerous in these samples that when estimates of local diversity were extrapolated to include all tropical moist forests in the world, a figure of thirty million species was obtained. Research is in an even earlier stage on the epiphytic plants, lichens, fungi, roundworms, mites, protozoans, and other, mostly small organisms that abound in the treetops. Other major habitats that remain poorly explored include the coral reefs, the floor of the deep sea, and the soil of tropical forests and savannas. Thus, remarkably, we do not know the true number of species on earth even to the nearest order of magnitude. My own guess, based on the described fauna and flora and many discussions with entomologists and other specialists, is that the absolute number falls somewhere between five and thirty million.

Each species is the repository of an immense amount of genetic information. The number of genes ranges from about 1,000 in bacteria through 10,000 in some fungi to 400,000 or more in many flowering plants and a few animals. A typical mammal such as the house mouse (*Mus musculus*) has about 100,000 genes. This full complement is found in each of its myriad cells, organized from four strings of DNA, each of which comprises about a billion nucleotide pairs. If stretched out fully, the DNA would be roughly one meter long. But this molecule is invisible to the naked eye because it is only twenty angstrom units in diameter. If we magnified it until its width equaled that of wrapping string, the fully extended molecule would be 600 miles long. As we traveled along its length, we would encounter some twenty nucleotide pairs or "letters" of genetic code per inch. The full information contained therein, if translated into ordinary-sized letters of printed text, would just about fill all fifteen editions of the *Encyclopaedia Britannica* published since 1768.

The number of species and the amount of genetic information in a representative organism constitute only part of the biological diversity on the earth. Each species is made up of many organisms. For example, the 10,000 or so ant species have been estimated to comprise 10^{15} living individuals in each moment of time. Except for cases of parthenogenesis and identical-twinning, virtually no two members of the same species are genetically identical, due to the high levels of genetic polymorphism across many of the gene loci. At still another level, wide-ranging species consist of multiple breeding populations that display complex patterns of geographical variation in genetic polymorphism. Thus, even if an endangered species is saved from extinction, it will probably have lost much of its internal diversity. When the populations are allowed to expand again, they will be more nearly genetically uniform than the ancestral populations. The bison herds of today are biologically not quite the same—not so interesting—as the bison herds of the early nineteenth century.

HOW FAST IS DIVERSITY DISAPPEARING?

No precise estimate of current species loss can be made because, first, the number of species of organisms is not known even to the nearest order of magnitude. And second, even in simple isolated ecosystems, which are most tractable to analysis, diversity reduction depends on the size of the island fragments and their distance from each other, factors that vary enormously from one country to the next. And third, the ranges of even the known species have not been worked out in most cases, so that we cannot say which ones will die out when the tropical forests and other species-rich habitats are partially eliminated.

However, scenarios of reduction can be constructed to give at least first approximations if certain courses of action are followed. Suppose, for example, that half the species in tropical forests are very local in distribution, so that the rate at which species are being eliminated immediately is approximately this fraction multiplied by the rate-percentage of the forests being destroyed. The rate of tropical forest destruction is now reasonably well known, thanks to improvements in satellite scanning and increasingly accurate ground surveys. By the late 1970s, according to estimates from the Food and Agricultural Organization and United Nations Environmental Programme, 76,000 square kilometers, or nearly 1 percent of the total cover per annum, were being permanently cleared or converted into the shifting-cultivation cycle. The absolute amount is greater than the area of West Virginia or the entire country of Costa Rica. In

effect, most of this land is being permanently cleared, that is, reduced to a state in which natural reforestation will be very difficult if not impossible to achieve. By the present time the reduction could easily be 100,000 square kilometers a year.

Let us conservatively estimate that five million species of organisms are confined to the tropical rain forests, a figure well justified by the recent upward adjustment of insect diversity alone. The annual rate of reduction would then be $0.5 \times 5 \times 10^6 \times 0.007$ species, or 17,500 species per year. Given ten million species in the fauna and flora of all the habitats of the world, the loss is roughly 10^{-3} species per species per year. How does this compare with extinction rates prior to human intervention? The estimates of extinction rates in Paleozoic and Mesozoic marine faunas have ranged according to taxonomic group (e.g., echinoderms versus cephalopods from 0.1 to 1 species per species per million years, or 10^{-7} to 10^{-6} species per species per year). Let us assume that on the order of ten million species existed in these earlier times, in view of the evidence that diversity has not fluctuated through most of the Phanerozoic eon by a factor of more than three. It follows that both the per-species rate and the absolute loss in number of species due to the current destruction of rain forests (setting aside, for the moment, extinction due to the disturbance of other habitats) would be about one to ten thousand times that prior to human intervention.

I have constructed other simple models incorporating the quick loss of local species and the slower loss of widespread species due to the insularization effect, and these all arrive at comparable or higher extinction rates. It seems difficult, if not impossible, to combine what is known empirically of the extinction process with the ongoing deforestation process without arriving at extremely high rates of species loss in the near future.

The current reduction of diversity thus seems destined to approach that of the great natural catastrophes at the end of the Paleozoic and Mesozoic eras—in other words, the most extreme for 65 million years. In at least one important respect, the modern episode exceeds anything in the geological past. In the earlier mass extinctions, which some scientists believe were caused by large meteorite strikes, most of the plants survived even though animal diversity was severely reduced. Now, for the first time, due to deforestation, plant diversity is also declining sharply. The ultimate result is impossible to predict, but it is not something, I think, with which humanity will want to gamble.

WHAT IS TO BE DONE?

A great many creative scholars and policymakers from previously unconnected disciplines, have recently converged on the problems of international conservation. They foreshadow the collective enterprise likely to dominate the conservation movement during the twenty-first century. I will try to summarize the outlook very briefly in the form of seven trends or prospects, as follows.

1. A complete biotic survey. I am convinced that the needs of humanity in the context of the biodiversity crisis demand nothing less than a complete catalog of life on the earth. For how can we conserve and use our inherited biological wealth if we don't even know what it is? The beginning of wisdom, according to a Chinese maxim, is knowing things by their right names. Beyond that first step we will profit from a vastly increased study of the distribution, biology, and evolutionary history of each species in turn. The magnitude and cause of biological diversity comprise, in fact, one of the key problems in all of science. It can be said that for a problem to be so ranked, its solution must yield unexpected results, some of which are revolutionary in the sense that they resolve conflicts in current theory while opening productive new areas of research. In addition, the answers should influence a variety of related disciplines. They should affect our view of mankind's place in the order of things and open opportunities for the development of a new technology of social importance. These several criteria are very difficult to satisfy, of course, but I believe that the diversity problem meets them all. To attempt an absolute measure of life on the earth is a mission worthy of the best effort of science. Equally to the point, it has a time limit: if we wait much longer, there will be little left to study.

2. Ex situ conservation. The biotic survey should be accompanied by a more nearly comprehensive effort to build larger seed banks than now exist, as well as to expand populations of some of the most threatened species of plants and animals in zoos and botanical gardens. Central data centers, such as those now in existence for zoo animals, are needed to coordinate such activities and prevent entire loss of biotas and groups of organisms. For example, the staff of the Royal Botanical Gardens at Kew have begun a systematic program to study and salvage the remains of the endemic flora of St. Helena, including unique forms of trees that evolved from herbaceous composites. Individual countries can do a great deal more. National biodiversity centers can be built in individual countries at no great expense, in order to coordinate systematic surveys with more intensive biological research and germplasm preservation.

3. Combining conservation and economic development. Conservation is inseparably linked to the future of economic development by a form of mutualistic symbiosis. Biodiversity will be impoverished without the shaping of land use in a form that preserves it, and economic development will be hindered and eventually reversed if it omits the kind of environmental policy that reserves and uses biodiversity. Applied scientists and land management experts agree with near unanimity that the crucial step is the improvement of land already in use, in order to take pressure off the natural habitats. The surviving habitats (and they are perilously small in many countries!) can then be treated as a reservoir of biodiversity from which new species and genetic strains can be drawn for improved economic development. A host of such enrichment techniques are already in the planning or even operational stages, although still far from the levels needed to make a real difference. They include the combination of crop and noncrop species in mixes that reduce insect infestations and retain soil nutrients; the planting of "wood grass," fast-growing and densely packed trees that can be scythed like grass and require little or no replanting; lumbering of native forests along contoured strips to permit regeneration; and, not least, the promotion of portions of national parks and forests as economically profitable recreational areas.

4. Pressures from assistance and lending agencies. It is in the interest of each country in turn to use its natural resources so as to get a sustained yield rather than a short-term yield,

even when the latter may be very high. The question for the pure utilitarian is whether to take a tidy one-time profit or a vastly larger profit over generations of time. There is only one moral choice. To cut down a virgin rain forest may produce a few million dollars during a ten-year period, but then it is gone forever, the age-old patrimony of the country having been diminished by the loss of many of its native species, the soil having been impoverished, and the hydrological cycle and water tables soon to be altered unfavorably. The Agency for International Development, The World Bank, the Asia Development Bank, and other assistance and lending agencies have an obligation to the recipient countries, indeed to the world at large, to insist on project designs that protect the environment and ensure long-term yields.

5. Restoration ecology. A major effort of the next century will almost certainly be in this relatively new subdiscipline. The trend will be animated by the heart-warming idea that it is possible not only to hold on to some natural areas, but also to start to enlarge them so as to secure the preservation of biodiversity for all time. We can heal the world, in other words, and in so doing make it a healthier, more stable place for our descendants. National parks and biosphere reserves can be expanded. Natural ecosystems can be reconstituted in forms that both restore the original biodiversity and add to productivity in agriculture and forestry. Restoration ecology also promises to be an exciting branch of basic science. Each project is an experiment in the formation of living communities that scientists can study from start to finish, in effect making ecology a more predictive science.

6. Engagement by the social sciences. One of the many weaknesses of the social sciences is their failure to make realistic assessments of the environment, including biodiversity. They have virtually nothing to say about how behavior and economic health are related to the living world in which the human mind evolved over millions of years. In this respect neoclassical economics is bankrupt. Its quantitative models of optimization and equilibrium have no realistic measure to place on the value of the environment. Economists cannot factor in opportunity costs, the losses incurred when habitats are destroyed and species go extinct. They are unable to handle multiple margins outside a narrowly defined market economy. Psychologists, for their part, have never made a serious effort to study the relationship of mental development to the natural environment. They cannot answer the following basic question: Given a completely free choice, where do people really want to live, how do they feel about it, and why do they tend to develop in this way and not some other? Finally, sociology is so ideological and unaware of any environment except the "social" as to be almost useless in addressing the root problems of overpopulation and environmental degradation in the third world.

7. Aesthetic and moral reasoning. Environmental ethics, still a small and neglected branch of intellectual activity, deserves to become a major branch of the humanities during the next hundred years. In the end, when all the accounting is done, conservation will boil down to a decision of ethics based on empirical knowledge: how we value the natural world in which we evolved and now, increasingly, how we regard our status as individuals. We are fundamentally mammals and free spirits, not engines of economic and social progress, who reached our high level of rationality by the perpetual creation of new options. Natural philosophy and science have brought into clear relief the essential paradox of human existence. The drive toward perpetual expansion—or personal freedom—is basic to the human spirit. But to sustain it, to avoid the "conquest" of nature from becoming the destruction of nature, we need the most delicate, knowing stewardship of the living world that can be devised. Expansion and stewardship may appear at first to be incompatible goals, but the opposite is true. The power of the conservation ethic will be measured by the extent to which each of the two approaches to nature is used to reshape and reinforce the other. The time for defiance, Fairfield Osborn truthfully observed, is at an end.

Part I

TOMORROW'S WORLD

2

Population, Resources, and Environment in the Twenty-first Century

DAVID WESTERN

It is difficult to conceive any check to population which does not come under the description of some species of misery or vice.

MALTHUS   1798

Sometime between 1970 and 1985 the world will undergo vast famines—hundreds of millions of people are going to starve to death. That is, they will starve to death unless plague, thermonuclear war, or some other agent kills them first. Many will starve to death in spite of any crash programmes we might embark upon now. And we are not embarking upon any crash programme. These are the harsh realities we face.

EHRLICH   1967

If present trends continue, the world in 2000 will be more crowded, more polluted, less stable ecologically and more vulnerable to disruption than the world we live in now.

GLOBAL 2000   1980

If present trends continue, the world in 2000 will be less crowded (though more populated), less polluted, more stable ecologically, and less vulnerable to resource-supply disruption than the world we live in now.

SIMON AND KAHN, THE RESOURCEFUL EARTH,   1984

What in the world will the twenty-first century be like? The answer depends, as it has through the ages, on whether you listen to the Pollyannas or Cassandras. But, surely, you may argue, we have gotten better at predicting human affairs. Let me answer with another quote: "Asking an economist to accurately forecast next year's energy demand is like asking an evolutionary biologist what species will evolve next" (K. Arrow, reported by Kolata 1987). If we can't predict next year's economy, what is the point in trying to anticipate the fate of nature a century hence?

The exercise is not quite so futile as it may at first seem. For one thing, anticipating the problems faced by nature in an increasingly humanized world is not the same as making predictions about economics and geopolitics, for example. Where a socioeconomic prediction is relatively precise, based on specific models of human behavior and its response to future events, the aim of projecting the fate of nature is more a question of identifying plausible problems and opportunities to act soon enough. And there are several reasons why such projections might help to conserve our natural world where a lack of forewarning might condemn it.

In the words of John Gibbons, "If you don't change direction, you end up where you're headed." More to the point, not all forecasts are the haphazard guesses of Malthus's day. Demographic predictions are sound enough for life insurance agents to make a living and governments to predict student enrollments and the number of old-age pensioners years ahead. Weather forecasts are a good guide for daily dress and our weekend plans. Agricultural needs, water requirements, health care, and communications are planned decades ahead. Unless conservation is given the same attention, wildlife and habitat will be lost by default. The World Conservation Strategy and the International Whaling Commission agreements, however inadequate, suggest the value of taking a longer view.

Furthermore, the case for despair and indifference would be understandable if rooted in genuine futility. It is not. As population growth has slowed and production has soared, the growth mania of the industrial revolution has been tempered by the environmental concerns of today. Similar trends exist in many develop-

ing countries too. Need the transition take so long? Anticipation and action can, I suggest, make a difference. East Africa's great herds would have gone the way of the bison had preventive legislation not been taken to halt another massacre by colonial settlers. Looking to the future, changes in attitude based on foresight can improve the outlook for nature far faster than a slowdown in population growth.

Finally, preemption does not call for precise prediction. A guess at the risks can help focus research and training on methods of avoiding crises. Today, as with demographic predictions or weather forecasts, many more minds and better tools can help us look further and more insightfully into the future than ever before to save wildlife, the most vulnerable and least replaceable of all resources.

If this is reason enough to look at wildlife prospects in the twenty-first century, how do we go about it? First, the forces likely to affect the future of wildlife must be identified. Diamond (chap. 4) cites the Evil Quartet—overkill, habitat destruction and fragmentation, introduced species, and chains of extinction—as the dominant forces of destruction. Biologically, these are undoubtedly the archcriminals, but they are neither the sole nor ultimate factors. Pollution in the form of toxic waste, acid rain, pesticides, and herbicides kills countless animals and plants. Global warming, ozone depletion, and sea level rise may change the twenty-first century biomes and ecosystems catastrophically. A brief nuclear apocalypse may destroy most life long before then. Even so, these "downside" factors ignore the agents of nondestructive change—the species enrichment of fertilized lands (Green, chap. 18), the diversification of ecosystems through human activity such as burning, logging, grazing, landscape modification, species introductions, and habitat reclamation (Walker, chap. 12; Western, chap. 16). The list of proximate factors, overwhelmingly negative, is lengthy, but ultimately stems from human activity. Take, for example, the projected 20% species loss by the year 2000 (Global 2000 1980). The underlying assumptions, whatever their veracity, rest solely on predictions of tropical forest destruction by logging, farming, and ranching. The species extinction scenario, based on past trends in human activity, could easily and quickly be nullified by changes in land use practices (Myers, chap. 5). One way or another, humanity will inescapably be the arbiter of wildlife survival in the twenty-first century.

This is not to apotheosize ourselves, as conservationists often fear (Ehrenfeld, 1981), but to draw attention to the awesome power we have to save or destroy life on earth. Whether we have the will or wisdom to preserve millions of hapless species is another question. To win over public sentiment, the wildlife versus people myth must be shown for what it is: a clash of human values between those who care for wildlife and those who don't, no less than rock music fans and their critics. If development is about improving the quality of life, then saving wildlife qualifies as progress just as much as television and space exploration to the millions who flock to national parks. The preservationist who decries health care and famine relief on the grounds that they mean more people and less wildlife is as antisocial as the industrialist who poisons rivers and pollutes the air.

The real issue is whether we can meet the universal inalienable right to a better living and save wildlife too. In addressing that question, I will look at likely trends in human activity, consider the consequences for environmental welfare, and in the Conservation Agenda (chap. 33) I will suggest how to improve the outlook. Before looking at scenarios of the next century, however, it is worth reviewing the pitfalls of forecasting, as portrayed in conflicting views of our future.

GLOBAL OUTLOOK

Predicting the future world, once the domain of astrologers and soothsayers, palmists and conmen, took on a quantitative step with the publication in 1798 of Thomas Malthus' *Essay on the Principle of Population*. Contemporary models of the future have taken on labyrinthine complexity with the use of high-speed computers in the service of armies of analysts, but whether our vision is improved or impaired is debatable. *The Limits to Growth* (Meadows et al. 1972), *The Global 2000 Report to the President* (1980), FAO's Agriculture: Toward 2000

(1981), *The Resourceful Earth* (Simon and Kahn 1984), *The Global Possible* (Repetto 1985), The National Research Council's report on *Population Growth and Economic Development* (1986), *Sustainable Development of the Biosphere* (Clarke and Munn 1986), and other publications in recent years run the gamut from apocalyptic to supremely optimistic visions of the future. The future of wildlife is more uniformly dismal, as portrayed in Marsh's *The Earth as Modified by Human Action* (1864), Osborn's *Our Plundered Planet* (1948), Carson's *Silent Spring* (1962), Ehrlich and Ehrlich's *Population Bomb* (1968), Commoner's *The Closing Circle* (1968), Myers' *The Sinking Ark* (1979), and numerous other books. What can one conclude about the twenty-first century from the modern visionaries?

If anything, it is the lack of consensus on most matters. Malthus saw endless misery as the geometric power of population growth outstripped the arithmetic powers of food increase. He was wrong. In Europe today, the population is aging as birth rates fall below replacement, and food output is overhauling demand to the point where large tracts of land will be idled in the next century (Green, chap. 18).

Yet Malthusian visions of mass starvation and global misery still haunt the affluent West, though more as a backlash from third world poverty. *The Limits to Growth,* the earliest global computer model, sees relentless exponential growth in population, resource use, and pollution leading to the collapse of society early in the twenty-first century. Agricultural land will run out by 2005, precipitating a great Asian famine. *The World Integrated Model,* a later version, shows a steep rise in food prices causing widespread famine before 2000. *The Global 2000,* in a similar if less cataclysmic vein, predicts environmental degradation precipitated by price hikes in food and energy and shortages in basic commodities; destruction of 40% of the tropical forests by the turn of the century could wipe out 20% of all species. Though it skirts the question of global carrying capacity, the report sees nothing to contradict the U.S. National Academy of Sciences (1969) figure of ten billion people as the upper limit of what an intensively managed world might support with some degree of comfort and choice. Few, if any, of the crippling problems of population, food production, and environmental destruction can be solved soon by quick-fix technology or policy reforms.

The Resourceful Earth flatly rejects *The Global 2000's* conclusions. It sees fewer shortages, lower prices, a higher quality of life, and less environmental destruction in the twenty-first century. The opposing scenarios stem from different assumptions. *The Global 2000* has traditional supply and demand mechanisms leading to resource pillage. *The Resourceful Earth* believes the time-tested approach will continue to improve our lives and the environment. *Toward 2000* is cautiously optimistic, calculating the world's carrying capacity at four times the projected population ceiling of eight to fourteen million. Yet another analysis, produced by the 1986 Dahlem conference (Abelson 1986), sees no immediate global shortfall in minerals.

The Global Possible, spurning models altogether, shows how the developmental record can be used to support either an optimistic or a pessimistic view of the twenty-first century. The means to stabilize population within global carrying capacity, to improve the quality of life, and to clean up the environment are within our grasp, if we implement proven policies soon enough. Poverty must be eliminated, and the gap in wealth between rich and poor nations should be narrowed as a matter of priority, according to *The Global Possible.*

The NRC report, in much the same vein, takes the middle ground between *The Global 2000* and *The Resourceful Earth.* In its view, rapid population growth, though not the main cause of world problems, does contribute to human and environmental stress.

Finally, *Sustainable Development of the Biosphere* is less a look at the future than a prescription for balancing resource supply and demand. Like *The Global Possible,* it assumes that sensible action taken soon enough can avoid environmental disasters and improve the state of our environment.

Opinions about our future are as divided now as ever. Yet methodology and thinking are shifting. The highly aggregated global models using thousands of equations and voluminous data may predict repeated weather cycles reasonably well, but are notoriously unreliable in forecasting acyclical human affairs (McNees and Ries

1983), let alone projecting global welfare decades ahead. Most global models are based on an evolutionary paradigm, a steady "suprise-free" progression of events, where in reality changes occur unexpectedly and abruptly (Brooks 1986). The oil crisis in the 1970s, for example, produced a strong surge of energy conservation measures, and the 1950s London killer smogs led to smokeless fuel regulations. The trend is toward case studies of the incentives and constraints in development, and what it will take to avoid disasters and narrow the poverty gap between rich and poor nations. In the process, opinion on the future of humanity has shifted from the despair of *The Limits of Growth* to the cautious optimism of *The Global Possible.* In contrast, the outlook for wildlife looks even gloomier because of the crushing pressure of population growth and poverty on the biologically rich tropics.

POPULATION AND WELFARE

What, if anything, can we anticipate about future populations and welfare, given the divided opinions of pundits? While past trends are easily extrapolated, the switch points in population growth—the postwar baby boom, the 1960s fertility drop and the 1970s echo-boom in the developed world, and antinatal programs in China—make predictions rather uncertain (Coale 1983). Nonetheless, demographic patterns track economic development in most countries, with death rates falling rapidly in response to improved welfare, followed by a slower fall in birth rates. Demographic transition can be divided into four convenient stages (Alexandratos et al. 1983):

1. Slow growth in pretransitional societies due to high death rates offsetting high birth rates.
2. Rapid growth in transitional societies due to a high birth rate and falling death rate.
3. Growth rate peaks, then falls as birth rates drop.
4. Population stabilizes soon after birth rate falls to death rate.

We can look at global population projections in light of the model. Overall, world population

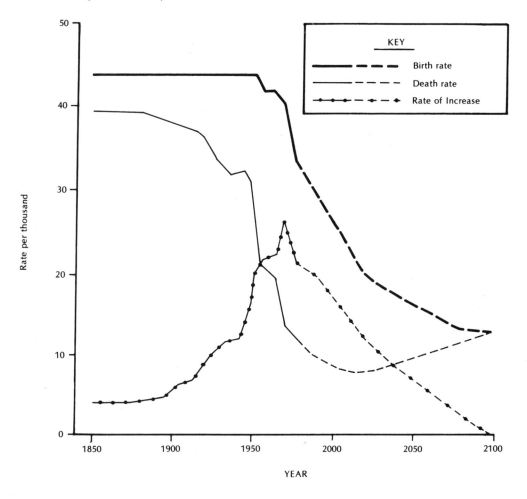

Fig. 2.1. Historical and projected birth and death rates showing the short and dramatic consequences on the rate of population increase. (After Coale 1983.)

growth peaked at 2.0% in the 1960s and fell to 1.7% in the late 1970s. The decline, a historical turning point, marks a global demographic transition to stage 3. The United Nations (1981) median forecast anticipates global replacement by 2025 and an ultimate population of 10.2 billion around 2100, a figure little over twice the present population, versus 33 billion had the 1960s growth rate continued (Coale 1983). Viewed historically, the high growth phase between the 1930 and 2025 will be remarkably short; no longer than a human lifespan (Fig. 2.1). But the light at the end of the tunnel should not blind us to the tremendous tensions of population growth and demographic transition. I will cite three examples:

First, the uncertainty in global projections hinges on how quickly third world fertility will decline in stage 3. Stationary population levels could be anywhere between eight and thirteen billion—a difference equal to today's total—depending on whether replacement birth rate is reached twenty years before or after 2025 (Repetto 1986). History is no guide to the third world demographic transition. Peak growth never exceeded 1.3% in the industrial nations, whereas in the developing world a rapid drop in birth rate due to improved health and nutrition has generated growth rates in excess of 4%. Stage 3 transition times, on the other hand, will be faster, on the order of 70 years or less, compared to 100 to 150 in developing nations (Chesnais 1979). Nevertheless, demographic transition is underway. Most of Latin America and Asia entered stage 3 before the 1980s, the Near East is presently entering that stage, and Africa, with a few exceptions, will enter it during the 1990s.

Second, global averages also disguise population concentrations arising from differential growth. A regional look at where population will grow through the twenty-first century, and to what extent, gives some idea of the pressure points (Table 2.1). Ninety-five percent of future growth will occur in the third world; Asia will account for half the total, Africa a quarter. In terms of present population, Asia will have two and a half times its numbers, Latin America three and a half, and Africa five and a half.

Finally, within nations, urban drift, which transformed Europe during the industrial revolution, is running at 3.7% annually (Hauser and Gardner 1980). Continued at that rate it will also transform the developing world from an agrarian to an urban society in half a century. The agrarian population will fall from 70% of the population presently, to 20% in 2050 (Beckmann 1984). This implies a mere 30% increase in rural population by 2050 and a rapidly falling population thereafter, but a 600% increase in urban population (U.N. 1981). The rural loss of population will be sooner in countries such as Kenya, where urbanization rates are especially high.

Together, these three points have profound implications geopolitically and environmentally. Geopolitically, the population center of gravity will shift east and south in the twenty-first century. The power of numbers will reside overwhelmingly in the tropics, where the popu-

Table 2.1. Distribution and Growth of Actual and Projected Population

	Total Population by World Regions (billions)					
	1980	%	2000	2050	2100	%
World	4.43	100.00	6.12	9.51	10.18	100.00
More developed	1.13	25.51	1.27	1.40	1.42	13.95
Less developed	3.30	74.49	4.85	8.11	8.76	86.05
Africa	0.47	10.61	0.85	2.17	2.59	25.44
Latin America	0.36	8.13	0.57	1.10	1.24	12.18
North America	0.25	5.64	0.30	0.36	0.38	3.73
East Asia	1.18	26.64	1.48	1.77	1.76	17.29
South Asia	1.40	31.60	2.08	3.20	3.28	32.22
Europe	0.48	10.84	0.51	0.51	0.50	4.91
Oceania	0.02	0.45	0.03	0.04	0.04	0.39
U.S.S.R.	0.26	5.87	0.31	0.38	0.38	3.73
World	1.70	38.37	1.39	0.36	−0.03	−0.29
More developed	0.68	15.35	0.40	0.07	−0.01	−0.10
Less developed	2.04	46.05	1.64	0.41	−0.03	−0.29
Africa	3.00	67.72	2.77	0.84	−0.03	−0.29
Latin America	2.38	53.72	1.92	0.52	−0.06	−0.59
North America	1.04	23.48	0.62	0.22	0.03	0.29
East Asia	1.24	27.99	0.89	−0.03	0.01	0.10
South Asia	2.17	48.98	1.53	0.30	−0.04	−0.39
Europe	0.34	7.67	0.15	−0.08	0.01	0.10
Oceania	1.44	32.51	0.92	0.19	0.00	0.00
U.S.S.R.	0.93	20.99	0.60	0.16	−0.06	−0.59

Source: Repetto 1985.

lation will increase from two billion in 1980 to seven billion by 2100; that is, from 44% to 70% of the world's population. Rapid growth and sluggish development are, however, likely to lead to a winter of poverty, especially in south Asia and Africa. Here, the potential for turmoil will mount as the gap between rich and poor nations widens, and the predominantly young and landless drift to towns and become the chronically unemployed. Economically, power is certain to move to east Asia, where industrialization and agricultural intensification are making enormous strides.

Urban drift is a mixed blessing. In Korea and Taiwan, for example, the booming agroindustrial economy is luring the young from the land at a time when agricultural intensification is making fewer demands on labor. In Africa, in contrast, the drift is often more push than pull, a move of desperation by destitute peasants (Sai 1984). The sheer magnitude of urbanization is incomprehensible. In 1950 only seven cities had more than 5 million people. By 2000 some fifty-seven cities had more than 5 million people. By 2000 some fifty-seven cities, forty-two of them in developing countries, will have exceeded that figure (Hardoy and Satherthwaite 1985). In 1950, Mexico City had less than 2.5 million people; by 2000 it will exceed 30 million. By then, Bombay's population will reach 17 million and Lagos's 10.5 million. The problems of such rapid growth are hard to imagine, let alone solve. How will municipalities handle the growth of shanty towns and slums, provide basic welfare services, control crime, dispose of mountains of waste, and avoid dense urban smog? No easy solution is in sight. Take, for example, energy needs. The energy concentration of such crowded third world cities may reach 30 W/M^2, far greater than New York City's 6.4 W/M^2, ruling out sunshine energy and biomass fuels (Beckmann 1984).

How many people inhabit the world late next century will depend on how quickly growth slows. The more immediate reason to slow growth is, according to advocates of control, to eliminate poverty and avoid environmental degradation. But, does rapid human growth actually slow development? Simon (1980) claims it does not. He finds no correlation between population growth and gross national product (GNP) per capita. Environmentally, rapid population growth, coupled with a slow increase in GNP,

may harm resources less than static populations with a rapidly rising GNP (Repetto 1986). In other words, the industrial world could continue to be the biggest threat to the environment well into the next century.

The NRC report also dismisses the notion that rapid population growth in itself is at the root of poverty, but does concede some costs, including lower worker productivity due to the dilution of capital diverted to education and health, poorer education, greater income disparity and sexual inequality, greater stress on cities and common property resources, and more pollution. Income is also likely to be lower. For a population growing at 3% annually, income would be 13% less per capita than for a population growing at 1% a year.

Less developed countries are taking population control seriously after some initial doubts (Vittachi, chap. 3). The outcome on global population in the twenty-first century is, however, indeterminate. Case studies support almost any scenario. Consider a few statistics: Some 2.4 billion of the less developed world's population is in sharp growth decline, another 100 million is in slow decline, and 800 million show no downturn yet. The break between two worlds, one increasing slower than 1%, the other faster than 2%, is large, with little middle ground (Brown and Jacobsen 1986). China, whose birth rate per thousand dropped from 34 to 20 in the last decade, shows what is possible; Japan's birth rate dropped from 34 to 18 between 1948 and 1958, and Cuba slowed its growth rate from 2.5% to 1% between 1960 and 1980. By contrast, Africa's population growth accelerated over that period. In South Africa, which has double the per capita income of Cuba, growth rose from 2.5% to 3.1%.

The slowdown in growth spans democratic and authoritarian governments and centrally planned as well as free-market economies (Repetto 1985). Contrary to conventional dogma, economic development is not a precondition of population transition, as China and Cuba show. In fact, the surprising point is the diversity of contexts in which population slowdown has occurred. In Thailand, where contraceptive use has increased from 14% in 1970 to 65% in 1980, most of the downturn is attributed to family planning and women's independence (Brown and Jacobsen 1986). Strong leadership, family-planning programs, the availability of contraceptives, and female emancipation seem to be the common elements of success (Repetto 1986).

In the opinion of third world governments, the real issue boils down to welfare and the quality of life, not simple head counts. Economically, the overall picture, like population slowdown, is improving. Incomes rose steadily by 3.5% over the last quarter-century (Repetto 1986), and from 1975 to 1985 rose to 4.1%, despite recession. Less developed countries showed faster than average income growth at 5% annually (Global 2000 1980). A 3.3% annual global increase is forecast through the rest of the century.

Other indices of welfare, including per capita food supplies, life expectancy, health, education, and access to clean water, also rose steadily in recent decades. Life expectancy in the developing countries, a good measure of diet and health, rose from forty-three to fifty-three years between the 1950s and 1970s (Simon 1984). Primary-school enrollment increased sharply from around 30% to more than 80% between the 1950s and 1980s.

Overall, the world has improved in this century, and there is no reason to doubt there will be further gains in the next. However, the figures obscure some harsh facts. Rapid population growth is eroding per capita income gains in developing countries, especially in Africa. The gap between the haves and have-nots is huge and widening. In 1985 per capita income in developing countries averaged $501, only 8.5% of developed country levels. The widening gap between the two worlds is likely to erode the biological wealth of the tropics in the process of heightening world tensions.

These projections are, however, no more than an extension of the past into the future. Actual variation in performance shows how fast conditions could improve or stagnate. Take as an example the range of cumulative change in per capita income between 1980 and 1986: China +58%, South Korea +34%, India +14%, Nigeria −25%, Phillipines −16%, Peru −11%. Despite the same starting level, South Korea's per capita income grew by 6.6% per year between 1960 and 1980, while Ghana's shrank by 1.3% per year.

Stagnation and recession, widespread in Africa and parts of Latin America, are the flash points likely to retard progress. Per capita food production is falling in forty developing countries, notably the unstable, e.g., Angola, Mozambique, Iraq, or Haiti. Other crises mar growth among the already poor. The 1973 and 1979 oil crises increased the proportion of export earnings many nations spent on fuel to between 30% and 50%, adding to an already staggering third world debt burden of $1.2 trillion in 1987. Sudan's external public debt is 79% of its GNP and Egypt's is 49%, conditions that strain relations between the rich and poor countries and between agricultural and rural populations as governments subsidize food prices to quell unrest.

Unrest and distrust erode progress in other ways too. Military expenditures worldwide grew at 15% per annum during the 1970s, a figure amounting to 40% of investments in scientific research. And again, the costs are often greatest in the third world. Africa's military expenditures in real terms increased from $500 million in 1971 to $4.5 billion in 1980; its standing forces grew from 141,000 to 441,000 as Sudan, Somalia, Ethiopia, Uganda, Chad, Libya, Morocco, Nigeria, Angola, Mozambique, Zimbabwe, and South Africa fought civil and national wars. The economic and social impact has been devastating. Crop failures and famine have worsened in many countries. Relief aid in Ethiopia alone amounted to $500 million in 1985.

Unchecked population growth, poverty, famine, civilian unrest, militarism, and ecological destruction are enough make the sunniest optimist wonder whether the hyperpopulated world of the twenty-first century will hold together. I suspect it will, but we cannot depend on rising incomes as a panacea for growth pains. Wealth is too spotty and increasing too slowly in the poorer nations to solve the most urgent human and environmental problems. A passive economic solution is not the answer for the twenty-first century. Instead we should take heed of lessons from China, Sri Lanka, Cuba, Zimbabwe, Costa Rica, and other countries of various cultural and political persuasion that have made great strides on low incomes. If infant mortality is used as an index of welfare, no correlation is found with per capita income up to $2,000. Improvements in food production, communications, basic services, education, health, and conservation of natural resources can be made for very modest sums. For example, infant survival can be doubled for about $2 to $4 per capita; community health programs spending $3.85 per capita reduced infant mortality in Haiti to 17% of the national average (Chandler 1984). The successful programs have in common the involvement of the poor themselves.

RESOURCES

The limits to growth are likely to worry futurists of the twenty-first century less than they did our predecessors from Malthus to Osborn, for the simple reason that population is poised to level off well within the capacity of the planet. The range of estimates pits the optimists against the pessimists once again. In 1969 the U.S. National Academy of Sciences calculated an upper limit of 10 billion living in some comfort in an intensively managed world. As recently as 1972, *The Limits to Growth* forecast widespread famine in the 1980s and worldwide population collapse in the early twenty-first century. *Toward 2000* says the world can support four times the projected total with available resources and technology. Hrabovszky (1985) thinks the total is closer to 150 billion, or some 47 billion at present U.S. living standards. Whatever the figure, and there is no way to calculate it without knowing future technologies, the twenty-first century should support its numbers quite comfortably. If there is the mass starvation forecast by *The Limits to Growth,* it is more likely to stem from social constraints and disorder than from limits to production. Overall, the trends support that conclusion. Between 1950 and 1980 world food output grew at 2.6% per year (Barr 1981). But again, those figures obscure as much as they tell and ignore the political and environmental setbacks.

On the bright side, food output in the developing countries grew 2.9% annually over the last 30 years, compared to 2.5% in the developed world. But, adjusted for population growth, growth in per capita food intake falls to 0.5% in the poorer countries and 1.4% in the wealthier. Worse yet, grain imports in the poorer nations grew 50%. The record is patchy within the third world. Over the last thirty years, per capita food output increased 30% in East Asia and 3% in South Asia and fell 12% in Africa. Sri Lanka's per capita output rose 54% and imports fell

50%, but Egypt's output fell 15% and imports rose 50%. In other words, the mixed signals on progress in population also apply to food production.

What about food production in future? The age of agricultural land expansion is coming to an end as intensive farming revolutionizes agriculture worldwide. Sixty percent of the gains in food output during the fifties came from newly cultivated land, some 138 million ha, all in developing countries. In the 1970s the contribution of new land fell to 25%, and the expansion of crop area to less than 1% annually (FAO 1981). Farming land actually shrank in a number of countries during the 1970s, by 1.7% a year in Korea, where output rose 4.6% annually; by 0.4% in China, where food output rose 4.5% annually; and by 0.2% in South Africa, where food output rose 6.8% annually.

Yield increases using available technology have a long way to go. *Toward 2000* estimates that the developing nations produce a quarter to a half the yield of developed countries for a wide range of crops. Average yields are even further below their potential—9% for wheat, 7.7% for maize, and 14% for rice, the three crops producing half the world's food.

Fertilization, pest control, waste avoidance, improved practices such as multiple cropping, new crop varieties, and irrigation account for most of the gains. Irrigated lands, for example, grew from 70 million to 100 million ha between 1960 and 1975 and yielded two to four times the output of rainfed agriculture (FAO 1981). On the whole, it is cheaper to intensify than expand cultivation. Research into the development of new and improved technology is the key to production gains. Mexico, for example, showed a 35% annual return on investments funding research into hybrid maize; India has posted a 63% annual return on agricultural research since 1960.

The expansion of agricultural land is slowing fast, despite half the world's potential cultivable land, which covers 3.2 billion ha, a quarter of all ice-free land being unused (Hrabovszky 1985). Agricultural land in Europe and North America may soon shrink rapidly if price subsidies are scrapped to reduce the food surpluses of intensified farming (Green, chap. 18). If so, the twenty-first century may see great tracts of agricultural land idled, a point of great significance for wildlife.

Will the fruits of intensified agriculture also quell land hunger in the third world? It seems likely from prevailing trends, barring social upheaval. The total additional land put under the plough by 2050 will be on the order of 250 to 500 million ha, according to FAO (1981), or a modest 15% to 30% increase. Other authorities (e.g., Crosson 1986) anticipate a steady expansion of agricultural land for years to come.

Producing enough food will be a trivial problem late next century when population levels off. The bigger concerns will be surplus production and health, personal and environmental. In fact they already are concerns for the developed and at least half the developing world, with good reason. Some 4.5 million ha of cropland, forest, and rangeland are lost each year to salinization, erosion, waterlogging, and urbanization (Myers 1987a). Worldwide, soils are thinning as a net 25.4 billion tons of topsoil are washed away. The United States is losing an excessive amount of soil on 44% and India on 60% of its croplands (Brown and Wolf 1984). The fertilizers, insecticides, feeds lots, and mass consumer markets driving up farm output are polluting streams and aquifers, eroding soils, causing widespread eutrophication, and producing bland meat and blander fruit and vegetables. We have sacrificed quality in the relentless pursuit of abundance, thrift, and supermarket convenience.

Intensive agriculture has its drawbacks, especially in the third world. Critics of the Green Revolution cite income disparity, dependence on high technology, environmental impact, and the cost of imports such as fertilizers, insecticides, and capital equipment as doing more harm than good to poor nations.

Yet realistically, there is no alternative to intensification, no matter what the agricultural Luddites claim. There is no going back to shifting cultivation and pastoralism. The world is too populous for that, much as subsistence farming would solve the unemployment problem. Besides, per unit of production, most peasant farming does more damage than intensive methods. Early societies, though sparse, left their mark indelibly on the Mediterranean Basin and the Middle East (Southwick 1976). And, if our present activity already consumes 50% of the world's primary production (Ehrlich 1986), intensification is the only hope we have of producing enough food with land left over for other uses, including wildlife.

Does this forebode the environmental disaster of *Silent Spring*? Not necessarily. Not if quality assumes equal rank with quantity. Ignorance and indolence are the only excuses for disregarding the environmental costs. Existing practices and biotechnological innovations around the corner give enormous scope for environmentally sound farming, if we care to harness them for qualitative improvements.

Conservation methods can improve the efficiency of fertilizers, insecticides, and water in the same way that oil shortages in the seventies increased energy-use efficiency. For example, only 5% to 10% of the fertilizer transported and applied on fields is used in plant growth and food production. Big improvements can be made in application methods by, for example, packing the seed with fertilizer prior to sowing (Wolf 1979). Similar methods can be applied to insecticides. Erosion can be slowed by standard control methods, as happened in Kenya after a presidential directive was issued to all district agricultural officers. The Blue Revolution in Israel improved water-use efficiency from 15 to 85% through drip and subterranean irrigation and the use of drought-resistant crops (Wolf 1979).

Improvements can also be made in crop production and farm technology. No-till agriculture, which can raise production, cut labor costs, save water, and reduce soil losses (Wijewardene 1978), may be practiced on 90% of U.S. croplands by 2010. Multiple cropping, intercropping, agroforestry, and integrated control are helping increase output, reduce input, and improve environmental quality by the application of ecological principles.

Finally, a genetic revolution which could radically change farming practices may be around the corner. The first genetically engineered product to boost farm production—ice-minus, a bacteria that reduces frost damage to crops—is already on field trial in California. What does that augur for the future? On the one hand, biotechnology critics fear the runaway synthesis of thousands of new organisms, some of which may prove lethal or destructive unless adequately screened before release into the environment. On the other, many scientists see the potential for a new era of ecologically adapted farming in which the plant could be tailored to the environment, rather than the reverse. The possibilities exist for selection of crops with higher photosynthetic efficiency; greater resilience to drought, salinity, alkalinity, and acidity; and improved nitrogen-fixing abilities. The nitrogen-fixing abilities of legumes can foreseeably be introduced to cereal crops to slash fertilizer bills. Allelopathic genes giving host immunity to specific farm pests can conceivably be spliced into commercial crops to eliminate insecticides. The possibilities are enormous. Their realization depends on research and development into new breeding methods, such as pollen and embryo culture and protoplast fusion (Wolf 1979). The dawn of a more productive, less destructive agriculture in the twenty-first century hinges on our demand for sustainable, benign farming practices.

Turning to energy resources, known reserves and feasible improvements in user efficiency should be sufficient to sustain demand well beyond the twenty-first century. Immediate concerns focus on oil and biomass shortages, the two energy sources most widely used today. Though the oil crisis of the seventies has receded temporarily, extraction costs are likely to rise steeply by the end of the century. Gains in efficiency due to the price hikes in 1973 and 1979 showed the value of conservation. Gross domestic product in the Organization for Economic Cooperation and Development (OECD) countries, for example, rose by 2.1% a year during the 1970s, despite a 0.3% annual fall in energy use (Repetto 1986), making the point that changes in efficiency can flatten or even reduce demand. The use of lighter alloys and ceramic and aerodynamic designing is expected to halve the 1975 average fuel consumption of 6 km/1 within a decade (Repetto 1986), to as low as 30 km/1 in the foreseeable future. Known oil reserves, 200 years of coal and gas reserves, and improvements in efficiency should give ample time for the development of new low- and high-tech energy sources, such as solar, wind, wave, geothermal, bioenergy, and nuclear fission and fusion, if the radioactive disposal problems can be resolved (Repetto 1986).

Future energy use will, however, be shaped as much by environmental issues such as acid rain, ozone depletion, rising world temperature, and radioactive contamination as by the quantity and price of resources. More attention must be given to energy-use efficiency as a way to reduce environmental impact, and to technological improvements in energy combustion,

storage, and waste disposal. Innovations in laser technology, superconductors, and energy storage could make light and electricity universal clean-energy currencies in the twenty-first century.

Energy use divides the world just as much as do wealth and health. While the developed world applauds the latest report on superconductor research, the third world peasant labors to collect enough wood to cook food and heat water. Biomass, mostly wood, accounts for 43% of all energy used in the developing world (Reddy 1985). The gap between supply and demand is widening fast. FAO (1981) believes that 100 million people suffer acute energy shortages and another 1 billion get inadequate supplies. The costs to human welfare, productivity, and environment are severe. Peasants over much of the world spend hours walking for fuelwood each day. Land cleared for cultivation further cuts down wood supplies. And, over much of the third world, especially in the arid regions, tree felling has contributed to desertification. In Kenya, wood consumption is four times annual production (Western and Ssemakula 1980), which leads to a depletion of woody vegetation around towns and along roads. It will take a concerted effort to plant fuelwoods and improve energy conservation methods to alleviate the third world's ecological and social problems caused by energy shortages (Reddy 1985).

I will not dwell on nonrenewable resources since they are relevant here only insofar as they impinge on conservation. In any event, most authorities do not expect the world to run out of any elements before 2050 (Goeller and Zucker 1984; Abelson 1986), giving time enough to develop new technologies to exploit lower-grade ores and bring some thirty new substitute elements into nearly infinite supply. Thirty-three of the sixty-five stable elements are likely to be available in nearly limitless supply by 2100 (Goeller and Zucker 1984). Prices should continue to fall in the future, as they have in the past (Simon and Kahn 1984).

The environmental issues raised by the extraction, consumption, and disposal of minerals are of concern to conservationists. Surface mining has done enormous localized damage to the environment. Rivers in Alaska have yet to recover from the 1920s gold rush; slag heaps from Welsh coal mines have stood bare and silent for decades; the extraction of bauxite and other minerals has destroyed great swathes of tropical forest in New Guinea. Those problems could magnify in the twenty-first century when the extraction of lower-grade ores forces miners to dig up larger areas of land. Recycling and reclamation practices will need to be in widespread use by then to slow the destruction.

ENVIRONMENT AND ENVIRONMENTALISM

Renewable resources—our water, air, soils, forests, grassland, and wildlife—are being used, abused, and destroyed as never before. We are beginning to change our climate, manipulate hydrological and biogeochemical cycles, usurp most of the earth's primary production, modify ecosystems, govern evolution, and sully the biosphere on a scale unimaginable to George Marsh when he wrote *Man and Nature: Or Physical Geography as Modified by Human Action* in 1864. Whether we adapt to resource scarcity or continue to populate, pillage, and pollute the earth depends on our wisdom and conscience.

The extent and scale of human impact in the twentieth century is staggering. Hardly an ecosystem or process other than deep crustal geological activity is untouched. We are changing the atmosphere, stratosphere, lithosphere, and hydrosphere worldwide. It would be pointless to belabor the ways in which we modify the biosphere, but a few examples should illustrate our perniciousness and show what is at stake.

Even the global geochemical cycles are speeding up as the by-products of human activity, including nitrogen, phosphorus, sulfur, and carbon exceed the background levels and recycling times of the major elements (Eisenberg and Harris, chap. 10). Take atmospheric carbon dioxide, for example. Preindustrial levels set by biotic respiration and decomposition varied between 200 and 300 ppm during the Holocene. Since the early nineteenth century, fossil fuel combustion has jumped from 265 ± 30 to 335 in 1981 (Cook 1984). If present trends continue, atmospheric CO_2 will double by 2025, producing a "greenhouse" effect which, by trapping incident radiation normally lost to outer space, will raise global temperatures by 3° C, elevate sea levels by 0.3 m to 0.6 m, and modify climate worldwide enough to affect agriculture; the subtropics would be wetter, and spring would be wetter and summer drier in the middle to high latitudes. In one scenario, the West Antarctic ice sheet could slip its landbase, raise sea levels 6 m, and drown the world's major cities.

The atmosphere is affected in other ways. Fossil fuel combustion and metallic ore smelting waft 75 to 100 million tons of sulfur into the atmosphere each year, more than it receives naturally from the oceans, swamps, and volcanoes (Postel 1984). The impact on the industrialized nations can be devastating. The gases acidify rainfall ten to twenty times normal levels. In turn, acid rain leaches soil nutrients such as calcium and magnesium, raises acidity, kills soil fauna, and devastates forests. Nearly 4 million ha of Europe's forests, an area the size of Austria, has been damaged by acid rain. Lakes and rivers are also acidified to levels lethal to fish and other aquatic life. West Germans are more concerned about acid rain than Pershing missiles, so devastating has its impact become.

Human wastes could be changing the atmosphere in a more disturbing way. Chlorofluorocarbons (CFCs), widely used in plastic foams, aerosol sprays, and as refrigerants, are reported to have thinned ozone in the stratosphere by 3% in the last decade. Less ozone means more radiation penetrating to earth, lowered crop production, and more skin cancers—as many as forty million extra cases over the next eighty-eight years—if present trends continue (Begley and Hager 1987).

The oceans, another global dumping ground, are also in trouble. Organochlorides (including DDT and PCB), detergents, oil, heavy metals, radioactive wastes, and other pollutants dumped into the sea may reduce annual unicellular marine algal production by 10% and the commercial harvest of marine organisms by twenty million tons (Patin 1982), though other evidence suggests little reduction so far (Holdgate et al 1982).

Lakes, rivers, and groundwater are also in trouble. Some thirty-three toxic chemicals are widely found in drinking water and wells throughout the United States, according to the

Council on Environmental Quality (Tangley 1984). A quarter of all groundwater sources are contaminated, most often by chlorinated compounds used in industrial solvents and by degreasers leaking out of surface impoundments and underground tanks.

Among other things, our impact on habitats and wildlife is also alarming, as detailed by Diamond (chap. 4), Myers (chap. 5), Olson (chap. 6) and Atkinson (chap. 7). Taken together, our accelerating global onslaught of the last hundred years would, projected over the next century, poses a severe threat to human welfare and the quality of life. Whether the doom and gloom prophesy becomes reality rests on another remarkable and counteracting upsurge in human activity—environmentalism.

Global thinking is a uniquely human trait. Before the twentieth-century push-button age put us in instant touch with grandma halfway around the world, brought the horrors of the Vietnam War, the triumph of the first space walk, the despotism of Idi Amin, the agony of Ethiopia, and the disaster at Chernobyl into our sitting rooms, before we could jet to Calcutta, Beijing, or Buenos Aires in a day, and before we could look back from the bleak face of the moon to see our tiny planet illuminated against the still blackness of space, we could remain blind to the world at large. Today, short of a lobotomy, one cannot ignore the latest twist in human affairs, the intricacies of the global economy—a sniff in the dollar and the yen catches a cold—or the environmental disasters. The world has shrunk to the point where we can, and must, think globally to size up the future. We can no longer close our minds to an oil crisis in the Middle East, starving children in Ethiopia, the teeming masses in Asia, mercury in our tuna sandwich, a radiation cloud from Chernobyl, eagle chicks dying of DDT, rhinos being poached to extinction, or tropical forests getting hacked back to tiny islands.

Subtly, our concerns and perceptions have widened to encompass broader human and environmental issues. A publicity explosion has showered the layman and scientist with environmental information. The number of environmental journals alone grew fiftyfold in a decade, from 13 in 1970 to 686 in 1980 (Holdgate et al. 1982). Just as important, the gap between science and lay reporting on key issues has shrunk and even reversed. Millions avidly follow the latest findings in the Antarctic ozone hole in daily papers even before it makes the science journals.

The publicity explosion is matched by the information explosion, a bewildering mountain of data collected on everything from geology to solar winds, from demography to public opinion about topics as disparate as the third world debt and this year's dress length. Data are gathered on the ground and remotely from satellite, stored in computer banks, transmitted around the world, and analyzed on supercomputers with sophisticated software packages that model global climate and hydrology.

In turn, the information explosion has led to breathtaking advances in the sciences and humanities. Yet, as bold and brilliant as the theories of relativity and quantum mechanics are, and as significant as the decoding of life's genetic code may prove to be, the greatest intellectual revolution is the humble notion of the biosphere. No other concept has such fateful overtones or will unify so many human endeavors. It is not so much the idea of the finiteness of our world as its vulnerability, its inability to soak up punishment and remain a benign living place, that makes the biosphere idea so inescapable. A scaled-up version of its intellectual precursor, the ecosystem concept, the biosphere notion gives us a framework for building a healthier, more sustainable world, a basis for coming together politically and economically to find common ground in managing the global commons. The notion of the biosphere, and the many examples from global warming to ozone depletion of how we affect it, compel us to think and plan on a scale inconceivable a few years ago.

Finally, knowledge and awareness have led to response. Whereas in the late nineteenth century the response was measured by a handful of conservation bodies, a few environmental laws, and a scattering of protected areas, by the 1980s it was hard to keep track of the many agencies and their activities. Thousands of local, national, and international groups throughout the world have lobbied successfully to improve environmental quality through legislation, education, and management. At first it took a crisis to generate response—the 1950s killer smogs in

London to bring in a clean-air act, the massacre of the great whales to introduce quotas, rampant wildlife commerce to clinch an international agreement on endangered-species trade, the Torrey Canyon oil spill to bring about tanker safety regulations. In recent years environmental response has grown from the local and reactive to the global and anticipatory. Global monitoring and assessment, set in motion by the International Geophysical Year (1957–1958), has been taken up by scores of international agencies, most of them under the United Nations family. International treaties, conventions, and declarations—such as the International Law of the Sea, the Mediterranean Treaty, the Convention on International Trade in Endangered Species (CITES), the Stockholm Declaration, and the World Conservation Strategy—reflect the widening concerns and responses. And, in a 1987 landmark agreement to protect the ozone layer, forty-nine nations undertook to cooperate on an environmental problem before it was conclusively proved harmful.

Such responses, though encouraging, are not nearly enough to slow, let alone reverse, the environmental damage in the next few years or even decades. What they do show is realization and hope, realization that more people need not be synonymous with greater degradation, hope that action, taken soon enough, can alleviate the impact.

THE FUTURE: IMPERATIVE OR CHOICE?

Does a study of trends and variations lead to any clearer insight on the future? Perhaps. We can probably reckon on the population doubling and growth slowing in the twenty-first century. We can also bet on a geopolitical shift from the northern industrial nations to the East and the tropics. More than likely our descendants will be more literate, healthier, wealthier, more mobile, and less rural than we are. Life will be more automated and communications instantaneous. Few people will be farmers and less land will be devoted to farming. Markets will be far more intricate and global. Change will be faster. Energy efficiency will be greater and lower-grade ores will be used. Global issues will be intensely debated and negotiated. All

environments will be more intensively managed. The quality of life is likely to matter more than it does today.

What of the surprises? No doubt unexpected innovations, technological hitches, political and economic alliances, wars, human and natural calamities, and dozens of other imponderables and improbables will change the steady trends into a ragged alternation of giant leaps and unexpected crashes. Depending on the direction of change, one can visualize a closing gap between rich and poor, a world on the mend as food production outstrips demand to the point of environmental issues taking precedents, or a world destabilized to the point of undermining the quality of life.

The outcome for nature is rooted in the rate and mode of economic and demographic transition, in technological innovations, and in environmentalism. Rapid demographic transition, increased wealth and welfare, education, the introduction of new benign technologies and environmental consciousness could quickly slow erosion, pollution, habitat destruction, and wildlife extinctions. The encouraging signals can be seen in rising life expectancies and improving welfare, in falling population growth rates, rising environmental consciousness, international environmental agreements, and localized improvements, e.g., the cleanup of Britain's Thames River, the spread of protected areas, and the recovery of endangered species such as the leopard and vicuña. Conceivably, environmental concerns could arise faster in the developing countries than they did in the developed. Indeed, they must if the tropical habitats and wildlife are to avoid the fate of the temperate latitudes. If not, the coming decades will see an unprecedented loss of tropical grasslands, forests, reefs, and their wildlife. The traditional reverence many societies have for nature will not be enough to preserve it unless channeled into action rather than mere concern.

Whatever else we can guess about the future, we know it will be different. How different and what our descendants will strive for are, for the most part, conjectural. Nature may find a lasting place in our spiritual and aesthetic psyche or pass like many modern fads. Yet, I suspect the best hope for all species is linked to a single, uncompromisable human goal—the improvement of human welfare. If our case is hopeless, we will cease caring about other species. If our lot improves, we will have more time, resources, and compassion to spare for the natural world. That path, rather than the alternative of poverty and decimation, could see nature emerge from an environmental bottleneck late in the twenty-first century. If it does, our descendants should be better placed than we are to rehabilitate the remnants. By looking ahead to anticipate the problems and opportunities, we may avoid the worst destruction and be prepared for whatever reconstruction is possible. Our future, and that of wildlife, is not an inevitability, but rather a matter of foresight, choice, and action. The sooner we put wildlife on the agenda for the twenty-first century, the greater the chance that it will find a lasting place in our world.

3

Demographics and Socioeconomics: The People Factor

TARZIE VITTACHI

In the next dozen years, by the year 2000, the world's population will reach six billion. This means that one billion children will be added to the present world population of five billion in that period, despite the most effective family-planning programs and the most stringent national policies. Since this increase of numbers is likely, even certain, unless some catastrophic misadventure intervenes, the most important concern on the global agenda is: what needs to be done to accommodate these newcomers, however importunate they might seem to people engaged in limiting fertility? Accommodating them, it is hardly necessary to say, involves not only physical space and shelter, but also access to food and water supplies, health and education facilities, transportation, recreation, and employment. The urgency of this concern is emphasized when another inevitability is recognized: Most of the increase will be in heavily populated nations and in the least developed countries which are already deeply enmeshed in the problems of poverty. (See Western, introduction to Part II.)

Unfortunately, because of the tendency to classify human problems in separate categories, the socioeconomic consequences of population growth have, by and large, been considered by population specialists, including many demographers, as a separate concern of the development specialists, who, for their part, regard population as an important factor in their field of work and not as the field itself. It is this cate-

gorical insulation which led to the sterile debate in the seventies between those who believed that economic development was the sole remedy for the ills of overpopulation and the zealots of fertility control, who argued that economic development in poor countries was being smothered by exploding population growth which, therefore, should be the primary target of the international community's development program.

The first international political conference on world population held in Bucharest in 1974, at which 138 countries participated, was, therefore, distinguished by being a nonmeeting of minds. The demographers who had ranged themselves alongside the family planners and the economists on the national delegations found that they had no common language in which to communicate with each other. The pivotal point of the occasion was established when John Rockefeller III, one of the patron saints of the family planners, told the nongovernmental forum, the people's tribune, which was meeting in parallel but some distance away:

I have changed my mind as I, like many others, dedicated to the population field, have learned increasingly how difficult and complex it really is. For many years a sense of urgency caused me to concentrate on the family planning approach. It was generally recognized in those days that industrialization led to low birth rates, but there were few countries that had the capital and the resources to industrialize, certainly to do so quickly. Family planning seemed simpler and more direct. It would save time and be relatively low in cost. . . . I now strongly believe that the only viable course is to place population policy solidly within the context of general economic and social development in such manner that it will be accepted at the highest levels of government and adequately supported. This approach recognizes that rapid population growth is only one among many problems facing most countries, that it is a multiplier and intensifier of other problems rather than the cause of them. It recognizes that reducing population growth is not an alternative to development, but an essential part of it for most countries. And, it recognizes that motivation for family planning is best stimulated by hope that living conditions and opportunities in general will improve.

There was jubilation in the development camp and sulking in the tents of those who believed that fertility control was the key to economic development. The irritation of the family planners was intensified by a lapel button being worn by every participant at the Youth Forum: "Look after the People, and the People will look after Population."

These statements contain the pith and essence of the reality of population growth and also of the few basic principles that must underlie the strategy of empowering people if the aim is to reduce fertility voluntarily. These principles include:

1.   People will not regulate their lives unless their lives seem to them to be worth regulating. This applies equally to attitudes and behavior in family planning, environmental sanitation, personal hygiene, and all such matters involving "personal" discipline.

2.   People are unwilling to change the traditional attitudes and values embedded in their collective consciousness as long as the practices that gave rise to those inner values remain unchanged. The clearest example of this is the fertility values common to all agrarian societies which persist in the communal culture of contemporary rural societies, though they coexist with industrialized societies where fertility values have changed in a changing environment.

3.   People are resistant to hortatory messages however authoritative their source or medium, until they understand the messages and their value for themselves and their families. Vertical messages do not become an integral and pervasive part of popular knowledge, attitude, and practice until "ordinary" people accept and practice them and communicate them horizontally, by word of mouth and by action in their homes and work.

For instance, the U.S. Surgeon General's exhortations against cigarette smoking, authoritative and even frightening as they were, had very little effect on common habit patterns until people recognized its danger for themselves and spread the word among themselves so effectively that public officials and commercial managers began to take action on their part to respond to the popular outcry.

For instance, the most sophisticated and persistent advertising by the infant formula industry failed to change the traditional breast feeding practice of rural women in the developing world. Some 98 percent continue to breast-feed their babies. The erosion of the practice has taken place in the cities and in the suburban "gray" areas where women who have daily work outside their homes and have no crèche facilities at the workplace and no time off after a child is born are impelled to resort to some sort of artificial feeding to be done by older children or neighbors. The dangers from infected bottles and teats and dilution of formula arise in these areas.

An example from government experience illustrates the principle briefly and clearly. A king may mint a coin with the authority of his image and royal motto. It may even have some inherent value from the metal used. It will be legal tender, but it will not become currency unless the people have uses for it and pass it from hand to hand.

4.   People should not be regarded as passive, inarticulate, rather mindless beings waiting with their hands outstretched for the favors of development to fall from above. They must be empowered to understand through credible, relevant, understandable knowledge so that they can become principal actors in the daily drama of their own lives, rather than passive recipients. The familiar "supply" approach to development—whether it involves population, environment, health, education, agriculture, or other fields of economic development—has been, and is likely to be, extremely costly in money, time, and effort except in centrally managed regimes where the writ of the rulers runs down to the smallest hamlet and no dissidence is tolerated. Since the human cost of this approach

is high, it is necessary to take a different approach—UNICEF calls it the "demand approach"—to bring about desirable social and economic action. When people understand the value to them of a recommended course of action, a demand for responsive reciprocal action from the "supply" system is generated. When that demand meets supply, there is development.

Experience in immunization is convincing. The international community in 1974 set 1990 as the target year for universal immunization. But as recently as 1983, no more than 20 percent of the children of the developing world had been immunized against the standard set of six diseases—diphtheria, whooping cough, tetanus, measles, tuberculosis, and polio. The goal of universal immunization by 1990 seemed chimerical, another mirage in the development desert. UNICEF took the demand approach to the problem, persuading national leaders to initiate action, while an intensive program of social communication through the news media and, even more important, the nonnews media—priests from every denomination, trade unions, peoples' movements, professional bodies, teachers, and nurses—spread the word in their communities so that entire societies were mobilized to have their children immunized. The result is that many countries large and small, such as Pakistan, Nigeria, Brazil, Colombia, Turkey, and Burkina Faso, have more than doubled their coverage of immunization in two years, and Indonesia, India, China, and others with large populations are now trying to reach previously unreached areas and achieve universal immunization by 1990. That target is no longer an illusion.

The brunt of the argument is that those who aspire to be agents of change—scholars, technologists, specialists in particular areas of social development, writers, social communicators, and program managers—need to realize that we have to change our own attitudes and the values governing our thought and action before we tread like importunate angels on the lifeways of other cultures in various stages of development. True, we have been saying this for many years but, alas, the way we proceed remains much the same as before.

The population field, for instance, pioneered social marketing. The Red Triangle devised for India as a telling symbol advocating the limiting of families to two or three children was a masterpiece of Madison Avenue techniques. That message was carried on the news media, on street hoardings, on posters carried by sandwich-boys, even on elephants. But it was a vertical message which essentially tried to sell contraceptives in a sellers' market and therefore was never horizontalized and accepted. The exception was the South, where the young female population had been given accessible free education for more than two generations. In the same period, accessible free health clinics were made available, so that within every 3 or 4 km there was a school and a health facility. With education and accessible health facilities infant mortality was reduced from 184 per thousand to below 50 between 1950 and 1975. And when people recognized, after a lag in time, that they no longer needed to build insurance-size families to be certain that fate would not take all their children away, they sought family planning services and contraceptives voluntarily. A buyers' market had been generated.

The lesson is plain: The problem of excessive population growth will not be solved in the uterus, but in the human mind. This lesson is valid in every field of development. Without the willing engagement of the people, sustained social change is a Sisyphean futility.

Part II
THE BIOLOGY OF CONSERVATION

Conservation Biology

DAVID WESTERN

Conservation biology, an emerging discipline, promises to help us decide what facets of nature to preserve, how to avoid extinctions, and and how to restore ecological damage. Its promise notwithstanding, the discipline has far to go, partly because, as in any young science, the application principles are still rudimentary, and partly because the biological issues must ultimately be integrated with other conservation values, such as aesthetics, economics, and recreation. However, with conservation becoming more concerned with saving threatened species and ecosystems, conservation biology will inevitably play a larger role.

Ideally, we should eschew any intervention in natural ecosystems. But, although technical ignorance means a few moments cursing when the car breaks down, it may spell extinction or irreversible disruption when the biological systems go awry. Unavoidably, ecosystems will need to be monitored more closely and managed more intensively in the future to prevent life's nuclear-powered systems "going critical."

The inevitability of more frequent and skillful action to save wildlife calls for a specialized discipline to bridge the gap between pure science and practical management, a discipline giving us guidelines on how to tackle the overwhelming complexity of ecosystems and the unmanageable number of needy cases. We need criteria for recognizing the biological boundary limits, for identifying species or ecosystems in trouble, and for distinguishing critical ecological processes and keystone species. In medical parlance, we need to distinguish the sick from the healthy, know what treatment to prescribe, and, on the preventive front, know how to avoid breakdowns.

Conservation biology is partly a response to a biological crisis, partly a crystallization of older disciplines drawn apart by specialization and rapid advances in the biological sciences (Soulé 1986). The discipline has grown from several areas of activity: from zoos setting up small captive stocks of animals endangered or difficult to obtain, botanic gardens and agriculture departments worried about dwindling genetic resources, forestry and fisheries and wildlife services charged with deriving maximum sustained yields, conservation agencies mandated to set up and protect nature sanctuaries, and biologists awakened by the disappearance of their study species.

Conservation biology has made a promising start by alerting conservationists to problems as diverse as inbreeding depression and insularization, as subtle as the loss of genetic heterogeneity and keystone species, and by prescribing a few simple principles for preserving species and ecosystems. Finally, and perhaps most significant, the discipline conservation biology has added an evolutionary dimension to conservation, alerting us to the long-term consequences of lost diversity, whether of genes or of species. The following chapters, and Soulé's summary (chap. 32), give us a glimpse of the role conservation biology has to play in preserving the wildlife, and what it will take to realize that potential.

Broadly, the aims of conservation biology are as follows:

1.   Provide scientific conservation principles.
2.   Identify conservation problems.
3.   Establish corrective procedures.
4.   Bridge science and management by making scientists responsive to the conservation problems and managers responsive to biological issues.

This section gives a sense of the discipline, its validity, controversies, potential, and limitations. It shows the discipline at work addressing the three most pressing issues in conservation—extinctions, biological diversity, and the maintenance of ecosystem processes. We read how biologists evaluate the problems, identify the causes, and grapple with the solutions. We also learn about shortcomings in the discipline and get some pointers for its development, as outlined by Soulé (chap. 32).

EXTINCTIONS

The goals of extinction biology, summarized by Diamond (chap. 4), are unambiguously simple—to predict extinctions, explain their causes, and prevent their occurrence. Patterns of past extinction and projections of the forces causing them predict the likelihood of future losses.

Historical evidence gives us every reason to expect an escalation of extinction in the coming decades. The only doubt is its magnitude, whether we face an "extinction spasm," (Myers 1985c) or not (Simon and Wildavsky 1984), whether the outcome is avoidable, and whether it poses grave risks or will impoverish our lives.

Over 90 percent of the post-1600 extinctions of amphibians, reptiles, and birds, and nearly a third of all mammals, occurred on islands, according to Atkinson (chap. 7). Islands provide a rich prehistorical and historical record for identifying extinctions and theorizing about their causes. MacArthur and Wilson (1967) established their far-reaching biogeographical theory from a study of island faunas. In the same tradition, Olson (chap. 6) and Atkinson dispel any notion that historical island extinctions were natural. The coincidence of extinctions and human invasions gives us clear insights into the magnitude of those losses and what makes species vulnerable. Virtually all oceanic islands have lost between 30 and 50 percent of their bird species to settlers in the last few millenia.

Diamond identifies the main extinction agents, the "Evil Quartet," as overkill (which has caused most extinctions so far), habitat destruction and fragmentation (the biggest future threat), introduced species (to which the island biota are especially vulnerable), and chains of extinction (the ripple effect through the community of species disruption and extinction).

MacArthur and Wilson's island biogeographical models have been widely applied in calculating extinction probabilities for habitat islands on continental land masses, a logical enough step if the same conditions hold. Global 2000 (1980) used such assumptions rather loosely to predict that 15 to 20 percent of all species will be extinct by the year 2000. The prediction rests largely on the fate of one biome, the tropical forests, which contain 50 percent of all species. Myers (chap. 5), in restating the predictions more precisely, concludes that we do stand to lose astronomical numbers of species in the coming few decades. Here is an example of controversy in conservation biology. Strong ctiticisms of this apocalyptic scenario have been made (Simon and Wildavsky 1984). Other reservations were raised during Conservation 2100 discussions. The extinction predictions involve several steps and assumptions—for example, the application of oceanic island models of extinction to mainland habitat islands, the assumption that species are at saturation prior to insularization, and predictions about the rate of habitat loss.

A sample of the questions raised at the conference underscores the difficulties of predicting species extinctions: Will habitat islands ever be as discrete to vagile species as oceanic islands? Can we conclude that forests are supersaturated, a point that Olson raises, considering that during the Pleistocene as little as 10 percent of today's forest survived for millenia in small, isolated refugia? Certainly we can no longer assume species saturation for the megamammals, knowing the large fraction lost during the Pleistocene. Have not the more vulnerable species been exterminated,

leaving a more resilient suite? And finally, what rate of forest loss can we assume, given the range of estimates (Sedjo and Clawson 1984), and can we assume a linear extrapolation of recent trends? The answers to this final, all-important question are economic and sociological, not biological.

The very fact of a debate highlights the uncertainties over the most far-reaching of all conservation issues. The implications of an extinction spasm are also debatable, among both biologists and nonbiologists. Are we at risk ecologically or materially? Would a 90 percent loss of forest be any more risky to the developing countries than it has been to Europe and the United States? Is the loss of millions of unknown insects and plants more worrisome than the loss of a large percentage of the megavertebrates during the Pleistocene extinction spasm? Such questions reach deep within and beyond conservation biology, into the realm of human values (Ralston, chap. 22).

The issue of extinction is so profound that biologists must be explicit in methodology and must set up testable hypotheses and predictions. Conservation biology should be the science, rather than the conscience, of conservation. This is not to deny the biologist his advocacy, or his emotional voice, for which Soulé (1986) argues eloquently, but to clarify the role of conservation biology, the subject, as distinct from the subjective conservation biologist. Diamond suggests a reversal of proof burden, from biologist to developer, in scientifically little-known areas. An assumption of "extinct until proven extant" in such cases has merit in cataloguing extinctions, but does not resolve the risks associated with a proposed development program, unless we go further to presume "doomed until proven otherwise." Such a

burden of proof would be unbearable economically and unacceptable politically in
developing countries. But, should conservation biology develop species vulnerability analysis to the point of predicting
extinction probabilities in any given context, it would provide a potent tool for shifting the burden of disproof to the development agent. That challenge underscores
Diamond's opening point, that extinction
biology is about predicting and confuting
species losses by directing action to the underlying causes.

When it comes down to confuting the
predictions, we are again on firm footing:
contain the Evil Quartet. Myers, switching
from predictive scientist to remedial advocate, suggests how to avert an extinction
crisis in the tropical rain forests.

EVOLUTIONARY POTENTIAL

Extinction is the last irredeemable breakdown in a concatenated series. Enormous
crippling damage to species and ecosystems can happen long before the finale.
Woodruff (chap. 8) points out the pitfalls,
from inbreeding and outbreeding to the loss
of adapted traits and learned behavior, all
of which reduce species fitness, adaptability, and evolutionary potential.

Vrijenhoek (chap. 9) looks at the genetic
problems of defining and maintaining evolutionary adapted units in the case of the
freshwater fish. His point is troubling. If
we don't know the basic taxonomy of species, or what criteria to use in defining conservation units, we are faced with a conun-
drum: genes may not be nearly enough. If
ecological rehabilitation is the ultimate
goal, we must also know the adaptive significance of a genome and conserve it in its

evolutionary setting, or some close approximation to it. More discouragingly, must
we, in ignorance of the relationships between genetic diversity, population size,
vagility, mating systems, and other life history traits, presuming they exist, fall back
on case-specific conservation? If so, only a
handful of species can be fully conserved
and restored biologically.

As Woodruff points out, we are developing methods to avoid the case-specific approach, but in reverse, through population
vulnerability analysis (PVA) (Salwasser et
al. 1984; Gilpin and Soulé 1986), a step up
from the gross extinction predictions discussed earlier. But vulnerability predictions do not tell us how to manage a threatened species in situ.

Conservation biology is most successfully applied to the management of small captive populations. Genetic theories, pedigree analysis to determine optimal
matings, and minimal viable population
(MVP) calculations routinely guide species
management in captivity and increasingly
in the wild. Looking ahead, Woodruff suggests that genetic engineering will soon offer more invasive and rapid methods of
eliminating deleterious genes and reconstituting diversity.

For wild populations, Eisenberg and
Harris (chap. 10) identify vulnerable
taxa—a level intermediate between the
gross numbers and PVA approach—by
looking at the sensitivity of life history
traits. Big intelligent mammals and top carnivores are likely to be eliminated first and
should be given conservation priority
since, in conserving them, we protect myriad species with smaller home ranges, higher densities, and greater resilience. For-
tuitously, these are the very species
conservationists regard as "flagships," the

charismatic drawing cards that elicit sympathy, raise funds, and help preserve large tracts of contested land.

Woodruff, looking into the twenty-first century, asks whether evolution will ever be over. His answer is a resounding no. Species may disappear, numbers may diminish, the conditions may change, but these same forces will trigger a new round of selection and evolution, albeit different from the past. What will those selective pressures be?

COMMUNITIES AND ECOSYSTEMS

The loss of a species (and even change in its relative abundance, ecology, or behavior) can have far-reaching implications for communities and ecosystems, depending on its ecological importance. That is the essence of the chapters by McNaughton (chap. 11) and Walker (chap. 12). Repercussions from single events can create disturbance cascades, as McNaughton shows in the case of rinderpest in the Serengeti and Walker in the case of barrier reef eruptions of starfish. Systems are, in other words, integrated wholes, as McNaughton illustrates in the improved efficiency with which plants use nitrogen and water when grazed. Here we find a common message in both chapters.

Confusion and disagreement arise most often over definitions and theories, and what they mean for conservation. McNaughton makes that point clear with reference to theories of ecosystem organization. If the reductionist theory of ecosystems, which holds that the properties at any level are derived from the summed properties of lower levels, is correct, then saving species is adequate. If the holistic

theory, which holds that each level has non-inclusive, unique properties, is correct, then gene pool preservation is, in McNaughton's view, a last-gasp effort which may save the fragments but not the organization. This Humpty Dumpty phenomenon is also alluded to by Woodruff.

Walker tries to unravel some definitional and theoretical confusion over ecosystem diversity and stability, which are both important conservation objectives and often, in practice, erroneously assumed to be congruent. Ecosystems have different dynamics, depending on subsystem interactions and external environmental forces, as Walker shows in three case studies—a weakly interactive, open system of African large ungulates driven by external episodic events; a strongly interactive and internally regulated community of kangaroos; and the Australian barrier reef invaded by crown-of-thorns starfish, a system whose dynamics are unresolved.

Theoretical weakness and disagreements over how ecosystems function, and inherent differences in how they do so, led to opposing and confusing messages for the conservation managers in later discussions (Lewin 1986). In practical terms, McNaughton advocates a laissez-faire approach to obviate the unforeseen repercussions of managing ecosystems. Walker questions whether all species are equally vital or desirable, whether we should worry about thousands of unnamed insects rather than the few charismatic large ungulates. The disagreement is profound, yet rests as much on philosophical interpretation as it does on scientific evidence.

A measure of agreement does, however, emerge. Diversity (species richness and equitability) and persistence of species, rather than constancy in composition, should be the twin objectives, which also neatly reconcile species and ecosystem conservation. Constancy, the unchanging state of ecosystems that managers so often pursue, is a will-o'-the-wisp, and usually counterproductive. On the contrary, we must maintain the instability which permits many species to coexist in complex ecosystems. The common denominator, and a useful rule of thumb for the manager, is: Maintain the internal processes and external agencies responsible for diversity and persistence; intervene to activate or simulate those forces only when the system would otherwise spiral beyond its normal boundary limits, or, at the species level, only when an ecologically critical or socially valuable organism is endangered. Both McNaughton and Walker

also make a valuable start in codifying critical and vulnerable processes.

The logic of saving species, communities, and ecosystems by maintaining the regime of processes on which they depend comes through clearly in both McNaughton's and Walker's chapters. Time is so short, McNaughton cautions, that we must identify and protect earth's major ecosystems now, rather than try to codify life's diversity, which Wilson (chap. 1) considers the first step. Add to that Eisenberg and Harris's justification for flagship species and Wilson's and Myers's concerns about the tropical forests, and some simple convincing guidelines do emerge. Most of them support the priorities common to many conservation organizations.

4

Overview of Recent Extinctions

JARED DIAMOND

This section of the book begins appropriately with a discussion of extinction, for extinctions are the events that the conservation movement aims to prevent. To have some estimate of the magnitude of the task ahead, we need to predict roughly how many extinctions are to be expected in the near future, where those extinctions are most likely to occur, and what will be their likely causes. As a basis for prediction, we can look at the numbers, locations, and causes of extinctions in the recent past and extrapolate the probable outcome if those factors continue to operate, taking into account probable changes in the intensity of those factors.

Our current concern with extinction is sometimes "pooh-poohed" by nonbiologists with the one-liner, "Extinction is the natural fate of all species." A moment's reflection shows that, even qualitatively, this claim is wrong: The fact that tens of millions of species exist today proves that the natural fate of many past species has been to evolve into new species (see Eisenberg and Harris, chap. 10). The other problem with this claim is quantitative: the current rate of extinction is far higher than the natural or background rate, because of effects of humans. Almost all well-documented recent extinctions are due in one way or another to humans. The reasons why the rate of extinction is accelerating are thus also obvious: There are more people now alive than ever before, and they have more potent tools of extermination than ever before, including not only guns but also pollutants and efficient means of destroying habitats. Even for birds, the group of organisms among which an extinction is least likely to pass unnoticed, the

rate of *documented* extinctions is close to overtaking the rate of discovery of previously unknown species (Diamond 1985a).

Among other groups of organisms, species are often barely discovered before being exterminated. For example, Gentry (1987) discovered, confined to one forested ridge in Ecuador, numerous plant species just before those species were exterminated by logging of the ridge. The insects of that ridge, and the plants of innumerable other logged ridges, were never described before being exterminated.

This chapter will briefly summarize the history of recent extinctions and then the causes of those extinctions. I shall conclude by discussing the type of proof required to document an extinction.

HISTORY OF RECENT EXTINCTIONS

It is often difficult to establish the causes of extinctions going on today. Not surprisingly, it becomes increasingly difficult to identify causes of extinctions as we go back further into the past (Martin and Klein 1984).

In the paleontological record, the first sets of extinctions for which human causation has been suggested are those associated with our colonization of previously unoccupied continents. Humans originated in Africa and spread to Europe and Asia around one million years ago. We have no clear evidence of man-related extinctions on these continents before the late Pleistocene, and there may not have been any: Human technology was simple and evolved so slowly that animals had time to evolve behavioral defenses. The situation may have been different when Australia was first reached by humans, already *Homo sapiens,* around 50,000 years ago. In the following millennia, Australia lost practically all its species of very large mammals (all except some kangaroos), its giant snakes and reptiles, and half of its large flightless birds. Whether humans caused these extinctions by hunting or fire is still quite unclear, partly because the exact timing of the extinctions in relation to the time of arrival of humans is unclear (Martin 1984).

A more incriminating, though still debated, case can be made for the impact of humans while colonizing North and South America, probably around 11,000 years ago. North America promptly proceeded to lose 73 percent of its genera of large mammals, South America 80 percent. One indication that humans had something to do with the extinctions comes from radiocarbon dating: Giant ground sloths and mountain goats in the Grand Canyon both went extinct 11,100 years ago, the time (within the accuracy of dating methods [a couple of centuries]) that human hunters arrived (Mead et al. 1986). Another, more direct type of evidence is the finding of fossil mammal skeletons with evidence of hunting or butchering by humans, such as the Escapule mammoth skeleton that has eight stone spearpoints among its ribs (Hemmings and Haynes 1969). However, unfortunately for modern archaeologists, the arrival of the Clovis hunting culture, which probably represents the first humans in the New World, coincides with the climatic upheavals at the end of the Pleistocene, and it is not certain that Clovis hunters really were the first humans in the New World. Thus, paleontologists and archaeologists continue to debate whether the extinctions of most of the New World's large mammals at the end of the Pleistocene were due to humans or to climatic changes.

The paleontological record provides more unequivocal evidence of prehistoric human causation of extinctions when we turn to man's colonization of oceanic islands within the past few thousand years. When the Polynesians reached New Zealand about 1200 years ago, all species of the giant flightless moas plus several dozen other bird species became extinct during the following centuries. Man the Exterminator left his calling card at numerous roasting pits excavated by archaeologists, which contain the remains of thousands of moas. As Olson summarizes (chap. 6), similar extinction spasms accompanied the arrival of humans at all other Polynesian islands investigated archaeologically, including Hawaii, Tonga, the Marquesas, Societies, Cooks, and Chathams, between 1500 and 3000 years ago. When Indonesians colonized Madagascar 1500 years ago, the casualties again included all species of large animals: the dozen largest species of the primate group called lemurs (including one of gorilla size), a hippopotamus, the giant flightless elephant birds, and giant land tortoises (Dewar 1984). Candidates for earlier extinction waves on islands are many mammal species (including dwarf elephant, hippopotamus, and deer) that disappeared from Mediterranean islands in the early Holocene, around the time that these islands were reached by humans, but details and causes remain uncertain (Martin 1984).

In the case of modern extinctions, there is certainly no doubt that the extinctions and human presence were contemporaneous. The species and subspecies of birds that have gone extinct since 1600 number 171, of which 155 are island forms (especially from Hawaii, New Zealand, the Mascarenes, and West Indies) that evolved in the absence of humans. Ten more of the avian extinctions occurred on the "New World" continents of North and South America, which were also free of humans until relatively recently. Among the "Old World" continents, Europe and Africa have suffered no extinctions, Asia only eight. (These statistics and the following data for mammals are from Table 38.4 of Diamond 1984a.) As for mammals, there have been 115 extinctions of species and subspecies since 1600, of which twenty-two have been on the West Indies alone, nineteen on other islands, and forty-four on the "newly settled" continents of Australia and North America. Of the twenty-nine recent mammalian extinctions in Africa, Asia, and Europe, twenty-six have involved large mammals, most of them victims of overhunting. Thus, most mammalian and avian extinctions during the last four centuries have involved populations newly exposed to humans or at least to Europeans, the humans with the most advanced arsenal of methods for exterminating. Let us now survey this arsenal.

CAUSES OF RECENT EXTINCTIONS

The arsenal of extermination has involved at least four sets of mechanisms: overkill, habitat destruction and fragmentation, impacts of introduced species, and secondary extinctions. Let us briefly consider each of these mechanisms—the "Evil Quartet"—and discuss how their importance has been changing with time (Diamond 1984a).

Overkill

Before the advent of agriculture, overkill—the hunting of animals at rates faster than they could reproduce themselves—was probably the main mechanism by which humans exterminated animals. It is suspicious that the great majority of the late-Pleistocene mammalian extinctions of North America, South America, and Australia involved large mammals, the preferred targets of human hunters. Overkill has also befallen plant species, such as the wine palm and various sandalwoods, logged for their sap or wood. Because animals exposed for thousands of years to a predator evolve behavioral means to minimize the risk of predation, victims of overkill tend to be naïve animals without any prior exposure to humans, such as the many birds and mammals exterminated on oceanic islands, or else animals previously exposed to some humans but now suddenly exposed to newly arrived humans with much more efficient hunting technology, such as the animals of North and South America and Australia that had survived Amerindians or native Australians but succumbed to Europeans. Compared to other mechanisms of extermination, overkill is now probably less important than formerly, simply because most of the preferred or susceptible victims have already been eliminated. However, there remain plenty of likely candidates for extermination by overkill in the near future, such as rhinoceroses, elephants, and whales.

Habitat Destruction and Fragmentation

Especially since the advent of agriculture, humans have been destroying natural habitats by clearing them for agriculture as well as for timber or domestic livestock. Other modes of habitat destruction have involved fire, draining of

wetlands, and destruction of vegetation by introduced grazing and browsing animals, especially goats and rabbits. Habitat destruction has accounted for about half of recent bird extinctions on the continents, and for most plant extinctions.

A habitat does not have to be completely destroyed to exterminate many species restricted to that habitat. In the past fifteen years there has been increasing appreciation of the effects of habitat fragmentation, the carving up of a former large expanse of habitat into smaller fragments separated from each other by alien habitats. If one looks at maps of the distribution of forest for almost any region of the world at various times during recent centuries, it is possible to follow how large tracts have been progressively subdivided into ever smaller fragments. Many species have difficulty dispersing across alien habitats. Since small habitat fragments contain fewer plant or animal individuals than do larger tracts, and since the risk of extinction of a population increases with decreasing population size, species with limited powers of dispersal are more likely to go extinct in ten small habitat fragments than in a single habitat tract of the same total area. Lovejoy et al. (1984), for example, has discussed experimental demonstration of the effects of forest fragmentation in the Brazilian Amazon. Among the many other well-documented examples, forest fragmentation eliminated eight of the twenty-three forest bird species of New Zealand's Banks Peninsula during the past century (Diamond 1984b) and twenty-one of the sixty-two bird species in a woodland on the island of Java during the past fifty years (Diamond et al. 1987).

Until recently, species losses due to habitat destruction or fragmentation have not been inordinate, because the destroyed or fragmented habitats have been those harboring modest numbers of species, such as various habitats on oceanic islands or else in temperate latitudes of the continents. Now, however, habitat destruction is extending to the most species-rich habitat on earth, the continental tropical rain forests, most of which will disappear at the present rate of destruction by the middle of the next century (Myers, chap. 5). That is why habitat destruction and fragmentation are rapidly taking the lead as causes of extinction.

Impact of Introduced Species

A third cause of man-related extinctions besides overkill and habitat destruction has been mediated by alien species that humans intentionally or unintentionally introduced to new environments and that proceeded to exterminate native species there. Almost all examples involve naïve victims: that is, native species with no prior experience of the introduced species in question or of other species functionally equivalent to the introduced species. I have already mentioned the devastation that introduced goats, rabbits, and other herbivores have wrought on island plants. This has occurred because most island plants evolved in the absence of mammalian grazers and browsers and lack the adaptations, such as thorns, spines, and unpalatable chemicals, evolved by continental plants long exposed to mammalian herbivores as antiherbivore protective devices. Similar considerations apply to animal victims (Atkinson, chap. 7). Introduced predators have accounted for about half of island bird extinctions. Rats and cats are the most notorious killers, and island birds the most notorious victims, in this regard. However, introduced birds themselves have been the exterminating agent in other cases, and in at least one case an introduced snake has been exterminating island birds (the native forest birds of Guam [Savidge 1984]). Introduced fish species have also had devastating effects on native fish in numerous lakes and rivers, partly by preying on native fish species, partly by competing with them. While herbivory and predation have been the most frequently documented mechanisms by which introduced species have exterminated native species, introduced diseases have also been important (think of rinderpest introduced from Asia to Africa, chestnut blight introduced from Europe to North America, avian malaria introduced from various sources to Hawaii, and smallpox introduced by Europeans to many other human populations). Competition between introduced and native species has also played a role in decline and extinction of natives.

As in the case of overkill, one might suspect that impacts of introduced species will decline as a means of extermination, on the grounds that most of the likely victims might be supposed to have already been exterminated. However, it may well be that the worst is yet to come. What may ultimately prove to be the largest number of exterminations chalked up by an introduced species at a single site is now underway in East Africa in Lake Victoria, whose cichlid fishes constitute one of the most diverse fish radiations in any lake on earth, and where an introduced predatory fish, the Nile perch (*Lates niloticus*), has already exterminated thirty-five native fish species and may well exterminate hundreds of others. Among the worst scenarios for native terrestrial species would be the introduction of monkeys from other Indonesian islands to New Guinea, one of the world's biological treasure-houses, or the arrival of Eurasian rats at oceanic islands still lacking them, such as Rennell Island.

Chains of Extinction

Species interact with each other, whether as predators, mutualists, competitors, herbivores, parasites, or pathogens. Thus, a change in abundance of one species is likely to lead to changes in abundance of other species (Pimm 1979; Diamond 1984a; Diamond and Case 1986a). Whenever one species is exterminated, its disappearance may lead to increases in abundance of other species (e.g., of its direct competitors and prey) and to decreases in abundance of other species (e.g., its predators, mutualists, and competitors of its competitors). For example, extinctions of Hawaiian honeycreepers led to the extinction or near-extinction of endemic Hawaiian plants of the genus *Hibiscadelphus*, which depended on the honeycreepers for pollination, while the decline and reproductive failure of the tree *Calvaria major* on Mauritius has been attributed to extinction of the dodo, which may have been its main seed dispersal agent. An example of the extermination of top predators leading to extermination of the prey of their prey has been happening on Panama's Barro Colorado Island, where the elimination of jaguars, pumas, and harpy eagles caused a population explosion of their prey such as monkeys and coatimundis, which in turn proceeded to exterminate several species of ground-nesting birds. An example involving humans as top predator illustrates how elimination of prey species by one predator may endanger a competing predator: human overfishing of the North Sea led to breeding failure in puffins dependent on the fish species sought by fishermen.

WHERE DOES THE BURDEN OF PROOF LIE IN DOCUMENTING EXTINCTIONS?

The various Red Data Books published by organizations such as the International Union for Conservation of Nature and Natural Resources or the International Council for Bird Preservation attempt to list all species in some taxon group known to be extinct or threatened. According to these tabulations, threatened species constitute only a small minority of the world's species: for example, 437 threatened birds out of more than 8,000 bird species worldwide (King 1981). Furthermore, documenting degree of threat is often difficult, and economists and others who wish to downplay the risk of an extinction crisis can easily dispute this case or that case, casting doubt even on the claim that 5 percent of the world's birds are threatened.

The implicit assumption of the Red Data Books and of governmental lists of threatened taxa is that positive evidence is required to support a claim that some taxon is threatened or extinct. That is, species are to be considered extant until proven extinct.

This assumption is the appropriate one for well-studied, easily observed taxa such as birds, in areas with many observers, such as Europe and the United States. Virtually every extant North American or European bird species is observed every year, and if it is not observed for a few years (e.g., ivory-billed woodpecker, Bachman's warbler), it immediately becomes a subject of intensive searches and debate. However, this assumption is clearly inappropriate for little-studied taxa, or for regions of the world with few trained field biologists (e.g., most of the tropics, where most of the world's species live). Large numbers of bird and mammal species were described in the nineteenth or early-twentieth century in remote areas of South America, Africa, or the tropical Pacific and have never been observed again since their description. In some cases we have strong reason to doubt that they exist, since their habitat has been totally destroyed, and in other cases we have no positive reason to believe that they still do exist. I cannot think of a case where someone has attempted to summarize how many of the species ever described in some rich tropical fauna or flora have actually been observed in recent decades. A recent study of Celebes and nearby islands made a specific search for, and failed to encounter, three fish species and one bird species belonging to endemic genera, but none of these species is listed in Red Data Books (Whitten et al. 1987). Bird surveys in the Solomon Islands by myself and others in recent decades failed to encounter several species of ducks and ground-nesting birds that were formerly described as common and that are now evidently extinct or near extinction, yet none of these taxa is mentioned in Red Data Books (Diamond 1987).

For most species of the tropics or other remote regions—that is, for most of the world's species—a more appropriate assumption would be "extinct unless proven extant." We biologists should not bear the burden of proof to convince economists advocating unlimited human population growth that the extinction crisis is real. Instead, it should be left to those economists to fund research in the jungles that would positively support their implausible claim of a healthy biological world.

5

A Major Extinction Spasm: Predictable and Inevitable?

NORMAN MYERS

We may well be about to witness a major extinction spasm. In many respects indeed, we are already into the opening phase of such an episode—that is, a mass extinction, in the sense of a sudden and pronounced decline worldwide in the abundance and diversity of ecologically disparate groups of organisms.

The ''background'' rate of extinction during the past 600 million years, viz., during the period of major life, has averaged, roughly speaking, one species every year or a little longer (Raup and Sepkowski 1982). Today the rate is surely hundreds of times higher, possibly thousands of times higher (Ehrlich and Ehrlich 1981; Myers 1987b; Raven 1985; Soulé 1986; Wilson 1987). Moreover, whereas past extinctions have occurred by virtue of natural processes, today the virtually exclusive cause is man, who eliminates entire habitats and complete communities of species in supershort order.

To gain some insight into the situation, let us take a lengthy look at tropical forests. These forests cover only 6% of the earth's land surface, yet they are estimated to contain at least 50% of all species (conceivably a much higher proportion [Erwin 1987]). Equally important, they are being depleted faster than any other major ecological zone. True, several other zones, notably coral reefs and wetlands, are being depleted even faster than tropical forests. But they do not harbor nearly so many species: the Caribbean is reputed to contain no more than 50,000 coral reef species, by comparison with perhaps 20,000 endemic tropical forest species in Costa Rica alone. So the outright destruction of coral reefs and wetlands would not contribute nearly so much to a mass extinction episode as would the elimination of tropical forests in just Africa, let alone in Asia, or in the richest region of all, Latin America.

TROPICAL FORESTS

There is general agreement that remaining tropical forests cover rather less than 3.6 million square miles, out of 6 million or so that may once have existed (according to bioclimatic data). There is also general agreement that between 30,000 and 37,000 square miles are eliminated outright each year, and that at least another 40,000 square miles are grossly disrupted each year (FAO and UNEP 1982; Hadley and Lanly 1983; Melillo et al. 1985; Molofsky et al. 1986; Myers 1980, 1984b). (These figures for deforestation rates derive from a database of the late 1970s; the rates have increased somewhat since then.) This means, roughly speaking, that 1% of the biome is being deforested each year and rather more than another 1% is being significantly degraded.

Tropical deforestation is by no means an even process. Some areas are being affected more than others. By the end of the century or shortly thereafter, there could be little left of the biome in primary status, with a full complement of species, outside of two large remnant blocs, one in the Zaire basin and the other in the western half of Brazilian Amazonia, plus a smaller bloc in New Guinea. Although these three relict sectors of the biome may well endure for a few more decades, they are not likely to last beyond the middle of the next century, if only because of sheer expansion in numbers of small-scale cultivators. As for the year 2100, it is difficult to see that much tropical forest will survive at all (except for isolated relicts and degraded fragments), if only because of population buildup and pervasive poverty. (For additional detailed treatment of these pressures on wildland environments, see Myers 1986.) This dismal scenario supposes, of course, that we shall not do a much better job on conservation of tropical forests; and fortunately, there is a rapidly growing awareness of the plight of tropical forests, of the problems that ensue in the wake of deforestation, and of the opportunities that exist to undertake expansive safeguard measures forthwith.

Population growth exerts its greatest impact on tropical areas in the form of communities of small-scale cultivators. Growth in the numbers of these communities occurs mainly through immigration rather than natural increase, i.e., through the phenomenon of the shifted cultivator. In the Philippines, numbers of slash-and-burn cultivators have been increasing during the past decade at rates that sometimes reach 10% per year (Cruz 1986). As a measure of how ultrarapid growth rates already affect tropical forests, consider the situation in Rondonia, a state in the southern sector of Brazilian Amazonia (Fearnside 1986). Between 1975 and 1986, the population grew from 111,000 to well over one million, i.e., a tenfold increase in little over ten years. In 1975, almost 500 square miles of forest were cleared. By 1982, this amount had grown to more than 4,000 square miles, and by late 1985 to almost 7,000 square miles.

It is this broad-scale clearing and degradation of forest habitats that is far and away the main cause of species extinctions, whether in the forests themselves or on a global scale. Regrettably we have no way of knowing the actual current rate of extinction in tropical forests, nor can we even make an accurate estimate. But we can make substantive assessments by looking at species numbers before deforestation and then applying the analytical techniques of island biogeography. So to help us gain an insight into the

scope and scale of present extinctions, let us briefly consider three particular areas, viz., the forested tracts of western Ecuador, Atlantic Coast Brazil, and Madagascar.

Each of these areas features, or rather featured, exceptional concentrations of species, with high levels of endemism. Western Ecuador is reputed to have once contained between 8,000 and 10,000 plant species, with an endemism rate somewhare between 40 and 60% (Gentry 1986). If we suppose, as we reasonably can by drawing on detailed inventories in sample plots, that there are between ten and thirty animal species for every plant species, the species complement in western Ecuador must have amounted to about 200,000 in all. Since 1960, at least 95% of the forest cover has been destroyed, to make way for banana and oil palm plantations, oil exploiters, and human settlements of various sorts. According to the theory of island biography, we can realistically reckon that when a habitat has lost 90% of its extent, it has lost half its species. Precisely how many species have actually disappeared, or are on the point of extinction, in western Ecuador is impossible to say. But ultimate accuracy is surely irrelevant, insofar as the number must total tens of thousands at least, conceivably 50,000—all eliminated in just twenty-five years.

Similar baseline figures for species totals and endemism levels, and a similar story of forest depletion (albeit for different reasons, and over a longer period), apply to the Atlantic Coast forest of Brazil, where the original 400,000 square miles of forest cover has been reduced to less than 20,000 square miles (Mori et al. 1981). Parallel data apply also to Madagascar, except that the endemism levels are rather higher (Pollock 1986; Rauh 1979).

So in these three tropical forest areas alone, with their roughly 600,000 species, the recent past must have witnessed a sizable fallout of species. Some may not have disappeared as yet, owing to the time lag in "equilibriation" or delayed fallout effects. But whereas the ultimate total of extinctions in these areas, in the wake of deforestation to date, will eventually amount in all probability to some 150,000 species (as an approximate estimate), we may realistically assume that already half, or some 75,000 species, could have been eliminated.

Deforestation in Brazil's Atlantic Coast forest and Madagascar has been going on for several centuries, but the main damage has been done during this century, especially since 1950, that is, since the spread of broad-scale industrialization and plantation agriculture in Brazil, and since the onset of rapid population growth among forestland-farmer communities in Madagascar. This means that a total of at least 50,000 species (perhaps many more) have been eliminated in these three areas alone during the course of the last 35 years. This works out to a crude average of almost 1500 per year—a figure that throws light on the independent assessment of Wilson (1987), who postulates a current extinction rate in all tropical forests of perhaps 10,000 species per year.

Of course many reservations attend these calculations. More species than postulated may still be "hanging on" before the relaxation effect of "islandizing" processes overtakes them. Conversely more species will presumably have been accounted for during the later stages of the thirty-five-year period than during the opening stage, that is, as human pressures have grown more intense. Whatever the details of the outcome, we can judiciously utilize the figures and conclusions to form a "working appraisal" of how far an extinction spasm is already underway.

Of course, and as noted, numerous extinctions are surely occuring in other species-rich areas such as coral reefs and wetlands, and we must take them into account insofar as the extinction spasm is truly global. But for purposes of this limited-scope review, let us concentrate on the main locus of current extinctions, tropical forests.

EXTINCTION RATES: THE FUTURE

As for the future, the outlook seems all the more adverse, though its detailed dimensions are even less clear than those of the present. Let us look again at tropical forests. We have seen what is happening to three critical areas. We can identify many other sectors of the biome that feature exceptional concentrations of species with exceptional levels of endemism, and that face exceptional threat of depletion, whether quantitative or qualitative. They include the Mosquitia Forest of Nicaragua; the Choco Forest of Colombia; the Napo center of diversity in Peruvian Amazonia, plus seven similar centers

(out of more than twenty centers of diversity in Amazonia) that lie around the periphery of the basin and hence are unusually threatened by settlement programs and various other forms of development; the Tai Forest of Ivory Coast; the montane forests of East Africa; the relict wet forest of Sri Lanka; the monsoon forests of the Himalayan foothills; northwestern Borneo; several localities of the Philippines; and a number of islands of the South Pacific (New Caledonia, for instance, with 6,530 square miles, which is smaller than New Jersey, contains 3,000 plant species, 80% of them endemic).

These twenty sectors of the tropical forest biome amount to roughly 400,000 square miles (two and a half times the size of California), or slightly more than one-tenth of remaining undisturbed forests. So far as we can best judge from their documented numbers of plant species, and by making substantiated assumptions about the numbers of associated animal species, we can reckon that these twenty areas harbor at least one million species of plants and animals combined—and in many of the areas, there is marked endemism. If present land use patterns and exploitation trends persist (they show every sign of accelerating), there will be little left of these forest tracts, except in the form of degraded remnants, by the end of this century or shortly thereafter. Thus forest depletion in these areas alone could well eliminate large numbers of species, surely hundreds of thousands, within the next twenty-five years or so.

Looking at the situation another way, we can estimate, on the basis of what we know about plant numbers and distribution, together with what we can surmise about their associated animal communities, that almost 20% of all species occur in forests of Latin America outside of Amazonia, and another 20% in forests of Asia and Africa outside of the Zaire basin (Raven 1985); that is, some one million species altogether, even if we reckon the planetary total at a minimum five million. All of the primary forests in which these species occur may well disappear by the end of this century or early in the next. If only half of the species in these forests disappear, this will amount to several hundred thousand species.

What about the prognosis for the longer-term future, to the effect that eventually we could lose at least one-quarter, possibly one-third and conceivably a still larger share, of all extant species? Let us take a quick look at the case of Amazonia (Simberloff 1986a). If deforestation continues at present rates until the year 2000, but then comes to a complete halt, we should anticipate a loss of about 15% of plant species and a similar share of animal species. Were Amazonia's forest cover to be ultimately reduced to those areas now set aside as parks and reserves, we should anticipate that 66% of plant species will eventually disappear, together with almost 69% of bird species, and similar proportions of all other major categories of species.

Of course, we may learn how to manipulate habitats to enhance survival prospects. We may learn how to propagate threatened species in captivity. We may be able to apply other emergent conservation techniques, all of which could help to relieve the adverse repercussions of broad-scale deforestation. But in the main, the damage will have been done. A major extinction spasm in Amazonia is entirely possible, indeed plausible, if not probable.

SYNERGISMS

Let us now turn to a further dimension of the extinction prospect, one that is almost entirely uninvestigated and yet could eventually prove to be the biggest factor of all. Actually it is something of a composite factor: the phenomenon of synergisms.

The main mechanisms of extinction—loss of habitat, above all, but also broad-scale pollution, introduction of predators/competitors/diseases, and overexploitation—tend to be studied in isolation from one another. We know much less, and we understand less still, about the dynamic interplay between the discrete mechanisms. When we consider the probable outcome of several mechanisms operating at once, we can reasonably surmise that many of their effects will amplify one another through synergistic interactions. This is mainly because, for instance, a biota's tolerance of one stress tends to be lower when other stresses are in operation. In turn, this means that the phenomenon of ecological synergism could well lead to an extinction episode with telescoped time frame, especially in the early phase, and in the longer term, to an extinction episode of even greater scale than is usually anticipated.

With respect again to tropical forests, what

are some synergistic factors at issue? The majority of species in tropical forests tend to be characterized by traits that leave them singularly susceptible to endangerment and extinction. Most exist at low densities (Gentry 1986; Gilbert 1980; Janzen 1975). Many are endemic (Gentry 1986; Janzen 1983; Terborgh and Winter 1983). Probably more important than both these traits, many species feature extremely narrow ecological specializations. For instance, abundant species of bees, wasps, moths, bats, and hummingbirds are obligate pollinators of their food-source plant species; much the same applies to frugivores and other mobile-link animals that interact with keystone-mutualist plants (Gilbert 1980; Gilbert and Raven 1975; Janzen 1975; Terborgh 1986). If, as a result of human disturbance of forest ecosystems, a mobile-link or a keystone-mutualist species is eliminated, the loss can readily lead to the loss of several other species. In certain circumstances, these additional losses can trigger a cascade of linked extinctions. There is a sizable literature (e.g., Dressler 1982; Howe 1982; Janzen 1979; Start and Marshall 1976; Terborgh 1986) with respect to certain trees, euglossine bees, wasps, bats, and other key species that could be severely reduced in numbers, if not eliminated outright (at the local level, at least), through logging alone, and whose demise could trigger extensive repercussions of biotic impoverishment.

These characteristics of tropical forest species predispose them to summary extinction even under normal circumstances. Under the impact of human intrusion, the characteristics become all the more pertinent. When a tract of tropical forest is reduced to fragments of isolated habitat, the process will generally lead to the extinction of more species by proportion to the original stock of species than would occur through the same process in a tract of temperate-zone forest (Burgess and Sharpe 1981; Lovejoy et al. 1984; Myers 1984b).

The biggest synergism of all, however, will surely lie with climatic change. In Amazonia, for instance, it is becoming apparent that if as much as half of the forest were to be safeguarded in some way or another (through, for example, multiple-use conservation units as well as protected areas), but the other half were to be "developed out of existence," there could soon be at work a hydrological feedback mechanism that would allow a good part of Amazonia's moisture to be lost to the ecosystem (Salati and Vose 1984). The outcome for the remaining forest would probably be a steady desiccatory process, until the moist forest became more like a dry forest, even a woodland—with all that would mean for the species communities that are adapted to moist-forest habitats. Even with a set of forest safeguards of exemplary type and scope, Amazonia's biotas would be more threatened than ever.

Still more widespread climatic changes, with yet more marked impact, are likely to emerge within the foreseeable future. By the first quarter of the next century, we may well be experiencing the climatic dislocations of a planetary warming, stemming from buildup of carbon dioxide and other "greenhouse gases" in the global atmosphere (Bolin 1986; U.S. Department of Energy 1985). The consequences for protected areas will be pervasive and profound. The present network of protected areas, grossly inadequate as it is, has been established in accord with present-day needs. Yet its ultimate viability will be severely threatened as vegetation zones, in the wake of a greenhouse effect, start to "migrate" away from the equator, with all manner of disruptive repercussions for natural environments (Peters and Darling 1984).

In addition, possible climatic dislocations are arising from the albedo effect, or increased "shininess" of the earth's surface in the wake of broad-scale deforestation. So far as climatologists can tell (Dickenson 1982; Henderson-Sellers and Gornitz 1984; Pinker et al. 1980), a not unlikely outcome is a decrease in rainfall in the equatorial zone.

Synergistic Consequences in Amazonia

Let us now look at the possible impact of synergisms on a single tropical forest region, Amazonia. Let us remind ourselves of the pioneering and apocalyptic calculations of Simberloff (1986a)—and note that he does not take account, beyond passing mention, of several (not all) of the additional factors just described. This means that a main part of the overall extinction episode in Amazonia could occur sooner than expected, perhaps much sooner. For instance, the "domino effect" of linked extinctions could start to exert its impact through (mere) disrup-

tion of forest ecosystems, that is, well before outright forest clearing occurs. Related to this is the factor of differentiated extinctions as concerns specialist species, such as predators and parasites. The demise of these specialists will remove some natural-control limitations of many prey and host species, including generalist species. These generalist species may then proliferate in numbers until they exercise destabilizing effects on other species in their ecosystems, thus leaving some of them less able to resist other threats.

Next, the question of centers of endemism. At least twenty-six of these centers have been identified in South America, more than twenty in Amazonia (Prance 1982). Several of the localities in question have been designated by governments of the region (for reasons that have nothing to do with their endemism values) as "development nodes." As we have seen in the Brazilian state of Rondonia, with one such center (Brown 1982; Prance 1982), the rate of deforestation is exceptionally high due to an ultra-rapid influx of settlers.

Third, the question of climatic dislocations could prove to be the most serious factor of all. Of the centers of endemism in Amazonia, nine are located in the southern border zone. That is, they lie in the region's fringe area that may well prove most susceptible to vegetation changes in the wake of climatic shifts, whether caused by disruptions to the hydrological cycle, by the greenhouse effect, or by albedo changes. Any of these climatic dislocations could start to make itself felt shortly after the turn of the century, and all could be inducing deep-seated modifications in forest ecosystems within another thirty years. More significant still for near-term considerations, even a marginal change could sorely exacerbate the survival outlook of species whose salient attributes include rarity and narrow ecological specializations.

In summary, these various mechanisms and factors will not only compound the impacts of each other, thus amplifying their collective and cumulative impact overall. They will also intensify the effects of the habitat loss repercussions as described by Simberloff. In other words, the total outcome could be much more pronounced, and occur far more rapidly, than postulated by Simberloff through his island biography model.

There is no need to comment on the urgent implications of all this for conservation policy and on-ground planning. But of course, conservation must be based on sound scientific understanding. So we might consider a research agenda to confront the conservation questions implicit in the phenomenon of synergisms. To my best knowledge, the amount of research underway on synergisms is scant indeed. In the main, ecologists cannot even identify all the dynamic interactions among the systems they know best, but what they do know is that in certain circumstances, a synergisms-induced upshot can be a whole order of magnitude greater than the simple sum of the component parts. So the "synergistic connection" will probably prove to be a major, if not the predominant, phenomenon at work during the extinction spasm impending. Herein lies a major research challenge—one might say an unusually creative challenge too!—for conservation biologists.

REPERCUSSIONS FOR THE FUTURE OF EVOLUTION

The foreseeable fallout of species is far from the entire picture of the extinction spasm underway. A longer-term, and ultimately more serious, repercussion could lie with disruption of the course of evolution, insofar as speciation processes will have to work with a greatly reduced pool of species and their genetic materials. We are probably being optimistic, moreover, when we call it a disruption. A more likely outcome is that certain evolutionary processes will be suspended or even terminated. To cite the graphic phrasing of Soulé and Wilcox (1980), "Death is one thing; an end to birth is something else."

From what little we can discern from the geological record, a "normal" bounce-back time may require millions of years. After the dinosaur crash, for instance, between 50,000 and 100,000 years elapsed before there started to emerge a set of diversified and specialized biotas, and another five to ten million years went by before there were bats in the skies and whales in the seas (Jablonski 1986). Following the crash during the late Permian, when marine invertebrates lost about half their families, it took as much as twenty million years before the survivors could establish even half as many families as they had lost (Raup 1986).

But this time the evolutionary outcome could prove yet more drastic. The critical factor is the likely loss of key environments. Not only do we appear likely to lose most, if not virtually all, of tropical forests, but there is also progressive depletion of coral reefs, wetlands, and other biotopes with exceptional biodiversity. These environments have served in the past as preeminent "powerhouses" of evolution, in that they have thrown up more species than other environments. Virtually every major group of vertebrates, and many other large categories of animals, have originated in spacious zones with warm, equable climates, notably tropical forests (cf. Darlington 1957). In addition, the rate of evolutionary diversification—whether through proliferation of species or through emergence of major new adaptations—has been greatest in the tropics, notably in tropical forests (Stenseth 1984). In addition, tropical species, especially tropical-forest species, appear to persist for only brief periods of geological time, which implies a high rate of evolution (Jablonski 1986).

Of course, tropical forests have been severely depleted in the past. During drier phases of the late Pleistocene, they have been repeatedly reduced to only a small fraction, occasionally as little as one-tenth, of their former expanse. Moreover, tropical biotas seem to have been unduly prone to extinction (Jablonski and Raup 1986). But the remnant forest "refugia" usually contained sufficient stocks of surviving species to recolonize suitable territories when moister conditions returned (Prance 1982). Within the foreseeable future, by contrast, it seems all too possible that most tropical forests will be reduced to much less than one-tenth of their former expanse, and their pockets of "holdout species" will be much less stocked with potential colonizers.

Furthermore, the species depletion will surely apply across most, if not all, major categories of species. This is almost axiomatic, insofar as extensive environments appear set to be eliminated wholesale. So the result will contrast sharply with the end of the Cretaceous, when not only placental mammals survived (leading to the adaptive radiation of mammals, eventually including humans), but also birds, amphibians, and crocodiles and many other nondinosaurian reptiles. In addition, the present extinction spasm seems likely to eliminate a sizable share of terrestrial plant species, at least one-fifth within the next few decades and many more by the end of the next century at the latest. During most mass-extinction episodes of the prehistoric past, by contrast, terrestrial plants have survived with relatively few losses (Knoll 1984). They have thus supplied a resource base on which evolutionary processes could start to generate replacement animal species forthwith. If this biotic substrate is markedly depleted within the foreseeable future, the restorative capacities of evolution will be all the more reduced.

These, then, are some dimensions of the extinction spasm that we can reasonably assume will overtake the planet's biotas within the coming century, indeed the next few decades (unless, of course, we move with due dispatch to implement conservation measures of suitable scope and scale). In effect, we are conducting an irreversible experiment of global scale with the earth's stock of species. The extinction spasm impending, with its numbers of species involved and the telescoped time scale of the phenomenon, plus the evolutionary impoverishment of the phenomenon, may result in the greatest single setback to life's abundance and diversity since the first flickerings of life almost four billion years ago.

CONSERVATION OF TROPICAL FORESTS: PROBLEMS AND OPPORTUNITIES

Let us look again at tropical forests and assess the scope for conservation responses to the impending extinction spasm. First, let us briefly review the main agents of deforestation and then consider some prospects for helping the situation.

Four main agents are at work (FAO and UNEP, 1982; Melillo et al. 1985; Molofsky et al. 1986; Myers, 1980, 1984b). First is the commercial logger, now accounting for an annual total of at least 20,000 square miles of gross disruption of tropical forests—but rarely destruction. Next is the fuelwood gatherer, whose overharvesting causes the loss of roughly 5,000 square miles and the degradation of about another 5,000 square miles per year. Third is the cattle rancher, eliminating some 8,000 square miles per year. Fourth is the slash-and-burn cultivator, destroying roughly 20,000 square miles and severely disturbing another 25,000 square miles per year. These figures add up to

more than the 70,000 to 77,000 square miles of forest converted per year as adduced in the figures presented earlier. But there is some overlap. The slash-and-burn cultivator often follows behind the commercial logger, using the logger's roads to penetrate deep into forest heartlands that otherwise remain closed to him—whereupon he adds to the disruption already imposed by the logger.

So the slash-and-burn cultivator causes more forest depletion than all three other agents put together. At the same time, he is the one who has most difficulty in adopting an alternative form of forest exploitation, that is, a form that proves less impoverishing to biotas. The commercial logger can readily switch to plantations (provided sufficient are established with due urgency—and plantations yield between ten and twenty times as much sustainable harvest of good-quality hardwood timber than does the natural forest). The fuelwood gatherer can avail himself of fuelwood plantations, in the form of village woodlots, tree farms, and the like. The cattle rancher can engage in a modicum of management, whereupon he can produce at least twice as much beef off existing pasturelands.

But such relatively simple and straightforward responses to forest depletion are not available in the case of the slash-and-burn cultivator. The problems he presents are much more complex and intractable; and they are far more variable, depending on ecological circumstances, cultural background, agronomic capacities, agricultural support systems, and the like. Nonetheless solutions are emerging, in the form of agroecosystem strategies that allow the cultivator to convert his agricultural lifestyle from a migratory into a stabilized, that is, stationary, affair; from extensive into intensive agriculture; and from wastefully inefficient to permanently productive agriculture. These solutions are becoming available in the form of agroforestry, tree crop cultivation, "home gardening," and other innovative agrotechnologies that could enable large numbers of cultivators to sustain themselves in relatively limited space, and to do so in already deforested lands.

It is with deforested lands that the key factor lies. Already between 2 and 2.5 million square miles have been deforested, the great bulk of it in the recent past. At a sustainable yield of 8 cubic meters per acre, we could grow all the tropical hardwood timber we need for projected needs in the year 2000, 400 million cubic meters, in just 160,000 square miles. We could take care of all foreseeable fuelwood needs in the humid tropics through plantations covering only 120,000 square miles. Through modestly improved management, we could produce twice as much humid-tropics beef without clearing another acre of forest for pastureland. At a rate of 5 acres per family of six persons, we could accommodate all 500 million people projected by the year 2000 to comprise shifted cultivators plus shifting cultivators, in no more than 650,000 square miles. The total area required would be well under one million square miles, or less than half the already deforested lands. True, much of the deforested lands are already taken for other forms of use. But huge areas remain virtually unoccupied, for instance, the 160,000 square miles of alang-alang grasslands and other depauperate vegetation types in formerly forested lands of Southeast Asia.

Of course one can juggle with these figures and come up with different combinations, alternative scenarios—whereupon the outcome will not always prove so positive and optimistic as the one just presented. Moreover, the figures cited represent preliminary and approximate estimates—nothing more, but also nothing less. The point is that there is much scope for us to get to grips with an apparently unpromising, if not hopeless, situation. There is nothing inevitable about tropical deforestation, even though the process is sometimes presented as moving inexorably toward its final gloomy conclusion. Nor is there anything unavoidable about a major extinction spasm.

Certainly, we shall lose a lot in the near future. The processes of forest depletion have worked up too much momentum for them to be slowed and stemmed, let alone halted, within a period of just a few years. But plainly, there is massive scope for maneuver. The cause is not lost: far from it.

6

Extinction on Islands: Man as a Catastrophe

STORRS L. OLSON

From a paleontological viewpoint, extinction is a pervasive, nearly inescapable natural process, though one that is hardly better understood than such phenomena as speciation. The threat of extinction has been among the primary motivators of the conservation movement, because most historic extinctions have been due to man and are thus regarded as unnatural and preventable.

If we look at historically documented extinctions, we find almost none of exclusively marine organisms. Although there is now great concern for habitats on continents, comparatively few extinctions have been documented in continental areas during the historic period. It is only when we turn to islands that man's negative impact on biotic diversity can be truly appreciated so far. Recognition of man-caused extinctions on islands can be traced back at least as far as the disappearance of the dodo (*Raphus cucullatus*) from Mauritius in the 1680s. Since then, many other species and populations of organisms have been exterminated on islands, as perhaps best exemplified by birds (Greenway 1958).

Because until recently there was no paleontological record for most oceanic islands, it was natural to assume that European man was chiefly responsible for the degradation of insular habitats that has resulted in historically documented extinctions. This, in combination with the "noble savage" fallacy, has led to a gross underestimation of the effects of man on insular biotas. Now, with the paleontological record being expanded to many more islands, we have sufficient data to hint at the true magnitude of the losses.

The most startling data have come from the islands of the Pacific. Bones of the gigantic flightless moas of New Zealand were discovered more than a century ago. Since then, much more of the previous avifauna of New Zealand has been documented from archaeological, swamp, cave, and dune deposits. The chronology of extinction leaves little doubt that the Maoris, through hunting and burning, have had a devastating impact on the biota of New Zealand (Cassels 1984; Trotter and McCullough 1984).

I have calculated the number and percentage of extinctions of resident land birds for New Zealand and the Chatham Islands, excluding species known or likely to have colonized the islands since the arrival of man. My systematic judgments are probably at variance with those of others attempting the same calculations, but the overall results would probably not be much different. I get figures of fifty-two extant resident species of land birds, of which at least nine are endangered. Extinctions in the historic period number twelve, and thirty-two species were exterminated prehistorically. Thus, 46 percent of the original fauna is now extinct and 33 percent of the fauna became extinct prehistorically.

A recently completed study of bird remains from late Holocene cave deposits in New Caledonia (Balouet and Olson 1988) documents the extinction of hawks, megapodes, pigeons, owls, a gallinule, and a snipe, in addition to the peculiar, gigantic, flightless galliform bird (*Sylviornis*). These fossils show that at least 25% of the resident species of nonpasserine birds of New Caledonia were exterminated prehistorically, almost certainly as a result of human disturbance. But the fossil faunas are demonstrably incomplete, and again, there are a number of species that have probably colonized the island since the arrival of man. Taking these factors into account, we have extrapolated extinction at at least 40% for nonpasserine birds. To this may be added the extinctions of a monitor lizard, a very peculiar crocodilian, and the horned turtle (*Meiolania*).

In the Hawaiian Islands, prehistoric man-caused extinctions were truly massive in scale (Olson and James 1982, 1984) and included large flightless geese, flightless ibises, many flightless rails, owls, an eagle, a hawk, a petrel, and many species of small passerines. Bones from archaeological sites, Holocene sand dunes, lava tubes, and sinkholes have so far documented the extinction of 50 species, equaling 51% of the total number of native land birds of the archipelago. This is in addition to the 17 species that became extinct in the historic period, so for the total avifauna yet known, 69% of the species are extinct. For the two islands with representative fossil faunas, prehistoric extinction was 69% on Oahu and 71% on Maui, where only 10 indigenous species of land birds were recorded in the historic period, all small arboreal passerines of the tribe Drepanidini. Of a total of 163 known island populations of endemic species of land birds, 82, or 50%, became extinct prehistorically, and 31, or 19%, became extinct historically, for a total of 113 (69%).

Archaeological deposits on remote and supposedly pristine Henderson Island in the Pitcairn group show that the island was once inhabited by Polynesians, who exterminated at least two species of pigeons, representing 33% of the total known land bird fauna, of which four species are still extant. These two species of pigeons are the same as, or very closely related to, species known historically from the distant Society and Marquesas groups (Steadman and Olson 1985).

Bones of pigeons, parrots, and flightless rails from Holocene cave deposits on the island of Mangaia in the Cook group have raised the number of species of land birds known on that island from two to ten, so that 80% of the fauna became extinct prehistorically (Steadman 1985, in press). Most impressive are Steadman's (in press) recent discoveries of extinct species of rails, pigeons, and parrots in purely archae-

ological sites on four of the thirteen islands of the Marquesas. Only eleven species of native land birds were known previously from the Marquesas, but the archaeological deposits now add at least seven species to the total, for a minimum avifaunal loss of 39% for the whole archipelago. Many of the species from these archaeological sites are not yet extinct but do not occur on the islands where their bones were found. The islands of Hiva Oa, Tahuata, and Ua Huka each have only four historically known species of birds, whereas the fossil record adds five, six, and nine species, respectively, to these islands, for local extinction rates of 55 to 69%.

On the island of Huahine in the Society group, only a kingfisher (*Halcyon*) and a warbler (*Acrocephalus*) are known historically, whereas bones from archaeological sites have now added at least seven species of rails, pigeons, parrots, and passerines, for an extinction rate of 78% (Steadman, in press). Other extinct species or populations of birds have been documented from archaeological sites in Tonga, Fiji, Wallis, Tikopia, and the Santa Cruz Islands.

Extinctions of birds following in the wake of European explorations in the fifteenth and sixteenth centuries have been documented both historically and paleontologically on islands in the Indian and Atlantic Oceans. The fate of the fauna of the Mascarenes, home of the dodo and the solitaire, which were large flightless pigeons, is all too familiar. On the small island of St. Helena in the South Atlantic, only one native species of land bird has survived, whereas fossil remains show that at least four others were probably present when humans first arrived in 1502 (Olson 1975). Many vertebrate extinctions have been documented in the West Indies, although good chronologies are lacking, so it is difficult to sort out environmental from human-induced factors. Nevertheless, we have documented through the fossil record drastic changes in the composition of vertebrate faunas of the Lesser Antilles that have taken place within the past 2,000 to 3,000 years, and these are almost certainly the result of man's interference (Steadman et al. 1984).

Although I have stressed land birds, the effects of man on seabirds have been just as dramatic. We know of the extinction by man of certain species of seabirds, as on St. Helena (Olson 1975), but most of the reductions have been in numbers and sizes of populations. The effects of man-caused removal of millions of individual predators from oceanic ecosystems within the past 2,000 years have never been calculated but should be of concern to fisheries biologists and others.

Organisms other than birds must necessarily have been affected by the nearly complete conversion of lowland habitats to agriculture throughout Oceania and elsewhere in the world. The only extensive evidence from the prehistoric record for anything other than vertebrates comes from land snails, where the same pattern of massive extinctions is discerned (see, for example, Christensen and Kirch 1986). Insects, other invertebrates, and plants have doubtless been just as severely affected. When extrapolation is attempted from the paleontological data, it must always be remembered that fossil faunas are almost invariably incomplete. The data I have presented here are only minima, and the degree of extinction is always greater, sometimes much more so, than indicated by fossils.

The fossil record has shown that most biogeographical data based only on the historic record of islands are so misleadingly incomplete as to be all but useless for determining species/area curves or the natural distributions of individual species. Theoretical studies of island biogeography founded on such data, including studies that have been used in planning reserves in continental areas, are thus not likely to be particularly accurate or meaningful (Olson and James 1982; Steadman 1986).

It is still too early to make any realistically quantified estimate of the impact of man on insular ecosystems. Too few islands have been sampled paleontologically, and, as noted, most samples are still quite incomplete. However, we can consider some examples that are illustrative of the scale of extinctions. Endemic species of flightless rails doubtless occurred on virtually every oceanic island in the world, with some islands having two or more species. Extrapolating from the number and size of islands in Oceania, we may expect that hundreds of species of flightless rails have been exterminated in the Pacific in the past 2,000 years or less. Exclusive of continental islands, New Zealand, and the Solomons, only fourteen species of flightless rails, of all the hundreds predicted, were recorded in the historic period in the Pacif-

ic, and all but three of these are already probably extinct.

About one-third of all the species of birds in the world are endemic to islands, and this figure is probably considerably underestimated by application of the so-called biological species concept, in which distinctive allopatric populations are considered as subspecies rather than full species. From the fossil record it is clear that species diversity of birds on virtually all oceanic islands was reduced by 30 to 50%, and sometimes much more, within the period of man's occupancy. Thus, perhaps as much as one-quarter of all recent avian species were eradicated within an instant of geological time. Add to this the thousands of extinctions of other vertebrates, land snails, insects, and plants that must have taken place contemporaneously, coupled with historically documented extinctions, and we are faced with one of the swiftest and most profound biological catastrophes in the history of the earth.

Unlike tropical rain forests, this catastrophic reduction in species diversity is not something that is projected into the future—it has already happened—and the remnants of insular biotas are continuing to be depleted at a very rapid pace. Previously it was thought that high islands had greater species diversity because of their montane rain forests. An important observation to emerge from recent studies, however, is that drier, more level, lowland habitats, the ones most susceptible to burning and clearing for agriculture, had greater species diversity than steep areas of high, wet forests. On islands, most species that persist in wet montane forests today do so not because this is their preferred habitat, but because it is the only habitat left that has not been too severely modified by man (see discussion in Olson and James 1982:42–49).

Can this knowledge be applied to continental areas as well? Have we perhaps underestimated the diversity of mesic and arid environments in the tropics for lack of appreciation of the prehistoric influence of man? These environments, as on islands, are more susceptible to alteration by man than are rain forests, and their biotas may have experienced as yet undocumented prehistoric man-caused extinctions. Campbell (1979) has shown that the desert west coast of South America harbored an extensive endemic avifauna that has largely disappeared since the end of the Pleistocene. These extinctions have been tied to climatic deterioration and increasing desertification, processes that have extended into the Holocene and up to the present, but that were also coincident with the arrival of man in that part of the continent. Can we really rule out the possibility that increased burning by man in habitats adapted to very little rainfall may have exacerbated and accelerated the process of extinction at the same time that the biota of the Pacific coast of South America was enduring climatic stress?

It seems to me that a historical perspective and much better knowledge of Pleistocene environments is absolutely essential to planning large-scale conservation efforts in South America. It is increasingly evident that neotropical rainforests are much less stable and of much younger origin than has long been thought (Campbell and Frailey, 1984). During the last glacial period, rain forests were greatly reduced in area, whereas the dominant habitat type was probably mesic or arid savanna (Lewin 1984). In some cases, areas that had been postulated as forest refugia were shown to have been savanna in the Pleistocene. Because the great biological diversity of South American rain forests about which we marvel today was sustained throughout the period when such habitats were much less extensive than at present, is it not essential to try to determine the location and extent of the late Pleistocene rain forests as a model for preserving modern diversity? And should we not also be equally concerned about conservation of habitats other than rainforest, which may be even more "fragile" and in the past may have been much more diverse?

Fossils have shown that the human-induced biological catastrophe predicted as the future of tropical rain forests has long been underway on islands and perhaps in less humid continental areas as well. From such studies it is increasingly evident that the element of time, the paleontological record, and human history are essential factors that must be woven into the fabric of any successful strategy for conservation.

7

Introduced Animals and Extinctions

IAN ATKINSON

Wherever man has colonized, there have been introductions of animals, either deliberate or accidental, often followed by extinctions, either total or local, of indigenous terrestrial plants and animals. Some of these extinctions have been a direct consequence of the introduced animals, which have usually been alien to the area of introduction. This chapter explores the extent and nature of this effect, its interaction with habitat loss, and ways to reduce such extinctions in the future.

EXTENT OF THE ALIEN ANIMAL PROBLEM

Many thousands of invertebrate species have been spread to all parts of the world by human activity. In the continental United States, for example, more than 1,500 insect introductions have been documented (Sailer 1983), and in Hawaii introduced insects comprise 28% of the islands' insect fauna (Simberloff 1986b). However, no documentation exists for most places and still less frequently are there studies linking extinctions of indigenous organisms to particular alien invertebrates (see "Some case Histories" below).

Data on causes of extinction in three groups of vertebrates are summarized in Table 7.1. These suggest that introduced mammals, including man as a predator (rather than as a destroyer of habitats), have been involved in more than 60 percent of these extinctions.

More than 176 species and subspecies of birds have become extinct throughout the world

Table 7.1. Causes of Extinctions in Three Groups of Vertebrates

Vertebrate Group	Place	Number of Species/Subspecies	Causes		
			Alien Animals	Other Causes	Unknown
Amphibian and reptile extinctions since A.D. 1600[a]	World	30 sp.	22	3	5
Frog and lizard extinctions or near-extinctions since A.D. 1000[b]	New Zealand	14 sp.	9	4	1
Bird extinctions or near-extinctions since A.D. 1840[c]	New Zealand	31 sp. + subsp.	23	2	6

Sources: [a]Honegger 1981
[b]Whitaker 1973; Worthy 1987
[c]Atkinson (in press)

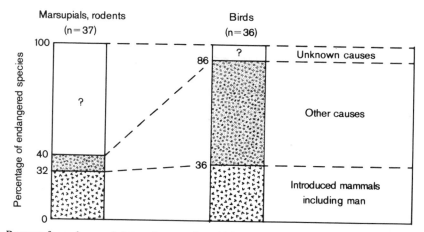

Fig. 7.1. Reasons for endangered status of mammals and birds in Australia. (Data from Burbidge and Jenkins 1984.)

since 1600 (King 1985). It appears that introduced predators, including man, were involved in more than half of these extinctions.

Data on currently endangered mammals and birds of Australia given by Burbidge and Jenkins (1984) suggest that alien mammals, particularly the dingo, the red fox, and the cat, are responsible for current declines in at least a third of cases (Fig. 7.1).

Alien animals have caused extinctions of indigenous plants as well as animals. For example, since the establishment of pigs, goats, and rabbits on Phillip Island, Norfolk group, between 1790 and 1840, there have been thirteen extinctions of indigenous plant species, including two endemic species, in the ensuing 140 years (Fullager 1978 and Fig. 7.2). It seems likely that the majority of these extinctions re-

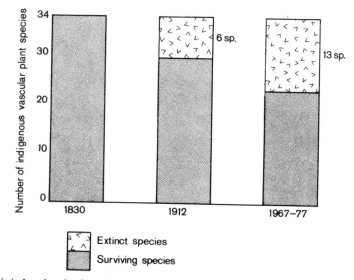

Fig. 7.2. Rabbit-induced extinctions of vascular plants on Phillip Island (190 ha), Norfolk Island group. The average rate of extinction between 1830 and 1977 was approximately one plant species every ten years. (Data from Fullager 1978.)

sulted from extensive grazing by rabbits, as pigs and goats had apparently died out by 1870. On Laysan Island in the Hawaiian chain, rabbits alone were responsible for eliminating twenty-six species of plants between 1903 and 1923 (Christophersen and Caum 1931), a rate of loss exceeding one species per year.

A few extinctions caused by alien animals can be associated with introductions of birds, or in one case a snake (Savidge 1987), but the vast majority are attributable to mammals. However, alien-induced extinction is largely an island phenomenon, one in which the greatest number of extinctions are associated with inhabited oceanic islands. More than 90 percent of the extinctions of reptiles and amphibians, and of land and freshwater birds, that have occurred since 1600 have been of island forms (Fig. 7.3). Even for indigenous mammals, which are not characteristic of oceanic island faunas, the percentage of island extinctions (29 percent) is high. This is, however, largely a result of the great changes in the mammal fauna that have occurred in the West Indies since man arrived there 4500 years ago: 37 species of flightless mammals have disappeared, an average extinction rate of one species every 122 years (Morgan and Woods 1986).

In contrast to island biotas, those of continents have suffered few extinctions as a result of introduced animals, leaving aside predation by man. The exception is Australia, where rabbits, pigs, sheep, and cattle have wrought enormous changes in the vegetation and three alien predators (dingo, red fox, and cat) have caused widespread reductions if not extinctions of small marsupials.

RATE OF ALIEN ANIMAL INTRODUCTIONS AND THE SPECIES INTRODUCED

A large number of alien mammals and birds have been introduced successfully to islands and continents. About 50 species of mammal have been introduced to continents (Lever 1985) as well as more than 100 bird species (Long 1981). On islands, about 80 species of mammal and over 300 species of birds have been introduced (Fig. 7.4, Appendix to this chapter). The rate of introductions to islands of both mammals in general and rats in particular has increased markedly since the 1850s (Figs. 7.5, 7.6). Introductions of mammals, particularly cats and rats, appear to have peaked during World War II as a result of the establishment of military bases on islands. The decreased rate of introduction since 1950 is probably not an indication of increasing effort to curb introductions. It more likely shows that many places, inhabited islands in particular, are now saturated with respect to the animals commonly introduced, i.e., goats, pigs, cats, and rats.

In spite of the numerous alien animals introduced to islands, most extinctions of island

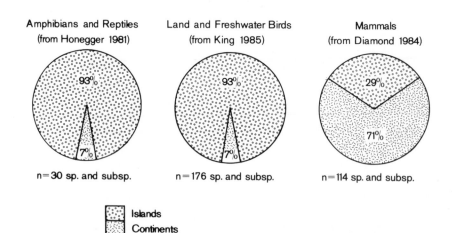

Fig. 7.3. Distribution among islands and continents of worldwide extinctions of several groups of vertebrates.

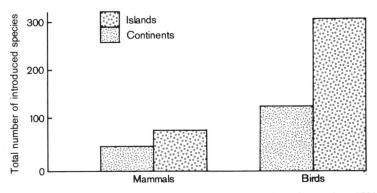

Fig. 7.4. Numbers of mammal and bird species introduced to islands and continents since 1700. (Data from Lever 1985; Long 1981.)

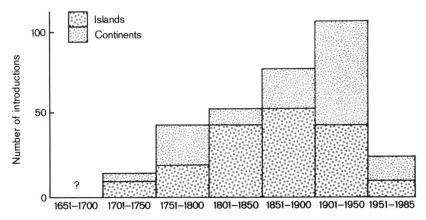

Fig. 7.5. Changes in the rate of mammal introductions to islands and continents between 1700 and 1985. (Data from Lever 1985.)

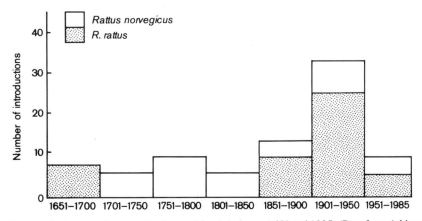

Fig. 7.6. Changes in the rate of rat introductions to islands between 1650 and 1985. (Data from Atkinson 1985.)

Table 7.2. Minimum Numbers of Island Groups Where Major Problem Mammals Have Been Introduced (excluding humans)

Species	Herbivore	Predator
Goat	45	
Rabbit	33	
Pig	51	51
Cat		65
Rattus rattus		66
Rattus norvegicus		45
Rattus exulans		39
Mongoose		6

plants and animals are associated with one or more of only nine alien species: goats, rabbits, pigs, cats, three species of rat, mongooses, and man as a predator, independent of any other effects he may have (Table 7.2). These are the major problem animals contributing to extinctions of indigenous plants and vertebrates. Alien invertebrates have also caused extinctions of native species, but these effects are poorly understood.

SOME CASE HISTORIES

Fire Ants in the Galápagos Islands

Ants are among the most ubiquitous of alien invertebrates in many parts of the world. The adverse effects of the cosmopolitan ants *Pheidole megacephala* and *Iridomyrmex humilis* on the insect faunas of Bermuda and Hawaii, following their invasions of these islands, have been described by Crowell (1968) and Zimmerman (1970). In the Galápagos Islands, another cosmopolitan species, the little red fire ant (*Wasmannia auropunctata*), was introduced in the early part of this century. It has spread to all inhabited islands as well as the higher parts of Santiago Island (Lubin 1984), and it continues to spread, most recently to Sante Fé Island.

Lubin's study showed that few other ant species can coexist with the fire ant and that where it occurred, populations of three species of arachnid were reduced or eliminated. Both flying and arboricolous insects were also affected by this ant.

The mechanism of species displacement by fire ants is not understood, although direct predation and competition for available food and nesting sites are involved. Fire ants are re-

stricted by extremes of temperature and humidity, but the ease with which they can be dispersed by people suggests they will extend their range still further in the Galápagos Islands, especially if the human population continues to increase.

Goats on Santiago Island, Galápagos Group

Goats, donkeys, cattle, and pigs have all become feral in the Galápagos Islands, where the only original land mammals were rats and bats. Dr. H. Adsersen (personal communication) estimates that 22 percent of the endemic plant species in the Galápagos group have declined significantly as a result of alien browsing mammals. Of these, goats have had by far the greatest effect.

Goats have been introduced to ten of the thirteen major islands in the Galápagos group and subsequently eliminated from four islands. They were established on Santiago Island (585 km^2) in 1813 (Hamann 1981) and now number in excess of 80,000 animals, together with much smaller populations of pigs and donkeys.

Probably no part of Santiago's original vegetation, other than that of steep, inaccessible cliffs, has escaped modification by goats. Regeneration of the major trees of the forest which formerly covered the island (*Bursera graveolens, Psidium galapageium, Zanthoxylum fagara, Pisonia floribunda*), together with that of many shrubs, has been curtailed for so long that the original forest has been replaced by an open parklike woodland over large areas. On the upper ridges of the island, forest has been completely replaced by herbfield and grassland. Stands of *Scalesia pedunculata* (Compositae) forest recorded early this century have been reduced to a few trees on steep cliffs. Two lowland species, *Scalesia atractyloides* and *S. stewartii*, both endemic to Santiago and its offshore islets, have been reduced by goat browsing to a few hundred individuals growing on cliffs inaccessible to goats.

Goats can reduce vegetation to a treeless state, particularly in areas of very low rainfall such as the Galápagos lowlands. During dry periods on Santiago, goats are in direct competition for food with land iguanas (*Conolophus subcristatus*) and giant tortoises (*Geochelone elephantopus darwini*). The former are apparently extinct on Santiago (pigs would also have been involved in this extinction), while the tiny remnant population of the Santiago subspecies of tortoise, earlier depleted by the hunting of buccaneers, whalers, and sealers, has little chance of recovery in the presence of goats.

These effects of goats on Santiago Island parallel what has happened on numerous goat-infested islands throughout the world. A notorious example is St. Helena Island in the south Atlantic. Cronk's (1986) study of the St. Helena ebony shows that when only a few individuals of a particular species have survived on inaccessible cliffs, the genetic depletion of the original population may make it impossible to recover the species in its former sense. The two surviving plants of ebony appear to be a dwarfed (1m) cliff ecotype, cuttings from which have not produced trees 4–5 m high, as originally recorded for this species.

Rabbits on Round Island, Mascarene Group

Rabbits have been liberated on about 700 islands throughout the world (Flux and Fullager 1983; Dr J. E. C. Flux, personal communication). The devastation by rabbits of Laysan Island (340 ha), Hawaiian group, and consequent loss of three species of the island's landbirds is a well-documented example of the effect of rabbits in causing extinctions (Warner 1963).

Rabbits were liberated on Round Island (151 ha), 22 km NNE of Mauritius, before 1810 and goats were introduced between 1844 and 1865 (North and Bullock 1986). Their combined effects eliminated the small area of hardwood forest originally present and greatly depleted the island's palm savanna, a lowland community now completely destroyed on Mauritius itself. Although goats were eradicated from the island between 1976 and 1982, rabbit browsing continued to prevent any significant recovery of the vegetation. The aging population of the commonest tree, the endemic lantan palm (*Latania loddigesii*), now virtually restricted to Round Island, continued to decrease rapidly. Two other palms, the endemic bottle palm (*Hyophorbe [Mascarena] lagenicaulis*) (now restricted to Round Island) and the hurricane palm (*Dictyosperma album* var. *conjugatum*) (variety endemic to Round Island), were re-

duced to eight and two individuals respectively by 1986 (Bullock and North 1982; Strahm 1986; D. V. Merton, personal communication).

However, unlike the main island of Mauritius, Round Island remained free of alien predators. Consequently it became a refuge for eight species of reptile, including two geckos, a skink, and a snake all extinct elsewhere in Mauritius, and a second species of snake, the endemic Round Island boa (*Bolyeria multocarinata*), whose survival is at present uncertain (Bullock 1986). The continuing depletion of the island's plant cover by rabbits was placing all these reptiles at ever-increasing risk of extinction.

In 1986 a three-man team led by Don Merton of the New Zealand Wildlife Service, and supported by the Jersey Wildlife Preservation Trust, eradicated rabbits from Round Island. By May 1987 the vegetation was making a spectacular recovery, assisted by an unusually wet season. Both lantan and bottle palms were regenerating; indigenous grasses, herbs, and vines had greatly increased; and the extensive soil erosion that had been a feature for many years had virtually ceased (Imboden 1987; D. V. Merton, personal communication).

A parallel success was achieved on Phillip Island (190 ha) of the Norfolk group (see section entitled "Extent of the Alien Animal Problem") in 1986 when rabbits were eradicated by the Australian National Parks and Wildlife Service (Hermes et al. 1986).

Pigs on Auckland Island

In 1807, pigs were introduced to Auckland Island of the subantarctic Auckland Islands group, 310 km south of New Zealand. They spread throughout the scrub, tussock-shrubland, tussockland, and herbfield communities of this 460-km² island and gradually destroyed a distinctive community of large-leaved subantarctic herbs composed of *Pleurophyllum criniferum*, *P. speciosum*, *Stilbocarpa polaris*, *Anisotome latifolia*, and *A. antipoda* (Challies 1975). These species are now restricted to sites inaccessible to pigs. More recent observations show that pigs in combination with goats are now threatening the survival of *Chinochloa antarctica*, a tussock grass which is a major component of low-altitude vegetation on the island (Campbell and Rudge

1984). What the original vegetation of Auckland Island looked like can only be judged from comparisons with neighboring islands, such as Adams and Disappointment Islands, that are free of alien herbivores.

Pigs are predators as well as herbivores. They take eggs, young, and adults of surface-nesting and burrow-nesting seabirds (e.g., Rudge 1976), and many terrestrial vertebrates such as reptiles, as well as numerous invertebrates, are eaten. Challies (1975) considered that pigs had their greatest effects on the seabirds of Auckland Island when pig numbers peaked between 1840 and 1865. Again, comparison with alien-free islands elsewhere in the group suggests that colonies of albatrosses, mollymawks, and smaller petrels have probably disappeared from Auckland Island as a result of pigs.

Cats on Ascension Island

Both cats and ship rats *Rattus rattus* were introduced to Ascension Island in the South Atlantic, but the evidence shows that cats alone have been responsible for the loss of several very large seabird colonies comprising many thousands of birds from the main island. These colonies included those of masked boobies (*Sula dactylatra*) and red-footed boobies (*S. sula*), both of which now breed locally only on the tiny Boatswainbird Island (4.6 ha) (Olson 1977; Stonehouse 1962). Breeding of the endemic Ascension frigate bird (*Fregata aquila*), the brown booby (*Sula leucogaster*), and the Madeiran storm petrel (*Oceanodroma castro*) is also now

restricted to Boatswainbird Island or other offshore stacks (Olson 1977). Although rats alone could have eliminated the storm petrel from Ascension Island in the absence of cats, they do not normally attack seabirds as large as boobies. The only extensive seabird colonies now remaining on Ascension are those of the sooty tern (*Sterna fuscata*).

Ship Rats on Big South Cape Island, New Zealand

The 1962 invasion of Big South Cape Island (930 ha), off the southern coast of New Zealand, by the ship rat (*Rattus rattus*) was followed by a catastrophic effect on the island's biota (Atkinson and Bell 1973). Within four years of rats establishing, four species of landbird were extinct (later rising to five) and a further four landbird species were severely reduced in numbers (Fig. 7.7). Seabirds were apparently little affected, although no proper studies have been made. The rat invasion also resulted in extinction of the last population of greater short-tailed bat (*Mystacina robusta*) (Daniel and Williams 1984) and extinctions of an unknown number of invertebrates, including a species of large flightless weevil (*Hadramphus stilbocarpae*) (Kuschel 1971).

Norway Rats on South Georgia Island

Norway rats (*Rattus norvegicus*) reached South Georgia Island in the South Atlantic early last

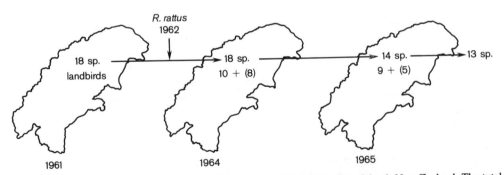

Fig. 7.7. Extinctions of landbirds induced by *Rattus rattus* on Big South Cape Island, New Zealand. The total number of landbird species at each date illustrated is the summation of those which had not decreased (numbers in parentheses) and those showing significant declines (numbers not in parentheses). (Data from Atkinson and Bell 1973.)

century, but have persisted there only in vegetated ice-free areas. Pye and Bonner (1980) found that Antarctic pipits (*Anthus antarcticus*) and South Georgia pintails (*Anas georgicus*) had become restricted in their breeding to rat-free parts of the island. Dove prions (*Pachyptila desolata*), blue petrels (*Halobaena caerulea*), South Georgian diving petrels (*Pelecanoides georgicus*), white-chinned petrels (*Procellaria aequinoctialis*), and probably white-faced storm petrels (*Pelagodroma marina*) are all preyed on by the rats but continue to coexist with rats on the main island (Murphy 1936; Pye and Bonner 1980). Populations of small seabirds, however, are much greater on rat-free offshore islands such as Bird Island (Payne and Prince 1979), suggesting that very significant decreases in the bird population of South Georgia have occurred since rats established.

Man and Pacific Rats in New Zealand

Extinctions of landbirds on mainland New Zealand after the arrival of Polynesians 1,000 to 1,200 years ago illustrate the combined effect of two introduced predators, man and the widespread Pacific rat (*Rattus exulans*) (Fig. 7.8). There were about thirty-five extinctions of landbirds between the time of Polynesian arrival and A.D. 1800 (Millener 1981; Cassels 1984; author's analysis), although further taxonomic

study may reduce the number of species of ratite birds (moas) below twelve, the figure accepted here. There may also be additions of species as the subfossil avifauna becomes better known.

About eighteen of the extinctions affecting larger birds can be attributed directly or indirectly to hunting by man. There is no doubt that hunting exterminated the moas (Anderson 1984), and as a result the huge eagle (*Harpagornis moorei*) that preyed on them was also lost. Other large birds, such as the two species of flightless goose and the New Zealand swan, are more likely to have disappeared from hunting than from loss of habitat.

The six smallest species of birds lost were mainly wrenlike forms or small rails that are most unlikely to have been eliminated either by hunting or by habitat loss. Their small size and frequently flightless state would have made them vulnerable to predation by *R. exulans*, a known predator of small birds (Atkinson 1985). This leaves eleven landbird extinctions at present unexplained. *R. exulans* is also considered responsible for extinctions in several other groups of land animals apart from birds (e.g., lizards and frogs in New Zealand) (Table 7.1).

Since 1800 and the arrival of Europeans there have been at least eight further extinctions of landbird species on the New Zealand mainland, although three of these survive on offshore islands.

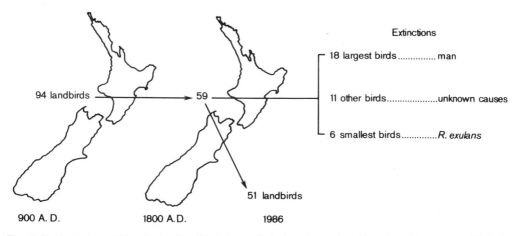

Fig. 7.8. Extinctions of New Zealand landbirds during the Polynesian period. (Data from Atkinson unpublished; Cassels 1984; Millener 1981.)

ALIEN ANIMALS AS A CONTINUING PROBLEM

From the case histories and examples discussed, it is apparent that the adverse effects of introduced animals extend from the tropics to regions as cold as south Georgia. Some of the resulting changes in biotas affected have been rapid, others slow and still continuing. But in no one case is the total effect of a particular introduction known, either qualitatively or quantitatively. All that is usually described are the most immediate and obvious effects of a particular alien animal following its establishment. Delayed effects are difficult to detect and measure, as is the network of indirect effects that follows the establishment of each new alien animal. The case of the Puerto Rican parrot (see section entitled "Nest Site Competition") demonstrates that even an alien animal as apparently benign as the honeybee can have dire consequences for indigenous organisms.

In spite of all that has been written about the serious impact of introduced animals, especially on islands, it is doubtful whether there is even yet any general appreciation of the problem, especially at government level. Introductions of alien animals still continue, and in some countries, New Zealand for example, pressures to introduce further alien predators and herbivores are often intense.

SPECIFIC EFFECTS OF ALIEN ANIMAL INTRODUCTIONS

Alien animals can exert one or more of several distinct effects in causing or contributing to extinctions of indigenous plants and animals. Predation and browsing have been most studied but some alien animals hybridize with closely related indigenous animals, compete for food, or nest sites, or introduce diseases. Any one of these effects may precipitate further changes that adversely affect indigenous organisms.

Predation

Indigenous animals of islands are well known for their tame or fearless behavior which makes them vulnerable to introduced mammalian predators. When such behavior is accompanied by a slow reproductive rate (infrequent breeding and/or small litter or clutch size), coexistence with alien predators is difficult. This is illustrated by the nocturnal and flightless kakapo of New Zealand, the world's heaviest parrot and the only parrot known to exhibit lek behavior (Merton et al. 1984). This incredible bird was formerly distributed throughout the main islands of New Zealand but was reduced in range after the arrival of Polynesians, possibly from the combined effects of hunting by man, predation on eggs and chicks by *R. exulans,* and habitat loss. Kakapo nest on the ground in small depressions or cavities and the female alone incubates and rears the young, leaving the nest unattended for long periods at night when feeding. Following the arrival of Europeans, kakapo were exposed to an ever-increasing array of alien predators: *R. norvegicus, R. rattus,* cats, pigs, dogs, stoats, weasels, and ferrets. At present the only remaining breeding population, comprising less than forty individuals, exists on Stewart Island, where its survival is threatened by cats and three species of rat. Transfers of kakapo to two offshore islands have been made, but breeding has yet to occur in these new populations.

Browsing and Grazing

Although goats have been the most devastating of alien herbivores, many other herbivores have been introduced to islands, including rabbits, pigs, sheep, cattle, horses, donkeys, monkeys, several species of deer and wallaby, Australian brushtailed possums, squirrels, and hares. If the browsing or grazing continues for any extended period, extinctions or near-extinctions of plant species are likely, for example, the reduction by goats of *Hebe breviracemosa* (Scrophulariaceae), an endemic plant of the Kermadec Islands, down to a single plant. The more general effect of alien herbivores, however, is to reduce habitat quality for indigenous species, thus making them more vulnerable to extinction from other causes (see section entitled "Environmental Chain Reactions"). A possibly important effect of browsers and grazers, although difficult to measure, is trampling, which can adversely affect plants and animals in a variety of ways.

Hybridization

Although recorded cases of loss of an endemic species through hybridization with a closely related introduced species are few, it has occurred at times. In the Seychelles Islands, the endemic subspecies of turtledove (*Streptopelia picturata rostrata*), has been largely replaced by hybrids with *S. p. picturata* introduced from Madagascar in the 1850s (Penny 1968). It has also been suggested that the endemic subspecies of cattle egret (*Bubulcus ibis sechellarum*) has been replaced by hybrids with the African subspecies, *B. i. ibis*, introduced in 1960 (Penny 1974).

Food Competition

The continuing decline since last century of one of New Zealand's rarest forest birds, the kokako (*Callaeas cinerea wilsoni*) (of the endemic wattlebird family Callaeidae) can be partly attributed to introduced predators and habitat loss. However, a study by Leathwick et al. (1983) provides strong circumstantial evidence that food competition is also involved in the decline. The study showed there was considerable overlap in the diet of kokako and of introduced possums (*Trichosurus vulpecula*), red deer (*Cervus elaphus*), and goats (*Capra hircus*), which occur throughout the range of kokako. Although a direct effect of this dietary overlap on adult mortality or breeding success of kokako has not been demonstrated, the fact that the introduced herbivores, particularly possums, feed on the most nutritious parts of plants eaten by kokako (e.g., fruit) makes it apparent that competition cannot be ignored as a factor in the continuing decline of kokako.

Nest Site Competition

The significance of nest site competition as a potential factor contributing to extinctions is shown in the study by Wiley (1985) of the Puerto Rican parrot (*Amazona vittata*). Overlapping preferences for cavity sizes of holes in mature forest trees used by this extremely rare parrot and by the introduced honeybee (*Apis mellifera*) have reduced the availability of nest sites for parrots. Nest site competition has subsequently been exacerbated by an increase in another indigenous cavity-nesting species, the pearly-eyed thrasher (*Margarops fuscatus*).

Introduction of Disease

There are many indications that diseases introduced by alien animals can contribute to extinctions of indigenous species. This effect, however, is even more difficult to investigate than that of predators. In a comprehensive study of avian malaria in Hawaiian land birds, van Riper et al. (1986) found malaria to be a major limiting factor currently restricting the abundance and distribution of native forest birds. They showed that the disease probably reached epizootic proportions sometime after 1920, following numerous introductions of alien birds from Asia, and suggested that some extinctions of forest birds subsequent to 1920 could be attributed to the disease. However, as these authors point out, malaria cannot explain the major decline of Hawaiian forest birds that began late last century. Although this has been attributed by Warner (1968) to a combination of malaria and avian pox, there is also circumstantial evidence to suggest that invasions of *R. rattus* were responsible (Atkinson 1977). In attempting to unravel the roles of such factors as disease and predators in contributing to extinctions, it is essential to ascertain as accurately as possible both the decline times of the affected species and the times of introduction of predators, disease vectors, and pathogenic organisms (Atkinson 1977).

Environmental Chain Reactions

The effects of predation, browsing, hybridization, food and nest site competition, and disease transmission by alien animals all have a direct impact on indigenous organisms. Such effects can also have indirect consequences that result from additional and sequential changes linked to the initial effect of the alien animal, that is, an environmental chain reaction. The study of *Powelliphanta* landsnails by Meads et al. (1984) illustrates this.

Powelliphanta is an endemic New Zealand genus of large, attractive landsnails that are both carnivorous and nocturnal, and which depend on high humidity for survival. Their typical habitat is deep forest litter associated with undisturbed forest. Populations of the ten species recognized are fragmented into subpopulations, sometimes of distinct subspecies, with some species and subspecies now approaching extinction.

Original predators of *Powelliphanta* were all indigenous birds. The establishment in New Zealand last century of three species of rats, as well as pigs, blackbirds (*Turdus merula*), and thrushes (*Turdus philomelos*), introduced additional snail predators and, in the case of the alien mammals, exposed the snails to kinds of predation to which they were not adapted. In addition, herbivores such as goats, deer, and pigs depleted the undergrowth and destroyed forest litter inhabited by *Powelliphanta,* thus reducing humidity near the ground, a factor of critical importance for snail survival. This depletion of the understory and ground cover also made the snails more visible and hence more vulnerable to predation. In this study, some of the severest predation was recorded in forest highly modified by goats, pigs, deer, cattle, sheep, and possums (K. J. Walker, personal communication; Meads et al. 1984).

Many other examples could be given of sequential reductions in habitat quality for indigenous species following introductions of alien herbivores. In Hawaii, for example, pigs eat the fruit and disperse the seeds of guava (*Psidium cattleianum*) (Stone 1984), an aggressive weed that has replaced large areas of native vegetation on many oceanic islands.

ALIEN ANIMALS AND HABITAT LOSS

Some species of alien animals, either singly or in combination, have brought about extinctions of indigenous species in the absence of any other environmental changes. More frequently, the effects of a particular alien animal are compounded by loss of habitat for the affected species.

The survival of a species, both short-term and long-term, is related in part to the genetic variability of that species (Frankel and Soulé 1981). The minimum number of breeding individuals required to maintain genetic variability without losses from chance demographic or genetic events has been called the minimum viable population size (MVP) for the species (Shaffer 1981; Frankel and Soulé 1981). Minimum sizes

of viable populations differ between species and between taxonomic groups and have been determined for very few species. However, related to this minimum number, and dependent on population density, is a minimum area of habitat required to maintain a minimum viable population. Unlike MVP, the minimum area of habitat required to maintain a viable population is not a fixed figure; it increases as population density decreases.

The effect of introducing an alien animal to a vulnerable population of indigenous plant or animal is to reduce the population density of the vulnerable species. This may result from any one or a combination of the specific effects of alien animals discussed earlier, including indirect adverse effects on habitat quality. Whatever adverse effects are operating, the area of habitat required to maintain the vulnerable species will increase.

The relationship between alien animals and habitat loss in causing extinctions can be illustrated by a hypothetical model based on the history of alien animal introductions to New Zealand during the European period (Fig. 7.9). Times of alien animal introductions, which are well known, are plotted on the x axis and area of habitat on the y axis. The continuous graph lines show the habitat area required to maintain minimum viable populations. The two broken lines show habitat areas actually available. In locality *B*, the available habitat is being lost at a greater rate than in locality *A*.

Species *X* of Fig. 7.9 was apparently unaffected by the introduction of Norway rats (*R. norvegicus*) but succumbed shortly after the introduction of cats in 1790. In this instance, species *X* was unaffected by habitat loss; predation by cats alone appears to have caused the extinction.

Species *Y* was variously affected by a series of alien animals that finally reduced its population density to a point where its requirement for habitat exceeded that available. (An alternative mechanism is that population density may be so reduced that surviving individuals are too far apart to find one another.)

Species *Z*, although at first unaffected by introduced animals, declined steeply following the arrival of *R. rattus* and then suffered further declines following the establishment of possums and German wasps (*Vespa germanica*). Because its requirement for habitat was increas-

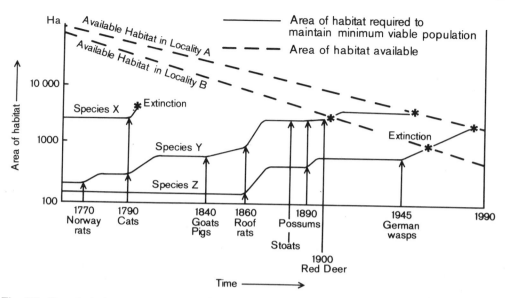

Fig. 7.9. Hypothetical model showing relationship between alien animal introductions and habitat loss in causing extinctions on islands. The model is based on the history of alien animal introductions to New Zealand during the European period, but the extinction curves are of hypothetical species chosen to illustrate differences in extinction patterns.

ing continuously following the arrival of wasps, it would be simple to lay the blame for the extinction of species Z on wasps. In fact, as with species *Y,* extinction resulted from the cumulative result of several alien animals interacting with habitat loss.

To be useful, a model must be tested with real data. Such an analysis would be most worthwhile for species still extant in order to gain a clearer picture of factors influencing their population density and area requirements for habitat. Whatever the merits of this model, it is clear that on islands it is the combined effects of alien animals with Man's destruction of habitats that is the most widespread process driving species to extinction. At least seventy-eight of the world's major island groups have species of indigenous plants and animals now at risk from the continuing interaction between alien animals and habitat destruction.

WHY ARE ISLAND BIOTAS SO VULNERABLE TO ALIEN ANIMALS?

The vulnerability of many island biotas to introduced animals appears to be largely a conse-

quence of the absence of mammals from most oceanic islands until the arrival of man. As a result, island plants commonly lack defensive features effective against the browsing of mammals, and island animals commonly lack behaviors effective against predation by mammals. Examples of these deficiencies in antipredator behavior among faunas of areas never reached by placental mammals are discussed by Diamond (1984a), Moors and Atkinson (1984), and Atkinson (1985).

SOME CRITERIA FOR DECIDING PRIORITIES FOR ACTION

Criteria are needed to identify both island species and biotas that deserve priority for restorative action.

Population Size

Species with very small populations have been shown to be at greatest risk from extinction (Terborgh and Winter 1980; Diamond 1984a), and clearly any small population that is also declining requires immediate action. However, if efforts were confined to saving small populations from extinction, for example, the black robin (*Petroica traversi*) of the Chatham Islands, other populations would not be prevented from becoming equally small. Thus a large population that is in steep decline deserves higher priority for action than one which is small but stable.

Where several species with small populations are at risk, a species that breeds or fruits only once every few years or has delayed sexual maturity will be at greater risk than those that breed or fruit annually and have rapid sexual maturation. Seed output per plant and litter and clutch size are further aspects of reproductive capacity that should be considered in deciding priorities, especially when alien predators are present.

Aesthetic Value

Particular plant and animal species are valued for their color, size, or interesting behavior. Large, warm-blooded vertebrates are usually more interesting to people than small invertebrates of nondescript appearance. A recovery program can be built around a single species of higher plant or vertebrate, whereas public support for conserving most mosses, liverworts, and invertebrates may only be possible by emphasizing protection of whole communities. Obsession with the conservation of a charismatic species need not become a problem provided it is used to increase awareness and support for protection of other species in the same habitat.

Taxonomic Distinctness

Given two threatened taxa of similar aesthetic appeal, one a species not closely related to other living species and the other a subspecies of an otherwise widespread and common species, it seems reasonable to give priority to the most taxonomically distinct form.

Endemic Species

Species that are endemic to an island group can reasonably be expected to receive priority for action ahead of other indigenous species that are also threatened. However, each case should be decided on its own merits. Some nonendemic island species are threatened throughout their range and therefore deserve priority action.

Trophic Level

Species at progressively higher trophic levels are progressively rarer. Thus, loss of one or two species from a high trophic level may result in loss of the whole trophic level. Theoretical models suggest that it is the most trophically complex communities that will lose most species when higher trophic levels are removed (Pimm 1982).

Number of Species at Risk

Biotas with many threatened species deserve a higher priority for conservation than those with fewer species at risk. Biotas with the greatest number of threatened endemic species may require a higher priority than those with few endemics at risk.

Human Pressure on an Island's Natural Resources

In the absence of any effective conservation policy, pressure to exploit the natural resources of an island in a nonrenewable manner will always be high where the human population is growing rapidly. Thus to some extent, the growth rate of the human population can be used as a criterion for measuring the magnitude of threat to an island's indigenous species and habitats. However, it would be wrong to assume that the biotas of uninhabited islands are therefore unthreatened. The recent proposals to use Henderson Island, Pitcairn group, as a family cattle ranch, if carried out, would certainly have resulted in introductions of alien mammals and placed the biota of this comparatively little-modified island at great risk.

Use of the Criteria

Many of the criteria cited involve value judgments and they should not be used in isolation from one another. Their greatest use may be in deciding priorities between species and islands within a single island group. In a global sense, the priorities are not difficult to identify. Every inhabited island has suffered introductions of alien animals and most have lost indigenous habitat. Few, if any, islands have a greater number of small and dwindling populations of endemic plants and animals, often of high aesthetic value, than Madagascar. But even on islands showing still greater extremes of modification, such as Bermuda, St. Helena, and Rodrigues, Mascarene group, there is still a need to identify conservation priorities and opportunities for restorative action.

THE FUTURE CONSERVATION OF ISLAND BIOTAS

With the biotas and biotic communities of so many of the world's islands now threatened with destruction, it is imperative that effective action be taken to conserve what remains for the twenty-first century. Outlined next are five initiatives for such action. These are not a sequence of steps so much as lines of action that should be pursued in parallel and integrated wherever possible.

Protection Plans

Many islands throughout the world, mostly uninhabited, remain still free or relatively free of introduced alien animals; some are also without alien plant problems. These islands must be identified and their conservation values assessed so that a priority list of islands requiring protection plans can be prepared.

The plans themselves should identify potential future pressures on habitats from development and detail the specific preventive actions needed to maintain such islands free of alien animals. One of the more difficult groups of alien animals to exclude, particularly from inhabited islands, are commensal species of rat. The problem is compounded by the difficulty, if not present impossibility, of eliminating rats from any large island where they have established. Recommendations on how to exclude rats from islands have been prepared by Moors et al. (in press). Preventive action appropriate for other species of alien animal should be developed and carried out as quickly as possible.

Research

There are still many islands for which there is no basic inventory of their species and communities. A biological survey should be the first priority for such islands.

Investigations of the biology of threatened

species will continue to be necessary, for if we do not understand why a species is declining, there is no scientific basis for restorative action.

A third research priority is to continue searching for new methods for eradicating alien animals and for improvements of existing methods that will allow eradication on larger islands than currently possible.

There is also a need to continue systematic and wide-ranging studies of the ecological history of individual islands, for only in this way can we gain a clear understanding of what has been lost and what might be reasonably regained through restorative action.

Translocation Strategies

Maintaining viable populations of endangered species of plants and animals in their original habitats should always be the primary objective in species recovery programs. Where this is not possible, for example with some threatened animals, at least three options remain: captive breeding; intensive management, such as supplementary feeding, of the wild population; and translocation to more suitable habitats.

Captive breeding and intensive management of wild populations, although sometimes vital, are only short-term solutions. If, however, suitable alternative habitats can be found or created, translocation may offer the possibility of long-term survival.

Strategies are needed that will disperse populations of vulnerable species to a greater number of islands and thus increase their security against both present and future threats. This technique has been in use with considerable success in New Zealand since the 1890s.

Some translocation strategies will need to be international in scope. In the Mascarene group of islands, for example, where would it be possible to establish a viable population of Mauritius parakeets (*Psittacula echo*)? This species is now reduced to eight individuals (D. V. Merton 1987, personal communication). Although Reunion Island has been suggested as a translocation site, a closely related parakeet has already become extinct there as a result of hunting pressure and habitat destruction. Some other island in the Indian Ocean, where there are fewer predators and a greater area of high-quality habitat, is required. The chance of saving the species from extinction, at least within its own biogeographical region, may be more important than battling impossible odds on its island of origin.

The question of long-distance translocations for endangered species is raised again by a recent study of Henderson Island, South Pacific (Steadman and Olson 1985), which formerly had a species of large pigeon, presumed to have been exterminated by Polynesians. This pigeon was closely allied to the "Marquesas" pigeon (*Ducula galeata*), which now survives only on Nuku Hiva in the Marquesas Islands, 2000 km northwest of Henderson Island. Steadman and Olson suggest that Henderson, now uninhabited, may be a suitable site for translocation of the endangered Marquesas pigeon. Whatever the merits of this particular suggestion, their study shows how paleontological investigation of extinct animals, a subject that some might dismiss as irrelevant to current conservation problems, can reveal new options for translocation.

No translocation strategy is complete without consideration of the biological consequences of such actions, both for species already present in the selected habitat and for the way in which a particular translocation may remove options for subsequent translocations of additional vulnerable species. Every translocation proposal should incorporate impact assessments of these effects.

Eradication Priorities

Priorities for eradication of alien animals from particular islands should be decided not on the basis of damage already done, but on the biological benefits that will result. These benefits need to be listed, and one of the more important will be the new options for translocating vulnerable species that may arise. For example, in the Chatham Islands, B. D. Bell and others have pointed out how Pitt Island (6200 ha), if maintained free of rats and cleared of certain alien predators, has the potential to secure the future survival of at least eight endangered birds of the Chatham group (Atkinson, in press).

During the 1980s there have been successful campaigns in New Zealand to eradicate cats from Little Barrier Island, 2817 ha (Veitch 1985), *R. norvegicus* from the Noises Islands, 22 and 10 ha (Moors 1985), and possums (*Trichosurus vulpecula*) from Kapiti (1960 ha) and Codfish (1396 ha) Islands. The eradications of

rabbits from Round Island (151 ha) in the Indian Ocean and Philip Island (190 ha) were discussed earlier. These various successes demonstrate that there are many more options for ridding biologically important islands of some species of alien animal than previously realized.

A poorly conceived attempt to eradicate an alien species from an island may result in temporarily increased numbers of the problem species. In discussing eradication, Merton (1978) stresses the importance of careful planning, the necessity to precede the operation with public relations programs that enlist support and reduce emotional or misinformed criticism, and the high level of dedication required by project personnel to achieve total eradication. As pointed out by Merton, eradication is often as much a psychological challenge as it is a physical and biological one, and without total commitment by field workers and those financing the project, eradication cannot be achieved.

As new and improved techniques for eradicating various alien animals are applied, it is important that this information be communicated widely. Dr. P. Cowan (personal communication) suggests that an international body such as IUCN should maintain a register of successful and unsuccessful eradication attempts with the names of people and agencies that can be contacted for advice.

Developing Awareness of Conservation Among Island Inhabitants and Their Governments

Crucial to the success of any plan to conserve the biotas and biotic communities of islands is the support and understanding of the local inhabitants (Kepler and Scott 1985) and the recognition that the limited resources of an inhabited island can support only a limited number of people at an acceptable standard of living. Support and understanding must be developed beyond the level of sympathetic interest to a point where there is pride and responsibility among the inhabitants for a heritage that is uniquely theirs. Without this responsibility, no amount of exhortations to conserve, no amount of research, and no plans for conservation action, will succeed. Equally, without acceptance of policies that limit the sizes of human populations on islands, conservation can have little meaning.

On some islands, the Galápagos for example,

there is a growing realization of the economic benefit to the inhabitants of conserving nature to promote the growth of carefully controlled nature tourism. On many islands, however, it is only recognition by the inhabitants that biological impoverishment will ultimately impoverish their lives, as has happened on Rodrigues Island (Gade 1985), that can halt or reverse the present degradation. Involving school-age children and other island inhabitants in imaginative programs of biological restoration, such as that effected in Bermuda by Wingate (1985), may be the best way of changing people's attitudes toward conservation.

Recent successful conservation and restoration programs demonstrate that a great deal more can be achieved. Governments must be fully informed of these successes so that they become more aware of the potential value these programs have for improving the quality of people's lives.

Appendix: Distribution of Introduced Feral and Commensal Mammals on Major Islands/Island Groups of the World

Islands	Goat	Rabbit	Pig	Cat	R. rattus	R. norvegicus	R. exulans	Other Introduced Mammals	Additional References
Atlantic Ocean									
Annobón*	(+)	+	–	+	?	?	–	Donkey, mouse, sheep	
Ascension	+	+		+	+	–	–	Sheep	Lloyd 1987
Azores Is.*	+	–	+	+	+	+	–	Cattle, dog, donkey, horse, mouse, racoon (*Procyon lotor*), sheep	Buden 1986; Campbell 1978
Bahama Is.	+	–	+	+	+	+	–	(Dog), mouse	Jones 1884
Bermuda Is.	+	–	+	+	+	+	–		Bannerman 1922; Dominguez and Bacallado 1984
Canary Is.	+	+	+	+	+	+	–	Barbary ground squirrel (*Atlantoxerus getulus*), *Capra lervia*, cattle, dog, donkey, dromedary, hedgehog, horse, mouse, mufflon, sheep	
Cape Verde Is.*	+	(+)		+	?	?	–	Green monkey, mouse, sheep	Dorst and de Naurois 1966; Fosberg 1983
Faeroe Is.*		+	+		+	+	–	Mink, mountain hare (*Lepus timidus*), mouse, sheep	
Falkland Is.	(+)	+	+	+	.	+	–	Argentine gray fox (*Dusicyon griseus*), cattle, dog, guanaco, hare (*Lepus europaeus*), horse, mouse, sheep	
Fernando de Noronha	–	–	–	+	+	–	–	Mouse	Wace 1986
Gough	–	–	–	(+)	–	–	–	(Dog), mouse, (sheep)	
Iceland*		–	–	+	–	+	–	Cattle, field mouse (*Apodemus sylvaticus*), mink, mouse, reindeer, sheep	Saemundsson 1939
Jan Mayen									
Madeira Is.*	+	+		+	+	–	–	Cattle, sheep	Fosberg 1983; Lloyd 1987
Martin Vaz					?	?	–	—	
Principé*	–	(+)	+		–	(+)	–		
Sable	–	+	+	+	–	–	–	Cattle, (fox), horse	Lockley 1964; Dr. H. Robertson, personal communication, 1988
Salvage	(+)	+	–	(+)	–	–	–	Mouse	
Sao Tomé*	–	–	+	+	+	+	–	Civet (*Viverra civetta*), mona monkey, mouse, weasel	Feiler 1984

Location							Introduced mammals	Reference
Shetland Is.	–	+	–	+	+	–	Brown hare, field mouse (*Apodemus sylvaticus*), hedgehog, mountain hare (*Lepus timidus*), mouse, stoat, sheep	Berry and Johnston 1980
South Georgia	(+)	–	+	+	+	–	(Dog), (horse), mouse, reindeer	Cronk 1986
St Helena	+	(+)	+	+	–	–	Cattle, mouse	
Svalbard*	–	–	+	+	+	–	Hare (*Lepus arcticus, L. timidus*), musk ox	Myrberget 1972
Trinidad	(+)	–	+	+	–	–	Mouse, sheep	Barth 1958
Tristan da Cunha	+	(+)	+	+	(+)	–	Cattle, (dog), donkey, (horse), mouse, sheep	Wace and Holdgate 1976
West Indies: Greater Antilles*	+	+	+	+	+	–	Cattle, collared peccary, dog, horse, mongoose, mouse, red agouti, rhesus macaque (*Macaca mulatta*), white-tailed deer, white-lipped peccary	Allen 1911
West Indies: Lesser Antilles*	+	+	+	+	+	–	Fallow deer, green monkey, hare, mona monkey, mongoose, mouse, opossum (*Didelphis marsupialis*), pale-fronted capuchin (*Cebus albifrons*)	Allen 1911; Marsh 1981
Indian Ocean								
Agalega*	+	+	+	+	+	–	Brown hare, horse	J.E.C. Flux, personal communication
Aldabra	+	–	+	+	+	–	(Dog)	Stoddart and Poore 1970
Amirante Is.*	(+)	–	(+)	+	+	–	Donkey	Jouventin and Roux 1983; Segonzac 1972
Amsterdam	+	–	+	+	+	–	(Dog), mouse, (sheep)	
Andaman Is.	+	–	+	+	+	+	Axis deer, cattle, dog, Indian buffalo (*Bubalus bubalis*), mouse, pig-tailed macaque (*Macaca nemestrina*)	
Ashmore Reef	–	–	–	+	–	–	—	Serventy 1952
Assumption*	+	+	+	+	?	–	Dog	
Astove*	+	+	+	+	?	–	Cattle	Newlands 1975
Cargados Carajos*	+	+	+	+	+	–	Dog, donkey	
Chagos Is.*	(+)	–	–	+	+	+	Mouse	Gibson-Hill 1947
Christmas	–	(+)	+	+	+	–	(Deer), mouse	Wood-Jones 1912
Cocos Keeling Is.	–	–	+	+	–	–	Bush pig (*Potamochoerus larvatus*), cattle, Indian civet (*Viverricula indica*), mouse, rusa deer, sheep	
Comoro Is.*	–	?	?	?	–	?		

(*continued*)

Appendix (continued)

Islands	Goat	Rabbit	Pig	Cat	R. rattus	R. norvegicus	R. exulans	Other Introduced Mammals	Additional References
Cosmoledo	+	+	–	+	?	?	–	Mouse, (sheep)	Bayne et al. 1970
Crozet Is.	(+)	+	(+)	+	+	–	–	Banteng (*Bos javanicus*)	
Enggano* (off Sumatra)	+	–	–	–	+	–	–	–	Malzy 1966
Europa	–	–	–	+	–	–	–	Horse	Racey and Nicoll 1984
Farquhar	(+)	–	–	+	?	?	–	Mouse	Battistini and Cremers 1972
Gloriosa Is.	–	–	–	–	?	?	–	–	
Heard and McDonald Is.	–	–	–	–	–	–	–	–	
Houtman Abrolhos Is.	–	(+)	–	+	?	–	–	(Dog), (sheep)	Fuller and Burbidge 1981
Kerguelen Is.	–	+	(+)	+	+	–	–	(Cattle), (dog), horse, (mink), moufflon, mouse, (mule), reindeer, sheep	
Lakshadweep (Laccadive)* Is.								Mouse	
Maldive Is.*	–	+	–	+	+	–	–	Mouse, musk shrew (*Sunchus murinus*)	Hill 1958
Mauritius	+	(+)	+	+	+	+	–	Black-naped hare (*Lepus nigricollis*), long-tail macaque (*Macaca fascicularis*), Indian grey mongoose, tenrec, rusa deer, shrew (*Sunchus murinus*), small Indian mongoose	
Mentawai Is. (off Sumatra)*					+	–	+		
Nias (off Sumatra)*					+	–	+		
Nicobar Is.*	–	–	+	+	–	–	–	(Axis deer), *Macaca fascicularis*	Watkins and Cooper 1986
Prince Edward Is.: Marion	–	–	+	+	+	–	+	(Dog), (donkey), (goat), mouse, (pig), (sheep)	Williams et al. 1979
Prince Edward Is.: Prince Edward	–	–	–	–	–	–	+	–	
Réunion	+	–	+	+	+	+	–	Coypu, dog, cattle, *Lepus capensis*, *L. nigricollis*, tenrec, mouse, red deer, rusa deer, *Suncus murinus*	Moutou 1983
Rodrigues	+	–	+	+	+	+	–	Cattle, Indian grey mongoose (*Herpestes edwardsii*), sheep	Gade 1985
Seychelles Is.	+	+	+	+	+	+	–	Black-naped hare (*Lepus nigricollis*), cattle, dog, donkey, mouse, (rusa deer), tenrec	Racey and Nicoll 1984
Simeulue* (off Sumatra)	(+)	–	(+)	(+)	+	–	+		
St. Paul	(+)	+	(+)	(+)	+	–	–	Cattle, mouse, (sheep)	Segonzac 1972
Tromelin	–	+	–	–	–	+	–	Mouse	Staub 1970

Location							Introduced mammals	Reference
Pacific Ocean								
Aleutian	(+)	+		−	+	+	−	Arctic fox (*Alopex lagopus*), caribou, cattle, deer (*Odocoileus hemionus*), dog, elk, *Lepus americanus*, mouse, musk ox (*Ovibos moschatus*), muskrat, red fox (*Vulpes vulpes*), sheep	Jones and Byrd 1979; Murie 1959
Antipodes	+	−	−	−	−	−	−	(Cattle), mouse, (sheep)	
Auckland	+	+	+	+	−	−	−	Cattle, (dog), (horse), mouse, (sheep)	
Austral* (including Rapa)	+	+	+	+	+	+	+	Cattle, dog, horse	King 1973
Baker	−	−	−	−	+	+	−		
Bonin Is. (including Seven Islands of Izu)	+	+	+	+	+	+	−	Deer, dog, sheep, sika deer, tree squirrel (*Callosciurus caniceps*)	
Campbell	(+)	−	(+)	+	+	+	−	(Dog), (cattle), sheep	
Caroline*	+	+	+	+	+	+	+	Dog, mouse	
Chatham	+	(+)	+	+	+	+	(+)	Brush-tailed possum (*Trichosurus vulpecula*), cattle, dog, horse, mouse, sheep	
Chesterfield	−	−	−	−	−	−	−	—	Cohic 1959
Clipperton	−	−	(+)	−	−	−	−	Mouse	Sachet 1962
Cocos	−	−	−	+	+	+	−		Snodgrass and Heller 1902
Commander	+	+	+	+	+	+	−	Arctic fox, mouse, red-backed vole (*Clethrionomys rutilus*)	
Cook	+	+	+	+	+	+	+	Dog, mouse	Hough 1975
Coral Sea*	−	−	−	−	−	−	−		
Desventurados							−	—	
Diego Ramirez	−	−	−	−	−	−	−	Guinea pig, sheep	
Easter*	+		+	+	+	+	+	Cattle, horse, sheep	Pernetta and Watling 1978
Fiji	+	−	+	+	+	+	+	Cattle, fallow deer, horse, Indian gray mongoose (*Herpestes edwardsii*), mongoose, mouse, red deer	
Galápagos	+	−	+	+	+	+	−	Cattle, dog, donkey, horse, mouse, (sheep)	Eckhardt 1972
Gambier*	+	+					+		
Great Barrier Reef*	+	+	+	+	+	+	−		MacGillivray 1928
Guadalupe	−	−	−	−	−	−	−	Mouse	Anthony 1925; J. R. Jehl, personal communication, 1988

(continued)

Appendix (continued)

Islands	Goat	Rabbit	Pig	Cat	R. rattus	R. norvegicus	R. exulans	Other Introduced Mammals	Additional References
Hawaii	+	+	+	+	+	+	+	Axis deer, cattle, dog, donkey, hoary bat (*Lasiurus cinereus*), horse, mongoose, mouse, mule deer, pronghorn, rock wallaby (*Petrogale pencillata*), sheep, Indian buffalo (*Bubalus bubalis*)	Tomich 1969
Howland	−	−	−	+	−	−	+	Dog, mouse	King 1973
Johnston	−	+	−	+	+	−	−		Kirkpatrick 1966
Juan Fernandez	+	+	+	+	+	+	−	Cattle, dog, donkey, horse, mouse, sheep, southern coatis (*Nasua nasua*)	Kunkel 1968; Torres and Aguayo 1971
Kermadec	(+)	−	(+)	+	−	+	+	—	
Kiribati (Gilbert)*	(+)	−	+	+	+	−	+		Perry 1980
Kiribati (Line)	−	−	+	+	+	−	+	Dog	
Kiribati (Ocean)*	+	+	+	+	+	−	+		
Kiribati (Phoenix)	+	−	+	+	+	−	+		
Lord Howe	+	+	(+)	+	+	?	(+)	Dog	Fullager and Disney 1974
Loyalty*	(+)	+	(+)	+	+	+	−	(Dog), mouse	
Macquarie	−	+	−	+	+	−	−	(Cattle), (dog), (donkey), (horse), mouse, (sheep)	
Malpelo	−	−	−	−	−	−	−	—	
Marcus	−	−	−	(+)	+	−	+		Sakagami 1961
Mariana	+	−	+	+	+	+	+	Dog, mouse, musk shrew (*Suncus murinus*), Sambar deer	Baker 1946; Barbehenn 1974; Savidge 1987
Marshall*	+	−	+	+	+		+	Dog, mouse	
Marquesas	+	−	+	+	+	+	+	Cattle, donkey, horse, sheep	Amerson 1969
Nauru*				+	+	+	+	Mouse	
New Caledonia	+	−	+	+	+	+	+	Cattle, donkey, dog, mouse	J.M. Williams, personal communication, 1987
New Zealand	+	+	+	+	+	+	+	Brush-tailed possum (*Trichosurus vulpecula*), cattle, chamois, deer (9 spp.), dog, ferret, hare, hedgehog, horse, mouse, sheep, stoat, tahr, wallaby (6 spp.), weasel	Warner 1948; Wodzicki 1950
Niue	−	(+)	+	+	+	−	+	Cattle, dog, sheep	Wodzicki 1969a
Norfolk	(+)	−	(+)	+	+	−	+	(Dog), mouse	Hermes 1986
Palau*	+	−	+	+	+	+	+	Long-tail macaque (*Macaca fascicularis*), dog, mouse	Barbehenn 1974

Pitcairn*	+	(+)	(+)	+			+	(Cattle), dog, mouse	
Pribolov		−					−	Arctic fox, mouse, musk rat (*Ondatra zibethicus*)	
Rennell and Bellona*		−			−	−	+		
Revilla Gigedo*				+	+		−	Deer, dog	McLellan 1926
Rotuma*		−	+			+	+		
Ryukyu*		−			?	?	−	Dog, Indian gray mongoose (*Herpestes edwardsii*), Siberian weasel, sika deer	
Samoa	−		+	+	+	+	+	Dog	
Santa Cruz (including* Swallow, Tikopia, Duff)		−	+		+		+		
Snares	(+)	−	−	−	−	−	−	−	
Society	+	−	+	+	+	+	+	Cattle, dog, donkey, mouse	
Solomon*		−	+	+	+		+	Mouse	
St. Lawrence	−	−	−		−	−	−	Arctic fox, reindeer	Jones and Byrd 1979
St. Matthew	−	−	−				−	Reindeer	Jones and Byrd 1979
Three Kings	(+)	−	−	−	−	−	−	−	
Tokelau	−	−	+	+	−	−	+	Dog	Wodzicki 1969b
Tonga		−	+	+	+	+	+	Dog, horse, mouse	
Tuamotu*		−		+	+	+	+	Dog, mouse	
Tuvalu (Ellice)*		−		+	+	+	+	(Mongoose), mouse	J. M. Williams, personal communication, 1987
Vanuatu (including Banks and Torres)*		−	+		+	+	+		
Volcano*		−		+	?	?	−		
Wake	−	−	−	+	+	−	+		King 1973
Wallis and Futuna*						+			

Sources: Basic sources of information used in compiling this list are Atkinson (1985) for rats, De Vos et al. (1956), Douglas (1969) for Pacific Ocean islands, Elliott (1972) for Indian Ocean islands, Flux and Fullager (1983) for rabbits, Johnstone (1985) for subantarctic islands and Lever (1985).

Islands without higher plants, such as those covered in ice, are excluded from this list, as are islands <50 km from continental coasts. New Zealand and New Caledonia are included because, notwithstanding their size, the history of their biotas is more similar to that of other islands than it is to that of continents.

*Islands or island groups for which information is known to be incomplete.

+ = mammal present; − = mammal not recorded; (+) = mammal no longer present; ? = rats known to be present but species unknown. An empty space in a column indicates that no information is available to the author for that particular mammal.

8

The Problems of Conserving Genes and Species

DAVID S. WOODRUFF

Species are fundamental units of nature and ecology. Their survival is critical if we are to achieve even modest goals of ecosystem and biosphere management for sustained development. Species are also fundamental units of the evolutionary process; they are pivotal organizational elements of biotic diversity. It is their innate ability to change, to adapt, that presents us with one of science's greatest challenges—safeguarding the future evolutionary potential of species. In this chapter, I shall review present species management strategies and problems, describe the development of species survival plans, and note deficiencies in the planning process. I shall offer a personal view of what needs to be done to facilitate species level conservation and point to numerous opportunities for increased interaction between academic researchers and applied biologists. The fundamental science and technology that can be brought to bear on species conservation issues are in urgent need of improvement. Because ensuring the continued evolutionary potential of many species will require far more active and intrusive management, I will conclude by examining the consequences of our failure to intervene in a timely manner. I will not belabor the obvious increase in extinction rates (see chaps. 4–7), but instead confront the proposition that, in the not too distant future, biotic evolution on this planet will be essentially over. Our actions or inactions, now and in the next century, are critical to determining the future courses of evolution; the prospects to be gained by accepting responsibility for the stewardship of this, Dar-win's (1845:378) mystery of mysteries, leaves no time for pessimism.

Species are comprised of groups of populations sharing intrinsic coadapted gene complexes and a common evolutionary fate. The populations of a species are often united by gene flow facilitated by species recognition cues and effectively separated from those of other species by reproductive isolating mechanisms. The conservation of species is twofold: First, it involves the conservation of the diversity of living species (Myers 1983a; Wilson 1985b, 1988). Second, it involves the conservation of the existing genetic diversity within each species to ensure its future evolution (Oldfield 1984; Orians 1988). Until recently, zoologists have concentrated on the former and botanists on the latter aspect of conservation; to get selected species of both plants and animals to the year 2100, we will henceforth have to pay increased attention to the second aspect—maintenance of the genetic integrity and evolutionary capability of species.

The magnitude of the task facing conservation biologists is daunting (Table 8.1). There are an estimated ten to fifty million species alive today (Erwin 1988). Just less than two million species have been recognized and named in a formal, taxonomic sense. For most of these recognized species, we know little more than what they look like and where they are found. Fewer than 10,000 species have been characterized ecobehaviorally, and closer to 1,000 of these have been examined genetically. If sound conservation is based on knowledge of the genetics, ecology, and behavior of a species, then we

Table 8.1. The Challenge Facing Conservation

Number of species extant in 1988	$>10^7$
Number of species formally described	10^6
Number of species characterized ecobehaviorly	10^4
Number of species characterized genetically	10^3
Number of species that are scientifically manageable in 1988	10^2
Number of species probably requiring interventive management by 2100	10^4

Note: Order of magnitude approximations

must admit that we are presently capable of managing the evolutionary potential of few more than 100 species. I estimate that the number of species requiring management (to a greater or lesser extent) by the year 2100 will be closer to 10,000.

The species that we have already selected for conservation efforts are a very heterogeneous group. Many were favored because they provide us with food, clothing, or companionship. The charismatic megavertebrates and certain flowering plants of unusual beauty, size, or antiquity have also received an inordinate share of our attention. Recently, a handful of previously unnoticed species have become the focus of major conservation efforts by those seeking to use their "rights to existence" to block exploitive development projects. Among the latter are the furbis lousewort (*Pedicularis furbishiae*), the snail darter (*Percina tanasi*), and the northern spotted owl (*Strix occidentalis*) (Ehrlich and Ehrlich 1981; National Audubon Society 1986b).

Although the majority of organisms still persist without human intervention, the ranks of those that depend on us for their survival are increasing rapidly. The technologies—broadly defined to include management systems and other means by which knowledge is applied—used to conserve species have been reviewed elsewhere (U.S. Congress, Office of Technology Assessment 1987) and are applicable at four different levels. First, many species are being managed where they occur naturally. The costs of conservation programs at this level are relatively low and usually benefit more than just the target species as management focuses on ecosystem maintenance. Included in this category are some food fish and migratory birds. At a second level are those species that now depend on parks and nature reserves for their survival.

Traditionally, management was passive or involved protection from poachers and natural disasters. Increasingly, however, managers must actively regulate population numbers and use such techniques as controlled burning and flooding to regulate community-level processes. Examples of this level of species conservation include California sea otters (*Enhydra lutris nereis*) and Indian rhinoceros (*Rhinoceros unicornis*) (Ladd and Riedman 1987; Martin et al. 1987). The third conservation level involves species that are now restricted to or heavily dependent on zoos and botanical gardens for relatively intensive care. Species whose survival presently depends on this level of intervention includes Père David's deer (*Elaphurus davidianus*) and the California condor (*Gymnogyps californianus*) (California Nature Conservancy 1987; Kohl 1982).

At the outset, it is important to note that the cost of a species conservation program increases from tenfold to 10,000-fold at each of these three levels of intervention (Conway 1986). For example, the cost of maintaining the whole Serengeti ecosystem is currently about U.S. $500,000 per annum; it costs the same amount to maintain viable populations of just five species of primates in North American zoos (Western 1987). It is obviously much cheaper and far more desirable from both economic and ecological viewpoints to conserve species in nature than in captivity. Furthermore, off-site conservation in zoos, for example, simply cannot accommodate breeding programs for the 2,000 species of terrestrial vertebrates expected to be dependent on such care in the next century (Soulé et al. 1986). Finally, there is a fourth level of species conservation, involving the cryopreservation of germplasm and embryos. Although this technology promises to be very useful for maintaining plant diversity off-site, it is presently irrelevant to the conservation of all but a handful of (domestic) animals (U.S. Congress, Office of Technology Assessment 1987).

SPECIES MANAGEMENT: PRACTICES AND PROBLEMS

Conservation practices are rooted in millennia of human experience, but I shall not attempt to review the vast literature of animal husbandry, plant propagation, forest tree, and wildlife species management here. Instead, I shall concentrate on the recent application of genetic and ecological theory to the management of threatened populations and species, the results of conservation biology's first decade.

Among the objectives of sound management are those practices listed in Table 8.2. The list is by no means comprehensive, and each practice is, in fact, complicated by unstated corollaries. For example, maintaining genetic variation may involve moving animals between isolated populations to simulate the effects of natural gene flow. Maintaining multiple populations also implies that individual populations are expected to go extinct with finite regularity, even if such catastrophes are stochastic and occur only once a century. Planning to ensure the persistence of the species as a whole cannot be based on mathematical models of single population genetics and ecology. Most species are patchily distributed; the resulting pattern is termed a metapopulation. Nevertheless, the list suggests that far more has to be done to save threatened species than simply providing them with a suitable habitat. For detailed justification of these and other management practices that will have to be implemented to conserve local coadapted gene complexes, the reader is referred to the references in Table 8.2 and to key reference books (Soulé and Wilcox 1980; Frankel and Soulé

1981; Schonewald-Cox et al. 1983; Soulé 1986, 1987) and the technical literature cited therein.

Despite the widespread recognition of the appropriate management practices, there are many problems impeding their application. The most pervasive is that of defining the size and structure of viable populations—populations or metapopulations that will retain 90 percent of their original quantitative genetic variation for 200 years (Soulé et al. 1986). Earlier attempts to define minimum viable population (MVP) size in terms of the theoretically derived effective population size (N_e) concept did not solve this problem. Thus, the argument that 50 unrelated individuals $(N_e = 50)$ were required for the short-term preservation of reproductive fitness to prevent a population from losing genetic variability through inbreeding is no longer accepted. Similarly, the more restrictive proscription that $N_e \geq 500$ is essential for the long-term protection of the adaptive potential of a population (Franklin 1980; Frankel and Soulé 1981) is no longer regarded as a useful rule-of-thumb. Despite the great importance of the effective population size (N_e) concept to conservation, it does not lead to magic numbers of 50 or 500. Species should not be abandoned simply because their numbers fall below such theoretically derived cutoff points, as was suggested in the case of Australia's orange-bellied parrot, *Neophema*

Table 8.2. Species Management Practices

Practice	Recent Discussion
Maximize effective population size (N_e)	Lande and Barrowclough 1987
Minimize the variance in population growth rate (r)	Goodman 1987
Attain viable population size as soon as possible	Foose 1983; Shaffer 1981
Equalize the genetic contributions of the founders	Frankel and Soulé 1981
Monitor and maintain inherent qualitative and quantitative genetic variability	Lande and Barrowclough 1987; Wayne et al. 1986
Reduce inbreeding or purge population of genes responsible for inbreeding depression	Ralls and Ballou 1986; Templeton and Read 1984
Avoid outbreeding depression	Templeton 1986
Maintain multiple populations (metapopulations)	Gilpin 1987; Lacy 1987
Avoid selecting for "type" or for domestication	Foose et al. 1986; Frankham et al. 1986
Facilitate natural behaviors including:	
dispersal and migration	Lewis 1986
social and breeding	Strum and Southwick 1986
Manage interacting species including:	
pollinators	Janzen 1986
prey species	Terborgh 1986
predators	Gulland 1987
parasites	Dobson and May 1986
competitors	Diamond and Case 1986a

chrysogaster ($N < 200$) (Brown et al. 1985) (the suggestion was rejected—Peter Rawlinson, LaTrobe University and Australian Conservation Foundation, personal communication 1987). It is worth remembering that Père David's deer (*E. davidianus*) and Przewalski's horse (*Equus przewalski*) both recovered from populations of less than 20 individuals.

Since the U.S. National Forest Management Act was passed in 1976, directing the Forest Service to maintain viable populations of the species in its care, attention has shifted to defining genetic and ecological thresholds for population persistence, thresholds below which nonadaptive, random forces prevail over adaptive forces (Soulé 1985). Shaffer (1981) defined a minimum viable population for any given species in any given habitat as the smallest isolated population having a 99 percent chance of remaining extant for 1,000 years despite the foreseeable effects of demographic, environmental, and genetic stochasticity and natural catastrophes. He described five approaches to determining MVP sizes: experimental, biogeographical patterns, theoretical and simulation models based on ecological variables, and genetic considerations. Subsequent workers have extended the concept to show how MVP size will vary with generation time, body size, population structure, geographical location within a species range, and expected persistence time. As Shaffer himself noted, the MVP size concept has important minimum area and minimum viable density correlates; the latter are particularly important for forest trees (Hubbell and Foster 1986).

A comprehensive or systems-level approach to estimating MVP size has been proposed and designated population vulnerability (or viability) analysis (PVA) (Gilpin 1987; Gilpin and Soulé 1986; Soulé 1987). PVA confronts some of the most difficult problems of ecology and evolutionary biology. PVA implicitly asks whether current theory leads to long-term predictions as to the probable persistence of populations and species. That it does not is simply a function of the complexity of the problems and the infancy of the approach. The synthesis of ecological and genetic factors (traditionally treated independently) in population models is difficult, because the interplay of the two is not well understood. The relationship between genetic variation, individual fitness, and popula-

tion viability needs elucidating. Similarly, endangerment or risk needs quantifying with respect to specified time spans. This latter factor is especially problematic, as random environmental fluctuations typically have very large effects on variation in population growth rates. Nevertheless, preliminary population vulnerability analyses lead to estimates of MVP sizes that are large (thousands of individuals) and necessitate very large reserves or multiple reserves with intensive management. It is clear that without interventive management, the largest mammals will not survive in even the largest parks and reserves. Grizzly bears (*Ursus arctos horribilis*) of Yellowstone National Park ($N < 200$), for example, have a low long-term probability of persistence despite their protected status (Salwasser et al. 1987).

Leaving analytical and theoretical problems of population vulnerability analysis aside for the moment, the manager is still confronted by numerous difficulties in applying the principles listed in Table 8.2. Data on the genetic variation of most species requiring conservation are simply not available. Yet the importance of maintaining genetic diversity in a population is clear; populations with low diversity are vulnerable to new pathogens and climatic change and have limited evolutionary potential. Studies of the positive relationship between heterozygosity and fitness in plants and animals are in general agreement on this important point (Allendorf and Leary 1986; Ledig 1986). Species with little detectable genetic variation, like the cheetah (*Acinoyx jubatus*), Arabian oryx (*Oryx leucoryx*), and Torrey pine (*Pinus torreyana*), may be highly vulnerable (Ledig 1986; O'Brien et al. 1985; Woodruff and Ryder 1986). Conserving genetic variability in managed populations requires the monitoring of allozymic and quantitative variation—monitoring procedures rarely carried out in captive populations, let alone in nature (Lande and Barrowclough 1987; Moran and Hopper 1983; Wyatt 1984). Such population genetic monitoring will also aid the manager in identifying situations where inbreeding exceeds 2 percent and is likely to become a problem. Such situations are often difficult to recognize in the absence of pedigrees, as the effects of inbreeding are often overlooked until they become severe (Ralls et al. 1979, 1986). The inbreeding problem is, however, likely to be of ever-increasing concern to conservationists as habitats become fragmented and populations smaller. The maintenance of genetic variation will increasingly depend on the artificial movement of organisms (or their seeds and gametes) between patches of the metapopulation. Although low rates of gene flow (one animal per generation) between patches may suffice to maintain qualitative genetic similarity, higher rates are required for quantitative genetic similarity (Vrijenhoek, chap. 9). Both the theory and the techniques of such population genetic manipulations require urgent development (Varvio et al. 1986). Former levels of gene flow, patch size, and turnover rate can, however, be estimated and used to guide management practice (Gould and Woodruff 1986; Slatkin 1987; Woodruff and Gould 1987).

Although genetic aspects of population management may be important in the long run, there is general agreement that, in a crisis, population ecology is more important. Yet even though the ecology of a species is easier to manipulate than its genetics, the conservation manager faces difficult problems. For example, reducing the variance in a population's growth rate and therefore the probability of extinction (Goodman 1987) requires the close monitoring of numerous biotic and environmental variables for several generations. Managers rarely have adequate longitudinal demographic data of the quality necessary for the identification of key or regulatory environmental factors. Without such data, the effects of natural catastrophes that occur with a frequency of once in every 50 to 100 years cannot be properly anticipated. The situation is even more complex for organisms that go through natural cycles of abundance. Existing management practices are poorly suited to such dynamic situations (Walker, chap. 12).

Another ecological factor complicating management arises from natural dispersal and migratory behavior. There are numerous cases where nature preserve boundaries are ill suited to the needs of the organisms and communities that now depend on them. Janzen (1986) describes a graphic example involving forty species of sphingid moths that pollinate flowers in the dry forest of Santa Rosa National Park, Costa Rica. These species migrate annually to spend the dry season in rain forest patches 15–50 km away from the park. The destruction of the rain forest will result in the extinction of the moths and, in turn, the plants that depend on them in the dry forest. Conservation management plans must be comprehensive enough to accommodate or artificially facilitate the normal dispersal behaviors of organisms and their mutualists.

DEFINING EVOLUTIONARILY SIGNIFICANT UNITS FOR CONSERVATION MANAGEMENT

If the goal of conservation efforts is to permit the continued evolution of species, then it is important to establish that the managed individuals or populations are conspecific. Currently, many operational conservation units are poorly defined, and the true evolutionary relationships of isolated populations treated as belonging to the same species are unknown. This is a serious problem, as the consequences of hybridization, termed outbreeding depression, can be just as damaging to a captive or a translocated population as inbreeding depression (Templeton 1986; Templeton et al. 1986). Unfortunately, traditional taxonomy, especially subspecific taxonomy, is a poor guide for managers seeking to avoid this problem. To illustrate the generality of this problem, I shall note its occurrence in a number of well-known mammals; other, less well-known groups are expected to present the conservationist with proportionally more problems.

Chromosomally distinct individuals and populations have now been identified in such diverse taxa as the squirrel monkey (*Saimiri sciureus*), spider monkeys (*Ateles* spp.), owl monkey (*Aotus trivirgatus*), orangutan (*Pongo pygmaeus*), dik-diks (*Madoqua spp.*), and okapi (*Okapi johnstoni*) (Benirschke 1983; Robert Lacy, Brookfield Zoo, personal communication 1988; Ryder et al., in press). In some cases (e.g., *Ateles*), the hybrids between these chromosomal types exhibit the effects of outbreeding depression; in other cases, the necessary analyses have yet to be performed. In the latter case, however, it is already clear that the Sumatran and Bornean orangutans differ in a number of other respects, and responsible zoos are removing hybrids from their breeding programs. Unfortunately, this sound management practice has not been adopted in the field, and orphaned Sumatran apes are being released in the Sepilok Reserve in Sabah, Borneo.

In some cases, the evolutionarily significant

units that conservationists need to work with correspond with traditional subspecies taxa; in other cases they do not. It is not at all clear which, if any, of the seven designated subspecies of African black rhinoceros (*Diceros bicornis*) now scattered in about seventy isolated populations have any merit as management units (Ashley et al., in preparation; Western 1987). Similarly, genetic and craniometric studies throw the status of the northern subspecies of the white rhinoceros (*Ceratotherium simum cottoni*) into question (AAZPA 1986; Merenlender 1986; Merenlender et al., in preparation). The resolution of these problems is important if conservation efforts are going to be targeted on appropriate management units. It is doubtful, for example, that the resources can be marshalled to conserve all five remaining subspecies of the tiger (*Panthera tigris*) (Seal 1985; Seal et al. 1987). If the northern white rhinoceros is not a separate species, are we justified in diverting relatively large amounts of conservation money to the protection of the last eighteen free-ranging individuals? Obviously, we are better off managing one species properly than diluting our efforts on numerous possibly ill-defined subspecies. But these decisions are never simple, and genetics alone will rarely dictate policy; there may be other compelling reasons to conserve regional or national varieties. The observation that the Asiatic lion (*Panthera leo persica*) is genetically extremely similar to the African lion (*P. 1. leo*) (O'Brien et al. 1987) does not indicate that efforts to conserve the Gir Forest Sanctuary with its remnant population of lions should be diminished.

It should come as no surprise, of course, that traditional subspecific taxa of terrestrial vertebrates are often inappropriate delimiters of evolutionarily significant units for conservation managers. If conservationists are to focus on natural units, they must recognize that evolutionary biologists abandoned the subspecies category many years ago (Wilson and Brown 1953). The vast majority of the subspecies recognized by zoologists were described long before the biological species concept was formulated. Subspecies, at best, may be useful taxonomic categories; they were never intended to be evolutionary categories of the type required for sound management (Wiley 1981).

If management efforts are to focus on species, then conservationists must also recognize that our understanding of the biological species as an evolutionary category has undergone considerable revision during the last decade (Atchley and Woodruff 1981; Barigozzi 1982; Templeton, in press; Vrba 1985a; White 1978). Although the frustrations with older species concepts led a minority to deny the existence of "species," there is little doubt that this taxon, unlike most others, has a reality and plays a fundamental role in biotic evolution. For many years, species were defined as "groups of actually or potentially interbreeding natural populations which are reproductively isolated from other such groups" (Mayr 1942). This orthodox view, which became known as *the* biological species concept, was correctly criticized for overemphasizing between-population reproductive isolation and the cohesive effects of gene flow.

Appropriately renaming it the isolation species concept, Paterson (1982) developed a positive inverse view, the recognition species concept, in which so-called isolating mechanisms are thought of as facilitating reproduction within populations. Species are thus defined as the most inclusive population of individual biparental organisms that share a common fertilization system (Paterson 1985). Although Paterson's concept has much to recommend it (Templeton 1987; Vrba 1985b) it shares a fatal limitation with the isolation species concept; it too, is inapplicable to fossils and asexually reproducing organisms, including many plants. A third view, the evolutionary species concept, in which species are made up of groups of populations that share a common evolutionary fate, accommodates asexual and self-mating taxa and fossils, but unfortunately has little operational utility (Templeton, in press). All three species concepts have difficulties dealing with reticulate evolution, natural hybridization, and interspecific introgression of mtDNA and nDNA (Barton and Hewitt 1985; Woodruff 1979). Although such phenomena were long recognized by botanists (plant species are often capable of exchanging genes with other members of a larger unit known as the syngameon [Grant 1981], it is only in the last decade that biochemical molecular genetic studies have revealed that animal species, too, are but imperfectly isolated taxa. In both plant and animal syngameons, however, the individual species maintain their often distinct, genetically based morphologies, and introgression is limited to only certain "compatible" components of the genetic system. Species are apparently capable of maintaining their genetic integrity despite such introgression (Woodruff and Gould 1980).

These realizations led Templeton (in press) to propose the cohesion species concept, which builds on the merits of the isolation, recognition, and evolutionary concepts. The cohesion species concept defines species as a group of organisms whose range of phenotypic variation is limited by genetically based cohesion mechanisms. Such mechanisms include gene flow and other phenomena which promote genetic relatedness, the genetic and developmental constraints on the origins of phenotypic variation, and the constraints on the evolutionary fate of genetic and phenotypic variation. Different species are to be expected to rely on different suites of cohesion mechanisms, but all organisms from across the spectrum of reproductive systems can be accommodated by such a cohesion species concept. Templeton's suggestion also has the advantage of focusing on the processes of speciation, the genetic assimilation of altered patterns of cohesion into cohesion mechanisms. As his ideas are tested, and as the molecular genetic dissection of species continues (e.g., Krieber and Rose 1986; Woodruff, in press), we can expect further refinement of the biological species concept. This will have a direct impact on the definition of many conservation management units. We should expect that, in the higher vertebrates, numerous allo- or parapatrically distributed populations (races and subspecies in some cases) will be recognized as semispecies or full species, taxa that merit conservation efforts under most existing regulations. Offsetting such increases in the numbers of species deserving attention, we can also expect the suppression of many more typologically defined subspecies. The evolutionary arguments for saving every infraspecific taxon will become increasingly hard to make as more is learned about the genetic cohesion of species.

In conclusion, both managers and theoreticians share a desire to identify phylogenetically related groups of individuals and populations. Progress in the use of allozymic and mtDNA variation and DNA fingerprinting suggests that within a decade this will be completely routine (Oxford and Rollinson 1983). As with the concept of N_e, however, it is unlikely that there will be any magic numbers; we should not expect multilocus genetic distances, for example, to automatically dictate taxonomic relationships and management policy (Nei 1987). As in the past, I would expect phylogenetically related populations to be characterized holistically, on the basis of the simultaneous consideration of genetics, morphology, ecology, and behavior. Nevertheless, we can expect more revision of the traditional taxonomy of the higher vertebrates during the next twenty years and a more stable, phylogenetically based taxonomy throughout the next century. This will greatly facilitate management programs both at the species and at the community level, where comparisons of local species lists are used to identify biodiversity "hotspots." Until then, we must treat each case individually.

SPECIES CONSERVATION PLANS

The few existing species management plans were developed by various government and nongovernment organizations and focus on a tiny, biased sample of the spectrum of biological diversity. Nevertheless, such plans provide a means of getting many species through the next century. I shall begin by reviewing some national planning in the United States and conclude with a brief review of some international planning efforts. Space does not permit a consideration of the many additional local and regional plans implemented or under development. I focus on U.S. government efforts, as they typify the high-technology, eleventh-hour listing and saving approach to species conservation. This approach and the alternative habitat preservation approach adopted, for example, by The Nature Conservancy complement each other. Both approaches are essential components in any national biodiversity conservation program. There is, however, no U.S. national program or policy for biodiversity, and the U.S. situation may not provide the best models for the rest of the world. Here, as in other countries, the different agencies involved are very variable in their commitment to conservation, and the whole enterprise is vulnerable to traditional political influences from pro-exploitation groups.

Within the United States, there are a number of federal government agencies that are directly concerned with preparing plans for species conservation. The responsibilities and activities of these agencies are reviewed annually in the reports of the National Audubon Society (1985, 1986a, 1987). The Fish and Wildlife Service (Department of the Interior) manages the 90-million-acre National Wildlife Refuge System and, through the Endangered Species Program, administers the Endangered Species Act. The ultimate purpose of the Endangered Species Act is to bring about the recovery of endangered and threatened species. Nine hundred thirty species had been formally listed by 1986, and about 60 more were added to the list that year, the additions drawn from a pool of over 1,000 species on the Category 1 backup list of taxa whose situations are well enough known to proceed to formal listing. The latter list is sometimes referred to by the acronym PETC (proposed endangered or threatened category), and for the purposes of biological discussions, most of its members should be regarded as if they are already formally listed. There are, in addition, another 3,000 species awaiting consideration. The Fish and Wildlife Service is charged with preparing recovery plans for listed species, and to date 223 of the 400 species listed as endangered or threatened in the United States have received some attention. Species and special groups for which national resource plans have been prepared include 8 mammals, 36 birds, 1 reptile and 11 fish, and regional plans are available for 36 more species. In addition, the Fish and Wildlife Service has responsibilities for the welfare of 831 species of migratory birds that are protected by 4 international treaties. Fifty-four of these species are receiving some degree of management attention. Unfortunately, the Fish and Wildlife Service has not yet been in a position to routinely monitor the status of listed species, or the effects of recovery plans, most of which are administered under cooperative agreements with the states involved. Nevertheless, at least 22 of its listed species are apparently recovering (Fitzgerald and Meese 1986). The Service has established two computerized databases to monitor all federally funded fish and wildlife research.

The Fish and Wildlife Service, with the National Marine Fisheries Service, administers the Convention on International Trade in Endangered Species of Wild Fauna and Flora (CITES) of 1973. The objective of CITES, to which 93 nations have agreed to adhere, is to ensure that trade will not cause the extinction of plant or animal species. The Convention has two important Appendices (Table 8.3) which are periodically revised: Appendix I contains the endangered species and species groups (e.g., all felids) whose commercial trade is prohibited. Appendix II contains a longer list of threatened species and species groups (e.g., all hummingbirds and 25,000 orchids) whose trade is restricted. As with any treaty, its success depends on the willingness of participants to implement its provisions. Problems with the unwillingness of some European member states to prevent the continued importation of Appendix I species and with Singapore (which was not a party to CITES until 1988 and chose to become a major transshipper of otherwise protected species and wildlife products) continue to frustrate the aims of the Convention. It is perhaps too soon to assess its overall effectiveness (Bean 1986).

The Forest Service (Department of Agriculture) administers 191 million acres of the National Forest System with more than 3,000 wildlife species, including 129 species listed by the Endangered Species Program in 1986. The National Forests Management Act requires the Service to maintain viable populations of the diversity of plants and animals under its care. To do this, the Service has selected "management indicator species" appropriate for various communities and regions of the country. Such taxa include species that are listed by the Endangered Species Program, species with special habitat requirements, species of special public interest, and species thought to be good indicators of changes in environmental quality. Selected spe-

Table 8.3. Number of Endangered and Threatened Species whose International Trade is Restricted or Regulated by CITES

	APPENDIX I (endangered)	APPENDIX II (threatened)
Mammals	179	303
Birds	133	618
Reptiles	52	340
Amphibians	4	7
Fish	7	15
Insects	0	49
Molluscs	26	5
Plants	87	c. 27,000

Source: Durrell 1986.

cies include three deer, elk, wild turkey, tree hole-nesting birds, resident trout, and anadromous fish. The value of the management indicator species approach can be seen from the fact that effective conservation of a key species like the northern spotted owl (*Strix occidentalis*) will in turn benefit more than eighteen other species of vertebrates restricted to the same old-growth forest community (National Audubon Society 1986b). The Fish and Wildlife Program of the Forest Service has recovery efforts for thirteen listed species under its care. In 1986, the Forestry Service installed the Endangered Species Information Tracking System for the 811 federally listed and PETC species of plants and animals that occur in the national forest system.

Managing over 300 million acres of public land, the Bureau of Land Management (Department of Interior) has hundreds of listed and PETC plants and animals under its care. By 1986 it had begun some level of management of forty-four of the listed species for which the Fish and Wildlife Service had prepared recovery plans. Active programs include the desert tortoise (*Gopherus agassizi*) and the desert bighorn sheep (*Ovis canadensis*).

With responsibilities for seventy-five million acres and one-third of the federally listed animal species, the National Park Service of the Interior Department has actively developed its conservation programs. The Service sponsored the influential U.S. Man and the Biosphere symposium and workshop, "Applications of Genetics to the Management of Wild Plant and Animal Populations," held in Washington, D.C. (Schonewald-Cox et al. 1983), and is developing a computerized database that contains inventories of plant species and threatened, endangered, and exotic species of animals in each park. The Service supports several species recovery projects, including the Peregrine Falcon Program.

Finally, the National Marine Fisheries Service administers the Magnuson Marine Fisheries Conservation and Management Act (1976). By 1987, the Service had implemented thirty plans, covering such species as the Alaskan king crab and such species groups as commercial and recreational salmon. Regardless of the merits of these plans, it is an indictment of the system that recent assessments of 140 stocks found that the majority were being overfished.

Nevertheless, these plans, and an equal number that are under development, are the first steps in conserving stocks of the 300 species of fish, crustaceans, and molluscs harvested annually by the United States, and are reversing the historical "tragedy of the commons" (Hardin 1968) pattern.

Space precludes a detailed discussion of the quality of the species conservation plans of the agencies cited. Some plans are supported by extensive research programs and are highly specific, whereas others involve little more than bland generalizations. Similarly, the implementation of the plans is very variable and is complicated by the large number of separate state and federal agencies involved.

Turning to the private sector, the Species Survival Plans (SSP) of the American Association of Zoological Parks and Aquariums deserve special mention. There are presently thirty-seven SSPs for the captive populations of selected species of prime interest to member zoos. Included are the orangutan (*Pongo pygmaeus*), lowland gorilla (*Gorilla gorilla*), Przewalski's horse (*E. przewalski*), and Asiatic lion (*P. l. persica*). Cooperating zoos agree to manage their animals in accordance with plans drawn up by participants and reviewed at annual meetings with the assistance of a species coordinator. Some of these plans are based on very detailed genetic analyses of the individuals involved. The procedure has had a direct and beneficial effect on the management of several endangered species and has resulted in an upgrading of the management policies for many others. Unfortunately, the list of Species Survival Plans is unlikely to grow much longer in the near future because of the limited resources (staff time and money) that can be devoted to such planning.

The development of such detailed plans for intensive management depends on the availability of data on the individual animals. For years, the Zoological Society of London has published lists of the occurrence of selected species in zoos around the world in its annual yearbook. The Society also coordinates about eighty international studbooks for captive populations. These are generally developed and maintained by individual staff members associated with leading zoos, and they vary in their quality and the frequency with which they are updated.

Another approach to the problem of establishing the essential database for intensive management is that taken by the International Species Inventory System (ISIS), founded by Dr. Ulysses Seal and based at the Minnesota Zoo (Flesness 1987, personal communication). In mid-1987, ISIS had computerized records of 75,000 individual vertebrates in 236 zoological parks in 19 countries. Although 182 of the zoos are in the United States, the system is now expanding internationally. Seven Asian zoos and one in South America have begun participating, and those in Australia and Britain have recently made commitments to enter the program.

A broader view of species conservation planning is taken by a leading nongovernmental organization, the International Union for the Conservation of Nature and Natural Resources (IUCN). The Species Survival Commission (SSC) coordinates the development of Action Plans by 94 Specialist Groups involving over 2,000 biologists and other professionals from 115 countries (Edwards 1987). Plans have been prepared for African primates (Oates 1986), Asian primates (Eudey 1987), antelopes of East and Northeast Africa (East, 1988). Additional plans are being completed for European bats, neotropical primates, canids, mustelids and viverrids, cats, cetaceans, sirenians, Asian elephants, African elephants and rhinos, Asian rhinos, equids, pigs and peccaries, North American bison, African rodents, lagomorphs, tortoises and freshwater turtles, marine turtles, mollusks, pteridophytes, and Mexican cacti and succulents (Stuart 1987). Plans for herons and cranes are being prepared in cooperation with the International Council for Bird Preservation and the International Crane Foundation. A plan covering European reptiles and amphibians is being prepared by SSC and the Societas Europaea Herpetologica.

In addition to the efforts of the various SSC Specialist Groups, the Captive Breeding Specialist Group oversees international cooperation among zoos and other organizations managing critically endangered species. The Captive Breeding Specialist Group, under the chairmanship of Dr. Ulysses Seal, has been actively concerned with such diverse challenges as the management of tigers and preservation of the last of the endemic Moorean land snails (*Partula* spp.). Additional specialist groups are active, but confronting taxa that are too large for the quick compilation of action plans (orchids, fish, butterflies), too poorly known (spectacled

bear), or are focusing on biogeographical rather than taxonomic units (Madagascar). IUCN has also sponsored the publication of a number of important sourcebooks on the status of endangered species (e.g., Davis et al 1986). Staff of the Conservation Monitoring Center, Cambridge, England, have since 1972 prepared Red Data Books for mammals, birds, reptiles, African birds, and swallowtail butterflies.

PROBLEMS WITH THE PLANNING PROCESS

This brief review of the problems associated with species management practices and species conservation planning points to a number of general dilemmas. As cooperative planning, based on genetic and ecological principles, is critical to the survival of many species and sound biosphere management, it is pertinent to examine the planning process itself. Despite the numerous short-term successes resulting from ongoing species survival planning, the processes by which these plans are developed are simply unequal to the challenge of the next century.

Among the flaws in the planning process are the following. First, there are clearly too few plans—hundreds when we need thousands. Second, the planning processes are often undertaken in a piecemeal fashion, with different government and nongovernment organizations taking on separate aspects of a particular problem. Each organization prepares its own database and has traditionally shielded its records from full scientific and public scrutiny. Records are thus usually studied by only a small fraction of the number of potential planning participants. Even when records are computerized, information transfer between such semiprivate databases and the larger community of conservationists is often slow. Third, the planning process itself is slow; most detailed plans take several years to develop. Subsequently, irregular and lengthy review processes make it difficult to revise planning documents in the face of rapidly changing circumstances. Fourth, the preparation of species conservation plans is expensive. It cost the Fish and Wildlife Service approximately $62,000 to place a species on the endangered species list in 1987. Similar budgetary and personnel constraints prevent the AAZPA from developing many additional Species Survival Plans. As presently conducted, biodiversity conservation planning efforts are inadequate, slow, and fragmented.

As noted in the introduction, present species planning processes suffer from a second general dilemma—they focus on a biased sample of biodiversity and overemphasize mammals and birds. Given that we will never enjoy planning resources equal to the task, the choice of species receiving attention is increasingly important. We cannot study "just any animal" but must concentrate on "the really extinct ones," to paraphrase Campbell's (1987) anecdote. Indeed, several workers have recently examined the question of whether we should concentrate on rare species at all (Frankel 1982; Hubbell and Foster 1986; Main 1982; Rabinowitz et al. 1986). Although strong arguments can be made to save phylogenetically unique species, more emphasis must be given to those ecological keystone species whose activities are critical to the maintenance of entire communities. Individual species thus become the focus of management efforts that will conserve whole communities (Myers 1987c; Owen-Smith 1987; Terborgh 1986). The question is not whether one pair of spotted owls is worth $16 million (the 1985 net value of the lumber that could be extracted from their home range), but what the societal value is of conserving this area of old-growth forest in perpetuity. Although I suppose one could calculate the instantaneous cash-out value of a species' extinction, it seems far more useful to think in terms of the net value of a species' persistence. Such considerations should be given increased emphasis in choosing species for conservation planning efforts in the future. Species conservation and community conservation are closely interrelated, and ecologically significant species deserve more attention in developing regional biodiversity management plans.

Finally, there are some serious institutional impediments to sound species conservation planning. Funding levels and bureaucratic inertia aside, in the absence of centralized planning, the individual organizations now involved are all limited in their responses to the biodiversity crisis. I will not belabor the litany of inherent woes. Parks may be doomed by their inability to sustain "frozen ecosystems" in the face of changing climates and uncontrolled edge effects. Zoo managers strive to find the ideal mix

of entertainment, education, and captive propagation to ensure the financial survival of their institutions. Research efforts in universities and government laboratories are contingent on short-term funding, while progress in conservation science is contingent on a longer-term commitment of public resources. All three types of institutions and their staff devote inordinate amounts of time to crisis intervention. Sound conservation planning might be better conducted under different circumstances.

In the forgoing sections I have perhaps implied that the planning process flows deterministically from the biological database. Nothing could be further from the truth; planning decisions are rarely simple and are usually made in complex multidisciplinary settings. Interinstitutional cooperation is essential, and new ways must be found to diminish traditional barriers to communication. Salwasser et al. (1987) describe one successful example of a complex cooperative program involving the grizzly bear (*Ursus arctos*). Another has resulted in the reintroduction of the extirpated Arabian oryx (*Oryx leucoryx*) (Stanley Price, chap. 20). Such cooperations involving government agencies, zoological organizations, research scientists, and private individuals are the essential mix of today's species conservation planning efforts.

SPECIES CONSERVATION IN THE NEXT CENTURY: WHAT NEEDS TO BE DONE?

Present commitments to species conservation are clearly inadequate. The processes of risk assessment and planning are unequal to both natural realities and public expectations. The dissipation of talent and resources in a crisis management mode are counterproductive in the long run. The problems of species level conservation are global and require a more integrated and professionally managed response. Circumstances have forced conservationists to "think cheap," and this has placed artificial constraints on their ability to mount appropriate responses to biosphere-level threats.

If we were really serious about species conservation, we might launch a Species Defense Initiative (SDI, this use of the acronym replacing current misuse for the Strategic Defense [Star Wars] Initiative). The goals of the program would include conserving selected species to prevent further environmental degradation. As existing institutions and volunteers are unequal to the magnitude of this challenge, achieving this goal will require bureaucratic changes at all levels. National and international conservation networks will require the support of more centralized authority than now exists in, for example, the United States. The SDI would require a planning policy shift toward maintaining the evolutionary potential of species. This will, in turn, shift the emphasis from simple censuses to determining the genetic quality of the managed populations.

Far more population-level intervention will be required to conserve most species. Much of the scientific support work for the planners and field managers might be shifted to national or regional centers staffed by geneticists, demographers, behavioral ecologists, economists, and other professionals. Not only will we have to train this corps of professional conservationists quickly, but far more effort has to be put into education at all levels. Public education is vital as species conservation regulations are still too often proscriptive. As species management will of necessity become more interventive, it is essential that the public be better informed as to why, for example, eradicating introduced species is required. Conservationists must come to terms with the "animal rights" movements (Short 1987). Public education is, in fact, pivotal to the success of the SDI; unless the wisdom of sound biosphere stewardship becomes more widely appreciated, governments, religions, and multitudinous other vested interests will continue to contribute to environmental degradation in both developed and developing countries.

What will the Species Defense Initiative cost? To prevent further biosphere degradation, I think that perhaps 10,000 species will need to be managed in the next century. How much, then, does it cost to manage one species? The National Audubon Society (1986b) proposed spending $2 million per year for fifteen years to develop a sound management plan for the northern spotted owl. The California condor recovery plan costs more than $1 million annually. Globally, 10,000 such projects might therefore cost $10 billion annually. This is more, to be sure, than the $4 billion budget of the U.S. National Institutes of Health, but a little less than the gross national product of Bangladesh and far

less than Americans spend on their pets annually. But perhaps the owl/condor model is misleading—the whole Serengeti can be maintained for $500,000 a year. Suppose, for example, we were to spend an average of just $2 million per species to ensure that each of the 10,000 species persisted for 100 years; the total cost would be $20 billion but the cost per year would be only $200 million. That is equivalent to about 0.1 percent of the value of annual U.S. imports and exports of an exploitive (nonsustainable) nature. Dr. Paul Ehrlich (presidential address, American Institute for Biological Sciences, August 1987) advocated gradually increasing the U.S. National Science Foundation budget for population biology to $4 billion per year—a figure halfway between my estimates. The important point is that none of these sums are prohibitive when seen in the context of the available global resources. World military spending currently runs at an absurd $2 billion per day (Myers 1984a).

It will take a decade, however, to reorganize national and international conservation networks and train the necessary professionals to mount such a Species Defense Initiative. In the interim period, the techniques they will need must be developed. Among the many challenging research problems are the development of a quantitative science for risk assessment based on population vulnerability analysis; the development of noninvasive tissue sampling techniques for molecular species identification, pedigree analysis, disease diagnosis, and monitoring genetic variation and load; the development of exotic animal propagation technology (reproductive biology, embryo transfer, cryopreservation, and so forth); the application of genetic enginerring to the problems of pest, parasite, and pathogen control. Field studies are also urgently needed to identify ecological keystone species in threatened communities. Unless we devote more thought to the choice of species for conservation, the present efforts to "list and save" may be ill placed (Norton 1986b). The proper identification of chosen species requires redoubled efforts to catalog biodiversity, and this last requirement brings us again, full circle, to confront the serious shortage of professional taxonomists. We also need to improve our theoretical understanding of species biogeographical ranges, for they will surely change dramatically as global climates change in the next century. For an extensive discussion of these challenging problems, the reader is referred to the report prepared by the U.S. Congress, Office of Technology Assessment (1987).

CONSERVATION OF GENES AND SPECIES AND THE FUTURE OF EVOLUTION

I have argued that the best way of taking care of genes is to take care of the species that carry them. Genetic conservation (Antonovics 1988) and conservation genetics (Woodruff 1988) are really two sides of the same coin. As on-site (in situ) conservation is greatly preferable to off-site (ex situ) conservation, I have advocated that we make major efforts to save selected species in nature. If we are successful, then we will also achieve our larger goals of biodiversity and community conservation. We will thus begin to reverse present trends of environmental degradation and realize the broader objectives of the World Conservation Strategy (IUCN 1980; Thibodeau and Field 1984). All this must occur during the next century.

But what if we fail? Is biotic evolution essentially over? What can we say about the future evolution of species? Those species that do not go extinct will suffer losses of genetic variation. Biogeographical ranges will become increasingly fragmented, and range fragmentation has a disproportionately large and negative effect on effective population size (N_e). Demographic and environmental stochasticity will drag many of the smaller and more inbred populations into the four extinction vortices identified in population vulnerability analysis (Gilpin and Soulé 1986). Many species will find their predators, prey, and competitors eliminated; they will live in simpler, disharmonious (sensu Davis 1986) communities whose composition is largely unpredictable. To exacerbate matters, the physical environment in which they live will be changing. Global temperatures and sea levels are expected to rise along with atmospheric carbon dioxide and particle content (Bolin 1986). All of these biotic and environmental changes constitute evolutionary opportunities to which surviving species may adapt. So evolution is far from over; in fact, the ecological theater may well stage some of the fastest microevolutionary plays seen in the last billion years. Whether any of it leads to a new wave of speciation to replace the biodiversity lost by ongoing habitat destruction will depend on what happens in the twenty-second century.

It is not difficult to imagine some of the consequences of the predicted loss of biodiversity. We will lose a world filled with beautiful, intricate interactions and make one for the less novel generalists. Whether such simplified ecosystems can support the planet's biogeochemical cycles remains to be seen. I agree with those who see a close relationship between the quality of the human situation and the integrity of nature (Lovejoy 1986; McNeely and Miller 1984). On the one hand, I share the fears of Chief Seattle (1854, cited in Myers 1984a): "What is man without the beasts? If all the beasts were gone, men would die from a great loneliness of the spirit. For whatever happens to the beasts soon happens to man." On the other hand, I am struck by the strengths that flow from knowledge and resourcefulness. In the last century, our single biggest discovery, as a species, was the process of evolution. In the present century, our greatest achievement has been the collective understanding of what that process and its product, the biosphere, means to our own survival. The challenge of the next century, then, is to apply that knowledge before it is too late. As human beings are the problem, so too must they, as a species, be the solution.

9

Population Genetics and Conservation

ROBERT C. VRIJENHOEK

Conservation efforts aimed only at the twenty-first century are little more than short-term crisis management. Although immediate action is necessary to save many endangered organisms, our species recovery plans must look to the thirty-first century and beyond. Planning only for the preservation of remnant populations, in the hope that they can someday be introduced into a better world, may be inadequate for their long-term survival. We must learn to accept a world that changes constantly as a result of natural and artificial processes. Widespread habitat destruction as a consequence of accelerating human activities has contributed to local extinctions and geographical fragmentation of a great many plant and animal populations. Will our descendants, a thousand years from now, remember us as exploiters and destroyers of the world's biological diversity? Or will we be remembered as the generation that developed an evolutionary conservation ethic? In this chapter, I argue that we should use our technology to understand the structure of genetic diversity in remnant populations of endangered species, and that it is our obligation to reestablish the patterns of migration and gene flow that we have disrupted.

Evolutionary geneticists who engage in conservation research are faced with some perplexing dilemmas. Worldwide, only a few laboratories are using state-of-the-art biochemical, molecular, cytogenetic, and biometrical methods to assess the genetic composition of threatened and endangered species. Genetic research is costly, and most of our time is spent in more fundable studies involving economically or medically important species, or on basic research that attacks currently popular theories. I am reminded of a colleague who is funded to study the population genetics and systematics of snails that transmit a debilitating disease to humans. On most days, his primary goal is to learn more about an undesirable species that we would like to eliminate or control. Yet on other days, he uses the same genetic methodologies to learn more about desirable species that we would like to save. There is a bit of schizophrenia in all of us engaged in conservation genetic studies, because the research effort must be supported by the largesse of our more fundable scientific projects.

To date, we have examined the genetics of only a few dozen endangered species. Every day, species are becoming extinct before we have even had a chance to see just how genetically different they were. To expand our research activities, and to recruit new investigators, we need better facilities and stable funding sources that would allow conservation genetics to emerge as a legitimate field of scientific investigation. Major zoological parks and conservation agencies should develop scientific collaborations with sophisticated genetics laboratories at nearby universities. Communication and collaboration between academic geneticists and applied biologists have already led to several comprehensive management plans for endangered species. I have had the good fortune to integrate basic population genetic studies with an ongoing species recovery plan for endangered fishes in the American southwest. I report here on some general concepts and methodologies that are the foundation of conservation genetics research, and I use our work with endangered fish populations as examples of their application.

ESTIMATING GENETIC DIVERSITY

Advances in biochemical and molecular techniques have made it possible to reveal genetic diversity in species for which traditional crossing experiments are not feasible. Geneticists interested in population structure have primarily used protein electrophoresis. This technique can reveal genetically determined differences in the size and electrical charge of proteins. One can also use electrophoresis to examine variation in the DNA directly, but these methods are difficult, requiring expensive equipment and chemicals. Electrophoretic studies of numerous plants and animals have revealed that a considerable proportion of the genes in a species are polymorphic, that is, they have two or more relatively common alleles (defined as variant forms of a specific gene). For example, in humans approximately 30% of the gene loci (defined as a specific position on a chromosome) are polymorphic (Lewontin 1974). The genetic diversity attributable to a gene locus is a func-

tion of both the number of alleles (richness) and the equitability of their frequencies (evenness). For example, imagine a situation in which three distinct alleles segregate at a hypothetical gene locus (Fig. 9.1). Diversity at a gene locus is defined as

$$h = 1 - \Sigma\, p_i^2 \qquad (1)$$

where p_i is the frequency of the ith allele. If frequencies of the alleles are even, diversity is maximized. In this case (A), $h = 0.67$. There would be a 67% probability that two randomly sampled alleles would be different. Since each individual in a population inherits a pair of alleles, one from its mother and one from its father, this is another way of saying that for this particular gene, 67% of the individuals in the population will be heterozygous (i.e., carry two different alleles: $A1/A2$, $A2/A3$, or $A1/A3$), and 33% of the individuals will be homozygous (i.e., carry a pair of identical alleles: $A1/A1$, $A2/A2$, or $A3/A3$). If allelic frequencies are not even, then diversity is greatly reduced. In the second example (B), $h = 0.18$; only 18% of the individuals will be heterozygous, the 82% will be homozygous. Diversity is also reduced by the loss of allelic richness. For example, having

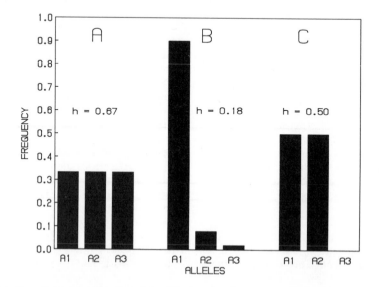

Fig. 9.1. Gene diversity, h, as a function of the richness of alleles and the evenness of their frequencies: (A) three alleles with equitable frequencies; (B) three alleles with inequitable frequencies; and (C) two alleles with equitable frequencies.

only two alleles at even frequencies (C), reduces h to 0.50.

The total genetic diversity of a species is also affected by the geographical distribution of its constituent populations. Barriers to migration and gene flow can subdivide natural populations into an assemblage of subpopulations that might differ genetically. Consequently, total genetic diversity (H_T) can be partitioned into two major components (Nei 1975:149–154):

$$H_T = H_S + D_{ST} \qquad (2)$$

where H_S is the average gene diversity within subpopulations [from equation (1)], and D_{ST} is the variance in allelic frequencies among subpopulations. H_S is equivalent to the average level of heterozygosity contained in individuals (assuming there is random mating within subpopulations). Dividing each side of the equation by the total, H_T, allows us to express these two components as proportions of the total variance.

The proportion of the total diversity contained in each component is largely a function of a species' ability to disperse. Migration and gene flow among colonies maintain genetic diversity within colonies and decrease the variance among colonies. For example, in humans, about 7% of the total genetic diversity is contained in the differences among the three major races, Caucasoids, Negroids, and Mongoloids (Nei 1975). Most of our genetic diversity (93%) exists within each of the major racial groups. This is hardly surprising, since we are a highly mobile species with a great propensity for spreading our genes. On the other hand, the Ord kangaroo rat, *Dipodomys ordii*, has not invented sailing ships or supersonic transports, and consequently, about 70% of its total genetic diversity involves differences among local populations (Nei 1975). The goal of conservation programs should be to maintain as much genetic diversity as possible. Both the diversity within and between constituent populations might affect a species' ability to respond to new evolutionary challenges.

Equation (2) can be extended to describe hierarchical subdivision of genetic diversity (Nei 1975):

$$H_T = H_C + D_{CS} + D_{ST} \qquad (3)$$

where H_C is the heterozygosity within local colonies and D_{CS} is the variance among local colonies within major subpopulations. For example, in the Sonoran topminnow, *Poeciliopsis occidentalis,* more than half ($D_{ST}/H_T = 52.8\%$) of the genetic diversity is attributable to the differences among three major subpopulations (Vrijenhoek et al. 1985). The remaining diversity is spread evenly between heterozygosity within local colonies ($H_C/H_T = 21.3\%$) and the differences among colonies within the major subpopulations ($D_{CS}/H_T = 25.5\%$). This genetic information is playing an important role in the recovery plan for endangered populations of the Sonoran topminnow in Arizona. I return to this subject later.

THE DYNAMICS OF GENETIC POPULATION STRUCTURE

Habitat destruction has led to increased geographical fragmentation of many species. Without natural migration and gene flow connecting remnant subpopulations, the relative contribution of H_S and D_{ST} to the total genetic diversity will shift as a consequence of genetic drift (defined as random [i.e., nonselected] changes in allelic frequencies). Prolonged genetic drift will cause a decrease in the heterozygosity within local subpopulations and an increase in the genetic variance among subpopulations (Fig. 9.2). The rate of drift is a function of the genetically effective size of local interbreeding populations, N_e. As an extreme example, imagine a large population that has been fragmented into isolated colonies, each with a genetically effective size of two. In approximately twenty generations, nearly all the heterozygosity within colonies will be lost and the variance in allelic frequencies among colonies will increase to its maximum value. This shift of diversity from H_S to D_{ST} is slower if subpopulations are larger, and of course it is retarded by migration among subpopulations.

The genetically effective size of local populations (N_e) is typically much smaller than the actual population size. Frankel and Soulé (1981:31–41) provide a helpful discussion of N_e as it applies to conservation biology. The breeding system (e.g., sex ratio biases, harem formation, inbreeding, high reproductive variance among individuals, and so forth) and fluctuations in population size over time reduce N_e to a fraction of the actual population size. For exam-

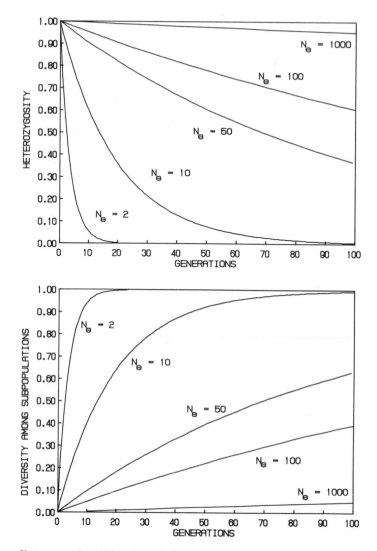

Fig. 9.2. Loss of heterozygosity within subpopulations (H_S/H_T) and increase in the diversity among subpopulations (D_{ST}/H_T) under genetic drift at varying effective population sizes (N_e). The equations used in generating these functions are discussed by Crow and Kimura (1970:328–329).

ple, if a population were propagated by mating nine females with one male in each generation, N_e would be equivalent to a population composed of only 3.6 parents. To maintain a high N_e, one should try to ameliorate conditions that lead to unbalanced sex ratios or high variance in the reproductive contributions of different females. As a general rule, conservation programs should strive to maintain the largest populations possible, to prevent the decline in heterozygosity and to avoid the negative consequences of inbreeding.

Total genetic diversity (H_T) does not necessarily change during the process of drift and divergence; its components may just shift from H_S to D_{ST}. New mutations and differential selection leading to local adaptation may accelerate this shift; however, these divergent processes may be counteracted by homogenizing processes. Stabilizing selection favors average characteristics, thus retarding divergence. In the absence of local differences in selection pressures, unimpeded migration and gene flow will eliminate the differences among local populations. For low levels of migration, however, populations will eventually reach an equilibrium level of genetic differentiation determined by the balance between homogenizing processes (gene flow and balancing selection) and divergent processes (mutation, differential selection, and genetic drift). The interactions among mutation, selection, and genetic drift are complex. Some instructive simulations of these processes and their effects on population structure are discussed by Allendorf (1983).

Equilibrium conditions are unlikely to apply to endangered species, however. Instead, endangered status is usually applied after a species is already in serious decline. Population sizes will be small and connections between remnant populations will be weak, leading inevitably to a decline in H_S and an increase in D_{ST}. If high rates of local extinction are opposed with a mindless restocking effort, the eventual result will be complete loss of diversity between subpopulations (Maruyama and Kimura 1980).

GENETIC DIVERSITY AND FITNESS IN LOCAL POPULATIONS

For species that ordinarily outcross in nature, the loss of heterozygosity during inbreeding generally is associated with inbreeding depression, a decline in viability, growth, and fertility (Falconer 1981). Inbreeding depression is a serious problem for zoo populations of many endangered species (Ralls and Ballou 1983). Several factors contribute to inbreeding depression: (1) an increase in the frequency of individuals that are *homozygous* for deleterious recessive alleles; (2) a decrease in the frequency of superior *heterozygous* genotypes; and (3) a decrease in genotypic diversity among individuals. Although the relative importance of these factors to fitness in natural populations is often disputed, breeding studies suggest that homozygosity for deleterious recessive alleles is the predominant cause of inbreeding depression (Wright 1977). Thus, it might be possible to breed zoo strains of endangered plants and animals that are largely purged of their deleterious recessive genes. Templeton and Read (1983)

suggested that selective breeding might work as a last resort for Speke's gazelle (*Gazelli spekei*). But such a strategy is risky because it requires the culling of many individuals from an already depleted stock. Great caution must be exercised in extrapolating the results of experimental inbreeding studies to endangered species (Hedrick 1987). Experience with animal breeding suggests that most inbred strains are prone to extinction.

Rapid losses of genetic diversity during colonization events (founder events) and during severe population crashes (bottlenecks) may also have detrimental effects on fitness. The history of human colonization has left an excellent record of founder events, many of which are associated with the expression of deleterious recessive traits (Cavalli-Sforza and Bodmer 1971). Extremely low genetic diversity in cheetahs (*Acinonyx jubatus*) may exist because of recent bottlenecks and inbreeding (O'Brien et al. 1985, 1987). Low heterozygosity within cheetah populations is associated with inbreeding depression—high juvenile mortality, a high incidence of morphological abnormalities, and low sperm counts. Also, little genetic differentiation exists between east and south African subpopulations. Local founder events have had a significant impact on fitness-related characters in desert topminnows of the genus *Poeciliopsis* (Vrijenhoek and Lerman 1982; see later discussion).

Evidence from electrophoretic studies of natural populations suggests that genetic diversity is often correlated with fitness (reviewed by Frankel and Soulé 1981; Mitton and Grant 1985; Zouros and Foltz 1987). Correlations between the heterozygosity of individuals and characters such as developmental stability, growth rate, metabolic efficiency, fertility, and survival have been observed in many plants and animals, but these correlations are not universal (Ledig et al. 1983). Although at present we do not understand the mechanisms behind an association between individual heterozygosity and fitness in natural populations, the safest strategy for conservation programs should be to maintain as much heterozygosity as possible.

The third consequence of loss of heterozygosity is the loss of genotypic diversity among individuals in a population. Differences among individuals, such as those governing the use of natural resources, environmental tolerances, and disease resistance, may influence the density a population can maintain. For example, extraordinarily high diversity exists for genes involved in the mammalian immune response. It has been suggested that the allelic diversity of immune response genes persists because of frequency-dependent natural selection (Clarke 1979). Imagine a species wherein one immunotype becomes very common. It would be fairly easy for a parasite, bacterium, or virus to evolve antigenic mimicry and escape immune surveillance by the common host genotype. As a result of its higher probability of infection, the common genotype would be at a significant disadvantage and therefore would decrease in frequency. According to this scenario, there would always be a premium on having a rare immunotype. It is easy to imagine how loss of immunological diversity might increase the vulnerability of endangered species to parasitic infections. Similarly, the dynamics of predator-prey interactions and interspecific competition may also have strong frequency-dependent components (Clarke 1979).

Efficient exploitation of heterogeneous environments may be facilitated by genotypic diversity. For example, the Colorado River sucker, *Catastoma clarkii,* exhibits a cline in the frequencies of two esterase alleles (Koehn 1969). One allele (*a*) is most frequent downstream in southern Arizona, where water temperatures are warmer on average, and the other allele (*b*) is most frequent in the upstream part of this river in northern Nevada, where water temperatures are colder. Tests of the relative activity of the enzymes produced by the three esterase genotypes revealed that *b/b* had the highest activity at low temperatures, *a/a* had the highest activity at low temperatures, and the heterozygote *a/b* had the highest activity at intermediate temperatures. The temperature-dependent activities of the three enzymes encoded by these genotypes correspond well with the distribution of the *a* and *b* alleles in the Colorado River.

Adaptation to fine-scale ecological differences in a patchy environment might also be facilitated by genotypic diversity, but examples of this phenomenon are limited (Hedrick et al. 1976). A population of diversified individuals can potentially exploit a wider range of habitats and food resources than a uniform population. Habitat destruction or introduction of exotic competitors might displace an ecologically diverse species from part of its range, but these factors are unlikely to eliminate it completely. However, loss of genotypic diversity in an endangered species may make it more vulnerable to competition interactions.

GENETIC DIVERSITY AND FITNESS IN DESERT FISHES

Over the past ten years, I have been studying changes in genetic diversity and fitness in topminnows of the genus *Poeciliopsis*. An advantage in studying these fish is that closely related sexual and asexual forms coexist in the same desert springs and streams of Sonora, Mexico. Thus we can monitor changes in genetic diversity of the sexual populations and use the asexual clones as genetically fixed controls. For example, in 1976 portions of a small stream containing these fish dried up during a severe drought. By 1978 the uppermost portion of this stream had been recolonized by topminnows that had survived in more permanent locations downstream, but in the process of recolonization, the sexual population had lost nearly all of its genetic diversity. The loss of heterozygosity apparently was due to a series of founder events that occurred when small numbers of fish (low N_e) established new upstream colonies during this two-year period (Vrijenhoek and Lerman 1982). A coexisting asexual form, being genetically fixed, had not lost any of its heterozygosity during the recolonization process. Reduced heterozygosity in the sexual species, *Poeciliopsis monacha,* was associated with markedly reduced developmental stability for eight morphological traits, as compared with the asexual form (Vrijenhoek and Lerman 1982). We have continued to study these populations and have since found that loss of heterozygosity in *P. monacha* also results in decreased resistance to anoxic stress, compared with the asexual form (Vrijenhoek, unpublished).

Our long-term studies of these fishes (1975–87) have also revealed a relationship between gene diversity and population dynamics. Prior to their local extinction in the headwater portion of this stream, *P. monacha* constituted about 80% of the fish, and the asexual form constituted 20%. However, after recolonization, the situation was reversed, with the asexual form now constituting the majority of the fish. The new frequencies (about 90% asexual and 10% *P. monacha*) remained stable for the next five years (1978–83), or roughly fifteen *Poeciliopsis* generations. Genetic diversity in *P. monacha* also remained low during this period (mean gene diversity, $\bar{h}$, equaled 0.01, averaged across four polymorphic loci). In 1983 I transplanted 30 pregnant *P. monacha* females into the study site, from a genetically variable population several hundred meters downstream in the same river ($\bar{h} = 0.44$). By 1985, $\bar{h}$ in the recipient population rose to 0.47. Most important, the proportions of sexual and asexual fish reverted to about 75% *P. monacha* and 25% asexual and have remained stable through 1987. It appears that the ecological relationship between *P. monacha* and the asexual form depends in part on the genetic diversity contained in *P. monacha*. Whether the competitive disadvantage suffered by the homozygous founder population of *P. monacha* was due to inbreeding depression, or to a loss of genotypic diversity among individuals, or both is unknown.

We were lucky that our long-term studies of genetic diversity and population dynamics in *Poeciliopsis* allowed us to discover this remarkable result. We need more long-term studies with experimental organisms to teach us how much of the dynamics of species interactions might be affected by genetic diversity in the participants. Is it possible that the loss of genetic variability associated with small population size in threatened and endangered species sets them on an accelerating "extinction vortex" (Gilpin and Soulé 1986)? One cannot perform such long-term monitoring or transplantation experiments with organisms such as cheetahs, pandas, or black rhinos. Thus, in order to develop realistic management plans for large, long-lived species, we must rely on basic studies of model organisms to examine the linkage between genetic diversity and population dynamics. In the meantime, it is prudent to maintain as much genetic diversity in our target organisms as is possible.

A MANAGEMENT PLAN FOR THE SONORAN TOPMINNOW

The population-genetic principles discussed herein have influenced the species recovery plan for the Sonoran topminnow, *Poeciliopsis occidentalis*. This small viviparous fish was once the most abundant native fish in lowland streams, springs, and marshes of southern Arizona (Hubbs and Miller 1941). Unfortunately, the past forty years of stream diversion, impoundment, and groundwater pumping have severely reduced and fragmented the native habitat of this fish (Meffe et al. 1983; Minckley and Deacon 1968). Furthermore, introduction of exotic species such as the mosquitofish, *Gambusia affinis,* reduced the Sonoran topminnow to the point that it was placed on the federal Endangered Species List in 1973. However, large and apparently healthy populations of this species exist across the border in Sonora, Mexico. An effective conservation program for this fish required knowledge of its genetic population structure throughout the Arizona-Sonora region.

We surveyed twenty-one populations of *P. occidentalis* from Arizona and Sonora for electrophoretic variation at twenty-five gene loci (Vrijenhoek et al. 1985). As previously mentioned, the genetic diversity in this species could be clustered into three main subpopulations (Fig. 9.3). Endangered populations in Arizona are composed mostly of Group I fish in the Gila River basin. An isolated headwater tributary of the Yaqui River near the Mexican border, in Douglas, Arizona, contains Group II fish. Partitioning of genetic diversity for this species revealed that 52.8% of the total diversity existed in the differences among the three groups. Although habitat destruction by humans and unnatural barriers to migration may accelerate genetic diversification among Arizona populations of these fish, the large differences between the three groups were established more than a million years ago (Vrijenhoek et al. 1985). In fact, endangered populations of Group I and II fish in Arizona had been recognized as distinct subspecies: the Gila topminnow (*P. o. occidentalis*) and the Yaqui topminnow (*P. o. sonoriensis*) (Minckley 1973). Restocking efforts in Arizona have avoided mixing between the subspecies (U.S. Fish and Wildlife Service 1983).

The species recovery plan for the Gila topminnow relied on a hatchery stock of *P. o. occidentalis* originally from Monkey Spring, a thermal springhead in the Gila drainage of southern Arizona (U.S. Fish and Wildlife Service 1983). Fol-

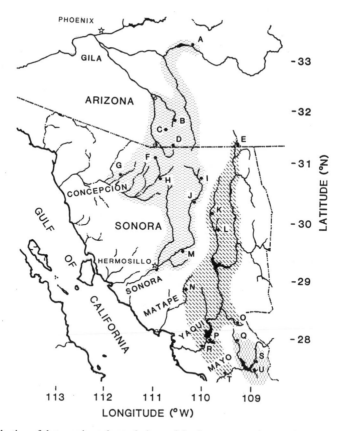

Fig. 9.3. The distribution of three major subpopulations of the Sonoran topminnow, *Poeciliopsis occidentalis*, in Arizona and Sonora. Subpopulation I inhabits the Gila River, the Rio de la Concepcion, and Rio Sonora. Subpopulation II is restricted primarily to the Rio Yaqui basin, although it extends into the Rio Matape and the lower Rio Mayo along the coastal plain. Subpopulation III inhabits the intermontaine tributaries of the Rio Mayo. The letters represent 21 localities from which samples were taken. For a list of collection sites, allelic frequencies, and heterozygosity estimates see Meffe and Vrijenhoek (1988). (Modified from Vrijenhoek et al. 1985.)

lowing some initial success with this stock, a plan for downlisting the species to "threatened" and eventually delisting it completely has been put into action. However, we recommended that use of this stock be abandoned for four reasons (Vrijenhoek et al. 1985):

1. It was completely homozygous for our electrophoretic markers.
2. It had very low fecundity compared with other Arizona populations of this species (Constantz 1979; Schoenherr 1977).
3. It may be adapted to thermally stable conditions, and therefore incapable of dealing with more variable conditions of desert streams.

4. The hatchery stock may have become even more inbred and selected for laboratory performance during its ten years under culture.

The first three reasons might be coupled if the Monkey Spring stock had become inbred, but even if they were uncoupled, each reason alone is sufficient to question its use in restocking efforts throughout the Gila drainage system. In its place we recommended using a natural stock from Sharp Spring for four reasons:

1. This population had the highest heterozygosity of any of the Group I populations in Arizona.

2. It was more fecund than the Monkey Spring stock (Meffe 1985).
3. Sharp Spring is a thermally fluctuating spring and stream habitat, and therefore, the fish might be able to establish themselves in a greater variety of habitats.
4. This natural population had not been captively propagated.

Following our recommendations, the U.S. Fish and Wildlife Service is now raising Sharp Spring *P. occidentalis* at the Dexter National Fish Hatchery in New Mexico (Brooks 1986). The starting stock involved 192 adults (176 females, 16 males). Because the topminnow females store sperm for several months and because most females are multiply inseminated under natural conditions (Leslie and Vrijenhoek 1977), the genetically effective population size of this propagule may have been twice this number. Current population sizes in the stock ponds at Dexter are sufficiently large that significant genetic drift is unlikely (J. Brooks, personal communication). We are continuing our electrophoretic screening of the hatchery stock to monitor the level of genetic diversity.

Current plans of the U.S. Fish and Wildlife Service involve experimental restocking with the Sharp Spring stock (Brooks 1986). Both the earlier Monkey Spring and the new Sharp Spring restockings will be monitored to assess their relative success in establishing viable, self-sustaining populations. In the light of our recent discoveries of a relationship between genetic diversity and population dynamics in *P. monacha* in Sonora, it would be interesting to test whether the more variable stock of *P. occidentalis* from Sharp Spring is more successful coexisting with exotic species such as *G. affinis* in Arizona. We are also continuing our laboratory studies with topminnows. An ongoing study of juvenile growth in several Arizona stocks raised under controlled environmental conditions revealed that Sharp Spring fish grow approximately 20% faster than Monkey Spring fish (Vrijenhoek and Sadowski, unpublished). We are not sure whether heterozygosity and fast growth in these fish are directly correlated with fitness, because the tradeoffs between fast growth, early reproduction, and different patterns of adult and juvenile survival can be very complex. Nevertheless, all our laboratory studies suggest that the genetically variable Sharp Spring stock is more robust and therefore is more likely to establish itself in restored habitats.

CONCLUSIONS

If human disturbance has artificially reduced gene flow by fragmenting habitats and destroying migration corridors, then perhaps we should intervene by reestablishing gene flow, at least within the confines of major subspecific groups. Certainly, we do not have the resources to save every remnant population of every endangered species. Our task in the twenty-first century will be to infer from genetic studies the major evolutionary subpopulations that existed prior to human disturbance. Where possible, we should maintain these groups, since they are the product of naturally divergent processes that might contribute to local adaptation. Indiscriminate hybridization between genetically discrete subpopulations may lead to outbreeding depression, a decrease in fitness attributable to negative interactions between differentially adapted genotypes (Templeton 1986). Yet we must be cautious in identifying major evolutionary groups. If our identifications are based solely on morphological criteria, we are likely to be misled by environmentally induced variation or minor genetic variation in external characteristics. Since it is the genetic integrity and evolutionary future of endangered species that we are trying to conserve, we must use genetic tools that characterize a larger fraction of the genome.

At the same time, we should strive to reestablish genetic connectedness between populations that have become fragmented as a result of human intervention. For example, habitat destruction has left only a few isolated populations of topminnows in Arizona. Should we attempt to preserve each of the remaining populations? Perhaps we should not, since some of these populations may already be suffering the consequences of isolation, genetic drift, and inbreeding. If we can document that human interference created the current disruptive circumstances, then our obligation is to reconnect remnant colonies. This can be accomplished by providing migration corridors or by manually transplanting individuals. An exchange of only one individual between populations per generation would be sufficient to maintain most of the allelic diversity in local populations without swamping the opportunity for local adaptation (Allendorf 1983).

From analysis of genetic population structure, we can roughly estimate the patterns of gene flow that created present-day population structures in our endangered species. From these estimates, we should be able to design species recovery programs that maintain or re-establish genetic connectedness between remnant colonies. To move into the twenty-first century, we must shed our current "preservationist" mentality (Frankel and Soulé 1981). We should, instead, take a reconstructionist role—to set things straight, rather than just preserve what we have disrupted in the first place.

10

Conservation: A Consideration of Evolution, Population, and Life History

JOHN F. EISENBERG AND LARRY D. HARRIS

We have been asked to consider the future of wildlife and plant resources in the year 2100 by examining three aspects of biology—populations, life history, and evolution. When one considers the variety of global environments from the marine benthos to the deserts of the Sahara, and when one further considers the scope of the three topics, it is obvious that we shall have to restrict our remarks to certain taxa and certain habitats that are illustrative of key principles, but perhaps not sufficiently comprehensive for a global inference.

SOME UNIVERSAL BIOLOGICAL PRINCIPLES AND THEIR IMPLICATIONS FOR CONSERVATION

The Consequences of Body Size for Terrestrial Organisms

When viewing organisms from the broad perspective, one of the most important influences on the survivorship of a species is expressed by the simple metric of body size. Bonner (1965) demonstrated that size, expressed as the length of an organism, and generation time covary positively. The generation time for a bacterium measuring 5 μ may be less than an hour, while a sequoia tree standing at 100 m height may have a generation time exceeding 1,000 years. Species consisting of large body sizes take a longer period of time to attain sexual maturity and generally live much longer. Hence there are greater

intervals between generations, and for any set interval of time, species with large bodies and long lives will probably respond to ecological change and evolve more slowly than species of smaller size (Fig. 10.1).

Mature, multicellular, terrestrial plants are for the most part stationary, and although they may grow in three-dimensional space, once rooted they are incapable of displacing themselves. However, plants have evolved numerous mechanisms for dispersing their reproductive propagules and in many cases have exhibited coevolution with animals, where animals act as dispersers of their seeds or transport their pollen.

Obviously, given the very real difference in basal area, more stems of blueberries (*Vaccinium* spp.) can be counted per unit area in suitable habitat than sequoia trees (*Sequoia gigantia*). Large plants need a larger area to maintain the same number of individuals than do smaller plants. Higher plants do not move as seedings or adults and can exist at higher densities than comparable-sized animals. Higher plants stand, and with the aid of sunlight and water, convert carbon dioxide into sugars, starches, cellulose, and lignin. Thus a conservation strategy for plant species may differ from that devised for animal species. Many relatively small preserves could suffice to protect plant species richness, and indeed the greater site specificity exhibited by plants compared to animals virtually dictates that the size and spacing

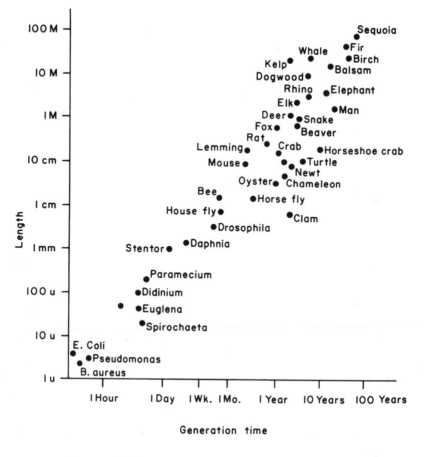

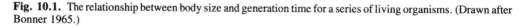

Drawn after Bonner

Fig. 10.1. The relationship between body size and generation time for a series of living organisms. (Drawn after Bonner 1965.)

of plant reserves must be tailored to different life history strategies and growth characteristics. This suggests that in terrestrial environments, it may be far easier to preserve even the largest tree species by strictly protecting several reasonably sized tracts of land. Conversely, it will be nearly impossible to protect species of large, terrestrial animals with a comparable strategy.

Animals are characterized by mobility, a capacity to move around and select appropriate microhabitats, or to course over the landscape and exploit the resources of numerous macrohabitats. Of course, some marine animal species such as sponges (*Porifera*) and sea anemo-

nes (*Anthozoa*) resemble plants in that they are sessile and fixed in space at certain stages of their life cycle. For terrestrial animals, the rate and area in which they move varies as a function of body size; the larger the species, the larger the home range (McNab 1963; Western 1979a). As a corollary of this, animals frequently and actively space themselves into recognizable dispersion patterns in order to reduce competition for resources. Thus, there is a strong tendency for the typical population density of a species to vary inversely with body size. The largest of the herbivores (i.e., the elephant) could never achieve the population density that smaller herbivores do, and typical density differences span about the same range as the weight differences (one million-fold).

It should be obvious at this point that small preserves (<5,000 ha) can preserve a great number of small organisms that have modest space needs and are able to exist at high densities within a restricted space. Larger organisms, especially large animals, face quite a different set of problems for long-term survival.

Some Space Rules for Terrestrial Vertebrates

Amphibians, by and large, are limited to moist areas because of their vulnerability to drying out in xeric environments. Almost all amphibians require freshwater for spawning; thus this entire class of organisms is, with a few exceptions, almost entirely water-dependent during part of their life cycle. Reptiles, on the other hand, by evolving the cleidoic egg, have freed themselves from dependency on aquatic environments for reproduction and range over a broader variety of terrestrial habitats. Both classes have in common the fact that they do not usually maintain a constant body temperature by shifts in metabolic rate. In addition, they both have low basal metabolic rates and do not require the same energy from the environment per unit body mass as do homeothermic birds and mammals. As a generalization, then, amphibians and reptiles can potentially exist at tenfold higher biomass densities than their homeothermic counterparts of the same body mass. Birds and mammals that are endothermic homeotherms need to maintain a high level of energy intake and as a result exist at relatively lower biomass densities than their reptilian and amphibian counterparts of the same size class and trophic class. For example, the giant tortoises (*Geochelone*) of Aldabra Island can exist at a density far exceeding a comparably sized mammalian herbivore such as the capybara (*Hydrochaeris hydrochaeris*) (Hamilton and Coe 1982). Aside from the reptile and amphibian specialists that become vulnerable when their microhabitats are in very limited supply, it is fair to say that the lower densities of birds and mammals predispose them to more frequent local extinction events when compared with their reptile and amphibian counterparts. This is most evident on islands (Case and Cody 1983).

It is clear to most biogeographers that species richness is a function of land area. All environmental variables being equal, the greater the area, the more species one finds. Island biogeography has also demonstrated that islands close to continents have a higher species richness than islands widely separated from the continents. Thus, a large island near a continent has more species than does an equidistant small island. Also, a large island distant from the more contiguous continents has a lower species richness than an island of comparable area near to a major continent and part of the continental shelf. This implies that at glacial maxima with lowered sea levels the near island will connect with the mainland.

The number of species on an island is the result of an equilibrium between successful colonization rate and local extinction rate. Colonization success is high when the island is relatively unoccupied, but with a greater colonization success rate, subsequent colonization attempts have a reduced probability of success. The later colonization events have a higher probability of being unsuccessful or going extinct in a short span of time. Protected areas in a "sea" of development are like islands, hence the success of applying the principles of island biogeography to the analysis of faunal stability in national parks. These parks are becoming more and more like islands as land is cleared around them (Cody 1975; MacArthur and Wilson 1967; Wilson and Willis 1975).

The Consequences of Phylogenetic Affinity and Trophic Specialization Within the Mammalia

The interval between a female's birth and the production of her median daughter may be represented by the term τ. This is roughly equivalent to a generation. The net reproductive rate (R_o) is a measure of the total number of femal offspring left behind by a cohort of females in a generation (Andrewartha and Birch 1954). To convert from time as measured in generations to time as measured in years requires the division of the former by the latter ($r \simeq ln R_o \div \tau$). Thus r, the instantaneous rate of increase, can be calculated from the following average life history characters: age at first reproduction, annual age-specific birth rate, and age at last reproduction

(Cole 1954). Although there is a strong inverse relation between the instinsic rate of increase (r_m) and body size, there is a great deal of scatter around the regression line, and this is in no small measure attributable to phylogenetic differences (Robinson and Redford 1986). For example, primates show a slope similar to the average, but all primates have a low r_m relative to other mammals; rodents and ungulates have a higher r_m than most other mammals. Edentates show a disjunct position with anteaters and sloths having low reproductive rates, and some species of armadillos having relatively high rates (Fig. 10.2). As a generalization, the low instantaneous rate of increase of primates would cause them to be slow to recover from population declines induced either by catastrophic events or by habitat destruction. On the other hand, some ungulates and rodents have the potential to rebound more rapidly from such disasters (Robinson and Redford 1986).

Home range size of mammals is directly related to body size, but again there is a great deal of scatter (McNab 1963; Western 1979a). Strict carnivores have a relatively large home range

relative to their body size, whereas herbivores have smaller home ranges. The net consequence is that within a defined habitat type for any given body size, herbivores can live at higher densities than carnivores, and it follows that the preservation of large carnivores will require very large tracts of land to maintain an intact ecosystem in the face of possible environmental perturbations. Interestingly, large anteating forms seem to require much larger areas relative to their body size than do comparably sized herbivores (Eisenberg 1980).

The interplay of trophic level, life history strategy, and size suggests the following. Large terrestrial carnivores are extremely vulnerable to extinction events. Consider the extirpation of the wolf (*Canis lupus*) and the puma (*Puma concolor*) east of the Mississippi River in the United States. Large herbivores are also vulnerable. Regardless of trophic strategy, species having an extremely low fecundity will recover slowly from catastrophic events or habitat destruction. Primates, large ungulates, some carnivores, and some edentates fall into this category of vulnerability (Eisenberg 1980, 1981).

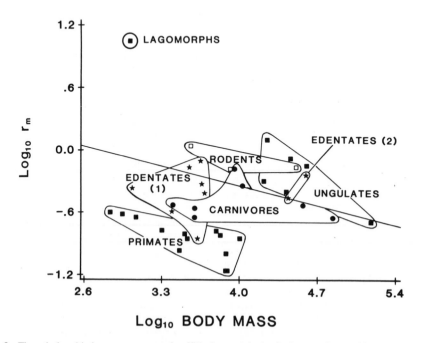

Fig. 10.2. The relationship between taxonomic affiliation and the intrinsic rate of natural increase (r_{max}). $\log_{10}$ body mass of thirty-nine neotropical forest mammals is related to $\log_{10} r_{max}$ values (Robinson and Redford 1986).

THE IMPORTANCE OF LIMITING RESOURCES AND VULNERABILITY FOR EXTINCTION: TWO CASES FROM THE SOUTHEASTERN UNITED STATES

We should add a very special category of vulnerability: a species dependent on some highly specialized, but scarce resource. The organism may be a masterpiece of adaptation, but vulnerable because of one requirement within its habitat that must be met. An example would be the Mexican free-tailed bat (*Tadarida brasiliensis*) in the southern United States. This form is highly mobile and can range widely in its feeding, but is absolutely dependent on a cave with the appropriate temperature and humidity for passing the day and rearing its young. Natural caves were the original source of refugia. If, for some reason, caves became unavailable to them, such as through commercial exploitation and mining, then the species could go extinct (Humphrey 1985).

This brings us, then, to the question of human activities in the exploitation of resources and occupancy of space that impact on what otherwise are beautifully adapted forms. The harvest of young pine trees (*Pinus* sp.) in the southeast has inadvertently produced a decline of the red-cockaded woodpecker (*Picoides borealis*). This woodpecker needs a tree of a certain diameter in order to successfully excavate a nesting cavity. Furthermore, it is the only North American woodpecker that requires a living tree in which to build its nest cavity. By seeking a rapid economic gain, pulp and timber companies have been harvesting pine trees in the southeast at a relatively young age. This is especially true of those stands in the southeast sandhills that mature slowly. The net result has been a decline in the availability of suitable nesting cavities for the red-cockaded woodpecker and an overall population decline throughout the southeastern United States (Porter and Labisky 1985).

EXTINCTION EVENTS: WHAT CAN THEY TEACH US?

Extinctions: Priorities and Process

When one looks at the broad pattern of mammalian evolution, one will notice that through time species have come and gone. Within any given lineage one can distinguish what, for want of a better name, may be termed "chronospecies." The temporal succession of species within a lineage is the result of gradual evolution, and what may appear to be an extinction is really the replacement of one species by the descendants now recognized through evolutionary process as a new species. This succession of species within a lineage is not true extinction.

What should be important to biologists is the recognition that there are distinct, unique lineages; within the Mammalia, some of these go back over 60,000,000 years. They are so different from one another that we give them recognition as higher taxonomic categories, such as orders. When the descendants of one of these lineages become very limited in number and eventually disappear, it is an extinction event of an order of magnitude different than the disappearance of chronospecies or sibling species.

Extinctions: The Record

Van Valkenburgh (1985) has analyzed niche specialization among carnivore communities found within past and existing guilds. If major lineages are not eliminated during an extinction event, it is clear that communities can reconstitute themselves with morphological forms reflecting similar adaptations at future times. In other words, there is some reality to our concepts of adaptive radiation and successive replacement of faunal assemblages by new faunal assemblages that are similar in form and function. This should not lead to complacency. Some life forms will replace communities that are being eliminated at the present time, but the replacement is possible only if the major lineages are still intact. Even so, the order of magnitude of faunal turnover may be at least 10,000,000 years before equivalent replacement, given that the available habitat is equivalent.

Considering mammalian faunas, Webb (1984) has presented the most recent, comprehensive analysis of North American land mammal extinctions. Six major extinction episodes have occurred during the last 10,000,000 years. The largest was in the Late Hemphillian, 5,000,000 years ago; and the most recent event was in the Rancholabrean, approximately 10,000 years ago, at the end of the Wisconsin glaciation period. Webb concludes that the extinction episodes are highly correlated with the terminations of glacial cycles. Large vertebrates were exceptionally vulnerable at the termination of these glaciation periods, and vulnerability was correlated with latitude; that is, large mammals at high latitudes were extremely vulnerable during these major climatic shifts.

The Fossil Record: Who Will Inherit the Earth?

If we confine ourselves to mammals, the fossil record from Florida has this to offer. Throughout the Pleistocene there have been at least four major and eighteen minor glaciation events in the Northern Hemisphere. Glaciation events correlate with shifts in sea level and the redistribution of plants deriving from global climatic change. Widespread and local extinctions result, but in the past, given enough time, extinct communities have been restored in terms of species richness through emigration and/or the evolution of new species from isolated, refugial populations. Since 10,000 B.P., however, stocks have been irrevocably lost from both North and South America, not to mention the Old World and Australasia (Webb 1984). Are past extinction events a guide to the future?

The modern terrestrial mammalian fauna of peninsular Florida includes forty-nine native species, fourteen of which are bats. If we exclude bats, we are left with thirty-five species, thirty-one of which are less than 10^5 g in body weight (i.e., $<10^2$ kg). Twenty-four of the thirty-one are less than 10 kg. This group of twenty-four includes ten browsers and/or grazers, five omnivores, and two carnivores (see Table 10.1).

In contrast, let us consider the attributes of the species that went extinct between 12,000 and 8,000 B.P., again excluding the Chiroptera. There were forty-two species of nonvolant land mammals at the beginning of the interval (Vero) (Webb 1974). Twenty-two species that were less than 100 kg in body weight survived through the Vero period to modern times. Seventeen species that were greater than 100 kg in body weight became extinct. Of the latter group, eleven were large browsers and/or grazers, three were large omnivores, and four were large carnivores (Figs. 10.3 and 10.4). The conclusion is obvious: The large herbivores

Table 10.1. Terrestrial Mammal Extinctions and Survivals in Florida

Size	Gz	Br	Rh	Gr	In	Om	Ca
A. Extinctions Between Vero and Modern							
1							
2	1		1				
3							
4						2	
5	1					1	1
6	3	3				2	3
7	2	1					
Total	7	4	1			5	4
B. Survivals from Vero to Modern							
1					1		
2			1	3	2(6)		
3	2	1	1	1		4	2
4						3	2
5		1					2
6						1	
7							
Total	2	2	2	4	3(6)	8	6
C. Modern[a]							
1					2(5)		
2	1			6	2(9)		
3	1	1	1	3		5	2
4		1				4	2
5		1					2
6						1	
7							
Total	2	3	1	9	4(14)	10	6

Source: A and B from Webb and Wilkins 1984.
Size: Numbers refer to maximum mean weight as logarithm to the base 10.
Trophic categories: Gz = grazer; Br = browser; Rh = rhizovore; Gr = granivore; In = insectivore; Om = omnivore; Ca = carnivore.
Number in each cell equal total species for that size and trophic category. Numbers in ( ) are species of *Chiroptera*.
[a]Pre-1900.

and the associated predators and scavengers were maximally vulnerable to (a) the combined effects of climatic and subsequent vegetational changes, (b) the closure of the gulf coastal, savanna corridor through sea level rise, and (c) the reduction of the land area of the peninsula to one-half of its former size. Humans may have played an insignificant role in the extinction events of peninsular Florida, but may have had a significant impact elsewhere.

RETROSPECTIVE

Leaving aside the focus on Florida, there was a net trend over the last 15,000 years toward a loss

50 Miles

Fig. 10.3. Some members of the extinct megafauna of Late Pleistocene, Florida. Note the larger land mass of Florida prior to the glacial melt. (Subjects not drawn to scale.)

smaller herbivores; with the demise of large herbivores, there was a loss of large predators in North America. Although overall it appears from the fossil record that large mammals are more vulnerable during extinction episodes, small mammals may be very adversely affected, especially during periods of cooling or during periods of major floristic changes associated with dramatic climate shifts. During the Late Hemphillian extinction period, small mammal species (<5 kg body weight) accounted for 40 percent of the total extinctions. This was the largest proportion of small mammal extinctions recorded by Webb during a 10,000,000-year interval (Webb 1984).

Unlike South America and other continents, the shape of North America causes a major reduction in continental area as glacial ice moves southward from the higher latitudes. During glacial maxima, there is not only a shift in climate and a displacement of the biota southward; there is also a major compression effect. This area reduction effect is comparable to, but precisely out of phase with, the shrinkage of land bridge island areas during glacial maxima. Survival of temperate-zone, large mammals is disfavored during glacial minima. Although ice-free land areas become available habitat, the climatic changes and associated vegetation changes force the megafauna to either retreat

Fig. 10.4. Some examples of the extant mammalian fauna of Florida. (Subjects not drawn to scale.)

north or seek montane refugia. During the period from the Hemphillian to the present, large mammal extinctions were frequent in North America. Some extinct species (e.g., *Bison*) were replaced from surviving stocks in Asia via the Bering land bridge as a new cycle of glaciation events occurred. These Eurasian stocks survived in the more extensive interglacial refugia found in Asia. To this day, the heterogeneous habitats of western Sichuan and Tibet support a relict, Pleistocene megafauna, including the yak, *Bos gruniens,* and the wild ass, *Equus*

(Hemionus) kiang, to mention only a few (Han and Xu 1985; Seidensticker et al. 1984). Until very recent times the Mongolian high plains supported large ungulates such as the wild horse and camel. With the current, impending demise of the large ungulates of central Asia, the possibility of a reconstitution of the North American megafauna during the next glacial dims and disappears. The extinction process in central Asia during the last 10,000 years was indeed the result of mankind's activities.

MANAGEMENT CONSIDERATIONS

Knowledge of the Status of Populations— Critical for Decisions

Clearly, what we need to retard the events that could transpire by the year 2100 is information on the status of vertebrate species and a monitoring system to give us an indication when a species appears to be in trouble (Humphrey 1985). Only if we know there is a problem can we attempt a solution. The solution we effect will be dependent on how much we know about the species' biology. Environmental monitoring and single-species studies can help us divert problems before they become critical; however, this is a labor-intensive, extremely expensive solution. The least expensive solution is to manage at the ecosystem level, thereby attempting to preserve through time the entire assemblage of species. Ultimately, this requires the maintenance of very large tracts of land, especially if one considers the top carnivores to be essential components of the ecosystem and worthy of maintenance. The alternative approach is to manage diminutive reserves in the hope of saving in perpetuity those smaller species with smaller space requirements. Clearly, some compromise will become necessary in the future.

All indications suggest that the large herbivores with vast requirements of space and the large carnivores that traverse the landscape are the most vulnerable components of an ecosystem. It is possible to be optimistic about the large herbivores because they are more tractable in terms of management in enclosures. It is probably not a coincidence that large herbivores were among the earlier species domesticated by neolithic peoples. On the other hand, large carnivores, especially those that are solitary, present a different challenge.

Wemmer et al. (1987) summarize the problem confronting the tiger (*Panthera tigris*). Although the tiger in Nepal and India is currently protected in a variety of preserves, the parks are relatively small and scattered. The barriers to gene flow set the stage for inbreeding depression, and local extinction in the small parks is virtually a certainty. Only a concerted effort to move male tigers from park to park can avert the problem; this dramatizes the fact that small parks are, at best, living museums.

Global Climatic Change: A Genuine Possibility

Schneider and Londer (1984) have presented a comprehensive documentation of how climate and the biota interact. Sea level changes have occurred over the last 180,000,000 years. Although short-term fluctuations can be noted, the long-term trend through the Cretaceous was for higher sea levels with a subsequent climatic deterioration during the Tertiary. Concomitant with this trend has been an alteration in the surface temperature of the earth, with an increase during the Cretaceous followed by a fluctuating decline from the Oligocene to the present. The most recent trend (12,000 B.P. to present), however, has consisted of increasing surface temperature and an accompanying rise in sea level.

Although the causes of climate change are debatable, the use of fossil fuels and the subsequent accumulation of CO_2 in the upper atmosphere may well be contributing to the "greenhouse effect." While uncertainty prevails with respect to long-term forcasting of global climate, human activity is undoubtedly contributing to overall climatic change, and the ability of human technology to cause climatic change is a rival to natural causes that we poorly understand. To the extent that we can predict the features of climatic change and identify human causes, we should design conservation strategies accordingly. As we look forward to the year 2100, we must not be complacent about the location of our current reserves. What might now appear to be marginal habitats for certain communities could well become optimal habitats in the future. A shift of only a few degrees in global temperature or an increase of 200 mm of annual rainfall can change currently marginal xeric habitats into habitats suitable for increased populations of species we wish to protect. Flexibility must be the byword in park planning, and "writing off" certain populations as marginal could be counterproductive to the continued maintenance of biotic diversity. On the other hand, the contemporary penchant for locating wildlife refuges along the coasts will pale in effectiveness as sea levels continue to rise and inundate massive acreages.

As an example of mamalian populations that have been considered marginal, we might point out the desert bighorn sheep (*Ovis canadensis*) of the southwestern United States and the populations of African elephants (*Loxodonta africana*) isolated in southwest Africa and in the Central African Repbulic and in Chad. In both cases the populations exist in what now appear to be marginal habitat and are to some extent relicts that have managed to exploit a suboptimal habitat based on a learned, living tradition. From time to time it has been suggested that these populations do not deserve conservation efforts since they occur in suboptimal habitat. But we encourage all workers in conservation to consider the very real prospect of global climatic change and to attempt to maintain what we already have in our hands. Given the dynamics of our global ecosytem, it would be premature indeed to write off any population of an endangered species.

Lest the preceding scenario seem wildly speculative, we note the recent publication by Haynes et al. (1987). They documented that in 1978, the first modern germination of plants occurred in the eastern Sahara. This event was triggered by the first measurable rainfall recharge event since the beginning of the thermonuclear era.

Do Large Mammals Count in the Long Run?

Much of the world's biological diversity (species richness) is contributed by small organisms such as the protozoa, bacteria, mosses, and grasses. Setting aside many small preserves selected with an eye toward maximizing habitat variability would most likely succeed in preserving these smaller forms of life. In order to preserve larger, unique forms of distinct evolutionary lineages, large areas must be set aside. Critics could claim that advocates of large preserves are hopeless romantics.

We may be classified at the moment as hopeless romantics, but from our perspective, a lifetime of dedication to conservation cannot be dismissed by trivial criticisms. Ultimately, the management of intact ecosystems mandates a tolerance for the potentially destructive (viz.,

human interests) elements of the community. Technology offers a false hope for salvation. Medical technology has certainly extended the prospect of life beyond the biblical three score and ten, but what is the expense of this victory to the next generation? In the great human economy of the globe, does it profit anyone that we live four months more, if five elephants should die, or one ounce of gold should be mined to augment the "stockmarket" by 0.0002 point? Think about it! We have thought about it, and we have no ready solutions. We are the victims of our own compassion for each other.

Management-Based Multiple-Use Concepts

Many conservation efforts in the twenty-first century will have to be integrated with some forms of human activity. The case of the red-cockaded woodpecker, discussed in a previous section, brings home the point that management is not necessarily incompatible with the preservation of a target species. All too often, management decisions are an outcome of political consensus, and the species' needs are lost in the shuffle. When management is executed without regard to the biological needs of a species, the results can be misguided and counterproductive. Harris (1984) has suggested a scheme whereby logging efforts can be compatible with the preservation of an ecosystem. His application of a long-rotation cutting scheme to the evergreen forests of the Pacific Northwest could stand as a model for plans where multiple uses of forests are contemplated. Of course, the recommendations for an evergreen forest in the Pacific Northwest of the United States cannot be applied to any other place in the world without the requisite research to determine habitat needs, regrowth of forest, and so forth. The value of Harris's book, however, is in the model it suggests, and such efforts should be encouraged wherever forest utilization as a renewable resource and preservation of the animal life within the forest are primary goals (Eisenberg and Harris 1987).

11

Ecosystems and Conservation in the Twenty-first Century

S. J. MCNAUGHTON

PLACES SET ASIDE

—what good heed Nature forms in us! She pardons no mistakes.
Her yea is yea, her nay, nay.

EMERSON 1836

As we look forward to conservation in the twenty-first century, it is well to remember how recent and fragile is the idea that humans should preserve as well as conquer nature. Formal conservation of natural resources by a society can be traced to the creation of Yellowstone National Park by the United States in 1872, which followed by eight years the creation of Yosemite as a reserve administered by California. Although British and European royalty had maintained shooting preserves for their exclusive use, the establishment of Yellowstone as a conscious act of preservation through social policy marked a dramatic change in collective attitudes that had consequences continuing to the present and, I hope, will continue beyond 2100. Isolating areas from human impact and development was a unique, and indeed, revolutionary idea. Early policymakers recognized the vulnerability inherent in that isolation. That their policy decisions led to the current predominant American view of reserves is indicated by the fact that hunting and settlement by nonpark personnel

were *de facto* prohibited by Moses Harris, the U.S. Army administrator of the park, beginning in 1886, fourteen years after the park was set aside and long before such policies became legally explicit (Haines 1977; but see Hales, chap. 13). Poaching continued to be a problem well into this century (Houston 1982), so the general social consensus leading to designation of certain areas as national parks was not, and is not, universally shared. Park management policy in the United States included predator control, culling of large herbivores, and fire control as standard procedures until recently, so management was largely interventionist. Existence of *cordon sanitaires* around parks was generally an accidental by-product of creation of parks within larger federal landholdings.

The current critical juncture of tropical conservation, therefore, reflects conflicts in social attitudes and inequalities of resource allocation (Iltis 1983b; Lewis and Kaweche 1985; Mares and Ojeda 1984; Western and Henry 1979) identical to those present during development of the

109

U.S. national parks system. The crisis is not new, but the magnitude of the problem, the heterogeneity of jurisdictional bodies, and the rate of human impact on natural areas are much greater now than during development of the U.S. parks system. The variety of habitats now being affected is also unprecedented, ranging from mountains (Eckholm 1975) to tropical rain forest (Gomez-Pompa et al. 1972) to desert streams (Vrijenhoek et al. 1985). Not only are conservation problems rooted in historical, sociological, and economic factors (Mares 1986), so also there are economic, social, and moral reasons for conservation (Ehrlich and Ehrlich 1981; Westman 1977), and it has been cogently argued that developed nations have an economic interest in preserving natural areas in economically less developed nations (Iltis 1983a). The idea of nature as a spiritual as well as material resource can be traced at least as far as Emerson (1836). The theme of this chapter is that sound policy should consider conservation in an ecosystem context, cognizant of all life forms characteristic of natural ecosystems and of indirect interconnections between organisms through both their physical and their biotic environments. A chapter such as this must, of necessity, take many licenses with the richness of scientific thinking, and the cautious reader should remember that the views expressed are my own, not necessarily those prevailing in ecology.

THE NATURE OF ECOSYSTEMS

One of the founders of modern ecology, S. A. Forbes (1887, 1925), head of the Illinois Natural History Survey, wrote that a lake "forms a little world within itself—a microcosm within which all the elemental forces are at work . . . [so that] whatever affects any species . . . must have its influence of some sort upon the whole assemblage." Almost four decades later, Tansley (1935), a founder of the British Ecological Society, argued that there is "constant interchange of the most various kinds within each system, not only between the organisms but between the organic and the inorganic. These *ecosystems*, as we may call them, are of the most various kinds and sizes" (emphasis in original). Furthermore, there is a "universal tendency to the evolution of dynam-

ic equilibria. . . . The more relatively separate and autonomous the system, the more highly integrated it is, and the relatively greater the stability of its dynamic equilibrium. . . . [Ecosystems] develop gradually, steadily becoming more highly integrated and more delicately adjusted in equilibrium." Humans, Tansley argued, are "an exceptionally powerful biotic factor which increasingly upsets the equilibrium of preexisting ecosystems and eventually destroys them, at the same time forming new ones of very different nature. . . ." Although few ecologists today might embrace the degree of integration explicit in both Forbes's and Tansley's remarks, the ecosystem concept has, nevertheless, remained a central idea in ecology. An ecosystem is now commonly defined as all of the organisms and their environments co-occurring in time and space, with no explicit recognition of the aspects of interaction and control discussed by Forbes and Tansley.

One of the most important features of ecosystems that must influence conservation policy is that they are open systems. Unlike molecules in a perfectly insulated container, ecosystems are leaky to energy, to chemicals, and even to organisms themselves. It is impossible to set aside an area sufficiently large as to be self-contained; there will always be spillover between reserves and surrounding areas. This can be a blessing if that spillover is regarded favorably by humans in adjoining areas, or a curse requiring careful management if humans consider spillover detrimental to their interests.

Natural Hierarchy

A hierarchy is a body of entities or processes arranged in a graded fashion; Tansley (1935) explicitly placed ecosystems in a hierarchical structure of nature (Fig. 11.1) since they "form one category of the multitudinous physical systems of the universe, which range from the universe as a whole down to the atom." Both ecology and conservation biology concentrate primarily on levels of organization between the individual and the ecosystem, although physiological ecology may extend as far as the biomolecule level and applied ecology as far as the biosphere level. Within nature's hierarchical structure, ecosystems seem the largest practicable unit at which conservation policies can be directed.

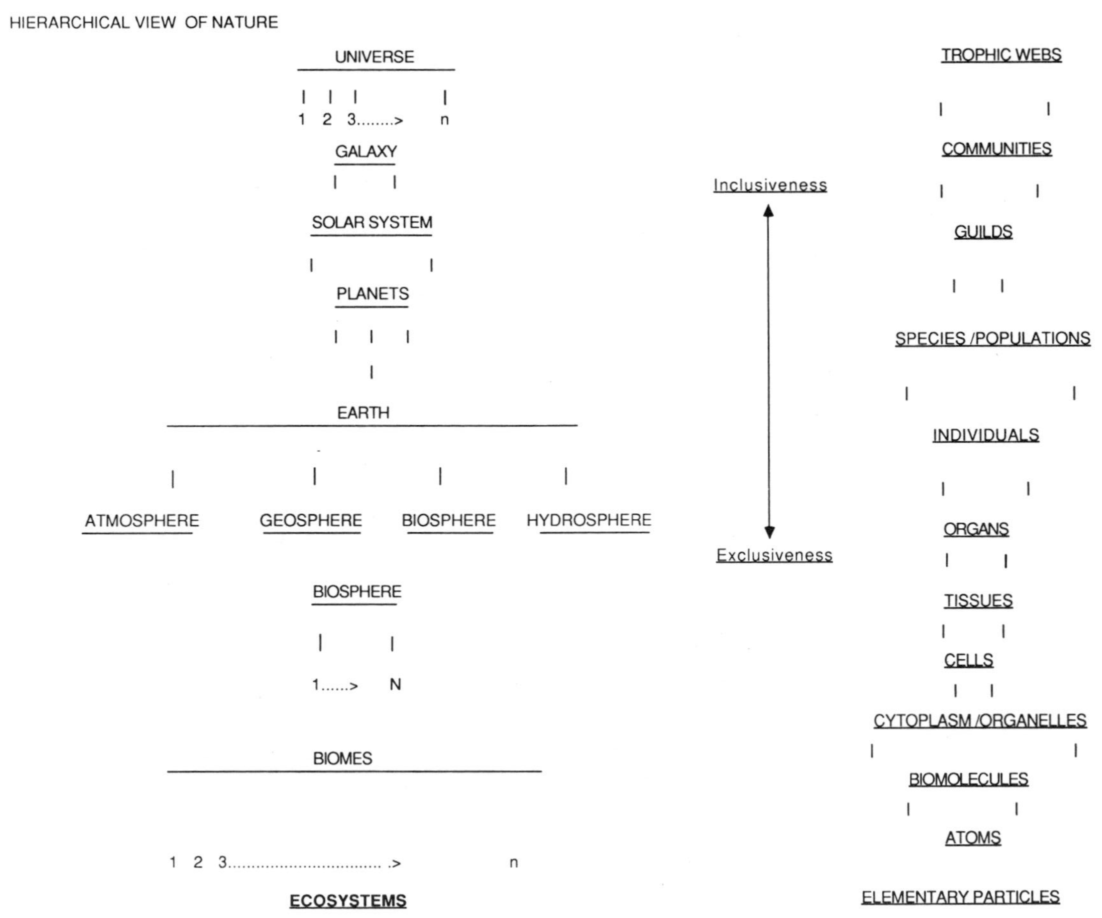

HIERARCHICAL VIEW OF NATURE

Fig. 11.1. Within a hierarchical structure, conservation biology is concerned primarily with levels of organization between individuals and ecosystems.

Although it borders on an ontological problem, it is important to recognize that there are two fundamentally different, though not wholly mutually exclusive, views of the meaning of hierarchical organization (for a general perspective, see Ashby 1956, Koestler 1967, Wiener 1948; for an ecological perspective, see Allen and Starr 1982, and, particularly, Schoener 1986, Ayala and Dobzhansky 1974, Engelberg and Boyarsky 1979, Margalef 1968, McNaughton and Coughenour 1981, Odum 1977, Salt 1979). One view, often associated with a reductionist approach to scientific problem-solving, is that the properties of an entity at any level in the hierarchy are a summation of the properties of less inclusive entities; Salt (1979) referred to these as collective properties. The alternative view, commonly associated with a holistic approach to science, holds that each level has unique properties, called emergent properties, that are characteristic of, and can only be learned by studying, that level.

Whether the world is reductionist, with only collective properties of importance, or holistic, with emergent properties of importance, is significant to conservation policy. If it is reductionist, preservation of gene pools by the presently feasible method of captive breeding or such currently infeasible, but not implausible, methods as development of DNA banks and recovery of DNA from existing tissues of extinct species would allow conservation to preserve biotic diversity even in the face of the current destructive rampage of humanity (Conway, chap. 19). If it is holistic, preservation of gene pools will not necessarily preserve nature if we are unable to reconstruct its structure and dynamics merely by rereleasing representative gene pools into nature at some future time. That is, if ecosystem organization depends on the development of specific, dynamic relationships between organisms interacting through the food web and the physical environment, merely storing genotypes for subsequent reintroduction may not reestablish the original ecosystem if emergent properties have been disrupted. Suppose, for example, that a sort of genetic Noah's ark were established to preserve the large mammalian species of tropical regions where rampant poaching and habitat deterioration threaten them with extinction. If those genetic stocks could be preserved until 2100, and if rational conservation policies had been established by

then, would release of those genetic stocks back into whatever habitats then remained allow reconstruction of the ecosystems of which they were once members? Does the wholly laudable reintroduction of bison into remnants of natural prairies in North America recreate the native prairie ecosystem? Since learning is an important component of environmental relations in more complex animals, and lower life forms may disappear with the ecosystems that contain them, gene pool preservation is best regarded as a last-gasp conservation strategy capable of preserving fragments of nature, but not necessarily its organization.

Ecosystem Organization

Ecosystems are organized by the patterns of resource acquisition, that is, feeding patterns, that the organisms they contain have evolved (Fig. 11.2). The simplest view of structure is to consider food chains, linear patterns of resource flow from soil and atmosphere to plants to herbivores to carnivores. A cluster of interconnected food chains is a food web. A food web characterizes the pathways through which energy and chemicals flow through an ecosystem. Energy is transferred through food webs principally as bonds between carbon atoms—C-C bond energy. That bond energy, at its most abundant form in lipids and carbohydrates, is utilized at each step in a food chain for two principal functions. One function is maintaining the organisms present at that step; the energy expended for that purpose is called maintenance respiration. The other is creating new organisms or organism mass, referred to as growth respiration. The total living mass present in an ecosystem at any given time is biomass; change in biomass through time is productivity.

There are two fundamentally different types of food webs: those based on living tissues, commonly called grazing food webs, and those based on dead tissues, commonly called detritus food webs. Grazing food webs are most important in aquatic ecosystems where much of the plant growth, called primary productivity, is consumed directly by animals. Detritus food webs are most important in terrestrial ecosystems where much of the primary productivity is unconsumed and dies before being eaten.

Energy flow is hierarchical within and between organisms. Transfer between organisms

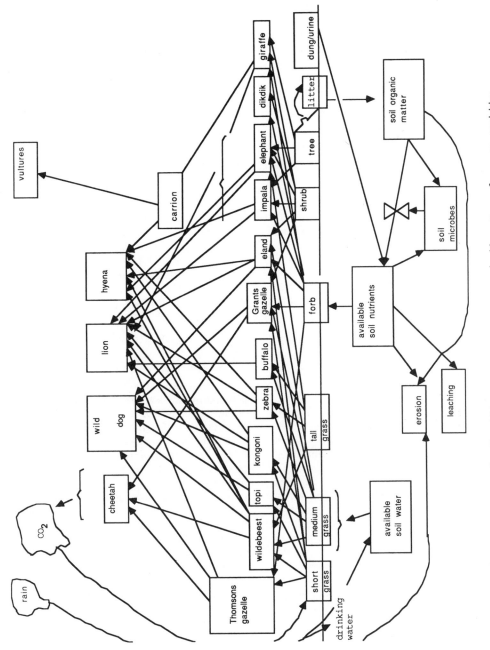

Fig. 11.2. Diagram of an East African savanna ecosystem, organized by patterns of resource acquisition.

takes place primarily as C-C bond energy, but much of the work within organisms is accomplished by the high energy of phosphorylated chemicals, for example, as the terminal phosphates of adenonsine triphosphate (ATP). As work is done through respiration, the chemical constituents of molecules are both recycled internally and returned to the environment in inorganic forms; respiration releases carbon dioxide and water, with the former returned to the environment and the latter largely retained. Carbon dioxide released to the environment can then be recycled as plants take it up in the process of photosynthesis to produce primary productivity.

Respiration is the generator of work in organisms, and that work may be used to maintain what is present in the face of the entropic tendency of all structures to decay, maintenance energy, or to generate more living mass and structure, growth energy. Some chemicals are returned to the environment continuously, but many are conserved against this loss and are recycled to the environment only upon death or as excretory wastes. Dead organisms and wastes enter detritus food webs in which microorganisms are major constituents. Without these microbes, about which little is known in natural environments, and which conservation does not consider at all, the ecosystems we seek to preserve could not exist.

Energy flow and chemical cycling are intimately coupled and weld aboveground and belowground organisms, large mammals and microorganisms, into a functional system (Fig. 11.1). These circular causal pathways, in which origin is impossible to assign to a given element (Hutchinson 1948), are both manifestations and causes of ecosystem organization. Neither is possible without the other although, in general, while all ecosystems must be open to energy, they may be open to chemicals to extents that vary depending on how tightly chemicals are cycled internally. Erosion, leaching, volatilization, and animal movements can transport significant quantities of chemicals, as do anthropogenic processes (i.e., air and water pollution). By 2100, most patterns of energy flow and nutrient cycling will have been profoundly modified by humans, even in reserve areas.

Conservation at the ecosystem level, then, must seek to preserve the basic trophic structure

of an ecosystem and the patterns of energy flow and nutrient cycling resulting from that structure. A striking feature of biotic diversity is that convergent evolution in similar habitats at geographically widespread localities has produced similar life forms from distinct hereditary lines. Preserving coniferous forests in North America, South America, and New Zealand would conserve quite different genetic lineages. Conversely, widespread species commonly achieve that broad range through intraspecific genetic differentiation (McNaughton 1966).

Interventionist management may be used to either modify or maintain ecosystem structure and dynamics, although this often has not been explicitly recognized. Predator control programs, herbivore culling, and other management techniques are fundamental interventions that necessarily modify ecosystem structure and processes. Controlled burning for fire or habitat control is also a fundamental intervention in ecosystem processes since it volatilizes large quantities of carbon, nitrogen, and sulfur from the vegetation burned, releasing nonvolatilized elements in forms that may be readily available to support plant growth (Rundel 1981).

Spatial Scale in Ecosystems

Ecosystems are part of a larger, natural hierarchy. But they also have internal hierarchical organizations relevant to conservation planning. Foraging by large mammals, whether herbivores or predators, ranges in scale from the level of geographical regions to the organs of food sources (Laca and Demment 1987; McNaughton 1983; Senft et al. 1986). Migratory herbivores that often dominate the food web in grassland ecosystems move over large areas in the course of an annual cycle. During these movements they may range over tens of thousands of square kilometers, occupying different regions in different seasons. At this macroscale, foraging may be genetically programmed by evolution (Senft et al. 1986). At the mesoscale of resolution, landscape types within regions may be selected on the range of weeks to hours. On the microscale of swards within landscapes, patches of vegetation to feed on may be chosen on a time scale of minutes. Finally, food selection will take place on a time scale of seconds for bites within patches (Laca and Demment 1987). Foraging at this level may be partially innate but much of it is also probably learned. Ecosystem reconstruction through release of captive genotypes may be only partially successful if transfer of learned behavior between generations is an important component of resource utilization, predator avoidance, or other adaptive behaviors.

Conservation can operate at many spatial scales, depending on the natural phenomena to be conserved. This has long been recognizd in the design of reserves of different sizes to meet different objectives, as is evident elsewhere in this volume. Also apparent is that we have insufficient information on the life histories of many species to make intelligent choices about reserve size, configuration, and the possibility of corridor connections to create a large, interconnected reserve out of many small reserves.

One approach to scale is to provide reserves of sufficient size to provide the habitat required to support the species with the largest required area. This, then, would provide numerous smaller habitats within which other species could exist. Since predators commonly have larger ranges than herbivores and range generally increases with body size (McNab 1963), predator-based reserves can serve as umbrella areas protecting many other species with smaller spatial or habitat requirements.

CONSERVING THE HIDDEN
BUT INDISPENSABLE

Conservation policy is generally blind to the two classes of organisms most important to human welfare: plants and microbes. These are the crucial, indispensable components of every ecosystem; human society, life itself, is based on them. Plants are essential to ecosystems because they are the most abundant organisms capable of capturing the sun's energy in forms that are stable and transferable through the food web. Microbes are essential because they recycle the elements that plants must have to effect energy capture. The simplest self-contained ecosystem must, at the least, contain these two components. Yet they are largely, for plants, or solely, for microorganisms, ignored in conservation policy.

Much has been written in this book about the dire future for tropical diversity and, indeed, relatively undisturbed ecosystems everywhere.

I believe it will be difficult to convince policymakers or the general public that it is in their self-interest to preserve the diversity of tropical insects, or, perhaps, even of primates. On the other hand, a cogent, convincing case can be made that the preservation of potentially useful plants and microbes, presently unknown, is in the self-interest of all human beings (Ehrlich and Ehrlich 1981). Plant domestication beginning about twelve centuries ago made possible the modern, industrial society. Similarly, the discovery of antibiosis by microbial chemicals less than a century ago led to the modern healthcare systems that protected humans in a modern, population-dense, heavily urbanized world, contributing to the current crisis of conservation.

Energy in the human diet is obtained largely from a mere handful of grasses domesticated early in human history. So, also, the number of animals upon which agriculture depends is a shadow of animal diversity in the biosphere. Had aurochs survived the domestication of cattle, it is possible that they could represent a gene pool of hardiness and pathogen resistance that could be introduced into domesticated cows. The precarious nature of the genetic ancestors of domesticates is documented by the important rediscovery of teosinte, a presumed progenitor of maize that had been believed extinct (Iltis et al. 1979). Reanalyses, based in part on this rediscovered species, led to a new hypothesis of maize origin that is both scientifically important and of practical significance (Iltis 1983b). In the absence of the wild plants, it is unlikely that these strides of understanding could have been accomplished. Further agricultural development leading to increased crop yields could be a major contributor to conservation if it brought food supply in developing countries into balance with population, releasing land currently under cultivation to ecosystem reconstruction. Land degradation and soil erosion work opposite to this opportunity, diminishing the potential yield of arable lands (Brink et al. 1977; Pimental et al. 1976), but potentially releasing degraded land to conservation purposes.

The discovery of marine hydrothermal vents less than a decade ago was associated with the discovery of groups of organisms, previously unknown, with unique physiological and biochemical properties (Arp and Childress 1981; Cavanaugh et al. 1981; Felbeck 1981). These ecosystems are supported by chemosynthetic microbial production associated with hydrothermal fluids in such diverse locations as the Galápagos Rift, the East Pacific Rise, and the Juan de Fuca Ridge, and cold sulfide seeps on the Florida Escarpment and in the Gulf of Mexico (Grassle 1985). Sixteen previously unknown families of invertebrates have been identified. These discoveries indicate that our knowledge of the biosphere is far from complete.

INTEGRATIVE MECHANISMS AND POTENTIAL TECHNOLOGY

Tropical biotas, from rain forest to coral reef, are frequently highly diverse and often manifest exceptionally complex ecological interactions. The chemicals that mediate such interactions and mechanisms of biotic integration that create systems of the type Forbes (1887) and Tansley (1935) believed ecosystems to be (McNaughton and Coughenour 1981). The trophic structure of an ecosystem does not arise out of the mere crashing together of organisms, as molecules in a flask collide with one another. Instead, feeding patterns are due to specific stimulus-sensor-effector relationships that have evolved over eons to govern food choice. Many of these are mediated by chemical properties of organisms that could have immense economic potential. The potential importance of such chemicals is demonstrated by the accidental discovery of antibiotics by Fleming and the industry that developed from that discovery. An impressionistic list of ecological interactions mediated by chemicals of potential economic importance includes:

a. the production of shark-repellent chemicals by marine fish (Tachibana et al. 1984);
b. the first bacterium known to both digest cellulose and fix nitrogen, which was isolated from the gland of Deshayes in six species of terdinid bivalves (Waterbury et al. 1983);
c. soil-borne epiphytes on plant roots that suppress plant diseases (Schroth and Hancock 1982);
d. a plant flavone that induces the expression of nodulation genes in *Rhizobium* bacteria (Peters et al. 1986);
e. a chemotactic chemical inducing a specific

nitrogen-fixing association of cyanobacteria and bacteria (Paerl and Gallucci 1985);
f. an aphid alarm pheromone produced by wild potatoes that repels aphids (Gibson and Pickett 1983);
g. the widespread occurrence of skin compounds in frogs and toads that interact with Na^+/K^+-dependent ATPase (Flier et al. 1980);
h. defensive secretions of arthropods (Eisner and Meinwald 1966);
i. plant alkaloids sequestered by butterflies that protect them from predators (Brown 1984);
j. coral reef invertebrates toxic to fish (Bakus 1981); and
k. the revelation that the long-employed dyestuff from cochineal insects is a potent feeding deterrent to ants (Eisner et al. 1980).

The vast diversity of chemical interactions in nature could be of major potential economic importance through their agricultural, industrial, and medical applications (Myers 1976).

These interactions are mediated by chemicals that are, either directly or indirectly, gene products. It is inconceivable that all such chemicals have yet been discovered or that they will continue to be subject to discovery if the ecosystems where they evolved are destroyed. There can be little doubt that biotechnology and gene cloning have the potential to create new technologies releasing us from our dependence on such limited and fast depleted technologies as those requiring fossil fuels. But in this day of biotechnology and gene cloning, it is imperative that we recognize that there must be useful genes to clone. We are still far from understanding genetic expression well enough to design genes; we will be dependent on the genes that evolution has designed for the foreseeable future. To assert that we now know what organisms to save is to assert that all that is useful that can be discovered has been discovered.

Allowing the destruction of biotic diversity will vastly impoverish the bank of genes currently stored in living organisms. One of the most diverse freshwater fish communities known, in Lake Victoria, is going extinct due to the introduction of Nile Perch (Baerl et al. 1985). Large, conspicuous animals may still be preserved by captive breeding, but the plants, microorganisms, invertebrates, and other largely indiscernible organisms that have evolved in the same ecosystems are unlikely to survive if the ecosystems they inhabit are destroyed. The coupling between animal and plant extinctions is demonstrated by evidence that a major tree on Mauritius is following into extinction the dodo (*Raphus cucullatus*) that fed on its seeds and facilitated their germination (Temple 1977). If the spasm of extinction predicted elsewhere in this volume does occur between now and 2100, we will have wasted a resource much more precious than fossil fuels. We will have wasted the information that evolution has been creating and storing for eons.

BIOTIC CONSERVATION

Plants can be conserved and bred in botanical gardens after their natural habitats are destroyed, just as animal captive breeding programs may play a major role in future programs to conserve animals. But while research and thought is now being directed toward determining the degree of genetic variation in animal populations in natural environments, as is evident elsewhere in this volume (Vrijenhoek, chap. 9), little is known of the extent and importance of genetic variation in natural plant populations. There are few plant communities for which even a rudimentary quantitative estimation of species diversity, a fundamental type of genetic variation, has been determined. There are major genetic gradients within grass species in the Serengeti region that are related to both climatic and biotic gradients across the ecosystem (McNaughton 1979, 1984). Genotypic differentiation within species includes such fundamental traits as growth form and such fundamental physiological properties as nutrient uptake capacity and regulation of that capacity by the defoliation regime experienced (McNaughton and Chapin 1985). These represent fundamental adaptive traits of such potential economic importance to agriculture that their preservation might be of great future significance. Since so few species in natural ecosystems have even been examined for traits of potential adaptive or economic importance, designing collection and culturing techniques to preserve them at the present is unlikely to be

successful. Therefore, an umbrella reserve is much more likely to preserve them than depending on garden cultures or the type of germplasm banks that have been employed for crop plants (Harlan 1975).

Studies of the Serengeti ecosystem indicate that the effects of grazing are not limited merely to direct interactions between plants and animals. The level of infection of grass roots with symbiotic mycorrhizal fungi was positively related to grazing intensity in Serengeti grasslands (Wallace 1981). These symbionts could facilitate nutrient and water uptake, alleviating stress from both factors under heavy grazing conditions. Serengeti grasses also make more efficient use of nitrogen in urea than in inorganic forms, an obvious adaptation to nutrient cycling through animal wastes and an apparently unique trait among plants (Ruess and McNaughton 1984). And, as in the mycorrhizal pattern, soil microbial biomass potential and resultant mineralization potential were positively correlated with the mean annual grazing intensity that a site experienced (Ruess and McNaughton 1987a). Finally, ammonia volatilization can be a major source of nitrogen loss from ecosystems where large mammals are a conspicuous component of the fauna (Woodmansee 1978), but the Serengeti ecosystem is highly conserving of nitrogen due to effects of the grazers on the microbial community and plant form and function (Ruess and McNaughton 1987b). Aboveground grazing can also have a regulatory effect on belowground microbial consumers (Ingham and Detling 1984; Ingham et al. 1985). Thus, large mammals have a wide variety of effects, both direct and indirect, on the organisms that coexist with them, ranging from the plants that are their food sources to the microbes essential to recycling nutrients required for energy capture at the plant level. It seems likely that elimination of those animals would have drastic effects at almost all ecosystem levels.

DISTURBANCE CASCADES IN ECOSYSTEMS

Patterns of change in the Serengeti region in historical time suggest that not only the large mammals but also the ecosystems they occur in were affected drastically by the great rinderpest pandemic that swept the continent in the late nineteenth century (McNaughton 1988). Those changes include a primary effect of the pathogen on ungulate populations; early records suggested 95 percent mortalities among severely affected species (Lydekker 1908). Many humans were plunged into abject poverty by this disaster and human populations were further decimated by accompanying human diseases (Ford 1971). An increase in fire frequency and intensity associated with forage accumulation in the absence of grazing may have had an immediate effect of destroying seedling and sapling size classes in tree populations. Repeated burning, however, results in bush encroachment (Trollope 1982), so a major secondary effect was probably conversion of savannas into bushland and then woodland. This increase in arborescent cover led to an increase in tsetse (*Glossina*) abundance, acting as a further deterrent to recovery of pastoral human populations (Ford 1971). Predator and scavenger populations would have obtained a surfeit of food during commencement of the pandemic, but then would have been confronted with drastically reduced food supplies as the plague ran its course. Additional tertiary effects were probably modifications of the genetic properties of grasses (McNaughton 1979, 1984), as the principal consumer changed from grazers feeding on them primarily during periods of active growth to fire, which consumed their tissues when they were largely dormant. Quarternary effects probably involved a modification of soil nutrient pools as fire volatilized large quantities of carbon, and lesser quantities of nitrogen and sulfur, releasing mineral elements to the soil in readily available forms.

Interconnected interactions in ecosystems through evolutionary time led to chains of indirect effects producing mutual adaptive complexes (Wilson 1980) among the myriad co-occurring organisms at many different trophic levels (McNaughton 1985, 1988). The Serengeti ecosystem eventually came to the state described upon its discovery just after the great pandemic had swept through. The great nomadic herds, then much reduced in numbers, spent the entire wet season on the open Serengeti Plains. Zebra and gazelle densities approached and exceeded, respectively, the abundance of wildebeests. Large areas of the system were unexploited by herbivores and fires were extensive and frequent. Elephants were absent, predators were comparatively sparse, as were scavengers, and ecosystem state departed markedly from what it had been before and what it was to become after rinderpest was controlled in the mid-1960s. But we must beware of wholesale arguments that everything is connected to everything else in nature. Cascading cause and effect in ecosystems depend on the strength of interactions within those ecosystems (Paine 1980).

Paine (1969) identified as "keystone" species predators high in the trophic web that control the communities below them. Other ecologists have described "critical" species at various positions in the trophic web that may be essential for an ecosystem to maintain its fundamental structure and process integrity. Critical species can often be inconspicuous members of the flora or fauna. A mollusk in Atlantic estuaries, for example, is responsible for less than 1 percent of the energy flow through those estuaries, but processes about 15 percent of the phosphorus and about one-third of the environment's particulate phosphorus each day (Kuenzler 1961a, b). Deciduous trees may be insignificant components of the biomass of coniferous forests, but the rapid decomposition of their leaf litter may make them much more important in nutrient cycling than their abundance suggests (Witkamp 1966). The occurrence of critical species of minor importance in numerical abundance suggests that a rational conservation strategy leading to 2100 requires conserving ecosystems rather than just species.

Ecosystems may be characterized by dynamics involving breakpoints of environmental change associated with thresholds of response which, once passed, lead to a drastically different stable state (May 1977). The impending spasm of extinction could, therefore, be associated with much greater ecosystem change than those direct extinctions resulting from human activities. Indirect effects propagated through the trophic web and physical environment could lead to collapses of entire ecosystems once breakpoints are exceeded. Not only the magnitude of ecosystem modification is important, but also the position of that modification relative to thresholds. In plain fact, such thresholds have not been characterized quantitatively, to my knowledge, for any natural ecosystem, but both theory and the qualitative behavior of stressed ecosystems suggest that they may be important (May 1977).

CONSERVING ECOSYSTEMS: TOWARD THE TWENTY-FIRST CENTURY

The general thesis of this chapter is that except under the catastrophic constraint of impending extinction of any given species, the best conservation strategy over the next century is to preserve whole ecosystems of sufficient size and habitat diversity to maintain representative trophic structures and critical species. We cannot casually and passively accept development policies, whether formally stated or *de facto,* that allow the destruction of total ecosystem types, whatever their geographical extent and location.

As a first policy, World Heritage Sites should be provided with the financial and material resources necessary to protect them. The Serengeti National Park, for example, has been and is under a potentially devastating assault from poachers that has all but eliminated the black rhinoceros, reduced the elephant population by 90 percent, and effectively exterminated buffalo in the northwest and topi in the southwest. In the absence of an effective commitment from economically strong nations, the developing nations simply lack the resources necessary to preserve major ecosystem types into the twenty-first century (Iltis 1983a; Western and Henry 1979).

Second, those parks which do not constitute effective ecosystems should be upgraded, where feasible, by annexation of surrounding areas to provide the spatial scale necessary to constitute relatively self-contained units. But, at the same time, we should understand that ecosystems are naturally open systems, so total self-containment is impossible. Research attention should also be directed toward determining whether reserves that may constitute subecosystems (e.g., the panda reserves in China) are degenerating because they are not total ecosystems. To the extent that degeneration is evident, conservation policies should be modified by the methods outlined elsewhere in this volume (e.g., corridors of connection in Harris and

Eisenberg, chap. 17) to weld subsystems together.

Third, representative areas of sufficient scale should be established in all the earth's biomes to preserve characteristic trophic structures and the integrity of ecosystem processes. Scientists currently recognize approximately fifteen to twenty major biome types, but there also are a number of additional communities of smaller spatial extent but ecological distinctiveness, such as estuaries or hydrothermal vents, that should be preserved. At the least, major terrestrial biomes should be preserved or recreated on each of the continents or islands on which they occur (or occurred). In addition, representative freshwater ecosystems should be set aside on each continent, and marine ecosystems protected in each ocean.

It has been argued persuasively in this volume and elsewhere that much of the earth's biotic diversity resides in the wet tropics and that most of that diversity may disappear well before 2100. While cataloguing that diversity is a major responsibility of field scientists (Wilson, chap. 1), preserving it is of even greater importance. I believe field scientists have a major responsibility to develop an agreed-upon list of what the earth's major ecosystems are, identify specific localities where representative examples of those ecosystems yet exist or might be recreated, and work assiduously for public policies in all nations that will preserve or, as necessary, recreate those ecosystems.

Among the most effective conservation organizations in the United States, in my view, is the Nature Conservancy. It is particularly effective because its policy is simple, but effective: preserve places and the organisms therein. In the absence of such a straightforward, workable policy on a worldwide basis, conservation in 2100 may be a dead issue, because it is no longer meaningful. Bewailing the loss of tropical diversity, in the absence of convincing, compelling policies to arrest that loss, will accomplish nothing. Conservation biology must be a curious, but attainable, blend of research on how preservation is best accomplished and activism to implement policies based firmly on the understanding that develops from research. Perhaps it is no accident that the Nature Conservancy had its origins in the Ecological Society of America. The conference Conservation 2100, and others like it, have demonstrated that field biologists are dedicated to both understanding how to conserve and making judgments about what should be conserved. This is again a fusion of science and policy that was evident when the Nature Conservancy developed from the Public Affairs Committee of the ESA. But we should not be misled; the time is too short for implementation to wait until research has provided all the answers. Forceful, interim solutions are required now. An ecosystem catalog, and an ecosystem-based conservation policy, could be such an interim program.

Unanimity is not required to implement effective conservation policy; Moses Harris proved that over a century ago. But a consensus that can be effected by persons in key positions is required, as Harris also demonstrated. By analogy with ecosystems, keystone and critical persons are required for conservation in 2100 to be more than an apparition. Those persons must, on the one hand, provide tangible and convincing evidence that conservation is important and, on the other hand, determine what should be conserved and how it is to be conserved. A *critical-places* strategy, based on ecosystem types representative of the earth's existing biotic diversity, could accomplish this objective. Future generations may value those of this generation who enunciate and implement effective conservation of biotic diversity, just as many in this generation revere those of past generations who developed the concepts and programs that made national parks a reality.

CODA

1. Natural ecosystems are structured as food webs organized by feeding modes and the resultant processes of energy flow and chemical cycling. This organization makes them reservoirs of genetic diversity, most of which is currently undescribed.

2. Much of that diversity is in plants, microbes, invertebrates, and other organisms that conservation policy cannot address explicitly since little is known of them. Diversity includes differentiation within species as well as differences between species.

3. Some of the most valuable organisms for potential human utilization are inconspicuous in nature.

4. Diversity represents an irreplaceable storehouse of information produced by evolution over eons.

5. That storehouse is of potentially immense practical significance to humans through direct use and the twenty-first century technology of genetic transfer.

6. Humans cannot create diversity but they can conserve it.

7. Genetic diversity cannot be retained, for all practical purposes, without preserving the ecosystems of which it is a part.

8. The earth's ecosystem types should be categorized.

9. Representative types of each ecosystem in both terrestrial and aquatic habitats should be preserved in as great a variety of locations as is technically and financially feasible.

10. Conservation to 2100 should be based on a policy of maintaining representative food webs and ecosystem process, so management should be as noninterventionist as is feasible but as interventionist as is necessary to achieve that objective.

11. In the absence of the genetic diversity that can be preserved in ecosystems, further evolution of all organisms will be largely precluded except through artificial mutagenesis.

12
Diversity and Stability in Ecosystem Conservation

BRIAN WALKER

The physical and chemical environment of the world is changing. Whether we like it or not, owing to marked changes in the global carbon budget and in regional hydrological systems, and to quite natural longer-term changes in the world's temperature regime, the physical base of the biological systems we wish to conserve is being altered. For this reason alone, it is necessary that conservationists move away, once and for all, from the preservation view. We cannot preserve exactly what we now have, even if it were desirable; and the question, therefore, is what do we want to conserve, and how do we maintain as high a level of diversity as possible?

In a strategic sense, most objectives of conservation areas include "to maintain high species diversity," and in a tactical sense, most management activities are aimed at stabilizing the ecosystems concerned—preventing dramatic changes. So it is appropriate to consider diversity and stability, both in a scientific way, because these two notions are perceived as being important aims of conservation.

It is unfortunate that the two terms have been used in very different ways, and have been interpreted differently in purely scientific and in general conservation terms. As just implied, diversity and stability are generally taken to be desirable goals to achieve in conservation, but when one attempts to put them into operational terms, things become less clear. I cannot review here the vast literature that the relationship between diversity and stability has generated.

Some of the historical developments are given by Robert McIntosh (1985), and an overview of current developments can be obtained from May (1973), Orians (1974), Goodman (1975), Halfon (1979), Ulanowicz (1979), Connell and Sousa (1983), Pimm (1984), Weins (1984), and De Angelis et al. (1985). I shall give only a brief summary of current views as a basis for considering the significance of the topic to conservation.

DEFINITION OF TERMS

Since confusion about stability and diversity stems from differences in the use of these terms, it is necessary to state how they are used in this chapter.

Diversity

When used on its own, the word *diversity* is taken to be synonymous with alpha- or species diversity within a community. High diversity means lots of species and high equitability (i.e., an even spread of the total numbers or biomass among the species). The number of species per se is referred to as "species number" or "species richness." (In the conservation literature, diversity is often used to describe richness.) The rate at which species change across the landscape is known as beta-diversity. Community diversity is the counterpart of alpha-diversity, but refers to the numbers and proportional amounts of different communities. Patchiness refers to the sizes and relative distribution of communities. Beta-diversity, community diversity, and patchiness all contribute to spatial heterogeneity. (Community diversity and patchiness admittedly require prior definition of what constitutes a community.) Complexity refers to the species interactions and the structure of the trophic web—the number of levels, the number of species in each level, and their connectance (proportion of possible interspecific interactions).

Stability

The term *stability* has been used in many different ways. Orians (1974) described seven meanings and attempted to rationalize the problem, but unfortunately the term continues to be used in contradictory and confusing ways. In broad terms, it is given two distinctly different meanings.

In the most common usage, it is the same as Orian's (1974) "constancy" and refers to the degree of change in the abundance of the system's components over time (i.e., in stable systems, the abundances of the species do not change much). The observed constancy may, in turn, be due to the fact that the system has a constant environment or it may be due to internal, stabilizing, negative feedback mechanisms which enable the system to remain constant under pressure from a changing environment. Connell and Sousa (1983) refer to the latter type of constancy as "resistance," and it is important to note that stability in this sense can only be evaluated relative to variation in environmental change (or external pressure) over time.

Discussion of degree of change requires consideration of another system property relating to dynamics, namely, "resilience." Resilience, too, has been used in different ways. It has been used to describe the rate at which a system returns to its equilibrium following a perturbation (Pimm 1984), but although resilient systems generally exhibit rapid change, it is used here in the sense of Holling (1973) and Walker et al. (1981) to indicate the degree to which a system can be changed and still recover (referred to as "amplitude" by Connell and Sousa [1983]). It can only be considered in relation to an equilibrium state of a system, and it describes the size of the domain around that state from within which the system will tend to change toward the

equilibrium. Once one of the system variables (at least) has changed so much that it places the system beyond the domain of attraction, the system then changes toward some new state. The new equilibrium state may constitute different amounts of the same variables, or it may involve a change in the variables (species) themselves. This leads us to the other, broad use of the term *stability*.

The second meaning of stability, here called "persistence," refers to the integrity of the system's species composition over time. In a stable system, all species persist, whereas in an unstable system one or more species will be lost or gained with time. Stability is therefore a qualitative measure of the constancy of species composition, and it again needs to be considered in relation to persistence under a constant versus a fluctuating environment (or other external pressure.)

The confusion in definitions has led to confusion in interpretation of cause and effect. Diversity is sometimes seen as the desirable outcome of stability (used in the constancy sense), and stability (persistence) is sometimes regarded as the desirable consequence of high diversity (which in turn is taken to be some complex feature of richness, diversity, and connectance).

CURRENT BELIEFS ABOUT DIVERSITY AND STABILITY

At the risk of oversimplifying the issue, the notions about diversity–stability relations can be summarized as follows:

1. The original hypothesis relating diversity to stability (persistence) was based on the choice of flow pathways in the trophic structure (MacArthur 1955). Replacement of the diversity of flows by the diversity of species (which is easier to measure) has prevented the estimation of what is perhaps an essential requirement for ecosystem self-regulation, a property that Ulanowicz (1979) has called the redundancy of the community structure, and which is related to the choice of alternate pathways.

2. The early belief that an increase in diversity or complexity resulted in increased community stability was not well founded. It may sometimes happen, but there is

no necessary connection. May (1973) demonstrated that in model systems increased complexity per se reduced stability (in the persistence sense of the word), and others (e.g., Pimm 1984) agree that the more complex or diverse a system is, the less likely it is to retain all its species in the long term. The long-term stability of complex systems that are at or near equilibrium depends on a particular kind of diversity and on special feedbacks in the system.

3. Much of the original theory relating diversity to stability arose from analyses of systems that were assumed to have strong interactions, and interpretation of the theory was based on the outcome of the system when it had achieved equilibrium (or alternatively whether it could achieve equilibrium). Subsequent work has demonstrated that there are a variety of types of dynamic behavior, including (i) the stable point equilibrium system; (ii) the classic stable limit cycle of predator/prey models; and (iii) "loose" equilibrium systems (De Angelis et al. 1985), also called "density-vague" systems by Strong (1986), in which the dynamics are bounded but within the bounds the system variables show little preference for particular values; and finally, (iv) unbounded, neutral or nonequilibrial systems.

Connell and Sousa (1983) considered the evidence necessary to establish the existence of equilibria in natural ecosystems and, after reviewing the published accounts of natural ecosystem or community dynamics, concluded that there is so far no evidence that systems with multiple stable states exist. Furthermore, although there are some indications of natural systems having equilibrium states, they are difficult to demonstrate.

4. Most ecosystems are comprised of a number of subsystems. If the subsystems are stable (persistent) and if the interactions between the subsystems are weak, then the ecosystem as a whole is stable (Siljak 1979).

5. Spatial variability and the presence of refugia and reserves promote both persistence (e.g., Hassell and May (1973) and constancy (Walker et al., in preparation).

6. In the long term, stable (constant) environments promote stable systems which allow a gradual increase in species diversity (Pielou 1975).

7. In the short term, instability of the environment promotes increased species diversity by allowing unstable mixtures of species to persist. If the environment is too variable, then species numbers again decrease, and this has led to what is known as the "intermediate disturbance hypothesis," which states that maximum species diversity is attained at some intermediate level of disturbance.

8. Resilient systems generally have low constancy, and the most important point in resilience theory is that the degree of resilience is related to the degree of disturbance and change. If a particular kind of disturbance or stress is alleviated or damped, then the system itself changes and is in the future less able to withstand such a disturbance. Maintenance of resilience therefore requires periodic disturbance.

9. Interpretation of observed ecosystem dynamics is confounded by time and space scales. What appears to be a system off its equilibrium at one time scale may appear as a fluctuation at another. The population age structure of a species at one spatial scale may indicate instability, but over a larger area, the different patches may constitute a balanced age distribution.

10. Controversy over equilibrial versus nonequilibrial behavior is causing unnecessary confusion. It is better to focus instead on the relative importances of internal community processes and external or environmental determination in system regulation; whether the system has strong or weak biological interactions and whether these interactions cause the system to tend toward preferred values. Since there is little or no evidence of real ecosystems ever being in equilibrium, the notion often confuses rather than helps our understanding.

DIVERSITY AND STABILITY IN CONSERVATION AREAS

I assume now that the primary goal of conservation is diversity of species (including high richness) and the persistence of all these species. The significance of this for conservation policy and management can be summed up in two statements:

1. The most complex and desirable ecosystems that we wish to conserve are markedly unstable (nonconstant), and achieving our conservation goals depends on their remaining that way. It is the continued instability of these systems which allows for the continued coexistence of their many species, whether or not the systems have strong internal regulation.
2. The consequences of this are sometimes counterintuitive, because a confused interpretation of the stability-diversity literature has resulted in managers equating "constancy" with "good" and management of conservation areas is therefore sometimes counterproductive.

I shall use examples from three different ecosystems to illustrate this:

African Wildlife Systems

The central Savuti channel section of northern Botswana's Chobe National Park serves as the prototype, though a very similar picture could be drawn for most of the other large wildlife areas of the subcontinent. The area is treasured by conservationists because of its high diversity of large ungulates and the high numbers of large predators. The question is: What kind of management policy is needed to maintain this diversity into the 2100s?

The general structure of the system is presented in Fig. 12.1. The essential features which allow for the continued existence of a high diversity of so many large ungulate species (and therefore of predators) are as follows:

1. The system is spatially very diverse, and animals use different parts at different times. Those parts far from dry-season water points provide emergency forage during drought years, and the stocking density (biomass) of ungulates is far below that which the vegetation biomass could support in an average year.
2. It is an open system, into and out of which there is considerable movement of migratory species. The zebra (*Equus burchelli*) migration is the largest, but wildebeest (*Con-*

nochaetes taurinus) and tsessebe (*Damaliscus lunatus*) also exhibit considerable seasonal movements and buffalo (*Syncerus caffer*) undergo strong seasonal concentrations and movements within the area. Joos-Vandewalle and Owen-Smith (in preparation) have shown that on the ±100 km² of the central Savuti grassland the numbers of these animals vary annually from virtually zero (for all species) to 16,500 zebra, 2,500 buffalo, 1,500 tsessebe, and 600 wildebeest. Zebra and buffalo are there during the rains, tsessebe are there during the dry season, and wildebeest are more variable. Elephant (*Loxodonta africana*) numbers can be high, and their density depends on surface water.

3. The strength of biological interactions is variable and weak. Attempts to estimate feeding overlap, and competition for resources between any pair of species is invariably disrupted either by one of the species moving out of the area, or by the sudden influx of large numbers of other ungulates. Predation is strongly opportunistic (Viljoen, personal communication), and connectance is both qualitatively and quantitively highly variable. Conditions are never constant long enough for strong biological interactions to develop. It is meaningless to attempt to derive average parameter estimates for an interaction matrix, so the notion of a stability analysis is meaningless.
4. The system is driven by external, episodic events—in particular the supply of surface water in the Savuti channel (the only major dry-season water supply), drought, fire, and (at least in the past) disease. The Savuti channel, when full, carries water from Angola via the Linyanti swamps and empties into the Savuti marsh (currently a grassland). It was full in the late 1800s, dried up around the turn of the century and remained dry until the mid-1950s, was full until 1982—and has been dry since then.

The size structure of *Acacia* woodlands (Walker and Joos-Vanderwalle, in preparation), the most highly preferred habitat in the area by ungulates and tourists alike, indicates that, in population dynamics terms, these woodlands are completely unstable and are, quite naturally,

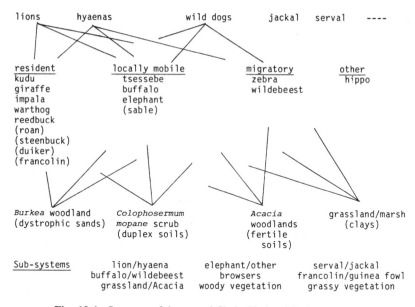

Fig. 12.1. Structure of the central Chobe National Park ecosystem.

declining. There is no regeneration, due to a high browsing pressure by a large variety of animals, and the stands of *acacias* consist of mature, even-aged trees which are drying as a result of old age and elephant damage. The woodlands became established during the early years of this century when two rare events coincided: The channel dried up and the rinderpest epidemic decimated many of the ungulate species. Elephants are not affected by rinderpest, but Cumming (personal communication) suggests, on the basis of early written accounts of the region, that elephant numbers in the area were greatly reduced by hunting before the end of the century. The combination of these events reduced browsing pressure long enough to allow the extensive stands of *Acacia* spp. to develop. Regeneration of the woodlands will require some similar combination of events to remove browsing pressure long enough to allow germinating seedlings time (ten to fifteen years?) to grow to a "safe" size. In the absence of such a period, the species of *Acacia* will persist as isolated trees or in small groups, since enough individuals will continue to make it through the establishment sieve. But the large woodlands will not persist. What we observe today, the co-occurrence of lots of elephants and extensive *Acacia* woodlands, represents a very narrow window in time and is apparently not sustainable (Fig. 12.2). Culling of elephants alone is unlikely to lead to regeneration of the woodlands. Both elephants and other browsers that select young *acacias* will need to be reduced to very low levels for the required establishment phase. The question, of course, is whether the managers and tourists are prepared to accept a ten-to-fifteen-year period with virtually no animals to see. However, we still do not know enough about the dynamics of *Acacia* spp, and it may well be that there are combinations of conditions (rainfall, lack of fire, spatial movements of ungulates) that will allow regeneration at moderate ungulate levels. This highlights the need to recognize the importance of timing and of episodic events when contemplating management intervention in this type of system.

In the Chobe ecosystem, the subsystem of trees (in general) and grasses is undoubtedly equilibrial, as demonstrated by Knoop and Walker (1985) for a similar savanna, and a change in one vegetation component will induce a change in the other. However, the subsystem of large herbivores is much less interactive, and changes in one may not induce changes in the others. Long-term changes in the key herbivore species (those which can significantly influence vegetation structure and composition), such as

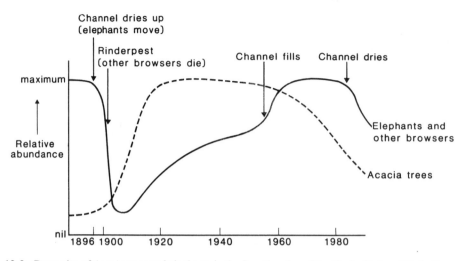

Fig. 12.2. Dynamics of *Acacia* trees and elephants in the Savuti region of the Chobe National Park, Botswana.

elephant and buffalo, will lead to changes in others, but in the short term this is difficult to demonstrate, and the externally induced changes in these key species preclude any particular change from lasting long enough for the effect to be felt.

Apparently, in southern Africa's magnificent, diverse wildlife ecosystems, the large herbivore subsystems are at best loose-equilibrial systems, and their high species diversity depends on continued change and disturbance. Unfortunately, conservation management is often intuitively opposed to this. No one likes to see animals die of thirst or splendid trees get burned in a fire, but preventing these processes increases the risk of future severe problems. Ungulate mortality following a severe drought has been shown to be severe and much higher in areas where artificial water points have allowed access to previously "reserve" grazing areas, than in areas where this had not occurred (Walker et al., in preparation). Management often seems intuitively aimed at stabilizing the system (preventing numbers from getting too high or too low) and spreading things evenly over the area (reducing spatial heterogenity). Both these activities are likely to be counterproductive in terms of both constancy and persistence.

Australian Arid Grazing Systems

Kangaroos in the arid zone are remarkably well adapted to the variable environment in which

they live. Under good conditions, adult females have a young at heel, a pouch young attached to a teat, and a diapausing blastocyst. As soon as the pouch young leaves the pouch or dies (i.e., as soon as suckling stops), implantation of the blastocyst occurs. About thirty-three days later (in red kangaroos) the young is born and moves to the pouch. Postpartum oestrus follows and the female conceives again (Tyndale-Biscoe 1973). The function of this delayed implantation is that when the pouch young dies under drought conditions, there is always another ready to take its place. The population therefore responds very rapidly to an improvement in food supply.

Caughley and associates (1987) have examined the combined dynamics of the vegetation and the kangaroos in the Kinchega National Park of New South Wales, and this example is taken from their work. Kinchega is a fenced area of 440 km² and has a mean annual rainfall of 235 mm. The vegetation is mainly *Atriplex* species and Chenopodiaceae scrub, with shrub areas, mainly of *Mareana* sp. The herbaceous layer is a mixture of annual grasses and forbs.

There are two very common kangaroos, the red (*Macropus rufus*) and western gray (*Macropus fuliginosus*); and two uncommon, the eastern gray (*Macropus giganteus*) and the wallaroo (*Macropus robustus*). All four are of similar size. The two uncommon species are limited by habitat association. Caughley et al. (1987) have determined the numerical response func-

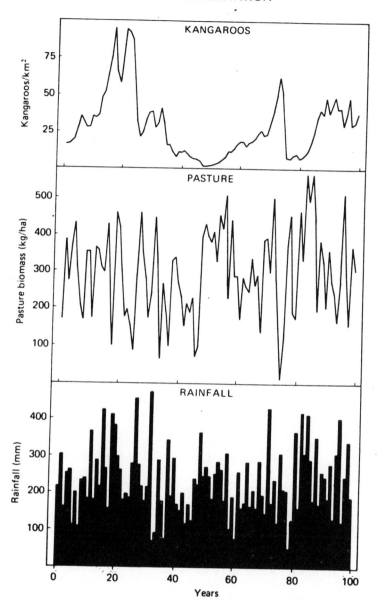

Fig. 12.3. Simulated changes in rainfall, pasture biomass, and density of red kangaroos at Kinchega National Park, New South Wales. The rate of change in kangaroo density is a function of pasture biomass. (From Caughley et al. 1987.)

tions between vegetation biomass and kangaroos, and the relations between vegetation biomass and rainfall. The composite picture is presented in Fig. 12.3 for red kangaroos, for a 100-year period, based on the model that has been developed. The important points, for this analysis, include:

1. The system is strongly interactive and seems to be strongly internally regulated. The relation between pasture biomass and rate of change in the kangaroos is very strong and rapid. The change in actual kangaroo numbers (which is the product of rate of change and existing numbers) only ap-

pears not to be dependent on vegetation. The net effect is a very nonconstant system due to a very variable rainfall. If rainfall is held constant, the system comes rapidly to equilibrium. The system is therefore one in which the dynamics are strongly directed toward a target, but in which the target is constantly moving.

2. The very low constancy of vegetation has no effect on the diversity of large herbivore species, and vice versa. The relations between stability and diversity are unimportant, if they exist at all, and are not an issue in the conservation management of Kinchega.

3. Any five-year period, taken on its own, would give a completely erroneous impression of the dynamics and ''trends'' of the kangaroos and would probably lead to inappropriate management responses.

The Great Barrier Reef

A major concern of coral reef conservation in the Great Barrier Reef of Australia is what to do, or not to do, about the crown-of-thorns starfish (*Acanthaster planci*) problem. The crown-of-thorns starfish preys on coral, and every now and then, in some places, it reaches very high levels and kills most of the coral and therefore leads to a loss of all the many other species associated with a coral reef. There is a belief that the problem may have become worse in recent times.

There are at least two views about the starfish dynamics. The more conventional view (e.g., Potts 1981) is that the dynamics represent episodic outbreaks of starfish which are a response to natural disturbances, such as severe storms and terrestrial runoff, which enhance larval recruitment. Pollution from agricultural and other development may exacerbate the response. The outbreaks are confined to certain sections of the reef, and some of these could be influenced by terrestrial developments.

The other view, developed by Bradbury et al. (1985a, b), is that the starfish and coral dynamics conform to a stable limit cycle. The basis of this interpretation is as follows:

Owing to the archipelago nature of the reef, time lags are introduced into the rates of coral development and starfish infestation, and there is evidence (admittedly based on using the states of different reefs in an area to represent the trajectory of a single reef) that for some sets of reefs, the pair-wise dynamics of the coral and starfish represent what Bradbury and colleagues call a qualitative stable limit cycle. In addition, it appears that other subsets of the reefs conform more to the qualitative counterpart of stable point equilibrium, or metastable, states owing to differences in the predator/prey interactions and a variety of other possible reasons. Different kinds of dynamic behavior are therefore possible and are apparently evident in different sections of the reef.

It is important to note that this interpretation of starfish-coral dynamics still needs to be validated. It is based on the use of different states of the system in space to infer dynamics in one place over time. This is problematical, as has been shown in studies of plant succession. However, if Bradbury and his colleagues are correct, then it has important conservation implications. Management intervention, based on a notion of episodic outbreak, would tend to remove starfish when they become very abundant, and if the limit cycle model is correct, this would push the system inward (from the top of the cycle, as in Fig. 12.4). Such a displacement could run the risk of bringing the system within the domain of attraction of a metastable state—the state Bradbury et al. call chronic infestation—with abundant starfish and moderate amounts of coral. It would be very difficult to change such a reef, and there is evidence of such states persisting for several years. The metastable state of coral and starfish would support a lower diversity and

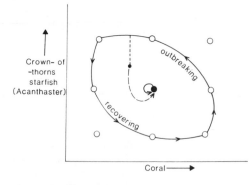

Fig. 12.4. Proposed qualitative stable limit cycle of crown-of-thorns starfish and coral in the Great Barrier Reef. (From Bradbury et al. 1985a.)

abundance of other species than well-developed coral.

For those parts of the reef where this dynamic behavior is deemed to occur, some proportion of the area will always exhibit a crown-of-thorns starfish outbreak, and the actual proportion will depend on the relative rate which the system takes to move along various parts of the cycle. A single equilibrial state does not exist, and attempts to induce one would be counterproductive.

It is not known which of the interpretations of starfish dynamics are correct, and as Potts (1981) has emphasized, conclusions drawn about the causes and effects of outbreaks must still be regarded as tentative.

IMPLICATIONS FOR CONSERVATION POLICY AND MANAGEMENT BEYOND 2100

Before we reach the year 2100, the changes in the world's atmosphere and the human pressures on conserved areas will have highlighted the futility of trying to maintain completely "natural" areas as they exist today. If they are not to join the remainder of the completely replaced, or at least extensively altered, ecosystems, then we must plan on their being multiple-use areas, in which conservation is one of the uses. We need to learn how to maintain what we want in "used" ecosystems. The three examples cited in this chapter illustrate that natural ecosystems may exhibit very different kinds of dynamics—weakly interactive, open "loose" systems (Chobe); strongly interactive but very variable (Kinchega); and either episodic or strongly interactive in a stable limit cycle (Great Barrier Reef). In the absence of a proper and full understanding, what does a manager of a conservation area do? The following are some suggestions:

1. Maintain the elements of change and heterogeneity. Discard the notion of some idealized state for the ecosystem, and allow change to occur. In order to maintain ecosystem resilience, it is the ecological processes in ecosystems which we need to conserve, not some particular state of the system.

In addition to the fact that persistence of all the species in an ecosystem requires mainte-

nance of system resilience, the persistence of any particular species depends on its maintaining a high (intraspecific) genetic diversity, with an associated diversity of physiological and behavioral traits enabling it to be an adapted and adaptable species. This again requires changing conditions and spatial heterogeneity. The widespread urge among conservation managers to stabilize ecosystems, and to spread the biota evenly over the areas they control, is likely to be counterproductive.

2. Focus attention on the ways in which the ecosystems concerned are influenced by external events. Most of the systems we wish to conserve are complex and species-rich. Apparently, such systems have only weak internal regulation, and focusing attention on the biological interactions of the upper trophic levels is less likely to achieve the goals of conservation than understanding and responding to the major, usually episodic external events which have an overriding influence on the system.

3. Recognize the need for a long-term perspective of the dynamics of a system in order to establish a policy with regard to responding to change. In the example of kangaroo dynamics (Fig. 12.3), the 30-year "trend" from year 20 to 50, taken in isolation, could well lead to a drastic and inappropriate action on the part of management. Any particular five-year view would give the wrong interpretation and would also lead to a poor management response. Likewise, a 100-year perspective is necessary to formulate a conservation policy for *Acacia* woodlands and elephants in northern Botswana.

4. Develop the theory of loose and nonequilibrial systems and systems that have only weak internal regulation. The methodology for analyzing and understanding the dynamics of complex ecosystems of this kind is inadequate. This suggestion is clearly aimed at research, but such an understanding is essential if management is to succeed in its conservation goals, since managers base their actions on their own mental models of the dynamics of the systems they manage. At present, these mental models are too often incorrect and sometimes confused interpretations of the theories developed from analyses of closed-equilibrium mathematical models.

5. To reduce the complexity of the problem, break the ecosystem down into component

subsystems that are relatively internally strongly connected, but loosely connected to one another—for example, the grass-wildebeest-lion and the flower-bee-bird subsystems. Focus management on those in which problems are evident. As a means of identifying the problem subsystems, identify the problem species and work outward from them.

6.   Establish whether thresholds are likely to occur in ecosystem changes and intervene only when such thresholds are approached. The species composition and the essential structural and functional properties of equilibrial systems will persist, provided the amounts of the species and other system variables (e.g., grass cover) remain within safe bounds. For some systems, the bounds may be beyond any likely changes, but there is some evidence (e.g., Knoop and Walker 1985) that exceeding certain levels can lead to change in system function, which makes recovery to the original domain of change very difficult. The methodology for analyzing systems in this context is poorly developed.

7.   "Open" systems are more stable (persistent) than "closed" systems. In operational terms for conservation areas, this means paying attention to boundaries. Changes in the nature and opaqueness of the boundaries, usually as a result of changes outside the area influencing emigration and immigration, will have marked effects on the internal dynamics. Changes in boundary conditions may have to be compensated for by corresponding management intervention in the species concerned inside the conservation area.

CONCLUSION

Conservationists, both applied and theoretical, are too preoccupied with animals and with their effects on one another. In the context of conservation, this is misleading and inappropriate.

Conservation of complex communities depends on maintaining the processes that determine their dynamics. It is the diversity of these processes which is important, not the diversity of the species per se. The rates of all the processes vary, quite naturally, over time, and what is needed is to maintain the regime of processes.

The most important processes involve the abiotic part of the system (mineral and water cycling). Changes in the nature and amounts of predation, competition, herbivory, migration, emigration and immigration, and so forth are important and will lead to changes in community composition. However, changes in the hydrological cycle (Tinley 1978, Walker et al. 1981) or in the interactive processes of the mineral cycle (McNaughton 1983) are likely to have more profound effects on the structure of the system.

Conservationists should spend less time worrying about the persistence of particular plant or animal species and begin to think instead about maintaining the nature and diversity of ecosystem processes.

Part III
CONSERVATION MANAGEMENT

Why Manage Nature?

DAVID WESTERN

In the last section we looked at conservation from a biological viewpoint. In this section we look at it through the eyes of managers, planners, and sundry practitioners.

The silver lining in the cloud of despair over the rapid erosion of nature is the rising public concern. The fate of wildlife depends on how fast that concern spreads and on the action it leads to. In acting, we must know when and how to step in to avoid doing more harm than good. For example, a number of animals, such as the Nakuru hartebeest and Madagascar coucal, have become extinct in recent years through inaction, a reprehensible policy when survival is at stake.

Conservation management is about knowing when and how to intercede as the case for doing so becomes more compelling. In this section we look at the three strategic weapons in our conservation arsenal—protected-area management, conservation-based rural development, and ex situ care and biotechnology.

Protected areas, lands set aside exclusively or primarily to conserve wildlife, date back little more than a century. Today, they cover 4.25 million km², an area

half the size of the United States, or 2.8 percent of the earth's surface. IUCN's goal is to include a cross-section of all major ecosystems in the protected area system, a task which calls for a total of 13 million km², or some 8 percent to 10 percent of the earth's land surface. While strategically this should rank as a top conservation priority, there are several reasons why conservation-based rural development and ex situ care and biotechnology will become indispensable complementary strategies.

First, the 3,500 protected areas are too small and widely scattered to avoid massive biological hemorrhage if immured by humanity. Second, as Hales (chap. 13) points out, human enjoyment, not biological conservation, was the driving force behind the parks movement, leading to a preoccupation with objects rather than processes, with the scenic spectacles of the Grand Canyon and Ayers Rock rather than the less inspiring American prairies or Hawaiian lowland forests. As a consequence, few parks were designed biologically. Finally, as Hales also notes, the protectionism of North American parks and developed nations does not sit well in the developing world, where ejecting people to protect wildlife often does more harm than good. McNeely (chap. 15) makes that point more forcefully and echoes the message of the Third World Parks Congress in Bali, 1982; protected areas in developing countries will survive only insofar as they address human concerns.

Design shortcomings and the need to show tangible returns weaken the biological viability of protected areas. McNeely argues that protected areas can be strengthened by satisfying many needs, among them wildlife and resource protection, recreation, tourism, education, research, cultural survival, and rural economic development. That means, as he points out, treating conservation as a human rather than biological issue. We should explore new ways to use resources sensibly in the face of land pressure—the source of the problem—rather than treat the symptoms with scientific bandaids. Ugalde (chap. 14), envisioning what it will take to secure an ideal South American park system in the next century, again sees the solutions more in human issues outside the park than biological ones inside.

As persuasive and pervasive as those arguments are, we cannot lose sight of what happens to wildlife within parks while the problems beyond them are being resolved. Ironically, the multiplicity of purpose advocated by McNeely, and already widely practiced, may, in the process of broadening the case for protected areas, lead to a conflict of interest and confusion of purpose, with wildlife losing out. Tourist congestion, recreational impact, overharvesting of resources, and the inevitable societal changes as traditional cultures meet and clash with the modern world, all place an added burden on wildlife and its managers.

Hales, in looking at multiple-use planning and concentric zoning, finds both solutions fail in most cases to protect wildlife, either because zoning divides a small cake yet further, or because economics generally prevails over aesthetics.

Ugalde suggests that protected areas be expanded to include a cross-section of all habitats, be made "user-friendly," especially to the local and national citizenry, and promote the sustainable use of resources. To achieve these improvements, conservation managers will need to improve their skills in visitor interpretation, mass communication, education, and biological management.

Earlier McNaughton (chap. 11), in pointing out how the livestock-borne disease rinderpest triggered off a century-long disturbance cascade in Serengeti, and Western (chap. 16), in showing how savanna parks are modified by an invasion of elephants fleeing poachers, demonstrate that even Africa's enormous ecosystem parks are not free of human influence. This is reason enough to adopt the second strategy of conservation-based rural development. Another more cogent argument is made by Western, reinforcing the point stressed by all four papers dealing with the protected areas—if we can work out cohabitation principles in the 95 percent of our world we consider the exploited human realm, the protected areas will become less important in the twenty-first century; if not, they will be overwhelmed. Rough lands, wastelands, water catchments, rangelands, deserts, swamps, and other sparsely occupied areas make up most of the earth's surface, harbor most of its wildlife, and offer us the sole chance of avoiding a biotic cataclysm.

Need wildlife disappear from the rural

lands and be confined solely to protected areas in the twenty-first century? Western suggests that if we adapt conservation to local circumstance—culturally, economically, and politically—it need not, a message that comes across clearly in the chapters by Harris and Eisenberg (chap. 17) and Green (chap. 18).

Examples drawn from the tropical savannas illustrate how wildlife, by adding 30 percent to livestock incomes, is on the increase on ranchlands in southern Africa. The turnaround stems from a policy change, from protectionism to utility, with regard to wildlife on private lands. In the tropical forests of Southeast Asia, selective felling and shifting cultivation, practiced thoughtfully, are compatible with wildlife conservation. Birds and primates can survive in secondary forest, albeit in different proportions, if disturbance is moderate (Johns 1985). Harris (1984) makes a similar case in advocating long-cycle felling around core area reserves as a solution to species extinction in temperate forests. The opportunities exist. With imagination and research and development into new ways of balancing conservation and exploitation as envisaged in the World Conservation Strategy, protected areas need not be the sole or even the best hope for wildlife in the twenty-first century.

Should we be at all sanguine about conservation beyond protected areas, considering the pressures wildlife will experience in the twenty-first century? Perhaps not. Yet Western (chap. 16) suggests that rural environments will not deteriorate universally; here and there improvements can be expected, especially in the third world, as agriculture intensifies and populations migrate from rural to urban centers. We capture a hint of such a scenario in Green's chapter, focusing on the future of Britain's rural landscape in the wake of demographic and agricultural transition to steady-state levels.

Green reviews the historical demise of wildlife in Britain as population increased and agricultural output expanded. Three major phases of agriculture—beginning in the Neolithic with the near eradication of woodlands, continuing with the enclosures of the seventeenth and eighteenth centuries, and, after a brief recession during the nineteenth century, culminating in the twentieth-century drive for self-sufficiency in food through intensified production—have taken their toll on Britain's wildlife. Yet in some respects, in the tapestry of pastures, meadows, heaths, and woodlands, if not in the number of species, the changes have created habitats arguably more diverse than the extensive woodlands they replaced. The wildlife losses in Britain also prompted conservationism, foreshadowing the growing international movement in response to the worldwide threats to nature in the twentieth century.

Agricultural intensification, as inimical as it is to wildlife, may be its ultimate salvation too, according to Green. Like North America, Britain and Europe are entering an age of overproduction, with the mountains of grain and lakes of milk already costing over twenty billion dollars a year in subsidies. With further productivity increases on the horizon, as much as one-third of Britain's agricultural land could be redundant by the turn of the century. If we play a careful hand and designate rural lands as heritage reserves, cultural landscapes, and productive agricultural lands, Green suggests the twenty-first century could see a recrudescence of countryside conservation in Britain.

How that can be achieved is the subject of intense debate. Green, noting the incompatibility of species diversity and intensive agriculture, argues for a polarized strategy in which high-production farming is concentrated on the better-quality land, and the remainder retired for conservation. Here, disturbance from fires, rotational grazing, and coppicing will be needed to arrest succession to woodlands and maintain species diversity. The British case may hold wider relevance for conservation in the twenty-first century, following the global demographic and economic transition (Western, chap. 2).

The strategy of last resort, the crisis response, when damage control within protected areas and rural-based conservation measures fail, is ex situ care and biotechnology. Ex situ care means managing a species out of its natural state. Biotechnology means technical manipulation of species or ecosystem processes to enhance survival and reestablishment. The battery of tactics being used to combat extinction and ecosystem degradation is impressive, as Conway (chap. 19) and Stanley Price (chap. 20) illustrate.

For example, scientific breeding programs are helping zoo managers to retain genetic diversity and minimize inbreeding depression in scores of endangered species, including Przewalski's horse, the Arabian oryx, and the Siberian tiger. Reproductive rates are now artificially boosted by polyovulation, artificial insemination, cross-fostering, hormonal manipulation, cryopreservation, and behavioral stimulation. Borrowing the reproductive apparatus of a Holstein cow to boost the population of the endangered gaur was the stuff of science fiction a decade ago. Behavioral manage-

ment is improving reproductive success and infant survival of gorillas, cheetahs, and rhinos in captivity and the rehabilitation of the Arabian oryx and black rhino in the wild. Ecological studies are helping us restore, reclaim, and regenerate habitats and ecosystems damaged by strip mining, waste disposal, and pollution.

Ex situ care and biotechnology did not start out with a conservation mission, but rather adapted zoo and livestock husbandry techniques to endangered-species management. Were it not for zoos and botanical gardens, many species, including Père David's deer, Przewalski's horse, and the California condor, which survive only in captivity, would now be extinct. But there is more to ex situ care than saving the pieces in what amounts to living museums. There is the far more daunting problem of reassembling the fragments, of rehabilitating species in the wild and restoring ecosystems to a normal functional state. In the last section, McNaughton (chap. 11) made this point in arguing that an ecosystem is more than the sum of its parts, and Walker (chap. 12) pointed out the need to understand the internal interactions and external disturbances responsible for the complex workings of ecosystems.

The ultimate goal of crisis management is to tide over a species or ecosystem through periods of human-induced stress, and to reinstate them as closely as possible to their former state. In other words, ex situ care and biotechnology should be the handmaiden of in situ conservation. Captive populations should aim to mimic and replenish wild stock and alter them as little as possible. We must be sure that the genetic breeding programs imposed in captivity do not produce ideal geneologies for avoiding inbreeding or the maintenance of genetic diversity at the expense of species survival and evolution within natural ecosystems.

Saving the pieces and recreating the world's many and complex ecosystems is akin to all the King's best minds charged with putting Humpty Dumpty together again. It simply cannot be done, not now, and perhaps never. Conway and Stanley-Price give us good reasons why. Two examples should help illustrate the problems.

1. Ex situ carrying capacity. According to Myers (chap. 5), hundreds of thousands of species will go extinct in the next few decades. How many can we save in captivity? Conway (1986) estimates that we can currently support fewer than 1,000 of the 20,000 plus vertebrates (minus fish) in adequate numbers to preserve 90 percent of their genetic diversity for 200 years. But what of the 5 to 30 million invertebrates? It would cost on the order of fifty million dollars annually to sustain the 200 primate species alone. In contrast, it costs half a million dollars to conserve thousands of animals and plants in the 15,000 km^2 Serengeti National Park (Western 1986). Space and cost preclude ex situ support for more than a tiny fraction of all species.

2. Rehabilitation. Stanley Price, from his experience in rehabilitating the Arabian oryx to the wild, stresses the time, cost, and skill needed to rehabilitate a species even when its ecosystem is intact. Animals dumped into the wild without rehabilitation programs are likely to fail. Few great apes have been successfully reintroduced to the wild. Kleiman et al. (1986) have elsewhere detailed the difficulties of reintroducing the golden lion tamarin into Brazil's remnant Atlantic forests. Only three of fifteen animals survived an intensive rehabilitation effort involving retraining in foraging skills prior to release. Conservation education, follow-up research, and often habitat restoration add to the difficulties. Technical manpower and costs are likely to severely limit rehabilitation efforts.

The technical problems and costs are far greater when it comes to the restoration of habitats destroyed by agriculture or the reclamation of land stripped by open-cast mining. Reforestation efforts may hinge on cultivating and reconstituting the mycorrhizal fungi and on critical factors that influence their formation, in order to reestablish the biogeochemical cycles between forest litter and tree roots. We do not yet have the skills and funds to restore complex ecosystems or badly degraded lands. Some of the technical problems and promising solutions have been reviewed in recent publications (Cairns 1986; Jordan et al., in press).

These and many other problems limit what ex situ care and biotechnology can accomplish in conservation and, as Conway states, give us every reason to use them sparingly as a last resort.

In conclusion, provided all three strategies—protected area management, conservation-based rural development, and ex situ care and biotechnology—are thoroughly explored and sensibly used, the triad should give us a well-stocked arsenal for tackling conservation problems well into the twenty-first century.

13
Changing Concepts of National Parks

DAVID HALES

There are two ways to consider the relationship between parks and surrounding areas. One is to consider whether the values for which parks were created must have some direct physical or biological link with surrounding land uses. The other is to ask whether public and political support for park values will continue if parks are not managed in ways that are demonstrably beneficial to other land uses and thus to people outside the park. The chapters in this section consider both aspects.

The issue is further complicated by the potential range of opinion about the primary values of parks. A universal answer may be difficult to find. Some views will be human-centered; others resource-centered. Both will have ample ammunition for their arguments. From either perspective, the central question of this section concerns the ability of parks to contribute to "conservation," and the conditions under which those contributions may be maximized. I shall provide some definitions and an historical perspective for the discussion.

When we talk of "parks," we are referring to approaches to protected-area management most characterized by Protected Area categories I, II, and IV of the Commission on National Parks and Protected Areas (CNPPA) of the International Union for the Conservation of Nature and Natural Resources (IUCN 1984a). This approach, or "movement," as its proponents would style it, began with the interest in Yosemite and Yellowstone in the United States some 125 years ago, although these developments and the evolution of the concept have been influenced by previous efforts to set aside

areas as hunting preserves for the rich and royal. Since then, approximately 500 places, encompassing approximately 425 million ha, have been considered worthy of governmental recognition and protection by over 120 countries (IUCN 1985). The reasons for that "protection," its degree of restrictiveness, and the competency with which it is provided vary greatly.

Much of the energy and philosophy of the parks effort have derived from its North American heritage. Four aspects of that heritage are particularly important to our discussion.

The North American antecedents of today's "movement" were little concerned with "conservation" as we seem to be using the term in this volume—the protection of wildlife populations that retain meaningful evolutionary potential. The goal or mission of North American park systems was the preservation of scenic beauty and the protection of natural wonders so that they could be enjoyed by people (Harris and Eisenberg, chap. 17). The famous 1916 Act of Establishment for the U.S. National Park Service (NPS) gives as a mission directive the words of Frederick Law Olmsted, "To conserve the scenery and the natural and historic objects and the wildlife therein, so that they can be enjoyed by this and future generations." In what is very close to an official history of the National Park Service, William Everhard defines "true conservation philosophy" as preserving historic places and "setting aside" places of unique natural beauty (Everhard 1972).

The Yellowstone Act, as originally passed by Congress, barred only "wanton destruction" of animals, allowing hunting and other consumptive uses of wildlife. Although this policy was soon changed for Yellowstone, the NPS had no explicit and uniform policy to direct the management of wildlife resources until the 1963 Report for the Advisory Committee on Wildlife Management (Leopold Report) established as a goal that "natural" parks should "represent a vignette of primitive America." To many resource managers in the NPS, the term *carrying capacity* still refers to the ability of humans to tolerate each other, not to resource constraints.

Moreover, none of the U.S. National Parks in the contiguous forty-eight states, except possibly the Everglades, was brought into the system primarily to protect its fauna and none are managed with that as a primary or overriding goal. With the exception of Alaska, no attempt has been made to develop unit boundaries on the basis of habitat or coherent natural systems. To the limited extent that goal is met in the United States, it is through the refuge system of the USFWS, or private efforts such as those of the Nature Conservancy.

Second, inherent in the development of the North American systems is the concept of "setting aside" "special" places to protect them from the ravages of ordinary use. In the words of the first leader of the NPS, "keep the established sites safe from invasion, and purge the established sites of private holdings" (Everhard 1972). In other words, park boundaries were to be walls against which profane activities would founder, providing within sanctuary to the human spirit. Others continue to see in this heritage the essence of the parks movement, the separation of the sacred from the mundane (Engel 1983).

The third relevant element of this heritage is the emphasis on providing for the "enjoyment" of the visitor. To quote Everhard again, "if it is granted that parks are set aside for people's enjoyment, then a phrase used by the Park Service, 'Parks are for People,' would seem to be a self-evident truism." The assumption was, of course, that the park areas set aside had little or no economic value, and that human recreational use of the resource was compatible with the preservation of the area. Carefully excluded from the working definition of "people" are those who would make "nonpark" use of the resources, uses not oriented to the enjoyment of the values for which the unit was set aside. In

North America and in other places, park management has catered to humans and the human demand for convenient access to "nature."

The fourth element is the perception that protection of natural treasures is not only an appropriate but a necessary governmental role to be energetically pursued by the highest national authority. The American experience was formed by the frustration resulting from the inability of state and local governments to protect resources from degradation. Local interests were seen as competitors and adversaries, and subnational governments were (and are) mistrusted as inadequate and weak trustees of resources of national significance.

Inherent in the origins of the National Park concept, then, are the basic contradictions which have characterized its history. The purpose of parks was to provide enjoyment and inspiration to humans. The means of doing so was to draw a boundary around the elements that were enjoyable or inspirational and preserve them unchanged. The agency by which this was to be accomplished was the national government.

These aspects of the early North American parks experience have served as centers around which the international dissemination and application of the parks concept have resolved. Through the middle of this century, the themes were persistent and insistent:

protect natural phenomena for public enjoyment (in the natural state) from human exploitation. (Machlis and Tichnell 1985)

The "natural phenomena" to be protected, particularly in Africa and Asia, clearly came to include some species of wildlife, but mostly larger mammals which captured the imagination of Europeans and North Americans often as targets for hunting or as objects to be placed in zoos. Internationally, as well as nationally, parks were object-oriented, rather than process-oriented.

These themes still dominate most formal definitions of parks. For example, according to the current definition of the Internationl Union for the Conservation of Nature (IUCN), "parks" are legally designated areas wherein natural or cultural phenomena of national significance are protected from exploitation for private gain so that they can be enjoyed by the public. In practice, however, in most of the countries of the world, the principles and the reality of parks were evolving. A look at the last two World Conferences on National Parks is instructive.

In 1972 the Second World Conference on National Parks met in Grand Teton National Park in Wyoming, United States. A cursory glance through the proceedings reveals the dominance of the meeting by North Americans and Europeans, and a closer examination reveals an almost exclusive focus on the "traditional" concerns of the national park movement, the preservation of natural landscapes and their use for recreational (and educational) purposes (Hales 1983).

With rare exception, the perspective of those gathered in Wyoming in 1972 was that of one standing on the boundary of a park looking inward. Although one speaker cautioned that the "heritage argument upon which United States conservationists often rely so strongly, was one likely to be shared by a very small part of the population and only in a few countries" (IUCN 1974), these dissonant remarks had little impact on the proceedings. The recommendations of the Conference were clearly aimed at protecting the integrity of existing areas and increasing the number of protected areas.

Ten years later the third World Conference, now called the World National Parks Congress, convened in Bali, Indonesia. A banner, prepared by the host government, spread the words "Parks for Sustainable Development" across the front of the room used for the general assembly. A cursory glance through the program for this meeting reveals the heavy influence of park professionals from developing countries; closer examination reveals an emphasis on pragmatic approaches to resource conflicts, approaches that are as diverse as the countries represented. The monolithic, North American–dominated national parks movement, so omnipresent in 1972, was almost absent in 1982. The perspectives had changed. No longer is the view from the border inward; the debate was whether one should focus outward from the border, or whether borders exist at all.

The major conclusion from these deliberations, according to the IUCN, is that "if conservation is to succeed, it must become part of humanity's adaptation to the living environment, part of the human ecosystem" (IUCN 1983). In other words, the future of the protected-areas movement in most parts of the world will be determined by the extent to which its proponents can demonstrate its direct relevance to human concerns. The "heritage argument" had in fact been found wanting by representative professionals from around the world. The voices of 1982, so different from those of 1972, told us that parks should no longer seek "hard and fast boundaries," that there was need for "flexible transition" from more intensive uses to a protected core, and that protected areas must not be regarded as "isolated islands" (Segnestam 1983). We were reminded that parks and game reserves are "in almost all cases, or will eventually become, surrounded by land modified . . . by humans" (Wilcox 1983), and that "it is a mistake to suppose that a protected area can be isolated, through park managers' fiat, from its hinterland" (Myers 1983b). This prospect "that areas designated for nature conservation may in the future exist as islands surrounded by lands used intensively for the production of food and other necessities for human survival has caused serious concern that these areas may be inadequate to provide for the survival of the species originally contained within them" (Dasmann 1983). Dasmann concludes:

[C]ertainly no system of parks and reserves will survive, if we attempt to set up systems of protected areas, no matter how well distributed, within a system of land use that otherwise is contributing to the degradation of soils, exhausting the productivity of renewable resources, and relying on heavy inputs of agricultural chemicals to compensate for a deteriorating resource base.

In response to these perceptions, various approaches were proposed, from Lusigi's "conservation unit" (Lusigi 1983) to national land use planning (Garratt 1983; Olembo 1983; Segnestam 1983). In all of these approaches, the national park was seen as a nonmanipulated core around which increasing amounts of manipulation would occur—concentric zoning, if you will. In this manner the park core would be protected, human needs would be met, and conservation and development could coexist. If this is possible, we should be able to have our cake and eat it too. It may well be, however, that the situation is more complex and the answers, in practice, more elusive.

Emerging from Bali, we find two distinct views of the purposes of national parks: the environmentalist establishment view and the international conservation establishment view. One view, considered more traditional by North Americans, argues that the purpose of parks is human enjoyment and inspiration and enlightenment, recreation in its fullest sense. The promotion of biological diversity or the provision of watershed protection may result from the presence of the park, but the park's continued existence must not be contingent on providing these values. Many see these recreational or spiritual values as even more important in the future. To them, parks are refuges for the human spirit, sources of renewal, catalysts for national and regional pride, bearers of cultural identity—"places where we can touch what we have been and which can help us see that which we can become" (Hales 1983).

Another view is that the heritage argument is persuasive only with small sectors of society; other, more quantifiable and utilitarian, contributions to human society will be critical to the survival of parks and, thus, must be included in the "basic park values" as legitimate management goals, not just incidental by-products. This multiple-use approach is to achieve all its goals by use of concentric zoning. The park core will be protected, human needs will be met, preservation and development will coexist across a series of barrier zones so designed that all the purposes of each will be attainable. The concentric-zoning approach allows other conservation values to coexist with North American traditional park values.

There are contradictions in both views. The environmental establishment view posits "natural" wild areas, while the areas we have to work with, even ones as large as Yellowstone, are manifestly artificial, resulting from human actions. From a biological and ecological perspective, it is apparent that the units already designated are not large enough to maintain evolutionary and ecological processes which would occur in nonfragmented reserves. Since we cannot rely on "nature" to maintain systems if provided a sanctuary in which to do so, then to the degree that we wish to preserve the status quo within parks, human manipulation must become far more active and interventionist. We may well have reached the point where the preservation of natural systems in parks will be dependent on the human ability to synthesize its process.

The practical difficulties inherent in conserving for enjoyable use also remain unsolved. In order to get sufficient political support for the designation and protection of parks, a substantial public constituency is increasingly necessary. The building of these constituencies for "fortress parks" has depended on selling or marketing them in ways which have created expectations and demands that cannot be met without substantial intervention and manipulation of the resources to be set aside. Moreover, the values provided by this approach are difficult to sell in places where basic sustenance is a daily concern. Therefore, we find that the strongest supporting constituents of traditional parks in developing countries are citizens of developed nations.

We find ourselves in a position akin to that of Hank Morgan, Mark Twain's Connecticut Yankee, who tried to put all that he valued inside a fence of technology, only to realize that his sanctuary was a trap. Because we believed that our walls would protect our parks, we are now at risk of finding them to be prisons rather than fortresses. Park boundaries have become the Maginot Line of preservation.

On the other hand, concentric-zoning approaches, satisfying as they may be in concept, have proved difficult to apply. Even with adequately designed and effectively managed buffers, they may only retard the process of insularization. Even productive buffer zones remain vulnerable to demands for more intensive use as technological capabilities increase their economic value or as human needs and numbers insinuate themselves. Concentric-zoning approaches are successful at protecting park values only to the extent that they are core-dominant; that is, activities in outer zones must be limited by compatibility with activities of inner zones. Activities that would be acceptable if there were no parks must be restricted, or the argument must be made that compatible uses are superior economically.

The second approach is a dangerous double-edged sword; if we choose one activity over another on economic grounds, how do we respond when a third activity is proposed and its economic value exceeds that of the first? The first approach is but a new version of the heritage argument and is feasible only if there is sufficient political will. Political will is more likely if there is public understanding and support. Complex and utilitarian approaches are more likely to engender confusion than enthusiasm.

It is also important to note that the implementation of a concentric-zoning approach will require a significant increase in the amount of land and water dedicated to conservation management. This will require exercising some degree of control where control is not now exercised, and often it will also require changes in authorities and jurisdictions of existing government agencies. All of this must be accomplished in the face of rapid change and increasing pressures.

Thus we find ourselves in a major dilemma. By overemphasizing the special, we sacrifice too much of the necessary. If we overemphasize the necessary, we will lose the special. We face the future with conflicting visions. I have taken the opportunity in the last four or five months to meet a wide range of our professional colleagues and ask them to share their dream of the future. Some see parks as places to confront nature on its own terms; others see parks as natural versions of Disneyland, yuppie playgrounds: safe, scenic, and sanitary. Some see tourists as essential components of future systems; others see them as neocolonial invaders, encased in plastic and polyester. Some see parks as critical units of an international system, monitored by international agencies and managed by a cadre of certified professionals. Others see park units meeting the needs of local people and controlled by them, for better or worse. Some want a rational, scientific system with the human hand and mind replacing evolutionary processes; others want a system of nonmanipulated areas, elments of world heritage, oriented to the provisions of human inspiration, and they remind us that all we have really learned in 100 years of scientific management is that yesterday's scientific answers were wrong. Some see parks as positive vestiges of yesteryear, a link with our past, protectors of cultural diversity. Others see parks as genetic reservoirs, a heritage for the future, protectors of natural diversity. As I consider these mixed visions, I must conclude that the key element in considering our proposition is not answering whether integration of parks and surrounding areas is important, but how integration should occur, and to what degree.

As we consider this question, a caution or two may be in order. The discussion of "integrating" must be honest and realistic. A central principle of conservation is that pigs don't fly. We cannot demand of parks that which they cannot give, and we cannot treat their maladies in isolation from their basic causes. We must return to Ray Dasmann's point: park values cannot survive in a hostile environment, nor can our support for parks save our societies from otherwise irresponsible behavior. At best, parks are holding actions, as Michael Soulé puts it, "200-year islands," which can serve as holocene refugia (McNeely, chap. 15), not only for plants and animals, but for dreams as well. Parks, if they are successful, are bridges between the past and the future.

It is legitimate and necessary to discuss the principles and tools of integrated management as methods by which the life of these refugia can be extended. But let us not expend all our energy fighting among ourselves; in the long run, our agenda is mutual. It is likely that no answers or approaches are universally applicable. Methods must be selected based on goals that are explicitly stated and based on realities of the cultural and natural environments in which they will be employed. Institutions that evolve in one place will not always succeed in another; in fact, they may be counterproductive. Our allegiance must be to values, not to institutions which are mere vehicles for promoting those values. Let us use whichever park protection approaches work in specific local situations, while turning our united attention to causes rather than symptoms of habitat destruction.

Population growth, irresponsible consumption and waste, nuclear proliferation, unrestrained technology, industrial poisoning, gross inequities between rich and poor are all examples of basic problems conservation must address. In the final resort, success in defending park values depends on the courage and competence with which those who support these values unite with and support those forces in society which will make walls and buffering unnecessary. Revisiting and refighting old arguments about the purpose of parks holds little value. What is needed is a synthesis, a statement of purpose which grows out of the past and will give relevant guidance to the future. That purpose for the next hundred years must be to provide sanctuaries to preserve elements of our current world that we wish to pass on to our children. Individual cultures, indeed different regions within larger countries, may seek to preserve a variety of values. This diversity is not only acceptable; it must be sought after.

Succeeding periods of glaciation pushed the ancestors of all living things into small islands and spaces. When the glaciers retreated, life emerged to recolonize the world. We face such an event. Masses of humans and human activities are the glaciers of our era. We are forcing much of the world's living diversity into smaller and smaller islands. The more we push, the more threatened these life forms become. The more we lose, the poorer we become. What we do not consciously save on those islands may well not accompany us into the future.

The islands will carry more than various elements of biological or genetic diversity. They will also contain the elements of human experience necessary for establishing a bond of comprehension and unity between our children and our parents. It has been said that if we do not preserve wild nature, our children will never forgive us. That may be true, but an even worse fate is in store: our great-grandchildren will not care—they will have no way to comprehend what was lost. They will be indifferent to that which challenges and excites us, and makes us wonder, and gives meaning to our lives. They will not grieve, no matter what choice we make. If we fail and if they still live, they will build a new human experience, comprised of different elements than ours. The essence of being human

will have changed. This may not be a bad thing; we have no right to impose certain experiences on them. But we do not have the right to deprive them of the opportunity to choose, either. What modern conservation must conserve is not just trees or birds, but options. The right to choose the nature of our own lives is the most important of human rights.

The goal of parks and protected areas is to contribute as much as possible to the range of choices available to the children of the future. They cannot choose the impossible or dream the unimaginable. In this very real sense then, the physical reality of our parks is linked to the spiritual reality of our humanity. Parks are collections not of objects, but of synergetic biophysical processes, including human perception and experience. Parks result from, and give birth to, our dreams.

We now run the very real risk of discontinuity, of fraying, even breaking, the thread of human experience. This could be done by nuclear war. It could also come from the loss of biological diversity. We need parks as living vaults to protect our living treasures. At the same time, we must also confront and roll back destructive pressures, for the treasures cannot live in vaults for very long. The stakes could not be higher, for if we fail, there may be no children to "come out and wonder," or worse, children, but no sources of wonder.

14

An Optimal Parks System

ALVARO F. UGALDE

We must be very cautious and humble when trying to imagine the future. We still know little about human nature and about nature in general. But based on present knowledge, trends and conditions, and on the fact that the twenty-first century is only a decade away, we can make educated guesses in some areas and brave assumptions in others. Many scenarios are possible, but here is what I would see in an optimal parks system in the twenty-first century.

I assume that by the year 2100, humans will not have dared to use nuclear weapons even on a minor scale. My basic dream, then, is that mankind will still exist, and that the biosphere of spaceship earth will be functioning, and if somewhat more despoiled than today, then at least with no irreversible damage. Furthermore, I hope that by the year 2100 there will be no nuclear arsenals, less military spending, and several "disarmed democracies" like Costa Rica, using their resources in a more intelligent way to improve health, education, recreation, and the biosphere generally.

My second hope is that, well before the year 2100, mankind will have arrived at a much better distribution of resources internationally, nationally, and locally. For this to happen, we must first become a much less wasteful society, with a new code of ethics. "What is needed is an ethical approach to planet earth, our only home, with all its diversity, and above the concept of our country first" (Budowski 1986). The selfish genes will have to give room to the survival of the gene pool. The North-South differences in energy and resource consumption and the wealthy-poor gap must be brought to acceptable minima.

I like to think that we can achieve some kind of "social pact" or "settlement for survival," by which humans would make a major collective decision to practice intelligent tinkering with the biosphere, remembering, as Leopold cautions, that "the first rule of intelligent tinkering is to save all the parts" (Forsyth 1982). I have the feeling that we are losing many parts very rapidly. The losses must be brought under control as soon as possible, wherever feasible.

It is now unavoidable that the twenty-first century will be a much more populated world. Costa Rica will double its present population of 2.5 million in twenty-five years, and I see no way to change that. I hope that by the year 2100, humans will have begun to get a strong handle on the population growth of an already plundered planet. But as a consequence of the increase in human numbers, there will no longer be unknown frontiers. The earth will be a totally managed world, from cities, to agriculture, to national parks.

One vision that keeps recurring, although I hope it never crystallizes, is that of an earth much more battered and less natural than today. In Carl Sagan's cosmic calendar (Sagan 1977), hardly one cosmic second (500 of our years) has gone by since Christopher Columbus named my country Costa Rica, the "rich coast." Yet in the last fifty years, roughly one-tenth of one second of the cosmic year, we have destroyed 70 percent of our natural ecosystems. Within ten years, when most, if not all, of the forests outside are gone, the loggers and public will realize the value of our national parks.

Janzen (1986) is already writing about the biology of the survivors. By 2100 he thinks that only 10 percent of the original tropical ecosystems will survive. That figure may be too high, considering the destruction in Costa Rica.

Thus by the year 2100 we will see fewer species, very few (if any) self-contained ecosystems, and less soils. In Costa Rica, roughly 680 million tons of soil per year get washed into our rivers and oceans through inappropriate land use practices, (CONICIT 1984). We can expect less predictable rain patterns, less permanent and clean freshwater, less diversity of natural landscapes, fewer nonrenewable resources, and a growing human dependency on renewable resources. We seem close to a hopeless, no-win situation, but I am sure that by adopting a more hopeful stance, we can avoid the fulfillment of our worst premonitions.

In this kind of scenario it seems that from now on, things will get progressively worse for several decades into the twenty-first century before they begin to improve. The cost of improvement may be very high, but humanity will be eager to repair its spaceship.

While the plundering will still go on for a while, I feel that man is also arriving at a much better understanding of the functioning of his mind and of the biology of human nature. By the year 2100, I hope we will be much better at predicting the future and shaping human attitudes. I hope that we will use this power intelligently, that we will become a wiser species, with a better handle on our aggressive drives.

At the same time, the scarcity of nature will make humanity much more curious and conscious of its value, of the mysteries of life on earth, and of Man's inescapable dependency on a healthy planet. We will realize, and I hope we do so soon, that the future of nature depends on us, that we create its problems and hold the remedy to them, and that we can change course.

The twenty-first century will, I hope, witness the integration of several areas of human activity, such as ecology, economics, engineering, sociobiology, anthropology, politics, the arts, and religion. Humanity will begin the rediscovery of the remains of its own planet, and the sciences, especially those dedicated to the understanding and intelligent management the biosphere, will flourish.

Humanity will someday thrive on a better understanding of the planet's potentials and limitations. It will be more appreciative of nature, less afraid of it, and less aggressive toward it. I hope that the twenty-first century will witness the onset of a golden age of exploration of earth's ecosystems, or rather, of what will be left of them.

Scientific and nature-oriented tourism will flourish, along with respect and reverence for nature. This, of course, will impose challenging situations and opportunities for the national park services of the future.

Frankly, I find it difficult to think of a more optimal parks system and service than thinkers such as Kenton Miller have described (Miller 1980a, b). If the park services of today were run as he envisions, people in the twenty-first century could have more options open to them.

The greatest differences with today's world will probably be that the political battles over what and how much to save will be over. The park systems will be accepted and justified, but under great pressures for visitation, research, education, and recreation. The scientific community will likely be intensely active in the management of parks and in biological restoration of species, communities, ecosystems, and other life processes. The general public will also be very involved in scrutinizing management, probably more closely and sentimentally than park managers care for. So, the park systems of the future will need to be efficiently managed. Their personnel will be less occupied with protection, and more with the management of their natural resources and with enabling the park's staff to be aggressive communicators and excellent teamworkers. Park staff will be more scientific and education-oriented.

As Miller (1980a,b) and other conservation biologists advise us, an optimal parks system should include, as far as possible, representative samples of the biological regions, ecosystems, natural communities, and species of the country. Parks should protect a nation's ecological diversity, its genetic wealth, and its wildland life-support systems and processes. And even though self-contained ecosystems are difficult to establish and maintain today, it is necessary to begin biological restoration as soon as possible. This is one type of knowledge that we urgently need. An optimal parks system must strive to save all the parts without exception. As

McNeely says: "The more species survive today, the more material there will be for designing the human ecological niches of the future" (McNeely 1986).

An optimal parks system should be planned and managed comprehensively, which entails plans for each park, a national systems plan, and its integration into the country's overall development planning process. Park services should take special care to train and promote the professional staff in all areas of the parks program. They should have efficient organization, clear and respected lines of authority, good teamwork, and be efficient at public communication.

The parks service should also monitor and evaluate the effectiveness of the system, with special emphasis on objectives and management for integration of the parks into the development process. The service should turn itself into a spokesman on behalf of wildlands.

Managers must learn to think and work in terms of systems: energy systems, nutrient systems, ecosystems, national wildland systems, regional park systems, global wildland monitoring systems, and so on. They must learn a way of thinking that integrates parks locally, nationally, and internationally with other human objectives.

Several specific points must be addressed in order to conserve nature for the future:

1. We must possess the knowledge to get the national parks and conservation philosophy embedded in our socieities as a new kind of institution, heavily linked to education, to aspects of everyday life, and to local economies. We must learn how to nationalize conservation at the local and national levels by creating and maintaining strong conservation capabilities in the public and private sectors. We must also establish more efficient ways to collect and handle data pertinent to management (Janzen 1986). Humanity also needs this information for a better understanding of nature.

2. One challenging question that needs more discussion is how to choose priorities when we cannot save all the parts. How do we save parts that are becoming increasingly separated? The parks of the next century will be shrunken, highly managed fragments of nature. We are beginning to realize that hardly any park is a self-contained ecosystem, and that most will lose species if ecologically isolated (Harris and Eisenberg, Chap. 17). We need to know how to meld the skills of park managers and ecologists. I would like to see all biologists, in fact all humans, turned into conservationists. As Janzen says: "If biologists want any tropics in which to biologize, they are going to have to buy it with care, energy, effort, strategy, tactics, time and cash" (Janzen 1986). Since the surviving species and habitats will depend largely on the national parks, an optimal parks system must provide excellent opportunities for their intense study and manipulation to see what they offer humanity. I adhere to the call for a massive resource infusion into the taxonomy and classification of tropical organisms, without which "the rate of acquisition, synthesis, and use of knowledge about tropical wildlands will stutter and move so slowly that the world at large can hardly be blamed for viewing wildlands as a featureless blot on the agroscape" (Janzen 1986).

3. Park managers must soon learn how to influence the outside world. Human populations are growing fast, soils are being eroded, watersheds are being destroyed, forests are dwindling, and our waters, air, and soils are being polluted. The national parks are created in perpetuity. We must see that they do not fall prey to lack of information or political myopia. The national park managers and institutions must play an important role in promoting the intelligent use of all natural resources. Intelligent use will come when the state of life on earth becomes a concern for all disciplines of human endeavor. Society needs food and shelter, and those needs should be universally met. But need we do so at the expense of our descendants? We can improve the efficiency of food and wood production on more productive lands without ruining them or destroying the life-support systems on less productive areas (Green, chap. 18).

4. The parks of the twenty-first century will need excellent communicators. How do we get our messages across to the adults who are making decisions today, and to the children who will make them tomorrow? I agree with Janzen when he says that "within 10-30 years (depending on where you are), whatever tropical nature has not become embedded in the cultural consciousness of local and distant societies, will be obliterated . . ." (Janzen 1986). Although we might agree that environmental education is es-

sential in this regard, our school systems and our awareness campaigns transmit the message painfully slowly compared to our alarming capacity to destroy our environment. Conservation needs a massive injection of modern communications technology to reach a mass audience. I have seen presidents, cars, cigarettes, and many less worthy items than life on earth sold through these means. We also need funds. It means getting biologists, ecologists, psychologists, educators, and media specialists, among others, working together as a team. What do we tell people first, second, and third? How do we say it and with what intensity and frequency? (Crystal, Chap. 31) How do we foster a true personal interest, a change of attitude, and a collective decision to conserve nature? Today, the national parks and other wildlands in many countries are often "paper parks." Some are not actually there, and many are seriously threatened. Several are being lost to logging, poaching, poor management, and lack of human and financial resources. We must learn to stop the degradation of all national parks and other protected areas. We must set solid national and international precedents on efficient park management and establish public respect for them. If we do not, the new additions to the systems will only be waiting to be destroyed. We must get the conservation movement on the offensive; we must be optimistic and successful. But we must also be brave, speak out, and explain our position again and again.

5. We must make parks what Janzen calls "user-friendly" to personnel, neighbors, scientists, and visitors. It is especially urgent that we accommodate concerned neighbors and local communities in the management of the parks. Most parks depend on their support, and their actions can greatly enhance or imperil their future. Most neighbors around third world parks are extremely poor. We need to make sure that parks provide appropriate benefits for them and compensate them when their traditional activities are no longer possible. Local populations can, if sympathetic to a park, buffer it from the outside world. Most important, we should make sure that the national parks do not exaggerate the gap between "the haves" and "the have-nots." Janzen calls for an effort to use the wildlands for raising the intellectual quality of life of those living in the surrounding agroeco-

system in the tropics. He says that if we offer people the ecological stories of animals and plants, we will not only gain their attention, but also instill a sense of values for wildlands. Perhaps we should study how people and schools become integrated through the parent-teacher associations and try to adapt the mechanisms to our national parks.

6. Society must allocate more resources to the park services and to other public agencies and private groups in charge of wildlands. These groups need more funds and other support. There is a devastating gap between the responsibilities these groups have been given and the resources they have. A concerted effort between governments, international development agencies, foundations, and the philanthropic community is necessary to close the gap. If national parks could get 1 percent of present military spending, the future would look much brighter for our descendants.

7. In turn, the people who work for these agencies must learn to act selfishly. They must be dynamic, efficient, and dedicated. They must understand that their job, along with the scientists', is to integrate the parks into the users' world. If they do not, then they are not building an optimal parks system for the people of the twenty-first century.

We must find better ways to accomplish a stronger participation of industrialized nations in the conservation efforts of developing countries (Pearl, chap. 29). The international economic situation calls for shared responsibility. But the poor countries must also understand that they have a direct national interest in ensuring the health of their environment. They must do their homework, they must show their commitment, and then, proudly, ask for help.

Finally, we must acquire the knowledge to change the popular concept of national parks and conservation. Most people see the parks as distant, pretty places for tourists, scientists, and biologists. They consider conservation a movement to halt development. A special effort is needed to explain and clarify park concepts; otherwise people will not see that the problem involves all of us or recognize that its solution is also in our hands.

Technically speaking, most people living today will live to see the beginning of the twenty-first century. But in reality, what the world will be like in the next 100 or 114 years depends on what we do today. To me, the twenty-first century is already here, and I feel as much a part of it as I feel part of the twentieth century. Within our lifetime, biological diversity has suffered an attack of such devastating magnitude that our time may well be known as "the dark ages of life on earth." But I strongly believe that our generation still has the opportunity to change course, to initiate an era of enlightenment in the understanding of the relationship between man and nature.

15

Protected Areas and Human Ecology: How National Parks Can Contribute to Sustaining Societies of the Twenty-first Century

JEFFREY A. MCNEELY

How many national parks will there be in the year 2100? I probably will not be around to find out, but my best guess is none. What a defeatist attitude, you might protest in alarm. Quite the contrary, I would respond. By the year 2100 nature may well be conserved reasonably well *without* national parks as we know them today, just as nature was conserved without national parks in most parts of the world just a generation or two ago.

Yet I hate to think what today's world would be like if our predecessors had not had the foresight to establish national parks and take other far-reaching conservation measures. In many parts of the world, areas that have not been protected have essentially lost their natural character. The areas that have been established as national parks serve a number of specific functions for the benefit of human society, ranging from tourism to watershed protection to wildlife conservation, and these have helped national parks become part of our collective consciousness. But we should recognize that the very success of national parks is a reflection of our inability to harmonize with our natural environment. Indeed, we would not need national parks if we did not have such an exploitative relationship with nature. It was only with the coming of an industrial age, fueled by energy from natural ecosystems long extinct—that is, oil and coal—that human greed started to radically exceed human need. And when natural

ecosystems started to be exploited to provide goods and services to people living far beyond the local ecosystem, it became necessary to have national parks. National parks, then, might be seen as part of the adaptation of *Homo sapiens* to an ecological niche which covers the globe.

Our distinguished colleague Ray Dasmann (1976) illustrated very clearly the ecological difference between modern industrial societies and all those which have gone before. International trade and global patterns of consumption have made us "biosphere people," he suggested, drawing our support not from any one local ecosystem, but from the entire capital of the world's living matter. This is in stark contrast to "ecosystem people," such as the hunter in rural Sumatra who lives within the constraints established by his local ecological conditions. Consuming planetary resources through rapid and inexpensive trade and communications, biosphere people can bring great amounts of energy and materials to bear on the exploitation of any one ecosystem, abandoning it when it is no longer sufficiently productive.

But how secure are the supplies of resources that support the ecological niche of biosphere people? When George Schaller was studying mountain sheep and snow leopards in the Hindu Kush a few years ago, he once came upon a tiny village nestled in a small valley just above 10,000 feet. With usual Pakistani hospitality, some villagers invited him into their compact, snow-covered hut to share a dinner by firelight consisting of tea and boiled potatoes. This was a meeting of a field scientist who was a biosphere person, supported by goods and services from around the world, and villagers who were still ecosystem people with only sporadic contact with the outside world. "There was no trace of Western culture to distort the evening," Schaller said. "Here it was easy to see the excesses of civilization in perspective, to realize the value of simplicity. I would not want to return to such an existence, but made aware of the waste in one's own life one makes a silent promise to conserve. My ancestors lived like this. And perhaps some day my descendants" (Schaller 1979).

Ray Dasmann pointed out that at the 1972 Stockholm Conference on the Human Environment, "there seemed to be tacit agreement that truth, for purposes of the conference at least, would be set aside for acceptable fiction. The truth that the biosphere and its resources are limited and that population growth and consumption of natural resources as a result must be limited was ignored. The fiction that nations can continue to develop to ever-higher levels of material consumption without limiting their populations was widely approved" (Dasmann 1973).

One could argue that this fiction of sustainable growth and development is necessary because no government today could stand on a platform of decreasing consumption for the general populace. But perhaps it is time that conservationists carry the message more forcefully to the public. On biological and ecological grounds, continued growth of the human population and continued expansion of per capita GNP are utterly unsustainable.

If we agree, as I think we must, that the modern industrialized human ecosystem cannot be sustained, at least at its current profligate level of consumption of both nonrenewable and potentially renewable resources, what will replace it? Will it be a "golden age," where new sources of energy have been found, where genetic engineering has enabled us to reach new and unprecedented levels of productivity and recycling, where mechanisms have been found for attaining new ways and means for people to work together in harmony, where we are all efficient biosphere people, and where all land use is under conscious human control? Or will it be a case of "back to the stone age," where we all

once again become ecosystem people, following the collapse of the international monetary system, the exhaustion of oil supplies, the extinction of many of our most cherished fellow creatures, the radical reduction in human population, and the reclamation of agricultural land by nature? Or will it be even worse: "back to the ice ages," following a nuclear exchange?

I shall not attempt to predict the future, because it does not seem that any of the possible scenarios is significantly more likely than any other. The only thing that seems certain is that a fundamental change in the relationship between people and nature is required if life on earth is to prosper. History suggests that such a fundamental change is unlikely to come easily or peacefully, or in a planned manner.

Not knowing the future should not freeze us into inaction. On an individual level, we do not know whether tomorrow our house will burn down or we shall win the lottery. But we make personal decisions that optimize our chances of adapting to whatever comes, by taking care of our health needs, having a good education, putting something in the bank, having children, and taking out insurance. Similarly, irrespective of what the future may bring, societies can take steps to prepare. We need to maintain a healthy environment, learn how natural ecosystems work, maintain the maximum possible diversity in natural ecosystems, and maintain the maximum diversity in human uses of living natural resources.

Conservation serves certain timeless functions in supporting humanity. Some of these functions have been met in "biosphere societies" by national parks, but the same functions are met by other mechanisms in "ecosystem societies." These functions, I suggest, are prerequisites for all healthy human cultures and will be required in any sustainable human society of the future. Whether national parks or some other conservation mechanism is most appropriate for meeting its conservation needs will depend on the characteristics of each of the human societies of the future.

SOME FUNCTIONS OF CONSERVATION

National parks in the United States are considered by most Americans as wonderful places to go for a vacation, where nature in the raw can be experienced from the comfort of one's own automobile. But national parks throughout the world are far more important than this—they address a number of major concerns of human society (see MacKinnon et al. 1986 for more details). This section identifies a few of the functions of conservation and suggests how national parks address these functions in "biosphere societies." These include not only the industrialized countries, but also the tropical countries whose forests and wildlife are being depleted to meet the demands of distant markets. In order to explore the notion that the functions of conservation have stood the test of time, these mechanisms will be compared with means by which the same functions are met in "ecosystem societies."

Respecting the Symbols of the Relationship Between People and Nature

Throughout the world, ecosystem societies have acknowledged their dependence on nature by including animals among their sacred symbols, and even today, many cultures use animals to symbolize certain fundamental beliefs about reality. In Indonesia, for example, the banteng and the tiger appear together on the *gunungan,* the large, triangular shadow puppet that represents the universe in all its complexity. The triangular shape is Mt. Meru, the holy mountain of the Hindus, where the tree of heaven grows. On the *gunungan,* this tree is filled with monkeys and birds, symbolizing the complex world of nature created by the Supreme Being. Underneath the tree, at the center and widest part of the *gunungan,* the tiger and banteng stand in balanced opposition above a small house with ornate doors. But the doors are closed, representing the difficulty humans have in attaining peace of mind. Only by balancing the opposing emotional forces can this desired state be attained. The tiger and the banteng symbolize the way Indonesians reconcile the contradictions inherent in human life. Other nature symbols, such as the naga serpent as the representive of water and the garuda as the representative of the sun, are prominent in tropical Asia, irrespective of the dominant religion.

In biosphere societies, animal symbols are still strong. The British lion and the American bald eagle are obvious examples. National parks are the habitat of these important animal symbols, but perhaps more important, they also symbolize the wild world of nature, the opposite of the urban life which many people find so stressful. This symbolism is communicated to the public through films, commercials, photographs, calendars, and many other media. Judging from the popularity of these symbolic representations of nature, they must be helping to keep the stresses of urban dwelling within bearable bounds. So while biosphere people and ecosystem people have utterly different relationships with nature, both have found nature symbols to be important.

Respecting Religious Links Between People and Nature

Religion and nature is a huge topic, but the important point to make in this short discussion is that nature has been the fount of most religions. Religions help to explain the power of nature, the unexplainable events that happen despite the best efforts of humans to avoid them. Mother Earth as both the producer of all life and the ultimate receptacle of death is often considered the first diety, but both sun and water were probably also very early subjects of veneration. Throughout the tropics, rural people who are in closest contact with nature are firm in their belief that all living things have spirits, and that these spirits can be helpful or harmful depending on how they are treated. The belief in nature spirits in many cultures has provided a brake on overexploitation of natural resources. When complex rituals are required for chopping down a tree, for example, then trees are only taken when really necessary. The belief that animals have spirits that are in no significant way different from human spirits also helps underline the essential unity between human and animal.

When reinforced by peer pressure and limitations of technology, nature spirits effectively kept human greed under some sort of control. But once purchasing power became the driving force, and firearms and chainsaws became freely available, the pressures for exploitation were often too strong to be resisted by ecosystem people eager for the goods of the biosphere. To counteract this impulse for consumption, biosphere societies developed national parks as the method of choice for controlling overexploitation by attempting to ban *any* exploitation. Many national parks have incorporated natural areas which were important in the religions of the ecosystem people living nearby, and several national parks—Mt. Everest in Nepal for one—still have important religious values for local people. While national parks are seldom given any particular role in the organized religions of biosphere societies, the awe, humility, and respect for nature that many people feel in national parks may be a more fundamental religious experience than that found in the more usual man-made houses of worship.

Ensuring the Productivity of Wildlife

Ecosystem people have always had ways of conserving wildlife. Although it can be argued that much of this conservation was due to limitation of technology and low population levels, the fact remains that once societies had lived long enough in their habitat to understand the systems they were dealing with, conservation became part of their culture. It is only when there are basic shifts in the ecological niche of people that wildlife suffers. An excellent example is the near-extinction of the American bison due to railroads, hunters, farmers, and barbed wire after over 30,000 years of sustainable use by America's first colonizers. Of course, it is not only industrial man who fills a new niche. The waves of extinctions following the first human arrivals in Madagascar, New Zealand, Polynesia, and the Americas have been well documented (Olson, chap. 6; Martin and Klein 1984).

Despite the human capacity for exterminating other species, hunting seasons, ceremonies that randomize directions in which hunters travel, sharing of game, and many other techniques are found throughout the world and help to ensure that wildlife is not overexploited. Sometimes this is for the material benefit of people, as when game is harvested on a sustainable basis. In other cases, such as the respect shown to tigers by the forest-dwelling people in peninsular Malaysia, the benefit is primarily psychological.

When market pressures dictate that these traditional conservation means of ecosystem people can no longer function, or are perceived to no longer function, then measures such as national parks are required for conserving wildlife populations. Some endangered species, such as the Javan rhino, live *only* in national parks. Populations of other species, such as grizzly bears, may be largely within national parks. Popula-

tions of yet others, such as orangutans, may be largely outside of national parks, but the protected area is used to symbolize government commitment to their conservation.

Ensuring the Productivity of Vegetation

Since wildlife depends ultimately on habitats, and forests provide products, agricultural land, and harvested species, ecosystem people usually have ways and means of conserving vegetation. One of the best known is the former Sherpa custom of *shingo naua,* or forest guards, where several men from a village were elected to protect the forest, which protected the village. They had the power to prevent cutting of protected forests, determine where trees might be cut, inspect firewood stocks in people's houses, and level appropriate fines for transgressions. Their power was reinforced by annual celebrations, where the fines were paid; everybody had a party, and the perpetrators were subjected to good-natured ridicule by their peers (Furer-Haimendorf 1964).

In many countries, national parks have taken over the function of vegetation protection, not always with complete success. It has sometimes been necessary to institutionalize some exploitation of park vegetation. In Nepal's Chitwan National Park, for example, the local people are allowed into the park for two weeks each year to harvest thatch grass, worth some U.S. $600,000 per year to the local community. Since the natural vegetation around the park has been cleared in the past few decades as biosphere people opened up the wilderness, Chitwan now provides virtually the only source of thatch, the most important traditional roofing material in the region (Mishra 1984).

Protecting Water Supplies

Water is so important to people that all societies have taken steps to ensure its continuing supply. In the traditional rice cultures on Bali, for example, the sources of streams are protected by sacred groves, special ceremonies are conducted when irrigation water is taken out of the river, and water is considered a manifestation of the gods.

For biosphere people, water comes from the tap and is always there. But we also realize that ancient aquifers are being exhausted, water supplies are being polluted, and dams are being silted up. In countries such as the United States, water is being exploited as a nonrenewable resource, and the depletion of Pleistocene aquifers is becoming a serious problem in the arid southwest. National parks have an important role to play here, since natural vegetation cover acts like a sponge to regulate and stabilize water runoff. Deep penetration by tree roots or other vegetation makes the soil more permeable to rainwater, so that runoff is slower and more uniform than on cleared land. As a consequence, in areas around national parks, streams continue to flow in dry seasons, sediment content of the water is reduced, and floods are minimized in rainy weather. In some cases, these hydrological functions can be of enormous value. For example, the Canaima National Park in Venezuela safeguards a catchment feeding hydroelectric developments, which will save the nation an estimated U.S. $4.3 billion annually in fossil fuel (Garcia 1984). On recognizing the importance of the watershed protection function of Canaima, the Venezuelan government tripled the park's size to 3 million ha to enhance its effectiveness.

Providing Tourism and Recreation

Tourism is a lot older than Club Med and package tours to the Serengeti. Societies have always had destinations of particular spiritual value that certain parts of the population visited during certain times of the year, or at certain times of their lives. Hunters and gatherers often moved in large and complex migratory patterns, not too different from the movements of biosphere people from Paris to the south of France every August, or the movement of Americans from the cities to the national parks in the summer.

The importance of tourism and travel for ecosystem people was once brought home to me in the upper Barun Khola of Nepal, where I thought I was exploring virgin land. A cave high up on an apparently inaccessible cliff looked interesting, so with three Sherpas, some ropes and pitons, and considerable courage and exertion, we climbed up to the cave like intrepid pioneers. Approaching the mouth of the cave with care, expecting to hear the growl of a bear or the scream of a yeti, we were devastated

when the cave turned out to be a shrine, which barefooted local maidens visited to make offerings to help them bear children.

Biosphere people have developed national parks for mass tourism, transferring foreign exchange from one country to another and stimulating local industries—hotels, restaurants, transport systems, souvenirs, handicrafts, and guide services. The value of national parks for tourism is likely to become ever greater as the availability of other wild recreation areas is further reduced. But the tourism of biosphere people is fickle, depending on oil prices, prosperous economic conditions, political stability, and a whole host of other factors beyond human control. While tourism for biosphere people is an important function of national parks, it is a weak justification unless ecosystem people living around the park have other reasons for conserving nature. A park that is designed primarily to serve foreign tourists faces serious problems when the tourists no longer come, as has happened in Uganda (Kayanja and Douglas-Hamilton 1984).

Conclusions

I have highlighted only a few of the many functions of conservation in order to illustrate their timeless nature and how ecosystem people and biosphere people use different means to address these functions. National parks make many other contributions to human welfare as well, including monitoring living natural resources, ameliorating local climate, providing a reserve of resources for periods of disastrous social upheavals, forming and protecting soils, providing opportunities for training, research, and education, stimulating local employment, preserving breeding stocks, conserving traditional and cultural values, and many others (see, for example, MacKinnon et al. 1986).

We should recognize that our whole attitude toward nature affects the weighting we give these various functions, so our industrial society tends to give more weight to utilitarian functions, while nonindustrial societies often give more weight to spiritual, symbolic, or aesthetic values. But together, these multiple functions add up to a considerable contribution to human social, ecological, and economic welfare.

LIMITATIONS TO THE NATIONAL PARK APPROACH

While the national parks of biosphere people make crucial contributions to some of the universal functions of conservation, the American model of national parks does not always translate very well in the tropics. In fact, it is difficult to find national parks that are effectively meeting all the functions for which they were designed. In a sample of 100 parks from 49 countries, Machlis and Tichnell (1985) identified 1,611 specific threats to the parks. For example, some 76 percent of the parks reported illegal removal of wildlife, and this figure increased to 95 percent in the tropics.

If the functions of conservation are indeed universal, then surely society needs to examine how national parks can meet these functions more effectively. Entire books have been written about this subject (see, for example, Sax 1980 and McNeely and Miller 1984), so I will highlight just two problems.

Control of National Parks

The official definition of a national park includes words to the effect that they are not materially altered by human exploitation and occupation, and that the highest competent authority of the country having jurisdiction over the area has taken steps to prevent or eliminate, as soon as possible, exploitation or occupation in the area (IUCN 1985). The central government, in effect, is asserting that it can control the land better than any local authority. This attitude is fully understandable for a "biosphere government," which needs to promote the flow of goods and services over a wide area and to extend its control as broadly as possible. In the tropics, the colonial era was followed by a period when governments needed to assert their political viability, requiring strong central governments to consolidate their power. National parks were sometimes used as mechanisms for extending central government influence into the most distant and least secure parts of the country.

As we begin to move into the postindustrial age, governments need to think more in terms of ecological and economic viability; this will often require a decentralization of power. Conservation will not necessarily suffer. In Central America, Houseal et al. (1985) have found that "native peoples have devised sustainable long-term land use practices combining migratory agricultural practices with aboriculture and wildlife management. . . . Their mixed agricultural and forestry systems produce more labor, more commodity per unit of land, are more ecologically sound and result in more equitable income distribution than other practices currently being imposed upon their lands. There are no other land use models for the tropical rain forest that preserve ecological stability or biological diversity as efficiently as those of the indigenous groups presently encountered there."

Boundaries of National Parks

By their very nature as legally established units of land management, national parks have boundaries. Yet nature knows no boundaries, and recent advances in conservation biology are showing that national parks are usually too small to effectively conserve the large mammals or trees that they are designed to preserve (Harris and Eisenberg, chap. 17). The boundary post is too often also a psychological boundary, suggesting that since nature is taken care of by the national park, we can abuse the surrounding lands, isolating the national park as an "island" of habitat which is subject to the usual increased threats that go with insularity (see, for example, Olson, chap. 6; Soulé and Wilcox 1980).

Boundaries have also separated people from nature. National parks "have not drawn us into a more thoughtful relationship with our habitat," says park interpreter Kevin Van Tighem (1986). "They have not taught us that land is to be used frugally, and with good sense. They have encouraged us to believe that conservation is merely a system of trading environmental write-offs against large protected areas. They have more than failed, in fact; they have become a symptom of the problem." Park managers in many parts of the world therefore have a "siege mentality," feeling encroachment from all sides. "The romantic vision of parks as protected paradises," say Machlis and Tichnell (1985), "is widespread and, ironically, may threaten the permanence of national parks. This purely preservationist approach, where parks are considered 'fortresses' under siege, invincible or soon eradicated, carries great political risks. It requires an essentially militaristic defense strategy and will almost always heighten conflict.''

ENSURING THE SURVIVAL OF PARKS

Accepting that the functions of conservation are essential to human welfare, what can be done today to ensure that national parks can more effectively carry out these functions? What other conservation mechanisms are required to supplement the national park idea? What can be done today to build the foundations for a healthier tomorrow? The general answer is that biosphere people need to learn to behave more like ecosystem people. The ecological niche of biosphere people is certain to change as its energy base changes, and logic suggests that by the year 2100 people will depend much more closely on renewable resources than they do today. The following four general principles may help ease the transition from the current nonsustainable exploitation of the biosphere to a healthier harmony with local ecosystems. They will lead to various sorts of actions adapted to local situations.

Shifting Control over Resources

Ecosystem people have long recognized that diversity is the key to their survival, using a wide range of means to wrest a living from a reluctant environment. Mixed systems, transhumance, terraces, agroforestry, local varieties, hunting and fishing, and the forestry/agriculture/wilderness interface are essential to rural cultures. This diversity needs to be maintained as a matter of highest importance. What works in one place will not necessarily work in the next valley, and small or rich countries have different imperatives than large or poor ones. A series of local adaptations based on local cultural diversity is required, not a "universal elixir" to solve all conservation problems.

Most of us are comfortable being biosphere people, but we should also recognize that living like ecosystem people would be much more secure. While we depend on a broad range of goods and services that are far beyond our control, and sometimes even our comprehension,

ecosystem people are more closely linked to the productivity of their local ecosystems. Therefore, protected areas should be designed and managed in ways that contribute to the well-being of the people living around them, and which help encourage biosphere people to understand their dependence on natural ecosystems.

Conservationists should make use of traditional cultural approaches to species and habitat conservation and try to rekindle these where possible. Cultural diversity often parallels ecological diversity, and local traditional adaptations are often the most environmentally sound. In the past, long-term cultural stability has shown that local people are fully able and competent to enforce regulations for the benefit of their community, so it seems appropriate that the people who are most directly dependent on nature should reassume the custodianship that was traditionally theirs. In some areas, it would be possible to establish management units under the control of local village councils, and local people should serve on the advisory board of each protected area. Key points are that local responsibility should follow local institutional patterns, and that it is better to strengthen local institutions than create new ones.

Expanding the Concept of Protected Areas

The question is no longer whether conservation is a necessary part of social and economic development, but rather how conservation can be achieved in the face of constantly increasing demands from an expanding population of biosphere people. Natural habitats and wildlife should be maintained wherever they occur, but at least in the short term, national parks and other protected areas provide the most secure means of conserving samples of natural ecosystems. Protected areas will never be more than a small proportion of what formerly were natural areas, yet they must satisfy the habitat requirements of threatened species and meet certain basic human needs.

Linking protected areas together with human needs can support ecologically sound development which takes on practical meaning for governments and local people. In order to demonstrate how protected areas can contribute to sustaining society, Miller (1980b) devised a set of twelve broad objectives which can guide management decisions. To accommodate this wider range of management objectives without giving up any of the important gains made by national parks and other strictly protected categories, IUCN (1978, 1984a) devised a system of eight categories of conservation units of which the national park is just one.

A series of case studies illustrating how a range of complementary protected-area categories can enable governments to meet their responsibilities for protecting nature while providing for human development on a sustainable basis is presented in McNeely and Miller (1984). But by themselves, protected areas will never be able to conserve all, or even most, of the species, genetic resources, and ecological processes they were established to protect. The best answer to this dilemma seems to be to select and manage protected areas to support the overall fabric of social and economic development—not as islands of antidevelopment, but rather as critical elements of regionally envisioned harmonious landscapes. Through a planned mix of national parks and other types of reserves amid productive forests, agriculture, and grazing, protected areas can serve biosphere people today and safeguard the well-being of future generations of people living in balance with their local ecosystems.

Seeing Conservation as Primarily a Human Problem

Most of the speakers at the conference Conservation 2100 were ecologists or biologists. Meetings on national parks are dominated by protected area managers. But this chapter has illustrated that conservation is far more a *social* challenge than a *biological* one. Natural scientists, to their great credit, have led the conservation movement, but it is now time to enlist a far broader constituency, including anthropologists, sociologists, theologians, politicians, economists, historians, and others.

Conserving Both Cultural Diversity and Biological Diversity

Ecosystem people throughout the world have developed ways and means of conservation which are interwoven into their cultural fabric (see McNeely and Pitt 1984, for a series of case studies and McNeely and Wachtel, 1988, for a detailed discussion of Southeast Asia). As nations are built, literacy becomes widespread, mass media become more effective, and new biosphere cultures are formed. Conservation needs to become part of every possible section of the national development process and thereby part of the new national culture, rather than just a discrete responsibility of a wildlife or national parks department. Conservation is too important to leave to scientists or managers. But those who are now leading the conservation movement would do well to incorporate human concerns more effectively in their discussions with politicians and those who are making decisions that affect the future of us all.

CONCLUSION

The aim of this chapter has been to communicate how important national parks are to our biosphere society. Why, then, do I think that national parks may be extinct by the year 2100? If we have somehow figured out how to overcome our political obstacles, reduced our population, and attained a "golden age" that allows us to be biosphere people without destroying the environment, then I expect that our descendants will see a spectrum of more knowledgeable, carefully controlled, and carefully tailored human influences on local ecosystems which allows both the maintenance of biological diversity and the continued prosperity of *Homo sapiens*. National parks as we know them today will have merged into far more flexible and adaptive land-use techniques.

If, on the other hand, our future does not allow us to continue being biosphere people, then as ecosystem people we will not *need* national parks. But until people learn to live with nature, or are forced to live with nature, we need national parks more than ever. Wildlife and biological diversity are resources too valuable to lose. The people of the year 2100 will judge our success in creating "Holocene refugia" by the diversity of both natural resources and human adaptations that we are able to pass on to them. Our consumerism will surely be harshly judged by future generations. Let us do everything possible to ensure that our efforts at conservation receive a better verdict from our descendants.

16

Conservation Without Parks: Wildlife in the Rural Landscape

DAVID WESTERN

Nature, like taste, is subjective. In the broadest sense, nature means the realm of animals and plants. But does it also mean, as many Western cultures would have it, the absence of humans and human activity? Not necessarily. Many Asian and African cultures do not distinguish between the natural and human realm, with good reason; there is no clear-cut separation. Areas are more or less occupied, but seldom vacant. Wilderness, though not exclusively a Western concept, is meaningless to many societies living side by side with nature.

Whether we think humanity is a part of nature or not affects our view of its future. If we take the more traditional, less anthropocentric view, the outlook for nature is not so bad. Many, perhaps most, species can survive the future world where human activity will be far more pervasive and habitats more disrupted. The extinction-prone species, live or genetically encoded, can always be saved some other way, in zoos perhaps, or cryogenically (Conway, chap. 19). But for the purist, the advocate of natural ecosystem preservation, the outlook is bleak.

Is one view any more valid than the other? In fact, are the two views mutually exclusive? I have raised the human and nature issue because it is central to how we perceive our future, and how we think nature fits into it. What I hope to show is that our future, and nature's, is likely to be better for those with a less purist, more third world view. The segregationist and integrationist views are, moreover, complementary.

The parks and reserves help to conserve a less altered, more confined nature, and the regions beyond help to conserve a more altered, less confined nature. We should not continue to ignore wildlife outside parks. The human realm occupies 95% of the earth's surface and will one way or another affect the future of nature far more than the diminutive parks. Conservationists have ignored the non-park areas in favor of saving nature by segregating it from humanity. The trouble is that species segregation, like racial segregation, gives the subordinate party, nature, small fragments of usually inferior land.

Wildlife beyond parks has been left to hunters and ignored by conservationists as too unnatural to merit serious attention. But consider the facts. We expect the 2.8% of our land surface set aside as nature reserves to protect the planet's ten million or more species of plants and animals. Is this realistic? Almost certainly not. Rather late on, we are learning of design problems and other threats which will whittle down the biological wealth of nature reserves. For example, with perhaps fewer than 5% of all living species described scientifically (Wilson 1985a), millions of unknown species could be left out of reserves. Knowledge alone may be insufficient to save species where the human threats are formidable. Species are especially prone to extinction from the insularization of reserves (Harris and Eisenberg chap. 17; Diamond and May 1976; MacArthur and Wilson 1967). Poaching, pollution, and other factors also threaten reserves (Machlis and Tichnell 1985). Another little-appreciated problem—the simplification of reserves because of the removal of diversifying factors such as burning, shifting cultivation, and livestock—is equally troubling, as I show later. And, because we are so hazy about how ecosystems are assembled and operate (Strong et al. 1984), we could lose as many species to mis-timed and misinformed management as we lose to habitat fragmentation and hunting. Finally, human factors, ranging from shortage of funds, manpower, skills, and equipment to politics and outright hostility, threaten nature reserves. Few countries can remedy these problems immediately. The prospect of conserving more than a modest number of species in zoos is also gloomy (Conway 1986). Overall, our existing conservation practices will be inadequate in the twenty-first century. A public increasingly worried about its own future in a shrinking world is unlikely to give more space to wildlife. To meet the challenges of the next century, we need new solutions for conserving wildlife.

If we must look beyond parks, we need to start by establishing a few fundamentals. How important is wildlife outside parks? How does it survive? How are non-park ecosystems different from park ecosystems? What are the implications for conservation? These are a few of the questions I will explore in one biome, the East African savannas, before considering the broader prospects and challenges.

PARKS AND NON-PARKS: AN EAST AFRICAN COMPARISON

The East African savannas warrant special attention for several reasons. Only here do we find, more or less intact, the rich megafauna that was exterminated elsewhere in recent millennia. This is reason enough to protect the remnants. In addition, the problems wildlife face in the savannas—rocketing human numbers and severe land pressures (Myers 1972)—are especially formidable. To make matters worse, the large savanna carnivores and herbivores need more land than other mammals. So if we can save wildlife here, the odds are better than even that we can do so in less problematic areas.

To understand how wildlife is doing outside parks and might fare in the future, we need to establish the following:

1. The numerical distribution of species nationwide.
2. The absolute and relative abundance of species in and outside parks.
3. The ecological links between animals in and outside parks.
4. The reasons for species differences outside and inside parks.
5. The anticipated impact on wildlife of societal or landuse changes.

Wildlife is still found over most of East Africa. Indeed, all but a few species are more common outside parks than within, whether in Sudan, one of Africa's poorest nations, or Kenya, one of its wealthier.

Data from aerial large herbivore counts over the entire 700,000 km^2 Kenya rangelands (Andere et al 1980), which covers 40% of the country, illustrate the point (Table 16.1). All species other than elephant, rhino, and wildebeest are more numerous outside parks. Of nearly two million animals in the rangelands, three-quarters live outside parks. Absolute densities inside and out cannot be validly compared, because most wildlife range occurs in the arid north, whereas most parks are in the wetter south. We can get around this problem by normalizing for rainfall (Fig. 16.1). Here, data for fifty-three ecosystems in eastern Africa, covering over 700,000 km^2 about 40% of the rangelands, shows human and wildlife productivity under similar conditions in and outside parks. I use production (Western 1983a) as a measure of biological importance. Four points relevant to wildlife survival emerge:

- Both wildlife and livestock production increase with rainfall.
- Combined livestock-wildlife production exceeds either individually.
- Livestock production exceeds wildlife production where both coexist.
- Livestock competition reduces wildlife production outside parks.

Subsistence herding does reduce wildlife production, though it is difficult to say to what extent. It could be in the order of 50% (Fig. 16.1). But, if we discount elephant production in

Table 16.1 Distribution of Wildlife in and Outside Parks and Reserves Within Kenya's Rangelands.

	Species	Total Number		% Outside Parks
		Rangelands	Parks	
Browsers	Gerenuk	55,600	1,909	3
	Ostrich	39,700	3,037	8
	Giraffe	77,600	8,499	11
	Lesser Kudu	19,200	3,637	19
	Rhino	350	189	54
Mixed Feeders	Grant's Gazelle	331,100	40,394	12
	Eland	51,300	7,847	15
	Impala	253,700	72,131	28
	Thomson's Gazelle	244,200	88,109	36
	Elephant	30,000	17,500	58
Grazers	Grevy's Zebra	7,900	111	1
	Water Buck	18,200	1,958	11
	Hunter's Hartebeest	7,500	1,500	20
	Topi	138,600	31,897	23
	Oryx	74,800	20,357	27
	Buffalo	85,600	25,053	29
	Kongoni	59,300	19,839	34
	Burchell's Zebra	182,500	73,216	40
	Wildebeest	207,400	112,605	54
		1,884,558	529,788	

Estimates of total numbers are taken from Andere et al. (1980). (Estimates for parks and reserves are from figures available on each area.) Grevy's zebra numbers are low in parks because the population ranges widely in arid northern Kenya, where there are few protected areas. Heavy poaching has increased the relative number of elephants and rhinos within parks.

parks, where numbers are artificially high because of hunting compression (see later discussion), wildlife production losses due to livestock competition might be minor (Fig. 16.1). Further, there is no evidence of species displacement. Non-parks have as rich and diverse a fauna as parks (Fig. 16.2). Pastoralism may alter and even severely degrade savannas (Brown 1971), but since it does not eradicate habitat in the way clear felling and burning does forest, wildlife survives and seems to do well in free competition with livestock (Western 1973). Indeed, pastoralists, who reached East Africa over 3,000 years ago, have helped shape the modern savannas. During this time no large herbivore has, to our knowledge, gone extinct. What of the differences in parks and non-parks fauna? There are several. I will touch on three.

First, only elephants, rhinos, and wildebeest are more numerous in parks than outside. Second, browsers are relatively more abundant than grazers outside parks. Third, the reverse is true inside parks. These differences are not simply an artifact of park design, of selection for spectacular plains game, as data from Tsavo National park show (Cobb 1976). Though originally bushland, Tsavo Park, like most others in East Africa (including Amboseli, Meru, northern Serengeti, Mara, and Ruaha), has been transformed to grassland (Laws 1969).

Two related reasons linked to human activity explain the differences inside and outside parks. First, elephants and rhinos, both valuable commercially for tusks and horns, are poached more heavily outside parks. Woodlands are transformed to grasslands by the resulting elephant compression (Laws 1970). Grasslands support hot fires and further inhibit woodland regeneration. Second, high livestock densities outside parks reduce grass cover and fires and often indirectly encourage woody growth. Wildebeest are exceptional. The extraordinary numbers in one ecosystem, the Serengeti-Mara, account for their greater abundance in parks.

These observations give cause for both concern and optimism: concern because even these enormous savanna parks are demonstrably being altered by human activity outside their boundaries, optimism because wildlife is so abundant outside parks, despite neglect. What, if anything, can we anticipate about the future of East Africa's wildlife? We can get an idea of what is possible, though not inevitable, by looking at wildlife survival on the commercially de-

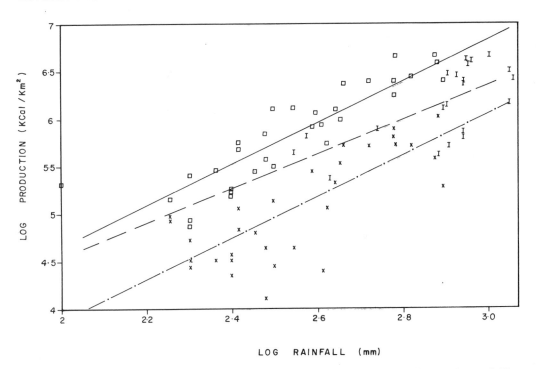

Fig. 16.1. Production figures for wildlife and livestock plotted against rainfall for fifty-three ecosystems in East Africa. The productivity of mixed wildlife and livestock ecosystems is greater than wildlife production in national parks where livestock are absent. All regressions are significant and significantly different from each other in intercepts ($p < 0.05$) but not in slope.

veloped rangelands, which foreshadow the fate of most savannas.

In South Africa and Zimbabwe, where commercial ranching is relatively sophisticated and has been underway for decades, and in some areas for centuries, wildlife is still common and generally on the increase. Wildlife is also doing relatively well on commercial ranches in East Africa, but we still have little information on how it is affected ecologically and what this implies for conservation in the longer term. Such data as there are lead me to believe that wildlife extermination is neither inevitable nor imminent in the savannas. Rather, I see some hope, provided there is action—action calling for policies and practices, strongly enforced, that benefit landowners, build up public awareness and support, and reduce poaching.

In conclusion, the savanna parks are greatly affected by human activity and may be a very limited solution to maintaining the wealth and diversity of savanna ecosystems. The time has come to look beyond them to the human realm, to see what options exist.

BEYOND PARKS: THE UNREALIZED POTENTIAL

Most wildlife still survives outside parks. The most diverse biome on the earth, the tropical moist forest, supports a rich fauna even under moderate exploitation, such as shifting cultivation and selective felling. In Southeast Asia, for example, Johns (1985) finds that commercial forests support as great a diversity of birds and primates as primary forests, though in different proportions. The method, level, and frequency of timber harvest affect how drastically the wildlife community is altered. A good deal of attention is being focused on how to simultaneously use and conserve forests (Harris

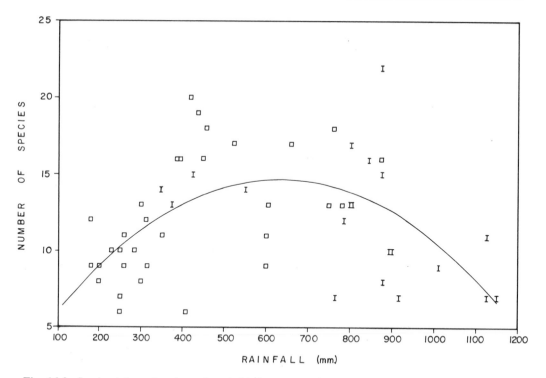

Fig. 16.2. Species richness (numbers of species) in large mammal ecosystems of East Africa shows a parabolic relationship with rainfall, but ecosystems dominated by livestock (□) are no poorer in species than national parks (I) where livestock are absent.

1984). Further research into harvesting practices based on patch dynamics in natural systems could further benefit wildlife in exploited forests.

Examples can be drawn from virtually every biome. I shall cite several from various habitats and land-use systems to illustrate the importance of the human realm to wildlife:

• Forests reserves have many uses, including timber production, firewood, pulp, water catchment, erosion control, genetic raw material, hunting, hiking, tourism, and outdoor recreation of all sorts (Myers 1984b).
• Rangelands support abundant wildlife. Commercial harvesting, sport hunting, and tourism help maintain wildlife alongside livestock, especially in the Americas and Africa.
• Deserts are often suitable wildlife habitats, despite human pressures. Oil revenues have accelerated the urbanization process in much

of North Africa and the Middle East, reducing human dependence on deserts in the process (Stanley Price, chap. 20). Here, wildlife could increase, given adequate protection from poaching and some justification from sport hunting and tourism where necessary.

• Wetlands have hydrological, waste-assimilative fisheries, wildlife, and aesthetic values. Estuaries are usually nutrient-rich habitats important in commercial fisheries. Reservoir, dams, and impoundments have many different values, from purely commercial to aesthetic (Greeson et al. 1978).
• Montane regions are often too rugged to be commercially exploited, yet are valuable water catchments which double as wildlife habitat (Green 1981).
• Arable lands, despite obliterating most natural habitat, can also support wildlife in tree windbreaks, hedgerows, reservoirs, and copses (Green 1981).

- Urban parks and greenbelts are also receiving serious attention as wildlife habitats (Simons 1985).
- Even degraded and abandoned lands can be turned back to wildlife habitat through natural succession and reclamation.
- Finally, zoos, zoo parks, and private estates and ranches are playing an ever-larger role in wildlife conservation (Conway, chap. 19).

WHY WILDLIFE SURVIVES ALONGSIDE HUMANITY

Why does wildlife do so well beyond parks, often under intensive exploitation? There is no simple answer. In one of the few quantitative efforts to explain a species' conservation status, Burrill et al. (1986) showed that of the many geographical, land-use, socioeconomic, political, and conservation factors examined, civilian disruptions, and in a complex way, socioeconomic indices, best predict elephant status in Africa. Elephants are increasing at 2.5% a year on average under stable governments, while decreasing by 16% annually under unstable governments. And although the more developed African nations have lost a higher percentage of their original elephant populations, they are doing a better job now of preserving them than less developed nations. Literacy, wealth, and protective measures all help preserve elephants.

Development may affect wildlife in another way. Wildlife is often relatively safe among traditional and industrial societies and particularly vulnerable in the transitional stages. The explanation seems to be that safety in traditional societies stems from cultural strictures on hunting practices and the limitation of primitive weapons. Societies in transition abandon traditional constraints, acquire modern firearms, and, in an atmosphere of uncertain land and natural resource ownership, go for quick profits. Finally, once ownership is settled, laws instituted and enforced, and awareness generated, the remnant populations are better protected. Though a useful generalization, wildlife survives alongside humanity for many other reasons, including:

1. Profitability. Many species are profitable. Pastoral societies often supplement livestock produce with game meat. Similarly, in Zimbabwe and South Africa, commercial ranches are profitably combining beef production and wildlife utilization. Between 1975 and 1979 for example, over 24,000 large mammals of twenty-one species were profitably moved from parks to private ranches in South Africa (Hanks et al. 1981). On average, ranchers who utilize wildlife increase farm income by 30%. The greater production of combined wildlife and livestock use of rangeland (Fig. 16.1) is widely recognized and increasingly exploited.

2. Zero-cost species. Many species do not compete with livestock, and therefore are not worth eliminating.

3. Hardy species. Other species are too fugitive, naturally rare, or otherwise too costly to eliminate.

4. Areas unused, little used, or abandoned. Large areas are too far from water, too intractable for livestock or humans, too disease-ridden, or too subject to disruptive warfare to be heavily occupied.

5. Ecological complementarity. Some species, such as the elephant, improve habitats for livestock.

6. Pleasure. Yet other species are pleasurable to the landowner, at a cost affordable to him.

7. Indifference. Many landowners are simply indifferent to wildlife, especially in low numbers.

8. Cultural, ethical, legislative, or political restraints. In most countries wildlife is owned by the state and cannot be eliminated at the landowner's whim. Pressure from special-interest groups and close government scrutiny also commit landowners to species preservation.

PUTTING THE PRINCIPLES TO WORK

Out of expediency, conservation policy and practice is slowly changing as the limits to reserves and the prospects beyond them become more compelling. For example, IUCN (1982) now recognizes eight protected-area categories, including managed resource areas and anthropological reserves. Such brazenly exploitative goals might appear to dilute the concept of strict nature reserves. Not at all. The nature reserves remain intact. The new categories skirt the limitations of parks by appealing for conservation in terms people understand. A few short years of oil shortage convinced a profligate generation that conservation had relevance to modern economies just as much as it does to traditional societies.

Giving a human face to conservation is catching on fast. The World Conservation Strategy (IUCN 1980) promotes nature protection through the concept of sustainable development. National parks have also been promoted under the rubric "Conservation for Sustainable Development" (IUCN 1982). The new charter aims to maintain life-support systems and essential ecological processes, to preserve genetic diversity, and to ensure that wildlife and natural habitat use is sustainable. In an ironic twist, the new philosophy links conservation to development by invoking interdependency, thus reversing the age-old dogma that nature is the victim, development the archenemy. The idea that conservation is progress, not antidevelopment, is finally winning support (Western 1985).

There is, however, a catch in the new philosophy, for if nature reserves are expanding, they are doing so increasingly by serving human interests first, wildlife second. And, in reality, the World Conservation Strategy is not new, except to a generation or more of biologists and preservationists weaned on the idea that nature sanctuaries are the Holy Grail of conservation. Sustainable use has its roots in early European forestry practices, and later, in the United States, in the doctrine of maximum sustained yield. In India a century ago, millions of hectares of forest reserve were established to produce *"in a permanent fashion, the greatest possible quantities of that material which is most useful to the general public"* (Vedant; 1986 italics added). Yet those policies did not protect India's forests (Vedant 1986), any more than the same sentiments echoed in the World Conservation Strategy can in similar, more prevalent circumstances today (Western 1985). Poverty, ownership uncertainties, and the crushing necessity to replace useless with useful species defy the logic of conserving diversity for its own sake. The modern agricultural revolution, responsible for such enormous prosperity in the West, succeeded by narrowing food webs to boost productivity of the few crops useful to

humanity (Green, chap. 18). Progress in the developing world also depends on high-production, low-diversity agriculture, though one hopes to a lesser extent.

Given that a mere twenty of the 350,000 plants on earth supply most of our food, sustainable use is not a sufficient argument for conserving diversity. Other justifications, for example Myers's (1984b) pharmacopoeia argument for protecting tropical forests, have been advanced for protecting biological diversity. All are utilitarian, or future-valued, and fall victim to necessity when the poor decide to consume today what they must to have any future whatever. The more tangible utilitarian arguments, such as water catchment, erosion control, maximum sustainable production of food and utilities, and so on, merely restate commonly shared development goals, which stand or fall when necessity and desirability clash (Western 1985).

We must look more closely at why conservation, whether of renewable resources or of wildlife, succeeds in some cases and fails in others. There is a great deal to learn from the record about what options to try in the future.

CONCLUSION

The extermination of wildlife has, until now, had more to do with hunting and human attitudes than inexorable land pressures. So, for example, many more large mammals were exterminated by the comparatively few hunters in the late Pleistocene (Martin and Klein 1984) than at any time since. Europe lost 30% of its large mammal genera, North America 73%, South America 80%, and Australia 90% (Stuart 1986). Over 33% of the mammals and 43% of the birds known to have become extinct since 1600 also were eliminated by hunting, which accounts for an even higher portion, some 43%, of all presently endangered mammals (Fisher et al. 1969). Habitat loss has been far less destructive, accounting for around 20% of the 194 vertebrate extinctions since 1600 (Nilsson 1983). It will, however, become a decisive factor, as habitats fragment in the coming decades, unless countermeasures are soon taken (Diamond, chap. 4).

Sanctuaries have been successful to the point of blinding us to other options. They are an attractive, simple solution requiring no complicated policies, no intricate social or economic formulations, and virtually no management. Management is, in fact, something of an anathema. Only the simplest legislation and management—largely antipoaching measures—are admissible. Sanctuaries have been especially successful in the third world, particularly where land pressures are minimal and tourism is profitable.

Such a seemingly ideal and simple solution is not enough. Humanity is the crux of the wildlife threat, and therefore of its solution, too. A generation of biologists and managers raised to believe that segregation is the sole solution has ignored the humanities and social sciences and poorly prepared itself to manage wildlife in an increasingly human world. Unlike the national parks movement, which advocates strict conservation standards for reserves, irrespective of national differences (IUCN 1982), wildlife conservation beyond the parks can only succeed by adapting philosophy and methodology to local conditions, whether cultural, economic, religious, or political. Human self-interest, tolerance, curiosity, or just plain indifference may decide whether wildlife survives.

Land beyond parks is the best hope and biggest challenge for biological conservation. Here are a few pointers to what is involved in realizing their potential:

1. Research. What species do (or do not) survive outside parks, where, and why? How do non-park ecosystems differ from parks, and what are the evolutionary and conservation implications?
2. Management. How can the major ecological imbalances, either in parks or outside, be corrected? Is that desirable, or realistic?
3. What incentives exist or can be introduced to encourage conservation on private, public, and communal lands?
4. How do existing policies and laws, including land and wildlife ownership, commercial rights, cropping, hunting, and trade regulations, affect wildlife conservation outside parks? How can they be improved?
5. What institutions implement policy, and what improvements are needed?
6. How do international aid, the development agencies, business, and conservation bodies help conserve nature? How can each contribute more?
7. How do external factors such as agricultural pricing subsidies, veterinary policies, and land demarcation affect wildlife, and can those practices be changed advantageously?
8. What recreational demands for wildlife are anticipated? How should they feature in planning and policy decisions?
9. How can education and extension programs widen the conservation support for wildlife?
10. How can one ensure that local populations benefit preferentially from wildlife returns?
11. What areas face increasing, stable, or decreasing land pressure? How can plans for wildlife conservation benefit from such projections?

The shortcomings in nature reserves are reason neither to reduce effort in them nor to view them fatalistically as our sole hope. The shifting emphasis and broadening scope of modern conservation merely illustrate what is abundantly obvious and undeniable, that wildlife has more chance allied to humanity than divorced from it. A twenty-first-century wildlife-human alliance practiced over much of the globe will give wildlife far more chance than it has in parks, and the best hope of avoiding mass extinctions. Unless we take a wider, less purist view of conservation, all hope will devolve on parks. As a result, species extinction rates will skyrocket, and ex situ Band-Aid measures will be overwhelmed. The best way to stop the domino effect of species loss is to work out the principles and methods of human-wildlife cohabitation.

17

Enhanced Linkages: Necessary Steps for Success in Conservation of Faunal Diversity

LARRY HARRIS and JOHN EISENBERG

BACKGROUND

Efforts to conserve biological diversity should neither deny nor overlook the importance of cultural diversity encoded in value systems. Historical patterns of resource limitation have shaped underlying cultural values, which have, in turn, led to the development of significantly different strategies toward the conservation of wildlife and nature. Although there is not a one-to-one correspondence, cultural values are frequently reflected in the institutional policies of the nations or states that embody a cultural group or groups (see Tarak, chap. 26). Many resource conservation programs were institutionalized during the late nineteenth and early twentieth centuries, a time of widespread colonialism. Thus, perceptions of resources and resource limitations in the homeland undoubtedly were factors that motivated and shaped the approaches to resource conservation in the colonies.

Our combined international conservation experience exceeds fifty years in as many predominantly tropical and subtropical countries. We have witnessed and studied the strengths and weaknesses of dozens of colonial, national, and state conservation policies and feel that some reflections on successes may be in order. Our present location in Florida provides the benefit of working among one of the world's most affluent and rapidly growing human populations while residing near to and working among the Western Hemisphere's economically poorest but rapidly growing states. We hear in one ear that wildlife conservation cannot succeed because of too much human population growth due to affluence while hearing in the other that it cannot succeed because of too much poverty and squalor. Yet, we believe that a conservation paradigm can be developed that has the capacity to bridge such social and cultural differences.

From among the spectrum of colonial powers and the cultural values represented by them, two fundamentally different and juxtaposed philosophies seem to underlie most early conservation strategies (see also Hargrove, chap. 21). A utilitarian approach that put greatest emphasis on the instrumental value of resources was evident in the nineteenth century. German hunting reserves in East Africa, the Theodore Roosevelt philosophy behind the establishment of a U.S. refuge system principally for migratory game birds, and the Gifford Pinchot philosophy that shaped the policies of the U.S. Forest Service are examples of this view. The simple phrase "wise use without abuse" seems to encapsulate this philosophy and approach. It incorporates a management philosophy based on the premise that regenerated furbearers, fisheries, or forests are not importantly different from unexploited ones, and that the essence of ecosystems such as old-growth forests and wetlands can be maintained or recreated by appropriate management. Little if any significance is attached to the internal contradiction in the phrase "wildlife management.'' (i.e., can it be wildlife if it is managed life?).

Near the other extreme lies the second philosophy and approach, which puts greatest emphasis on the intrinsic value of nature in a wild state. This philosophy follows directly from European Romanticism (e.g., Goethe, Schiller, Rousseau) and its American counterpart, expressed by Emerson and Thoreau and embodied in the National Parks movement by John Muir, Fredrick Law Olmsted, and others. Throughout much of the world, National Parks (and State counterparts) are maintained as pristine enclaves of nature under a no-management philosophy. Tourists are solicited, and while great ecological imbalances and perhaps even species loss may result from no management of the park ecosystems, great emphasis is attached to making the resource available to tourists. Because deep-seated cultural values of landowners were frequently disregarded when the land was originally appropriated, and because parkland and resource use by local agrarians is generally prohibited, the parks philosophy frequently creates hostility between traditional land-user groups and the national administration.

With maturation of the wildlife conservation movement has come several distinct modifications and developments to these basic nineteenth-century approaches. Although rarely institutionalized at the national level, the natural-areas movement has achieved prominence in the latter part of the twentieth century. Unlike parks that place heavy emphasis on people, tourism, and recreation, this philosophy attaches greatest value to the maintenance of native flora and fauna even if it means virtually complete closure to human usage. But without the resources of national governments to appropriate large land areas, natural areas are, on average, much smaller and more isolated than federal parks, forests, and wildlife refuges. This predisposes the areas to lower effectiveness as large vertebrate conservation areas.

Subsistence hunting is no doubt one of the oldest and most deep-seated forms of wildlife utilization. The Canadian fur industry represents an early and successfully institutionalized subsistence utilization scheme, but only in recent decades has this philosophy become widely sanctioned and institutionalized as a wildlife conservation strategy (Darling 1960; Huxley 1961; Leopold 1959). The key characteristic of this approach is development of widespread but regulated agrarian uses of wildlife so that its value is kept sharply in focus by the people who live and work close to the land and the habitat.

A fifth and most recently developed approach targets commercialization and husbandry as a central means of wildlife conservation. Dassmann (e.g., 1964) has long been a champion of this approach, and it now has numerous advocates (e.g., Eltringham 1984; Webb et al. 1987). Although certain applications of this approach may be advisedly integrated with any of the other approaches, a contradiction of thought and purpose is ever lurking in the concept of wildlife husbandry. The degree to which the species are wildlife, in the strict sense, is reduced in proportion to the degree that they are husbanded. Not only is the wild setting quick to give way to the artificial; behavioral, phenotypic, and ultimately genetic changes in the wildlife species themselves beg the purpose of conservation in the first place.

Yet other fundamentally different (ex situ) approaches (e.g., zoological parks; see Conway, chap. 19) are assuming increased importance as biodiversity is increasingly stressed. The evidence is accumulating that no single approach has either sufficed until now or will suffice in the future and that even the combination of approaches has not been adequate to date. Biodiversity continues to erode and be lost at all levels, ranging from within-species genetic diversity to among-species communities and higher-level faunal and floral assemblages.

Because each approach is usually subscribed to by a different agency or organization, much greater linkage between authorities and organizations will be necessary in the future. Unfortunately, little to no central integrative authority or leadership exists, and all too often, the personnel of one program or approach express hostility toward the others. In many cases, competition between agencies and authorities significantly impedes the overall conservation effort.

In the final analysis, integration of philosophies and approaches must occur on the landscape among its human inhabitants. The need for movement is one characteristic that distinguishes most animals from most plants. With some exceptions, the distance moved increases as body size increases, and it is frequently this movement by large vertebrates that causes both conservationists and nonconservationists great concern. For this reason, physical linkages throughout the landscape also will be increasingly called for, as will strategies that attempt to bridge the gap between "their animals" or "their actions" encroaching on "our areas" or "our freedom."

Specific applications of the overall strategy will need to be developed for each region and each cultural milieu. We report on wildlife resource exploitation and conservation in two greatly different circum-Caribbean states, Florida and Haiti, to provide examples of the broad dimensions of the approach. We have chosen to analyze these two because the comparisons and contrasts are so vivid. Both states have peninsular geographies in the subtropical latitude, albeit one the western tip of an island and one the southern tip of a continent. Both were discovered and impacted nearly 500 years ago, and both have experienced significant periods of Spanish colonial rule. Both have high human population growth rates and nearly 500-year histories of faunal and floral resource exploitation. But most important, we believe they represent the extremes of human population affluence and poverty and the extremes in wildlife conservation programming. We believe that a strategy that applies under such diverse economic and social conditions will be widely applicable throughout the world.

RELEVANT HISTORY AND PREHISTORY OF HAITI AND FLORIDA

Colonization

The year 1492 represents a turning point when Spain was simultaneously released from 800 years of Moorish rule and became the dominant colonial power in the New World. The age of "Conquistadors" followed within months of the "reconquista." Inasmuch as portable firearms were not yet available, large dogs (*Canis familiaris*), bred specifically for human combat, were an implement of the conquest. Thus, in 1493 killer dogs were released against Amerindians as a show of force, and within a short time the dogs' New World population had expanded and began to range freely (Varner and Varner 1983). Unlike the small, barkless, frequently toothless dogs that were attendant to the Amerindians, these large European breeds exerted high protein demands in an already protein-poor

insular setting. Free-ranging (feral) dogs thus became the first and only large mammalian predator on the Caribbean islands. There is some evidence that they had devastating effects on native species (Morgan and Woods 1986; Varner and Varner 1983). Swine (*Sus scrofa*) were also introduced in 1493, and the attendant infectious diseases began to wreak havoc on native human and wildlife populations alike (Crosby 1972; Lawren 1987; McNeill 1976; Sauer 1966, 1971). The combination of factors, including, at least, human slavery and slave exports, introduction of infectious diseases, and resource depletion, virtually exterminated the native Taino Indians of Hispaniola within twenty-five years of contact (Deagan 1987). Save for the animal waifs released by the wrecked and dismembered Santa Maria in 1492, the domestic dog and pig were the first overt introductions into the New World. To our knowledge, the Taino Indians represent the first extinction. West African slaves were quickly introduced as a labor source to compensate for the extirpated Amerindians, and a new culture was substituted for an old.

Spain maintained control over Haiti until 1580, when the costs of the struggle to maintain a mercantile colony became overwhelming and the area was abandoned (Hoffman 1980). The vacuum left by the Spaniards was filled by French adventurers who captured the feral and highly abundant introduced cattle (*Bos taurus*) for sustenance and sale. They roasted the meat over open fires or "boucans" and gained rapid notoriety as "boucaniers" (Craton 1962). France gained control by 1650 and exercised colonial power until 1802, when Haiti became the second independent republic in the Western Hemisphere (Fig. 17.1). During the past 165 years a predominantly despotic and dictatorial rule has galvanized Haitian doubts and suspicions of the exploitative policies of colonial, social, and bureaucratic power.

In 1513 Ponce de Leon sailed along the eastern seaboard of North America and claimed Florida as a possession of the Spanish crown. But not until 1565 was a permanent Spanish enclave established on the North American continent (north of Mexico). During the intervening 52 years, Spain, the strongest colonial power of the day, witnessed the death of its first six Conquistadors attempting to explore and settle Florida and the Southeast (Sauer 1971). During that

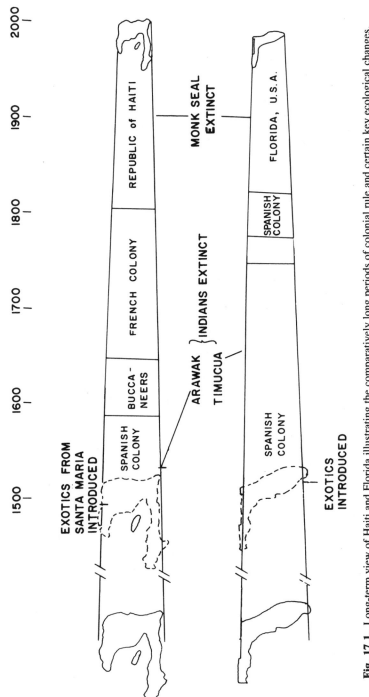

Fig. 17.1. Long-term view of Haiti and Florida illustrating the comparatively long periods of colonial rule and certain key ecological changes.

169

same time, scores of galleons wrecked on off-shore reefs (Peterson 1965) and no doubt bilged dozens of exotic species into the surf and onto the continent. The combination of slave raids to the mainland, the several expeditions including the massive DeSoto expedition of 1539, the French Fort Caroline established in 1564, and the permanent Spanish settlement dating from 1565 meant that the full range of European, Caribbean, Mexican, and even some African plants and animals were candidate introductions. "To a notable extent, the whole migration of Spaniards, Portuguese, and the others who followed them . . . depended on their ability to 'Europeanize' the flora and fauna of the New World . . . . and it was irrevocable in both North and South America by 1550" (Crosby 1972:64).

Cattle, hogs, horses (*Equus caballus*), donkeys (*Equus asinus*), sheep (*Ovis aries*), goats (*Capra hircus*), barking dogs, chickens (*Gallus domesticus*), sugar cane (*Saccharum afficinarum*), the orange (*Citrus* spp.), and the coconut (*Cocos nucifera*) were all introduced and had opportunity to become fully naturalized for 200 years prior to the King of England's official natural history investigation by John Bartram in 1765 or William Bartram's later survey (Cruickshank 1986). Ironically, the policy for numerous Florida parks is to recreate faunal and floral conditions "as they existed when William Bartram first [*sic*] saw them." At present about one-third of the peninsula plant species (R. Wunderlin, personal communication) and 7.5 percent of Florida's free-ranging vertebrate species are exotic.

Almost as dramatic as the demise of the Taino of Hispaniola, the Timucuan Indians of East Florida suffered rapid decimation and were perhaps the first mainland taxon to be eliminated (Deagan 1978, 1985).

With the exception of 21 years of quiescence under English rule (1763–84), Florida remained a Spanish colony for 287 years and thus did not gain independence as an American territory until 1821, 19 years after Haiti's independence. In the year 2108 (120 years from now) Florida will have been part of the United States for as long as she was a Spanish colony (Fig. 17.1).

Resource Exploitation

Since a major reason for Columbus's initial exploration was the establishment of trade centers and the acquisition of material resources, it is not surprising that resource extraction was both fast and dramatic. Although considerable emphasis was directed toward gold, silver, and precious stones, both the value and tonnage of biological products were as great as mineral exports (Chaunu and Chaunu 1957:vols. 6–7).

Because there were no native terrestrial vertebrates of exploitable size or abundance on the Caribbean islands, Monk seals (*Monachus tropicalis*) and marine turtles (Chelonidae) that were large, abundant, and concentrated on feeding shoals and breeding grounds suffered the heaviest exploitation and dietary staples and export commodities. This is evident from de Leon's 1513 visit wherein certain Florida keys were named Las Tortugas

because in the short span of one night they took one hundred seventy turtles from one of these islands, and they could have taken many more if they had wished to do so, and also they took fourteen seals and they killed many pelicans and other birds which totaled five thousand (from Herrera 1935, in Larson 1980:163).

So while the island terrestrial faunas were repeatedly assailed as depauperate, both the mainland and marine faunas produced "vast numbers of birds, including infinite numbers of parrots . . . and the turtles are infinite and huge and excellent to eat" (Cueno 1495, in Gerbi 1975).

Although the Spaniards apparently did not exploit Florida's mainland resources as heavily as they did Haiti's, products such as white-tailed deer skins (*Odocoileus virginiana*) were a major component of the tribute system imposed on the Indians of "La Florida," which until 1690 extended north to Virginia. Throughout much of the eighteenth century, deer hide exports brought greater returns to the major southern ports than all other commodities combined (Wing 1965). Because traffic involved as many as 100,000 skins per major port per year, it is little wonder that the American vernacular for dollars became "bucks" and big skins meant "big bucks." With the technology for meat preservation relying principally on salting, even the preservation of meat in the northern colonies was dependent on Caribbean salt for curing (Craton 1962).

But plant resources gripped both aesthetic and commercial interests even more than did the animal life. Already in 1494 it was observed that the pines (*Pinus* spp.) yielded "very good turpentine with which we cured some of our wounded." Resin from one of the native gum trees was so notable that the genus was scientifically named liquid amber (i.e., *Liquidambar*) and the common name became sweet gum (*Liquidambar styraciflua*). The expansive pinelands were not viewed so much as a forest as a warehouse of vertical mast poles and naval planking; they soon became world renowned as Naval Stores (Tyson 1956), and by 1910 over 50 percent of the world's trade in turpentine and resin was shipped from Florida ports (Chapin 1914). Shiploads of Brasiletto (*Caesalpina vesicaria*) and other shrub and tree species along with cochineal (*Coccus cacti*) were extracted and shipped to Europe for use as dyes.

Faunal Extinction in Perspective

Environmental conditions in Florida and the West Indies have been changing dramatically and persistently since the Pleistocene. Any serious evaluation of the faunal consequences of the 500 years of European settlement must be viewed against this coincident environmental change. Not only has the climate warmed and become more mesic, the sea level has risen approximately 90 m (Cooke 1939; Fernald 1981). These changes have, in turn, caused a series of related environmental shifts. Consequent to the 90-m rise in sea level:

• The land area of the Florida peninsula and the former Greater Antilles land mass (including Bahamas) has been reduced by approximately 50 percent.
• The formerly contiguous islands, such as the Bahamas and Florida Keys and the more closely articulated of the Greater Antilles, have become increasingly distant and isolated, one from another, and from the mainland itself.
• Throughout most of Florida (i.e., the coastal lowlands), the topographic relief has been reduced by nearly 75 percent (i.e., 90 m loss compared to less than 30 m presently). Even considering the highest present elevations, the loss of topo-relief has been nearly 50 percent (i.e., sea level rise of ca. 90 m compared to present high point of ca. 100 m).
• The broad coastal corridor that circumscribed the Gulf of Mexico has been topographically diminished (Fig. 17.2), with its

more open savanna vegetation now substantially altered and obstructed by closed canopy forest (Delcourt et al. 1980; Marshall et al. 1982; Watts and Stuiver 1980). In total, the coastal corridor has been severed. Webb and Wilkins (1984) have identified the gulf coast corridor as Florida's principal faunal exchange route, and thus its closure had the effect of subdividing and isolating numerous pancoastal populations, for example scrub jays (*Aphelocoma coerulescens*), caracaras (*Caracara cheriway*), burrowing owls (*Athena cunicularia*), and fence lizards (*Sceloporus undulatus*).

• Higher sea levels have probably caused a commensurate rise in the water table underlying the coastal plain (Watts and Hansen 1988). This may explain the greatly increased dominance of cypress during the last 5,000 years. Combined changes in climate, colonization by Amerindians, and an increase in incidence of fire are correlated with expansion of pines and their increased dominance of the coastal plain during the last 5,000 years (Delcourt et al. 1980; Watts and Hansen, 1988; Watts and Stuiver 1980). These geographical and ecological changes provide the backdrop for recent changes in faunal communities. The continuing rise in sea level of perhaps 50 cm per century (2.5 m since Columbus) and the continuing loss of species are not independent of the longer-term dynamics.

Webb and associates (Marshall et al. 1982; Webb 1974; Webb and Wilkins 1984; S. D. Webb, personal communication) have analyzed the paleontological record of Florida and have established that approximately 150 species of mammals (nonmarine) have resided in Florida during or since the Pleistocene. Although only 32 of these species (21 percent) remain, recent immigrations bring the present terrestrial mammal fauna to 45 species (see Eisenberg and Harris, chap. 10). Webb and Wilkins (1984) report the ascendance and demise of 113 mammal species from five representative Florida sites and thus provide a database for analysis. When coupled with data for known local extinctions during historical time (among mammals, Monk seal, bison [*Bison bison*], and red wolf [*Canis rufus*]), the total pattern can be reviewed.

Morgan and Woods (1986) have conducted paleontological and historical analyses of the re-

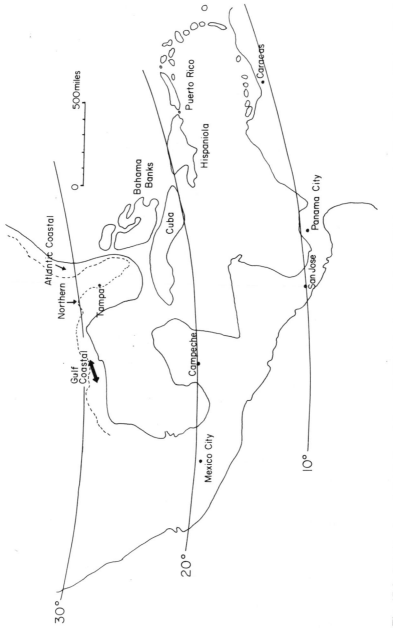

Fig. 17.2. Relative size and distribution of circum-Caribbean land areas during the Pleistocene sea level low. The dotted-line profile of present-day Florida illustrates the magnitude of land area reduction and closure of the wide Gulf-coastal corridor that has accompanied the post-Pleistocene sea level rise.

cent land mammals of the West Indies. Again, their data show that post-Columbian extinctions represent a major component of the total mammalian faunal collapse that has occurred. Post-Pleistocene extinctions are dramatic, but so too are the extinctions during historical time. The extinction process is continuing today.

Although weights of the now extinct species cannot be known precisely, the use of allometric equations based on skeletal measurements allows assignment of each species (both extinct and extant) to one of seven logarithmic weight classes (a < 0.01 kg $< b < 0.1$ kg $< c < 1$ kg $< d < 10$ kg $< e < 100$ kg $< f < 1,000$ kg $< g$). A direct and linear relation between the percent extinction and body size of Pleistocene Florida mammals results (Fig. 17.3). Whereas 100 percent of the very large animals ($>1,000$ kg) have gone extinct, there is no fossil evidence that any of the very small species (<0.01 kg) have gone extinct. Although there is a strong covariance

with body size, very high percentages of the browser-grazer (85 percent) and grazer-browser (79 percent) trophic groups have gone extinct (Eisenberg and Harris, chap. 10). Perhaps this is related to the shift from palatable flowering plant species that dominated the woodland savanna of Pleistocene Florida to the more closed conifer forests (cypress [*Taxodium* spp.] and pine) that have come to dominate during the last 5,000 years.

Numerous Pleistocene mammals of Florida, (for example, armadillo (*Dasypus* spp.), peccaries (Tayassuidae), tapirs (*Tapirus* spp.), and jaguarundi (*Felis jaguarundi*), were of tropical origin and affinity, while others, such as mastodons (*Mammut americanum*), were of temperate origin. A significantly ($p < 0.05$) higher proportion of those of tropical affinity have gone extinct than have those of temperate affinity. Perhaps this derives in part from closure and obstruction of the circum-Caribbean coastal

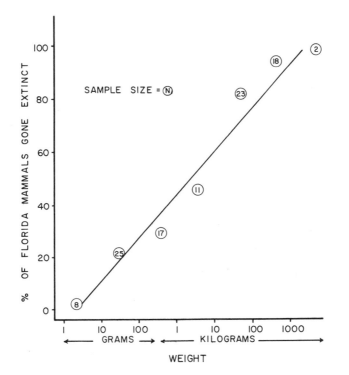

Fig. 17.3. Post-Pleistocene extinction rates for Florida mammal species based on five representative sites reported by Webb and Wilkins (1984). Percent extinctions are calculated for weight classes on the basis of the total number of species (extinct + extant) assigned to each class (*N*).

corridor (Harris 1985; Webb and Wilkins 1984).

As early as 1855 de Condolle observed that "the breakup of a large landmass into smaller units would necessarily lead to the extinction or local extermination of one or more species and the differential preservation of others. . ." (in Browne 1983). This concept has since been referred to as faunal relaxation (Diamond 1972, 1973; Terborgh 1974, 1975). The overall pattern of mammal species loss from Florida and Hispaniola is consistent with predicted faunal relaxation due to the rising sea levels, shrinking land areas, loss of topographic relief, and increasing isolation. Thus, without laboring the circumstances of each of the "recent" extinctions, the overall pattern is consistent with principles of island biogeography (MacArthur and Wilson 1967).

Whereas 92 percent of the recent terrestrial (nonvolant) mammals of Hispaniola (and thus Haiti) have gone extinct, the comparable figure for Florida is only 44 percent (Table 17.1). Thus, even though the percentage loss in Florida's land area is much higher than the land area loss from Hispaniola per se, the physical connection with the mainland has been a definite advantage for survival. This notion is supported by the immigration data, which reveal that Florida's mammalian fauna has been significantly buoyed upward by new colonists, while no new species are known to have naturally colonized Hispaniola (Table 17.1).

A much lower percentage of volant forms has gone extinct from both Florida (17 percent) and Hispaniola (10 percent) than have nonvolant or terrestrial forms (44 and 92 percent, respectively). This suggests that the degree or mode of movement is an important factor in long-term survivorship of mammals. The ultimate dire consequence and the severity of the relaxation phenomenon for mammals can best be portrayed by noting the occurrence of indiginous terrestrial mammal species on the largest of the Greater Artilles. On Cuba, approximately 115 thousand km^2, five terrestrial mammals remain. Hispaniola, about 78 thousand km^2, maintains two species into the 1980s, while Puerto Rico (3400 km^2) no longer supports any native terrestrial mammal species (Morgan and Woods 1986).

CURRENT CONDITIONS AND OPPORTUNITIES

Perhaps more than any other conservationist, John J. Audubon was able to bridge the 1000 km between Florida and Haiti. Having been born in Haiti in 1785, it was Audubon's mid nineteenth-century paintings of Florida's birdlife and the 1905 murder of an Audubon Society Warden in

Table 17.1. Approximate Number of Land Mammal Species Known from the Recent Paleontological and Historical Records of Florida and Hispaniola

	Post-Pleistocene c. 7000 yrs. B.P.	Extinct. (−)	Immigr. (+)	Present (=)
Florida[a]				
N.V.[b]	48	−21(44%)	+4	=31
V.[c]	6	−1(17%)	+9	=14
				45
Hispaniola[d]				
N.V.	25	−23(92%)	+0	= 2
V.	20	−2(10%)	+0	=18
				20
West Indies[c]				
N.V.	76	−67(88%)	+0	= 9
V.	59	−8(14%)	+0	=51
				60

[a]To increase comparability, Florida data are drawn just from the Vero site, which is considered to represent approximately 7,000 years before the present (Webb and Wilkins 1984).
[b]Nonvolant (terrestrial) species.
[c]Volant (airborn) species.
[d]Hispaniolan data are derived from Morgan and Woods (1986).
[e]Data for all of the West Indies, which are provided here as corroborative background, are also derived from Morgan and Woods (1986).

the Everglades that riveted national attention on the trade in egrets and the demise of south Florida's plume bird (Ciconiformes) population (Pearson 1937). What had been a growing, but largely unstructured conservation spirit until that time suddenly became institutionalized and official. The first U.S. National Wildlife Refuge was established in behalf of the pelicans of Florida's east coast (Pelican Island N. W. R.) in 1905, and the first national forest in the eastern United States was established at Ocala, Florida, in 1907 (Ocala N. F.).

During the last eighty years a combination of local, state, federal, and private efforts have combined into a complex structure of organizations and programs involved with conserving Florida's biodiversity resource. At least five state agencies (Game and Fish, Natural Resources, Forestry, Environmental Regulation, and Community Affairs) administer regulatory authority, while at least four federal agencies (Fish and Wildlife, National Parks, Forest Service, and Defense) administer large tracts of public domain land, and at least five nongovernmental organizations (NGOs) retain paid professional staff to work toward wildlife conservation programming. Thus, aggressive proactive planning and land acquisition programs aimed at rare and endangered species habitat now complement the more reactive programs that characterized former times. Combined state and federal land acquisition programs have allocated approximately one billion dollars for the purchase of conservation-oriented land within the state of Florida during the last three decades (Table 17.2).

Public domain land in Florida now consists of about 250 parcels totalling 3.1 million ha. An additional 65 parcels of nongovernmental conservation organization land totaling 40,000 ha are also committed to natural areas management. U.S. Government holdings account for 65 percent of the total area committed to renewable resource conservation. But more important, 100 percent of the very large parcels ($>10^5$ ha) and 65 percent of the parcels greater than 10,000 (10^4) ha in size are federally owned. This means that in the not too distant future, large, wide-ranging species such as the Florida panther (*Felis concolor*) and black bear will be largely restricted to six refugia consisting of federal land. More common and early-successional species will occur throughout the landscape, but special attention will need to be given to the insular subpopulations of terrestrial mammals lest the phenomenon of faunal relaxation continue its inexorable post-Pleistocene trend.

In Haiti, conservation programming is somewhat less aggressive and successful. While many European governments established effective parks and conservation reserve programs in their colonies throughout the world, it seems worthy of note that none resulted from Spanish colonialism in the New World. Nor were any official or notable programs implemented by the French during their rein over *Saint Domingue* (present Haiti), nor did any national program derive from the Haitian government until the mid-twentieth century (C. Woods, personal communication; Westermann 1953). Programs aimed at the conservation of Haitian patrimony date only from 1955. The official designation of National Parks that will meaningfully address biodiversity follows from a decree published in 1983 (Woods and Harris 1986). Two 2,000-ha parks, Morne La Visite and Morne Macaya, were implemented in 1986, and the size of Parc National Pic Macaya has been significantly expanded for enhanced watershed protection.

It is no simple coincidence that the primary rationale for establishment and/or perpetuation of the large conservation reserves in neither Florida nor Haiti has centered on wildlife per se, but rather, has been oriented more toward the commodities of water and wood (Table 17.3). The establishment of Everglades National Park in Florida might seem to contradict this, but from the outset it was the more nebulous "Everglades Ecosystem" and its wilderness values

Table 17.2. Approximate Total Area and Average Parcel Size (000's ha) of Principal Publicly Owned Land in Florida That Can Serve as Biodiversity Islands in an Otherwise Developed Landscape

	N	$\bar{X}$	Total
U.S. Dept. of Agriculture			
Forest Service	3	156.2	495.5
U.S. Dept. of the Interior			
Park Serivce	10	94.5	944.6
Fish and Wildlife Service	24	7.7	185.8
U.S. Dept. of Defense		86.2	258.8
State of Florida			
Game and Fish Comm.	15	27.9	418.2
Division of Forestry	20	7.5	149.2
Dept. of Natural Resources	116	1.7	194.5

Table 17.3. A Comparison of Salient Characteristics of Florida and Haiti as Pertains to the Conservation of Wildlife

	Florida	Haiti
Human population	11×10^6	5×10^6
Percent annual growth rate	4	2
Predominant location	urban	rural
Hard-surface roads (000's km)	150	<1
Percent of forest acreage liquidated	50	99
Publicly owned conservation lands (million ha)	3.1	0.003
Government agency responsible for large reserves	USDA USDI USDOD	USAID
Commodities most responsible for initiation of reserves	water/wood	water/wood

that catalyzed active programing within the National Park Service. Expanded protection to include surrounding lands has been hinged on water management and water conservation, and only indirectly on wildlife.

Equally noteworthy is the fact that in both Florida and Haiti, the conservation of large tracts of land that will serve the needs of large mammals or entire ecosystems has depended on U.S. government agencies (in Haiti it is USAID; see Table 17.3). Thus, one might conclude that state and private conservation programing are critically important in shaping cultural values, regulating wildlife use, and perhaps guiding decisions, but an outside agency or force that is removed from local resistance is generally necessary to institutionalize the effort. All too rarely is the conservation of wildlife and biodiversity demonstrably in the best interest of local inhabitants of an area. Herein lies the key to effective conservation programing in contrasting states such as Haiti and Florida. Haiti now has federal legislation, two significant national parks, and an emerging system of natural and cultural resource conservation sites. Outside support from donor countries and nongovernmental organizations (e.g., UNESCO) may well be able to provide the necessary financial support. But without programs to generate local acceptance and support for what appear to be imperialistic restrictions on land and resource use, we believe the efforts hold little promise of success. In the words of

one authority, "Not only do they already know the ecological advantages of trees, they are less interested in nutrient flows or soil flows than in desperately needed cash flows. . . ." This same advisor goes on to suggest that we should "strive for a linkage between two preexisting anthropological patterns. . . ." (Murray 1987a:324). We agree.

FRAGMENTED LANDSCAPES AND FRAGMENTED EFFORTS

At 4 percent per year, Florida's human population growth rate is one of the fastest in the world. Over 300,000 new residents per year move into the state. And while the present statewide population density is only half that of Haiti's, the two will be equal within two decades (Fig. 17.4). Along with Florida's 12 million permanent residents, about 34 million tourists visit the state annually. Half of these tourists arrive by automobile, and 10 million automobiles are registered in the state; thus there exists a great need for highway expansion. The total mileage of primary and interstate highways has increased at the rate of 7.4 km per day for the last 50 years, i.e., from 26,000 km in 1937 to 53,000 km in 1987 (Fla. Dept. Transport. Statistics). Highways of any kind, and especially high-speed highways, are known to have a serious impact on mobile wildlife species that are impacted directly (e.g., Adams and Geis 1981; Case 1978; Wilkins and Schmidly 1980), and on other species that incur indirect effects such as aversion, toxic poisoning, or habitat fragmentation (Leedy 1975). With respect to mammals, highways may represent a more serious isolating mechanism than even a body of water (Oxley et al. 1974). Thus, the combined effects of rapidly expanding present population centers, establishment of new towns and cities, construction of high-speed and high-density roads, and the development that occurs along these roads is fragmenting Florida's landscape and natural habitats more than any area that we know of. Formerly expansive tracts of forest, range, and wetland habitats are now highly dissected and increasingly isolated by the human-dominated features mentioned. Even though existing parks, reserves, and natural areas in the state now exceed 300, fewer than 10 are greater than 1,000 km² in size. This is well below the mini-

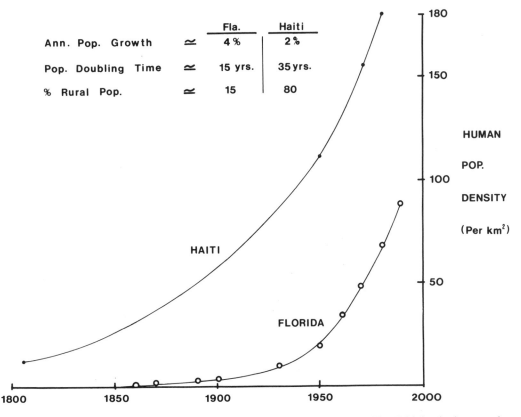

		Fla.	Haiti
Ann. Pop. Growth	$\simeq$	4 %	2 %
Pop. Doubling Time	$\simeq$	15 yrs.	35 yrs.
% Rural Pop.	$\simeq$	15	80

Fig. 17.4. Human population density, growth rate, and related characteristics. The Haiti density is presently twice as great, but Florida's population growth rate is twice as great as that of Haiti and therefore the conditions will change rapidly. The important fact that Florida's population is primarily urban allows a high percentage of land area to be committed to natural resource conservation.

mum size necessary to maintain viable populations of mammals such as black bears (*Ursus americanus*) (Fig. 17.5) unless focused and intensive habitat and population management is practiced.

Seven species of nonhuman land mammals greater than 25 kg in size remained in Florida well into historic time. Of these seven, three (bison, Monk seal, red wolf) have been locally or irrevocably extirpated, two (manatee (*Trichechus manatus*), Florida panther) are listed as endangered, and one (black bear) is listed as threatened. The white-tailed deer remains widespread throughout the state, but the island form of this species (Key deer: *O. v. clavium*) is listed as endangered. It is easy to classify the wolf, panther, seal, and black bear as nominal car-

nivores; the manatee, deer, and bison are clearly herbivores.

Variables other than trophic category better explain the demise and/or threat to long-term survival of these species. Population fragmentation and the amplified mortality that results from wide-ranging movements through a human-dominated landscape or else numerical concentration near specific points of resource concentration (seal and manatee) seem to be critical factors. It is hardly surprising that collisions with motor vehicles constitute the greatest known mortality source for Florida panthers, manatees, Key deer, and black bear throughout most of the state of Florida. Whether species-specific or more generic in nature, successful large-mammal conservation plans will need to

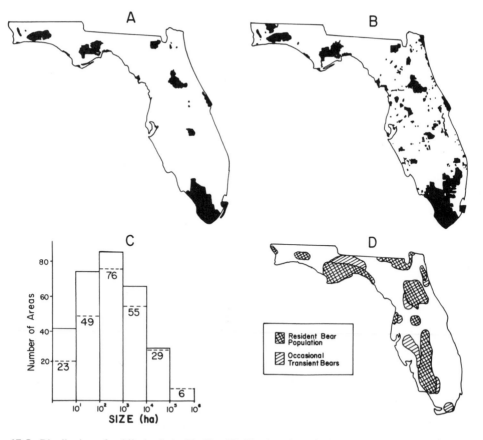

Fig. 17.5. Distribution of public lands in Florida. (A) The location of large federal land holdings; (B) the location of large tracts of both state and federal lands; (C) the distribution of public lands by size class, showing that while the majority of state-owned tracts are less than 1,000 (10^3) ha, very high proportions of the large tracts suitable for mammal conservation are federally owned. Florida panther distribution is presently restricted to the large tract of public land in south Florida, while the black bear distribution (D, modified from Brady and Maehr 1985) is increasingly fragmented and centered on large federal tracts.

aim at reducing the consequences of fragmentation and habitat island effects.

The largest continuous tract of publicly owned land in Florida, about 1 million ha, occurs in the Everglades Region of South Florida. Everglades National Park is complemented by the Big Cypress National Preserve, the Loxahatchee National Wildlife Refuge, expansive water management districts, the Fakahatchee State Preserve, and a newly authorized Florida panther National Wildlife Refuge. In total, more than 60 percent of the land area in the southern six counties of Florida is now in public ownership aimed at resource conservation. But with an average home range of more than

50,000 ha (USFWS 1987), a maximum of twenty of the highly territorial Florida panther males could exist in this area. This is well below the viable population size necessary to maintain genetic integrity.

Thus, the ultimate paradox exists: The human population of Miami Beach approaches the highest density on earth, 5,400/km², while the surrounding region has perhaps the highest proportion of land surface committed to resource conservation of any area on earth. The human inhabitants require more water, the Florida panther is in serious danger of extinction, and the natural ecological functions of Everglades National Park seem seriously compromised

(Kushlan 1987). But we believe there is a solution that will enhance the ecological integrity and security of the park, maintain the Florida panther, yet not detract from the human sector or quality of life. We believe it is roughly the same prescription that is called for in Haiti.

PROPINQUITY: GETTING IT TOGETHER

The Oxford English Dictionary (1971 ed.) defines propinquity as "nearness, closeness or proximity (a) in space, (b) in blood kinship, (c) in nature, disposition, belief, or association, or in time." The term is commended by both its breadth of connotation and the specific denotations, for in our judgment most serious threats to indigenous wildlife in Florida, Haiti, and elsewhere derive from (1) the fragmentation of habitats and isolation of faunal enclaves, (2) alienation of the relevant people from both the use and protection of the wildlife resource, and (3) uncoordinated and frequently competitive activities of the authorized agencies and conservation organizations. Evidence is mounting that the most critically threatened forms of wildlife on earth (i.e., large mammals and birds, intrinsically rare species, or those that must move long distances) can neither be contained nor be maintained solely within parks and reserves that are isolated from their naturally functioning landscapes or the adjacent human populations that must tolerate their presence. The means for natural wildlife movement, dispersal, and genetic interchange must either be provided for in the natural environment, or else continuous and expensive efforts toward relocation and genetic transfer will need to be provided artificially. Even under the best of circumstances, isolated parks and preserves, as we know them today, are not adequate to maintain viable populations of most large mammals. It is also beginning to appear that the acreage committed to conservation may be a less important variable than the configuration of that acreage in the landscape. In our view, at least the following direct and indirect linkages must be greatly enhanced in order to maintain viable wildlife communities to the year 2100.

Linkage (or Closeness) in Space

Local extinction and recolonization now appear to be more important as ecological processes than heretofore recognized. During former times, when natural dispersal and recolonization routes were open, neither the frequency nor the consequences of local extinction were clearly apparent. In landscapes dominated by unplanned human population growth, critical animal dispersal routes are severed. This has the compound effect of amplifying the negative encounters between humans and dispersing animals, amplifying mortality rates beyond sustainable levels, diminishing gene flow, and preventing recolonization of viable habitats.

Physical habitat linkages throughout the landscape can be created by several means. Wildlife dispersal corridors that build on society's more fundamental need for flowing water and wood conservation are an important planning strategy (Harris 1983, 1984; Noss and Harris 1986). Underpasses that allow, and drift fences that facilitate, the movement of organisms around and across human obstructions such as cities and highways are important tactical devices (e.g., Harris 1985; Leedy and Adams 1982). The aggregation, concentration, and elimination of intrusive isolating forces such as railroads, powerlines, water and fuel pipelines, canals, and effluent drainages away from centers of biotic diversity become increasingly important as human populations become more dense.

Implementation of habitat transition zones around parks that can serve as two-way buffers between the human and native wildlife population centers will greatly reduce the negative encounters while facilitating the positive cultural linkages (Harris 1984). The effective size of any given natural area for wildlife can be increased by focused habitat and wildlife management in these multiple-use buffer zones surrounding the biodiversity natural-areas islands (Harris 1983, 1984).

Linkage (or Closeness) with Local Cultural Values

In addition to physical space, plants and animals need protection from overexploitive and/or malicious forms of mortality. Vandalism and related acts, including poaching, arson, the cutting of nest trees, nonchalance about wild fire, and the denial of wildlife access to critical resources such as water, are documented forms of local resistance to wildlife conservation programing that occur in Florida as well as Haiti. Resistance and resentment frequently derive unnecessarily when it is construed that the rights of animals are being elevated higher than those of local human constituencies.

Just as land-use planning and zoning around parks and preserves can increase their effective area, culturally compatible land and wildlife use can effectively lower the viable population threshold of rare species by increasing survivorship and decreasing the probability of local extinction. Wildlife occurrence on, and access to, wide expanses of habitat that occur on private land can be bartered for by managing public-owned lands surrounding the parks so as to provide services badly needed by local residents. Although monetary rebates are frequently employed as the exchange resource, this is only one of many services that managed public lands can provide. In his efforts to develop a successful reforestation scheme in Haiti, Murray (1987b:235) found that "the income-generating tree itself, not an artificial incentive, was the prime engine of peasant enthusiasm." We believe that it will be unproductive to look for a generic reward scheme since the cultural group surrounding each park may well be different. Efforts should be directed at determining the needs, wants, and anxieties of the specific cultural groups surrounding each park or preserve (see Marks 1984).

The south Florida panther recovery effort may well depend on the degree to which the private landowners perceive success in saving the panther as a direct threat to their own future interests. The Seminole Indian tribe no doubt has quite different expectations and concerns about saving panthers than do the large incorporated and/or private ranchers in the area. Yet, grazing, hunting, and several other low-intensity resource uses within the Big Cypress National Preserve and related buffer areas, as well as assurance against undue land-use restrictions on their own private lands surrounding the preserves, are common desires. Covenants that ensure resource use within the public-owned but managed buffer areas and continued land use on the private-owned contiguous acreage around the preserves appear to be a necessary social linkage to increase both quantity and quality of panther habitat, and ultimately save the panther. We believe that demonstrated compatibility between panther conservation and other land and resource uses in south Florida is also necessary before there will be widespread support for reestablishment of a free-ranging subpopulation in north Florida.

One way that local support for conservation can be accomplished is by creating participatory management (e.g., Amboseli Park in Kenya; Western 1976). Despite its many advantages, this approach has some disadvantages, and generally has not succeeded in achieving national goals. A second approach assumes that the authority for management lies with a central government, but that the activity of management hinges on a local participatory structure. Not only does this approach link the local employment and economic well-being to the success of conservation, it provides a mechanism for translating national and international goals into local action. A scenario for how this model could be applied to the Haitian parks follows. Unemployment and cash flow are chronic problems, especially in rural Haiti. International and national support funds should be used initially to employ rural Haitians in the implementation and management of the parks. Five days' salary could be paid for four days' work, such that the individual Haitian would receive a salary for his or her four days work while the fifth-day salary would go to a local governing council. Thus, incentive and participation are created at two local levels. The national authority gets the benefit of the local labor supply from individuals while in effect purchasing security and involvement from the local governing council. The local authority (council or cooperative) gains monetarily, but only in proportion to the labor of individuals. This could create both incentives and rewards for efficient and skillful management at the level of the local council. Finally, individual landowners or tenants surrounding the parks may be rewarded for damages that accrue from, and/or their positive activities directed at, effective conservation in and around the park. Such a model creates the mechanism for participation at all levels, ranging from the individual landowner or tenant to the national and international support agency. Surrounding agrarian land tenants would, of necessity, be allowed land use and sustenance use of resources such as grazing, fuel, wood, and water that derive from a managed land buffer surrounding the parks.

Linkage (or Closeness) Among Agencies and Approaches

As we review the record, we see that nowhere has a single approach worked successfully to conserve biodiversity. Moreover, we suspect that even the combinations of approaches that have been used to date will not suffice for long in the future. In our experience, there are few examples of prolonged or consistent interagency cooperation resulting in two or more of the different approaches (e.g., parks and forest management or hunting) being successfully employed. We believe the time for leadership that transcends the authority of individual agencies has come, and that nothing short of greatly enhanced interagency (complementary approaches) efforts will suffice in the future. Because it is difficult (if not impossible due to statute) to establish institutional authority above the level of national departments or ministries, we suggest that nongovernmental mechanisms may be necessary. Murray (1987a) believes that leadership by a nongovernmental organization (NGO) is necessary in order to establish a successful agroforestry scheme in Haiti.

Numerous ''think tank'' institutes and centers with resource management and conservation agendas exist, but to date, none seems to have directed full attention to developing strategies for biodiversity conservation. We believe a new generation of multiagency cooperative regional centers is called for.

One efficient and expedient means of integrating philosophies and activities among agencies and potentially competitive interests lies in the regional landscape. Regional plans that are aimed at Biosphere Reserves (e.g., Gregg and McGean 1985; Wood 1984), Multiple Use Modules (Harris 1983, 1984), or a similar strategy and are undergirded by landscape ecology principles (e.g., Forman and Godron 1986) are recommended. Many examples of clusters of parks, forests, refuges, and natural areas could be cited as focal points for beginning the process.

Perhaps the single greatest advantage of choosing regional clusters of parks and reserves as rallying points is that all three types of linkages (physical, cultural, institutional) can be implemented simultaneously.

The approach can be applied equally well in the affluent south Florida environment around Everglades National Park or in the poor rural hinterlands of Haiti. We believe it is the single best way to achieve propinquity and that, in turn, will be the most effective conservation strategy to the year 2100. This management can be directed to favor certain species by enhancing the habitat or prey base for predators, while being directed against other species such as exotics.

18

Conservation in Cultural Landscapes

BRYN H. GREEN

THE EVOLUTION OF THE LANDSCAPE

Very little representation of natural ecosystems remains in much of northwestern Europe. In Britain, one of the most densely populated and intensively exploited European countries, nearly 10% of the land is urban, 10% forest, and 80% farmland (Fig. 18.1). Most of the forest is planted, but a large part of the farmland is rough grazings, mainly of unsown, seminatural ecosystems. This landscape is essentially the product of three major periods of agricultural change. All have led to substantial habitat and species loss, but have also created new, seminatural ecosystems, some of them rich in species. Despite, therefore, having suffered nearly all the adverse environmental impacts currently causing concern in many parts of the world, much of the British landscape is still remarkably rich in wildlife.

The widespread clearance of the native, broad-leaved deciduous forest climax vegetation of the lowlands began with the colonization of Neolithic peoples and their farming technology around 3000 B.C. Recent advances in aerial survey and archaeological interpretation make it clear that in Britain early clearances were much more extensive than previously supposed. The Romans certainly found a predominantly open, settled, and farmed landscape, which they reclaimed further, especially by drainage of the extensive wetlands which still remained in the river valleys and estuaries. By Norman times, most of the forest had gone; from William the Conqueror's Domesday Sur-

vey of 1086, it is estimated that perhaps only 15% of the land was left under trees (Rackham 1980). The great mammals of the postglacial forests went with the trees. The wild ox, or aurochs (*Bos taurus*), ancestor of domestic cattle, and possibly the European bison, or wisent (*Bison bonasus*), were probably lost in the Bronze Age; brown bears (*Ursus arctos*) and beavers (*Castor fiber*) may have survived almost until the Normans. In continental Europe, the forests and their animals survived longer. The last aurochs died in the Jaktorowska Forest in Poland in 1627 (Szafer 1968); wisent narrowly escaped extinction and, like bears and beavers, still precariously survive today.

Despite these losses, the Medieval rural economy arguably generated ecosystems in many respects richer in wildlife populations than the forest they replaced. Croplands were limited in extent, and domestic stock maintained vast open expanses of heath, moor, and grassland which were naturally colonized by plants and animals of open habitats forming tundra, steppe-, or prairielike plagoclimax ecosystems. Poor livestock husbandry and ineffective means of predator control meant these ecosystems maintained very large predator populations (Ruiz and Ruiz 1986). Some indication of their numbers can be gotten from churchwardens' and later gamekeepers' records (Pearsall 1950), or from a visit to Scotland or Spain, where large numbers of stock are still maintained in more remote and mountainous areas. In lowland Britain, such ecosystems persisted until the seventeenth and eighteenth centuries, when agricultural innovations, particularly effective drainage and the use

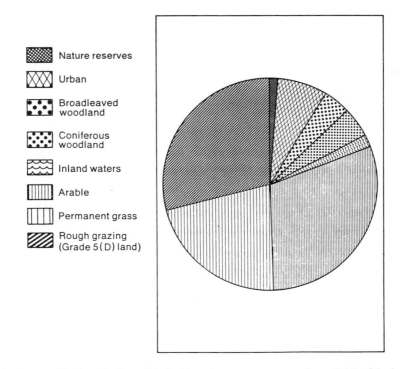

Nature reserves

Urban

Broadleaved woodland

Coniferous woodland

Inland waters

Arable

Permanent grass

Rough grazing (Grade 5(D) land)

Fig. 18.1. Pattern of land use in Great Britain. Note that nature reserves take up 0.8% of the land surface.

of crop rotations, enabled much of the rough grazing land to be enclosed, agriculturally improved, and brought into more intensive production. In 1696, an early land-use survey showed that uncultivated rough grazings covered more than a quarter of the land surface of England and Wales; by 1901, their extent had been more than halved (Best 1981). Coupled with the advent of more effective firearms, great losses of plants and animals ensued. Storks (*Ciconia ciconia*), cranes (*Megalornis grus*), great bustards (*Otis tarda*), ospreys (*Pandion haliaetus*), sea eagles (*Haliaeetus albicilla*), wild boar (*Sus scrofa*), and wolves (*Canis lupus*) became extinct and many other species almost so. Even common species such as the buzzard (*Buteo buteo*) greatly declined (Fig. 18.2).

It was these losses of species and habitat that led to the beginnings of the British conservation movement toward the end of the last century. The Commons, Open Spaces and Footpaths Preservation Society was founded in 1865, the

Royal Society for the Protection of Birds in 1889, and the National Trust in 1895.

At around this time, however, home agriculture went into recession, cheap food being imported from overseas. A pleasant, patchwork mosaic countryside of unintensively managed small farms, hedged fields, pastures, meadows, heaths, and woods abounding in populations of common plants and animals and rich in recreational opportunity resulted. It is this type of countryside which is regarded as typically English and which many people now look back to so longingly. The wartime drive for self-sufficiency and postwar agricultural improvements and an increasingly state-supported drive for greater production led to the rapid conversion of much of it into larger-scale landscapes dominated by arable cultivation. It has been estimated that in Britain between 1949 and 1984, 80% of the remaining limestone grasslands, 50% of lowland mires, 30% to 50% of ancient woodlands, 40% of lowland heaths, and 30% of upland moors were lost or significantly

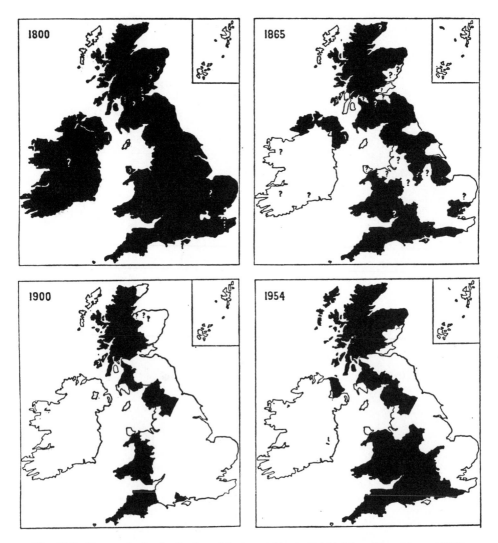

Fig. 18.2. Changes in the distribution of the buzzard in the British Isles. (From Moore 1987.)

damaged (Ratcliffe 1984; Fig. 18.3). In England and Wales, the overall loss in seminatural vegetation between 1947 and 1980 has been 25% (Countryside Commission 1986). With this loss and fragmentation of habitat, ten species of flowering plant, three or four species of dragonfly, and one species of butterfly have become extinct. Many other species, including 149 plants, 13 butterflies, 11 dragonflies, four reptiles and amphibians, 36 breeding birds, and several mammals, especially bats and the otter, have seriously declining, or endangered populations.

These losses of habitats and species have been largely responsible for a resurgence of the conservation movement, reflected in the burgeoning membership of voluntary conservation organizations (Fig. 18.4).

Now we again seem to be on the threshold of an agricultural recession caused by overproduction. It is estimated that some 10% of agricultural land in the European Economic Community countries is presently surplus to food production requirements (EEC 1985), and in the United Kingdom it has been forecast that by the turn of the century, conceivably as much as one-

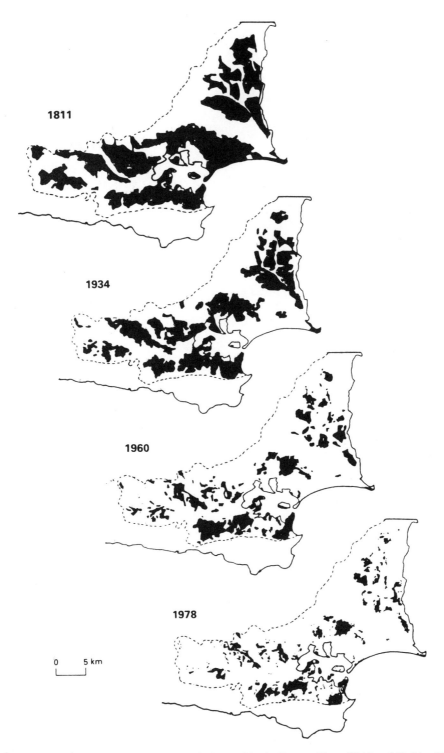

Fig. 18.3. Loss and fragmentation of heathland in the pool basin, Dorset. (From Webb and Haskins 1980.)

Membership of countryside recreation organisations (mainly from Countryside Commission 1978).

	1950	1960	1965	1970	1972	1975	1977	1984
County Nature Conservation Trusts	800	3 006	20 960	57 000	74 815	106 759	115 328	155 000
Royal Society for the Protection of Birds	6 827*	10 579		65 577	128 528	204 997	244 841	380 000
National Trust	23 403	97 109	157 581	226 200		539 285	613 128	>1m
Ramblers' Association	8 778	11 300	13 771	22 178	25 818	31 953	29 541	44 000
National Federation of Anglers			394 653	354 901			446 136	
Royal Yachting Association	1 387	10 543	21 598	31 089		36 368	52 140	
British Field Sports Society	27 269	20 250	18 401	20 965		43 000	55 000	
Wildfowlers' Association of Great Britain and Ireland				21 255		30 815	34 412	
British Horse Society	4 000	6 000	10 000	17 000			25 500	
Pony Club	20 000	30 000	29 000	33 300		45 500	49 500	

*1955.

Fig. 18.4. Membership of countryside recreation organizations, 1950–2000.

third of agricultural land may no longer be needed (Edwards 1986). By 2100, it may well be that the growth in the world's population will have forced us into finding ways by which this overcapacity in the agricultural industries of the developed world can be used to help feed all the world's peoples. For the foreseeable future, however, it seems that apart from emergency food aid, economics and the need for security of supplies dictate that most staple foodstuffs will be largely produced where they are consumed.

STRATEGIES TO CONTROL FOOD SURPLUSES

There are two main ways by which supply of foodstuffs can be brought more into line with demand. Either farms and farmers can be taken out of production, or, alternatively, all farmers could be encouraged to produce less efficiently than technology permits. The future of conservation in man-made landscapes in Europe depends crucially on which of these strategies, or what mix of them, is pursued under the Common Agricultural Policy.

Economists tend to favor the "efficient" strategy of concentrating farming in the hands of low-cost producers (Marsh 1986), but almost everyone else, including most conservationists, favor the other approach. Generally, this is because of the perceived virtues of the small family farm, including hard work, self-reliance, and financial prudence; and because their large numbers make small farmers a major political force in many European countries. Specifically, to conservationists, small farms seem to offer the opportunity of a return to the pleasant prewar countryside, with more wholesome food being produced in a more sustainable way, in particular with much less use of polluting agrochemicals (Lowe et al. 1986). There is undoubtedly room for moves in this direction, but ecological principles seem to dictate that the best prospect of a countryside rich in wildlife is to adopt the alternative, more polarized strategy whereby efficient production is concentrated on the better-quality agricultural land and the remainder retired, either partially or completely, from agricultural production.

THE ECOLOGY OF PRODUCTION AND DIVERSITY

Retiring farmlands is a better strategy for conservation because high-production, herbaceous ecosystems are almost invariably poor in species. Under fertile conditions a few, vigorous, wide-tolerance range plant species can usually competitively exclude most others (Fig. 18.5). Since many animals, particularly invertebrates, are dependent on particular plants, animal diversity also declines. Extremely infertile sites are also poor in species, and maximum diversity seems to be attained, therefore, in intermediate conditions of fertility (Grime 1979). Croplands are analogs of early seral communities such as reedswamps, dominated by opportunist and competitive species. Crop plants are likewise mainly those that can respond to the increased fertility which the farmer supplies—they have been called ''dung-heap superweeds''—reflecting the probable origins of some of them. Relatively few of these species are able to respond and dominate in fertile, mesic conditions. Thus eutrophicated ecosystems and even large geographical areas often contain a few such species with large populations and many other species with small populations. It has been estimated, for example, that 30 species of the British avifauna of 426 species account for 75% of the total bird population (Fisher 1951). Common species are rare, and rare species are common!

This was a noticeable feature of a recent comprehensive analysis of the flora of the man-made landscape of the Sheffield region (Hodgson 1986). Common species were wide-ranging (Fig. 18.6) and associated with habitats of high fertility, which were often also highly disturbed

and of recent origin (Fig. 18.7). These common species were better represented in the more evolutionarily advanced families of flowering plants (Fig. 18.8). Perhaps this is because environments where there are abundant free, inorganic supplies of the major nutrients (nitrogen, phosphorus, and potassium), in their forms needed for plant growth, were rather scarce in nature until human intervention. They naturally occur mainly in sites flushed with the products of erosive processes, for example in river valleys, in animal dunging areas, and where unavailable nutrients are released through fire or other disturbance (Tilman 1986).

It is no coincidence that agriculture evolved in such river valleys and, until the invention of crop rotations and synthetic fertilizer, was only enabled to move away from them by exploiting animal dung or by fire. In doing so, it has greatly extended fertile environments and favored the adaptable species best able to exploit them. Rare, narrow-tolerance-range species adapted to more specific environmental conditions have, in contrast, suffered. Fertilizer added to species-rich pastures, for example, leads rapidly to species loss. A traditional English pasture might contain as many as forty species of flowering plant and twenty species of butterfly; an agriculturally improved pasture ideally contains only one plant species—the crop—and no associated butterflies at all (Moore 1977). But it is much more productive. Fertilizer use in Britain since World War II has increased two- to sevenfold on arable land and up to fortyfold on grass (Fig. 18.9). The objectives of the farmer and the conservationist are thus fundamentally, diametrically, and irreconcilably opposed. The farmer wants high production and therefore low-diversity ecosystems, preferably monocultures; the conservationist usually wants diversity, and therefore low-production ecosystems, which are often infertile or stressed in some other way.

This makes the integration of wildlife conservation into the management of farmed landscapes extremely difficult. Environmental damage and loss of species is intrinsic, not incidental, to the maintenance of heavily productive ecosystems. If the maximizing of production is a major objective, then species loss is inevitable, however sustainable the means of exploitation might be in terms of maintaining other environmental resources such as soil or water. The

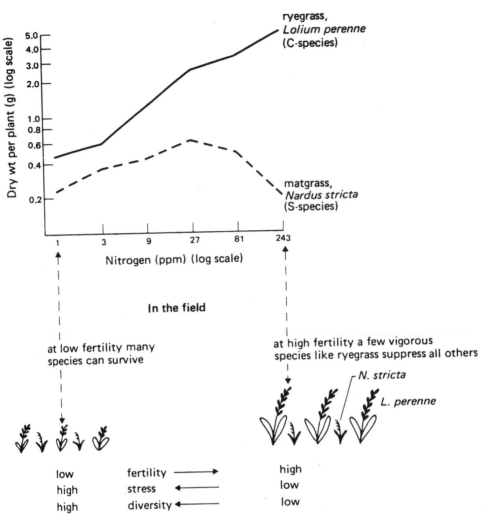

Fig. 18.5. Competition and diversity: variation in yield of grass species in sand culture with different levels of nitrate nitrogen. (From Green 1985.)

British countryside rich in wildlife and scenic beauty of cherished memory was the product of half a century of neglect by a depressed agriculture and before that by old kinds of farming very different from modern agriculture. Mixed arable and livestock systems with traditional rotations made such farming sustainable, but only at very low levels of production. Before the advent of synthetic fertilizers, the great imperative in agriculture was the severe limitation of cultivation by infertility. Enrichment of farmland by flooding alluvial areas and manuring it with dung was pivotal to the old rural economy. Vast areas of downland and heathland outfields or "waste" were needed as the fertilizer factories for the limited productive infields. Folded stock was the mechanism by which the nutrients were transferred as dung. They grazed the outfields by day and dunged on the arable at night. It is estimated that the ratio of outfield rough

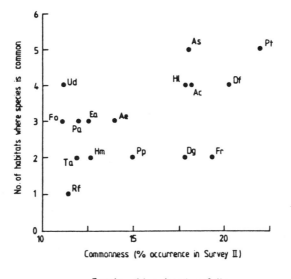

Species abbreviated as follows:

Ac	*Agrostis capillaris*	Hl	*Holcus lanatus*
Ae	*Arrhenatherum elatius*	Hm	*Holcus mollis*
As	*Agrostis stolonifera*	Pa	*Poa annua*
Df	*Deschampsia flexuosa*	Pp	*Poa pratensis*
Dg	*Dactylis glomerata*	Pt	*Poa trivialis*
Ea	*Epilobium angustifolium*	Rf	*Rubus fruticosus* agg.
Fo	*Festuca ovina*	Ta	*Taraxacum* agg.
Fr	*Festuca rubra*	Ud	*Urtica dioica*

Fig. 18.6. An estimate of ecological amplitude for the most commonly recorded species in the Sheffield region. (From Hodgson 1986.)

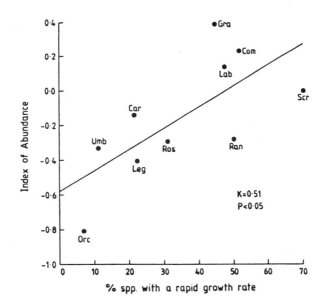

Fig. 18.7. The relationship for the major families of the Sheffield region between IA and the proportion of polycarpic perennials with a rapid growth rate. (From Hodgson 1986.)

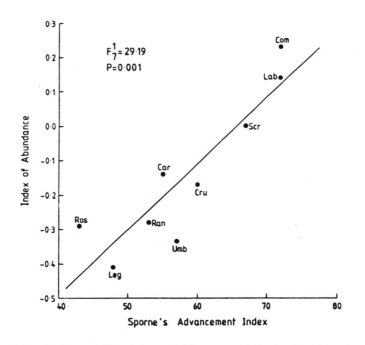

Fig. 18.8. The relationship between IA and Sporne's Advancement Index for the polycarpic perennials in the major dicotyledonous families of the Sheffield region.

INORGANIC FERTILISERS: UK CONSUMPTION

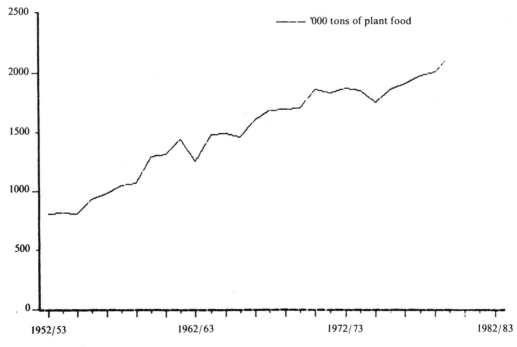

Fig. 18.9. Inorganic fertilizers: UK consumption. (From Capstick 1986.)

grazing to infield cultivated land needed to be of the order 3–11:1 (Gimingham and De Smidt 1983). The outfields were literally laid waste by this process of plundering their fertility, and the whole system depended on their slow recovery by the processes of nutrient accumulation which accompany natural succession (Green 1972). The fertility of woodlands was also run down by grazing and the cropping of timber and underwood (Rackham 1980).

The species richness of these outfield ecosystems was a direct result of this impoverishing degradation and resultant infertility. Today, whether hedgerow, roadside verge, farm pond or copse, or extensive heath or down, they are more likely to be subject to the very opposite process of nutrient enrichment from fertilizer drift and runoff, enclosed grazing, or natural succession.

The small size of natural and seminatural habitats in cultivated landscapes makes them particularly vulnerable to such edge effects, and since they are often effectively habitat islands in what is essentially a biological desert of agricultural land, they are subject to the rules of island biogeography. A study of English woods in agricultural landscapes has, for example, shown that in order to find all 50 or so lowland woodland birds at reasonable levels of probability, the wood must be greater than 100 ha in size. Most farmland woods, indeed many nature reserves, are much smaller than this (Moore and Hooper 1975).

HABITAT MANAGEMENT

Their low production and isolation combine to make it very difficult to maintain habitats such as down, heath, marsh and coppiced woodland, which were the products of a rural economy now in decline. Left ungrazed, or uncut, they are subject to the processes of natural succession and change to secondary woodland with the loss of their characteristic species (Fig. 18.10). Since secondary woodland is generally not as uncommon, conservation objectives usually focus on maintaining the more open ecosystems (Green and Townsend 1986). The intensity of disturbance, indeed degradation, by cutting, grazing, or burning needed to maintain their vital infertility and provide suitable niches for species requiring open conditions is poorly appreci-

ated by many conservationists schooled in the equation between environmental protection and sustainable, productive resource use. Many such areas, even nature reserves, have thus, through a process of benign neglect, been allowed to lose many of their characteristic species and change to commoner scrub or woodland ecosystems.

Species richness is probably maximized at intermediate disturbance frequencies, and community composition depends on the scale, pattern, and phasing of perturbation in relation to the autecology of individual species (Sousa 1984). The relatively long-cycle, small-patch disturbance of traditional land uses such as coppicing and rotational grazing simulated natural perturbations, such as lightning fires, erosion, and windthrow, creating richer ecosystems than the either completely unexploited or the overexploited ecosystems all too typical, respectively, of nature reserves and modern farming or forestry (Green 1986).

A RURAL LAND-USE STRATEGY

Genuine multipurpose use of the countryside, with productive agriculture incidentally creating and maintaining land rich in wildlife and recreational opportunity, as it did in the past, may thus no longer be possible. But land zonation is still possible between productive and protective uses, long ago recognized as inevitable by Odum (1969), at different scales, including the small-field scale which many people regard as multipurpose use. Rural land-use strategies are required which make proper provision for the protection and management of amenity areas, integrated with compatible land uses, including appropriate kinds of agricultural production.

In Britain it has been suggested (Green 1981; O'Riordan 1983) that the present multiplicity of protective land designations might be replaced by the following tiered system of rural land zoning:

1. Heritage, reserve, or sanctuary areas where wildlife and landscape protection, in places with some access for people to enjoy these things, would be the exclusive land-use objectives.

2. Cultural landscapes where conservation

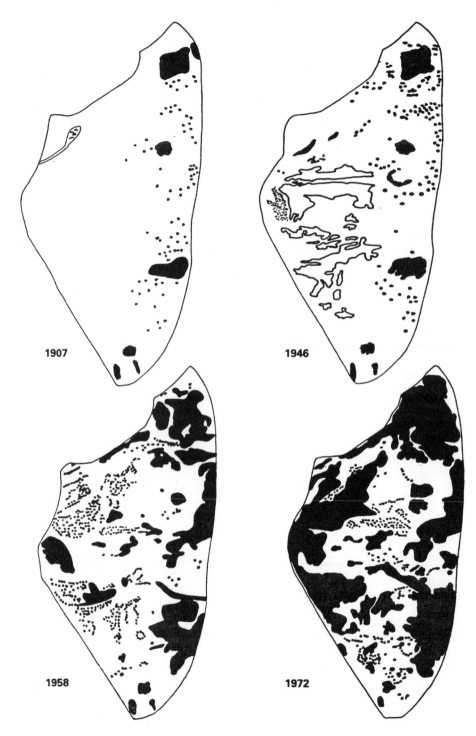

Fig. 18.10. Tree colonization at Hothfield, Kent. Drawn from Ordnance Survey 1: 2500 maps and aerial photographs. (From Green and Townsend 1985.)

objectives would be primary, but traditional and other environmentally benign kinds of farming, or other land uses, would continue; to help maintain conservation values, generate products of value to the economy, and help sustain rural livelihoods.
3. Productive lands where food production would be the primary objective, but where wildlife and landscape conservation access would be important secondary objectives.

Although there is no formal commitment to such a system of land designation in Britain, land planning and management is beginning to fit into this pattern. But many challenges remain if such a strategy is to be successfully implemented.

In heritage areas, which, it is estimated, ought to cover some 10% of the land (Ratcliffe 1984), the main difficulties are going to stem from their relatively small size and isolation. To protect their natural habitats and species populations, every effort will have to be made to buffer them from productive landscapes by means of intervening cultural landscape areas (Fig. 18.11). Even so, species loss will probably be inevitable. Although some species may recolonize naturally, as has been the case with the osprey in Britain, the populations of more specialist species will probably have to be maintained by restocking and reintroduction. This has recently been successfully achieved with the sea eagle on the Isle of Rhum National Nature Reserve in the Scottish Hebrides (Love 1983). It has been proposed that this is a perfect location for the reestablishment of all the large species lost to Britain, including bear, beaver, wild boar, and wolf (Nevard and Penfold 1978). Such replacement of species to reconstitute more complete ecosystems would be an exciting scientific experiment that could reveal much about their dynamics of great potential application to their management and exploitation. Such complete ecosystems, with their full complement of spectacular large mammals and birds, would also be a considerable amenity attraction, briding a gap between present protected areas (and their rather invisible fauna of small animals in their native ecosystems) and the popular, if incongruous, assemblages of large, alien animals in safari parks and zoos. Many small habitat creation and introduction programs of species such as attractive flowering plants, butterflies, and reptiles and amphibians are already underway. In recognition of this, the Nature Conservancy Council has produced a set of introduction policy guidelines (Green 1979).

In productive lands opportunities for integrating conservation objectives are rapidly expanding as the need to maximize production declines. Achieving such integration will be important, since food production will remain the major land use, even though needing in the future to occupy less, perhaps 50%, of the total land area. Trees and copses can be established in uncultivated corners to replace hedges lost in field amalgamation; irrigation reservoirs and drainage sump ponds can help substitute for lost wet areas. Unsprayed field margins have been demonstrated by Game Conservancy research to benefit not only the partridges favored by the farmer for his shoot, but many other species as well. The Countryside Commission has established demonstration farms to help promote such agroconservation, and it increasingly forms an important element of extension advice to farmers from the Ministry of Agriculture. An independent, privately financed Farming and Wildlife Trust has been established by farming and conservation organizations exclusively to provide such advice through a growing team of county advisers. Much has been, and remains to be, achieved by this approach, but it can never ensure the maintenance of the large tracts of heath, moor, down, and marsh which traditional farming once sustained. This must be the role of specific measures in cultural landscape areas.

Such cultural landscape areas represent the biggest departure from established land-use planning and management in Britain. If current predictions are fulfilled, they could eventually cover some 20% of the land. In a countryside with so many demands on it, multipurpose use must inevitably remain the cornerstone of land-use strategy. But before any piece of land is allocated to more than one use, the compatibility between these uses must be clearly established (Fig. 18.12). Many extensive land uses, such as military training grounds, reservoirs, mineral workings, and golf courses, can be surprisingly compatible with wildlife conservation. Flooded gravel pits have been a key factor in the recovery of the great crested grebe (*Podiceps cristatus*) and spread of the little ringed plover (*Charadrius dubius*) in Britain (Fig.

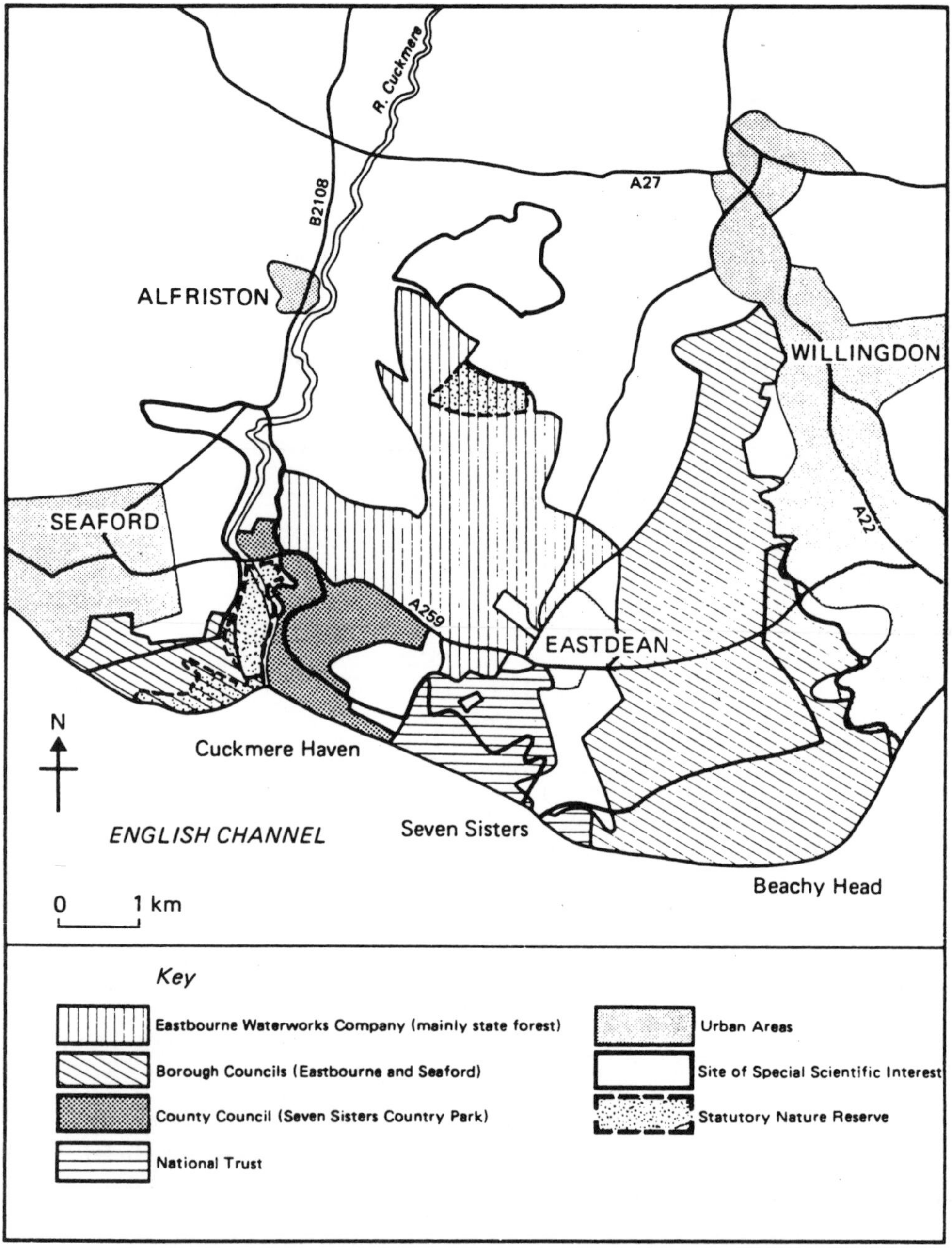
R. Cuckmere
B2108
A27
ALFRISTON
WILLINGDON
SEAFORD
A22
A259
EASTDEAN
N
Cuckmere Haven
ENGLISH CHANNEL
Seven Sisters
Beachy Head
0 1 km
Key
Eastbourne Waterworks Company (mainly state forest)
Borough Councils (Eastbourne and Seaford)
County Council (Seven Sisters Country Park)
National Trust
Urban Areas
Site of Special Scientific Interest
Statutory Nature Reserve

Fig. 18.11. The Sussex Heritage Coast. Public land ownership. (From Green 1975.)

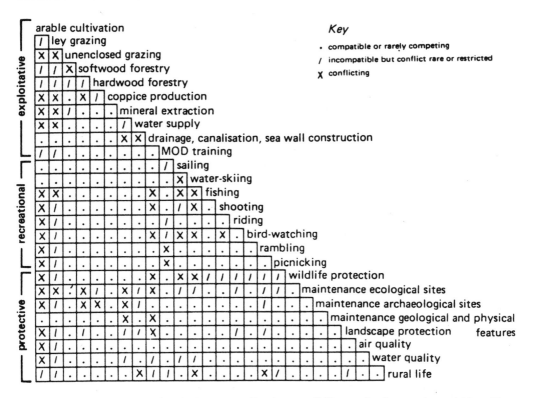

Fig. 18.12. Multipurpose land use in the countryside. A compatibility matrix of competing activities. (From Green 1977.)

18.13). A recent survey of golf courses in one English county showed their rough and semi-rough terrain to contain important representation of some seminatural ecosystems and the best population of a nationally rare species of a ground orchid, *Himantoglossum hircinum* (Green and Marshall, in press).

While modern intensive farm practices are not so readily compatible with conservation of wildlife and landscape, surviving traditional forms of husbandry still are. Means are thus now being actively developed to compensate farmers who are prepared to forgo maximizing the profitability of their enterprises in order to protect seminatural ecosystems such as heath, moor, down meadows, and marsh. This usually means them retaining, or returning to, relatively unprofitable traditional husbandry systems rather than converting to, or staying in, more intensive grass or arable crop production. Similar compensation through management agreements has long been available for farmers prevented from undertaking such activities in Sites of Special Scientific Interest and National Parks. The important differences in the new proposals are that the agreements will be optional, not compulsory, and that the money will come, not from conservation, but from agricultural support funds. Legislation to promote these new "environmentally sensitive areas" where the scheme will operate is now part of the Common Agricultural Policy of the EEC and promises to be a seminal new instrument for promoting both agricultural and environmental policy. Habitats requiring some low-intensity farm management will be maintained and some of the overproduction of surplus foodstuffs checked. The switching of agricultural funds from production to environmental protection will help sustain farm livelihoods in areas where this is vital to local economies.

But some abandonment of farms and continued outmigration from remote rural areas seems inevitable. Other mechanisms of "set-

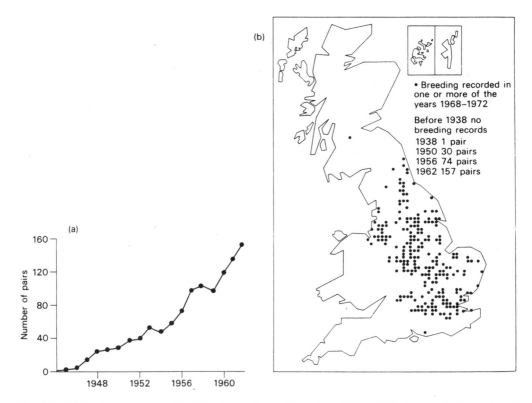

Fig. 18.13. The changing range of the little ringed plover, *Charadrius dubius*. a) The increase in the number of pairs summering in Britain. (After Murton 1971.) b) The increase in the range related to habitat change, especially as a result of the increasing number of gravel pits. (After Moore 1977.)

ting aside" land from agricultural production will offer further opportunities for greatly extending natural areas, perhaps even to wilderness through complete abandonment of other uses. We may again see the white arable of the chalk hills reverting to greensward, pasture to woodland, and drainage systems being allowed to decline and the land flood back to fen and marsh. Determining where this might most appropriately take place in order to maximize ecological potential and maintain the capacity of productive areas is a problem already being addressed by ecologists and economists (Fig. 18.14). Reducing soil fertility residual from agriculture (Marrs 1985) and controlling the steadily increasing levels in precipitation derived from industrial and car exhausts will be a vital prerequisite to the reestablishment of such ecosystems and to the maintenance of the integrity of low-fertility ecosystems free from invasion of strongly competitive, nutrient-demanding spe-

cies. Bracken (*Pteridium aquilinum*) is such a species which is already spreading rapidly in European heaths and moors. Rodhe and Rood (1986) suggest that nitrate in precipitation doubled in Europe between the late 1950s and early 1970s, having already doubled since the 1850s. Together with the growing use of fertilizers, this widespread eutrophication of the environment is likely to be the major threat to species and ecosystem protection in cultural landscapes in the future.

CONCLUSIONS

The great challenge to conservationists in the next century in cultural landscapes is going to be to define precisely what their objectives are and how they may be achieved. Farmers used to very professional advice from agricultural advisers are already beginning to demand it of

KEY

1 : , 2 : , 3 : , 4 : , >4 :

Fig. 18.14. Evaluation scheme for environmental factors favoring selection as a "set-aside target area."

conservationists. They, however, are still mainly and rightly preoccupied with more negative, reactive approaches to defending pristine ecosystems and will have to adjust to the transformation of conservation from a vague maxim guiding other land uses to a positive land use in its own right. Furthermore, they must accept that its objectives and practice may often be far removed, sometimes diametrically opposed, to those of more productive farming and forestry; or even, indeed, to broader concepts of conservation as sustainable resource use where high-production, low-diversity ecosystems are the overwhelming objective of maximum-sustained-yield resources management.

The need for persuasive arguments to promote environmental protection, together with the realization that only relatively small, and perhaps inadequate, areas are ever likely to be specifically managed primarily for conservation, has led its proponents to embrace the concept of sustainable resource exploitation into a modern, integrated conservation ideology. Thus, the World Conservation Strategy (IUCN/ UNEP 1980) is based on the ideas that (1) conservation and development are interdependent, and (2) adverse environmental impacts are incidental rather than intrinsic to resource exploitation and can, therefore, be avoided, or reme-

died, by appropriate levels of exploitation and measures such as environmental impact analysis. This policy is clearly the one most likely to succeed in protecting the environment in a world in which continued massive resource exploitation is inevitable. In its promulgation, however, two important ecological considerations must not be overlooked. First, ecosystems that can bear continuous heavy exploitation of utilizable material, without artificial inputs, are rather scarce in nature and commonly poor in species. Second, many ecosystems considered desirable on conservation grounds are extremely unproductive and naturally disturbed. Prescribed disturbance and degradation of ecosystems is vital to the survival of many species. The objective of the conservation land manager will often be to make one blade of grass grow where two grew before!

19

The Prospects for Sustaining Species and Their Evolution

WILLIAM G. CONWAY

In biological conservation, ex situ care and biotechnology are crisis responses to the threat of extinction. Their principal values in species preservation rest in a potential to make up for lost biological and ecological functioning, hence to enhance species and populational carrying capacity. They are also valuable tools for ecological education and essential to any hope of nature restoration following catastrophic change. Their potentials for preserving or reinstating basic ecological services are largely unexplored.

Ex situ care is the management of populations of wild plants or animals away from their natural distribution. Its techniques include capture, translocation, propagation, storage, replacement, and some kinds of ecological support. Biotechnology in the context of biological conservation, seeks to modify or utilize some aspect of the biology of a taxon, community, or habitat, using the paraphernalia of modern animal husbandry, ethology, ecology, genetics, and reproductive physiology on behalf of its preservation. In these terms, "evolutionary potential" represents the maintenance of some proportion of original genetic variability and thereby some option to express it, whether or not guided by humans.

In what follows, key assumptions are that the next 100 years will be a time of unprecedented anthropogenic change; that virtally no large terrestrial wild animal will persist long into the future unless looked after in some way by hu-

mans. Challenges to survival are expected to range from global warming to extremely severe habitat fragmentation, contraction, and chemical disruption. The value of ex situ care will depend on its ability to increase populational and species-carrying capacities in response to: (1) insufficient habitat for most large species; (2) protected areas in separated pieces too small or too unstable to sustain viable populations of the plants and animals they seek to protect; (3) reliance by the majority of wild vertebrates on habitats outside of nature reserves; and (4) proliferating human land uses powerfully changing form and shape. The practicality of highly intensive conservation approaches depends on the survival of economically vigorous and interested cultures in areas relatively secure from the modifications taking place elsewhere for significant periods.

Large vertebrates, especially those which conflict with humans, will usually have to be the principal focus of intensive care and management programs, while spectacular colonies or gathering places of wildlife will have to be protected in refuges or monitored and cared for in newly intensive ways.

The techniques of ex situ care and biotechnology (ESB) are presently used to sustain populations of such varied and economically important forms as screwworm flies, geraniums, rainbow trout, corn, firs, and dairy cattle. They are flexible and widely applicable. The world population of introduced domestic terrestrial vertebrates is about ten billion, including three billion ruminants (Myers 1984b), an ex situ technology degrading many ecosystems. By contrast, the uses of these techniques to preserve biological diversity have usually been narrow actions of last resort started so late that much diversity has been lost, as with the California condor and the black-footed ferret.

CURRENT PROGRAMS OF EX SITU CARE AND BIOTECHNOLOGY

Many kinds of ex situ and biotechnology preservation efforts are coming into use; several are listed here by technique and species. They range from networks of botanical institutions dedicated to preserving alive every endangered U.S. plant (Office of Technology Assessment 1986) and zoological gardens seeking to preserve critically endangered animals (Conway 1978, 1980a, 1980b, 1982) to the relocation of Arabian oryx in Oman and Asiatic elephants in Sri Lanka, or the construction of nest ledges for oilbirds in Trinidad. Their successes include the reintroduction of Galápagos giant tortoises in nature and interspecies embryo transfers from gaur to domestic cow and bongo to eland in captivity, and egg transfers from peregrine to prairie falcon and whooping crane to sandhill crane in the wild. They include the artificial incubation of Mauritius pink pigeon eggs and "head-starting" ridley sea turtles, and they utilize artificial insemination and cryobiology. All seek to expand animal carrying capacity or to strengthen populations.

Each technique has been utilized with the species cited on a long-term or experimental basis. The list is suggestive, not comprehensive.

- *Short-term propagation and reintroduction:* golden-lion tamarin, cheetah, red wolf, American and European bison, Arabian oryx, dama gazelle, dorcas gazelle, red-fronted gazelle, onager, Andean condor, bald eagle, peregrine, Hawaiian goose, Lord Howe Island wood rail, European eagle owl, Mauritius pink pigeon, Galápagos giant tortoise, Galápagos land iguana, Ash Meadows amargosa pupfish.
- *Long-term propagation:* lion-tailed macaque, Siberian tiger, Père David's deer, Eu-

ropean bison, Przewalski's horse, brown-eared pheasant, Edward's pheasant, Guam rail, Guam kingfisher, Bali myna, white-naped crane, addax, slender-horned gazelle, scimitar-horned oryx, gaur, Grevy's zebra, Puerto Rican horned toad, Chinese alligator, Madagascar radiated tortoise, Aruba Island rattlesnake.

- *Relocation, transplantation:* koala, mongoose lemur, aye-aye, brown lemur, chimpanzee, gorilla, squirrel monkey, wooly monkey, spider monkey, common marmoset, black rhinoceros, white rhinoceros, red deer, white-tailed deer, mule deer, moose, Tule elk, bighorn sheep, musk-ox, pronghorn antelope, roan antelope, mountain goat, African elephant, more than 400 species of birds, and many reptiles and amphibians.
- *Fostering, cross-fostering:* peregrine, bald eagle, whooping crane, masked quail, polar bear (captive), many species of waterfowl, pigeons, cranes (in nature and captivity), and passerine birds in captivity.
- *Artificial incubation:* gharial, Siamese crocodile, Chinese alligator, green turtle, ridley, hooded crane, whooping crane, white-naped crane, and many other birds, reptiles, amphibians, and fishes.
- Artificial rearing: hundreds of species of most vertebrate groups.
- *Artificial insemination:* alligator, ocellated turkey, brown-eared pheasant, whooping crane, squirrel monkey, gorilla, yellow baboon, giant panda, guanaco, Speke's gazelle, addax, gemsbok, bighorn sheep.
- *Embryo transfer:* gaur, banteng, bongo, eland, mouflon, common zebra, Przewalski's horse, cottontop marmoset, yellow baboon.

Only about 20 of the 20,000 edible plants known provide most of the world's food today (Vietmeyer 1986), a remarkably vulnerable situation. Official and long-established plant "gene banks" (seed and germplasm storage facilities, clonal plantations, seed orchards, and rare-breeds farms), which attempt to sustain the genomes of domestic and wild plants as a hedge against extinction, are grossly incomplete and underfunded, (Office of Technology Assessment 1986; Perlas and Rifkin 1986; Sun 1986a,

1986b). Although we hear much of experimentation with agricultural plants, ranging from intense selection to cloning and gene insertion, serious attempts to preserve a major representation of botany's genetic building blocks, either in nature or ex situ, are discouragingly rare—and we do not yet know how to preserve many seed plants, even of crop species.

The management needs of wild animal gene banks are even less understood. They have received little scientific study or government support, except for that directed toward animals used in biomedical research, are complicated to operate, and, thus far, include very few species (Conway 1985a). They face daunting research costs, for most of what is known about their management has been worked out with a few domestic animals, often with little applicability to wild species. Conservationists are a long way from storing condor and crocodile seeds in a paper bag on a cold shelf. Nevertheless, intensive programs for animals are proliferating. The following is a representative list of technologies, focusing on animals.

- habitat modification or restoration
- animal rehabilitation
- translocation
- genetic and demographic management
- disease treatment, prevention, control
- intrapopulational management (dominance, competition)
- interspecies management (predation, competition)
- long-term propagation and short-term propagation
- selective breeding
- rearing a species from one sex
- introduction and reintroduction
- nutritional management
- artificial insemination
- embryo transfer
- cross-species trophoblast inner cell mass chimeras
- cryobiological ova, sperm, embryo, seed, and tissue storage
- artificial and surrogate incubation
- embryo sexing, embryo splitting, egg enucleation, cloning
- induced hibernation and diapause
- artificial rearing
- cross-fostering

- inducement of oestrus, musth, superovulation, contraception
- reproductive cycle management
- biochemical and surgical sexing

The enormous damage caused by ill-advised animal introductions is legend. It is less known that translocations in aid of threatened animal populations within or near their original ranges are often rewarding. The South African Wildlife Department has translocated some 30,000 animals in a largely successful effort to restock denuded former ranges, provide more room for wildlife populations, and move animals from areas of incompatible development to areas reclaimed for refuges (Hanks et al. 1981). Through translocation, the New Zealand Wildlife Service has saved from extinction taxa as diverse as South Island saddlebacks and Chatham Island snipe. Cornell University's Tom Cade is reestablishing the peregrine in eastern North America (Cade 1984), and U.S. game biologists have moved species as varied as turkeys and moose.

Captive propagation followed by reestablishment is most likely to be successful (1) when it can be of short duration, and genetic or physiological changes in founding stock are minimal, and (2) when the cause of decline may be temporary, such as overhunting or introduced predators, disease or competitors, rather than gross habitat destruction (see Fig. 19.1). For example, the Australians rescued the Lord Howe Island woodhen and restored it to much lost habitat with a predator-control, propagation-release program that raised woodhen numbers from less than 30 to more than 200 in four years (Fullager 1985). The FWS Patuxent Wildlife Research Center has bred and reintroduced several threatened birds (Erickson 1980), and the New York Zoological Society successfully initiated the reintroduction of American bison to newly created western reserves early in this century. Today, a dramatic reestablishment program for the Arabian oryx in Oman is underway (Stanley Price 1986 and chap. 20).

In zoos, a newly collaborative effort has resulted in the propagation of thousands of animals, including several of species extinct or very rare in nature. Most of the great terrestrial predators and the large ungulates are now bred regularly. Zoo propagators have recently

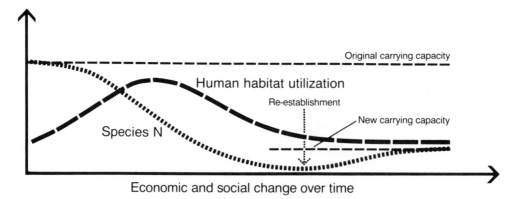

Fig. 19.1. Short-term ex situ care may enable future reestablishment of some species as human land use changes.

awakened to the genetic challenges they face (Ralls and Ballou 1986) and are providing new insights to field biologists concerned with critical problems in the preservation of small populations. During 1985, 90 percent of all mammals and 72 percent of all birds added to the 215 collections participating in the International Species Inventory System were bred in zoos (Flesness 1987). In fact, at least 19 percent of all the living species of mammals and 9 percent of all the birds have been bred in zoos during the past few years (Conway 1986).

LIMITATIONS OF EX SITU CARE AND BIOTECHNOLOGY

Despite these successes, the applications of ESB to sustaining diversity, like the chances of securing large nature reserves, are severely limited. By definition, proposals for ex situ care respond to diminished populations and insecure in situ care (Fig. 19.2). They relocate threatened animals or plants from their place of origin as a means of preventing total loss and because the technology to sustain them locally is unavailable. Nevertheless, coming from a wealthy agency or conservation group to an impoverished LDC, such proposals may seem as warmly helpful as an English curator offering Melina Mercouri a free pass to visit the Acropolis at the British Museum. From recent efforts to initiate ex situ programs for black-footed ferrets, California condors, and Sumatran and northern

white rhinoceroses, it is clear that such offers may not be greeted enthusiastically, no matter how well intended or costly for their authors.

On one hand, an ex situ or relocation program may remove the last local stimulus for preserving a threatened habitat; on the other, it may win local support for wildlife protection. When reestablishment of a wild species is proposed, controversy may be even greater, especially when the subject is a big predator capable of eating domestic animals—or people. Besides, most captive collections have not yet been developed with reintroduction programs in mind. They are not yet ready to provide animals, nor is the veterinary community ready for the international movement of animals needed for most restitution programs.

The very diversity conservation seeks to sustain affects its manipulation in unpredictable ways (Diamond 1986b; Ehrlich 1986). We do not know what the extinction or restoration of one species will do to others. In biotechnology, we are especially ignorant about nutrition, reproductive physiology, and the technology of reintroduction. Years of expensive research will be required before we will be able to employ such high-technology aids as embryo transfer or even artificial insemination (AI) with more than a handful of genera (AI has been successful with scarcely twenty wild mammals), to say nothing of the cold storage and transfer of usable zygotes and embryos.

Ex situ care is not an option for great whales of enormous appetites and vast space require-

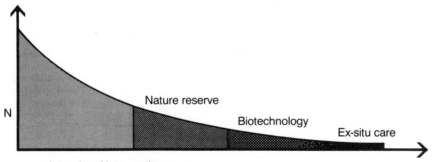

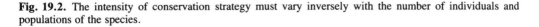

Fig. 19.2. The intensity of conservation strategy must vary inversely with the number of individuals and populations of the species.

ments any more than for tiny invertebrates with bizarrely complicated life histories, or unique animal spectacles such as great seal and penguin colonies or vast wildebeest and shorebird migrations, although intensive supportive techniques are likely to prove increasingly important to them.

The basic requirements of animal care, housing, and financial support impose foreseeable caps on intensive long-term breeding efforts in captivity. Excluding fishes, the total number of vertebrates, mammals, birds, reptiles, and amphibians in zoos is only about 539,000 (Fig. 19.3), a measure of zoo room.

Genetic diversity is lost each generation at a rate inversely proportional to the effective size of the population. For this reason, maintenance of genetic variability in a closed population, be it a zoo or an isolated nature reserve, depends on effective population size, the time period over which variation must be maintained, and the generation length of the population.

Much zoo room, especially that for birds, is unsuitable for propagation. Perhaps half of the total could be available for long-term breeding programs. Because it is desirable, for genetically and demographically viable populations, to maintain at least 100 to 300 individuals of each taxa (but see Woodruff, chap. 8), less than 1,000 of the 20,000+ mammals, birds, reptiles,

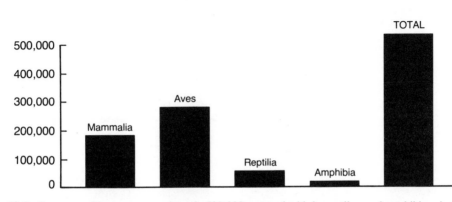

Fig. 19.3. Zoo space. There are approximately 539,000 mammals, birds, reptiles, and amphibians in the 635 collections known to house these animals (Olney 1982; Wagner 1982).

and amphibians could be cared for on a *long-term* basis with current technology and facilities (Conway 1984). But these will be critically important taxa whose preservation could make possible the survival of many others.

In 1984 it was recommended, in a preliminary way, that zoos trying to sustain long-term animal populations start out by designing collaborative management programs so as to retain about 90 percent of original variation for 200 years and begin each population with as many founders as possible (Soulé et al. 1986) (Fig. 19.4). Similar heuristic advice is relevant to some nature reserve management. Because of differing generation times, a population of long-lived white-naped cranes could require a very small genetically effective population (N_e), while a short-lived striped grass mouse might require a quite large one to preserve 90 percent heterozygosity after 200 years. But, for demographic and stochastic reasons, "minimum viable populations (MVPs)" will often be more than twice N_e (Frankel and Soulé 1981).

Planning for only 200 years may seem too brief a period of concern. For evolutionary biologists used to thinking in terms of geological time, the rapidity of human impacts on environment makes conservation biology a sobering discipline, one whose goals may seem ephemeral in the face of megatrends such as population increase and global warming—or evolutionary change. After all, the natural life of a species can often be five to ten million years (Diamond 1984a; Raup 1986). Thus, the likelihood of genetic change in small populations, even under the most rigorous management, may seem great—but probably not in the critical time period of concern.

Intensive intervention strategies will usually be dealing with slow-breeding forms at population levels and with management technologies which preclude rapid evolution. While ex situ programs are unresponsive to the "Red Queen Hypothesis," which holds that a population must continue to evolve in concert with its ever-changing environment in order to persist, genetic drift is far more powerful than selection in small populations of slow-breeding forms in reserves or zoos (Frankel and Soulé 1981). Consequently, drift can more easily be minimized in captive programs. In any event, uncommon large wild vertebrates in nature will not keep

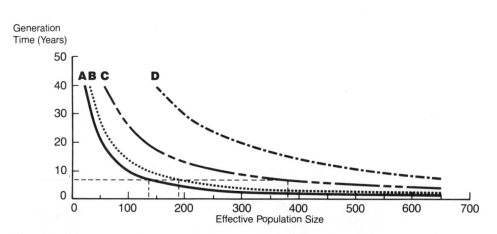

Fig. 19.4. Population size, founder size, generation time, and preservation of diversity. Relationship between effective population size, generation length, and founder group size required to maintain 90 percent of original genetic diversity for 200 years. (A) No founder effect; (B) twenty founders; (C) eight founders; (D) six founders—assuming immediate expansion of founder groups with no loss of diversity. (Modified from graphics prepared by M. Soulé and J. Ballou.)

pace either. And intensive techniques will be more, not less, relevant in the face of rapid change. Nor is it clear how relevant the preservation of original variation may be in a particular instance of adaptive response, as the untoward success of many animal introductions illustrates (Atkinson, chap. 7).

Given the fact that there are so few spaces for long-term captive populations, choosing the species to fill those spaces is not a trivial exercise (Fig. 19.5). There are, for example, about 1,785 big-cat spaces available in North American zoos (Foose 1983). How shall these be ap-

portioned among Persian leopards, Sumatran tigers, Indian lions, snow leopards, and their kin? The task is further confused by uncertainty about what representation of a genetic lineage should be sustained. A monotypic species? A race of a species? A population? Besides, many traditional subspecies designations are not consistent with more recent biochemical, geographical, and behavioral evaluations, and existing taxonomy oftens fails to represent "evolutionarily significant units" (Conway 1985b; Woodruff, chap. 8).

Yet another limitation is the high cost of high-

Fig. 19.5. Choosing what to care for is not a trivial exercise.

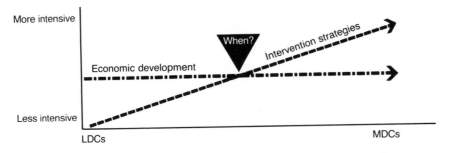

Fig. 19.6. In situ use of high technology is impractical at low levels of economic and technical capability.

technology approaches. They require expensive expertise, continuing research, logistical support, and rigorous supervision. At low levels of technology and government capability, preserving habitat is the only realistic way of preserving species (Western 1986) (Fig. 19.6).

Although conservationists often worry that ex situ programs will compete with preservation in nature, support from different sources is commonly restricted to different purposes and that accessible only to ex situ or biotechnology programs is not likely to be lost to biopreservation. Conservation's task is to find synergistic ways of tapping different sources of support. Zoos and research and humane organizations, for instance, may have access to municipal funds and donors otherwise impenetrable to international conservation.

The lessons of conservation biology (MacArthur and Wilson 1967; Schonewald-Cox et al. 1983; Soulé 1986; Soulé and Simberloff 1986) suggest that small isolated populations will rarely survive without artificial help, so how can the potentials of ex situ care and biotechnology be improved?

LOOKING AHEAD: EX SITU AND BIOTECHNOLOGY STRATEGIES FOR THE FUTURE

Two challenges head the agenda of conservationists working with ex situ care and biotechnology: (1) to develop the science, technology, and institutional resources necessary to sustain selected taxa in a manner responsive to the impacts of change, and (2) to find ways to use their specialties to bring home to the public the significance of accelerating extinction and to create stronger support for biological conservation.

Uncompromising antimanagement attitudes characterize some otherwise well-informed conservationists, while the idea of a technological fix often excites popular writers. For conservationists, especially wildlife or refuge managers, knowing when and how and when not to call for the technologies of intensive care is a new requirement.

Securing Taxa

If ex situ care and biotechnology strategies are to buy time for gravely threatened taxa, priority targets should be identified before their populations and diversity have diminished to near extinction, and existing programs should be revised to accommodate them within present capacities. Scientific tools and capabilities should be extended as rapidly as possible.

In the light of very limited resources, choosing which approaches to take and taxa to save requires a more participatory and supportable decision process. Biotechnology applications, be they disease control or selective culling, captive care of habitat modification, provide many possibilities for misunderstanding and mistake. Whether it be inducing a condor to lay more eggs, enhancing the survival of a rare warbler by reducing a population of parasitic cowbirds, or protecting rare plants by controlling their predators, it is clear that the programs developed must be responsive to biological and political criteria. Ecological questions concerning eventual biomass and synergistic effects, disease, competition, and food supply all challenge release efforts. Will a reintroduction play a significant role in ecosystem change or stasis? Will helping to restore a desired ecosystem through seed dispersal, vegetation modification, or predation be compatible with economic-political concerns?

Decision theory and sensitivity analysis are formal tools for analyzing decisions under uncertainty that have been developed for business management (Raiffa 1968). Using "decision trees," "parameter estimates," and "sensitivity analyses," these essentially participatory techniques can improve communication, facilitate better use of growing information bases, and identify priorities for research, management, and propagation (Maguire 1987). They are a natural extension of the process developed for U.S.-type "recovery plans" and "environmental impact statements" and come much closer than "cost-benefit," "minimum standards," or the popular "triage" approaches (Bennett 1986; Conway 1980a; Myers 1979) to providing the negotiating tools needed to make the complex scientific and political processes of conservation work together.

Whatever the process, genetic "eggs," foreign or local, should not be left uncared for in insecure baskets. International biotechnology resources should be moved and concentrated where they are most needed.

Advancing the Science and the Options

In species preservation, ex situ care and biotechnology have the potential to respond to both intrinsic and extrinsic problems (Soulé and Simberloff 1986). Theoretically, they can utilize otherwise nonreproductive individuals, insert lost diversity into isolated populations, and even reestablish a species from one sex (Diamond 1985a; Gyllensten et al. 1985). Intelligently used, relocation, reintroduction, and captive propagation may one day sustain many taxa when transitory economic or cultural activities threaten and may provide support in marginal habitats or where modified lands are left fallow (Mathews 1986, but see Anon. 1986a; Cowan 1965; Geist 1985; Grieg 1979; and Stanley Price, chap. 20 concerning the hazards of translocation). They have the potential to make "too-small" nature reserves useful and to sustain equilibrium between species, and they are the only possible response to global climatic change. However, their potential effectiveness varies with different taxa, between ectothermic and endothermic forms, between polygynous and monogamous taxa, and even between those employing lek strategies and monogamous species. They also vary with habitat preference and relationship with well-known domestic forms.

When preservation choices have to be made between different populations of the same taxa, new biochemical tools for the analysis of genetic variability may help managers make a decision. In zoos, such techniques have enabled the separation of the lineages of Borneo and Sumatran orangutans and Asiatic and African lions.

Habitat restorations will need original "keystone species" to help reestablish and sustain ecosystem structure and stability, such as major predators and large herbivores, or plants that are important as breeding or feeding sites (Gilbert 1980; Soulé 1985), and gene banks can provide some of them. ESB will be needed to restore coevolutionary relationships and to replace natural opportunities for genetically and demographically essential dispersal between isolated population fragments. Individuals may be transferred from captivity to nature and even from sperm or embryo banks to wild dams when social and territorial structure prevent simpler animal transfers.

For many threatened large species, the peregrine, most large lizards, turtles and tortoises, rhinos, deer, wild asses, desert antelope, and the black-footed ferret, adequate habitat is present. But protection is lacking. Ex situ refuge for a human generation or two may enable species reestablishments even after extinction in nature, when local educational, economic, and cultural progress may encourage their return. Many, perhaps most, such species are wide-ranging and capable of using habitats greatly altered by agriculture.

Ex situ gene banks are safe from local disease outbreaks. In 1984, twenty of the remaining sixty Javan rhinos died of an unidentified disease (Anon. 1984a). The Meeteetse black-footed ferret epizootic would not have been so devastating had a captive reservoir existed (Dobson and May 1986; May 1986). For very small populations, gene banks allow genetic and demographic imbalances to be dealt with, generation times to be prolonged, and consequent selection and drift minimized, or genetic expression of each family line to be maximized. Sometimes even highly inbred populations can be sustained (Templeton and Read 1984). Small captive populations can be managed so as to retain a greater degree of original diversity than can their wild congeners in numbers several times larger (Frankel and Soulé 1981). Where the biotechnology of long-term cryopreservation of embryos and zygotes can be combined with AI and embryo transfer, founder heterozygosity may be retained for long periods and these techniques offer hope of enlarging the carrying capacity of *long-term* captive reservoirs.

Limited carrying capacity, more than all other problems, restricts the preservation potentials of captive gene banks. The relevance of game ranching to expanding capacity is not yet clear (Anon. 1986b; Geist 1985) but is clearly deserving of intensive study.

Short-term propagation programs, such as those now underway for Guam rails and kingfishers (pushed into extinction in 1984 by the introduced brown tree snake), permit care for more taxa. Restorations not accomplished quickly run the risk of losing relevance to local conservation objectives. Where possible, ex situ programs should be developed within an agreed-upon time frame during which the authorities concerned should initiate practical programs to enable species restoration within a few generations.

Research is needed to find better ways to reestablish wild animal populations in translocations or from captivity, to monitor them, and to determine when help is needed, and what kind. The lessons of captive management can sometimes be applied to the design and care of otherwise inadequate reserves, some of which will have to be targeted to the care of especially threatened species and many of which are destined to be so intensely managed as to be megazoos. There is a newly compelling need to tie together the developing science of ex situ care with field biology, and to find better tools for predicting the results of restoration efforts.

When a species' historical homeland is so changed that there is no foreseeable chance of its survival in nature or immediate reestablishment, we are left with four options to secure its survival: (1) sustain it in captivity for ethical and educational reasons and for a preservation of future options; (2) manage it in semicaptivity on intensely cared-for parks or ranches, where the species is suitable, for the foregoing reasons and those of economics; (3) introduce it some place near its historical range—say the California

condor in the Grand Canyon where it nested 12,000 years ago. Finally; and (4) place specialized species in a wholly new geography where habitat is adjudged appropriate and possible adverse effects can be avoided or controlled—say whooping cranes in Idaho, saddlebacks on New Zealand islands.

New ways of retaining biodiversity outside of reserves, even outside of "nature" in lands modified by humans for other purposes, are worthy of study: ways of increasing species on agricultural land, abandoned mine sites, dam-created marshes and lakes, cooling ponds and even deserts. It is nonsense to overlook expanding habitats where humans are modifying rivers, lakes, marshes, and forests (Western, chap. 16).

After all, domestic and exotic animals and plants will continue to be distributed in ill-considered and selfish ways to serve mankind's momentary economic and aesthetic purposes. Is it unreasonable to consider carefully planned introductions on behalf of biological conservation? Why allow these biological black holes to be populated by accident and default when the need to sustain diversity is begging for space?

Expanding Conservation Support

Conservation's agenda requires a serious commitment to the founding and support of plant and animal gene banks. They are essential insurance for the protection of specialized species of limited geographical range and crucial in habitat restoration; zoo gene banks are still administered largely by unpaid volunteers. Vanishing species must be accorded new status in international agreements and public perceptions, nothing less than a new international convention providing them with priority treatment in international dealings and special protection in the face of expanding land use and in time of social strife.

Zoos and botanical gardens, historically seen as educational and recreational institutions, are becoming mankind's primary contact with living diversity. They already exist and are critically located in world centers of human population and decisionmaking, many in third-world nations. They have conspicuous physical bases caring for live animals—"flagship species"—around which the case for restoration and preservation can be built. And most have municipal underpinnings of support not otherwise available to conservation. Thus they are uniquely positioned to act on behalf of society as centers for conservation research and ex situ preservation. It is time for them to be overtly devoted to the maintenance of vanishing species and to become more compelling tools in the essentially cultural effort to link human communities with natural communities, to play a more productive role in shaping the fundamental human values essential to the preservation of natural life.

Biotic diversity is much more than species diversity, and intensive biotechnology programs are weak and limited tools. But they are as significant to the preservation of biological diversity as the fragments of nature they can save and restore that other kinds of conservation efforts cannot.

20

Reconstructing Ecosystems

MARK R. STANLEY PRICE

INTRODUCTION

The extinction of plant and animal species, either from their wild environments or totally from the face of the earth, is of much concern to biologists. While analyses show patterns in the types of species or communities which are most vulnerable, one conclusion is inescapable, namely, that extinctions from the wild will continue and probably accelerate. Another concern of conservation is maintenance of the earth's genetic richness under artificial conditions, if this is the only way to ensure its perpetuation. Zoo managers and directors are now aware of their obligations to manage their stocks of endangered species, as the objectives and methods of captive propagation plans become increasingly unified in both theory and practice (Ralls and Ballou 1986). The effort invested in improvements in reproductive technology is directed toward the same end.

By comparison, the science of restoring communities to a previous or relatively natural state is in its infancy. This may become an ecological growth industry, but now is the time to develop the techniques and gain experience before wild populations are further reduced and while species related to those which are endangered or extinct are still available for comparative study.

The theme of "reconstructing ecosystems" encompasses both the restoration of whole plant and animal communities and the reestablishment of the smallest or least significant organism in its ancestral habitat. Examples of plant community reconstruction, rather than re-

habilitation, after industrial dereliction (e.g., Cairns 1986), are few. The native flora of St. Helena Island is now being restored through international effort to clear "exotic weeds" while growing and bulking endemic species in overseas botanic gardens for replanting on the island (Anon. 1984a). An ambitious project to restore 700 km² of coastal dry forest in Costa Rica through intensive management has been proposed (Janzen 1986).

So far, more effort has been expended on restoring the animal component of natural communities, and this chapter will concentrate on them. The emphasis is on large vertebrates because (1) most experience lies with this group, and (2) 2,000 species of large, terrestrial vertebrates will require captive breeding, and hence be potential candidates for reintroduction, within the next 200 years (Soulé et al. 1986).

The techniques of reintroduction on which the very success of the effort may depend, are not considered here. The case histories referred to in this chapter are an eclectic selection to demonstrate the increasing range of scientifically planned management exercises, which have been documented properly. By no means have all been total successes, but their increasing number and scope, and the generalizations they provide, may allow assessment of the role of animal transport and release as a scientific tool for restoring communities. This chapter makes some generalizations about the animals and their habitats that promote the chance of successful releases, the reasons and benefits of reintroductions. It also considers the interface between captive-breeding programs and reintroduction projects.

MOTIVES FOR REINTRODUCTION

Just as there are many different types of activity described by "reintroduction," so the motives for reintroducing animals or managing ecosystems vary widely. Developed countries in particular hanker for the ecosystems or communities of some past period. While McNaughton (chap. 11) laments the absence of a true North American prairie grassland despite its former huge area, attempts at recreating historical ecosystems have been made in South Africa (Anderson 1986) and in Israel. Proposals have been made for the recreation of a northern palearctic mammal fauna on a Scottish island (Yalden 1986), and the Costa Rican dry forest project is an initiative in ecological and cultural restoration. The reconstruction of coral reefs is a special case, because once an appropriate, artificial physical substrate exists, recolonization occurs naturally through immigration and larval settling (Goodwin and Cambers 1983). More often, a key species in a community is missing, and its replacement is proposed to repair the damage, subject to habitat conditions being suitable and the species meeting with public acceptance, in the case of predators. This has been the case with the European bison and Arabian oryx, the lynx in many parts of Europe, the sea eagle in Scotland (Love 1983) and the griffon vulture in France.

The reinforcement of wild populations has been proposed because captive populations were exceeding zoo carrying capacity. This resulted in carefully planned releases for the golden lion tamarin (Kleiman et al. 1986) and the Jamaican hutia (Oliver 1985). It is felt that certain types of animals "would be better off in the wild." This has led to the rehabilitation and release of chimpanzees (Brewer 1978) and orangutans (Aveling and Mitchell 1980), well-planned releases on islands of groups of chimpanzees of very varied origin (e.g., Borner 1985; Hannah and McGrew, in press), and the rehabilitation of captive-bred carnivores such as lions (Adamson 1986), tigers (Singh 1984), and cheetahs (Pettifer 1980). In some of these cases, the introduction of one or a few animals is a marginal reinforcement of an existing population and would be irresponsible if it resulted in any outbreeding depression. A peregrine falcon population in the northeast United States has been reestablished (Barclay and Cade 1983) and the otter population of southeast England reinforced with captive-bred animals (Jefferies et al. 1986) because the specific cause of former extinction or decline, namely persistent pesticides, was known to have become a lesser threat.

Direct exploitation of released captive-bred animals may be an adequate motive. For many years this has been so with the release of reared game birds, albeit not of endangered species, for hunting. This is also one motive for efforts to breed large numbers of houbara bustards for release in several countries of the Middle East. Some reintroduction projects have several purposes. The small-scale release of the red squirrel into Regent's Park, London, has the serious research aspect of why the native red has been replaced through much of England by the introduced gray squirrel (Bertram and Moltu 1986). The project is in and around the London Zoo, allowing the public to see in nearly natural surroundings a species whose disappearance is generally regretted, and it draws attention to reintroduction projects. Finally, it hopes to serve as a model for reintroduction techniques which are as applicable on this scale as for large animals in remote places. The motives in some reintroductions may be only barely biological, but legitimate nonetheless. The Père David's deer has been returned to its native country, China, where it will live in seminatural, enclosed conditions while the search continues for available natural habitat (Jungius and Loudon 1985).

THE VALUES AND BENEFITS OF REINTRODUCTION PROJECTS

A successful reintroduction has many benefits, and different people may perceive these in different ways; for example, they may be influenced by whether they live in the reintroduction area or not. Several categories cover the main benefits.

A reserve or area with a nearly complete community of plants and animals is intrinsically most satisfying. This is adequate reason for returning species to the wild and is the conclusion of Conway's (1986) argument in favor of captive propagation that "[although] depleted reserves would certainly remain invaluable, . . . the Mountains of the Moon without Mountain gorillas seems like saving the husk without the kernel." This argument is most relevant in the case of the large, conspicuous species which were probably never very abundant, such as condors, vultures, oryx, and Przewalski's horses. Such animals are the most likely reintroduction candidates.

A returned species restores ecological processes. This is obvious in the case of specialist species, such as scavengers like the sea eagle, griffon vulture, and perhaps one day the California condor. Although it is difficult to demonstrate quantitatively the impact of a restored species on community functioning, there are many examples of the changes following selective removal of key species, such as the population dynamics of fish and other krill eaters following the near-total removal of blue whales (Laws 1985). The reintroduced species can provide the stimulus for improved environmental awareness. In Brazil, the golden lion tamarin project's public education activities have identified the prime environmental concerns of the local people. Efforts to protect the tamarin and its habitat are linked to maintenance of the area's resources for the future (Kleiman et al. 1986).

Conservation effort concentrated on the reintroduced species while it is still at low numbers and vulnerable may effectively safeguard larger areas of surrounding habitat than can be actively protected, and at the same time protect other animal species. In the case of Oman's Arabian oryx project, the visible effort of protecting the oryx herds has had a ripple effect so that the law forbidding hunting of the Arabian gazelle is respected over an area over 20,000 km². This ensures one viable population of this gazelle in south Arabia.

Reintroduction projects can have a major role in the local economy and community life. The Arabian oryx project employs bedouin in their tribal area without requiring a complete break with their pastoralism. Because of their knowledge of the desert and its ecology, no one else could track and monitor released oryx to their standard. Employment on the project uses the skills of the pastoralist, while teaching new ones. On a small scale, it prevents a drift to larger population centers in search of work, a common problem in contemporary desert societies.

The project camp with facilities for acclimatizing and preparing immigrant oryx for release in central Oman has become a focus for tribal social life and assistance in an area of low population density and very sparse services. The forms of assistance provided are many and varied, but are at negligible cost to the project, or at some slight cost to project staff when they must entertain or care for visitors. In any event, the cash cost of developing this role is far outweighed by the reputation of the project and the reciprocal obligations it engenders for past help. The camp also serves as a desert research center and meteorological station. Through the cost of the camp and staff, an oryx in Oman is more expensive to maintain than in an American zoo (Conway 1986), but for the Oman government it is an effective way of creating rural employment and a small desert center for a seminomadic population.

SPECIES BIOLOGY AND ITS IMPLICATIONS FOR REINTRODUCTION

For a successful reintroduction, the methods used must exploit the animal's biology. In addition to a detailed knowledge of the species, an understanding or insight into how the animal perceives its environment is needed. This may be critically important when the reintroduced animals are first released into an unenclosed area. Major considerations include the following:

Social Organization

The most productive animals in captivity are probably those living in their natural social groupings (Kleiman 1980). Western lowland gorillas in captivity breed better in social groups that mimic those of the wild (Schmidt 1986). A major objective of release programs, whether of wild-caught or captive-bred animals, is now the prerelease attainment of the species' correct and stable social organization. This principle has guided the successful releases of captive-bred Arabian oryx (Stanley Price 1986), European otters (Jefferies et al. 1986), golden lion tamarins (Kleiman et al. 1986), and the translocation of complete troops of wild baboons (Strum and Southwick 1986). Many release failures, in which the animals scatter explosively into strange habitat, can be ascribed to ignoring this simple precept. The problem can arise in slightly different form where logistics or resources prevent translocation of entire groups of very large animals, such as elephants (Anderson 1986).

Size

Enough collations of life history data for animal taxa have been made to deduce general ecological correlates of brain and body size, age of maturity, reproductive rate, longevity, group size and social organization, range size, and diet type and quality (e.g., Clutton-Brock and Harvey 1980; Jarman 1974; Mace 1981; Western 1979a). Such principles can aid captive management, but they may be critical to the design of reintroduction techniques and their success.

A large antelope, such as an oryx, is a coarse grazer and has simple dietary requirements. A small species, such as a duiker, requires a more complex and richer diet (Thomas et al. 1986), so that its cost per unit biomass in captivity is greater. Its small social grouping will require more holding units for a given number of individuals, but the composition of the large species will have to be manipulated in confined areas to avoid damaging aggression.

Genetic management of the smaller species is easier and cheaper, while the N_e/N ratio for the larger species will be adversely affected if a few "successful" males are allowed to breed preponderantly (Mace 1986). Active rotation of males is the solution (Wemmer 1983). The longer generation time of the large species, however, requires a smaller captive population to maintain a prescribed proportion of genetic variability over a defined period. Thus maintenance of the large species' population for genetic criteria is again cheaper (Conway 1986).

This example oversimplifies, because many medium-sized antelopes are polygynous, with more than one type of social group. This complicates their management both in captivity and in the wild after reintroduction. However, large species are cost-effective for zoos, and their simple food requirements and lower food density suggest their transition to the wild would be less hazardous.

Home Range Size

The relationship between an animal's home range size and its "reintroducibility" is not sim-ple. A species with a naturally small range because of a dense food supply is liable not to move away from a release site to search for adequate food. Successful reintroduction will depend on accurate matching of the release area's resources with the species' requirements.

If the animal's food supply is dispersed but clumped, it will have a larger home range. Where the food occurs predictably at a certain place each year or season, such as ripe fruit on forest trees, the animal must locate each food source once and remember its location from year to year. In contrast, where the food supply is not only scattered but unpredictable in place from year to year, such as the grazing of a desert oryx, the species will be an explorer. It will move widely in search of food, responding to environmental clues such as the sight and smell of distant rainstorms and wind-borne information. Released birds of prey disperse widely in search of food. Such exploring species will be easier to reestablish in the wild, even if monitoring is more difficult.

Life Cycles

Species with complex life cycles, such as many invertebrates, will be difficult to reestablish because of their very specific and essential interactions with other species in the community. In England, the reestablishment of the large blue butterfly, *Maculinea arion,* has just started following intense research (Thomas 1980). The young caterpillars eat the flowers of a single plant species, but older larvae are removed from the plants by one ant species to its underground nests where the grubs feed on ant larvae for nine months. The ant colonies must occur above a certain density in the butterfly's habitat. Their density is affected markedly by grazing pressure from livestock and rabbits and by agricultural practices, and the manipulation of these factors has to precede any possible increase in butterfly numbers. In a simpler situation the reestablishment of another English butterfly, the swallowtail (*Papilio machaon*), failed because of its dependence on one food plant (Dempster and Hall 1980). This plant population declined to an inadequate level as its fenland habitat dried out through drainage of the surrounding farmland. Many invertebrate species are very intolerant of habitat modification, and their successful reintroduction will depend on sophisticated environmental management.

HABITAT TYPE AND REINTRODUCTION

Just as animal size and species ecology were relevant to reintroduction prospects, so habitat requirements influence the methods of reintroduction and the chances of success. To demonstrate this, Table 20.1 lists those aspects which are relevant to the reintroduction of an animal species into the contrasting habitats of a tropical forest and a desert. The illustrative animal types would be an arboreal primate, of which there are many potential species for reintroduction, and an antelope, such as the Arabian oryx.

The habitat factors point out the gross differences between a desert and forest, and they suggest that the animals released into the forest will encounter far more obstacles to their successful establishment. Management aspects of the two reintroductions again show that monitoring in the desert will be much easier, which translates into greater cost-effectiveness per animal or more detailed information about them, or both. The overall simple conclusion is that the oryx will be better off because the desert's main problems stem from its harsh and unpredictable climate, against which physiological and behavioral adaptations provide protection as long as enough food is found. Despite the forest's superficial appearance of providing an easy living from luxuriant resources, the released animals are forced to interact with many hostile species, whether toxic plants, disease pathogens, predators, or competitors. These animals are more vulnerable while acquiring the

Table 20.1. Tropical Forest and Desert Compared for Implications for Successful Animal Reintroduction

	Forest	Desert
Habitat		
Flora	diverse	less diverse
Fauna	diverse	less diverse
Plant 2y compounds	common	rare
Animal niche width	narrow	broad
Diet composition	mixed fruit, foliage	mixed grass, herbs
Food dispersion	scattered, very localized in time and space, but predictable between years	scattered, unpredictable between seasons but larger clumps
Diet quality	changing quickly	quality maintained longer
Animal diet	highly selected	little selection
Diet development	much learned	little learned
Habitat structure	complex	simple
Habitat vulnerability	high	low
Habitat rehabilitation	long-term, very expensive	unnecessary except on very local scale?
Climate	predictable, effects partly buffered by structure	unpredictable and extreme
Problems faced by reintroduced species		
Interspecific competition	high	low
Original niche	occupied/partitioned among other species	vacant
Disease challenge	high	low
Food shortage	relative	absolute
Predation risk	high	low
Management of reintroduced animals		
Group size	small	large
Number of groups	high	low
Ease of monitoring	low	high
Carcass location	poor	good
Size of reintroduction area	small-large	very large

skills and experience to cope with these hazards than is the desert species with its problems.

Reintroduction success may also depend on the species' tolerance to an altered habitat. An unselective grazer such as the American bison or a wide-ranging desert animal, accustomed to search for scattered resources, is likely to be relatively unaffected. Forest species will tend to be more susceptible to habitat disturbance, although the responses of rain forest bird species to selective logging can be tentatively correlated with some aspects of each species' ecology (Johns 1985). This type of analysis may help predict which species can be reintroduced successfully.

One habitat type for which special considerations apply are islands. It is clear that their animal species are especially prone to extinction (e.g., Olson, chap. 6) through a variety or combination of factors. This vulnerability may indicate greater problems in their reintroduction: between 1960 and 1978, 1,761 captive-bred Hawaiian geese were released onto the islands of Hawaii and Maui, but in 1978 the population was not yet self-supporting without continuing releases (Kear and Berger 1980).

INSTITUTIONAL ASPECTS OF REINTRODUCTION PROJECTS

Most captive-breeding centers are in the Western world, and not in the countries where reintroductions are current or proposed. Captive-breeding programs on one continent require cooperation and coordination (Conway et al. 1984), and long-term agreements between the producers and users of the animals to be reintroduced should be mandatory.

As two contrasting examples, all Arabian oryx in the United States were under the management of the World Herd trustees from 1963, when this herd was created. A total of eighteen oryx had been either committed or delivered to Jordan and Oman by 1981. At this point, just when the captive population was large enough to discuss options and priorities for the animals, the trustees dissolved themselves, ownership of the animals reverted to the zoos holding them, and animals were available for trade rather than for legitimate reintroduction schemes. Only in late 1986, with the prospective development of an AAZPA Species Survival Plan for the spe-

cies, is there a management authority with which Oman can communicate. In contrast, the golden lion tamarin benefits from a Cooperative Research and Management Agreement to which all owners and holders of animals must belong (Kleiman et al. 1986), and which has allowed a large increase in numbers and genetic diversity, with a comprehensive research program on the species and its requirements. Further agreements bind the U.S. institutions and the Brazilian authorities where the reintroduction takes place.

Such formal arrangements are essential, because the reintroduction of captive-bred animals to establish a population will involve repeated releases over many years. Project planning should allow for this, ensuring that the animals will be available at the appropriate times. Releases of peregrine falcons (Barclay and Cade 1983) and whooping cranes (Kepler 1978) were delayed until adequate annual supplies of captive-bred birds were guaranteed.

DURATION OF REINTRODUCTION PROJECTS

The duration of an actively managed reintroduction project will depend on the rate at which a genuinely independent population is established. This will depend on the performance of the released animals, their overall rate of increase, and the rate at which batches of further immigrants arrive. It is a mistake to equate the act of releasing animals with their reintroduction: for the animals, their release signals only the beginning of their testing time. Thus reintroduction projects are inevitably long-term, and the resources for them should, ideally, be guaranteed before they are begun.

One specific point is important. When captive-bred animals are released, they have no body of social experience or traditional knowledge of their new habitat. This has to develop anew through the experiences of the founders. Only with the next generation of animals born in the release area will individuals again learn about their environment from birth. Thus the founders and their first offspring are extremely valuable and must be protected until a body of traditional knowledge has accumulated. Where a truly wild existence depends on specific knowledge of the area, the process of exploration may take several generations. For instance, the wild oryx in Oman have not yet discovered any of the small natural water sources along an escarpment 25 km from the release site, despite a total home range of over 2000 km². Until at least one source is found, their pattern of movement and distribution will be influenced by the occasional need to drink at the release site.

One general corollary may be that animals at the edge of their historic range might have survived in a relatively hostile environment only through possession of peculiar behavioral adaptations or responses, the result of greater experience. Reintroductions should, therefore, be made into optimal, rather than marginal, habitat to reduce this type of requirement for survival. A further corollary of essential survival experience in a population is the gravity of the decision to remove from the wild the last individuals of a remnant population. Their genes can be returned at some future time, but their experience is lost totally and has to develop again.

ADEQUACY OF CONVENTIONAL BREEDING PROGRAMS AND ZOOS

There is now a consensus that for long-term viability of a captive population, the objective should be the retention of 90 percent of the founding genetic variability for 200 years (Soulé et al. 1986). Alternative propagation plans for preserving genetic diversity or for adaptation to captivity have been published (Foose et al. 1986), but the mere maintenance of genetic diversity may not be adequate investment in animals whose descendants are to face release to the wild. While strenuous efforts must be made in captivity to avoid unconscious selection between animals or their gradual domestication (Frankham et al. 1986), no one can yet say what the reaction of captive-bred animals may be to their original, natural environment after 200 years and many generations in captivity. There is evidence that the small rodent *Peromyscus maniculatus bairdi* lost some hereditary control of habitat selection after twelve to twenty generations in captivity (Wecker 1070). A colony of European storks has now been established in France in which the annual winter migration to West Africa has been deliberately suppressed (Renaud and Renaud 1984). The first golden lion tamarins released in Brazil failed to respond

to danger or a predator (Kleiman et al. 1986). Was this due to lack of exposure to danger while young in captivity or because of genetic change? If too much selection has acted in the captive phase, the desired reintroduction may be merely the introduction of a feral population.

While the dangers of unconscious selection modifying behavior in captive populations, to the eventual detriment of reintroduced animals, are well known, it may also be difficult to avoid morphological changes. The gut length of red grouse shortened after six generations in captivity because of the artificial diet fed (Moss 1972). How would such birds have fared in the wild? For captive herbivores, a diet of correct quality and natural physical form may not be adequate: Arabian oryx born in the desert and grazing from weaning have larger hyoid structures, which suggests a different tongue action from captive-born animals fed cut food.

One partial solution to the problem of long-term unnatural selective pressures in captivity is suggested for the group of large terrestrial animals, such as polygynous antelopes, which require most demographic management in captivity (see previous discussion). If more large, nonexhibit satellite breeding areas could be set aside as a low-cost management option (Doherty 1982), their larger area might allow relatively normal expression of the animals' social behavior. The reproductive contribution from different males would certainly be skewed, as in the wild, but the breeding males would have become so through male-male competition rather than through the artificial selection of an egalitarian breeding program. Animals bred and reared under these conditions, and subject to selective pressures more similar to those of the wild, might be more suitable candidates for reintroduction. This argument would favor protected breeding areas in a species' natural range, such as the secure sanctuaries for the black rhino now necessary in Africa.

If a captive colony and a more naturally breeding population can be maintained with only a little genetic exchange between them, this may be a better technique for maintaining animals for reintroduction than the maintenance of maximum heterozygosity alone (Hedrick et al. 1986). Such a change of emphasis in captive breeding is consistent with the general trend of zoos to keep more individuals of fewer species (Ralls and Ballou 1986) in recognition of their obligation to maintain viable populations of the most endangered animals. The development of large breeding areas would allow zoos to escape the physical limitations of those facilities which were designed for displaying many species with little imitation of their habitats.

Captive breeding programs should obviously avoid artificial selective pressures. Even if it were possible to mimic natural selection to obtain wild-type genotypes, these might not be the correct genotypes when the species is reintroduced. Habitats change through time (and logically must have changed upon extinction of any species). The Oman desert changed in the period between the extinction of the last wild Arabian oryx in 1972 and the first reintroduction in 1982. During this interval, the local bedouin became motorized, joined the cash economy, and started to enjoy the benefits of modern society. Patterns of land use have changed, and not all are necessarily adverse for the reestablishing oryx, but selection on the captive-bred animals in the desert may already favor different genotypes from those of ten years ago. This is one argument for minimizing the time between extinction and reintroduction. The longer the captive-breeding phase, the greater will be the selection forces and mortality among the reintroduced animals, requiring more founders to be tested in the wild before viable animals survive. The number of founders required will depend on the species' pattern of mortality, and in simple terms, whether it is a relatively r or K strategist.

Conclusions

The successful reintroduction of animals to their native habitat, as one tool in restoring ecosystems, involves far more than the species' biology alone. Many relevant aspects, such as project planning, the selection of founder animals, inbreeding in the wild, veterinary and transport implications, and release techniques, have not been discussed in this chapter. Nonetheless, a few general conclusions can be made concerning species "reintroducibility."

Those species which will always be rare in natural communities, either because they belong to higher trophic levels or because they are specialist species occupying narrow niches, will be difficult to reestablish. During their reestablishment, they are liable to face greater competition in their efforts to regain their original niche or develop a new one.

The reestablishment of species whose survival in the wild relies much on learned behavior patterns, such as feeding techniques and food selection, which cannot be taught in captivity, will be difficult. Limitations in the learning ability of captive-bred individuals that are released as adults may significantly reduce viability in their native habitat.

Species that can be identified as "explorers" because of their food distribution are likely to be good candidates for reintroduction.

Species with complex life cycles or specific requirements will be difficult to reestablish because of their essential interactions with other species in the community.

These four aspects of species biology, which increase the problems of reintroduction or reduce its chances of success, resemble in many ways those factors which make a species prone to extinction in the first place. If this generalization is true, it demonstrates that conservation priority lies in the maintenance of habitats in their near-undisturbed states. This confirms the conclusions of other chapters in this volume.

While loss of habitat has always been the main cause of extinctions, the prospects for reintroduction of species that were eliminated by direct persecution are much brighter. Some of the reasons for vulnerability to extinction by mankind may allow successful reintroduction. For example, the Arabian oryx is large, very conspicuous, lives in herds in open country, is most reluctant to run, and when running has little endurance. This caused its extermination through motorized hunting, but these same features are exploited in effective management and monitoring for its reintroduction. The same points apply to the bison species and, hopefully, to Przewalski's horse in due course. By the same token, while it is easy to eliminate scavenging birds such as vultures, the sea eagle, and condors by poisoning, their reestablishment is facilitated by the easy provision of an artificial food supply to maintain some fidelity to the release area.

These animals are large and very visible members of less diverse communities. Such species generate great public interest, and as they are the most "reintroducible," they should be given priority in any reintroduction proposals. The conservation movement needs visible examples of constructive conservation in action, and each reintroduction is a declaration of optimism that wild communities will thrive into the future. However, reintroductions are expensive even where feasible, and conservation re-sources must be partitioned wisely and objectively between habitat protection, captive breeding alternatives, and reintroduction efforts. Do the foundations now exist for a more rational basis for this task?

Part IV

CONSERVATION REALITIES

The Human Side of Conservation

MARY C. PEARL

In the preceding chapters, we have heard from wildlife experts, both theoreticians and practitioners. We have learned that a major, man-made extinction spasm is underway, and that therefore the underlying goal of conservation biology must be to mitigate the effects of human actions. We also learned that the most difficult task of wildlife management is to create accommodations between short-term human economic needs and the needs of wildlife. In the next set of chapters, we focus on human society and return to a theme articulated at the outset by Vittachi (chap. 3): the most important concern on the global agenda is what people need to do to accommodate our burgeoning numbers while maintaining the supporting base of natural resources, including wildlife. Effective messages, powerful enough to influence cultural practice, are best spread horizontally among ''ordinary'' people. To conserve the earth's biological resources to the year 2100 and beyond, we need a broad base of people's support and action. Only a large, international citizenry with conservation values and concerns can ensure that wildlife management and social action at various levels of government and through the efforts of nongovernmental organizations will succeed.

One of the first tasks in the creation of this citizenry is to reexamine traditional ethical principles and values of diverse cultures to incorporate environmental values and needs. In the first section that follows, ''Human Values'' (Chaps. 21–24), three ethicists and a scientist/historian examine the bases for an environmental ethic in American society. Hargrove traces the roots of the academic field of environmental ethics, a relatively new branch of professional philosophy. In the last decade, environmental ethics has become increasingly relevant to conservationists' concerns, as they seek a potentially popular rationale for saving wildlife. Environmental ethicists have identified two major and contrasting concepts of nature and an ethical approach to its protection. Is nature valuable for its own sake without regard to its usefulness to people? If so, the implication is that preservation and conservation arguments can be developed which are independent of cultural parameters and human valuation. Rolston (chap. 22) argues passionately for this view of life: every biological organism, he states, is per se a conservationist, defending its life. Therefore, a culture's conservation goals ought to encompass all the earth's biological processes, including those that precede and exceed the human presence. The opposing view is held by instrumentalists, who believe that the value of nature lies only in the minds of human valuers. Out of this view comes a belief that environmental arguments are culturally grounded in aesthetic taste for natural landscapes, much as we have an interest in and concern for works of art, as well as the belief that conservation must be justified by the practical value of wildlife to humans. Both variants of the instrumentalists' approach were reflected in Hale's and McNeely's chapters (13 and 15) on the purpose of national parks.

Norton (chap. 23) rejects the debate between intrinsic and instrumental valuers of wildlife as a dilemma that will not be settled until well into the next century and suggests that American society focus on a more tractable question: the moral consequences to human beings of destroying nature. Environmental ethics, according to Norton, should be concerned with the cultural sickness and arrogance that reduces all values to consumer values when wildlife is considered exploitable. Ehrenfeld (chap. 24) points out another flaw in Western culture that mitigates against a conservationist ethic: the failure to value diversity because of that society's preoccupation with the general rather than the particular and the power that an understanding of general laws has brought to many areas of inquiry. The purpose of conservation is to preserve natural diversity, and we cannot summon the will to preserve what we fail to value. All contributors to the discussion on environmental ethics agree that the chances for the success of conservation are inextricably linked to a shift in current human values.

Despite the discouraging news of our current lack of a pervasive, unifying conservation ethic in Western society, the good news is that the search for such an ethic is underway, and conservation activists and wildlife managers are beginning to understand that conservation ethics is as impor-

tant to their profession as medical ethics is to the medical profession: it can offer specific guidelines for managers faced with difficult choices, providing a rationale according conservation action public acceptance. Western societies are not alone in rekindling a search for a cultural basis for conservation. Efforts are underway in India, Thailand, and Sri Lanka (Davies 1987; de Alwis, personal communication). George Schaller (1986) has noted that every culture and every religion has its distinctive concepts linking humans to the natural world. These concepts could be a great force in local conservation.

Like physicians facing dilemmas in the application of scarce medical resources or dealing with ethical problems resulting from advances in technology, wildlife managers must act even in the absence of a mature, culturally embedded ethics system. In the section ''The Role of Planning'' (chaps. 25–28), two park system managers, a UN official, and an expert in conservation legislation relate the view from the trenches. In his overview of the planning process, Olindo (chap. 25), like many managers from emerging nations, sees no viability within his culture for the notion that conservation arguments should be developed independent of human valuation and societal parameters, a position conservationists from the North are increasingly coming to understand (Hales, chap. 13; McNeely, chap. 15). If we are to insist on the right of wildlife to coexist with human activities outside of parks, we should allow reverse utilization of protected areas by external interests compatible with wildlife. In the twenty-first century, Olindo sees negotiated and integrated land use as the only successful strategy for maintaining wildlife inside and outside parks. Competitive adverse impacts of wildlife on other economic activities will have to be compensated. At the same time, he urges that we protect diverse habitats and include diverse, seemingly tangential issues in our plans, regardless of whether we see current human benefit, because of our role as stewards of nature for coming generations. In the future, uses about which we are ignorant will be found if we have preserved a true diversity of habitats and possibilities in our current plans. He also suggests that in planning for the future, conservationists link with their countries' economic and political planners, a theme expanded by Bean (chap. 28). On the international level, Olindo notes the increasing number of conventions, many toothless, concerning wildlife. Fellow Kenyan Reuben Olembo (chap. 27) spells out in detail some ways to work toward the creation of more effective mechanisms for the planning and administration of environmental protection action common to groups of nations.

Tarak (chap. 26) draws on his experience as the developer of the national conservation strategy for Argentina to state some features common to all nations planning such a strategy. The same environmental problems crop up everywhere, from soil erosion to lack of conservation of genetic diversity by commercial cultivators. We also share our goals: the maintenance of biological diversity and ecological processes, and the sustainability of human activity through wise allocation of resources. Achievement of these goals implies a major change in cultural attitudes and social behavior by a vast number of inhabitants of a nation, and it is here where a strategist must practice the art of coalition and consensus-building in a manner geared to his own country. The key is to broaden the author-

ship of a national strategy to ensure that all critical constituencies have a stake in its realization.

Even the best-laid conservation plans are only as good as what they can accomplish in a world of clashing agendas. Conservationists are rarely called upon to create even a piece of a country's overall domestic plan; much more frequent is the necessity to compete with other interests to influence legislation or directives by governments at best unconcerned with environmental issues. The challenge to conservationists in every country is to become a more effective and enduring political force, seen as embracing the basic desires and values of the majority of its citizens. An American environmental lawyer, Bean (chap. 28) sees the primary task for conservationists and legislators in the coming century as defining solutions to environmental problems that preserve or improve environmental quality while allowing continued growth in the standard of living.

If this painless growth in the standard of living is in fact possible, it can only come through broad public recognition of every nation's economic dependence on the earth's living resource base. A major problem in both the United States and the USSR (Goncharenko, personal communication) is the failure of economic planners to consider the health of the environment in their planning. We need vastly increased efficiency in resource use and substitution of scarce resources by more common and more readily renewable materials. In the absence of any international code of conduct for multinational industries, currently we must rely on market forces to achieve this. The quest for efficiency and sustainability through technological advances is one way in which institutions in developed nations can promote conservation in the developing world.

But perhaps the largest impact of the developed nations on tropical ecosystems has been through massive economic development schemes, funded by multilateral development banks, that have characterized recent decades (Rich 1985). As World Bank official Lee (chap. 30) points out, a development bank's first obligation is to seek to stabilize the world's grossly inequitable economic situation. Yet measures taken to bring rich and poor nations into closer balance must not continue at the expense of the very environment that makes all development possible. If the World Bank's newly adopted wildlands policy to promote sound environmental resource practices in its development projects is effective and imitated, it will have served as a turning point in world conservation efforts. Whether a major financial institution can incorporate goals foreign to its central professional structure is questionable (Pearl, chap. 29). Conservationists will need to monitor the success with which the World Bank meets its new goals, because past history is not encouraging. In 1980, the World Bank and eight other multilateral aid agencies formed a Committee on International Development Institutions on the Environment (CIDIE) under the auspices of the United Nations Environmental Program. Subsequent studies (e.g., Sierra Club 1986) reported that CIDIE's mandate to promote environmental analyses of funded bank projects was not translated into action.

Multilateral banks are not the only international actors in conservation efforts; government aid agencies and nongovernmental organizations are other institutions that can promote concern for natural resource man-

agement and environmental protection. The U.S. Agency for International Development (USAID), one of the U.S.'s assistance instruments (others include the Overseas Private Investment Corporation, the Peace Corps, the Export-Import Bank, the Trade and Development Program, and many more, all poorly if at all coordinated), is the world's largest development aid agency, and the one with the most explicit conservation program. Pearl (chap. 29) discusses USAID's strengths and weaknesses and speculates on the direction of it and other aid organizations over the long term. Although there is concern over the relatively small amount of aid given worldwide for environmental protection, just the 330 million dollars in USAID's 1987 budget request for forestry, environment, and natural resources projects still dwarfs the amount private organizations can muster for international wildlife conservation. Last year, the largest network of NGOs, the Worldwide Fund for Nature (WWF), spent a total of 50 million dollars on its programs (Bohlen, personal communication). All the other private organizations put together perhaps add another 10 million dollars to this figure. The most effective role for private organizations may be to act as watchdogs of the high-budget activities of the governmental aid agencies of the developed nations and as advisors to assist less developed countries in leveraging aid funds for protecting biological diversity. The current and growing number of training programs (e.g., the newly created Program for Studies in Tropical Conservation at the University of Florida, Gainesville, or the Wildlife Conservation and Management Training Program at the National Zoological Park of the Smithsonian Institution, both in the United States) directed at tommorrow's conservation biologists in less developed nations is another means for the developed nations of the temperate realm to promote tropical ecosystem conservation.

One major failing on the international scene is any one source tracking the distribution of conservation moneys and activities around the world. Contributors include international bodies (the UN system: UNEP and its cooperating bodies, including the FAO, ILO, UNESCO, UNICEF, and others; the International Union for the Conservation of Nature [IUCN]; international conventions, such as the Convention on International Trade in Endangered Wildlife Products [CITES] and the International Whaling Commission [IWC]; multilateral aid banks, multinational corporations, and international networks of nongovernmental private organizations), governmental bodies (national, regional, local), and a plethora of lobbyists, special-interest groups, independent conservation biologists, and journalists. The challenge for the future is for people throughout these interacting levels to find ways to work synergistically. A first step would be a mutual awareness of activities.

The mission for expanding participation in the human side of conservation in the next century can be summed up in the word *education*. People can be educated to understand what the continuation—or destruction—of wildlife means to their future and that of their descendants and may be persuaded to act on their resulting concern in ways respectful to the diversity of life and to their own cultural mores. One effective means of communication, second only to Vittachi's (chap. 3) "horizontal" messages, is the mass media, television in particular, because of its ability to present striking and memorable visual images of current issues. We can expect, as video technology advances and transmission equipment becomes ever more compact and inexpensive, that this medium will continue to permeate ever more extensively even the most remote populations. Crystal, in his chapter on the coverage of conservation crises by American broadcasters (chap. 31), draws on his experience as the president of a major television news network and producer of a nightly international news program to explain why the extinction spasm, global warming, and other environmental catastrophes rarely appear on this pervasive information medium. The lesson for conservationists is complex; conservation biologists must be more willing to speculate intelligently to the public on the causes of environmental decay, and to share their moral and emotional concern as human beings over the implications of their findings. Journalists, on the other hand, must recognize that a crisis is not any the less urgent for building silently and must find ways to communicate the importance to everyone of environmental issues that do not currently fall into the existing categories of what constitutes "breaking news."

21

An Overview of Conservation and Human Values: Are Conservation Goals Merely Cultural Attitudes?

EUGENE C. HARGROVE

Historically, environmental ethics can be traced back to a history of ideas largely independent of the history of philosophy, beginning with the aesthetic appreciation of nature in the seventeenth century. As people traveled over the Alps in the 1680s, they found that they had strange new aesthetic feelings toward mountains, an appreciation of the sublime, the awesome, the powerful. In the eighteenth century these feelings broadened to include the picturesque, natural landscapes in between the beautiful and the sublime. This kind of picturesque travel experience was strongly supported by a landscape painting tradition arising out of a technical interest in representation. As landscape painting became more realistic, it encouraged an appreciation of natural scenery. Likewise, the importation of foreign plants and their placement in botanical gardens awoke an interest in foreign natural scenery and comparatively in local scenery. The creation of zoological gardens produced the same effect. These developments were also closely associated with the scientific study of nature in the natural-history sciences. Unlike physicists and chemists, who dealt with abstract or hypothetical entities which had no aesthetic properties, naturalists catalogued, classified, and studied properties of natural things which were also of interest to painters, poets, and landscape gardeners. The aesthetic appreciation of nature was, in fact, built into

their training: in order to prepare themselves to illustrate their work, they took art lessons in landscape painting. By the middle of the nineteenth century, all of these developments came together as the foundation of the nature preservation and nature conservation movements (Hargrove 1979, 1987; Nicolson 1963; Nash 1973). These historical considerations have direct bearing on the question of whether conservation goals are merely cultural attitudes. They are cultural attitudes beyond any doubt. All that remains to be discussed is the word *merely*.

Since the aesthetic tradition linking the natural history scientist with the artist and poet no longer plays a significant role in the professional life of biologists and other environmental scientists in this century, value issues in conservation often seem mysterious, if not obscure. Loss of value sensitivity in naturalists has resulted from the attempt to be scientific on the model of physics and chemistry. Today environmental scientists are taught that facts are scientific, and values are not. Although this shift away from value concerns is characteristic of twentieth-century environmental science, it has its roots, nevertheless, in the nineteenth century. Darwin, for example, in his autobiography complained that his mind had "become a kind of machine, for grinding out general laws out of large collections of facts," and that as a result, he had gradually lost the ability to appreciate art, literature, and music—only some appreciation of fine scenery remained (Darwin 1958).

Before the twentieth century, philosophers played virtually no positive role in the history of ideas leading up to what is now called environmental ethics. Philosophers were involved in the study of the sublime, but dropped out when the focus shifted to the picturesque. Only Emerson and Thoreau are customarily cited as early philosophical influences on environmental philosophy, and neither is considered to be an important figure in the history of philosophy. The reason why philosophy as a professional discipline has no place in the tradition seems to be at least twofold: (1) The Greek notion of metaphysical permanence made "real" objects indestructable, thereby eliminating a need for concern about the preservation of the environment. (2) Academic skepticism about whether we can know the world exists generated debates about epistemology and metaphysics which made professional philosophy of the last 300 years incompatible with preservationist and conservationist concerns. In order to deal with environmental issues philosophically, one must be willing to accept, first, that the environment exists; second, that it can be damaged and destroyed; and third, that human action and restraint from action can make a difference. Mainstream philosophers today are only reluctantly conceding that there may be environmental problems with traditional philosophical perspectives, and acceptance is still far from unanimous.

Contemporary professional interest in environmental ethics is indeed only a very recent phenomenon, beginning in the late sixties and early seventies, and the idea that there is a need for professional philosophical work in the subject has developed only slowly in the minds of those people who are now important figures in the field. Philosophers who work in environmental ethics, moreover, have to risk the scorn of colleagues and, if they are untenured, the potential loss of their jobs. We live in a period characterized by what is called the "pure/applied" debate. Applied ethics or applied philosophy, of which environmental ethics is a part, is viewed by pure philosophers as something akin to prostitution. Many pure philosophers believe, or claim to believe, that medical ethics, professional ethics, animal rights, environmental ethics, nursing ethics, and so forth, will ruin

philosophy and perhaps even bring about the end of Western civilization!

Just as there are critics of environmental ethics within philosophy, there are many outside as well. People who try to read recent work in environmental ethics frequently complain that they have difficulty understanding what is being said. One of the reasons for this is that environmental ethicists spend a lot of time discussing historical philosophical positions. There are three reasons for this preoccupation with the history of philosophy. First, philosophers commonly use historical positions as guideposts or as rules of thumb to sort through contemporary issues. This approach allows philosophers to proceed more efficiently. If they did not maintain a historical perspective, they would probably senselessly rediscover all sorts of philosophical positions over and over again, with each generation pointlessly spinning its wheels. The second and most important reason for the strong focus on the history of philosophy is that environmental philosophers almost universally hold that major errors were made in the history of philosophy which promoted improper attitudes and values still widely held today. They are trying to point out and correct these errors. And finally, there is a very practical reason: in order to keep their jobs, and thereby be able to continue doing research, environmental ethicists must produce work that other philosophers, if they approach the material with an open mind, may consider professional. Until environmental ethicists are supported by the environmental affairs community in the way that medical ethicists are supported by the medical community, there will be no environmental ethicists doing case studies.

Although this third reason will become unimportant when the "pure/applied" debate is over, the first two reasons will continue to apply. It is, therefore, not very likely that there will ever be a time when it will be possible to read environmental ethics research completely out of the context of the history of philosophy, although eventually most references may be to other contemporary work. Thus, some familiarity with major historical figures and their basic positions will always be useful to a reader of environmental ethics literature.

In addition to the difficulties with *understanding* environmental ethics literature, there are also complaints about the *relevance* of the work being done. This difficulty is really a perceptual problem, for, although it may not always be readily apparent, most work in environmental ethics has practical implications. Almost any informal survey of environmental ethicists will reveal that nearly everyone who writes in the field has environmentalist interests—and therefore has an understanding of or feel for the ethical issues involved. The applicability of work in environmental ethics, nevertheless, is often obscured by the fact that, unlike medical ethics, environmentalists are usually not really asking philosophers how to make particular decisions, but rather how to justify what they already feel they ought to do. Basic environmental attitudes were already fully established, for all practical purposes, by the middle of the nineteenth century. These attitudes made themselves apparent through behavior, especially through political action. These attitudes and the behavior associated with them, however, preceded their justification. One of the main tasks of environmental ethics is belatedly to provide these justifications. This activity involves sorting through various conceptual confusions. It is an attempt to reorder our intellectual, philosophical, or ethical traditions so that they are compatible with these new attitudes and behavior. And finally, it involves an evaluation of our new attitudes and behavior in order to determine whether they are really what we *ought* to think and do. Once we have determined the possible justifications for them, we may decide that we ought to change our behavior and attitudes in some ways.

The animal liberation movement provides an easy example of what is required. In the middle of the nineteenth century, it became clear that most people in North America and northern Europe had concluded that it was morally wrong to inflict unnecessary suffering on animals. Attitudes and behavior had changed. Most of the argumentation, however, was emotional and sentimental, and the century ended without anyone having established clearly why it was morally wrong to mistreat animals. The task of the animal liberation movement in the last decade has been to sort out the justification, and there are a number of conflicting possibilities. For example, (1) it could be wrong to mistreat animals because they have a right not to suffer, or (2) it could be wrong because humans, who used to have the right to do whatever they wanted to

animals, have now had that right restricted: they may still do a wide range of bad things to animals, including killing them, but only for good reasons and with attention to reducing suffering. In the first case animals have been brought into the moral community as either moral agents or moral patients. If this justification is commonly accepted, it will eventually lead to additional changes of attitude and behavior as the rights of animals are extended. In the second case, the focus is not on the animals at all, but on the moral character of human beings—a good, moral person no longer does certain things. One might, for example, say that treating animals well is good practice for treating other humans well. In this case, the animals are not part of the moral community, only morally considerable entities, things that a moral agent ought to take into account in making moral decisions and moral actions. Unlike the first case, there is less chance of additional change in attitude and behavior—a correction in our moral practice has been made. That is, the first justification may someday contribute to the abolition of all animal experimentation. The second would most likely only contribute to changes in the manner in which such experimentation was carried out.

In looking for justifications, the philosopher is acting much like a tailor or clothing designer with a customer who already has something in mind, but cannot fully articulate it. The end product is judged in terms of the degree to which the philosopher meets or exceeds the environmental customer's expectations. Philosophy itself is often conceived in two very different ways: (1) as a creative activity in which the end product is something like an intellectual work of art, or (2) as an attempt to reach general agreement in such a way that the end product (when properly explained) makes sense to ordinary, educated people. Environmental ethics is philosophy in the second sense, since it is trying to account for ethical attitudes in a way that will eventually meet with the approval of the practitioners in environmental affairs.

There is, however, still plenty of room for additional misunderstanding. When a nonphilosopher looks at a piece of writing in environmental ethics, he or she may conclude that the writer fails to deal with very basic issues and focuses instead on strange and esoteric ones. This is usually an error. Environmental ethics deals with two kinds of harms: harms to human beings and harms to nonhumans and the environment in general. To the degree that environmental problems involve the first, harms to humans, there is no need for new work in environmental ethics at all: Traditional ethics, which has always recognized that actions contrary to the health and welfare of humans are wrong, is in all such cases more than adequate. It is only when we move on to harms to nonhumans and the environment that the need for new principles and concepts arises, for in many cases protecting nonhumans and the environment may be opposed to the interests of all or many humans and may, in fact, endanger their health and welfare. The concern may even be more aesthetic than ethical, not concerned with harms at all. The emphasis that philosophers place on these issues does not mean that they fundamentally misconstrue the nature of environmental problems. Their job is not to solve environmental problems as such, but to provide guidance with regard to the philosophical or ethical issues that cannot be considered in terms of traditional principles and concepts alone.

Because of all these difficulties with environmental ethics, it is, of course, not easy to see whether any progress is being made. Nevertheless, if one looks closely, it is possible to discern that the debate in environmental ethics has achieved some positive results. First, animal liberation has been carefully distinguished from environmental ethics. Writing a decade ago did not sharply separate these positions. In 1980, however, J. Baird Callicott, in a paper called "Animal Liberation: A Triangular Affair," showed convincingly that the basic intuitions, behavior, and principles involved in environmental ethics are incompatible with an animal rights or animal liberation approach (Callicott 1980; see also Worren 1983). Whereas animal liberation is concerned with the individual interests and rights of animals and humans, environmental ethics is concerned with the protection of species and natural systems, a concern that is not necessarily focused on the welfare of the individual animals and plants involved. Today, no one who is aware of this debate would try to propound an environmental ethic based on animal liberation principles. While they may not be completely incompatible, they are at a minimum complementary ethical positions dealing with different ethical intuitions and behavior.

Second, environmental ethics has thoroughly examined and dismissed the claim, frequently made by Aldo Leopold and many conservation biologists, that nature has some kind of right to exist. Such a position would be feasible if an environmental ethic could be constructed on animal liberation principles so that we always acted to preserve the rights and interests of every living organism in every species and in every ecosystem. To do so, however, would be inconsistent with our basic behavior toward wildlife and natural systems, as long as we continue to want wildlife to interact naturally. Put simply, the good of the species or the system is not often, and indeed is usually not at all, compatible with the interests of individual plants and animals. Only when a species becomes endangered does our behavior toward it come close to being rights respecting behavior. If we want to discuss ethical rights seriously, then we need to alter our behavior radically. If we want to continue our current preferred behavior toward nature, then we need a new theory (Norton 1982a; Watson 1979; for a discussion of rights of future generations of humans, see Norton 1982b).

What this new theory might be is still very much a matter of debate, and even the terminology is up in the air; but since it is very relevant to the discussions in this section, it is important to sort out some of the issues involved. At the most general level, we may say, using a term invented by Kenneth Goodpaster, that we want to minimally identify nature as being morally considerable, that is, worthy of being considered by a moral agent in moral decision making (Goodpaster 1978). The problem of moral consideration leads directly to a problem of value. In finding an appropriate ethical theory of justification, we need to determine in just what sense morally considerable entities are valuable. There are two general perspectives. First, these entities may be valuable instrumentally or intrinsically. They are instrumentally valuable if their value is in their use to human beings or some other beings. They are intrinsically valuable if they are valuable for their own sake, without regard to their use. Second, they may be valuable anthropocentrically or nonanthropocentrically. They are anthropocentrically valuable if their value is derived from human judgment or valuation or from human use, interests, or needs. They are nonanthropocentrically valuable if their value is completely independent of human judgment or valuation or of human use, interests, or needs.

It is possible to arrange these terms so that we have the following possibilities: anthropocentric intrinsic and instrumental value and nonanthropocentric intrinsic and instrumental value. The first two are tied in some way to human judgment or to human use, interests, and needs. The second two are not. In general, there is a desire among environmental ethicists to develop a theory that is nonanthropocentric, so that the value of natural things will not be dependent on some reference to human beings. A position based on such values would be a very strong justification for the preservation and conservation of nature and natural things, since it would be independent of cultural parameters and all human valuation. The values would be *in* nature itself, not merely in the minds of humans. Despite the desirability of a theory based on such values, however, it is theoretically difficult: Such a theory would be incompatible with traditional value theory, and there is no guarantee that ordinary people would make the transition from a valueless world of fact, the common view today, to one in which both values and facts exist in the world independent of human valuation.

Although for a long time the quest has been exclusively for a nonanthropocentric theory, recently a new possibility, called "weak anthropocentrism" (Norton 1984), has been suggested. According to the proponents of weak anthropocentrism, although strong anthropocentrism might have only bad behavioral consequences for environmental ethics, weak anthropocentrism, on the other hand, has the same practical consequences as nonanthropocentrism and, moreover, is philosophically less complicated and can be used productively as the foundation of environmental ethics until an acceptable nonanthropocentric theory is available.

In the chapters that follow, two by philosophers and one by a conservation biologist, these distinctions play an important role. The first philosopher is Holmes Rolston III, who is strongly committed to the quest for a nonanthropocentric theory. The second is Bryan G. Norton, who is the originator of the weak anthropocentric position. The conservation biologist is David Ehrenfeld, who will present a practical example—he will discuss attitudes toward diversity.

It is impossible to predict in advance just what the principles of environmental ethics will be in 2100. Those principles will depend in part on possible changes in moral sentiment of the peoples of the earth and in part on the direction that mainstream professional philosophy takes in the coming decades. There is also the possibility of cross-cultural borrowing. More than a decade ago one philosopher argued pessimistically that we need not concern ourselves with the formulation of any principles for environmental ethics, since such activity would "rest on the presumption that our descendants will still delight in what now delights only some of us and did not delight our predecessors" (Passmore 1974). Such a position, I believe, underestimates, first, the close relationship between developments in environmental ethics and the historical development of an interest in and concern for nature in Western civilization and, second, the comparative philosophical and cultural resources in other world traditions that are likely to have a favorable impact. Changes in philosophical and ethical perspective do not take place very quickly and are slow to disappear. There is, for example, a basic unity in all the philosophical writings in Western philosophy over the last 300 years, and environmental ethics is in part an outgrowth of and in part a reaction to this body of philosophy material. Given the glacial speed at which philosophy changes its basic paradigms, we can reasonably expect people in 2100 to still have a concern for nature, one which is still intelligible to us, though perhaps more refined, but based, nevertheless, on the work that is taking place today. The following papers are a step in that direction.

22

Biology Without Conservation: An Environmental Misfit and Contradiction in Terms

HOLMES ROLSTON III

CONSERVATION IN BIOLOGY AND PHYSICS

We can launch this exploration at what may seem an unpromising point: by distinguishing between conservation in physics and in biology. In physics, conservation is a natural law and takes place willy-nilly. In classical physics, energy is neither created nor destroyed but conserved through transformations. Likewise with matter. In relativistic physics, though the one may be transformed into the other, matter-energy is conserved in the interconversions. Likewise with spin, charge, momentum, or baryon number. Conservation in physics is an impressive feature of nature; much elegance and mathematical symmetry depend on it. In a sense, it is something humans can value; it adds aesthetic beauty to our world. But in the usual sense, when we say that values are conserved, we mean, for example, that the numerical amounts on both sides in an equation remain the same, reflecting certain automatic natural phenomena.

Sometimes in physics, statistical minima or maxima may be maintained, as when a light ray travels over the shortest path, or when a reversible system, after fluctuation or disturbance, returns to an equilibrium. All these things happen without anyone looking out after them. A group of concerned physicists, gathered to guarantee conservation goals, would be confused.

Anticipating conservation in biology, we note that a merely physical object has nothing to conserve. Though conservation takes place during the various events that happen to a rock—being heated by the noonday sun, being eroded by the rains—the rock conserves no identity. It changes without conservation goals. An inert rock exists on its own, making no assertion over the environment and not needing it. When high waters run into a lake, the exit streams shift in flow; the lake level rises and later subsides to its former level. But the lake is conserving nothing.

CONSERVATION IN ORGANISMS

Biological organisms, by contrast, conserve an identity, an anatomy maintained over time by a functioning metabolism. They have a life, whereas physical objects do not. Organisms are self-maintaining systems; they grow and are irritable in response to stimuli. They resist dying. They reproduce. They can be healthy or diseased. They erect a careful, semipermeable boundary between themselves and the rest of nature; they assimilate environmental materials to their own needs. They gain and maintain internal order against the disordering tendencies of external nature. They keep rewinding and recomposing themselves, while inanimate objects run down, erode, and decompose.

Life is a countercurrent to entropy, an energetic fight uphill in a world that overall moves thermodynamically downhill. Organisms suck order out of their environment; they pump out disorder. In physics entropy is not conserved; it increases. In biology organisms must locally fight this increase: a conservation of negentropy.

The constellation of these life characteristics is nowhere found outside organisms. A crystal reproduces a pattern and may restore a damaged surface; a planetary system maintains an equilibrium; a volcano may grow in countercurrent to entropy. A lenticular altocumulus cloud, formed as a standing wave over a mountain range, is steadily recomposed by input and output of airflow. But any mechanical precursors of life fail to integrate into the pattern that we call an organism. Or perhaps we should say that over evolutionary time they did, and that there emerged something greater than the physical precedents: life. The organism is vitally more than physics or chemistry.

The "genius" of life is coded into genetic sets, which are missing from minerals, volcanoes, clouds. An organism is thus a spontaneous cybernetic system, self-maintaining, sustaining and reproducing itself on the basis of information about how to make a way through the world. Some internal representation is symbolically mediated in the coded "program" held forth, in motion toward the execution of this goal, checking against performance in the world, using some sentient, perceptive, or other responsive capacities through which to compare match and mismatch. The cybernetic controlling program can reckon with vicissitudes, opportunities, and adversities that the world presents.

Causes are pervasive in physics; conservation persists through causal chains. But something more than causes, if (sometimes) less than sentience, is operating within every organism. *Information* is superintending the causes, and without this information the organism would collapse into a sand heap. This information is a modern equivalent of what Aristotle called formal and final causes; it gives the organism a *telos*, "end," a kind of (nonfelt) purpose. All this cargo is carried by the DNA, essentially a set of linguistic molecules. Humans artificially impose an alphabet on ink and paper, but living things long before were employing a natural alphabet, imposing a code on four nucleotide bases strung as cross-links on a double helix. A

triplet of bases stands for one of the twenty amino acids, and thus by a serial reading of the DNA, translated by messenger RNA, a long polypeptide chain is synthesized, such that its sequential structure predetermines the bioform into which it will fold. Ever-lengthening chains, logical lines, like ever-longer sentences, are organized into genes, like paragraphs and chapters, and so the story of life is written into the genetic library.

The genetic set is thus really a *propositional set*—to choose a deliberately provocative term—recalling that the Latin *propositum* is an assertion, a set task, a theme, a plan, a proposal, a project, as well as a cognitive statement. From this it is also a *motivational set,* unlike human written material, since these life motifs are set to drive the movement from genotypic potential to phenotypic expression. No book is self-actualizing. Given a chance, these molecules seek organic self-expression. They project a life way and claim the other as needs may be, an assertive claim. Unlike the physical rock, existing on its own and making no claims on its environment, coyotes must eat. The biological organism must claim the environment as source and sink, from which to abstract energy and materials and into which to excrete them. It "takes advantage" of its environment.

The DNA representing life is thus a *logical set,* not less than a biological set. Coding the logic of a life that is carried on not only at the molecular, genetic level but equally at the native-range, environmental, phenotypic level, organisms by a sort of symbolic logic make these molecular positions and shapes into symbols of life. The novel resourcefulness lies in the epistemic content conserved, developed, and thrown forward to make biological resources out of the physicochemical sources. An open cybernetic system, with an executive steering core, is partly a special kind of cause-and-effect system and partly something more: a historical information system discovering ends so as to make a way through the world, and a system of significances valuing operations, pursuits, resources.

Even stronger still, the genetic set is a *normative set;* it distinguishes between what *is* and what *ought to be.* The organism has a biological obligation thrust upon it. This does not mean that the organism is a moral system, for there are no moral agents in nature apart from persons. But the organism is an axiological system. The

DNA is a set of *conservation molecules*. So the organism grows, reproduces, repairs its wounds, and resists death. The physical state that the organism seeks, idealized as its programmatic form, is a valued state. The living individual, taken as a "point experience" in the interconnecting web of an ecosystem, is per se an intrinsic value. A life is defended for what it is in itself, without necessary further contributory reference—although, given the structure of all ecosystems, such lives invariably do have further contributory reference.

Warblers preserve their own kind; their program is to make more warblers; they consume (and regulate) insects and avoid raptors. They have connections in their ecosystems that go on "over their heads," but what is "in their heads" (and in their genes) is that being a warbler is a good thing. Organisms have their standards, fit into their niche though they must. They promote their own realization, at the same time that they track an environment. They have a technique, know-how. Every organism has a *good-of-its-own;* it defends its kind as a *good kind*. In that sense, to know what a kind is is also to know what a good-of-that-kind is. As soon as one knows what a yellow-rumped warbler is, one knows what a good yellow-rumped warbler is. One knows the biological identity sought and conserved.

Biology can mean two different things. It can refer to the science that humans have produced; this appears in textbooks, in theories of kin selection. Such biology goes on during laboratory exercises and field trips. This is a subjective affair in human heads. Take away humans, and biology, like the other sciences, disappears. Biology can also refer to the life metabolisms that appeared on the earth long before humans. Such biology is an objective affair out there in the world. Take away humans, and this nonhuman biology remains. Biology in the latter sense is primary, and on it biology in the former, secondary sense depends. In the primary sense, biology without conservation is impossible, a contradiction in terms, a condition that can exist in the actual world only temporarily, since it will be self-defeating and selected against. Biology without conservation is death.

Conservation in biology both is and is not a natural law. Conservation is required for survival; but, unlike physics, conservation may fail. The law of life is do or die; that disjunctive law is maintained without fail. But conservation occurs only when a bio-logic drives a will-to-live. Conservation in physics pervades the universe as natural law. Conservation in biology has to defend a local, earth-bound self-organization. This difference introduces alternatives into biology. When humans appear, this further introduces options and moral decisions. What this means for biology in the secondary, humanistic sense is a conclusion toward which we are headed.

CONSERVATION AND ELABORATION IN ECOSYSTEMS

Conservation of Spontaneous Biological Community

The conservation of biological identity within organisms is evident, the first law of life. Turning to the outside environment, however, we may be prone to think that nature conserves nothing. From the skin in, the organism is a model of conservation; all its parts are integrated into a whole with the end of conserving life against threats in the environment. From the skin out, the environment is sheer conflict, with opposing forces pressing to disintegrate the unwary life. Or, the environment is utter indifference; ecosystemic forces are nonbiotic (wind, weather, solar energy, geomorphic processes); ecosystemic materials are inert (rocks, soil particles) or dead and decaying (humus, scat).

By contrast with an organism, we may first say that ecosystems are not cybernetic systems. They involve only stochastic processes—equilibrating systems where one form of life preys on or pushes out another. All the cybernetics lies in the individual organisms; ecosystems are nothing but these organisms locked in contest with each other, placed in a setting of nonbiotic forces. This indifference and hostility of the environment is precisely why organismic conservation can fail.

Yet there is more. Is anything conserved in ecosystems? Unlike organisms, ecosystems have no control center, no genome, no brain, no self-identification. There is no *biological identity* to conserve, yet *biological community* is conserved. In fact, we find in ecosystems not only the conservation of biological processes over long periods of evolutionary time, but their elaboration and diversification. True, an ecosystem is not an organism; it has no tight, centered biological identity. It is not an individual. But, at the other extreme, an ecosystem is not a fortuitous juxtaposition of unrelated organisms. It is a web of interdependent life, with some subsystems and components more closely, others more loosely interrelated. An ecosystem is a selective system in which natural selection results in a sufficient containment for the component species. Mutations that prove beneficial (= of value for life) are selected; species that fit a niche are selected, via selection of individual organisms. All the component individuals fight for their own conservation and for that of their kind, but nothing can win except under the requirement that each winner have a satisfactory fit. Otherwise all lose; individuals die, species remain rare or go extinct.

Ecosystems yield results that go on "over the heads" of any of the component organisms. Ecosystems have no centered cybernetic control, much less do they deliberately conserve anything. Nevertheless there is the generation of an order that arises spontaneously (though systematically and inevitably) when many organic units interact, each projecting its own program. We tend to think that such order will be of low quality because it is uncentered and not purposive, without any single center of experience. But, on the contrary, such order can be of high quality just because, in result, many diverse kinds of things with their widespread skills, biological identities, and evolutionary achievements are integrated into a pluralist community.

A human culture is another example of the spontaneous generation of order, seen when language or markets arise, or when arts and sciences develop to which many performers contribute each by pressing his own career, nobody overseeing the whole. A culture would be quite poor under the tyranny of one mind; it is richer, more diverse, more complex because it integrates 100,000 minds. One person can appreciate only a fraction of the wealth of a culture. Likewise a biological community would be quite poor if restricted to the accomplishments that can be contained in a single natural kind. How much richer is the community with 10,000 species where the system is a cybernetic transformer that interweaves diverse organic achievements.

Perhaps in moving from organisms to ecosystems we have slipped back toward something like conservation in physics. Mass, energy, spin are conserved by blind laws; analogously, natural selection, conserving adapted fitness, is a blind, noncybernetic law of nature. There is nothing organismic about selection; no life is being conserved. The homeostatic forces in an ecosystem—by which, for instance, insect outbreaks are damped out, or by which succession is reset and the forest regenerated after a fire—are stochastic forces not significantly different from the homeostasis that after a flood returns a lake to its former level. The forces of conservation in physics are causal forces, and so also, one may first say, are the forces of conservation in ecosystems.

Yet the matter is not so simple. Natural selection is an odd sort of causation. It posits, first, random mutations. These random variations make a difference only as emplaced in the genetic set of an organism with a survival drive, located in an ecosystem. Natural selection, although nonconscious, is still a force that picks the few out of many options, picks the best adapted for their ecosystems, selects for biofunction. Nowhere in physics or chemistry do we meet a causal or other conservative force of this kind.

Indeed, we now find a natural pressure that favors biofunctional efficiency in community, a positive, prolife force in this respect, however groping, blind, or indifferent it may otherwise seem. There is something extraordinary, from the viewpoints of physics and chemistry, about a causality that operates statistically to select A over B because of increased adaptive fit. Physics talks of conservation in forces and fields, but biology introduces something new: the conservation of fitness in community, keyed to information about how to make a resourceful way through the world. Unlike a warbler, a rock in its environment has neither a fitness nor an ecology there.

When conservation in physics and chemistry is not inevitable (not of mass, energy, spin, etc.), what is maintained is the statistically more likely: stochastic processes that result in minima or maxima that are probable (such as the stablest geomorphic system) in a world constantly tugged toward entropy. Conservation in ecosystems can involve such stochastic elements, but there is more. In the biotic realm, the selection over time is improbable from the viewpoints of chemistry and physics, that is, the rare and less likely mutation but novel and more fit life structure, were random or even physicostatistical factors alone to govern what persists in time. The system selects for life forms that are novel in their diversity and complexity.

The conserving system generates new species, as well as conserving existing ones that remain fit in their environments, and we have nothing like this in physics and chemistry. This process too is statistical; there are fluctuations upward and downward, but it is biostatistical. Nor do we think that biostatistical conservation, because it is statistical, reveals no laws of nature.

Randomness and Evolutionary Development

Ecosystems are the least understood level of biological organization, and evolution at the systemic level is the most incomplete part of evolutionary theory. Unfortunately, biologists have little theory explaining the elaboration and development of life. John Maynard Smith, a principal theorist, says that we need "to put an arrow on evolutionary time" but we get no help from evolutionary theory. "It is in some sense true that evolution has led from the simple to the complex: procaryotes precede eucaryotes, single-celled precede many-celled organisms, taxes and kineses precede complex instinctive or learnt acts. I do not think that biology has at present anything very profound to say about this" (1972:98). "There is nothing in neo-Darwinism which enables us to predict a long-term increase in complexity" (1972:89).

Indeed, a widespread doctrine is that increasing complexity in the process is random. The evolutionary ecosystems that result on the earth, including the humans produced by them, says Stephen Jay Gould, another principal theorist, are "chance riches" (1980). Everything is "the fragile result of an enormous concatenation of improbabilities, not the predictable product of any definite process" (1983:101–102). Jacques Monod, a Nobel laureate, insists, "Pure chance, absolutely free but blind, [is] at the very root of this stupendous edifice of evolution. . . . The tremendous journey of evolution over the past three billion years or so, the prodigious wealth of structures it has engendered, and the extraordinarily effective telenomic performances of living beings, from bacteria to man . . . [are] the product of an enormous lottery presided over by natural selection, blindly picking the rare winners from among numbers drawn at utter random" (1972:112–113, 138). Humans can value what they have received by chance, but it is hard to see how ecosystemic nature could be conserving or elaborating anything, if the outcome is all by chance.

On the other hand, equally prominent biologists think—in the phrase of Melvin Calvin, another Nobel laureate—that there is some "selectivity intrinsic in the structures" that lures the ascent of life (1975:176). Life is "a logical consequence" of natural principles (1975:169). George Wald, another Nobel laureate, says, "This universe breeds life inevitably" (1974:9). Manfred Eigen, still another Nobel laureate, concludes "that the evolution of life . . . must be considered an *inevitable* process despite its indeterminate course" (1971:519).

L. v. Salvini-Plawen and Ernst Mayr (1977) claim that sight or photoreceptors have evolved independently at least forty times; that seems evidence of selection for perceptive complexity. It also seems plausible, in at least some lines, that other forms of sentience (hearing, smelling) will be selected for, as will locomotive ability and even intelligence—where these convey survival power. In some niches and up to the point of overspecialization, the more complex will be better able to deal with the shifting vicissitudes of a complex environment.

Even those who doubt any trend toward complexity are forced to concede a trend toward expansion, though often they do not realize that biology has hardly any more theory that explains expansion. Life might have achieved a few simple forms and stagnated. But it did not. G. G. Simpson, a paleontologist, though denying any upward trends and noticing that there are periods of contraction as well as of expansion, concluded that there is in evolution "a tendency for life to expand, to fill in all available spaces in the liveable environments, including those created by the process of that expansion itself. . . . The total number and variety of organisms existing in the world . . . has shown a tendency to increase markedly during the history of life" (1964:243, 341).

R. H. Whittaker, a founder of ecosystem theory, finds, despite "island" and other local saturations and equilibria, that on continental scales and for most groups "increase of species diversity . . . is a self-augmenting evolutionary process without any evident limit." There is a natural tendency toward increased "species packing" (1972:214). Aldo Leopold, a founder of conservation biology, says, "Science has given us many doubts, but it has given us at least one certainty: the trend of evolution is to elaborate and diversify the biota" (1949:216).

It is certainly true that there is randomness in evolutionary nature. But it is not random that there is diversity. Four billion species (the total number over evolutionary time) do not appear by accident. Rather, randomness is a diversity generator, mixed as this is with principles of the spontaneous generation and conservation of order. Nor is it random that there is advancement. Rather, randomness is an advancement generator, supported as advancement comes to be by trophic pyramids in which lower ways of life are also conserved. We do not wish to cast out the randomness, or the conflict, but we need to recast both in a bigger picture.

There is a sort of pushup, lockup, ratchet effect that conserves the upstrokes and the outreaches. The accelerations and elaborations are selected for, not in the sense that all life forms are accelerated or elaborated, but in the sense that the later in time, the more accelerated the forms at the top of the trophic pyramids, and the more elaborated the multiple trophic pyramids of the earth. Some groups dead-end in extinction, but most evolve into something else. There are some wayward lines, but, through it all, there is remarkable conservation. Simpson says, "Few, if any, of the broadest and most basic types have ever become extinct. . . . All main types represent abilities to follow broadly distinctive ways of life, and the earlier or lower persist along with the later and higher because these latter represent not competitors doing the same sorts of things as their lower ancestors but groups developing distinctively new ways of life" (1964:341).

Biomolecular Conservation and Species Elaboration in a Prolific System

At the molecular level, where the story taking place at the molar level is recorded, the cytochrome *c* molecule has been conserved through its modifications from molds, to moths, to humans—over one and one-half billion years. Glycolysis, used in every cell and especially crucial in the blood and the brain, has been preserved since before there was oxygen in the atmosphere. Myoglobin, which evolved before hemoglobin, was both preserved as a separate molecule and transformed and modified into one of the subunits of the hemoglobin molecule. The genetic coding used for synthesizing protein molecules is at least two billion years old, conserved in essentials, modified in details. The three-letter code used now seems to have evolved from a two-letter code, both storing the information by which, in various life forms, billions of different kinds of proteins are keyed.

The difference between a handful of mineral dirt and a handful of humus lies principally in the fact that the humus—containing seeds, spores, pollen, insects, worms, invertebrates, fungi, bacteria—has a billion years of heredity in it, recorded in a trillion bits of information. A handful of mineral dust might be the same on Jupiter or Mars; the handful of humus is bound into the earth's history. It is a handful of biological conservation.

Some will say that none of this biomolecular conservation is assignable to ecosystems; it results from conservation forces inside individual organisms. Ecosystems are epiphenomena that arise when individuals interact, nothing over and above their member parts. Accordingly, conservation takes place only in organisms. Individuals defend only their own kind. What is stored in their genes is information about how to make their particular species of way through their world, nothing more.

Yet events in a community of adaptive fitness transcend any individual and species, because in addition to the conservation, coded at the genetic level and enacted at the phenotypic level, there is an elaboration of kinds in an increasingly richer and more diverse community. The particular, individual stories recorded in the biomolecular events are substories of a bigger story. Everything is what it is in relation to other things, and the genetic stories are as much of relational roles as of individual integrities. Nature treats individuals with short lifespans. Never long conserved, they are born, hatched, sprouted, die. Even sequoia trees are ephemeral on evolutionary scales. What is longer conserved is really the species, the form of life, instantiated in individuals, transmitted through the genes, kept as long as it fits its environment.

What is still longer conserved is the biological community, in which species come and go, with the community too at length transformed over geological time through species turnover. Species increase *their kind;* but ecosystems increase *kinds,* superposing the latter increase onto the former.

Seen over such spans of time, the biomolecular conservation records this ecosystem elaboration. It is true that mutations taking place at the molecular level provide an innovative principle, the supply side of the novelty. It is equally true that, on the retention side, what gets conserved is tested at the molar level for its fit into niches in an ecosystem. And the whole ecosystem churns incessant, kaleidoscopic novelty.

When conservation is transformed into elaboration, nature becomes liberal as well as conservative. Nature seems to make as many species as it can, to maximize species. Despite the pressures toward efficiency that constrain each kind, the overall display of kinds is profuse. This conservation and elaboration in ecosystems, like the biology in organisms, takes place prior to and independently of the human presence. The biologist finds these to be objectively satisfactory communities, that is, communities making and maintaining satisfactory places for millions of species. The ethicist, in a subjective judgment matching the objective process, finds such ecosystems to be imposing and satisfactory and wishes to conserve them. What this means for human conservation biology is, again, a conclusion toward which we are headed.

CONSERVATION IN CULTURE

Conservation of Cultural Goals

Humans are a unique species. Humans are in the world *cognitively* at linguistic, deliberative, self-conscious levels equaled by no other animals. Humans are in the world *critically,* as nothing else is. Only humans can consider, reflect upon, be right or wrong about the way they are in the world. Humans are in the world *ethically* as nothing else is. Animals are wholly absorbed into those niches in which they have such satisfactory fitness, but humans can stand apart from the world and consider themselves in relation to it. Humans espouse world views, as can nothing else; they have options in these world views. Humans are only part of the world in biological senses, but they are the only part of the world that can orient themselves with respect to a theory of it. The animal has only its own horizons; humans can have multiple, even global horizons. Animals have a habitat; but humans have a world. Humans are, in this sense, eccentric to the world, standouts in it.

This cognitive, critical, ethical importance in humans is matched by their ecosystemic unimportance. Humans have little biological role in ecosystems—in the sense that were they subtracted from oak-hickory forests, or African savannas, or Asian steppes, those ecosystems would not be negatively affected; rather they would be improved. Humans are not important as predators or prey; from an ecosystemic point of view the early humans played little role in the food chains or in regulating life cycles. They are a late addition to the systems, and their cultural activities (except perhaps for primitive tribes) only degrade the system, if considered biologically and ecologically.

Has this species without a typical role some apical role? What is the standing of those who stand on top? The most important answer is that humans are to develop *cultures;* we are set to that task by the hand and the brain, by the options we have cognitively, critically, ethically. Humans superpose culture on biology. Man is the political animal; he builds a *polis,* a city-state.

A culture too is a cybernetic system and must conserve the information by which it is maintained. In important respects, a culture is more like an ecosystem than an organism; it is decentralized and loose—a community, not an individual. In culture, however, conservation of information is not genetic but neural. Acquired, Lamarckian information can be transmitted. This takes place through the conservation of ideas, sponsored by the brain, coded into its memory circuits, selected because these ideas are in some sense culturally functional or significant. Such information can be stored in agricultural, industrial, political, scientific, artistic, and religious traditions. In literate societies such information can find its way into books.

One thing a culture must preserve is its knowledge and technology in the natural world, because a culture, by definition, rebuilds that environment. A culture cannot persist without a resource base, without resourcefulness, without behaviors toward nature that protect the culture. Humans too must play the survival game; they must capture values in nature. Humans can and ought to conserve their own (worthy) kinds of life.

If the conservation and elaboration of their cultures is the only human role, it follows that conservation goals are merely cultural attitudes, with nothing owed to biological processes beyond. It is perfectly permissible for such goals to maximize the cultures they serve. Indeed, it is pointless to do more, since there are no other values to which conservationists are obligated. True, cultures are responsible beyond themselves to other cultures, so that conservation goals will have to be negotiated interculturally. But such intercultural goals will still be nothing but cultural attitudes, although resulting from multiple cultures. All goals will maximize culture, with nature nothing but an instrument for the maximizing of culture. Goals will defend only the collective human interest.

Moral Fitness and Biological Conservation

What is the standing of those who stand on top? One answer is that one human role is to admire the ecosystems they culminate. They ought to be ideal observers, using the excellent rationality peculiar to their niche so that rationality functions as more than a survival tool for defending their cultural forms of life. Mind forms an intelligible view of the whole and conserves ideals of life in all their forms, with the ecosystemic processes that sustain these biological ideals.

Humans can begin to comprehend what comprehends them; in this lies their paradox and responsibility. Their world views may lead them to resourceful use of or responsible care for other species. Humans can be superior to nonhumans in their resource use, or in their self-actualization or cultural definitions. They can also be superior in loving nonhuman others, perhaps even as themselves. The human capacity for an overview of the whole makes us superior and imposes strange duties, those of transcending human interests and linking them up with those of the community of life on the earth. Humans can see and oversee not just their own, biological, species-specific conservation, with its emergent cultural conservation. They can see and oversee the ecosystemic conservation, diversification, and elaboration. They can admire the global story, the natural history, the biospheric conservation. Therefore, humans have a grander, more comprehensive, more responsible role.

Anything less would stunt humanity because it would not reach genuine human transcendence—a transcending overview caring for the others. Anything less would be nothing but a cultural attitude, since it failed to transcend culture and to understand the biological values, or to count morally the forms of life, that lie beyond culture.

But this requires of humans a new level of fitness. The concept of fitness is intially biological, but it can be extrapolated into morality. Appropriate conduct fits the situations encountered. In both biology and ethics, life demands suitable behavior—right actions. A black-footed ferret's behavior is *right* (or good) in its grasslands niche; a person's conduct is *right* (or good) when he or she conserves the ferret. In a way, this equivocates on terms such as *fit* and *right*. The first use means nonmorally adapted to an ecosystem; the second use counts ethically a species imperiled by human encroachment. Still, granted that animals are not reflective moral agents, the question arises as to what critical, reflective moral agency, when it occurs, contributes to human fitness? Perhaps when humans are moral in their cultural attitudes, this is functionally analogous at a higher level to the nonmoral fitness of animals in habitat. Both are questions about a life form being good-of-its-kind, good-in-its-kind-of-place, about being in a good kind of place, and these add up to the question of well-placed value.

"Every living thing," claimed Bertrand Russell, "is a sort of imperialist, seeking to transform as much of its environment as it can into itself and its seed" (1974:30). Such "self-seeking" is only part of the truth, even in the biological world. Every species, every organism is a sort of maximizer, defending its own program and seeking in reproduction to leave as many copies of itself as it can. Coyotes try to convert as much of the world as they can into coyotes; oak trees would make the forest into nothing but oaks. That is the survival of the fittest. Always replace another kind with one of your own kind—that is what the "selfish" genes say about conservation goals.

Yet that is not the whole picture. Nature has

not equipped or inclined any one form to transform very much of the environment into itself and its seed. Each life form is specialized for a niche, limited to its own sector, and so woven into a web that it depends on many other species in a dynamic biomass. Animals with locomotion, especially the specialists, seek their own preferred habitats and avoid others. Plants flourish in some soils, adapted to particular moisture and light conditions, and ill fit others. Recent biology has emphasized not so much aggrandizing conquest as it has adaptedness, habitat fittedness, efficiency. If not checked from within, a species' genetic impulses are checked from without by ecosystemic forces that keep every living thing in community. Would-be imperialists cannot dominate the world; they can gain only situated environmental fitness. Would-be maximizers can be no more than optimizers. What is increased over evolutionary time is not the population of any one kind, but diversity and richness in kinds.

All this is premoral, so what are we to say when, at the top of the ecosystemic pyramid, there emerges *Homo sapiens,* so powerful and unspecialized that, culturally evolving to where humans now are, we can almost transform the earth into ourselves and our seed? Must we, should we, unleash these selfish genes to develop the last acre in our interests? Must we set conservation goals that only defend our cultural attitudes? Should we maximize our natural kind or our kind of culture? Should we capture and fill up all the niches? Always convert a nonhuman into a human, or a human resource, insofar as possible. Or does some other behavior yield a better-adapted environmental fitness?

The answer lies in nature's simultaneously equipping us with a conscience coupled with our power, neither such power nor conscience appearing in nonhuman creatures. Humans are the creatures that have evolved a conscience. This conscience can wisely direct the magnificent, fearful power of the brain and hand. Conscientious human activity ought to be a form of life that both fits and befits, however much it also elaborates and extends, what has previously, premorally been the case. An environmental ethic tries to maximize conscience in order to maximize fitness in the environment.

Taking the global view, humans will max-imize not merely themselves and their cultures, but they will couple this with conserving the richness of kinds that has been achieved in ecosystems, conserved over billions of years. Humans ought to be integrated into the world ethically. Were the human species to use its conscience only to defend its own form of life, we should have the paradox that the single moral species would act only in its collective self-interest toward all the rest. There is something morally naïve about an anthropocentrism that takes the human reference frame as an arbitrary, yet absolute end and conserves everything else relative to its utility.

Several billion years' worth of creative toil, several million species of teeming life have been handed over to the care of this late-coming species in which culture has flowered and morals have emerged. Ought not those of this sole moral species do something less self-interested than to count all the produce of an evolutionary ecosystem in terms of conservation goals that are merely cultural attitudes? Ought not *Homo sapiens,* if true to their specific epithet, value this host of species as something with a claim to care in its own right? Have we not a biological obligation thrust upon us?

We conclude with a return to biology, this time not as an objective process in the natural world, but as a subjective process in scientists' heads—a cultural process. This subjective side of biology, too, must be a good fit. It can first seem that humans ought to pursue biology in order to exploit nature to build culture. Like other organisms, humans conserve, and ought to conserve, only their own kind. But what kind of biology would this be? A logic of life with no love for life beyond the human scene, no will for the fauna and flora to continue for what they are in themselves? A logic of life insensitive to situated environmental fitness? A logic of life in which only humans count? A logic of life in which the conservation goals are nothing but cultural attitudes?

Nonhumans in their biology can conserve only their own kinds, but humans have a more comprehensive, moral role in their conservation of biological values. Otherwise their biology without conservation is a contradiction in terms, as well as misfit in its environment.

23

The Cultural Approach to Conservation Biology

BRYAN G. NORTON

One lazy Saturday afternoon I was walking on the beach on the North end of Longboat Key, Florida—the last unspoiled strip of beach on that once-beautiful island. The currents in Longboat Pass had shifted and were dumping sand in a crescent spit out into the Gulf of Mexico. The new sandbar was forming a tidal lagoon. As I walked along on the sandbar, I came face to face with an eight-year-old girl as she clambered from the lagoon onto the ledge of the sandbar. She was cradling a dozen fresh sand dollars in her arms. Looking past her, I saw her mother and older sister dredging sand dollars from the shallow lagoon. They walked back and forth, systematically scuffing their feet through the soft sand. As they dislodged the sand dollars, they picked them up and held them for the little girl, who transported and piled them by their powerboat that was beached on the sandbar. A pile of several hundred had accumulated on the sand by the boat.

"You know, they're alive," I said indignantly.

"We can bleach 'em at home and they'll turn white," the little girl informed me. I could hardly argue with that.

"Do you need so many?" I asked.

"My momma makes 'em outta things," she explained.

I pressed my case: "How many does she need to make things?"

"We can get a nickel apiece for the extras at the craft store," the little girl replied.

Our brief conversation ended, as suddenly as it had begun, in ideological impasse. As I wandered away, muttering to myself, I turned over and over in my mind what I should have said to the little girl. Our discussion on the sand had posed, in microcosm, the problem of environmental values.

I might have talked to the little girl about sustainable yields and tried to get her to worry about whether there would be sand dollars the next time she came to the beach. That's what I was trying to get at when I asked if she needed so many. But, when I asked how many she needed, I'd already granted the utilitarian value of sand dollars. If one is worth a nickel, more will be worth dollars. I didn't want to object to the exploitation of the sand dollars merely on conservationist grounds; I wanted to say more, that the sand dollars are more than mere commodities to be measured in nickels.

I had encountered what David Ehrenfeld has aptly described as the conservationist's dilemma (Ehrenfeld 1976, 1978). To give "economic" arguments in terms of sustainable yields is to admit that species have value as commodities. And it is difficult to rein in exploitation once it is admitted there are profits to be made, for, in our society at least, the value of commodities is described by the adage "More is better."

Ehrenfeld has accordingly chosen the other horn of the conservationist's dilemma. He says that, by reason of their long-standing existence in nature, other species have an "unimpeachable right to continued existence" (Ehrenfeld 1978:208). This is an appealing position. It expresses the deeply moral intuition I felt when I saw the pile of green disks drying in the Florida sun and evokes the revulsion we feel in response to apartheid and other abominable discriminations against races of humans. Philosophically, however, this approach is beset with enormous problems. Rights have, historically and semantically, been ascribed to individuals. Could I, with a straight face, say to the little girl, "Put them all back, each and every one of them; they have a right to live"? I'd have felt silly because I knew this industrious family would not be moved by speeches for sand dollar liberation, however eloquent. Worse, I'd have been a hypocrite. These discoid echinoderms surely have no greater rights than the red snapper I had enjoyed for lunch.

Nor is it easy to transfer the concept of individual rights to species and ecosystems. Individual rights surely have something to do with the fact that individual organisms have a "good of their own" (Taylor 1986). But what is the corresponding "good" of a species? Is it good for the species of sand dollars to be left alone in the lagoon or is it better for little girls to exert adaptational pressure so the species will be prepared for greater exploitative challenges in the future? Should we put a fence around the lagoon to keep out all predators, including little girls? Or should we let sand dollars face, as all truly wild species must, selectional pressures (Norton 1987)?

While references to rights of wild species are appealing and may be rhetorically useful as propaganda, most philosophers now agree that appeals to rights of nonhuman species do not provide a coherent and adequate basis for protecting biological diversity. Many philosophers have therefore concluded that when environmentalists speak of rights, they really mean that wild species have *intrinsic value* in some broader sense, a sense that does not require that we attribute rights to them (Callicott 1986a). What is important, on this view, is that wild species are valued *for themselves,* and not as *mere instruments* for the fulfillment of human needs and desires. This view is attractive in many ways, but it is extremely difficult to explain clearly. Does it mean that other species had value even before any conscious valuers emerged on the evolutionary scene? Could species be valued by no valuers? (See, for example, Rolston 1986, chap. 22; Taylor 1986.)

Or does this view that species have intrinsic value mean only that all conscious valuers should be able to perceive it (Callicott 1986a)?

But what if some people, such as the little girl and her family, fail to see it? Do we simply accuse them, metaphorically, of moral blindness? Or can we somehow explain to them what this intrinsic value is and why they should perceive it (Norton 1987)?

My point in asking all of these questions is not to prove that intrinsic value in other species does not exist. It may. I hope that someday we will be able to show that it does. In asking these questions, and emphasizing their difficulty, I am trying to refocus attention on a related, but importantly different question: Can appeals to intrinsic value in nonhuman species be made with sufficient clarity and persuasiveness to effect new policies adequate to protect biological diversity before it is too late? With some experts projecting that a fourth of all species could be lost in the next two decades, I fear not. As a philosopher, I can perhaps say in modesty what would appear to be carping criticism if said by someone else: philosophers seldom resolve big issues quickly. We are still, for example, struggling with a number of questions posed by Socrates. It seems unlikely that the issue of whether wild species have intrinsic value will be decided before the question of saving wild nature has become moot. There are, then, two separate debates about environmental values. One debate is *intellectual,* the other is *strategic.* The first debate concerns the *correct moral stance* toward nature. The second debate concerns which moral stance, or rationale, is likely to be *effective* in saving wild species and natural ecosystems.

Important environmentalists have addressed the second debate and taken a pragmatic approach to rationales for environmental policy. For example, Aldo Leopold advocated a biocentric ethical system, hoping to undermine the human arrogance that reduces nature to an instrument for human satisfactions (Leopold 1949). But he decided, when entering the public policy arena, to rely on human-centered reasons. In one of his early essays on conservation policy, Leopold outlined a non-human-centered outlook on nature, but then said, ". . . to most men of affairs, this reason is too intangible to either accept or reject as a guide to human conduct." He proceeded to argue for conservation on the basis of concern for future generations of humans (Leopold 1923; Norton 1986a).

Similarly, Rachel Carson's career as a writer began with beautiful books on the sea. There, she used the ecological idea that all things are interrelated and interdependent to question human-centered attitudes and human arrogance. But, when she saw that the wild world she loved was threatened by persistent pesticides, she wrote *Silent Spring* (Carson 1962). In that book, she used the same ideas of interconnectedness to argue that spreading persistent pesticides indiscriminately in the environment places *humans* at risk of cancer and other debilitating illnesses. William Butler, who was the Environmental Defense Fund's counsel when the DDT case was argued in hearings before the Environmental Protection Agency (EPA), told me in an interview that they first presented evidence that wildlife was being killed by DDT, and that it was by no means clear that the case to ban DDT would prevail. But when they introduced into the hearings evidence of human effects, Butler reports that their arguments were attended to, and DDT was banned (Butler 1986).

To those who are uncommitted to environmentalism (and this includes many important decisionmakers), appeals to intrinsic values in nature and to rights of nonhumans appear "soft," "subjective," and "speculative." We can accept this fact of political life, without agreeing with it. Whatever the answer to the intellectual question of whether nonhuman species have intrinsic value, I agree with Leopold, Carson, and Butler that human-oriented reasons carry more weight in current policy debates. Given the urgency of environmental degradation and the irreversibility of losses in biodiversity, it would be equivalent to fiddling while Rome burns to delay action until the achievement of a positive social consensus attributing rights and intrinsic value to nonhuman species.

In the remainder of this chapter, I shall therefore concentrate on the human, cultural reasons to preserve species. I shall emphasize two points about these human reasons. First, these reasons are far broader, deeper, and more powerful than is usually recognized. Both environmentalists and their critics tend to emphasize, when focusing on human reasons for preservation, the commercial and commodity-oriented concerns about saving species (see, for example, Myers 1983a; Prescott-Allen and Prescott-Allen 1985). But this approach ignores a vast range of important cultural, aesthetic, and social reasons for a preservationist policy. Second, I would like to emphasize that, at least in the short run,

there is hardly any difference in the public policies that would be advocated under a broadly cultural, human-centered value system and the policy advocated by a biocentric value system. Both world views imply that we should do all we can do to save species and representative ecosystems.

Before I explain why I say the cultural and biocentric views have apparently identical policy implications, I must emphasize the breadth of human values that are served by wild nature. To do that, I want to return to the scene on the sandbar. There I was, facing Ehrenfeld's conservationist's dilemma while talking to an eight-year-old. I tried the respect-for-life approach as well as the conservation-for-future-use approach. The little girl wasn't buying the right-to-life approach; and the conservationist approach, by admitting that sand dollars are commodities to be exploited, admitted too much. It may be useful to set aside philosophical abstractions for a moment and consider the microcosmic situation on the sandbar strategically. I wanted the little girl to put most of the living sand dollars back. How could I accomplish that end?

If I have the chance again, if I run into another little girl with too many sand dollars, I think I'll become a labor organizer on the beach. I'll raise the question of child labor. I'll ask the little girl if she's having fun. "Wouldn't you rather build sand castles?" I'd say. Or, better yet, I'd ask her if she'd like to get to know a sand dollar. I'd pick one up and show her its tiny sucker feet and let her feel them knead her hand, almost imperceptibly. I'd explain how, with those tiny feet, the sand dollar pulls itself through the sand by tugging on many individual grains. I'd tell her how the sand dollar picks up particles of sand with its teeth, and digests the tiny diatoms that cling to the particles as they pass through its alimentary canal.

Sand dollars and many other echinoderms, such as sea urchins and starfish, have five sections. The little girl might be surprised to note that they share their pentagonal structure with us, in that we have one head, two arms, and two legs. But I'd point out that the sand dollar's five sections are all the same. They have evolved a less differentiated nervous system. Their behavior is consequently less complex than ours, and I hope the little girl will see that different species have evolved different adaptations to deal with quite different situations. The ancestors of sand dollars, beset with many predators in lagoons, invested in armor, rather than mobility. But I'd try to get her to see that our mobility isn't necessarily better; what works depends on the situation.

I hope, by the time we talk about all those things, the little girl will be distracted from her task of bleaching sand dollars for nickels and that she will prefer live sand dollars to dead ones. Ehrenfeld's conservationist's dilemma encourages us to face a bipolar choice: Will we value sand dollars as commodities to be used or will we attribute to them rights and intrinsic value and thereby respect them as worthy of our moral concern? In fact, these are not the only two alternatives, and the dilemma posed is a false one. By focusing on the little girl's attitudes and behavior, we can see a third alternative: The environmentalist's case for preserving wild nature can be expressed in terms of human culture.

The beach was being used that afternoon not just as an opportunity for exploitation: it was also being used as a schoolroom—the little girl was being taught that the value of beaches is a commodity value. In the process of teaching children that sand dollars are mere commodities to be exploited, we also teach them that children are mere consumers. The reduction of little girls to mere consumers follows inevitably upon the reduction of sand dollars and other wildlife to mere commodities. When all of nature is subdued and made mere commodities in our economy, we will have destroyed our only symbols of freedom. When the commercial world view entirely takes over, sand dollars will be mere commodities, and little girls in search of nickels will be mere consumers. Like other domesticated species, they will obediently seek the products that are glamorized in media advertising. The manipulative culture of capitalistic commerce will have become all-pervasive, and the greatest losers will be children who have lost the ability to wonder at wild, living nature.

And the reduction of children to mere consumers is unfortunate for *human* reasons—it represents a contraction of the child's value system. Whatever we believe about the intrinsic value of sand dollars, we can say that, when the little girl lost her chance to *wonder* at the living world of sand dollars at the bottom of lagoons, she was impoverished. The little girl's experience at the beach that Saturday was merely a manifestation of a broader cultural phenomenon. When little girls look at sand dollars and see nickels, they are expressing the same attitude as developers who look at unspoiled beaches and see condominium sites. The beach is shelled, fished, sand-dollared, and used as a tanning salon. But is it appreciated for its real value? Do we cherish its ability to contrast with, and call into question, our everyday world of commerce and profit-making? Hardly at all. Here, we can apply Roderick Nash's point that recreation and tourism involve a search for contrasts (Nash 1986). If all of our beaches are seawalled, boardwalked, and lined with pizza stands, how will they contrast with our roadways?

When we teach little girls to encounter sand dollars as mere opportunities to make nickels, we impoverish childhood experience. And, as that process is repeated throughout our culture, we impoverish our culture. We begin to see nature as a mere storehouse, rather than as the context in which our culture, our struggle to maintain a niche in nature, has developed and will develop. And we forget that our future, as well as our past, depends on our integration into the broader processes of life-building and niche-carving.

The struggle of sand dollars to survive in newly formed lagoons provides a symbol of our struggle to survive as self-determining creatures. The sand dollars must, in the face of hostile and predatory forces in the lagoon, negotiate a niche. In doing so, they create a tiny colony of life, a community that is supported by, and in turn supports, other forms of life. While the Darwinian revolution in biological science has undermined many of our older metaphysical, religious, and spiritual beliefs, it has also pointed out a new direction for understanding human life and the place of humans in the great experiment of evolution. Our species has emerged from the same processes that created sand dollars. Our natural history is, in a sense, contemporary with us; every species illustrates an alternative means of sustaining life. Every wild species is a repository of analogies that inform our ongoing struggle to survive. In the same way that we might learn to avoid errors of past cultures by studying cultural history, we can learn to avoid ecological disasters by studying the natural history of other living things.

The little girl was being cheated out of valuable experiences. She exchanged an afternoon of discovering nature for a few nickels. On this point, I'm sure, Ehrenfeld and I are in agreement. But I do not accept the implication that the only alternative to valuing wild species as nickels is to say that they have intrinsic value: they can also be valued as occasions for expanding and uplifting human experience.

If our culture proves incapable of preserving other forms of life in the wild, we will lose our only means to understand the great mystery of life's emergence and diversification. We will doom ourselves and our descendants to ignorance of the roots of our existence. The reduction of human valuing of wild nature to mere commodities, to mere objects to be exploited, doubly undermines human values. First, it narrows and cheapens human experience. The little girl entirely missed the mystery and wonder of living beaches. Second, that attitude is destroying the possibilities for future children to experience wild beaches and to expand their horizons of valuing. If we do not change this attitude, and the trends it promotes, there will be no more beaches where little girls might learn the wonder and value of living sand dollars. Those trends will have, and already have had, dreadful consequences for our culture. The valuing of solitude, the value of experiencing unmanipulated ecosystems, the value of seeing nature as a larger enterprise than our search for economic gain are all threatened by the attitude that sand dollars are mere commodities.

I've tried, then, to explain why the cultural approach to valuing biological diversity is broad, deep, and powerful. It is broad, because it appeals to the values of diversity, contrast, solitude, and so forth that commercial culture is in danger of forgetting. It is deep because it digs below the shallow tendency of our culture to reduce all things to the mere value they will bring in a marketplace. Finally, it is powerful because it addresses the question: What sort of world do we want our children and grandchildren to experience? If we extinguish wild nature, we will extinguish with it our ability to wonder; we will have extinguished a part of our consciousness. We might, of course, decry the passing of wild nature because we will have failed to protect intrinsic values residing in other species. But we can as well, and less controversially, decry the loss of richness from the human experience.

Now I would like to apply this cultural rationale for saving species to policy issues. What

policy would be pursued if one believes in the cultural value of wildlife and natural ecosystems?

I believe it is important to emphasize the *contributory* value of wild species. Economists who try to measure commercial and other economic values for species and environmentalists who emphasize the aesthetic-cultural value of species both tend to underemphasize the contributory value of species. Species do not exist in isolation. Most species function as important parts of ecosystems and therefore contribute to the support and sustenance of other species (Norton 1987). If one values a wild grass because it provides an opportunity to develop a perennial hybrid of corn, or if one values a sighting of a rare whooping crane, one must value not just those species, but the entire fabric of life on which those species depend. Similarly, we cannot place a value on a little girl discovering the wonder of living sand dollars without valuing the beach where sand dollars live. Economists and ecologists cannot tell us how to save economically and aesthetically important species without saving the ecosystems on which they depend. This is especially true of culturally valuable species. A dead sand dollar on a dissecting tray cannot provide the same experience as a living sand dollar with sucker feet kneading a little girl's hand. If we are to save the experience of nature, we must save that experience whole (Fowles 1979). The species we never notice, like the tiny diatom that nourishes the sand dollar, must be appreciated along with the sand dollar and the red snapper. If we are to save the experiences that enliven and enlighten our culture, then we must save whole ecosystems and all the species that contribute to them. It is difficult to see what believers in the intrinsic value of species would advocate, in addition to this policy.

The debate about policy regarding biological diversity, the debate about what ought to be done, is best seen as a *strategic* debate, largely independent of the *intellectual* debate about whether wild species have intrinsic value. If we recognize the full range of human values served by wild species, we will adopt as a policy goal an attempt to save all wild nature. Admittedly, we will fail in this idealistic goal—the task is too large and our culture has evolved a set of commodity-oriented values that push us inexorably to alter habitats and to threaten wild species. But pious assertions that species, dying out around us, have intrinsic value will make them no less extinct. My point is that a policy of saving as many species as possible is the logical implication of either a non-human-centered value system *or* a human-centered value system which recognizes the full range of human values. It is true that if our culture perceived species as intrinsically valuable, we would do more to save wild species. But it is also true that if our culture perceived the breadth, depth, and power of human-oriented values of species, we would do more to save them. Given this context, the debate about intrinsic values in nature should be seen as an intellectual one and the task of saving species should be addressed strategically. We need not first prove that wild species have intrinsic value and *then* begin working to save them.

An analogy may illustrate this point. Suppose a family must move across country and fit all their belongings in their station wagon. In the end, they find they cannot fit both the television and the large, old family Bible in the space available. One family member suggests they go to the pawn shop and determine which is more valuable and take the commercially valuable item. Another member might be affronted by the treatment of the family Bible, with its record of births and deaths recorded in the hand of patriarchal ancestors, as a mere commodity. This family member might insist the Bible has intrinsic value and should therefore be saved. A debate ensues and the trip is in danger of being delayed. But a wise member of the family cuts through the problem by pointing out that the Bible is valuable as a symbol of the family's struggle and unity and that seeing and touching the ancestral record will be valuable *for the family and its offspring*. If this point is made, that the Bible has irreplaceable value for building the family's character, the question of what to do need not wait upon agreement concerning its intrinsic value. Rather than standing on the sidewalk discussing the intrinsic value of family Bibles, the family should leave the television, pack up the Bible, and discuss intrinsic value en route. Similarly for saving wild species. Given the powerful case for saving species as a cultural need, it makes very little difference to policy whether those species are also attributed intrinsic value.

Cultural attitudes determine the values we ex-press and pursue. If we develop a healthy attitude toward nature and experiences of nature, we will act to save wild species and natural ecosystems. I have tried to emphasize the depth, the breadth, and the power of these attitudes and rationales for saving nature based on them.

I suspect that there is an underlying fear among American conservationists that if conservation goals are based on cultural attitudes, we have no right to work to save wildlife in other lands inhabited by other cultures. If the cultural value of wildlife were limited to American values, this limitation might pose a problem (see Regan 1981; Sagoff 1974). But all cultures relate to nature and derive important symbols from the unique communities of wildlife that grace their countryside. Further, if we believe in evolutionary theory, all cultures have evolved in a context of natural systems and can learn their place in the natural world by paying attention to their natural heritage.

A possible corollary to the concern about international action to save wildlife is the thought that perhaps we Americans, as citizens of an advanced industrial nation, have no right to impose what we have learned about evolution and the interdependence of living things upon other nations with different ideas. It is correct to say that we have no right to *impose* our knowledge and related attitudes, just as we have no right to impose our commercial attitudes on them, just as we have no right to export our idea that true civilization requires a fast-food restaurant on every corner and a herd of cattle on every hectare of formerly forested tropics. But at the same time, we cannot deny our role as world leaders in cultural opinions, as well as in economic organization. What we can do is act responsibly as leaders of world opinion to make available our science, our understanding of evolution, and the importance of that understanding in achieving a modern, but healthy, attitude toward human culture and its context in natural ecosystems. If we do that, if we develop a healthy attitude toward the natural world at home and share that attitude with people of other cultures, we will have gone a long way toward preserving the natural world and, more than incidentally, a place for a truly human and humane existence in that world.

24
Hard Times for Diversity

DAVID EHRENFELD

The appreciation of diversity has fallen on hard times in Western and Western-influenced societies. The spirit that moved Botticelli to incorporate at least thirty different species of plants in his canvas entitled *Spring,* painted in 1478 (Taylor 1963), the spirit that prompted Shakespeare to mention enough animal and plant species in his plays to provide source material for entire books (e.g., Rohde 1935), and the spirit that gave Thomas Jefferson delight in compiling his great collection of comparative vocabularies of fifty different American Indian languages (Koch and Peden 1944), if it has not vanished, has been effectively sublimated and suppressed in our day. In its place is the pseudodiversity of the sort that one finds on the menu of a Chinese-Polynesian-American restaurant, the ersatz variety that is the hallmark of a world culture that was described a few years ago as residing "everywhere and nowhere" (Trow 1984).

What has caused the decline of the love of diversity and is causing the decline of diversity itself is, not surprisingly, the ascendancy of its opposite: uniformity. In terms perhaps more readily understandable to scientists, we have abandoned our fascination with the specific in favor of a preoccupation with the general and

I dedicate this paper to my teacher, the late Archie Carr, one of the greatest conservationists of our time, and to my friend Wendell Berry, who wrote in 1977, "The land is too various in its kinds, climates, conditions, declivities, aspects, and histories to conform to any generalized understanding or to prosper under generalized treatment."

the generalizable. This is the Age of Generality (Ehrenfeld 1986a), and every month that passes sees it more firmly entrenched as the official way of seeing the world and dealing with the world.

Why is generality in the ascendancy? There are two reasons, I believe, which taken together are all but irresistible. The first is that generality confers power. Much of the control we have over the external world is related in one way or another to our discovery of general laws and principles of physics, chemistry, and biology, an explosion of knowledge that is essentially modern. Our ability to manipulate the world, beyond the dreams of the alchemists, is new—that the control is almost always flawed and self-destructive is, for the moment, beside the point: we humans are poor at giving up power once we get a taste of it (Ehrenfeld 1986b). Not that knowledge of the specific isn't valid and sometimes useful—rather, it doesn't very often help us control the world. Penicillin was discovered because of specific observations, but antibiotics as a class belong to the world of applied general theory. If the specific is involved in the modern scientific-technical process, it is usually at the beginning, and not for long. The most powerful and active frontiers in science and technology—nuclear weapons and counter-weapons, and genetic engineering, to cite two examples—have, at heart, little to do with specificity or diversity.

The second reason why generality is in and specificity and diversity are out is that in a world bent on manipulation and control, the study of specificity is too slow and tedious, and the maintenance of diversity is too expensive to be tolerated by the people who make decisions. Both the study and the appreciation of the particular, of diversity, take time, and time is money. The trouble with differences and particularities, from the economic point of view that prevails today, is that there is no general rule for coping with them. except, perhaps, to ignore them.

The purpose of conservation is to preserve natural diversity: A fundamental problem and paradox of conservation is that Western men and women no longer value diversity, and because of their preoccupation with the general and the power that an understanding of general laws brings, we are committed to the kind of exploitative approach to nature that places diversity in jeopardy. [This is truly a Catch-22 situation, or, to use Bateson's terminology, a double bind.] Our new-found love affair with generality and general laws, and the resulting power to change the earth, has enabled us to destroy biological diversity at an astonishing rate, but it has simultaneously caused us to lose interest and respect for the specific and the people who study it, and that prevents effective conservation.

This same ascendancy of generality and the cult of uniformity that goes with it has almost completely taken over the one-time home of diversity, the science of biology itself. No longer is diversity celebrated for its own sake; no longer do we see, for example, graduate students who have staked out as their primary life's work a taxonomic group, such as mayflies, or cyprinodonts, or the Betulaceae; at least we don't see very many of them. Now the work is organized around general questions and themes, such as "endemism" and "foraging strategies." Without such generality, at least as a cover, few biologists can hope to find employment and support. Any academic biologist in any large university can testify to the sheer political power of that most general of all modern biological discoveries, the universal genetic code. So powerful, indeed, is this particular generality (and its derivatives) that it has all but obliterated the once-prized distinction between pure science and technology, between the academic and the industrial worlds. Is it any wonder that there is a scarcity of top-ranked graduate students who are committed, for instance, to the study of the Chiroptera per se, and precious few jobs for those who are, except maybe in the field of bat control.

Even within biology, diversity is now valued primarily for its general usefulness and the useful generalities we can extract from it. As my philosopher friends would say, it has lost its intrinsic value, and now has only instrumental value. This has led to a host of secondary problems within conservation. As long ago as the late 1940s, Aldo Leopold (1966), who certainly appreciated the intrinsic value of the natural world, nevertheless began in his essay "The Land Ethic" to link the idea of the conservation of diversity with the idea of global survival. Diversity fosters stability. This idea took hold and spread among the scientific and lay communities until 1973, when Robert May called it in question among ecologists if not among lay conservationists. The troubles of the biosphere are real and pressing, but they are not all related in an obvious way to the loss of diversity. It is not necessarily true, for example, that if a continuous vegetative cover comprised of 500 different species of plants will prevent soil erosion in a particular region, then 10,000 species would do a better job.

Sagoff (1985) has described the scientific errors that conservationists have committed in the effort to demonstrate the general usefulness of the conservation of diversity, and while I disagree with some of his biological interpretations, his point is well taken. In the long run, this insistence on claiming a general, instrumental need and value for every last species and variety is only going to get us into trouble. Moreover, it is symptomatic of the kind of exploitative viewpoint that got diversity in trouble in the first place. In my book *The Arrogance of Humanism* (1981), and at the recent BioDiversity Symposium in Washington (1988), I explained why this sort of economic valuing has failed as a conservation strategy, and having made the point already, I won't elaborate further.

Another secondary problem of conservation caused by the turning away of science and society from the specific to the general can be seen in the emerging discipline of conservation biology. With some trepidation, I feel obliged to point out that there is a widespread obsession with a search for general rules of scientific conservation, the genetic code of conservation so to speak, and this finds expression in very general statements about extinction rates, viable population sizes, ideal reserve designs, and so forth. Some of this work is useful and interesting, as described in this book. Yet this kind of generality is easily abused, especially when the would-be conservationists become bewitched by models of their own making. When this happens, the sight of otherwise intelligent people trying to extract nonobvious, nontrivial general rules about extinction from their own polished and highly simplified versions of reality becomes a spectacle that would have interested Lewis Carroll. Generality is nice when you can get it: it's neat and tidy, it's easy to learn, it's easy to remember. As guardians of diversity, however, it behooves us to keep in mind the nature of our ward: several million species whose distinction is their differentness, further subdivided into innumerable populations each with its separate history and unique environment. We should not be surprised when different conservation problems call for qualitatively different solutions. With practice, we may even learn to welcome this challenge of diversity the way we now welcome the challenge of generality. But like it or not, this is the way life is—just as ecologists have learned that the once smooth and shiny picture of plant succession must yield to the warty irregularities of local history and local environmental discontinuities, so we too will have to learn that there is not going to be a short handbook of conservation biology—at least not one that works. Our genetic code is likely to remain as elusive as the Holy Grail.

Conservation is inextricably linked to human values—linked in its methodology and linked in its chances of success. Until science and society regain a fascination with diversity, with differences, with uniqueness, and with exceptions, all in their own right, there will continue to be a shortage of taxonomists, there will continue to be new methods of cutting down tropical rain forests faster, there will continue to be an accelerating loss of species despite all the science, land, and money that conservation can muster.

True, we cannot unlearn exploitative technologies. Nevertheless, the prevailing human value systems of an age can change in response to need and unknown factors, sometimes surprisingly quickly, and perhaps not by any deliberate acts of individuals. The love of diversity is now under a cloud, but it has not gone away—there would be no zoos, botanical gardens, or natural history museums if it had. The world, I believe, is in the process of starting to discover that the disastrous effects of exploitative generality can be curbed and moderated by a judicious applica-

tion of diversity of all sorts. Whether we refer to the failures of global economic systems, of vast forest monocultures, or of continent-wide irrigation systems, the cure resides in the various correlates of diversity: local or here rather than widespread or elsewhere, smaller rather than larger, many ways rather than one way, slow rather than fast, personal rather than impersonal, particular rather than general. And this is another paradox, but a pleasant one: There is a general instrumental use for diversity after all. It is not that thirty million species are all ecologically necessary to keep the biosphere intact; rather, if we relearn how to value this diversity for its own sake, we will automatically discover that we are no longer destroying the world.

In *The Natural History of Selborne,* the fourth most frequently published book in the English language, Gilbert White (1788–89 (1977)) began his fifth letter to Thomas Pennant with the phrase ''Among the singularities of this place.'' It was the genius of White that immortalized such specificities as his accounts of the way golden-crowned wrens hang from branches, of the number of spines in the dorsal fin of a loach, or even of the diameter, in yards, of the pond near his town. However it required more than White's genius to make the book so popular for 200 years. It required the human ability of his readers to value and prize the *singularities* of a place. That trait still exists, but lies dormant in most people, although it can easily be awakened. It is a prime task of conservation to find ways of arousing it again.

As an optimist, I look forward to a world where the genius of a Gilbert White or a Linnaeus can thrive alongside the genius of a Watson and a Crick. This isn't nostalgia, it has not happened before. It will require one of the most creative advances of recent human history. I hope that conservationists can help bring it about.

In conclusion, I want to apply some of this rather abstract theory to a real issue: the matter of tourism. I will also continue a theme begun by Western, Harris and Eisenberg (chaps. 16 and 17).

Having dedicated this chapter to Wendell Berry, it is fitting to close with him. While staying at his farm in Kentucky a number of years ago, I had several occasions to use his outhouse. The only decoration in that outhouse, I could not help but notice, was a large poster with the words ''Help Stamp Out Tourism.'' It surprised me at the time, and I didn't quite understand it, especially knowing that Wendell is a card-carrying conservationist and that his magnificent book on American agriculture, *The Unsettling of America,* was published by the Sierra Club.

Now, some years later, I think I understand the poster. What it says is that as long as we think of nature as always something somewhere else, something with which we have no enduring particular and personal relationship, then nature has no chance to survive, and conservation will be little more than a pleasant waste of money for the semi-enlightened rich and a source of employment for a few conservationists, a long retreat with occasional successful skirmishes.

Tourism may be the other, benign side of the nature exploitation coin, but it is still an exploitative relationship with nature; it is not, except in the most transitory and ephemeral way, a participatory relationship.

So I have a proposition of my own, one that is no more impractical than some of the propositions we have already discussed.

Proposition: One should earn the *right* to be a tourist, to go somewhere else to view nature, and the only way to earn that right is by knowing the particular nature in the place where you are coming from. You can see someone else's nature after you have learned about and lived with your own, wherever that may be—on the banks of the Kentucky River or in the vicinity of Manhattan. Tourism should be a reward for right living, not a substitute for it.

The New York City area, home of the conference on which this volume is based and the institutions that sponsored it, was mentioned only once, in passing, during the conference.

Yet only seventy miles to the south is America's first National Ecological Reserve, the New Jersey Pinelands, a million-acre ecosystem of which only one-third is in public ownership. A pioneering plan is now being developed to coordinate the protection of such fragile sites as the remarkable dwarf forests, or Pine Plains, with the regulated development of peripheral zones. And a few hours' drive to the north are the Berkshires of Connecticut and Massachusetts, where the development of an internationally recognized local currency, based on a cordwood standard, promises to help promote the conservation of private forest lands in a novel way. As these two examples show, the best conservation often begins at home.

If visitors to national and foreign parks knew the diversity and problems of diversity where they lived, they would be an asset to management, a source of ideas and helpful experience, not themselves a problem or a burden. And if this seems hopelessly visionary, let me cite the case of Israel, where each year a nongovernmental agency, the Society for the Protection of Nature in Israel, brings more than 30 percent of the nation's schoolchildren and many adults to all the representative ecosystems and ethnic systems of that tiny country, where they are taught about them in great detail. For many Israelis, the diversity of their landscape and human cultures has become a specific part of their national identity.

One part of our answer to the Age of Generality has to be that we must learn or relearn the specific details and intricate functions of our own habitats and find ways of teaching them to the people around us.

25

Overview: A Planner's Perspective

PEREZ OLINDO

So far in this volume, we have dealt with various aspects of conservation in national parks and outside national parks. We have discussed the various aspects of what we see and what attracts us, and we have also discussed the genetics of plants and animals, which are aspects we don't see and therefore may have had little appreciation of. Conservationists of ages past have been indicted for being preservationist. I accept that indictment on their behalf because I was with them and I was one of them. But there was a reason why we wanted to preserve natural areas. We were convinced that even the best players in the world need a field in which to play. I was privileged to attend the First World Conference on National Parks in 1962, when I was studying in the United States. I was also able to attend the Second World Conference on National Parks in 1972; there is something that I can tell you about those conferences: the people who took part in them were very concerned with the state of the environment. In corridors to the conference hall and during coffee breaks, the participants got together and talked; they were confronted with issues they did not know how to solve. Having been an actor in the realm of the environment for over twenty-five years, I have been able to see a transformation in conservation from a species approach to environmental management and a systems approach; here we are considering "biosphere people" and "ecosystems people" (McNeely, chap. 15). Despite everything, we have to give credit to those who wanted to preserve natural areas for their beauty and for their intrinsic values, and we also have to be grateful to those who promoted tourism; I'm not a pro-moter or strong supporter of tourism, but at that time the decisionmakers and the politicians needed reasons why vast areas of wilderness were to be protected against human pressure for land, for other economic activities. I have looked carefully at the list of contributors to this book. I do not see politicians or the political view adequately represented here; I do not see the planners. I do not see the economists. Elsewhere the politicians, planners, and economists are plotting how to utilize space on the face of the earth, while we are here thinking how to save and protect those same areas. We must appeal for an integrated approach, a broader incorporation of disciplines in planning, if what we have to protect is to be protected. If we believe that natural areas are doomed by fragmentation, then there is hardly any need for us to make an effort.

During the sixties, Americans confronted the problem of migratory species of birds and animals. The question was whether the biology of environmental rehabilitation by humans would be understood by the birds migrating at night at high altitudes. Americans collected money, their government cooperated, and nesting areas were reconstituted for water birds and for grain-eating birds. Interestingly, those bits of fragmented wetlands, small lakes, and areas of broken nature that had been reconstituted by human beings were recognized by the wild birds in migration! If the preservationist had not set aside areas that would today be used by geneticists, what would be used today by this or any other discipline of biology? What areas would today be used by poets and philosophers to interpret for us a deeper meaning in nature, to enrich our lives? Surely, we would have lost something irretrievably! I am one of those people who advocate the acquisition of what visually appears to be different in representative geographical belts. I believe in protecting something for its own sake. I agree it may not have meaning to me, but there are millions alive who are entitled to different feelings and interpretations. I think the conservation community has a duty to protect, even in the narrow sense, what appears different and therefore promotes the concept of diversity in nature (Ehrenfeld, chap. 24). Someone said we should protect the tropical forest because maybe some plant will provide us with the chemicals needed to cure a disease in the future: What is wrong with that? We may not find those chemicals, we may not find the message that is tied up in these communities of plants and animals today or tomorrow, but I think we have a duty to set aside, to promote, to protect diversity as we learn about it.

I was intrigued by the story of the mother and child who were walking on a beach doing something—killing sand dollars—that did not please one of the previous writers (Norton, chap. 23). I have had a different experience on a beach. I took my children to the coast of the Indian Ocean and put them on the beach. I moved back and made sure that they did not go into the ocean and expose themselves to danger, and I watched them build castles of sand: first they built, and then they broke the castles down, and I realized that the imperfection of knowledge looms around us all. My children were trying to build castles but were missing the point each time because the binding medium was absent without them knowing. It is the same with scientists. We have the materials for a perfect future available in nature. We try to put them together sensibly and we convince ourselves of our own theories, so much so that even when reality has eluded us, we come to believe in these theories. I think that future generations have a right to have the same intellectual freedom. But for that to happen, we have a duty to provide them with a natural environment in which to pursue knowledge of nature, and that can only be achieved if we ally ourselves with the decisionmakers. If they cannot come to us, we have to go to them, and together we must save representative ecosystems.

This century, the success in environmental conservation has been measured in the number of national parks and reserves that have been declared and protected by law. I think that even in the coming century, the measure of our success will also be on the basis of what we help to protect to promote diversity. I am convinced that extinctions are inevitable. But if the knowledge we achieve through research, through planning, and by removing conflicts and contradictions can slow down extinctions, we will have contributed to the conservation of our natural environment. I was one of those people who tenaciously protected national parks as areas in which only human beings could go as a privilege. I do not regret that. Western made a reference to the increased productivity that is achieved when wild animals and domestic stock are run together (Western, chap. 16).

Do the national parks of the world have a purpose for us? Is it our wish to increase productivity in those parks, or can we practice that through integrated planning, by making opportunities and developing policies that can achieve that objective in areas beyond the national parks? I know that as our wildlife migrates, it competes with other economic activities in lands adjacent to national parks. In years gone by, we resisted sharing the revenues accruing from national parks with our neighbors. That was a serious mistake while the animals continued to migrate outside the national parks. Whether birds or mammals, we expected them not to be molested by farmers. We did not expect them to be molested even at the expense of human life. That was unreasonable. I think that Vittachi (chap. 3) has a message for us. If those at the grass roots can understand what we are trying to achieve, if the people can see where we want them to reach, they will respond. I therefore have come to the conviction that it may be necessary to negotiate the security of the migratory species of wildlife with the people with whom they impact. Those people are a part of the natural setting. They have a right to exist, and we must also guarantee that existence if we are to save what we have in the protected areas.

How do we plan for animal communities which depend on ecosystems that go beyond sovereign borders? I'm not an advocate of a unitary management group, but we have moved in that direction, by the negotiation of international conventions to protect various activities and various interests. What bothers me is the complacency of certain sections of the conservation community, which consider these conventions as an end in themselves. Once a country has signed or acceded to a convention, we have not followed the matter to make sure that the provisions of those conventions are implemented to the best of our knowledge, to the best of our ability, and for the future security of natural areas. We have to ensure that these conventions are made active and do not remain the passive documents they are today.

We have been talking about conservation of biotic diversity. At the present time, in the setting of rampant economic disparity around the world, we ask a country like Kenya to protect representative areas as national parks and reserves. We ask a country like Rwanda to set aside habitats to protect the mountain gorilla. At the same time, the government of Rwanda is telling its nationals not to return home because there is no more land for them. How shall we convince these people that the gorilla, for which certain areas of their motherland have been safeguarded, do not enjoy greater rights to it than themselves? Economic disparity is threatening the viability of small sovereign governments, which convention forbids me to name. But if these countries are allowed to disintegrate, how will we protect those natural areas within their current borders which the international community holds dear? Conservationists in the developed countries will have to address issues which are at the moment not seen to be directly related to the natural areas we want to protect (Lee, chap. 30). They have to address themselves there to issues that are thousands of miles away from home; they have to address issues that at this moment look irrelevant to the process of conservation. Only by including a diversity of issues can minds meet on protecting diversity.

The superficial differences promoted within the ream of humanity are unnecessary. If the world acts as one, and it is one, the conflict over shared resources should be behind us by the twenty-first century. I'm not promoting a world government, but we need peace in order to achieve the survival of the world as we know it today. Let me share with you a feeling from the third world. Not too long ago, two very good gentlemen were having breakfast together. They are not supposed to be very good friends. So one said to the other, "If you do this, I'll move closer to you," and the other gentlemen said, "Yes, I'll do it," and they went on and on. The second gentlemen agreed to almost all the demands made. The world was led to believe that these two people were moving closer and that they would shake hands and be friends. The handshake that never was would have brought the world closer to lasting peace. The gentleman who was calling the shots turned around to his advisors and asked them what was wrong. He felt there must have been a trick from the other side! We lost an opportunity in Reykjavik to negotiate lasting peace, a loss that has grave implications for the appropriation or misappropriation of a large proportion of the world's natural resources. I hope and pray that these two world leaders will meet again soon and agree and shake hands and redirect those resources that go into armaments to strive toward the protection of the one world we all have to live in.

In the following section, we shall tackle the various aspects of planning with the objective of protecting the earth. We shall get a national perspective from Arturo Tarak, from Argentina, and later, we shall have an international perspective from my colleague Reuben Olembo, from Kenya, and last but not least, Michael Bean, of the United States, will give us the legal perspective which must be addressed if the security of those areas we set aside and aspire to protect are to be guaranteed through the twenty-first century.

26

A National Perspective

ARTURO TARAK

Slightly over a year ago, I was asked to develop the national conservation strategy for my country. I was immediately faced with a wide range of conflicting issues. Was I to develop yet another document to be stacked onto tons of paper already stored in bureaucratic government offices? Certainly not. So what was I going to do? Could I do it all by myself? Clearly not. What was the scope, the real "universe," as the statisticians would say? I almost felt as if the scope of the mandate were the real universe. This chapter is an attempt to organize usually distant or disparate concepts and fields of knowledge in order to aid the practicing conservationist in becoming aware of his methods in thinking out choices for action. It is based on my personal experience; I shall draw on cases to illustrate the conceptual issues I have faced.

I cannot imagine 2100 as anything but very different from the present time; that is almost all that I can imagine. I doubt that the present distribution of world power will persist as it is today. I don't expect nations or governments as they function today to continue. In fact, there may even be major changes in the underlying paradigms for development of conservation. Communications will continue to improve, technology will continue to expand, and the world will be even more interconnected; therefore, a large proportion of human culture will have planetary dimensions. How does one plan a conservation strategy for the next 100 years with such a degree of uncertainty? All I can do is relate what steps we are taking to promote a long-term conservation strategy right now in Argentina.

THE COUNTRY: A DESCRIPTION OF BIOPHYSICAL AND SOCIAL CHARACTERISTICS

Argentina is fairly large: Its continental territory covers 2,791,810 km² (INDEC 1984) ranging from 21° 46′50″ to 55° 58′35″ south latitude and from 26° 15′15″ to 49° 33′00″ west longitude. Though most of its territory lies beyond the tropic of Capricorn, a small portion lies within the tropical region. Throughout evolutionary history the massive western Andes have provided a seemingly infinite source of physical and biological variation. The Andes have had a major effect on loessic soil formation on the eastern extensive plains along the Chaco, Pampas, and Patagonia. The range is also a major element in the macroclimatic configuration of the territory. Otherwise the climate is mainly temperate owing to its oceanic character (Burgos 1970). There are 11 neotropical terrestrial biogeographical provinces in Argentina, one of the antarctic domain (Cabrera 1976), two marine regions, and two freshwater regions (Menni et al. 1984). The diversity of species follows the diverse geography; rough estimates indicate that there are 976 species of birds recognized in our territory (Olrog 1984), 300 species of mammals (Olrog and Lucero 1980), 250 species of reptiles (Freiberg 1977; Peters and Donoso-Barros 1970; Peters and Orejas-Miranda 1970), 312 amphibians (Cei 1980), 400 species of ferns (De la Sota 1977b), and 1,760 genera of flowering plants (Hunziker 1984).

Politically, Argentina is constitutionally organized as a republic, with a representative federal form of government. There are twenty-two provinces, one national territory, and the federal capital. The provinces exercise a lot of power over how resources are used; 90% of the decisions about how forest, wildlife, fisheries, soil, and water resources are used are made by the provinces.

Argentina is very unevenly populated. The 1980 national census indicated a population size of 27,947,446 (INDEC 1984), with an average population density of 10.1 inhabitants/km^2. Of this, the urban population constitutes 18,458,000, representing 79% of the total population: 8,435,000 live in cities larger than a million inhabitants (INDEC 1984). However, more than half of Argentina's population is concentrated in a narrow strip 150 km alongside the Paraná River, just north of the federal capital, Buenos Aires. Densities vary from 14,650.8 people per km^2 in Buenos Aires and 1,859.6 people per km^2 in greater Buenos Aires to as low 0.5 people per km^2 in Santa Cruz province.

Population growth is low: 1.610% for 1980, 1.583% for 1985, with a predicted drop to 1.46% for 1990 and 1.176% for 2000 (CELADE 1984). The predicted percentages for the urban segment of the total population are 85.84% for 1990 and 88.02% for 2000. The dominant culture is Western European in origin, Spanish-speaking, and mainly Catholic. This doesn't really fit in with the population growth patterns of other Catholic, Hispanic countries, which just shows that one cannot make general statements about almost anything. Most of the society is westernized, although there are pockets of native cultural areas: the northwest with Incan influence where Quechuan is spoken, western Patagonia with Araucanian influence where Mapuche is spoken, the Chaco where there is a conglomerate of Chacoan tribes, and Corrientes and Misiones where Guaraní is spoken.

THE ENVIRONMENTAL PROBLEMS AND GOALS IN ENVIRONMENTAL CONSERVATION

Despite the very distinct physical and social attributes of each nation, the problems one faces in developing a national conservation strategy are the same as in other parts of the world (see IUCN 1980, 1984b). Although each province has a particular combination of environmental problems, the problems themselves are the same and include soil erosion problems, salinity problems, mismanagement of rivers and wetlands, mismanagement of native forest and range-lands, pests and weeds, mismanagement of commercial and recreational fisheries and hunting, mismanagement of leftover rural vegetation, mismanagement of mining and extractive industries, mismanagement of nature conservation and of water conservation, insufficient recycling, misexpenditure of energy, lack of conservation of genetic diversity by commercial cultivators, huge urban impact through development, overcrowded large cities, deleterious impacts from outdoor recreation and tourism, air and water pollution, and destruction and impoverishment of the visual environment. The goals of conservationists are also the same worldwide: maintenance of biological diversity, maintenance of ecological processes, maintenance of the sustainability of human activity through the wise allocation of resources (see IUCN 1980). Wonderful goals: Can we achieve them? How?

OBSTACLES IN DEVELOPING A STRATEGY

Developing a conservation strategy is a formidable task if one is hoping that the strategy is actually going to achieve its own stated conservation goals. The main reason is that any real conservation achievement implies a major change in social behavior by a vast number of inhabitants of a nation. Therefore, the preparation of any strategy to develop such conservation goals should include large numbers of individuals and organizations, since only a broad array of authors can ensure appropriate changes in social behavior in a pluralistic society. I'm stressing this point because most conservation efforts have not focused on trying to change human social behavior, although this kind of effort is applied in other areas of human endeavor. People try constantly to manipulate each other's behavior through political propaganda, commercial advertisement, interest groups lobbying at political strata, and in many other, more subtle ways.

To illustrate these concepts and how they usually occur in an interconnected fashion, I present three current cases:

Case 1

In 1978 I participated in developing a training program for the national park rangers. Having a formal training background in the biological science ourselves, the planners assumed that anybody would be able to impress upon visitors and students a conservation ethic (Tarak 1979) and therefore be a good ranger and a good park interpreter. After a lot of effort was expended in developing successive curricula and practical training that gave a nationwide knowledge of Argentine nature, the rangers did learn a lot about wildlife. However, much to my amazement, their stored information was not transferred to the general public. We investigated the problem with psychologists and found that the rangers had great difficulty in establishing communication with the public at large. Basically, their motivation for becoming rangers was to get away from society and the modern world, not to integrate into society. Yet this was exactly what the parks system was implicitly asking them to do. The reason why they did not teach or transfer any knowledge is that they just did not have the attitudinal and behavioral skills required for communication.

We therefore started a special program for training rangers. Two psychologists ran workshops on communication skills, which had an immediate effect on the system. For example, in the Iguazú national park rain forest in the northeast, we had poaching problems with homesteaders just next to the eastern border of the park; these people were poaching for food inside the park. There was no way the rangers could effectively halt poaching; it was an economic necessity for the local people. The rangers developed an educational program for the homesteaders. Rangers brought the homesteaders' children into the park and gave them a simple short course in the wildlife biology of the park. They developed strong personal ties with these children; the children went home, told their parents what they had learned, and brought their fathers into the park to participate in the education program. It was clear to the rangers operating the program that they did not share the same value system as the illiterate parents, but the parents were really fascinated with what was

going on with their children; this was the first time in their history that someone had done something for their children. As a result, they agreed to respect the park hunting restrictions and poach somewhere else, outside the park. It was hoped that eventually some would act as assistant wardens at that border.

Case 2

About four years ago, two young naturalists from the Museum of Natural History of Buenos Aires discovered that just outside the port of Buenos Aires there was a wonderful fragment of nature. An expansion site for government administrative offices of the former military regime, it had been abandoned and was filled with wildlife. More than eighty species of birds were there nesting or just passing through, and pampas grass was growing (one can actually take a picture of the city skyline against the pampas grass today). It was obvious that this should be declared a city reserve, since the nearest national park is located more than 400 km northeast of Buenos Aires. Here was an excellent opportunity for developing the concept of a city nature reserve particularly geared for nature awareness through environmental education workshops, as well as a good site for birdwatching or the development of such activities. After two years of discussion among the various private conservation organizations on the importance of getting the reserve declared, nothing was done. Everybody in the organizations agreed it was very important to preserve the place. However, the architects' and engineers' lobby had a great interest against this happening because the area was also an ideal place for city development. Furthermore, there was a city councillor willing to promote this development and get appropriate legislation passed in the City Council.

Meanwhile, we conservationists developed environmental education programs with schoolteachers at the site to enlarge our own constituency. Newspaper articles about our work started to appear. The problem was that each conservation group wanted to put forward its own institutional goal at the expense of the greater goal. Finally, when this didn't work, five representatives, one from each organization, were brought together and went through five team development sessions where my role was that of group coordinator. Roles were analyzed, and tasks assigned; interpersonal conflicts were resolved, while we maintained an explicit awareness of our decision-making process. At all times, the focus was kept strictly on the very specific goal of obtaining reserve status for the fragments of nature. Some members of the team were very influential in local politics, and others were influential in the private sector. The group achieved the preservation of the park by working together. The City Council voted for the reserve, using among other arguments the existence of Gateway National Park in New York. The park was initially vetoed by the mayor, but it was overridden by the City Council, because of the amount of public support we had raised. Today, the area is a city park with arrangements with the National Parks Administration to provide rangers, the Natural History Museum to provide scientific expertise, and the Education Ministry to provide educational programs for schoolchildren.

Case 3

In 1977, I developed a conservation project for vicuñas in the province of Jujuy (Tarak 1978). Later, during the military government, only the aquatic environment was included in the national system as the Laguna de Pozuelos Natural Monument, which provided the unique aquatic system full protection. The basis for such protection is manifold. It is the major feeding site for two species of flamingoes (*Phoenicoparrus andinus* and *P. jamessi*) as well as many other waterfowl. Also, it is a major stopover site for migrating shorebirds that use the Andean route (Myers et al. 1987). The lake had minimal local use: waterfowl egging during laying season and recreational boating during a religious festival by local lakeshore inhabitants. The lake does not provide any freshwater for the llama or sheep herds since it is saline, and some years it almost dries up during the winter dry season.

In 1984, the local legislature overruled the previous military regime's decision of handing over its jurisdiction to the national government. However, because legally the federal government had taken possession of the area, in fact nothing happened: the park is still operating. For the province of Jujuy it was only a question of principle. To make that question a fact it would have had to win a federal suit at the Supreme Court, disrupting the nation-province relationship on dubious grounds—it hardly could be maintained that the traditional egging is a cultural need since the local inhabitants of native origin already have adopted mostly Western habits: they own cars, speak Spanish, and benefit from the social security system. The same could be said of participants in the Catalina Festival speedboat contest.

There are formidable obstacles to achieving conservation goals. They can be organized into the following categories: philosophical, ethical, psychological, educational, organizational, sociological, legislative, scientific, and political.

Philosophical

Is present epistemology, with its clear positivism and reductionism so highly effective for Watson and Crick in developing the double-helix model for DNA, still applicable to other aspects of human knowledge and endeavor that are relevant to conservation? I don't think so (see Deutsch 1986; Toulmin 1982). Are there any other philosophical systems that could lend us a hand in trying to solve these multiple problems? Some Eastern philosophies could be relevant (Cheng 1986; Hargrove, chap. 21); they come from societies that had to deal a long time ago with some of the problems listed, and they have had to manage some form of sustained yield and conservation of at least some of their resources. Philosophical discussion in this volume (chaps. 21–24) is largely limited to contemporary Western thought. Cultures are not static systems, nor are ecosystems static systems—people change, and we export and import ideas and views. We may not realize, for example, that some of our views that originated 2,000 years ago in ancient Greece were not originally Greek; they may have come from India or China.

Ethical

As conservation biologists, we have only begun to look at ethical problems (Rolston 1981). One is that societies do not have homogenous ethical structures. Although there is probably a lot of research to be done in every country, because ethics are culturally determined, Kohlberg (1981) lists six universal stages of moral development, and psychologists speak of stages of individual cognitive development. Kohlberg (1981) finds a high correlation between cognitive and spiritual development. Religion has had a profound effect on the development of secular ethical systems. The World Wide Fund for Nature has recognized this already in some parts of the world (Palmer and Bisset 1985). In September 1986, for the first time in world history, representatives of the numerically leading religions met in Assisi and issued an Ecumenical Call for global stewardship. Probably there is a need to revise religious concepts of mankind's place in nature embodied in each dogma with present actual religious experience within each spiritual tradition (see Jung 1984). This has been proposed already for the Christian tradition (McDaniel 1986) and is part of wider change among religionists worldwide (Hargrove 1986).

Psychological

I think it is relevant here to use an operational tool proposed by Lynton Caldwell (1984); the concept of the earth as contrasted with the world. The former refers to the biosphere, including humans as a biological entity. The latter is the fantasy construct made by each individual and eventually by society about the earth, which is obviously very far from being the earth itself. Each one of us, because of perceptual problems, has a reduced vision of the earth as it is. The way we reduce our perceptions is one of the major problems we are facing all over the world. The way we make decisions about the earth, which is such a large system, from such reduced perception, is a major problem and an underlying issue throughout this volume.

Some time ago I created my own system of nature awareness development as an operational tool (Tarak 1979). It is possible that there is a correlation between different stages of moral, spiritual, and nature awareness development. The reason that I am making this point is that we do not operate with society at large, but with distinct individuals, and we have to be able to relate to each of them in an appropriate fashion and be able to negotiate with them according to their own value systems. This is particularly important: In negotiation over land use, for example, misinterpretation can lead to other problems. Culturally, we lack a capacity to look be-

yond stereotypes to understand the singular; this problem was raised by David Ehrenfeld (chap. 24). Generalization as a principle or a habit interferes with our ability to find a creative solution to a particular, singular problem.

Educational

The question of whether something is knowledge and the question of whether it is teachable were held by Plato to be mutually dependent (Holland 1980). Probably, our traditional form of education of separate, distinct, disconnected disciplines will not develop the kind of thinking/reasoning pattern of the systems type (West Churchmann 1979). There are many more forms of intelligence than what we usually describe. Howard Gardner (1983) speaks of seven forms of intelligence. We tend to overvalue verbal and logical intelligence, minimizing the importance of many other forms, such as spatial, musical, or interpersonal intelligence. Interpersonal forms of intelligence can be extremely relevant to nature awareness. Extended awareness can be a key to other forms of education. The concept of human development may be a key issue in solving some of the educational/environmental problems (Nudler 1984).

Looking at case 2, the result is something I thought would never be the outcome of the course of action. It is clear that effective interpersonal relations were key. One can have the best intentions, but the results don't always follow a logical sequential pattern. What you have to provide to wildlife managers is a wider awareness and capacity to deal with different types of people.

Organizational

One of the characteristics of Latin America is the problem of the lack of awareness of organizational behavior. In Argentina there is an absolute lack of individual and social experience in organizing anything. We lack appropriately trained people with an understanding of roles, an understanding of what leadership is all about, and an understanding of stewardship. Equally critical is the training of environmental managers so that they can detect key obstacles and the nature and extent of intervention needed; this requires an intuitive/rational approach, as outlined by Mintzberg (1971). In conservation, organizational training is a critical problem, particularly because in an emerging nation we have to deal with the rest of the world initially at a disadvantage, since part of the economic transactions that have a direct effect on the environment (forestry, extended agriculture, fisheries, etc.) will put special demands on the system, and only trained managers will reduce unnecessary inefficiencies due to bad organization.

Case 3 shows that a small, adequately organized group is all that is required to get a conservation issue across to a large citizenry. Taking into account the enormous population, it is a major conservation achievement if one looks at it in terms of social behavior modification.

Sociological

Environmental issues are becoming major social issues in Argentina. At present, there are approximately 700 nongovernmental environmental groups, which shows the amount of general awareness. Another example is the number of nature publications now available with a local focus. Of a sample of 40 bird books published between 1920 and the present, 25 were published after 1970 (Christie, personal communication). Nature field guides are best sellers (e.g., Narosky and Yzurieta 1978, with about 7,000 sold already). There are local guides in various provinces (to mammals, Lucero 1983; birds, Clark 1986 and Nores et al. 1983; even snakes, Miranda et al. 1982 and Olmedo and Carrizo 1984; and wildflowers, Brion et al. 1987). Basically, to get any conservation strategy going, one must develop a network with as many environmentally concerned citizens as possible. How do networks operate, how do ideas flow across a network? How weak or strong must ties be to allow a network to be operational? (There is a whole subdiscipline of sociology, network analysis: see Knoke and Kuklinski 1982; Marsden and Lin 1982.) I would like to see someone doing network analysis on conservationists.

Legislative

In the area of legislation, networks can be extremely important. The groups of environmental lawyers working in the system have already managed to change some of the provincial constitutions in Argentina. For instance, the people of the province of Neuquen have the right to a healthy environment already written into their constitution. This constitutional right opens enormous opportunities for litigation, since it can provide for case court rulings that will allow specific jurisprudence to develop.

Scientific

A serious obstacle to conservation is gaps in scientific knowledge (Tarak and Canevari 1983). Throughout chapters 4 to 12 various aspects of scientific inquiry pertinent to conservation are examined. However, in my country perhaps the most important handicap is a very poor information base. We have no comprehensive resource inventory, and the status of most species is unknown or almost speculative (Cabrera 1978; Christie 1983; De la Sota 1977a). The entire flora of Argentina is unknown in amount, distribution, or status. In addition, we do not know the degree of habitat destruction, although it is quite intense (see Randle 1981). There are, however, patchy local information sources (Burkart 1979; Cabrera 1983; Correa 1977; Mares et al. 1981). The effect of weeds on the environment is only partially known. Olrog and Lucero (1980) mention at least seventeen species of exotic mammals, of which quite a number have become a major nuisance. Wild boar (*Sus scrofa*) is a serious pest in at least three different National Parks (Lanin, Palmar, and Los Alerces), and the technologies for eradication are either unknown or very costly.

Political

Obviously, a conservation strategy is a political problem, since it concerns the management of people. One should not be discouraged if certain politicans are not interested; it's still a viable political issue. By this I mean that if that particular politican is not interested, his opponent will be. What one needs definitely is a wider constituency. If one looks at case 3, it is quite clear that the real issues at stake are not those actually enunciated: in this case federal versus provincial power. In other words, one cannot take political issues as gains or losses: it is the process that counts.

At the international level similar issues occur. However, there is a tradition of binding national will through multilateral conventions that influence internal decisions. In that sense, the 1940 Pan-American convention was critical in the defense of the Argentine National Park System (Lyster 1985). At present, there is a proposition to develop an inter-American conservation system (Martinez 1987) through the Organization of American States that will implement the world conservation strategy regionwide. This shows that from a political perspective, the appropriate action may occur at almost any level, ranging from city all the way to international agreements. In this sense, international networks could play a critical role in national strategies.

THE CONSERVATION STRATEGY

At present, I am trying to develop the national conservation strategy operating from five different provinces. Since the way resources are used is constitutionally a right belonging to the provinces, it is politically critical to get organizations and governments at the provincial level involved from the outset. This will avert resentment toward the central government and a feeling of federal imposition that can seriously jeopardize a project of this kind. That is the reason I am working from a rural province myself, rather than in the capital city, Buenos Aires. Second, the choice of the provinces of Tucumán, Corrientes, Córdoba, Mendoza, and Río Negro obeys the following criteria: All have major universities where one can develop the scientific backing for the project; all have NGO activity and some tradition in environmental issues; and

each represents a province from a different biogeographical and political region.

At present, the plan is to develop in each chosen province three task groups and a coordinating team: (a) a scientific task group with the responsibility to prepare the database and the permanent assessment of the environment (Conservation Foundation 1984); (b) an environmental education group that will be in charge of assisting provincewide programs and developing conservation awareness among children; and (c) an environmental management group that will coordinate the participation and activities of local NGOs in helping map management alternatives with various social actors. Finally, a planning group will develop the strategy per se and relate with the task groups. Initially, a low profile and confidentiality is effective, and ideally the strategy group should have private backing so as not to appear linked to any particular political party that may be in power.

I close with a cautionary word about the use of the concepts discussed here at multiple levels. They may be applicable at one scale but not another. I am not sure that I am going to be successful in creating an effective conservation strategy. I am not sure that I am going to fail either. One needs specific targets and goals, and one has to be deterministic in terms of goals and opportunistic in terms of taking whatever comes. When I get terribly upset about what is going on, I have a prayer which I keep next to my wristwatch. It says, "God, give me the serenity to accept the things that I cannot change, the courage to change those that I can, and the wisdom to recognize the difference."

27

International Perspectives in Conservation Planning

REUBEN J. OLEMBO

One concluding event of the 1970 European Conservation Year was a conference organized by the Conservation Society of the United Kingdom, entitled "Conservation 1970." The motive and rationale for convening that conference were strikingly akin to those which have led Wildlife Conservation International to propose "Conservation 2100" as a fitting commemoration to the pioneering work and vision of Fairfield Osborn. One of the speakers at Conservation 1970 was Colin Hutchinson, and since what he said has validity today as we approach the twenty-first century and forms an excellent introduction to this topic, I shall quote his words. He said, "Mankind faces no problem more serious than mastering the ability to live within a finite environment," and then he went on to talk about how this could be achieved through conservation planning. He outlined fundamental elements of conservation planning to be ideas, action, and people. "We must," Colin Hutchinson said, "have ideas as a framework for what we must do; we must have a range of administrative skills and techniques, coordinated into effective action; and we must understand people and their behavior, because it is they who will have to act and who will be affected most."

Hutchinson was speaking at the European Conservation Year preparatory to the impending United Nations Conference on the Human Environment, held in Stockholm in 1972. Concerns about environmental deterioration and degradation, which had been gathering since 1945, peaked at Stockholm, which soon became the reference framework for the new resolve to institute adequate management procedures and practices for resolving diverse environmental issues.

Prior to 1972, discussions and analyses of environmental problems dealt with local or national issues, without considerations of overall policy ramifications, except perhaps in the United States. The Stockholm Conference not only legitimized environmental policy as a universal concern among nations, but also firmly implanted environmental issues on many national agendas where they had been previously unrecognized. Stockholm also reaffirmed the global ramifications to environmental action. Environmental problems commonly regarded as local, regional, or national may have international or even global implications because their physical reference and their ecological origins do not necessarily correspond to national boundaries. Some problems arise beyond the jurisdiction of any national government, thus making political solutions inherently international. Others may be localized in particular countries but are common to many others, and their international cooperative solutions represent efficient intergovernmental action. However, an issue can only be resolved internationally if it already has been recognized as such in the national sociopolitical milieu and has been accorded priority status through scientific, technical, and especially sociopolitical backup at that level. For it to deserve resolution, its urgency must be explicitly underlined in political terms, for policies are made or reaffirmed and implemented by people accountable to present, not future generations. Some issues, not always the most serious, must be dealt with in the shorter or medium term if they are to be resolved, or else all is lost. Protection of species at the brink of immediate extermination and halting irreversible ecosystem destruction are two examples with imperative for action now or be damned forever.

CRITICAL ENVIRONMENTAL PROBLEMS FOR COOPERATIVE INTERNATIONAL ACTION

Jurisdiction over the uses of international waters, especially boundary lakes and rivers, provided the earliest examples and forms of forging international cooperation on environmental matters. Migratory birds and animals also provided early impetus for cooperation. Since Stockholm, with subsequent coinage of populist catchphrases such as "Only One Earth" and "Spaceship Earth," coupled with a deeper scientific understanding of environmental processes and their relationships, the larger dimension relating to many other issues is beginning to be appreciated, each critical issue being weighed against its overall impact on the health of the environment. Nevertheless, as Lynton Caldwell (1984) points out, "critical issues as categorized by science do not always correspond to the perceptions and priorities prevailing in governments and international agencies." An issue must become sufficiently critical to its political constituency. The public at large must generally be aware of an environmental problem before it becomes a subject of public policy. A dilemma thus faces international environmental policy and planning, for international policymakers are only remotely identified with political-social constituencies, and that proxy relationship can mean many years in delayed action on a patently urgent international environmental problem.

Notwithstanding this dilemma, a consensus opinion gives a first approximation of issues of critical importance. *The Global 2000 Report* to the U.S. President (1980), UNEP's *World Environment 1972–82*, World Resources' *The*

Global Possible (Repetto 1985) and its companion sequel *World Enough and Time* (Repetto 1986), the Foundation for Reshaping the International Order's *Global Planning and Resource Management* (Dolman 1980), and Merril Eisenbud's (1983) review in Lauriston S. Taylor Lecture Series Number 7 are sources of some recent major analyses of current critical international environmental issues. Some arbitrariness and superficiality must, of course, be accepted in such analyses, because we are still in the rudimentary stage of the science and the technology required to expose all the issues in their full dimensions. Our information-processing capabilities, though expanding, are still limited. Also, we abysmally lack an understanding of human sociopolitical dynamics involved in our evaluation of environmental impacts.

Considerable consensus exists on the most significant environmental problems of our time and of the next twenty years. Satisfactorily tackling them affects relationships among nations, and the price of nonaction has worldwide implications. These processes are:

1. Loss and depletion of biological diversity, where the broad meaning is preferred to the more narrow concept of genetic loss (see chaps. 4–7). If present trends continue, 50,000 species a year will be facing extinction by the year 2000, and by 2050 one-quarter of the current stock will be lost.

2. Ecosystem and habitat disruption, destruction and loss of the productive capacity of crop and grazing land because of deforestation, soil erosion, soil salinization, and desertification. Some authorities quote the current annual rate of topsoil loss at 7 percent, predicting that the rate will accelerate to alarming proportions in the years ahead so that by the year 2000, the world will lose 676.5 million acres, or 18 percent of its arable land.

3. Pollution of air, water, soil, and biota by toxics and wastes of industrial processes, including radioactive materials.

4. The exhaustion or pollution of potable water. Severe water shortages are projected for at least thirty countries by the turn of the century.

5. Acidification, degradation, and depletion of forests and freshwater resources.

6. Environmental problems associated with

changing atmosphere chemistry and quality, which might ultimately trigger climatic changes.

7. Environmental drgradation associated with uncontrolled urbanization.
8. Energy issues, particularly those relating to the development and management of renewable energy sources.
9. The population, resource, and poverty equation (Western, chap. 2; Lee, chap. 30).
10. Disruption in biogeochemical cycles which might lead to the breaking up of linkages that permit regenerative capabilities of the biosphere, thus resulting in massive extinction of life on earth.
11. The global commons, particularly the oceans and their living marine resources.

I shall return to the last issue later, as I think, more than anything else, it will be the major platform for future debates and strategies in international environmental management of the twenty-first century. For the moment, I shall use the subject of tropical forests to illustrate how both national and international dimensions can coexist in a single environmental issue.

TROPICAL FORESTS: A NATIONAL ASSET AND A GLOBAL RESPONSIBILITY

The issues surrounding the fate of tropical forests vividly depict the emergence of the new global consciousness with regard to relations between nations, their natural-resources development activities, and patterns of international cooperation. This new consciousness has found expression in a number of concerns that are shared not just by policymakers and planners, but by the public at large throughout the world. The first is the concern about the disequilibrium between rates of change in populations and changes in resources, environment, and development, the disequilibrium which results in the depletion of the natural forest resources at a faster rate that it can be regenerated, leading to the ugly twin phenomena of deforestation and desertification, which in turn undermine development. The second concern pertains to the responsibility of present generations to provide for the well-being of generations to come. The third, but by no means the least, is the concern for what is observed to be the widely divergent

rates of forest resource use coupled with equally divergent capabilities to regenerate depleted forest resource capital. These concerns not only call for reconsideration of global cooperation and responsibility in resource management and conservation: They demand that a reconciliation of national and international obligations toward tropical forest use and conservation must first be made.

As a *national asset,* tropical forests form a prime, and often a primary, natural-resource base for development. As such, tropical forests constitute:

1. Habitat and home for millions of rural people. The number of people with direct dependance on forest products has been put at two billion, with those living in the forest at 200 million (FAO). Today some three million families live in the forest lands of the Philippines, one million in the forested uplands of Panama, and five million in Northeast Thailand (World Bank 1986).
2. A source of incomes (domestic, local, provincial, or regional).
3. A source of employment.
4. A foreign currency earner. In the case of Indonesia, which owns 9.54 percent of all the closed tropical forest resources of the world and 18.02 percent of the total forest ecosystems, the foreign currency earnings from forestry products rank only second to oil, and in 1980 prices, the total value of tropical forest exports from all developing countries totaled some U.S. \$8.4 billion.
5. A source for energy, building, and construction materials. Nine-tenths of all wood harvested in tropical countries is used for energy in the form of fuelwood, and by the year 2000, developing countries will need approximately 2.6 billion m^3 for this purpose annually.
6. Potential sources of land to be converted to other uses such as agriculture and horticulture, plantations, new settlements, and so on. Of Indonesia's 143 million ha of forest land, approximately 30 million ha have been earmarked for conversion to other purposes.

The global functions of tropical forests include:

1. An atmospheric purifier, maintaining the quality of the air we breathe;

2. A factor affecting global air temperatures;
3. A factor affecting global weather;
4. A factor affecting erosion, leaching, and other forms of soil-quality depletion or enhancement;
5. A genetic repository of wide biological diversity with great potential to meet future food and medical needs. The advent of genetic engineering should increase rather than diminish the value of tropical forests as a genetic reservoir from which the great wealth of genes still unknown to us can be used to create a vast array of useful products.

THE PLACE OF ENVRONMENTAL PLANNING AND MANAGEMENT

The application of environmental management strategies immediately encounters two diametrically opposed conceptions of a resource base that must be reconciled. The first views a resource base as a local asset for development; the second considers it a vital global ecosystemic factor that helps guarantee that the world remains livable for both the present and future generations.

Environmental Management Defined

A reconciliation of these two seemingly opposed views of an environmental resource problem could be found in the notion of environmental planning and management. Though its origins predate Stockholm, it was there that this concept became better crystallized to form the "drastically new concept of management" Maurice Strong noted in his review of the first year following Stockholm. Environmental management enlarges and reinforces the concept of environmental responsibility and encompasses the notion of sustainable development which emerged from the World Conservation Strategy in 1980. It can be defined as a systematic and scientific approach assuring harmony between natural and anthropocentric systems to minimize the adverse impact of human activities by matching ecological capability with societal goals and aspirations. Environmental management must attempt to resolve, in the most universally beneficial manner, conflicts that arise from the interaction of socioeconomic and natural systems, because, being systematic, it integrates all components into an effective and compatible mechanism. The essence of environmental management is that through systematic analysis, understanding, and control, it allows humanity to continue to evolve technology for the use of resources without profoundly altering or permanently damaging natural ecosystems.

For environmental management to be effective and systematic, it must consistently, within existing limitations of knowledge:

a. encompass all processes in unbiased perspective;
b. recognize and understand any processes or problems in the management structure and its component interrelationships;
c. handle interdependencies characterizing the process or operation as a whole;
d. design, build, and operate management systems which would serve as a means to manage any whole.

With this notion of environment management in mind, we can return to Colin Hutchinson's three fundamental elements of conservation planning and add additional ingredients, namely: priority setting; institutional mechanisms; and money and the political will to initiate, act, and persevere. I shall now discuss the importance of these basic ingredients of environmental management.

People and Public Support

Though perception of environmental quality may differ from place to place and from time to time, public environmental concerns will always remain as long as the problem is real. This makes the task of environmental management permanent, and since even successes create new problems, general public interest in environmental issues—no doubt with erratic highs and lows and with shifting points of focus—will remain a continuing factor of public opinion. People need to know the tradeoffs between action and side effects and must be given criteria to govern the changes they must make in their ways of doing things. If we ignore or fail to understand people and their behavior, success will evade us. If we are not to consign environmental action to the practice of a selected elite (those knowledgeable and in authority or elected representatives), we will have to regard the general public as so important that they must in all cases take priority in decision-making in resolving an environmental crisis. Education of the public is paramount in environmental management.

Ideas and Policy

Environmental management is a framework whose skeleton has to be fleshed out by knowledge from many fields so that the best alternatives for environmental decisions are available to the implementors. An overall policy defining the goals to be achieved by the proposed strategies is the kingpin of the framework and it must include the steps to sustain the proposed actions. At the global level, deficiencies and omissions notwithstanding, the World Conservation Strategy (IUCN 1980) has already been recognized as a first attempt at meshing ideas into a policy to address the multifaceted issues of natural-resource use and conservation faced by many nations, especially those in the developing world. *World Enough and Time* (Repetto 1986), a sequel to the World Resources Institute's *The Global Possible* (Repetto 1985), surveys successful management strategies for sustained development into the twenty-first century on the premise that with corrective action, the environmental challenges of the future are not unmanageable. The World Commission on Environment is expected to broaden the perspective and chart a policy framework capable of addressing 2000 and beyond and to articulate better linkage between environment and development.

Priority Setting

An environmental malaise seldom is due to a single cause, but may be a symptom or result of many diverse issues conspiring together. From a practical and economic point of view, it may never be feasible to tackle all these differing sources in a timely and effective manner. Consequently, priority-setting is essential to effective environmental management. However, planners need to state clearly the criteria they adopt in reaching these priorities, for in so doing, they gain political and public support for their proposed action, and in the criteria-setting, conflict resolution is inherently addressed. For-

tunately, the environmental management framework has built-in mechanisms for priority-ranking that should become sharper and better focused with improvement of the knowledge base. When priorities are correctly identified, action on one front promotes progress and strengthens initiatives on other fronts.

Plans of Action and Programs

A plan on paper is useless; it has value only when the benefits derived from its implementation are obtained. In order to attain results from action plans, the process of environmental planning must incorporate:

a. An education component. Without understanding of the need for action, and without commitment to that action, people will not contribute their effort, nor will they cooperate.

b. Coordination mechanisms. As environmental management benefits from and is carried through by multidisciplinary and interdisciplinary teams, coordination and control points should be spelled out clearly in the action plan so that the multidimensional aspects of the environmental problem-solving process move holistically toward an effective solution of the management problem.

c. Time frame and scales. Methodologies for environmental management vary with the scale and specifics of the environmental subsystems in question. Management effectiveness at the macrolevel is limited by national differences, outlook, geographical location, economic conditions, technological capacity, and proper availability and intepretation of environmental data. Global action plans must be aware of these limitations, just as they should take into account the fact that political segmentation and different national ambitions prevent any consistent international implementation of such plans. Realistic time frames are therefore to be incorporated into plans of action to avoid the damage that seeming inaction can engender among the enthusiasts or promoters of an environmental cause. Plans of action to combat desertification, to conserve marine mammals, to protect soils, and for sustainable development of fisheries and the most recent tropical forestry action plans are examples of current quests in environmental management at the international level. UNEP's recently developed Global Resources Information Data Base (GRID) will be an important resource for planners in the future.

Institutional Mechanisms

Environmental management requires sharpened responsibility foci, administrative skills, and techniques for dealing with environmental problems. Machineries for environmental action have taken many shapes at the national level, presumably because of the political and governmental structures on which they are based. The machinery created in the United States in 1970 by President Nixon is perhaps the best example at the national level of avoiding piecemeal responsibility, duplication, and the overlapping and proliferation of action points in environmental matters. UNEP was designated to be its mirror on the international front, but it has suffered from inadequate funding and understaffing. Many studies, such as those of Lynton Caldwell (1984), show that much reform is required, and it is for this reason that some proposals are expected from the World Commission on Environment and Development to strengthen the international institutional mechanisms so that they effectively address current environmental problems and those likely to emerge in the future. In the third world, more than environmental machineries are required: Building and strengthening of environmental protection and resource use capabilities are essential. The growth there of environmental NGOs, such as the African Network of Environmental NGOs (ANEN), should help, but much more still needs to be done.

Money and Political Will

The degree of commitment of any government to deal with an environmental crisis necessarily is a function of its total development perspective: Priorities assigned to environmental programs must fall within the overall frame of national priorities, whether these are established by long-term plans, pragmatic flexibility, or political opportunism. At the international level, the matter is further compounded by world power politics: East versus West, South-South

internal conflicts, and instabilities of North-South international economic relations. Even more fundamental are conceptual disagreements over basic issues of human well-being, such as economic growth, or what constitutes development. The disagreement over these terms is not just semantic, but conceptual as well as substantive. The notion of "sustainable development" that has grown out of the World Conservation Strategy, with its three bases of scientific realities, consensus on ethical principles, and considerations of long-term self-interest, could serve as a unifying theme for convergent international development strategies, and given a practical orientation, could become the cornerstone of environmental management. Then, financial resources generated at the national level could be coupled with foreign assistance to address systematically the priority environmental problems of our time and those likely to emerge in the future.

THE SPECIAL CASE OF ENVIRONMENTAL MANAGEMENT FOR CONSERVATION

From the preceding it is clear that environmental management is a framework with different application possibilities in an overall environmental policy context. This section considers ways to improve the efficacy of environmental management applied to conservation. As the battle for living resource conservation is likely to be won or lost in the third world simply because the largest proportion of the world's species exist only in these countries, they are the context of this analysis.

Living resources in third world countries are an especially important source of direct sustenance for their population, the basis for development, and in many cases a significant source of foreign income. It has already been pointed out that in the case of Indonesia, foreign exchange earnings from tropical forest products are second only to earnings from oil; in Kenya, tourism competes well with coffee and tea as a foreign exchange earner. An environmental management strategy for resource conservation therefore ought to address the following points:

a.   Causes and remedies for habitat destruction and transformation. When habitat is destroyed, wildlife loses food or shelter or other means of life support. In some cases, for want of appropriate and adequate food-source alternatives, humans compete with another species for a vital food source essential for that species' survival and sustenance.

b. Population growth and income aspirations. As the human population increases in most of the third world countries, hitherto unsettled lands are used for human habitation. In addition, the rising aggregate levels of consumption of goods and the need for jobs place mounting pressures on natural resources. No major reversal of this situation is likely to occur before we are well into the twenty-first century.

c. Influence of the marketplace. Although expansion of the market system and of markets for wild resource products can bring economic advantage, especially in earned foreign exchange, it can also result in greater exploitation of natural resources, particularly through absentee investors (be they local or foreign), and thus lead to less conservation. Exploitation of resources through absentee owners can rapidly sever the link between humans and nature and induce a laissez-faire attitude toward a crisis in conservation.

d. Information exchange and education. Greater emphasis needs to be placed on information exchange and dissemination of successful experiences of others, so that a collegial spirit permeates conservation efforts. International funds can have considerable catalytic and multiplier effects in creating solidarity in the conservation movement among third world countries. One needs, however, to guard against well-meaning, but inappropriate advice to third world conservationists, which often disregards traditional knowledge or local realities and which is given out of the social context of the conservation problem.

e. Equitable distribution of the benefits of conservation. If this economic issue with political implications is not carefully attended to, it can detract seriously from the gains in conservation. Equitability applies not only to the question of what accrues to the national treasury from foreign investment in a national resource, but also to what trickles down to the local population in a conservation area from the national receipts

from such things as selling natural resource products or tourism. Projects such as the pioneering work of David Western with the Maasai of Amboseli (Western 1979b) should be encouraged elsewhere. In relation to genetic resource conservation in situ, one needs to think of improvements in crop species and general agricultural productivity of the rural farmers in areas adjacent to the gene pools and to consider a wider sharing in the residual public benefits of conservation programs.

f. External aid and assistance. Grants and other forms of assistance from external sources are motivated by a wide range of factors and motives. Though conservation may be a basis of the external funds, it cannot always be taken for granted that its use will benefit living resource conservation. The emergence of the Committee of International Development Institutions on the Environment (CIDIE 1980) is a first step in analyzing compatibility between development assistance and environmental quality goals. Unfortunately, the principles enshrined in the CIDIE Declaration have yet to make a significant impact in practice. One reason is that third world countries lack the expertise to review carefully all proposed externally funded projects against recommended environmental standards, because there is no easy methodology to apply to the review.

TOMORROW'S ENVIRONMENTAL MANAGEMENT

The concept of the common heritage of mankind was originally launched in 1967 by Ambassador Arvid Pardo of Malta in the Twenty-second Session of the United Nations General Assembly during the discussion of an item on its agenda entitled "Examination of the question of the reservation exclusively for peaceful purposes of the seabed and the ocean floor, and the subsoil thereof, underlying the high sea beyond the limits of present national jurisdiction and the use in the interest of mankind." This concept was also obliquely referred to by Garett Hardin (1968) in his article "The Tragedy of the Commons." The concept became firmly internationalized when it was adopted by the United Nations General Assembly in 1970 "as a norm of international law." That it first applied to the seas and oceans and was given its first definition in the context of the negotiations of the Law of the Sea is no accident, for Plautus (cited 1928) had written in ancient time, "The sea indeed is assuredly common to all." Extending the concept beyond the seas to include other areas over which national jurisdiction is ambiguous or ineffective, Lynton Caldwell (1984) called it "international commons," concluding that "some forms of international cooperation in protection of the world's commons may be the ultimate requirement of human survival; in any case, they are essential to the maintenance of a healthy biosphere."

International cooperation in the environmental management of the global commons by rich and poor can be transformed as new international management regimes and strategies are forged. Opportunities for expanding the common heritage concept, and thus international resource management systems, exist in living resources, the atmosphere and outer space, and some unique international ecosystems. Opportunities also exist to apply the concept of the common heritage of mankind to areas and resources within national jurisdiction in which the legal ownership or tenure is ambiguous. An in-depth examination of the latter case was carried out at a workshop during the Ottawa World Conservation Conference. Examples of ambiguous tenure include pasturelands, inshore fisheries, irrigation water, community forests, and wildlife. The workshop agreed that the essence of common property management is the willingness of individuals to use resources in ways that respect the right of others in the interest of the sustainability of the resource and the welfare of the groups.

As it unfolds and develops, the concept of the common heritage will become a vital tool in resource conservation. However, on the basis of the lessons learned during the course of the long, difficult negotiations to apply its principles to the Law of the Sea, it is prudent to be aware of the pitfalls and, as we move toward the twenty-first century, make concerted efforts to clarify them. Some of these are:

a.   The legal institutionalization of the idea is still far off, and its definition is in some conflict with the classical and static concepts of private ownership and national

sovereignty, the latter being frequently invoked when the ugly phenomenon of tropical deforestation has been suggested for international resolution. The principles of common heritage could thus imbue reforms in the classical concept of ownership.

b.   Cooperation with industry and private management skills will be required as the technology and management skills that would be suitable to these tasks are yet to be fully developed, and the capital at the magnitude and levels necessary for full implementation is never available to international bodies and authorities.

c.   The international political and economic climate would have to improve considerably, and breakthroughs made in the many currently stalled East-West and North-South negotiations, such as the New International Economic Order and the Global Security arrangements, and in regional conflicts such as in the Middle East, Asia Minor, and Southern Africa.

GENERAL CONCLUSIONS

The trends in environmental issues and problems examined in the course of this analysis lead to a number of general conclusions:

1.   Scientific data are not available for a precisely accurate description of the nature, gravity, or imminence of critical environmental problems. However, approximations can be made for those problems on which we must act now or soon to avoid endangering the stability of the biosphere. We should be putting in place the policies and processes to redress them in an integrated and efficient manner because the time has arrived when humanity as a whole and nations individually can only continue to treat natural resources as if they were infinite at the peril of life on the earth.

2.   Since Stockholm, the political world has begun, albeit tentatively, to take up the task of planned environmental management at many levels of organization, and this will lead ultimately to permanent management of critical elements of the global environment—a task that cannot easily be defined yet, but can easily be identified as one in-

volving a jump in international cooperation. For this to happen, profound and pervasive changes in national and international attitudes, traditions, values, and organizations are needed.

3. Effective concern for the quality and health of global life-support systems will serve as an agent for, and lend legitimacy to, societal reform.

4. Environmental issues have implications for formal education, calling for public education and participation in environmental rehabilitation and conservation programs.

5. Professionals, especially ecologists, and private organizations have an important, conceivably critical role to play in global environmental management systems, especially in helping to overcome obstacles to cooperation imposed by conflicting political interests, official ideology, and bureaucratic inertia.

6. There is as yet no precise quantification of the costs of environmental management at various levels, but it certainly requires big financial outlays, thus raising major questions of budgetary, financial, and external assistance policies, which may require drastic changes in national and international economic and political relations.

7. The future security of wildlife and other living resources, the majority of which are to be found in the developing countries, will depend on designing well-balanced environmental management strategies which take into account several sociopolitical and economic factors, in particular respect for the traditional conservation ethics of the resource-owning country. External assistance should reinforce, rather than contradict, those traditions.

8. Current critical issues notwithstanding, the notion of the common heritage of mankind, further elaborated, defined, and expanded, will become a firm foundation for international environmental planning and management for resource use and conservation. To turn it into an effective operational instrument, profound changes will have to be made in the classical legal bases of property ownership, in international sociopolitical and economic relations, and in global institutions and machineries.

28

Conservation Legislation in the Century Ahead

MICHAEL J. BEAN

If one turns back the clock just a few years, to the eve of the Ninety-ninth Congress in the United States, one finds that the predictions made then about what that Congress would do in the area of conservation and environmental protection were anything but prescient. Few expected then that legislation to address what is perhaps our most serious domestic environmental problem—the destruction of forest and aquatic systems by acid rain—would fail to make any major headway in either the House or the Senate. Fewer still expected that fairly routine legislation to reauthorize the Endangered Species Act (1973) would be stymied or that the future of the Superfund program, Clean Water Act construction grants, federal pesticide reform, and other mainstays of the legislative framework for protecting our environment would be in doubt until the final days of the Congress. On the bright side, few foresaw that the 1985 farm bill would be the vehicle for sweeping agricultural reform to protect wetlands and other ecologically important, but agriculturally marginal, lands by eliminating crop subsidies when these ecologically important lands are brought into production.

That unimpressive record of divining the future in modest, two-year increments ought to give pause to anyone attempting to address the subject of conservation legislation in the year 2100. On the other hand, unlike shorter-term predictions, one can make assertions about the distant future emboldened by the knowledge that by the time they have been shown to be wrong, one will no longer be around to suffer any personal embarrassment.

In thinking about conservation legislation a century hence, it is important to keep in mind a rather fundamental, almost simplistic point. Legislation, like it or not, is made by legislators—not by biologists and certainly not by philosophers. Now that point is both sobering and tantalizing. It is sobering because it suggests the limits of how much one can expect from the legislative process. Anyone paying any attention to today's political races has very likely noticed the popularity of the somewhat mischievous tactic of surprising candidates in public fora with simple factual questions about current affairs. The object, apparently, is to make the candidates look like fools. It usually works. Still, most of the candidates manage to guess at least a few of the right answers. Imagine, however, a public forum in which candidates were asked similarly basic questions about science and the environment. You know the results. Is it any wonder, therefore, that legal developments seem always to follow, rather than anticipate, serious resource problems?

Thus, as much as one might like to envision a future in which those responsible for conservation legislation are genuinely well informed and knowledgeable about the substance of the environmental issues with which they will deal, the reality is likely to be quite different. One must recognize also that one cannot expect too much from legislation. There is, for example, in the United States, a federal law known as the Endangered Species Act. It is often described as the most comprehensive, far-reaching legislation for the protection of endangered species anywhere in the world, and perhaps it is. The purpose of the statute is to establish a program for the conservation of threatened and endangered species and to provide a means whereby the ecosystems upon which they depend may be preserved. Yet, after more than a decade of experience with that act, it is clear that most of the species within our very own country that should be protected under that act are not yet protected, many of the species that are formally protected have nevertheless continued to slip steadily toward extinction, and a relative handful appear to be making the recovery that is the act's ultimate objective. Much the same observation can be made with respect to the CITES treaty (CITES 1973). As Perez Olindo (chap. 25) noted previously, negotiating a treaty or passing a law is clearly not the end of the process; it is the beginning.

Now I mentioned that there is a tantalizing aspect to the fact that legislation is made by legislators. However little legislators may know about the basic biological underpinnings of the conservation controversies they must resolve, there is one thing they make a determined effort to know—the wishes of their constituents.

The demand for a quality environment, for clean air and water, for wilderness preservation, for wildlife protection, and for recreational opportunities in nature has grown, at least in the United States, as the general level of affluence and the amount of leisure time have increased. To the extent one is optimistic about continued growth in general economic well-being and available leisure time, one can expect an ever more active constituency in favor of conservation and environmental protection. Tomorrow's legislators won't ignore that constituency; they can't afford to—they're politicians.

If one accepts the basic postulates of what I have outlined thus far, one conclusion seems hard to avoid: Building a strong legislative framework for conservation in the next century will require, not so much legislators who understand and appreciate the basics of science and ecology, but rather a positive economic environment conducive to an enlarged, politically active constituency for protecting nature.

Often accused of being enemies of growth and advocates for lowering the standard of living as a way of securing a claimed better quality of life, conservationists may well find that their own future success, particularly in being an influential political constituency, is linked to continued economic growth—or at least to being able to find and advocate solutions to the problems of the future that are both environmentally sound and economically positive. More than merely embracing the rhetoric of growth is needed. The substance of growth must be reflected through ingenious approaches to long-bedeviling problems.

To cite a specific example (U.S. Congress 1985), one of the most rapidly growing areas in this country is southern California. The principal resource constraint to growth in the sprawling metropolis that stretches from Los Angeles to San Diego is water. The agricultural areas to the east, in the Imperial Valley, have already used up most of California's entitlement to water from the Colorado River through profligate practices encouraged by the availability of heavily subsidized water from federal reclamation projects. Los Angeles and the cities around it have therefore looked north to find the water needed for future growth. Their solution, for which an army of planners has been mobilized, has long been to build more dams on more rivers in the northern part of the state and to send the water stored in those new reservoirs south through a vast system of canals and aqueducts. Already 60 percent of the water that should flow into San Francisco Bay is diverted south.

From a conservationist's viewpoint, that dream is truly a nightmare. The free-flowing rivers of the north offer considerable aesthetic value and support important anadromous fisheries for commercial and recreational fishermen. More dams on rivers that flow eventually to San Francisco Bay threaten the salinity balance of the Bay and thereby pose a potential threat to the enormous productivity of the Bay and its delta. To damage these extraordinary resources so that an already overpopulated Los Angeles can add still more millions to its numbers seems insane, according to the conservationist's traditional calculus. In the face of such threats, the response of the conservation community has been consistent—fortify the barricades and fight each new dam proposal with fervent intensity. From the perspective of one not in that camp, the label *antigrowth* attaches quite easily to such efforts.

In classic contests of this sort, conservation forces have won some important victories. But they have also suffered their share of defeats, and not all of their victories will necessarily be long-lasting. The question, therefore, is whether there are solutions—as opposed to standoffs—that offer something of promise to both sides. If there are, being able to identify and embrace them will enable conservationists to shake the mantle of negativism. Exactly that is happening now (*Washington Post* 1985).

A good deal more water is potentially available for continued urban growth in southern California without the need to dam the state's last free-flowing rivers. It is evaporating from the fields of irrigated farmlands in the Imperial Valley, soaking through the bottoms of unlined irrigation canals, and being used to grow low-value, overabundant crops. These wasteful practices are part of the environmental cost of heavily subsidized water for irrigated agriculture. After railing unsuccessfully against such subsidies for many years, conservationists have taken a new tack. The cities of southern California can find the water they need for decades of growth in the irrigated fields of the Imperial Valley. By paying irrigation districts to line irrigation canals, put into place modern, efficient irrigation systems, and retire marginally productive, low-value cropland, the cities can obtain from those same districts the water thus saved at less cost, and certainly with less public controversy, than by building new dams on as yet undammed northerly rivers. Everyone becomes a winner in this new partnership; the cities continue to grow, farmers retain the benefits of their subsidies while modernizing their practices, and free-flowing rivers remain free. Even venture capitalists have moved in to broker the deals between farm and city. It is the type of solution that is beginning to be taken very seriously by all the concerned interests, and it is a growth-allowing solution that conservationists have played a key role in identifying and promoting. Conservationists have embraced the higher standard of living sought by development interests without sacrificing the quality of life.

There are other examples of the positive role that conservationists can play in shaping solutions that protect environmental quality while allowing for the continued economic growth that is very likely essential for the sustained effectiveness of the conservation movement. A very recent one concerns the chemical contamination of wildlife at Kesterson National Wildlife Refuge in California (Harris 1986). Again, irrigated agriculture has an important

role in this drama. The Kesterson National Wildlife Refuge is in reality a huge complex of evaporation ponds that receive water drained from beneath the irrigated farmlands of the San Joaquin River valley. A few years ago, grotesque abnormalities began to be noticed in certain of the waterfowl that nest at the Refuge. The cause, it was subsequently determined, was an unusually high concentration of selenium in the Refuge's water supply. Selenium is a naturally occurring element that, along with other salts, was being leached from the soils of the irrigated farmland.

Responses to the discovery of this alarming problem ranged the predictable gamut. Some environmentalists reflexively called for halting the flow of irrigation water to the valley farmers, thus putting an end to farming altogether in the region. Farm interests proposed bulldozing Kesterson and replacing it with a network of private evaporation ponds, thus substituting multiple smaller toxic ponds for one big one. Meanwhile, the Fish and Wildlife Service was kept busy with firecrackers and shotguns in a Keystone Cops effort to keep wildlife from getting anywhere near the wildlife refuge.

Is there a solution to this tragedy, one that does not require sacrificing waterfowl and other wildlife or putting an end to irrigated agriculture as the mainstay of the local economy? If there is, the conservation community ought to be its champion. As it happens, there may be, and it is environmentalists who have identified it. Using state-of-the-art, reverse-osmosis technology, the selenium-and-salt-laden drain water can be resalinated; the resulting concentrated brine can be used in solar ponds to produce modest amounts of electricity. Thus marketing of the end products of clean water and energy turns a toxic, wildlife disaster into a profitable means of sustaining existing agricultural investments while eliminating a chemical contamination problem of major proportions (Willey 1985).

If the solution proffered for the problem of Kesterson works, it may have application elsewhere. Selenium and related contaminants have since been found at a number of other western sites where irrigation drainage flows supply wildlife refuges. If the approaches taken by the conservation community require abandonment of irrigated agriculture, conservation will continue to be perceived as hostile to the economic well-being of a significant constituency of both national and state legislators. Creative solutions that address the economic needs of such constituencies while serving the interests of the environment are essential if the conservation community is to shape the legislative landscape into the next century.

The same principles apply in a myriad of other contexts. Certainly the most prominent environmental issue of the day is the problem of assuring safety in the disposal of hazardous wastes. Coastal and fishing communities are vociferous in their opposition to the burning of such wastes at sea. Land-based incinerators spark similar local controversies over virtually every siting proposal, and the difficulties of assuring no leakage into the groundwater seem likely to make disposal in landfills a thing of the past. Clearly, the long-run solution is to produce fewer such wastes by designing more efficient production processes and facilitating the creation of markets for the utilization of waste products. To the extent the conservation community embraces and becomes identified with such solutions, and not with unyielding opposition to every siting proposal, the greater will be its potential to influence future public policy and the legislation through which that policy is expressed.

Finding and promoting solutions that serve the twin ends of environmental protection and economic advancement are necessary for conservationists to make the conservation agenda appealing to the legislatures of the next century, if only because this will make their task easier by eliminating much of the contention between the conservation constituency and other influential political constituencies. In the century ahead, the primary legislative dilemma will likely be to determine how much authority for deciding conservation policy should be exercised by the legislature itself and how much should be delegated to other agencies of government, particularly expert administrative agencies. Most likely, even more so than in the current century, the role of the legislature will be not to articulate the fine details of conservation and environmental policy, but to outline in a rather general way the course of conservation policy.

Even if one assumes, as one probably must, that in the coming century legislators will be able to summon an extraordinary wealth of data and information to assess the environmental and economic consequences of the public policy choices before them, their capacity to absorb, comprehend, and question that data will be quite limited. The range of choices will likely have been delimited for them by the expert administrative agencies to which the responsibility for staying on top of the details of public controversy has been delegated. Complicating the legislature's limited capacity to stay atop an increasingly complex set of environmental information will be the growth of ever more sophisticated lobbies representing a myriad of competing interests: consumers concerned with controlling prices, business interests concerned with maintaining profit opportunities, regional interests concerned with geographical disparities, ethnic interests dedicated to preserving cultural uniqueness, and a host of others. For the success of conservation legislation in the year 2100, conservationists will have to be seen not as just one more in a varied pack of special interest lobbies, but as a social force capable of bridging and uniting those diverse interests. The key to that is identifying conservation solutions that embrace the basic desires and values of the larger populace.

29

How the Developed World Can Promote Conservation in Emerging Nations

MARY C. PEARL

A basic premise of this chapter is that wildlands and wildlife in the tropics are in everyone's interest to protect—not out of an exploiter's guilt for past overexploitation, or the moral obligation of rich to poor, or the narrow self-interest of a coterie of academic researchers and wealthy nature enthusiasts—but out of the direct economic self-interest of all nations. By the end of the next century, this belief will be a commonplace and a basic tenet of international economics—or we as global citizens will have failed to mitigate the worst extinction spasm in history, imperiling our own survival. Western (chap. 2) has described 100 years from now as a time when people will be more urbanized and more educated—in other words, in a better position to influence the actors in the increasingly intimate, instantaneously communicating network of the world's economy. This trend has begun, and already a slight shift in attitudes among the world's major economic agents is detectable. Whether environmental concerns can be effectively integrated into the professional structures of key institutions is uncertain.

World Bank President Barber Conable recently made a surprising statement for a banker: "Sound ecology is good economics. I believe we can make ecology and economics mutually reinforcing disciplines" (Conable 1987). The degree to which current reality is at variance with the belief he expressed represents a challenge to environmentalists and economists to change old assumptions to meet the next century with wildlife and wildlands in good shape. At present, the two disciplines share few common assumptions and do not even agree on vocabulary. As recently as 1984, a meeting of the World Bank designed to help ecologists and economists find common ground collapsed in failure (Holden 1987). Economists rejected the idea that natural resources can be finite and placed the burden of proof on scientists to show, first, that limits indeed exist, and then to delineate precisely where they lie. In rejecting explanations that use biological terms like *sustainability* and *carrying capacity,* the economists insisted that definitions must be made in economic rather than biological terms if they are to be used successfully to influence change in economic policies. One economist at the meeting summarized the very divergent concepts that ecologists and economists have about the nature of the physical world and the nature of technology. Basically, economists are more optimistic: At the meeting, they said that no evidence exists to tie high population density to low human welfare (but see Camp and Speidel 1987; Wilson, chap. 1), and they faulted environmentalists for failing to see that increasing scarcity evokes corrective responses in an economy, including unforeseen technological developments. To this, the conservationist would reply that in a truly free world economy, the marketplace rather than master planners would probably be a better allocator of increasingly scarce resources—but not in a world where one nation feels it can totally deplete another's resources.

Since that nonmeeting of minds, economists have grown more pessimistic and environmentalists more optimistic. Publications such as the report *Technologies to Maintain Biological Diversity* (U.S. Congress 1987) point to some limitations on what can be expected of technology, particularly as the biological diversity upon which some breakthroughs would be based erodes. At the same time, more sophisticated studies of the management of ecosystems have given environmentalists cause for more optimism than in the past about sustainable, multiple uses for wildlands (e.g., Repetto 1986). Rapprochement still lies in the future, however, and current economic practice usually fails to take the health of the environment into account. For example, many industries, governments, and multilateral development banks still calculate the economic return on an investment by discounting all profits to "present values" (Payer 1982; Sierra Club 1986). This means, for example, that given an interest rate of 4 percent a year, 96 cents will equal one dollar in a year's time; therefore, if a dollar is to be paid out in a year, the present value is 96 cents. It is easy to see how a sustainable, long-term forestry project with a long-term return on profit loses out to an unsustainable, short-term project under this calculus: the longer an investment takes to pay off, the lower its discounted present value. The practice also fails to take the depletion of resources—or even the cost of gross damage to the environment—into account. As a World Bank ecologist recently said, the most important task for the environmental movement is to "revamp orthodox economic methodology" (Goodland, personal communication). A first step is to translate ecological processes into terms economists can understand. Economists must become concerned not simply with short-term profits, but with maximizing returns over an indefinite period of time, which can only be accomplished by conserving the ecosystems from which the economy derives its resources and to which it consigns its waste products (Goldsmith 1987).

In the following discussion I explore the changes possible and likely over the next hundred years among three major economic actors affecting ecosystems and economies around the globe: multinational corporations, bilateral development assistance agencies, and multilateral development banks. The chapter concludes with a discussion of the catalytic role that educated citizens in industrialized nations can play in affecting policy and actions of these agents through participation in nongovernmental organizations.

MULTINATIONAL CORPORATIONS

Since the 1950s, multinational corporations (MNCs) have become increasingly active in the world economy. By the midseventies, intracorporate trade accounted for an estimated 25 percent of all trade; in 1982, investment in less developed nations (LDCs) by MNCs totaled $11 billion (Krasner 1985; Myers 1984a). Multinationals have become a primary means for the transfer of technology and capital across national boundaries (Krasner 1985). Not all countries benefit equally: Foreign investment in less developed nations is concentrated in countries with the most resources. However, despite the fact that resource-rich countries attract more investment, the general pattern over recent years within these wealthier LDCs has been for the share of extractive industries to decrease over time, and manufacturing, especially services, to increase (Krasner 1985). In other words, the more economically successful developing nation has as a springboard a good resource base, which is not depleted but instead becomes an increasingly smaller portion of the gross national product (GNP) as the country's technological expertise grows. Thus economic prosperity is linked to a lessening of exploitation of wildlife.

The lesson to be learned is clear: A third world nation should ensure that multinational corporations supply capital and technical training to facilitate the country's development (i.e., its transformation from a reliance on extractive industries to manufacturing and services) if they wish to do business within its borders. Since the term *ecodevelopment* was coined and gained acceptance in the mid-1970s, followed by the concept of *sustainable development* in the early 1980s, there has been growing realization among business professionals, in both the developing and industrialized world, that the destruction of the environment will demolish the very basis for economic growth (Gladwin 1987). Worldwide, technological advances have led to greater efficiency in use of raw materials in production. This trend will continue, and product manufacturers will also increasingly be able to make use of abundant materials rather than scarce resources in manufacture.

Until now, international arrangements related to the conduct of multinational corporations have been guidelines, rather than binding agreements, principally because governments of developing nations have, despite international and domestic weaknesses, been able to use their juridical sovereignty to regulate much corporate behavior (Krasner 1985). Yet unfortunately, the conduct requested often ignores the economic long-term self-interest of host nations in the areas of environmental protection and technology transfer. For example, a North-based corporation may retain the most profitable stages of production, while locating the less profitable (and less technology-intense) and highly polluting activities in the country producing the raw material. Another problem is that an MNC may bring jobs and markets to a country, but at the same time produce products that are inappropriate and a misallocation of resources (Krasner 1985). The degree to which a third world state can control the behavior of a multinational corporation varies with the relative bargaining power of the two. A corporation's leverage is that it can choose to go in or not or, once in a country, to pull out. A state's leverage is access to its territory, followed by control over laws that regulate economic activity. The power of less developed nations is greatest in the control of raw-materials extraction, and least in the area of manufacturing, primarily because of their difficulty in providing themselves with capital, technology, and access to markets. If a nation must rely on a corporation for these, it loses bargaining power. It is in the interest, then, of emerging nations to shift from a reliance on extractive industries to manufacture through more insightful regulation of MNCs and other international bodies.

A code of behavior for MNCs has been discussed since 1975 under the auspices of the UN Commission on Transnational Corporations. The Commission has as its goal the endorsement of a set of principles for the conduct of multinationals, starting with respect for the sovereignty of a host country and obedience to local laws

(Krasner 1985). Respect for the sustainability of harvest of living resources and the health of the host nation's biome are other principles that merit inclusion in the policy the UN commission is working on. The current draft of the document is flimsy with regard to wildlife; it simply encourages MNCs to obey the host country's laws relating to environmental protection (which are mostly nonexistent or nonenforced) and "take steps" to protect the environment (cited in World Resources Institute 1984). The creation of a strong, widespread international arrangement for multinational corporate behavior is essential for the protection of wildlife resources. Even if such an arrangement is a voluntary rather than binding code, uniform treatment of corporations all over the world would discourage competitive bidding for foreign investment, which can require nations to bargain away their wildlife resources beyond long-term sustainability. Furthermore, if a code were widely accepted over time, it would enter the corpus of customary international law and then be regarded as binding (Krasner 1985). Cooperative roles of government and business specifically in regard to environmental protection and wildlife conservation have been the subject of recent international conferences such as The World Industry Conference on Environmental Management (held in Versailles in 1984), which was sponsored jointly by UNEP and the International Chamber of Commerce, and a follow-up regional workshop in Thailand on the roles of business and government in environmental management in Asia and the Pacific, sponsored by UNEP's regional office, the World Resources Institute, and the Environment and Policy Institute of the East-West Center. Specific recommendations for a code of conduct have emerged from these and other meetings (Pearson 1987; World Resources Institute 1984).

While MNCs may be more environmentally damaging than local enterprises because they tend to be more capital-intensive, with production processes that are more energy- and synthetic-, and, hence, pollution-intensive, they nonetheless also represent a channel for transfer of productive and environmentally sound technology for several reasons (Gladwin 1987). They are often more in touch with environmentally sensitive innovations, they typically employ more professionally qualified managers and better-skilled workers than local enterprises, and the equipment they use tends to be more modern, more recently constructed, and more efficient in waste control management. MNCs can contribute to conservation by doing more than simply providing on-the-job training to host country national employees. Other methods of technology transfer include sharing with government agencies and local universities expensive environmental monitoring equipment and sharing with them results of local research, expanded beyond narrowly focused applications to issues of environmental protection and resource management (World Resources Institute 1984).

Along with the lack of a code of behavior for MNCs, there is no international body to hold corporations accountable for their day-to-day conduct. The best-known effort by developing nations to control the behavior of MNCs in their countries is that of the Andean Common Market (ACM), which consists of Bolivia, Colombia, Ecuador, Peru, and Venezuela. The ACM developed a coordinated strategy to rationalize production, to prevent competitive bidding among members, to ensure that corporations meet requirements for transfer of technology, and to direct transfer of corporate ownership over the long term to the host country. Failure to comply with requirements means denial of local capital markets and loss of customs-duty liberalization (Krasner 1985). In the future, if third world host nations are to better resist pressure from MNCs and their home country governments, regional markets like the ACM must grow in strength around the world, and nations with the same resources to sell (like the OPEC nations) must grow more sophisticated and cooperative in their dealings with consumer nations of the North. The more cooperative and consistent resource-selling nations become, the less able corporations will be to play one country against another, and the less likely will be interventions by industrialized states on behalf of their corporations, to the detriment of tropical biomes. However, corporations are not charities, nor are they agents of foreign policy; their overriding obligation is to their shareholders' pocketbooks. To stem the loss of biological diversity in the tropics, direct aid from the biologically depauperate but financially stable North is essential. This direct aid comes mainly from government agencies created especially for assistance to developing nations.

BILATERAL ASSISTANCE AGENCIES

Foreign assistance is sometimes humanitarian, but not purely altruistic; a nation's aid programs, as an arm of foreign policy, are designed generally to strengthen the donor nation's interests worldwide. Often, a donor's political need for quick visible results distorts criteria for assistance. As a result, few government aid schemes last longer than five years (Andrews 1986). By comparison, nongovernmental organizations are more successful in conservation planning, partly because they can more easily plan for long-term commitments. Another problem aid agencies have in general is the relatively large amounts of money spent in overhead costs. The United States' chief instrument for foreign assistance, the Agency for International Development (AID), calculates that it costs $120,000 per year to keep a foreign expert in the field, since the agency must pay for such diverse items as school fees for children, air fares and air freight, a large living allowance, administration in Washington, and so on (Andrews 1986). Such sums reduce the impact of already relatively tiny budgets set aside for conservation within a larger foreign aid package that has many objectives.

There are seven countries with aid programs in excess of one billion dollars per year. The aid program of the United States is the largest in absolute terms, is global in impact, and is also regarded as one of the most sophisticated (Cassen et al. 1986); it will therefore be the focus of this discussion. The next two largest donors, Japan and Germany, have a strong economic and commercial orientation to their assistance; Japan's geographical emphasis is Asia, while Germany concentrates on the poorest countries. The United Kingdom and France have programs chiefly connected with their former colonies, although the United Kingdom has the highest proportion of aid of any major donor going to the poorest countries. Canada and the Netherlands are notable for avoidance of tying aid to purchase of their own goods and services, and for generally giving a high amount as a percentage of GNP (Cassen et al. 1986). Among the smaller donors, the Scandinavian countries (Sweden, Denmark, Norway, and Finland) have been most sensitive to environmental concerns.

According to the Administrator of the U.S.

Agency for International Development, the goal of his agency is

to meet the basic human needs of the world's poor, and to assist the people of the less developed countries to help themselves through the creation of effective economic and social policies which encourage the development of local private enterprise, the participation of American business with local institutions, the transfer of appropriate technology and the reliance upon private voluntary organizations (McPherson 1985).

Indirect, but stated objectives (USAID 1985) include the political stability of less developed nations and the sales of U.S. goods and services (including, presumably, the services of American conservation biologists, lest they be surprised at resentment against foreign intrusion directed at their efforts as well as those of widget salesmen). However, within this framework, USAID has played a "splendidly pioneering role" (Myers 1985b) in promoting conservation of biological diversity.

A 1983 amendment to the Foreign Assistance Act required that USAID work together with other federal agencies to develop a strategy for the preservation of biological diversity, and in December 1984, the agency submitted a report to Congress that outlined biodiversity conservation issues and methods (USAID 1985). As an example of the fruit of this labor, USAID managers point to the setting aside of a new national park in Sri Lanka as part of the massive Mahaweli development scheme there (USAID 1985). However, it is ironic that this project should have been cited, since it has been fraught with difficulties. I found it a commonplace rumor in Sri Lanka that corruption exists in the handling of USAID funds for Mahaweli, and the important corridor between two sections of nature reserve land has already been eliminated in current plans. Comments received from USAID missions elsewhere suggest that problems exist in translating the general principles and recommendations of the agency into specific initiatives at the country level (U.S. Congress 1987).

Nonetheless, AID's innovative mandate to conserve biological diversity is a hopeful sign for future conservation, as AID's people on the ground in its 60 missions in LDCs around the world grow increasingly cognizant of the important role of wildlife conservation in develop-

ment. Conservation is not the background of most USAID officials (U.S. Congress 1987), but as USAID begins to interact with Conservation NGOs (USAID 1987 and see later discussion), its efforts to protect biodiversity will become more effective. In 1985, USAID produced natural resource profiles of over 20 client countries, which documented problems of pollution, overharvest, and habitat destruction, among others. As a result, for example, assistance to the Dominican Republic was redirected to soil and water conservation, reforestation, and energy conservation. With this promising beginning, the relatively tiny, shrinking allowance for USAID conservation assistance is a cause for concern. The 1986 budget request for USAID was just under five billion dollars. Of this sum, approximately 330 million dollars was designated for forestry, environment, and natural resources—less than 7 percent of the total budget, but a larger amount than had previously been allocated (USAID 1985). Unfortunately, USAID suffered a budget reduction of over 4 percent, with the natural resources division receiving a disproportionate 25 percent cut (Wolf 1987). Such cuts are particularly distressing if one compares natural resource conservation expenditures with the amount of foreign aid the United States devotes to military assistance—70 percent of all foreign aid spending. As Edward Wolf (1987) states, America "pays more to maintain American troops in Honduras, among the countries where deforestation is proceeding fastest, than it devotes to cataloguing and managing biological diversity worldwide." Congressional sponsors of biodiversity initiatives have been able to respond to reductions in conservation spending by earmarking specific funds within AID's appropriation for expenditure on conservation (USAID 1987). Nonetheless, the enormous deficit and need for massive spending reduction by the United States mean that America cannot be seen as a principal supplier of conservation funds to LDCs over the next century. Its role in promoting biological diversity in the tropics may be limited to pioneering methods that other wealthy nations may choose to follow.

It has been estimated, based on extrapolation from current rates, that Japan's industrial production will outstrip that of the world leader, the United States, in twenty years, and that Japan's GNP will bypass that of the United States in fifty years (Krasner 1988). Combined with the increasing economic muscle of the so-called "newly industrialized countries" (NICs)— Taiwan, Hong Kong, Singapore, and South Korea—the locus of lending power may have shifted dramatically from the West to the East by the next century. What does this mean for conservation, given that a number of Asian nations are not known for environmental sensitivity? Japan is currently in the process of defining itself as a world power. Given that it has a domestic myth of respect for the environment, Japan may choose to begin to export this sensitivity to nature as a statement of world leadership that is nonmilitary and nonpolitical, two positions it seeks to avoid (Krasner, personal communication). A characteristic of international behavior among the Japanese is great coherence in policy, together with flexibility and energy in its application. In 100 years' time, Japan may well be an effective leader in conservation of wildlife. Although it has been faulted in the conservation community for its lack of attention to the consequences of its short-term intensive exploitation of resources, a promising sign has recently appeared in Japan in the form of a more enlightened attitude toward the management of timber resources in the heavily depauperized forests of southeast Asia. At the inaugural meeting of the International Tropical Timber Organization in 1987, Japan pledged two million dollars for research on reforestation and sustainable management of tropical forests and signed an international trade agreement for timber that has built the goal of sustainability into its economic strategy—the first international trade agreement to have done so (Wolf 1987).

The NICs may follow Japan's growing international commitment to wildlife, not out of affection for Japan, but from a sense of what is appropriate international behavior from a developed nation. Taiwan, for example, started to set up its national park system as recently as 1980 and now boasts a large amount of protected land managed by one of the most highly educated park department personnel in the world. As the founder of the park system expressed it, developed nations have national parks and a citizenry that supports them. Since Taiwan has become a developed nation, it too must therefore have national parks (Chang, personal communication). By this logic of what constitutes a modern state,

Taiwan will begin to play a role in conservation of tropical forests outside its own borders, and will better monitor its trade in endangered wildlife.

MULTILATERAL DEVELOPMENT BANKS

Bilateral aid, from whatever source, is not the only way in which industrialized nations develop markets for their commerce while fomenting development in third world countries. There is also the vehicle of international development banks. An American law created in 1987 requires that USAID prepare a list every six months of planned development projects around the world that U.S. officials and private environmental groups say may harm local people or land (Press 1987). The first list mentioned problems of major soil erosion, massive or badly planned resettlement, and benefits to few at the expense of many in projects of the World Bank, the Inter-American Bank, and the African Development Bank. On the other hand, the World Bank has begun to emphasize the importance of wildlife protection in its projects. These banks have enormous potential for reorienting environmentally destructive development schemes.

Multilateral development banks (MDBs), like other banks, make loans, but are different in other respects. They lend all their money to governments and government agencies for economic development projects, because the primary objective of these banks is to modernize the international economy in its capitalist variant for the sake of its long-term preservation (Ayres 1983). Theoretically, lending policies are determined by a board of governors representing member countries. In reality, decision-making is delegated to a board of executive directors who vote in proportion to the amount of money their country gives to the bank. Major donors, like the United States, the United Kingdom, France, Japan, and West Germany in the case of the World Bank, appoint one executive director each, while other member countries are divided into groups that are each represented by one pooled executive director (Sierra Club 1986).

MDBs are a major force in international lending. In 1984, they provided U.S. $21.6 billion in loans and credits. Of that amount, nearly 70 percent came from the World Bank, with about 15 percent from the Inter-American Development Bank, and 11 percent and 4 percent from the Asian Development Bank and the African Development Bank, respectively. While the sum of MDB loans accounts for only a small percentage of the total North-South capital flow, and about a fifth of all official development assistance, every dollar that an MDB lends generates two to three dollars in cofinancing with other aid agencies, governments, and private investors. Furthermore, major projects in themselves generate investment (Sierra Club 1986). The MDB has another kind of power over borrowers: The good credit imprimatur it can bestow is a necessary prelude to access to private capital. This means that borrowers must comply with MDB loan conditions even if the loan is a minimal part of a much larger project, simply to be able to borrow from other creditors. Whether this power is used for the "good" (e.g., a requirement to replace an environmentally harmful pesticide with a relatively safe alternative) or the "bad" (e.g., a requirement to cancel a law requiring a multinational corporation to locate manufacturing as well as extractive facilities within the host country's borders) depends on the policies established by the bank, which in turn can be influenced by the taxpayers of donor countries pressing their representatives on the board of governors to monitor project approvals for compliance with principles the donor nations wish to promote. The present discussion centers on the World Bank because it has been a leader in acknowledging the environment, in part because of the powerful role the United States has in setting its policy. The other development banks also reflect the priorities of their leading donors. The Asian Development Bank (ADB), for example, is dominated by Japan, and the ADB loans are even more closely related to the trade interests and policies of Japan than the World Bank's are to those of the United States (Krasner, personal communication).

Pressure from U.S. citizens has played a role in influencing the actions of the U.S. executive director of the World Bank regarding environmental issues, and the lobbying efforts of conservation organizations in the U.S. Congress may have helped shape the thinking of former Congressman and current World Bank president Barber Conable. In June 1986, the World Bank published a new policy entitled "Wildlands: Their Protection and Management in Economic Development." This unprecedented official policy statement expressed the bank's commitment to seek to avoid damaging wildlife, mandating a new set of rules for guiding the development and approval of projects receiving a World Bank loan. They can be summarized in four points:

1. The World Bank will not finance projects that convert lands of special concern because they exhibit exceptional diversity or qualities providing environmental services (e.g., watershed protection). Lands "of special concern" would encompass national parks, biological reserves, ecological stations, plus undesignated or previously unprotected natural areas as well.
2. Projects will be sited on land that has already been converted to another use, rather than virgin tracts.
3. Any exceptions to 1 and 2 must be explicitly justified and, in any case, placed on less rather than more valuable wildland.
4. Whenever significant natural areas are converted for project use (significance is defined as over 100 km^2 or a large percentage of a smaller ecosystem), the bank will compensate for the loss of the area by funding the preservation of an ecologically similar area elsewhere. Furthermore, the Bank pledged to integrate wildland conservation into projects that depend on environmental services, including those that include activities in agriculture and land settlement, fisheries, forestry, transportation, water development, and—to a lesser degree—industry and mining (Fitzgerald 1986).

Nearly one year later (Conable 1987, cited in Holden 1987), the World Bank president announced administrative shifts and new projects to back up the promise of the Wildlands Policy. The status of environmental concerns at the bank was upgraded by the creation of a new Environmental Department, with a staff separate from those located within other departments. Furthermore, offices were created within each of the bank's four regional departments (Asia, Africa, Latin America, and Europe) with personnel to act as watchdogs and "scouts and advocates for promising advances in resource management.'' Finally, four new projects were created: first, an urgent country-by-country assessment of the most severely threatened environments in 30 developing countries, to be conducted jointly with member nations; second, a continentwide program to slow the spread of deserts in sub-Saharan Africa; third, a global program to promote the preservation of tropical forests (funding for forestry projects is to grow from U.S. \$138 million in 1987 to \$350 million in 1989); and fourth, in cooperation with Mediterranean countries, a cooperative effort to protect that sea's basin and coast. Of these projects, only the latter was progressing as of mid-1988 (Goodland, personal communication).

While the World Bank's new emphasis on the environment is welcomed by conservationists, some point to a basic problem that again reflects the huge difference in outlook between economists and ecologists. Whereas the World Bank's stated basic goal is to earn foreign exchange and create employment, an ecologist would change the basic goal to the conservation of the resource base of a country. Even with current reforms in place, the World Bank's new policy is aimed primarily at minimizing the ecologically adverse impact of projects that have other primary objectives, rather than at initiating projects which recognize that conservation of wildlife is itself a development objective (Parcells and Stoel 1987; Shabecoff 1986). As resources dwindle over the next century, it can be expected that there will be an evolution toward making resource protection a primary economic objective for a nation. There are two factors mitigating against such a shift in goals over the short term: First, as the failure of the human needs emphasis of the McNamara years revealed, the professional structure of the bank works against any goal but short-term enhancement of markets for international capital, despite full interest in and willingness to achieve other goals (Ascher 1983). Second, the priorities of the powerful members of the bank—the developed nations—reflect their large economic stake in promoting the expansion of big, short-term development schemes. While loans are made to developing nations, in reality most funds end up outside the third world. Of the World Bank's procurement disbursements (e.g., for machinery, consultants) until 1985, 80.7 percent went to developed countries and members of OPEC. A factor in this emphasis on the technology and products of the developed nations is the size and scale of most MDB projects. Large corporations are the beneficiaries of large, expensive engineering projects. Since it costs as much in staff support services to administer a \$500,000 project as a \$50 million dollar effort, an MDB will usually choose the larger scale. At the World Bank, this tendency has been especially pronounced since the big buildup in loans of the years when Robert McNamara was president (Ayres 1983). The result is that projects which cost relatively little, have local control, use local products, and employ many workers—and are thus potentially more ecologically and socially sustainable—are not funded (Sierra Club 1986).

What effect the World Bank's new policy will have on future projects will be seen in 1988 and 1989, when new projects have moved through the bank's planning cycle. A key factor will be how the criteria for justification of wildland conversion will have been put into practice, and how successfully local people and their stake in resource exploitation will have been included in bank projects. Some of the bank's harshest critics have pointed out that a typical loan for a forestry or fishing scheme has enabled entrepreneurs to increase the productivity of their employees by harvesting larger amounts of logs or fish, increasing the entrepreneurs' share of the harvest, depleting the local resources, and virtually robbing those who have traditionally taken a smaller harvest for their own or local use (Payer 1982). The World Bank has taken notice of this shortcoming. An economic advisor in the Projects Policy Department has said, ''We are dealing with complex behavioral issues here, and NGO's and bilateral organizations often have a better understanding of why things go wrong at the grass roots'' (Messiter 1986). MDBs currently lend almost exclusively through governments. Lending through NGOs may be a promising method for MDBs to act more sensitively to local people and ecosystems and thereby achieve truly sustainable development. The addition of NGOs as loan recipients will be fought by governments. The Inter-American Foundation found itself expelled from Brazil when it attempted to bypass the government (Ayres 1983). The growth and empowerment of NGOs through increased funding from MDCs is a task for the coming decades.

NONGOVERNMENTAL ORGANIZATIONS

In the United States alone, there are over 600 nonprofit organizations involved in development assistance abroad (Boynes 1978). Their total commitments are dwarfed by multilateral and bilateral assistance agencies: While development funds from private sources totaled 1.2 billion dollars in 1979, the World Bank lent ten billion dollars the same year (Ayres 1983). If we limit consideration to wildlife conservation, the sum is relatively even more miniscule; the largest conservation organization, the international network of Worldwide Fund for Nature (including WWF-US) spends roughly fifty million dollars per year (Bohlen, personal communication). Nevertheless, the grass roots experience of NGOs has positioned many of them to lead the way in implementing or designing projects for larger agencies to replicate in many locales over a wider geographical range. A new set of relationships should be established among NGOs dedicated to international development aid, education, and conservation, since the activities in these three areas can all be mutually reinforcing within a large-scale project. Furthermore, as Norman Myers (1985a) has pointed out, the initiatives required in these fields do not all call for infusions of money—much more can be done within the limitations of current economic commitments through shifts in policy. Supplying the rationale and impetus for such shifts is a task for NGOs. For example, NGOs can point out the causal links between increased access to education for women and lower birth rates and cultural practices which lessen pressure on the environment, or increased efficiency in use of fertilizer leading to much greater yields of grain and lessening of environmental and ecological damage to nearby bodies of water and fisheries.

The number of NGOs specializing in wildlife conservation in the tropics is growing rapidly in number and influence. In October 1986, a "Biological Diversity Technical Working Group" was established within the U.S. Agency for International Development to distribute 2.338 million dollars for new activities that assure conservation of biological diversity (USAID 1987). The method they used their first year (FY1987) consisted of matching grants to over fifteen NGOs, including the World Wildlife Fund, the International Union for the Conservation of Nature, the Belize Audubon Society, the Haribon Foundation of the Philippines, the Nature Conservancy, the New York Botanical Garden, the Missouri Botanical Garden, the African Wildlife Foundation, the Israeli Society for Protection of Nature, the Sri Lankan Center for Coastal Studies, the International Institute for Environment and Development, the National Academy of Sciences, and several universities. The number of universities with programs in conservation biology is growing; in California alone, since 1985, centers have been established at Stanford, University of California at San Diego, and San Francisco State University. By the next century, these and other programs may have matured into separate departments or even schools training many conservationists from developing countries and exchanging faculty with institutions in the tropics.

The network of NGOs and universities involved in protecting biological diversity in cooperation with bilateral and multilateral assistance agencies may grow even larger and more coherent in the future as a result of USAID's grant to establish a Consultative Group on Biological Diversity, which consists of such major nongovernmental granting foundations as the Ford Foundation, the C.S. Fund, the Alton V. Jones Foundation, the Geraldine R. Dodge Foundation, the Tinker Foundation, the Rockefeller Foundation, the Jessie Smith Noyes Foundation, and the Rockefeller Brothers Fund. In addition, as aid and lending agencies seek out NGOs, NGOs are actively pursuing support from them. The International Institute for Environment and Development, for example, raised over 2.2 million dollars in FY1987 from eleven different bilateral and multilateral aid agencies, the United Nations, and the World Bank (IIED 1987). The World Resources Institute recently collaborated with the World Bank and the United Nations Development Programme to create a global plan for tropical forests (World Resources Institute 1985). Institute 1985).

In the decades ahead, conservation NGOs may increasingly specialize in function, on the one hand, and form coalitions around important issues, on the other, in a more sophisticated relationship with government and multilateral agencies and consortia of major donors. NGOs in less developed nations have already begun to have special partnerships with one or more developed-nation counterpart organizations in the West, to have better access to these and other funding sources. Japan and the NICs (see earlier discussion) may become sources of funds for conservation in the future.

One of the great obstacles to conservation is the grossly inequitable distribution of wealth between rich and poor nations (Lee, chap. 30). Out of the current oppressive debt burden carried by many countries, however, has emerged a new opportunity for reduced debt coupled to natural resource protection. Hard currency donated to NGOs in wealthy nations for conservation purposes can be used to buy up a debtor nation's debt on the financial market at a large discount, which that nation can then agree to redeem with local (internationally worthless) currency to be used for wildlife protection. Several private U.S. conservation organizations have begun to use this method. With the total third world debt in excess of a trillion dollars, the money potentially available for conservation is enormous. The World Conservation Bank, founded in Washington, D.C., in 1987, aims to explore and extend the possibilities of the "debt swapping" technique, along with consideration of other financial vehicles, including blocked currencies and various international money markets, in order to free up money for wildlife conservation while at the same time reducing the indebtedness of poor nations (Sweatman, personal communication).

Another specialized activity for developed-nation NGOs that may increase in importance in coming decades is the carrying out of survival plans for endangered species by zoological parks, aquariums, and botanical gardens (Woodruff, chap. 8.) Clearly, the notion of an "ark" of animals continuing exclusively in captivity in a world devoid of wildlands is unrealistic, to say the least, and protection of ecosystems in the wild must be a paramount priority. Zoos are increasingly recognizing that alongside captive propagation must go in situ conservation and the development of a science of reintroduction and wild stock supplementation. Wildlife Conservation International, the field division of the New York Zoological Society, has pioneered implementation of the notion that captive propagation and field conservation, research and training of developing-nation conservationists are mutually complementary. Zoos in Frankfurt, Chicago, and Washington,

D.C., also sponsor field research on a smaller scale. As a consequence of the better education of zoogoers concerning the natural context in which exhibited animals live, other zoos will find that their memberships will support international conservation activities as a natural outgrowth of the zoos' reason for being.

CONCLUSION

The foregoing discussion has mentioned many direct ways in which the industrialized nations can promote conservation in less developed countries over the next century. Economic development could result in wiser natural resource and wild habitat management over the short and midterm, and in turn, conservation of resources could result in higher economic development worldwide over the long term. Essentially, then, the key role for multinational corporations, Northern governments, development banks, and NGOs is to continue to promote development in the South, but to inform that development assistance with consideration for the environment, and to muster the will to reallocate priorities to achieve this. Prosperous nations everywhere, including Asia, must begin to protect wildlife beyond their own borders, recognizing their self-interest in doing so. Beyond this recognition must come coordinated action, which would be the responsibility of donors and recipient nations alike. A poor country can easily be overwhelmed by too many actors creating a chaotic mishmash of attempts at ecodevelopment. For example, a variety of donors working on Kenya's water supply has resulted in the use of eighteen different designs of water pump, all of which must be run and maintained differently. It is not unusual for a poor country to have up to thirty official aid agencies and sixty NGOs working on projects within its borders (Cassen et al. 1986).

Individual citizen action through nongovernmental organizations is starting to alter the behavior of such powerful forces as the World Bank and USAID to reflect conservation values. It will continue to be individuals who will guide their leaders to the realization that peace and sustainable development, rather than military spending and accelerated resource extraction, is the true road to security and prosperity in the year 2100.

30
Conservation in a World in Search of a Future

JAMES A. LEE

The individual memorialized at the conference Conservation 2100, Fairfield Osborn, had unique talents and abilities that spanned both Wall Street and the very frontiers of the natural world. Equally at home in the Century Club in downtown Manhattan and the savannas of Africa, he referred to himself more often as a "naturalist" than an investment banker.

The son of an illustrious scientist, Henry Fairfield Osborn, he chose not to follow in his father's footsteps in becoming a scientist. But it can hardly be said he languished in the shadow of his father, for his own efforts on behalf of conservation won numerous accolades and honors. It is reasonable to assume, however, that his father and the retinue of scientists and scholars that were attracted to the elder Osborn were instrumental in developing his keen interest in the natural world. Long associated with the New York Zoological Society and founder of the Conservation Foundation, Osborn, in 1947, embarked on an effort to arouse the concern of peoples everywhere to the "accumulated velocity with which [man] is destroying his own life sources" (Osborn 1948). This was to become a crusade that would occupy his efforts until his death in 1969 at the age of 82 years.

His much acclaimed book *Our Plundered Planet* appeared in 1948, at a time when, as Osborn put it, "we are rushing forward un-

The views expressed in this paper are solely those of the author and do not necessarily reflect the policies and practices of the World Bank or its affiliates.

thinkingly through days of incredible accomplishment, of glory and of tragedy, our eyes seeking the stars—or fixed too often upon each other in hatred and conflict—and we have forgotten the earth, forgotten it in the sense that we are failing to regard it as the source of our life." Thus Osborn strongly expressed his concern about mankind's future on the earth. Clearly here also, was a man ahead of his time—a man undoubtedly characterized by many of his contemporaries as a "prophet of doom."

One can only wonder what his colleagues and associates on Wall Street must have thought and said about him—this investment banker talking and writing about the limits of the earth, the finiteness of resources and environments, the growing threat of overpopulation, and the specter of hungry people and a sick society. They, on the other hand, saw a whole new world to rebuild and develop after a long and devastating war. They saw mankind standing on the threshold of a new and exciting era with technology that promised liberation from want and toil. Whatever could possess that Osborn to see such a grim future when it was plain to every right-thinking person that the millennium was close at hand—well, almost that is, if that new United Nations did its job.

It is also interesting to note that Osborn's father was a lifelong friend of Theodore Roosevelt and, in fact, inspired and guided the construction of the magnificent memorial that depicts so well the life of the great explorer, sportsman, naturalist, and conservationist. Osborn himself was later to be honored by the Roosevelt Memorial Commission for his contributions to the cause of conservation. An ardent admirer of T. R., as was his father, Osborn probably shared Teddy's philosophy and views on such matters as the importance and role of conservation and resource management in the economic affairs of a great and growing nation. Certainly, Osborn would have supported Roosevelt's admonition to future generations inscribed on the walls of the American Museum of National History:

The Nation behaves well if it treats the natural resources as assets which it must turn over to the next generation—increased and not impaired in value. . . . *Conservation means development as much as it does protection.*

This chapter is about development and its relationship to environment as we approach the twenty-first century. While I shall examine this relationship particularly as it applies to the still developing countries wherein reside the majority of the world's peoples, I intend to comment on the role of international development agencies, private industry, and the media in the developed world as change agents.

The world of today would in some respects not be entirely familiar to Osborn—and yet he would quickly discern that the trend of environmental degradation and human suffering of which he warned has not abated. Quite to the contrary, it has grown dangerously precarious, as a spate of recent studies and reports attest (e.g., Elliott 1986; Harrison and Rouley 1984; Soulé 1986). They describe the world of the twenty-first century as being much more crowded, more polluted, ecologically less stable, and increasingly more vulnerable to disruption.

The World Conservation Strategy (IUCN 1980) is a document with which we are all very familiar. It conveys most vividly the dangers posed by the growing challenges to the earth's life support systems. It struck me, however, that given the vast and growing disparities between the "have" and "have not" nations, it is not enough merely to warn that mankind is in great peril of transgressing environmental outer limits—nor, on the other hand, to say complacently that mankind has the capacity, technological and otherwise, to push back the outer limits of a sustaining and nurturing environment. What is essential is to institute the requisite dialogue, mechanisms, and processes which give effect to both the warning stated in the World Conserva-

tion Strategy and to the notion of prudent use of technological capacity. And, of necessity, both sides must embrace the day-to-day lives of the majority of the world's peoples—many whose attempts to survive are, in fact, foreclosing their own future through irreversible degradation of the environment essential to their continuity.

Guy Mountforth once recounted an old Bedouin in the Jordan desert saying to him, "When I am hungry, a date palm gives me food. When my belly is full, behold, the tree is beautiful." Mountforth points out that "only when the great hunger in the Third World is assuaged, will its inhabitants be able to recognize the true value, let alone the beauty, of nature."

I think we need to recognize and understand that in the dialogue between the worlds of the affluent and the poor about such matters as economic and social development, population, and the environment, the points of view of each side are very different. On every count the contrast in values, in interests, in priorities, in capacities is marked. Much of what concerns you and me about the future and fate of the global environment still strikes no resonant chord in many parts of the developing world. Unless and until the practical outcome of these concerns can somehow be made to satisfy the perceptions, aspirations, and expectations of the majority of the world's peoples, they will remain just that—concerns. The goals of conservation, sound resource management, and environmental quality are almost surely *not* going to emerge as high priorities for the allocation of increasingly scarce financial resources in many developing countries in the immediate future. I say this because most of these countries are too deeply involved in their struggles to overcome their worsening economic and social problems to themselves give appropriate and timely attention to development strategies that include the environment as a pivotal element. Yet, as is pointed out in *The World Conservation Strategy* and other contemporary studies, attention to those environmental dimensions of development could be crucial in assisting them to achieve an improved measure of self-sufficiency and sustainable development.

International development assistance since World War II has always attempted to address problems of the human environment—the principal emphasis being on the poverty, disease, hunger, shelter, illiteracy, and unemployment associated with a low level of economic development. That purpose would seem to have been paramount up to the present, and I hope it will remain so tomorrow, although methods to achieve it are changing dramatically.

However, concern about the problem foreseen by Osborn, namely, a burgeoning population using up the world's environmental and renewable resources capital rather than living off the interest, has steadily mounted. It stands at the center of conservationists' concerns; it is the genesis of *The World Conservation Strategy*. The development process, as we have belatedly discovered, is not without its own threats to the environment's capacity for sustaining that development, and it has proved to be prejudicial to human health and social well-being on too many occasions. This fact has become, unfortunately, one of the clichés of our time. Constant warnings and alarms have become all too commonplace and have done relatively little to slow the pace of environmental degradation or to alter the patterns of development giving rise to it.

It is becoming abundantly clear that those who are charged with the responsibility for the world's economy must, likewise, be concerned about the declining state of the world's environment.

National economies and, indeed, the world economy depend on the ability of environmental systems and natural resources to sustain them. The integrity of the environment is essential to our being able to sustain economic development. Failure of our global environmental system translates into failure of our global economic system. Anything that threatens the integrity of the environment threatens the economy.

The deterioration of the world environment to which we are all witnesses (if, in fact, not contributors) represents a major deterioration of the human prospect.

Even at this moment, the resiliency of many national economic systems, and the international economic system itself, continues to be sorely tested. And disorder in the economy is increasingly threatening of order in the environment.

By every measure, the developing countries continue to face serious and growing economic problems, which promise to be exacerbated in the near to midterm. To cite just a few:

1. Rapidly growing populations that erase hard-won economic gains
2. Sharp increase in the current accounts deficit
3. Slowdown in the expansion of world trade
4. Growing protectionist tendencies
5. Depressing outlook for the exports of developing countries
6. Increasing costs of imports and technology
7. Continuing slow growth of most industrialized countries
8. Inordinate expenditures for national security purposes

The financing of these countries' large deficits has required a substantial rise in external borrowing at higher cost, and, consequently, the debt service burden for many has increased perceptibly in recent years. It is not expected that these large imbalances will be corrected quickly, and problems relating to external financing and debt are likely to persist. The plight of the poorer countries is particularly acute because they have limited recourse to interntional capital markets and are heavily dependent on declining official concessional assistance. Added to these burdens are overpopulation and the wave of rural-to-urban migration with its attendant strain on the provision of social services and employment. Political instability and social unrest further compound the international situation.

These factors of economic disorder in developing nations underlie the slowdown in the economic growth rates of the developing countries, giving rise to sharply higher unemployment with its associated social and political implications. They also reflect the climate of the international forum in which environmental concerns are seeking a hearing.

The immediacy and trauma surrounding these problems must, of necessity, command the attention and energies of national political leaders and those who are charting the economic growth of the affected countries. In countries where financial resources are scarce and growing more so, decisions concerning their allocation more often than not come down on the side of the traditional "more productive" elements of development. They also are targeted over the short term, that is, the immediate and the expedient as opposed to the longer view. However, the environment and its resources become of critical importance in the continuing attempts on the part of the developed and developing nations alike to find meaningful solutions to the world's economic ills.

What, then, can we do to reconcile the imperative for continued and expanded growth and the challenge it poses to the environment at all levels, locally and globally?

To paraphrase the foreword to *The World Conservation Strategy* (IUCN 1980), if the object of development is to provide for social and economic welfare, the object of integrating the environment into the planning and execution of that same development must surely be to ensure a capacity for sustaining it and supporting its future growth.

But, unless and until there is seen to be a demonstrable improvement in the lives of the growing numbers of the world's poor, the penalties of our collective failure will halt any real progress toward sustainable development. Thus our task, at a minimum, is to:

1. Recognize that economic growth in the developing countries is essential if they are to deal with both their human and environmental problems;
2. Act on the evidence that such growth, if properly planned, need not cause unacceptable and irreversible ecological penalties;
3. Assist the developing countries in their choice of a pattern of growth that offers hope of being sustainable;
4. Provide the external support required for that economic advance in the poorer countries by increasing the concessionary aid so urgently needed;
5. Plan and implement a new type of international assistance institution to promote public and private investment on concessionary aid terms to rehabilitate, protect, and manage the degraded environments of developing countries upon which the very future of their economies depend;
6. Mobilize the considerable resources of private industry here and abroad in a bold initiative to aid developing countries strengthen their own indigenous capacity for dealing with development-associated threats to their future;
7. Liberalize trade and dismantle inequitable trade barriers that penalize the poorer countries;
8. Encourage and support the media to overcome the apathy that still exists around the world to the growing threats to the environment, and what it portends for the human condition; and, finally,
9. Realize, above all else, that human degradation and deprivation on the scale it exists for the majority of the world's peoples constitute the greatest threat not only to national, regional, and world security, but to essential, life-supporting ecological systems upon which all depend—rich and poor, developed and developing.

The one "pollutant" that threatens above all others to destroy our environment, to rip apart our already badly frayed social fabric, to destroy the very essence and spirit of mankind is the permanent, pervasive condition of poverty.

To the extent that economic development fails to transfer the possibilities into realities; to the extent that billions of the world's poor see their lives, and that of their children, and generations yet to be born, being denied the slightest hope for something better—to that extent humankind sees more and more its image of the future as an illusion. Such peoples, bereft of hope now and for the future, are pressed to exact the last measure of sustenance from their surroundings.

"Parts of the earth," wrote Osborn, "once living and productive, have died at the hand of man. Others are now dying. If we cause more to die, nature will compensate for this in her own way, inexorably, as already she has begun to do" (Osborn 1948).

Osborn perceived accurately and early the cause-and-effect relationships, but he could have hardly anticipated their dimensions or the rapidity of their onset.

History will chronicle the final results of the interacting and conflicting triad of population, resources, and the environment. And it may very well record that the world's environment and its biota were not ensured of a future because of the collective failure of nation states to acknowledge in time the seriousness of the threat and embrace a strategy requiring a level of international cooperation that hitherto had been unattainable. Or, it may record that the expediency of individual national survival overtook all efforts toward balance and equity in a required deference to a common threat. For a growing number of the world's peoples, the options are narrowing. The culturally derived quest to develop and transform the environment is reflected in the 5,000 or so years of recorded history, but only *now* has the finiteness of that transformation become manifest. There are, indeed, limits.

I wonder how Fairfield Osborn might have concluded these observations, in this time, and given the international situation as I have attempted to portray it. We know he was a man of optimism. It is not likely he would have said (though with much justification), "I told you so." Rather, as a practically oriented man whose investment dealings dealt directly with the transformation of the environment and its resources, he probably would have said, "It cannot be, it must not be, the environment *versus* development. A *modus vivendi* must be reached. The demise of the environment threatens our need to develop, and that same development is likewise threatening the environment. Let us seek an accord, else we all lose."

The developed countries have made some significant gains over the last several decades in protecting, conserving, and managing their environment and its biota. To be sure, these gains are uneven in their distribution and affect, and much, much more remains to be accomplished. Whatever has been achieved needs to be vig-

ilantly guarded—vigilance cannot for a moment be relaxed.

And, when viewed globally, what is done or not done to address the growing political, social, and economic problems that have caused even the Secretary-General of the United Nations to state that we stand at the edge of international anarchy, will, in the final analysis, determine whether conservation even remains part of our prospective lexicon or is relegated to a description of the protection to be accorded the artifacts and other embodiments of an earlier society.

And so, to those of you who long ago mounted the ramparts in defense of the environment and to those just beginning the unending battle I say, reach out to the developers and transformers of the environment and seek not necessarily to stop but rather how better to proceed.

And, I would say to those who in many places have the responsibility for planning, or financing, or executing, or profiting from development—pay serious attention to what the global environmental barometer is telling you, for the forecast is ominous. Acknowledge that "environmental apartheid" can no longer and will no longer be tolerated.

If we can make this a visible agenda item of high priority for Conservation 2100, we will have taken the first big step toward a sustainable society befitting the dignity and rationality that I hope still characterizes humankind.

31

American Broadcast Journalism: Its Coverage of Conservation Crises

LESTER CRYSTAL

This is one of the few times when I am ready to say that it may not be a great pleasure for me to contribute to this volume. As a matter of fact, this has been a very troubling assignment for me; when I began my earnest preparation of my manuscript, I wish I had declined the invitation. I'm in a field that deals primarily with the "now" and the tangible. In fact, it can be argued that for those of us in daily journalism, it is a preoccupation and often an obsession; if we can't see it, touch it, show it, or hear it, we leave it for someone else to worry about. So here I am among some of the world's outstanding conservationists who are concerned primarily not about today, but tomorrow, not about what is certain, but what is uncertain. To make matters worse, the stakes for any of today's immediate issues, aside from nuclear war, pale when compared with the issues considered here. Frankly, I'd rather be at the television studio this afternoon at my job as executive producer of the "MacNeil-Lehrer Newshour" than facing the problem of how to preserve the environment for future generations. Today is much easier than the future, and the record of the mass media in alerting and educating the public to the need to manage and preserve the environment is spotty at best. So I don't think we have a lot to be proud of.

It is not all the media's fault; conservation is an extremely complex problem. But that doesn't make my task any more pleasant. I'd like to start out by sharing with you one of my most unpleasant memories. My first job as a journalist was as

a writer and producer for a station in Duluth, Minnesota, my home town. I was between my sophomore and junior years of college, more than thirty years ago. The biggest story of that summer, and I think of that year in the region known as the Iron Range, was the completion of a taconite-processing plant near a town called Two Harbors, Minnesota. It's still there, a small town on the north shore of Lake Superior less than an hour's drive north of Duluth. The plant was built and designed to crush and process low-grade iron ore known as taconite. The taconite was processed into pellets of high-grade iron ore for shipment to steel companies in Cleveland and Pittsburgh. Thousands of people had been hired or were about to be hired to mine the ore and operate the plant. In fact, a whole new community of homes, schools, and shops had been carved out of the pines and birchwoods near the plant; the little town was called Silver Bay, Minnesota, and shortly before the opening of the plant I went to Silver Bay to do a story. That plant, along with similar plants along the Iron Range, was expected to help restore the economic prosperity in the area. I filmed in the little town, talking to people, and focusing on the new community, particularly on the plant by showing how the ore was transformed into pellets. I remember rather vividly getting pictures of the waste of the process that was poured out into the lake. It was a gravity plant, so the taconite started up at the top of the hill as big low-grade iron ore, and as it worked its way through the plant, it came out as little pellets that went into the ships, plus a lot of waste that went into the water in Lake Superior. I was assured by the people representing the plant that the material in this waste would do no harm and would go to the bottom of the lake, where it would harden. I believed them; no one at the time disputed them. I wasn't asking very many hard questions. Many years later, it was discovered that the waste contained asbestos, and that the asbestos in the waste was polluting the water and may have been responsible for causing cancer in the surrounding communities. Suits were filed, and after a long, acrimonious battle, Reserve Mining was forced to bury the waste on land in a safe manner. This was not a proud moment in my career; I didn't question hard enough, I didn't press hard enough, and I was very young, or at least that's my excuse today. Also, the times were very different.

Today, the awareness of the environment is much greater and concern for it is considered vastly more important. Our capacity to measure the potential dangers of materials like taconite waste has improved, but in thinking back, and in covering stories like this over some time now, I realize that unless there is a smoking gun, unless the poison strikes quickly, the press, government officials, industry officials, and the public are unlikely to get very upset. Biologists are seeing signs of a massive extinction wave of species of plants and animals. This was reported in the popular news media along with the prediction that if nothing is done, all tropical forests could disappear in the next 75 years (Rensberger 1986). Many species, thousands of them still undiscovered, potentially containing new drugs or new food sources, will disappear with them. E. O. Wilson was quoted recently (Rensberger 1986) predicting that this could be one of the most extreme natural catastrophes in sixty-five million years. That's a strong warning. But no one has panicked—it has not galvanized the world's governments or the mass media; it received minimal attention in the major newspapers, not on the front page, less on television programs. The "MacNeil-Lehrer Newshour," I'm sorry to say, did not prepare a major segment on it. Why not? Partly because it's just too intangible, it's too "tomorrow"—the inevitability of the crisis is too uncertain.

The dilemma that we in the mass media face in trying to get the conservation biologists' message across both to the general public and also to the governments of the countries around the world is that we do an excellent job of affecting something that has happened, but we do very poorly at affecting things that haven't happened yet. We cannot convey the root causes of a problem before we can specify an effect. Unfortunately, only two issues—money and death—hold the public's attention and create the political willpower to force a major change in our society. Furthermore, both have to come within the time frame of the present and be close to home to have an effect. I know that's an oversimplification, but I don't think I'm that far off. What forced Americans to start conserving oil was not the warning that someday there would be shortages and therefore we needed to find alternative forms of energy; people in the field of energy had been doing that for years prior to the early 1970s; nor was it the warning that we were risking our security by depending so much on other nations for such a fundamental resource. Nothing happened until the cost was driven up so high that the burden on our life style (we didn't like waiting in line) and the burden on our pocketbooks (we didn't like paying U.S. $1.50 and more for a gallon of gasoline) became too much to carry. So we cut back consumption and we started to develop alternative forms of energy. Now that the demand has diminished, the supply is up, and the price is down, conservation and alternative supply efforts have slackened.

The energy crisis may be back before us as part of the 1988 presidential elections. I don't know if it's going to be that soon or not; on our news program, T. Boone Pickens predicted that the oil crisis would be back soon, yet at the moment, the United States is not preoccupied with it, nor is the press. Another very simple example is that despite all the warnings, many people still smoke cigarettes, because the tangibility of the consequences is not strong enough. Alarms and warnings about the dangers of pollution meant little until it could be seen and proven that people were dying. An example is the effects of toxic waste found in the community of Love Canal (Swan 1979), which got attention and action only after the resident families, the victims and the sufferers, could provide tangible proof of the danger and show the actual consequences. Millions of dollars can be raised when there is a famine in Africa taking lives before our eyes. We recently experienced another cycle of seeing famine and raising money through worldwide campaigns (Lando 1985), yet we cannot muster the long-term programs, funds, and willpower to deal with the solutions that might prevent that starvation. For years the United States has been putting off finding a solution for storing nuclear waste. There appears now to be some slow movement toward a solution (Fung 1984). It has taken an incredibly long time because no one is visibly hurt at this moment.

Attention and action come only when we citizens are affected in our pocketbook or in our lives literally. That's why it's so difficult to deal with conservation issues; the very nature of scientific evidence and knowledge is tentative and uncertain. Environmental concerns usually do not develop overnight, but build up over time, and cause and effect is tremendously complex. David Hales of the University of Michigan (personal communication) has said that the coalburning industry may not be solely to blame for acid rain. In my own mind, I'd finally come to the conclusion it probably was. Now I've learned that the cause of acid rain is broad and complicated; we may know the cause in a couple of years. When I think about the stories and programs we have done, and the political controversies we have covered in the effort to get some kind of solution to the problem of acid rain (Angier 1985), in light of our obligation to enlighten people about this problem, I am concerned. Even after years of dealing with the issue of acid rain, we're not quite sure what the cause is, which underscores for me the difficulty of meeting the responsibility our industry has to inform the public on highly complex issues. I've reviewed our files at "MacNeil-Lehrer" and tried to recall news programming when I was in charge of the NBC television network news. At "MacNeil-Lehrer," we've done a few programs on the greenhouse effect, and on the potential for a serious water shortage in the United States; we once devoted an entire half-hour program to the Oglalla Aquafer, an underground reservoir in the high plains that seemed to be in danger of drying up a couple of years ago (Matthews 1980). Afterward, when everyone realized that the real threat was about a hundred years away, one of the comments was, "We'll all be dead by then, why bother with that issue now?" I think that was said somewhat humorlessly, because the participants in the discussion weren't terribly interesting, but I think it points up vividly the difficulty those in daily journalism have in dealing with long-term environmental problems.

At NBC, I can remember improvising a documentary on nuclear waste (Angotti 1979), but most special programs on conservation and the environment dealt with the immediate problems and not the mid- or long-term future. Worse, the daily programs dealt solely with the present or the immediate past. After we did the program on nuclear waste, with some predictions of some serious circumstances, the sponsor of the program pulled out because the show was so controversial. Happily, the series continued. I haven't compiled a catalog of how all of the networks, public television, and cable news have covered the environment and conservation. I'm sure the documentary divisions and the magazine programs have dealt with the subjects within the context of long-term problems, but infrequently. As for daily broadcast journalism, we have dealt with it hardly at all. In your eyes it's probably a travesty. I'm very concerned about it, and I don't have any ready solutions.

I was recently faced with the issue of coverage of wildlife conservation when a group reported back from Antarctica about a hole found in the ozone layer. We were all prepared to do a segment on the news, because we expected we would finally get evidence that fluorocarbons released into the atmosphere was the cause. But the report that came back was not clear-cut in naming the cause. We had a brief but animated conversation about whether to go ahead with the story; we had an expert on fluorocarbons standing by in California, prepared to talk about the ozone break. We decided not to do the story because the preliminary report was too inconclusive, but to wait until the final report was complete. I had mixed emotions about our decision. Since we couldn't do something clear-cut, I was comfortable with delaying the story. At the same time, however, we had an important story of a building issue on something that the public needed to be informed about, and I had hoped I could report here on what a terrific job we'd done on that particular issue.

Another factor in the news business, among all the others that I've described, is that we spend a lot of our time on political problems between individuals or between governments. These issues are clearly important, but we are so wrapped up in them, partly through our training and our background, that when we have to deal with something that's harder to understand, like natural-resource conservation, which is also very uncertain, and somewhat intangible, we tend to shy away from it. Yet as those of you who live in America know, television can be very important in affecting public issues by affecting citizens' attitudes.

Television has both a megaphone effect and a dulling effect. By "megaphone effect" I mean the pervasive and repetitious dissemination of details about a particular issue that has caught the imagination of the public, the government, and/or the press. There is so much coverage of these particular issues that those in the news quickly become household names that would under circumstances ten or twenty years ago never have been so well known. I would guess that if you said the name *Daniloff* today, many people would recognize that name. There are so many discussion shows, and so many news programs, that there is hardly an issue that, once escalated enough, in and of itself doesn't become a media freak.

When Alexander Goldfarb was released from the Soviet Union, brought back by Armand Hammer, the plane landed at about 6:30 in the evening. Live cameras from all the networks were at the airport. Goldfarb was carried off the plane on a stretcher. The stretcher was wheeled over to a podium, raised up precisely to microphone height, and Goldfarb then held a news conference, with his son translating and his wife at his side. Then he was put into the ambulance and taken to the hospital. After that Armand Hammer had a news conference, then Goldfarb's doctor came up and had a news conference, then one of the family had a news conference, and finally Nicholas Daniloff had a news conference. This was all duly covered on the evening news programs, late news programs, and the following morning news programs. I describe this because it gives an example of the kind of attention that a particular individual, or issue, or story can get because of American television today.

Such attention can also have a dulling effect. How often can you show starving people in Africa without people finally getting inured to it? However often we go back and show it, the problem doesn't go away. We reach the point when people just tune out, and we can't just keep pounding them over the head with it.

There are some positive signs in media coverage of the enormous conservation issues today. The largest newspapers, magazines, and television organizations in America, at least, have people who spend their full work time reporting on science, conservation, and environmental issues; these people have developed strong knowledge in their subjects and excellent contacts in the various fields. They are respected and given consideration by their editors, publishers, and producers. However, their numbers are not growing in the late 1980s, and in fact may be diminishing a bit. Specialists in this area were created in the 1960s and 1970s, when the environmental movement was in full bloom. Now that environmental and conservation issues do not have such a crisis quality about them, at least in this country, and institutions have been created to deal with them, the environmental "beats" have disappeared in some publications and in some broadcast organizations or have become absorbed into general news reporting. We at the "MacNeil-Lehrer Newshour" have a full-time "beat" made up of a senior editor and two reporters who specialize in science, medicine, conservation, and the environment. I must admit, however, as I noted earlier, our concentration is more on today than tomorrow.

Technology may offer some hope for increased coverage of conservation issues; it is now possible to broadcast from virtually anywhere in the world. The satellite, microwave signal, videotape, and portable ground station have made all but the most remote locations in the world accessible to the television signal. If you can get physically to a location, you can broadcast from it. Networks that once were national are becoming international. The global village is becoming smaller and more and more tangible. It's still very costly to do this, but not as costly as it once was; not too long ago, it wasn't even possible. It's my hope that these kinds of advances will eventually help make the kinds of problems conservationists are concerned about and talking about more immediate and more tangible, and hence more newsworthy. The BBC has coordinated a series called "Only One Earth." It was done as an international coproduction, with three one-hour documentaries, eight half-hour special programs, and a global debate. That's an example of what can be accomplished, and what can be hoped for. Because of the new technology, we can now bring the examples of emerging countries' poverty, and the examples of natural resources in the environment being wasted, into the living room, but it's going to take some willpower and concentration and effort on the part of groups like Wildlife Conservation International and

others to force the media to pay more attention. It's going to require commitment and imagination on the part of people like me to respond, and my only concern is that the hurdles of uncertainty and intangibility are going to be extremely difficult to overcome. If not in this generation, in our lifetime, the consequences of our failure to disseminate broadly environmental conservation issues will be around here after we are gone.

Part V

AN AGENDA FOR THE FUTURE

32

Conservation Biology in the Twenty-first Century: Summary and Outlook

MICHAEL E. SOULÉ

The pressure on wildlands, on national parks, and on other kinds of protected areas can only increase. What do we know, and what do we need to learn in order to maintain as much biological diversity as possible? In this chapter, I attempt to summarize some of the material presented in this volume, including remarks made during discussions, both formal and informal. More general surveys of conservation biology have been published recently (Soulé 1986; Wilson 1988).

Beginning with extinction of species, we examine its causes at the level of population, proceeding then to its diagnosis and treatment at the level of community, then to the restoration and rehabilitation of such communities and ecosystems. Finally, I appeal for an opening up of conservation biology to the potential benefits of biotechnology.

EXTINCTION

We were shocked to hear from Diamond (chap. 4) that humans and their agents have already destroyed about one-quarter of the planet's species of island birds during the last 2,000 years. This fact, even if there were no others, should be

This chapter is dedicated to the memory of Deborah Rabinowitz, 1947-1987, a founding mother of conservation biology and a pioneer in the application of ecology to planetary welfare.

enough to give anyone pause. Additional evidence about the biological holocaust that our species is causing is provided by Atkinson (chap. 7), who discusses the fate of New Zealand animals.

Wilson (chap. 1) places the current extinction spasm in an evolutionary context, reviewing past evolutionary radiations and the massive extinctions in the fossil record. He also warns of annual losses of 10,000 species per year in the coming century. Myers (chap. 5) adds additional evidence for estimates of this magnitude. He suggests that at least three species a day are probably being lost now, and continuing habitat destruction probably will lead to an exponential rise in this rate to about 100 per day by early in the next century.

In absolute numbers, most of the extinctions will be insects—because about 98 percent of living species are insects. But other taxa will suffer greater relative losses. Among the most vulnerable groups are (1) primates, (2) large, rare species such as carnivores (Eisenberg and Harris, chap. 10), (3) ground-nesting birds, (4) flowering plants that depend on threatened animal mutualists for pollination, seed dispersal, and burial, (5) habitat specialists, (6) local endemics, and (7) species whose populations undergo large swings in abundance (Goodman 1987; Karr 1982; Leigh 1981).

In the recent past, most documented extinctions have occurred on islands or in islandlike habitats. Island species as well as those that inhabit long-isolated bodies of freshwater are vul-

297

nerable to the depredations of exotic (nonnative) predators, diseases, and competitors from continental biotas. These introduced, apocolyptic agents include cats, rats, goats, pigs, mongooses, snakes, snails, mosquitoes, fish, fungi, and invasive species of higher plants (Atkinson, chap. 7). Diamond (chap. 4) adds the three other members of the "deadly quartet" of factors that exterminate island species: namely, overkill by humans, habitat destruction, and the secondary effects of all these, such as reproductive failure in plants whose pollinators have been eliminated.

Islands are not the only vulnerable systems; the agents of extinction have established many continental beachheads as well. The main problem during the next few decades will probably be outright, direct habitat destruction on large land masses by humans and their agents. Ugalde (chap. 14) points out that all forests in Costa Rica outside of the boundaries of national parks will have been "converted" in ten years. Nothing is certain, however, and it is possible that a nuclear winter or more gradual kinds of climatic catastrophes could destroy more diversity than can bulldozers, chainsaws, and goats.

Another kind of habitat destruction, one that has received insufficient attention, is that caused by a rise in sea level, which in turn is one of probable effects of greenhouse warming of the atmosphere. The level is expected to be at least one meter higher by 2100, although experts disagree on the magnitude of the rise. In any case, a likely result will be great losses of coastal marshes and estuarine habitats (Titus et al. 1984). These habitats cannot migrate inland in many places because of the barrier of human-engineered structures that now abut the high-tide line. Tidelands and estuaries will be caught between a wet and dry place, and the consequences will be biological as well as economic.

THE VIABILITY OF INDIVIDUAL POPULATIONS

I turn now to the issue of causation: Why do populations go extinct? Sometimes the answer is obvious—the individuals are all shot. More often the issue is not this simple. Woodruff (chap. 8), Vrijenhoek (chap. 9), and Eisenberg and Harris (chap. 10) all address, in one way or another, some of the factors that determine the

viability or survival of individual populations. The subject has also been addressed recently under the rubric of population viability analysis (PVA) (Gilpin and Soulé 1986; Soulé 1987). PVA is an emerging branch of theoretical population biology; it attempts to integrate, using a systems approach, the complex interactions between genetic, demographic, environmental, and spatial-temporal (including metapopulation) factors that determine the extinction probabilities for populations of interest.

Vrijenhoek's work (chap. 9) has helped to clarify the genetics component by demonstrating the relationship between genetic variance and fitness. Eisenberg and Harris's (chap. 10) analysis of scaling factors, especially those related to body size and metabolic rate, provides a sound empirical foundation for observed patterns of population density and persistence. Similar allometric scaling has been used by Belovsky (1987) for calculation of extinction times. Such research will decrease the opacity of the demographic and environmental factors (Gilpin and Soulé 1986; Shaffer 1981) and their interactions.

What about 2100? All the authors agree that interventionist policies will be essential to save most rare organisms in the future. The reason for this is that the majority of nature reserves are simply too small to contain viable populations of such species, many of which are keystone species, ecologically. In general, we can safely predict that the rate of biotic and ecological simplification in reserves is inversely proportional to their size (Soulé 1986). In other words, the smaller the reserve, the higher its rate of "senescence," though there will be exceptions (Soulé and Simberloff 1986).

As a consequence, many rare species must be maintained in captivity during the coming "demographic winter" (Soulé et al. 1986)—the centuries-long interval during which humans will eliminate essential habitat for many space-intensive species. Although medium-size reserves have been temporarily successful in preventing the extinction of species such as the tiger in India, the population size of large animals in such reserves is often below the threshold for viability, and the level of inbreeding may reach dangerous levels. Eisenberg (1986) pointed out that average inbreeding coefficients in tigers are already at 33 percent in the Royal Chitawan National Park in India. To make matters worse, the personnel of reserves such as these have been attacked and killed by local villagers because the reserves sequester precious resources, and because the tigers kill people and livestock.

Reserves will disappear in many regions, and will be heavily poached and disturbed in others. Often, there will be no alternative but to move plants and animals around, or to remove them completely, appealing to institutions such as zoos and botanic gardens for sanctuary. The financial burden of such rescue efforts, however, is considerable; a rhino costs 8,500 dollars a year to keep (Conway 1986). Alternatives for the breeding of endangered species in zoos must be found. More will be said about this later.

Returning to PVA, my prediction is that the accuracy of estimates of minimum viable populations will increase dramatically in the next two decades. By 2000, we should not only have a mature theory of PVA, but there will be a solid body of field work and experimentation for the testing and refinement of the theory. Such an achievement is a necessary step, but not sufficient if we are to successfully manage the fragments of wildlands that will remain. An equally important research area is the study of community dynamics, the topic of the next section.

ISSUES OF SCALE: COMMUNITIES AND ECOSYSTEMS

Management prescriptions and techniques that are appropriate for very large areas can be disastrous for small ones. For very large reserves, for example, a single fire is not likely to burn the entire reserve at one time; hence, a big reserve provides its own buffering against certain kinds of catastrophic events. In other words, the more habitat space, the more likely it is that a given species will persist somewhere within the region, especially if recolonization of "empty" habitat patches can occur frequently. In addition, the requisite intensity of management (and therefore the cost) probably is inversely related to the logarithm of the size of the property (e.g., Soulé 1984b). Thus, many of the problems that managers must face are artifacts of the small size of the reserves that they manage. The manager of a small, isolated area must "prop up" populations of some species, while culling others, if he or she wants to prevent a gradual shriveling of the biota.

In this context, Walker (chap. 12) suggests that the best approach to management might be benign neglect, allowing populations to fluctuate, and permitting stable limit cycles, some lasting decades, to operate in such keystone species as fever trees and elephants. Such a passive approach, however, is a luxury of bigness and complexity, and of the continuity of institutions and policy. It is also a luxury of continentality (or "oceanality"), because the dependability of stable limit cycles is sensitive to stability in alpha (species) diversity and composition. Another reason for the relative stability of very large areas is that the larger the biogeographical region, the less susceptible it is to invasion by exotic species (Moulton and Pimm 1985). Walker also points out that intermediate levels of disturbance tend to promote diversity (Hubbell 1979).

The ideal conditions for passive management or benign neglect may rarely obtain, however. For example, the smaller the land mass, the more likely it is that exotic species will perturb it, driving some essential components to extinction. Pimm (1984) has suggested that the fragility of island communities may be autocatalytic in a kind of positive-feedback manner—in other words, the more the disturbance that occurs, the less stable the system. These observations illuminate the principle that the smaller the area, the more we must know about the species and their interactions if we are to manage effectively (Soulé and Simberloff 1986).

Matters of size and scale are also raised by McNaughton (chap. 11). He describes studies of the savanna system in East Africa. This work is an excellent example of how knowledge of subtle, but profound mutualisms can resolve management conundrums. He shows that for a grass on the Serengeti plain, it is better to be eaten and urinated on than to be ignored. That is, these communities are more diverse and productive when grazed. Furthermore, these grasses have evolved a unique capacity to use urea as a source of nitrogen. What might appear to be overgrazing, therefore, might not be. On the other hand, an optimal intensity of grazing in East Africa may be far too high for the Sahel, especially when the grazers (and browsers) are domestic animals. Stated another way, ecosystems will be less resilient where humans and their commensals are major players.

The time scale of ecosystem processes, and

the research that describes them, is also important. Many authors note the importance of detailed, long-term ecological studies. In the tropics, for example, results from a project described by Lovejoy et al. (1986) suggest the existence of extinction thresholds related to area.

HABITAT RESTORATION

Conservation and conservation biology will have to become increasingly opportunistic in the next century. As natural habitats disappear and, along with them, the opportunities for the establishment of new reserves within pristine habitat, our descendants will be faced with a surplus of degraded land and impoverished biotic communities. Thus, the scavenging and rehabilitation of degraded places may become the dominant activity of conservationists in the twenty-first century.

We already are seeing the beginnings of this transition. For example, agricultural productivity is surpassing the absorption capacity of the market system in some places. As grain surpluses pile up, land will be freed from plows and chemicals. Green (chap. 18) points out that the European Economic Community could take 10 percent of its farmlands out of production, and as much as one-third of the farmland in the United Kingdom may soon be surplus.

In the future we will see entire new industries based on the transformation of degraded and surplus lands. Wetlands and marshes that were drained for agriculture will be reirrigated and restored to something closer to their original conditions in order to provide wildlife for sportsmen, recreational sites for urban populations, as well as space for low-technology sewage treatment. As natural fisheries collapse from overfishing and pollution, new artificial ones will be created in regions that were formerly flood plains. On marginal and degraded uplands, ranchers will find it more profitable to "farm" wildlife for hunters than to run herds of sheep and cattle, especially in many overgrazed grasslands and savannas. Other degraded farmlands that were originally forested will be reforested and will once again become productive sources of fiber and other polymers.

Obviously, only a tiny fraction of such renaturalized lands will be returned to something like the conditions that existed before Europeans employed the saw, plow, bulldozer, canal, and levee. The pendulum, though, will swing back, and wildlife will have more *lebensraum*. The conditions that will permit these radical transformations are a relatively high standard of living and a stable or declining human population. These conditions already exist in parts of Europe and North America, though it may be centuries before they become the norm in many so-called developing countries. Nevertheless, it is apparent that the emphasis in conservation biology will gradually shift from the protection of quasinatural habitat fragments (there will be none left that aren't either protected or doomed) to the opportunistic construction of artificially diverse landscapes.

SPECIES REINTRODUCTIONS AND CAPTIVE PROPAGATION

Opportunism will also be the byword in the reintroduction of refugee species into seminatural habitats. We are being forced to acknowledge that habitat for endangered species is something to be created as much as it is something to be saved. Of course, there is no denying that the success of introductions depends a lot on the behavior of the species in question. In general, higher vertebrates will require more preparation and training than insects, but insects and plants may have much more specific habitat requirements. There are already several examples of successful reintroductions of species that were extirpated locally or entirely (Stanley Price, chap. 20).

Who will accomplish the necessary propagation, mate selection, and research? It is apparent that zoos and botanic gardens lack the resources to save and reintroduce the thousands of species that are likely to be orphaned due to habitat destruction (Soulé et al. 1986; Conway, chap. 19). The slack will be taken up, I believe, by new kinds of organizations, supplementing and partly replacing contemporary conservation advocacy groups. As wilderness-oriented groups gradually lose some of their *raison d'être* because all the wildlands that can be set aside are set aside, and because all the laws that can be passed are enacted, new groups of lay propagationists will emerge.

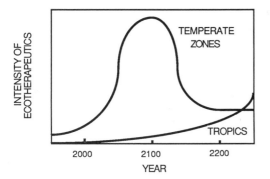

Fig. 32.1. Speculative curves suggesting the intensity of habitat rehabilitation and related activities in the future in the temperate zones (upper curve) and tropics (lower curve).

The new organizations will assume direct responsibility for specific taxa. Societies will spring up for such groups as lacustrine fish, bromeliads, primates, rhinoceroses, and parrots. But instead of merely being hobbyists and pet owners, the members of such groups will employ sophisticated husbandry and breeding practices, as do zoos today. The members of such groups will be linked by computer networks with scientists, veterinarians, and other specialists who will advise them on husbandry, reproduction, and related matters. Though successful reintroductions will be the major objectives of these societies, their energies will be spent mostly on the day-to-day challenges of propagation of their adopted species.

FUTURE BIOTAS

Soon, the distinctions between preservation, reintroduction, and restoration will vanish. In 2100, entire biotas will have been assembled from (1) remnant and reintroduced natives, (2) partly or completely engineered species, and (3) introduced (exotic) species. The term *natural* will disappear from our working vocabulary. This term is already meaningless in most parts of the world because anthropogenic fire, chemicals, and weather, not to mention deforestation, grazing, and farming, have been changing the physical and biological environment for centuries, if not millennia.

We are, even now, in the middle of revolu-

tionary changes that will continue to alter the composition of all biological communities and the ways that we manage them. As is usual in such revolutions, the pragmatic issues involved will probably overwhelm the ethical ones—the question will be what *can* be done, or what is cost-effective, rather than what *should* be done.

Reflecting further on the future, we might consider the north-south or temperate-tropical difference in the kinds of "ecotherapeutic" activities suggested in the preceding paragraphs. Based on demographic projections (Western, chap. 2) and on certain assumptions about the rate at which populations will decline following the plateau in human numbers (Soulé et al. 1986), we can assume that land will be made available for wildlife sooner in the temperate regions than in the tropics. As shown in Fig. 32.1, radical ecotherapies may peak in the temperate zone around the year 2100. We cannot be so sanguine about the tropics, where the demographic winter will be more severe and longer. By 2100, large-scale restoration of tropical lands may have hardly begun. (This discussion ignores the unpredictable demographic and ecological consequences of AIDS and AIDS-like epidemics.)

BIOTECHNOLOGY AND CONSERVATION BIOLOGY

The science and technology employed by twenty-first-century conservation biologists and managers will be vastly different from those of today. I suggest four categories of likely technological interventions:

1. The task of describing and classifying the millions of species that are still unnamed should be carried out with the collaboration of biomedical engineers, biochemists, and computer experts.
2. Molecular biologists, in collaboration with immunologists and epidemiologists, will solve the problem of exotic species in the next twenty-five years.
3. The problems addressed by conservation genetics, namely, inbreeding depression and the loss of genetic variability in small populations, will be solved with the tools of genetic engineering within a few decades.
4. In fifty years, it will be possible to maintain

or cache any species in a suspended, miniaturized state. The materials needed to regenerate entire biological communities will be stored in a single freezer.

These four points will be discussed briefly.

1.   It is an article of faith in conservation that the process of describing and classifying all the millions of unknown species will, itself, somehow help to lower the extinction rate. It may. People are more likely to stand up for named, classified species than for anonymous victims. But time is short and the taxonomists, hundreds or thousands of them (Wilson, chap. 1), would have to be trained. The major problem with the recruitment of such a taxonomy corps is the likelihood that it would be unemployed once the sense of emergency had passed, or sooner, if other crises or social priorities stole the limelight. Is there an alternative to the training of an ephemeral cadre of barefoot taxonomists?

The technology may already exist to produce the labor-intensive but necessary morphological and biochemical descriptions in ways that are more objective and faster, by orders of magnitude, than are conventional procedures. Techniques such as computerized axial tomography and nuclear magnetic resonance could be used to scan hundreds of specimens and display the external and internal anatomy in three dimensions in the time it would take a human to dissect and draw just one specimen. Automated biochemical methods can be used to screen, biochemically, plant specimens from frozen leaves. Computer programs could be written to compare specimens with those that have already been classified. Range extensions, faunal and floral lists, and the desciptions and names of new species could be electronically mailed to the relevant information centers, journals, and experts. Might not the investment of a few years and a few score million dollars on such a project yield much greater dividends for much less money, compared to the mobilization and training of a huge number of taxonomists whose job security would always be in doubt and whose working conditions might compromise their objectives?

2.   Exotic species have caused, and will continue to cause, incalculable damage to agriculture, commerce, and biological diversity. Now that biotechnology, particularly molecular biology and immunobiology, are making rapid strides in our understanding of genetic structure and disease resistance, it seems timely to recruit scientists with expertise in these and related fields to assist us in the search for solutions. By combining existing and "horizon" technologies, such as the production of sterile males, the production of genetically engineered, host-restricted pathogens, the artificial induction of genetic load, the repression of immunity, the manipulation of the genetic basis of reproduction, and the use of sexual attractants, it probably will be possible to eliminate most exotic species in less than a decade after the initiation of a program. Among the obvious candidates are Nile perch in Lake Victoria; predatory snails, rats, mongooses on many tropical islands; the Philippine brown snake on Guam; and kudzu in the southeastern United States.

3.   Today, we assume that the loss of genetic variability and the fixation of deleterious loci are irreversible and inevitable consequences of small, effective population size. The problem may not be so formidable in the near future. The insertion or induction of genetic variation, either by transfer from close relatives or by de novo synthesis, will offset many of the consequences of genetic drift. It appears likely that the cloning and transplantation of such genes will be possible in a few decades or less, pioneered by researchers in plant tissue culture and human genetic diseases. It will also be possible to excise or replace "bad" genes, probably during the early stages of development.

4.   Many conservation biologists, myself included, have stated that the ex situ preservation of an entire ecosystem, such as a tropical humid forest, is impossible. Certainly, it is true that at the present time, we cannot store, cryogenically, and restore the gametes or embryos of more than about a dozen species of mammals and birds, and there are many problems to be overcome in the storage of seeds of most tropical plants. Although the technology of embryo freezing and transfer is advancing rapidly, entire classes of organisms have, so far, been ignored in this quest. It seems foolish, therefore, to speak of preserving entire biotas ex situ.

Notwithstanding the mind-boggling diversity of many ecosystems and the technical difficulties still to be overcome, biotechnology is accelerating at a pace that could not have been foreseen thirty years ago, when the molecular structure of DNA was described. We cannot conceive in our wildest imaginings of the developments in another thirty years.

Some biologists might object to the idea of "cryoconservation" on ethical grounds. Purists will be horrified, no doubt, at the suggestion that entire communities, including insect pollenators, soil microorganisms, and parasitoids, might be put in a zip-lock freezer bag.

Part of this sentiment stems from the belief that it is evil to separate a species from its environment. Part stems from the belief that the transmission of "cultures" in animal lineages should be unbroken by a hiatus in captivity. A third argument against the development of such a technological fix is that the solution itself will become self-fulfilling—the existence of such technology might justify the destruction of the remaining vestiges of natural wildlands. These normative beliefs and psychological theories may explain why many well-meaning people object to the captive breeding of endangered species, even when this is the only alternative to extinction. Though we all agree that it is preferable to save the system in situ, I would argue that we should save as many pieces of the planet as possible and argue later about whether saving species by artificial means was in their best interests.

Obviously, ex situ storage is not the most desirable solution, even if it works. On the other hand, equally radical solutions would be tolerated if humans were threatened with extinction. Even now, for example, entire human communities are being resettled in Africa, Brazil, and Indonesia. In recent years, millions of people have voluntarily left their ancestral homes when local conditions became intolerable. Some governments are providing incentives as part of transmigration programs. What we do for ourselves, what many of our ancestors did for themselves, should not be categorically ruled out for other life forms. In any case, global climate change will necessitate the artificial transplantation of many plant and animal populations during the coming century, particularly in the tropics.

IS EVOLUTION FINISHED?

Has life on the earth come to the end of its evolutionary adventure? The situation cannot be summed up with a simple "yes" or "no." First, many lineages will become prematurely extinct, especially in the absence of vigorous campaigns for their protection. A disproportionate number of these species are large vertebrates, our closest living relatives and the likeliest candidates for sentient companionship and discourse in the future, barring a miraculous strange encounter with extraterrestrials.

Second, there is prima facie evidence that humans are changing the course of evolution in virtually all species. This is because we are altering the physical, chemical, and biological conditions throughout the entire biosphere. For the surviving species, the direction of evolution will change. In small, isolated populations, the direction is likely to be governed more by genetic drift, i.e., chance, than by natural selection.

Third, the rates of speciation (origination of new species) in many kinds of organisms could be drastically affected by anthropogenic confinement of populations. Radical constriction of ranges is happening to most species of large animals in the temperate and tropical zones. Because the persistence of small, isolated populations will often depend on artificial gene flow, the conditions for speciation will rarely be met. Hence, it is unlikely that new taxa of these animals will evolve during this current interval of universal anthropogenic disturbance (Soulé 1980).

At best, the planet's macrobiota is entering a kind of pause, an evolutionary lacuna, caused by the human usurpation of the land surface. For the survivors, the pause will last until the human population declines to a biologically tolerable level—a level at which land appropriated by humans is returned to nature, and extinction rates return to the (paleontological) background level. If this takes 500 years (Soulé et al. 1986), it amounts to only about 10^{-4} of a species' lifetime. That's the good news. The bad news is that a lot of species will have perished by the time the ark's gangplank is lowered.

In conclusion, human beings underestimate the rate of technological change. We also fear change. But whether we embrace or resist it, technological innovation will occur at an accelerating rate, if for no other reason than it is linked in the public mind with health, economic growth, and military defense. Since we have no choice but to be swept along by this vast technological surge, we might as well learn to surf.

33

An Agenda for Conservation Action

DAVID WESTERN, MARY C. PEARL, STUART L. PIMM,
BRIAN WALKER, IAN ATKINSON, and DAVID S. WOODRUFF

The diverse origins and aims of nature conservation give it secular appeal, though from the practical angle, its diversity and intangibility often become liabilities in the face of tangible economic interests. The deep inner peace we feel seated alone overlooking an empty sea or the sheer thrill that bubbles up uncontrollably inside us as we watch the restless energy of a million wildebeest criss-crossing the Serengeti plains is tangible enough to each of us. But such a deeply personal experience has little resale value in our materialistic world, unlike the market value of the once magnificent American prairie carved up into thousands of monotonous squared-off corn fields and millions of dreary tract homes.

The origins of conservation, whether spiritual, economic, or recreational, lie buried in ancient cultures scattered around the world. The modern movement encompasses the varied motives without always realizing our debt to our forebears or always doing justice to their motives. Hunting, religion, aesthetics, curiosity, adventure, recreation, entertainment, the rights of species, resource protection, science, education, economics, and many other reasons to save natural areas can be cited. Each new reason has added to, rather than replaced, others. From these small, localized beginnings, today's diverse global conservation movement is unified solely by a common interest in saving space and wildness.

The practice of conservation has also become more complicated in step with the widening reasons and expanding threats. A century ago, the biggest threats to nature—hunting, felling, and ranching—were fought off by laws, parks, and patrols (Hales, chap. 13). Later, when tourists began invading and destroying the parks, the answer again lay in protection on site. Today, however, the new threats, including ecological isolation, introduced species, ecosystem disruption, and global pollution (Diamond, chap. 4), cannot be tackled on site. Preservation by segregation is no longer sufficient when a park's very isolation can create a biological desert island.

Recognition that even the best protected parks are threatened by off-site factors (McNaughton, chap. 11) has directed attention to human impact on the biosphere generally. In the Western world, two measures, one based on intrinsic value, the other on instrumental value (Hargrove, chap. 21), are being taken to save nature. The intrinsic value means, by and large, changing public sympathy in favor of saving species in their own right. The instrumental view advocates saving nature by showing how rewarding it can be. The rich nations, which can afford the luxury of thinking decades ahead, are coming to see the fate of nature as a barometer of planetary health.

If modern conservation has its origins in the West, its shortcomings are being exposed most harshly in the tropics. Here, where population pressure and poverty are tearing down the richest and most intact ecosystems on the earth, conservation is in crisis. The Western concept of preservation by segregation is alien to societies evicted from their traditional homes and denied use of animals and plants within newly created reserves. Conservation is not an alien concept to the traditional societies (McNeely, chap. 15), but the harsh alien laws which give more rights to animals than people are resented. For the poor, family and kin come before trees and animals. Conservation must have tangible meaning if it is to win their acceptance (Olindo, chap. 25).

Among the worldlier of the developing countries a concern is growing that in the loss of forests and savannas something splendid is vanishing forever. Out of this concern, a pragmatic alternative to segregation and prohibition is emerging, rooted in the notion that conservation can help sustain water catchment, wood supplies, and other resources vital to rural societies. The idea that conservation can benefit the rural poor who usually lose out to preservation, however, gives no more than a reprieve for nature, unless population growth and poverty are checked.

The solution ultimately lies in tackling the root and not the symptoms of the problem. That means, foremost, improving human welfare, including health, education, unemployment, housing, population growth, and economic and social development (Vittachi, chap. 3; Lee, chap. 30). For natural resources, including wildlife, it means finding good reasons to conserve and resolving the sticking points, especially land and resource ownership, rights of access, decision, and control.

The long-term solution for the conservation of nature may lie in solving the human problems, but for many species and habitats, it will be too late. A biological crisis is in the making. Moreover, a window of vulnerability exists over the next century, even if we assume that growth will then slow, that food output will soar, that the rural farmers will migrate to the cities, and that benign technologies will replace the damaging ones. The crisis is forcing us to make choices, often snap decisions, about what to save and how. Conservation biology and conservation management are the scientific and technical responses to those uncertainties.

However, scientific knowledge and management skills to save species and restore ecosystems are the beginning and end point of a broad-fronted response. The knowledge must be communicated (Crystal, chap. 31), the ideas sold, the plans drawn up and integrated with other local national interests (Olembo, chap. 27; Tarak, chap. 26). In developing countries, it often means raising donor aid and technical support (Pearl, chap. 29; Lee, chap. 30). The lengthy process, from identifying a problem to launching a response, underscores the unavoidable complexity of modern conservation. Speed and flexibility, and sometimes endangered species, are sacrificed in the process. While the broad response is essential if it is to be effective, can it be achieved without falling victim to bureaucratic inertia and political dithering?

The issues touched in this book raise more questions than answers. In the Agenda for Conservation Action which follows, we spell out the central issues and gaps that must be addressed if conservation is to move beyond crisis responses to long-range strategies.

AN AGENDA FOR CONSERVATION AND DEVELOPMENT

The mixed progress on welfare and environment around the world gives ample scope for exploring the essentials of success (Western, chap. 2). Because the social and technical requirements for improvements on both fronts have been well covered in recent publications, notably *The Global Possible* (Repetto 1985) and *Sustainable Development of the Biosphere* (Clark and Munn 1986), this portion of the agenda will do no more than touch on some key socioeconomic and technological issues relevant to conservation.

Proven Solutions Within Existing Resources

Triggering the will. How do we convince people of the value of conservation? Vittachi, chap. 3) has outlined the concept of a demand pull among those we hope to influence. Birth-control technology, for example, is meaningless if contraception is abhorrent to a society. The change must emanate in the mind, not in the uterus, as Vittachi so compellingly points out. The advantages of change, whether in life-style or in outlook, must be demonstrated and accepted if well-intentioned projects are to succeed. As well understood as this point is, developers and conservationists alike often fail to apply it successfully, perhaps because of the cost and time involved, or because the approach differs from one society to another.

Why do the poor show so little interest in conservation? Their repeated rejection of what seems to us to be in their best interests means we are missing something. We must rethink the concept of vested self-interest in sustainable resource utilization among the disadvantaged. The tragedy of the commons, the tendency of individuals to exploit common property resources to the point of depletion, is the *bête noire* of conservation. How should we tackle it in the future? The answer lies in untried policies and untested practices which enable communal landowners to benefit individually from the group investment in conservation, much as the individual landowners benefit from self-investment. Figuring out how to generate such positive-sum games, how to benefit the community in the course of benefiting the individual, is the single biggest challenge to conservation. It applies to everything from personal health to planetary health and lies at the heart of checking runaway population growth, the greatest threat to the natural world in the twenty-first century. *Setting Policies*. Progressive policies, whether political, social, or economic, can quickly improve a society and its environment. By the same token, repressive policies soon check progress and create negative-sum games, in which the individual acts selfishly at the expense of society and environment. Several policy issues which impinge on conservation directly or indirectly need to be addressed:

1. Social. The most pervasive and egregious error in conservation has been the top-down philosophy, in which resource decisions are made nationally and imposed locally, regardless of social and cultural values. An historical legacy of colonial wildlife laws which run counter to national policies in newly independent states often makes matters worse. The rural poor resent losing control over their own resources. However, if control were fully vested locally and communally, resource abuse would worsen. How, then, can decisions and control over resources be localized without leading to overutilization? How, too, can conservation be linked to welfare improvement? Without that link, conservation will flounder on poverty and insecurity.

2. Economic. We have been characterized as a throwaway society weaned onto energy-demanding technology by cheap, abundant resources. In the mid-nineteenth century John Stuart Mill, realizing the unsustainable nature of our profligate ways, advocated technologies for living off nature's interest, rather than its capital. A few small steps in, for example, water and waste recovery have been made, but it will take radical policy shifts to save resources, especially soils, forests, and wildlife, in the coming century. Many governments actively encourage overexploitation by subsidizing energy and food prices. Pricing policies for natural resources must be reviewed with sustainability rather than political expediency in mind.

However, as with social reforms, economic policies for resource sustainability will be useless without economic alternatives. These include a diversification of markets within and among third world countries and the growth of appropriate and small-scale technologies geared to regional needs. The urban bias in economic policies, especially in Africa, must also be redressed. To alleviate food scarcity and pressure on marginal lands, farmers must be given more incentive to diversify and intensify output.

3. Political. Global political instability is a significant threat to human welfare and the environment. War, or the threat of war, whether military or economic, creates uncertainties about the future to the point of undermining long-term social, economic, and environmental planning. While one can argue that politics is not the concern of conservationists, the reality is that resource scarcity is often the source of instability. Resources are a political issue, just as politics is a resource issue. Conservationists, particularly in the third world, must develop the art of advocacy no less than the farmer or industrialist. Conservation must be argued more widely and forcefully in the international arena too, whether in regional bodies, such as the Organization for African Unity and the Association of South East Asian Nations, or globally through the IUCN, the UN, and other bodies.

High Technology/High Diversity

High-technology agriculture and industry will increase as population mounts in the coming decades. Though inevitable, it does not inevitably condemn the natural world. Provided high-technology systems are designed with environment in mind, a more benign technology could replace the smoke-stack bleakness of heavy industry (Western, chap. 2). That possibility hinges on advances in five areas:

- Intensification. Food production could overhaul demand in the third world in the twenty-first century, if investment in new crop varieties and farming practices is stepped up, particularly in Africa and Southeast Asia, where poverty will otherwise overwhelm nature. Whether intensification frees land for habitat restoration depends on economic policy, perhaps financial incentives, and land planning (Green, chap. 18).
- Efficiency. Modern agroindustry does not use resources efficiently. That must change as the demand for energy, water, fertilizers, and other resources goes up. Technological advances in conservation and recycling, as well as new products and processes, could give developing countries the means for greater self-sufficiency in resources.
- Adaptability. Genetic engineering in particular offers great promise in adapting crop varieties to local conditions such as salinity, drought, low nutrient status, and disease. Flexible production systems tailored to environment and society should be a key focus of research and development.
- Accessibility. Products and processes that can be cheaply and widely adopted in the third world will close the communications and development gap between rich and poor. For example, the plunging cost and rocketing data storage capacity of microcomputers will reduce the information gap between rich and poor nations, where good libraries are rare.
- Environmental standards. Few countries impose strict environmental standards on the impact of human activity. Such standards, whether applied to the impact of industry, agriculture, or settlement on our landscape, can only be set and met if society becomes aware and concerned enough to take action. Action raising awareness and precipitating action is covered in the section "Agenda for Conservation Awareness."

AN AGENDA FOR CONSERVATION BIOLOGY

The world is on the threshold of a catastrophic loss of biological diversity. Hundreds of thousands, possibly even millions of plant and animal species will be lost if current trends continue (Myers, chap. 5). There are four major causes of this loss of diversity—the so-called "Evil Quartet" (Diamond, chap. 4): (1) destruction and fragmentation of some habitats and pollution and degradation of others, (2) overkilling of plants and animals by humans, (3) introduction of alien animals and plants, and (4) secondary effects of extinctions—the extinction of one species caused by the extinction of another.

The first cause is clearly the most important. Even when apparently large reserves are protected, they may be spatially isolated. Each fragment may be too small to maintain viable populations and normal ecological processes (Harris and Eisenberg, chap. 17). Understanding the dynamics of very rare species is essential both in predicting which species are prone to extinction and in shaping the options for managing them. Many animal species have been hunted to extinction—the passenger pigeon in North America is a familiar example. Loss of these species may strike us solely as an example of gross human incompetence. But there are many species whose continued survival should have been in our own economic interest, but which nonetheless have been lost. The fisheries literature is replete with such examples (May 1984), suggesting that "overkilling" is not the simple issue it might seem.

We have moved many species around the world, sometimes deliberately, often accidentally. Some species, like the English garden birds introduced by New Zealand settlers, are merely quaint curiosities. Other introductions have been devastating. Goats, pigs, and rabbits on oceanic islands have sometimes removed nearly all the vegetation (Ebenhard 1987; Pimm 1987). A snake introduced to Guam has exterminated most of the island's bird species (Savidge 1987). A fungus introduced to North America all but eliminated the chestnut tree, once one of commonest trees in the forest. Understanding which species are likely to invade which communities and what effects they will have is another pressing need for conservation biology. Finally, there are secondary effects. The loss of a major food source can be expected to cause the loss of a species that depends on it. But species interact in complex ways, and the loss of certain species may cause the extinction of many others (Pimm 1982).

To reduce the magnitude of the loss in biological diversity, we have to halt the Evil Quartet. In this sense the solution is easy: We should not pollute, destroy, or fragment habitats, hunt species to extinction, or introduce exotics. We must accept, however, that our ability to intervene is greatly limited. Effective intervention requires, first, identifying where and how to act. Second, we must develop appropriate management strategies. Finally, we must identify research needs where we do not know how to intervene. We can intervene at a number of levels to prevent the extinction of a particular species or the loss of a particular community or to maintain vital ecosystem processes. We might ask whether we should place our emphasis on strategies to protect species, communities, or ecosystem processes, and to identify those which are most critical. However, the question is probably meaningless, for the strategies are not alternatives; rather, they are complementary. A species needing special protection reflects a fundamental failure to maintain the community in which the species occurs or the ecosystem processes that help maintain that community. Managing communities and ecosystem processes is one way to protect species.

Some species may be more appealing to us, and in protecting these charismatic species we may also, as a by-product, protect the communities in which they occur. Other species may have a more critical role in a community than others. Their loss may be more serious in terms of secondary extinctions. Similarly, the loss of some species may interfere with ecosystem processes. Put simply, managing species may be one of the ways in which we manage communities or ecosystems.

What are the priorities for preserving species, maintaining communities, and protecting critical ecosystem processes?

Extinctions

Where Are the Species? Identifying which species should receive conservation efforts is far from simple. First, we are far from having a complete catalogue of species (Wilson, chap. 1). Even with such a catalogue, we will often not know which species are endangered, especially in the tropics infrequently visited by ecologists. Despite our ignorance, we can often guess where endangered species are to be found from our knowledge about communities. We know which areas are being destroyed the fastest. And we know something about the biogeographical diversity of animals and plants. Most animal and plant groups show increased diversity as we approach the equator. Similarly, there are often more species in forests than in grasslands, more species on mainlands than on remote islands. Learning more about the detailed patterns of diversity may be the fastest way to identify where endangered species are to be found.

Which Species Are Vulnerable? Some species are more vulnerable to extinction than others. How can we determine the chances that a species will become extinct?

1. By far the most important factor is to determine population size: Rare species are much more likely to become extinct than common species. As an approximation, large-bodied species tend to be rarer than smaller species (and there are many more small species than large species). This means that large-bodied species will often be the most vulnerable (Diamond 1984a; Eisenberg and Harris, chap. 10).

2. But even for fixed population sizes and a given body size, there are differences in vulnerability. These differences can be related to a variety of natural-history effects. Some species may be more vulnerable to changes in the habitat, and other species may be able to recover from reductions in population less quickly than others. Some species will have population densities that vary more than others. Identifying extinction-prone species will require a good deal of knowledge about their natural history (Soulé, chap. 32).

Which Communities Are Vulnerable? Another priority in terms of identifying the endangered species is to identify the vulnerable communities. Some communities are more vulnerable than others because they are assembled in such a way that they are sensitive to the loss of certain species. Communities may be vulnerable because they readily admit species introduced by humans or because those introduced species have a great impact.

Ecologists have devoted considerable effort recently to trying to understand what determines whether a community will be invaded or not and what the attributes of successful invaders are (Mooney and Drake 1986). Some communities, like those on islands, are easily invaded because they contain relatively few species. The grasslands of the intermontane northwestern United States seem to have been more readily invaded by weeds than other grasslands because of historical differences in the grazing species to which the grasslands were exposed (Mack 1986). What are the effects of introduced species? The English garden birds in New Zealand cited earlier have had minimal impact. Other introductions have been devastating—goats or rabbits on various islands, for example.

Community vulnerability theory needs to be refined and tested, in particular for three sensitive cases (Pimm 1987):

1. Species introduced into predator-free or competition-free communities. Examples include the introduction of large herbivores to islands and predators that feed high in a food chain and themselves lack predators.
2. Highly polyphagous species, introduced to communities where they can eat a wide variety of plant species to extinction.
3. Species introduced into relatively simple communities where the removal of a few plant species will cause the collapse of entire food chains.

Which Species Are Important? Some species are likely to be much more important than others, and given that we probably cannot save all the species threatened with extinction, identifying "important" species becomes essential. What makes a species "important"? Clearly, species may be important because they are charismatic, like the rhinoceros, or economically important, like the coffee bush. From the biological perspective, it is the "keystone" species, those whose loss is likely to trigger the greatest number of secondary extinctions, that need to be identified. What rules, if any, govern keystone species? Such rules would be central to species and community vulnerability analysis. Several hypotheses need testing:

1. Removing a plant species from the base of a simple food chain destroys the entire system.
2. The loss of one of the several plant species utilized by a generalized herbivore in a more complex system would have much less of an effect, because the herbivore is not so dependent on one species.
3. Removing a predator from a monophagous herbivore reduces a plant's density, but

does not exterminate it. Special conditions are required for a predator to eliminate its sole prey before it, too, becomes extinct.
4. In a more complex system, the predator's absence may lead to a generalized herbivore exterminating all but the one resistant plant species, which then regulates the herbivore's numbers.

Clearly, special efforts must be devoted to identifying keystone species, because the fate of so many other species is tied to them.

Populations and Communities

Given that we have identified which species and communities are in need of intensive care, how should we go about preserving them? To answer this question, we need to address the problems faced by endangered species.

Why is the species endangered? The answer will sometimes be obvious. Preserving the species will involve removing the threat. All too often, however, the threat is irreversible habitat destruction leading to rarity and habitat fragmentation. What are the issues to resolve in preserving rare species and fragmented communities?

The Problems of Very Rare Species

1. Small populations often lose genetic variability and become inbred (Vrijenhoek, chap. 9). How can we maintain genetic variability? Promising methods for captive populations involve the development of computer techniques to provide optimal mating strategies for individuals of known pedigrees by preventing some individuals from contributing disproportionate numbers of young to the next generation. Such techniques might be applied to fragmented wild populations, where the individual subpopulations have only a sample of the genes in the total population. The difficulties in applying this procedure to wild populations are a challenge in themselves.

Some species, such as the cheetah, seem genetically more impoverished than others (O'Brien et al. 1986). The significance of genetic variability in natural populations—how it relates to population size, vagility, mating system, and so on—is a subject for further investigation.

2.   Small populations also have a much greater chance of extinction because of random demographic accidents or fluctuations, such as when all or many of the individuals die during a short period of time, the sex ratio becomes less than optimal, too great a proportion are non-breeders (e.g., the very old or the very young), and so on. How can vulnerability be reduced by, for example, moving individuals from healthy subpopulations to ones where local extinction has occurred or is imminent? Such metapopulation analysis needs fuller development as a tool in reducing the risk of extinction in species with a very localized distribution. The procedure has been carried out for the whooping crane in North America (U.S. Fish and Wildlife Service 1986).

3.   Some populations are clearly doomed to extinction unless they are brought into captivity. When such breeding programs are successful, there is the potential to return the species to the wild, provided that the cause of the extinction has been identified and removed. There have been a number of successful reintroductions of species, but many failures too (Stanley Price, chap. 20). What will it take to maintain and reintroduce species? (See "Agenda for Conservation Management.") If a species is to be successfully reintroduced, the species must (a) survive for a time at very low population densities and (b) increase despite the presence of potential competitors, predators, and diseases, and because the species can profitably exploit the environment. Considerations under (b) may not be a problem for species reintroduced to areas from which they were exterminated by, say, hunting, given that the species will no longer be hunted. But for species introduced to new areas, evaluating these factors may be difficult.

Considerations under (a) are certainly difficult. How likely is the population to survive the initial period of very low density? The answer to this question depends on how the introduction is carried out; in other words, we have control over the chances for survival of the initial population. Previous experience with introduced species shows that populations that are eventually successful often fail initially. Even when predators, parasites, competitors, and the physical environment are no impediment, success is not inevitable. The problem we face in designing an introduction can be stated quite simply. Suppose we have a limited number of individuals, X. Should we simultaneously introduce the entire population into one place or to several sites? If we do the latter, what is the smallest viable size of each group? The advantage of the first strategy is that we minimize the problems encountered by very small populations. The disadvantage is that such a strategy places "all one's eggs in one basket"—with the risk of its being the wrong one. Research is needed to provide the answer to this dilemma.

The Management of Critical Habitats. There are two key issues to resolve: first, patch design—the choices we may have in designing the fragments: money to buy land may be limited, but we may have some flexibility in how the areas are chosen; second, problems created by community fragmentation.

1.   We may often be unable to manage individual species, but we may have control on a larger scale of where we place our reserves. This has been the topic of extensive debate: whether we should put our efforts (and fixed land resources) into one large or several small reserves. Species diversity increases rather slowly with increasing area, so small reserves contain more species per unit area than large ones. But large areas often contain species not found in smaller areas—particularly large-bodied species that may require very large areas to maintain minimum viable population sizes. These large species may, coincidentally, be keystone species, on whose survival the nature of the community depends. Conversely, a large reserve may only sample a small part of the full range of communities to be found. Many carefully selected reserves may be an effective way of preserving species for given, limited resources. But these reserves must be of sufficient size to preserve viable populations of the species they were designed to protect. How do we optimally design reserves to accommodate viable populations and maximize species richness?

A fragmented reserve design may be imposed by outside factors. To overcome the problems of fragmentary reserves, we need to explore new ways of connecting reserves, whether by habitat corridors (Harris and Eisenberg, chap. 17), stepping stones of nonnatural habitat, or periodic genetic exchange (Vrijenhoek, chap. 9).

This will help reduce the isolation of the populations and so minimize the effects of low population size.

2. Fragmented habitats suffer from another problem in addition to their being small: They are surrounded by other areas that are modified, to a greater or lesser extent, by humans. This juxtaposition of man-made habitats with natural areas creates a special ecological problem, because man-made habitats are frequently readily invaded by the same set of species that have become commensals of humans worldwide. The fragmented natural areas become in ever closer proximity to these introduced species, and we have seen how introduced species can have a major effect on many other species in the community. The removal of introduced species may be essential for the survival of many species. Many plant communities are threatened by introduced herbivores, particularly on islands, for the reasons already discussed. The removal of these species may be accomplished by continued hunting or trapping, or through fencing. But other species—for example, smaller mammals, plants, and insects—may not be so readily controlled. We need to develop the science of early detection of potentially harmful invasive species if control is to be economically feasible.

What Are the Critical Ecosystem Processes?

Identification. The issues involved at the ecosystem level largely concern the identification of processes vital for the persistence of the system concerned. It is difficult to generalize, since a particular process that is important in one ecosystem may be inconsequential in another. However, several general guidelines to the identification of vulnerable ecosystem processes are worth exploring:

1. Determining the external agencies responsible for ecosystem dynamics. The primary determinants of most terrestrial ecosystems are the hydrological and mineral cycles. Ecosystems in which these cycles (and therefore the water and nutrient regimes) can be easily changed require special care. For example, the wetlands and hydromorphic soil systems (dam-

bos, vleis) of Africa owe their existence to impeded drainage. Where the impediment is due to a strong physical barrier (such as rock intrusions across drainage valleys), the system is relatively safe. If, however, erosion gullies dissect the drainage (as often happens), the system can be irrevocably changed by too much grazing or other prolonged loss of vegetation cover.

As an example of altered nutrient regimes, the small nature reserves in the wheat belt of western Australia are being subjected to increased nutrient levels through windborne soil from surrounding, fertilized lands. This has made the reserves vulnerable to invasion by alien plant species. Identification of the agents driving ecosystem dynamics is a top priority.

2. Stochastic events. There are particular events and times which are critical to the dynamics of ecosystems. For example, on only three occasions in the past 100 years have conditions been suitable for the establishment of new perennial shrubs in some arid regions of southeastern Australia. Likewise, the coincidence of a lack of surface water and the devastating effects of the rinderpest around the turn of the century in the Sauvuti region of Botswana's Chobe National Park gave sufficient time for acacia tree seedlings to establish and grow to a height safe from elephants and other browsers. Such a combination of circumstances has not happened since then. Recognizing such events or times is an essential part of understanding where to put conservation effort at the ecosystem level.

3. Ecosystem size and disruption. As a general rule, the smaller the area, the less likely it is that an ecosystem can absorb stress or disturbance through internal adjustments to regulating processes. In highly productive regions of the world, competition for use of resources has led to only small areas of previously large regions being maintained as natural ecosystems for conservation. Small areas require priority attention.

4. Boundary effects. The boundaries of most conservation areas are seldom natural. Fences, roads, and other barriers frequently cut off species from parts of their former range. This is most important when particular habitats or resources which are critical at certain times of the year, or for particular processes (e.g., breed-

ing), are cut off. "Open" systems are safer than "closed" systems. If boundaries are made tight, then responses such as emigration or immigration can no longer operate, so populations tend to build up to abnormally high levels and take longer to recover from low levels. There is also a reduction in gene flow if the area is small. The nature of the boundary is influenced by changes in the type of land use adjacent to the conservation area. Conservation areas with markedly artificial boundaries, which alter dispersal and the patterns and ratios of habitat types, deserve particular attention.

5. Ecosystem islands. The notion of completely isolated conservation areas is untenable in the long term. An important component in identifying areas for conservation priority is to consider the corridors between conservation areas—the kinds of transfers which currently take place and which previously took place. Attention to planning and management of the areas between conservation reserves may well be an important priority for many reserves.

AN AGENDA FOR CONSERVATION MANAGEMENT

We are eroding the biological wealth and diversity of our planet at an accelerating rate. The destruction is causing concern. For some, those concerns are tangible, a nagging worry that we are emptying nature's storehouse of useful products, or perhaps disrupting some delicate balance—atmospheric ozone levels, for example—which could harm us all. For others that loss is aesthetic, the extinction of a beautiful butterfly species, or the loss of wilderness and the sense of wonder and awe it inspires.

How much biological diversity will survive the coming decades depends on those concerns, tangible or otherwise, and on our responses to them. Appropriate action is what counts, for unless we know how to save the last eighteen northern white rhinos in Africa or how to return the Arabian white oryx to the wild, our concern is wasted, sometimes even counterproductive. Millions of well-meaning visitors eroding the walls of the Grand Canyon, shattering corral heads on the Great Barrier Reef, and hounding cheetahs in Serengeti attest to that.

This section deals with the question of what action is appropriate—when and how to manage nature. The decision not to act can be as devastating as bad action, more so when a species like the California condor would have disappeared as a result. The challenge is knowing when and how to intercede as the need to do so becomes more compelling.

We can conveniently think of three categories of management: conservation of protected areas, conservation beyond reserves, and ex situ management and technological manipulation when both fail, or in anticipation of that happening. This hierarchy follows from the most to the least natural management method, though in reality the distinction is often blurred. So, for example, we can build zoo-parks indistinguishable from nature or manage natural areas so intensively as to create superzoos. The distinction between natural and artificial is likely to blur more as we get better at mimicking natural habitats in large outdoor exhibits, at reconstituting ecosystems, and at corrective parks management.

Protected Areas

Protected areas will face such severe problems in the next century that few will survive without a great deal more protection and management. Biological losses will result from ecological isolation and poor protected-area coverage. Policy problems will arise from the multiplicity of uses and the tendency for tangible interests such as profit and consumption to override the intangible values of naturalness and nature (Hales, chap. 13). Disruption from human agencies such as poaching, encroachment, pollution, global environmental modification, exotic diseases, visitor pressure, antipathy, ignorance, and plain mismanagement will also imperil parks.

Despite the gloomy outlook, the prospects for protected areas can be improved by adding more land, by corrective management, and by integrated land use. These three points deserve special attention.

Expanding the Protected Areas.

1. Motivation. Talk of expanding the protected areas in a land-hungry world may seem starry-eyed, but astonishingly, the record shows new additions continuing apace. What justifies the additions, and what new reasons

can be used effectively in the future? What part does resource protection, recreation, economics, aesthetics, or altruism play in securing new sanctuaries?

The reasons are many. Culture, wealth, education, recreation, aesthetics, and land pressure, among other factors, all give grounds for conserving natural areas. But is motivation piecemeal, or does it arise predictably, shifting from the utilitarian to the aesthetic as societies progress? Will new lands become available as food production intensifies and exceeds demand? The motives for creating protected areas must be understood, broadened, and promoted through education and political persuasion. New reasons must be explored and adopted as attitudes and interests change.

2. Capability. Protected areas, always under attack from competing interests, must justify themselves and maximize the value of each new addition of land. How can this be done? Building the capacity to develop an optimal network is difficult. It involves two discrete steps: (a) biological evaluation, and (b) planning and implementation.

Biologically, which data and what criteria should guide the selection of priority conservation sites? IUCN's Commission on National Parks and its Species Survival Commission have both made a good start, despite the limitations of a small professional staff and a paucity of data. However, no unified criteria for choosing protected areas yet exist. Biological reasons range from protecting endangered species, like the giant pandas of Wolong, to the preservation of ecosystems, such as Serengeti, and natural spectacles, such as Patagonia's magellanic penguin colonies. Can ecosystem and species conservation be combined, or is it better, in some cases at least, to distinguish between the two?

Planning, the neglected interface between research and management, is just as vital. How can international, national, and local institutions improve conservation planning? How can they work together to give a global synopsis, on the one hand, and local detail, on the other? Such linkages do exist, but need to be greatly expanded. For example, UNEP's Global Environmental Monitoring System (GEMS), which looks at natural resources globally, usually from satellite imagery, and Kenya's Rangeland Ecological Monitoring Unit (KREMU), which monitors the country's animal and plant life from light aircraft and on the ground, do play exactly such complementary roles.

Apart from the technicalities of data collection, information exchange between institutions such as GEMS and KREMU is fundamental to good planning. How can data be collected, stored, retrieved, and circulated more quickly? IUCN's Conservation Monitoring Centre in Cambridge (U.K.) has made a start, but innovations in data management are needed to make such data universally available to planners.

Corrective Management. The need for corrective management of protected areas in the twenty-first century will be so great that we should anticipate the techniques and begin to develop them immediately. Several need attention:

1. Boundary adjustments. Modifications involving land exchange, connecting corridors, habitat stepping stones, and so forth need detailed research to pinpoint the missing elements critical to the survival of sanctuaries.

2. Legislation. Legislation and law enforcement to minimize human impact, whether poaching, visitor damage, or pollution, is a neglected instrument of corrective management, especially in the third world. How can deterrents to human abuses of protected areas be strengthened without unduly alienating public support?

3. Education. More desirable than policing, which in third world countries discourages visits by citizens, is education, whether outside the protected areas through school curricula, wildlife clubs, or the media, or within them by intepretative programs for visitors.

4. Balancing conflicting goals. Most reserves serve several functions, including recreation, wilderness preservation, species conservation, and watershed protection. Some uses are compatible: for example, wilderness trekking and watershed protection. Others, such as waterskiing and waterfowl conservation, are not. How can the conflicting uses be reconciled? Zoning is widely practiced, but not always practicable, especially where wildlife migrates seasonally. Another, more alluring challenge is the separation of recreation and conservation, with recreation zones located outermost. The opportunity still exists in most third world countries to classify protected areas for different uses, such

as intensive tourism, wilderness experience, research, strict conservation, recreation, and so on.

5. Biological management. When all else fails, imbalances can be corrected by moving animals in or out to maintain genetic diversity, for example, by culling animals to reduce overcrowding or introducing a diversifying agent, such as fire, to rejuvenate the community.

The intensive management of protected areas in the future is inevitable. What is in doubt is our ability to do so sensibly and opportunely. When should we intervene, and how? We need rules for safe intervention no less than a heart surgeon. Conservation biology must progress from a descriptive and predictive science to prescriptive management and give guidelines on when and how to intervene to save gravely threatened species and badly disrupted ecosystems.

Integrating Land Use. Many protected areas are too small and vulnerable ever to be fully revived by internal resuscitation. Most need external lifelines to larger ecosystems. Opening a park to lands beyond its boundaries breaks down the hard-edged boundaries at the root of its problems. How does one justify the external linkages? Several avenues are worth exploring:

1. Compatible land use. Encouraging land uses such as light- or long-cycle commercial forestry, ranching, game cropping, or sustainable fisheries around protected areas.
2. Compensation. Reimbursing landowners for the losses they sustain to protected area wildlife. In Amboseli National Park, for example, ranchers received grazing compensation for pasture lost to wildlife migrants.
3. Economic and social incentives. Involving local populations in returns, monetary or nonmonetary, from the protected areas, as in Zimbabwe, where villagers benefit from cheap meat culled from surplus elephants in parks and the adjacent lands.
4. Management participation. Involving local landowners and land users in decisions about resources which affect them. The Oubaigubi Bird of Paradise Reserve in Papua, New Guinea, is run by a village council on behalf of its population.

The examples are numerous, but each applies the principle of surrounding protected areas with compatible land uses and a sympathetic public. The approach, still in its infancy, is ripe for conceptual advances and novel applications.

Conservation in the Human Realm

Protected areas are a seductively simple way to save nature from humanity. But sanctuaries admit a failure to save wildlife and natural habitat where they overlap with human interest, and that means 95 percent or more of the earth's surface. Conservation by segregation is the Noah's Ark solution, a belief that wildlife should be consigned to tiny land parcels for its own good because it has no place in our world. The flaw in this view is obvious: Those land parcels are not big enough to avert catastrophic species extinction by insularization or safe enough to protect resources from the poor and the greedy. Simply put, if we can't save nature outside protected areas, not much will survive inside; if we can, protected areas will cease to be arks. The problems of conserving wildlife alongside humanity (Western, chap. 16) are as daunting as the opportunities are tantalizing.

Inventorying Nature. Wildlife inventories and research have focused on protected areas, partly because biologists want undisturbed study sites, partly because conservationists like to take stock of protected natural ecosystems rather than vulnerable modified areas. Nonetheless, in preparation for the coming decades, we must find out where and how nature survives and decide on priorities. This involves several steps:

1. Inventorying and ranking the ecological importance and vulnerability of species, habitats, and ecosystems outside protected areas. Governmental and international institutions, perhaps under a new commission modeled on IUCN's CNPPA, will need to collaborate on inventory methods, interpretation, and planning.
2. Resolving why those species and ecosystems survive without special protection and whether they are vulnerable in the face of impending changes in land use.
3. Producing criteria for ranking areas in terms of species conservation, biological diversity, and ecological function.

Sustaining and Enhancing Nature. New ways to sustain and enhance wildlife outside protected areas stand at the top of the conservation agenda. Four topics warrant special attention:

1. Strengthening and broadening the arguments for conserving wildlife in rural areas. The protection of water, soils, air, and genetic resources are modern reasons for conserving nature alien to the nineteenth century. Are there new reasons appropriate to the twenty-first century?

2. Balancing the conflicting uses of land. Diversifying the reasons to conserve also widens the scope for conflict. Wildlife viewing and hunting are incompatible, unless separated in some way. How can diverse uses by integrated more successfully? The problem arises in treating each sector separately for maximum gain, be it beef production, timber, or ducks for hunters, with little regard to the externalities, such as the cost of ducks to farmers. How can the conflicts in multiple use of land be averted and the mutual gains enhanced? Nonmonetary criteria and computer-integrated designs need investigation.

3. Halting land degradation. The heavy environmental costs of agricultural and industrial production due to poor technology, ignorance, negligence, and preoccupation with maximum short-term profit can be alleviated by improved technology, education, more stringent pollution laws, and better environmental assessments methods. The cleaning of the river Thames running through London shows what can be achieved. Several promising avenues lie ahead. In agriculture, genetic engineering could help adapt plant to environment, rather than environment to plant, by endowing cereal crops with nitrogen-fixing abilities and endogenous pathogens, alleviating pollution in the process. In forestry, new concepts such as long-cycle and light-harvest logging should help wildlife. In industry, high-technology production could mean less waste and lower environmental impact. The challenge is to create an environmentally compatible technology, not to stop it in its tracks (see "Agenda for Conservation and Development" and Pearl, chap. 29).

4. Repairing the damage. It will take a Herculean effort and novel skills to rescue the stressed ecosystems and endangered species of the twenty-first century. On a small scale, we can revegetate the Welsh slag heaps, reintroduce species like the Arabian oryx, and even reassemble ecosystems like Pilansberg in South Africa. But far more will be expected of restoration ecology and management in the coming decades. We must first keep the pieces and then learn how to reassemble them—the task of ex situ care and biotechnology.

Ex Situ Care and Biotechnology

As species become more endangered and ecosystems more impoverished by habitat fragmentation, hunting, pollution, and other human assaults, methods of keeping species artificially, maintaining and boosting their reproduction, and eventually returning animals to the wild will play a larger role in conservation. The time to learn those techniques is now, before the cascade of endangered species overwhelms our limited knowledge and physical capacity to deal with them. Père David's deer, Przewalski's horse, the Arabian oryx, and recently the California condor are examples of species kept alive in captivity after extermination in the wild. How many species can we save in captivity with existing space and technological limitations, and more to the point, how can we increase that capacity? What problems arise in keeping species in captivity and in returning them to the wild?

We are beginning to glimpse new opportunities and, simultaneously, sense frustrating inadequacies in saving endangered species and rehabilitating degraded ecosystems. The science of salvaging and repairing nature is in its infancy. To make ex situ care and biotechnology a powerful conservation tool means hastening to explore those new opportunities and shoring up the gaping holes in our scientific and technological superstructure.

The prospects opened up by scientific and technological advances are staggering, but our ability to grasp and harness them is hampered by technical uncertainties and lack of space, public awareness, and money. To play a significant role in species conservation, ex situ methods must develop on three fronts simultaneously: science and technology, enhancement of carrying capacity, and application principles.

Science and Technology. A number of broad,

interrelated science and technology topics need further development:

1. Ex situ animal care. The first priority, still a long way off, is to maintain and to breed all endangered species. Establishing self-sustaining captive populations of all endangered species calls for advances in everything from animal capture and handling, veterinary science, nutrition, behavioral ecology, and reproductive biology—what it takes to get animals reproducing naturally—to methods of enhancing their numbers and genetic diversity.

2. Maintaining a species's ecological and evolutionary potential. It is not enough to save an animal in captivity and turn it back into the wild at some future date. The high failure rate in species ranging from mouse to gorilla shows how difficult rehabilitation can be when learned or genetic traits have been lost (Stanley Price, chap. 20). A more onerous task is to maintain and ultimately restore a species to nature without loss of adaptability. Several topics bearing on rehabilitation science need special attention:

a. Criteria for defining how to deal with population variation. Natural variation among populations poses special problems for captive propagation. Ignoring variation invites inbreeding or outbreeding depression and the loss of genetic heterogeneity and locally adapted traits. Yet space limitations necessitate choice. To what extent should one homogenize populations or maintain their discreteness? Ideally, the answer is resolved case by case. But urgency and shortage of funds when species are in imminent danger of extinction call for generalized models to reduce the guesswork, and the risks, in taking emergency action on a shoestring budget (Woodruff, chap. 8).

b. Methods of detecting and replacing significant gene loss. Technological advances should be a boon to conservation geneticists struggling to quantify species and population characteristics and to identify deleterious genes which threaten highly endangered species. A far more ambitious goal is the development of technological skills to enable the biologist to map the entire genome, determine the function of each gene, and manufacture it synthetically. This would open up the ultimate goal—restoration genetics—the science of identifying and restoring genetic losses.

c. Rehabilitation science. While genes are in principle redeemable, learned behavior may not be. Realization that survival in the wild is a question of complex learned behavior as much as genotype raises the specter of species surviving in captivity without hope of returning to the wild. The techniques of identifying, preserving, and restoring the skills needed for survival in nature must be developed quickly to ensure captive propagation becomes a bona fide conservation tool, rather than an evolutionary black hole. Four challenges confront rehabilitation science: to identify species' survival strategies in the wild before they are lost; to retain those behaviors in captive populations; to develop pre- and postrelease techniques to reestablish them in the event that such adaptations are lost; and to purge rehabilitated species of deleterious behavior picked up in captivity.

Enhancing Ex Situ Capacity. With space for fewer than 1,000 vertebrates in numbers sufficient to avoid inbreeding, ex situ capacity must be expanded quickly to accommodate the endangered species fallout of the twenty-first century. Capacity can be expanded considerably and quickly if effort is directed to three key areas—live collections, nonliving collections, and public support.

1. Live collections. Until it is possible to store sperm, ova, and genes routinely, ex situ capacity will be set by how many live animals can be held in world collections. With zoo slots limited by space, cash, and manpower (Conway, chap. 19), it is time to look to novel solutions. For example, "megazoos," better termed species parks, which would maintain endangered animals in social and ecological conditions mimicking those in the wild, though perhaps in a different biome or on a different continent, could help avoid the loss of adaptive traits and obviate overt manipulation. Rhino sanctuaries on private ranches in Kenya and the 2,400-ha Canyon Colorado Equid Sanctuary in New Mexico, United States, are prototype species parks. Others could be established on abandoned agricultural lands.

2. Nonliving collections. The space limitation would be solved in terms or preserving genetic variation, if not adaptive genotypes, by innovations in storing biological material iner-

tly, whether in the form of sperm, eggs, or even individual genes. Such a technological fix could arise through advances in cryopreservation, seed storage, cloning, insertion of genes into genetic foster parents, and even laboratory synthesis of proteins from genetic maps.

3. Public and financial support. Further expansion of ex situ capacity is impossible without public support. Zoos and other agencies preserving wildlife in captivity must develop their education facilities and, through the media as well as sophisticated exhibits such as the Bronx Zoo's JungleWorld tropical forest exhibit, convince the public of their role in preservation and rehabilitation of endangered species. The greatly expanded metropolitan centers of the future could, through public support and financial input, make an even larger contribution to ex situ conservation programs. Closer ties between ex situ and in situ conservation by, for example, twinning zoos and national parks, financially and technically, would give greater credibility to captive management.

Application Principles. Space limitations, and the need to clarify how captive propagation can reinforce species preservation in the wild call for ex situ conservation guidelines and institutional collaboration.

1. Conservation guidelines. Until recently, animals in captivity were held for public exhibition and entertainment, not species preservation. Though zoos in particular now play a significant role in conservation, notably through the efforts of AAZPA and IUDZG, there is a pressing need for guidelines on how ex situ methods can contribute more effectively to global conservation, Genetic guidelines (Woodruff, chap. 8) on minimum viable population (MVP) sizes for captive animals are becoming widely accepted by zoos, even as population geneticists debate what constitutes MVPs for various species. Yet, if ex situ populations are to mimic in situ parent populations with a view to successful reintroduction, a far broader and more widely accepted set of policies and guidelines is needed, including:

a. Conservation policies that lay out the ex situ management role in global biological conservation and help to establish its priorities.

b. Genetic guidelines for selecting and maintaining populations able to respond to the changing environments of parent ecosystems.

c. Behavioral guidelines for maintaining traits essential to successful reintroduction.

d. Ecological criteria for maintaining a minimum viable community (MVC) of animals and plants from all major ecosystems.

2. Conservation coalition. With some notable exceptions, institutions involved in ex situ preservation have little contact with wildlife conservation, particularly in the third world. For ex situ preservation to be more applicable to wildlife conservation, there needs to be a forum, perhaps a greatly expanded version of IUCN's Captive Animal Specialist Group, in which conservation biologists, wildlife managers, and ex situ agencies can meet, exchange ideas and, set out guidelines.

AN AGENDA FOR CONSERVATION AWARENESS

The extinction crisis has reached the point where it is no longer possible for thoughtful people to consider the situation manageable by professional wildlife managers and park professionals alone. In order to conserve significant diversity in the earth's biological resources beyond the year 2100, action is needed by society as a whole. This section deals with the question of what new actions by segments of society traditionally unconcerned with the natural environment will be feasible and productive toward the goal of sustaining wildlife. Unlike the issues surrounding managing reserves or conducting biological research, few generalizations can be made, because every culture has produced a distinct set of attitudes toward nature. Therefore, one of the first key issues for those seeking ways to foster a more harmonious accommodation between land and people is to understand each area's cultural landscape. Given this caveat, one can usefully orient a discussion of human needs and wildlife survival into three categories of general goals: a reorientation of the fields of ethics and philosophy of education; a replacement of wildlife's peripheral status among competing agendas for a community's attention; and a reaccommodation between developed and developing nations in defining and then acting on what is effective aid for long-term sustainable development. It is easy to list these key issues; it is impossible to accomplish them given the gaps in our current knowledge. The discussion that follows points out some of the unknowns we must conquer on our way to the twenty-second century.

Human Values

Wildlife conservation values are not incorporated into mainstream Western and Western-influenced societies and are devalued in many cultures within emerging nations. While basic environmental attitudes were formed in the United States and Europe by the middle of the nineteenth century, Western society has yet to identify the ethical underpinnings of what many members of that society concerned with conservation of wildlife already feel they ought to do (Hargrove, chap. 21).

Environmental Ethics. The task ahead for environmental ethicists in the West is to evaluate environmental attitudes and the behaviors they foster to determine whether they are really what Westerners ought to think and do as members of their culture. This is not a simple problem. The mores of a society can shift quite rapidly if a convincing, culturally based rationale causes a significant number of people to shift their attitudes. On what basis will a conviction of the importance of protecting the diversity of life spread beyond the conservation community to the average citizen and the average multilateral aid bank director? The nascent field of environmental ethics has carved out for further analysis several promising perspectives on the value of wildlife (Hargrove, chap. 21). The first two points of view value wildlife in relation to human interest, use, and need:

1. Anthropocentric, intrinsic value. The first alternative states that wildlife has its own intrinsic value that in turn enhances human life. What are the prospects that this perspective can spread rapidly through societies that have become urbanized and distanced from nature?

2. Anthropocentric, instrumental value. The other alternative states that wildlife is only to be valued in terms of human use. This is the rationale expressed by many conservationists, who themselves are motivated by theory no. 1, to convince members of materialist societies to alter hyperconsumptive behavior in the interest of an even bigger payoff later. Can this argument effectively protect whole ecosystems when it concedes that life forms for which no human use is identified are expendable?

The two anthropocentric views just listed are by definition rooted in culture, and thus fomenting their global adoption requires rooting a respect for wildlife in a myriad of traditions around the world. However, the great advantage of the anthropocentric perspective is that it is compatible with most current ethics and religions and is thus perhaps a relatively easy philosophy for the average person to adopt or reaffirm. Western culture has evolved a set of commodity-oriented values that affect natural resources throughout the world, causing the alteration of habitats everywhere (Norton, chap. 23). But at the same time, there remains a full range of human values in all cultures that are served by the existence of wildlife, which can be forcefully promoted.

3. Nonanthropocentric views. The other principal set of perspectives is based on humans granting that there is a value to nature that resides within nature itself, and not simply in human minds; this value can be either completely intrinsic (Rolston, chap. 22) or reside in wildlife's value to humans and other beings. Mores based on these perspectives, the so-called nonanthropocentric view, have the advantage of being independent of all cultural parameters, and thus universally applicable. Perhaps by the year 2100, people may have moved through the more sellable anthropocentric arguments to a new plane, now culturally untenable, of seeking to conserve nature for its value beyond human reference.

Reexamination of Existing Religious Traditions. Both Hargrove (chap. 21) and Tarak (chap. 26) point out that cultural and philosophical resources in other world traditions are likely to have a favorable impact on the moral attitudes of Westerners toward nature. They are also, of course, key to the conservation of nature in non-Western societies. The task of identifying these resources is underway, not only outside, but within cultures where some non-Western attitudes of harmony with nature have been temporarily forgotten or suppressed.

Incorporation of Environmental Ethics into Education. Once identified, religious, ethical, and aesthetic perspectives on wildlife can be incorporated into programs of environmental education.

1. Childhood education. At present, very few schools incorporate issues of land and wild-

life use into their curricula, for several reasons. First is the lack of a consensus, based on cultural attitudes, of what is important and valuable about wildlife. Second, there is a lack of educators with the background to create multidisciplinary curricula that integrate ethical issues with biology.

2. Professional training. Field biology training is often available only at the professional or postgraduate level, where another obstacle to protection of biological diversity appears: the failure by current scientific tradition to embrace the challenge of diversity the way it embraces the challenge of generality (Ehrenfeld, chap. 24). In other words, professionals in wildlife science are encouraged to develop general theories about organisms or ideal dimensions for generic reserves rather than explore the uniqueness of various life forms or the problems peculiar to a specific habitat. While computer programs can take over much of the tedium of taxonomic work, for example, the lack of a love of diversity even among those charged to defend it perhaps contributes to the decline of diversity itself. A current gap in the philosophy of science results, then, from the rejection of inductivism.

Political Planning

Conservationists are not seen as problem solvers reflecting people's basic desires and values, partly because they too often do not recognize as relevant issues of the disparity of wealth (Lee, chap. 30) and political power (Olembo, chap. 27). The problem may be as basic as not knowing how to relate to the public at large, to economists, and to politicians (Tarak, chap. 26). Meanwhile, impatience mounts among supporters as conservationists create more new plans, while existing plans are not put into practice.

The Constituency for Conservation. A first task for conservationists working in the political realm is to broaden the constituency for wildlife protection (Tarak, chap. 26). In different countries, this requires different strategies. The inclusion of the countryside population, middle- and upper-class citizens, and wildlife managers is critical in building an effective constituency for conservation; conservationists in less-developed nations often come from too narrow a segment of society.

1. Rural people. In developing nations, a priority is to include the people who live in rural areas abutting wildlife reserves in the sharing of revenues generated by the parks, including short-term income from activities like tourism or sustainable harvests of wildlife products, as well as long-term anticipated gains such as watershed protection, climate stabilization, or protection of wild relatives of valuable cultivars. Revenue sharing is particularly important where neighbors are asked to tolerate losses due to emigrating wildlife and loss of opportunity to conduct traditional economic activity.

2. Middle and upper classes. In developed nations as well as undeveloped nations, broadening the constituency for conservation in the middle and upper socioeconomic classes is a necessary prelude to conservation legislation. The people who traditionally support wildlife conservation are generally those with affluence and leisure, so that there is a linkage between economic growth and the success of conservationists' goals.

3. Wildlife managers. Third world countries particularly need well-trained managers because they must engage in trade in natural-resource products with other nations at an economic disadvantage, placing a special strain on agriculture, forestry, and fisheries. At the same time, managers must also preserve their nations' underlying biological support systems. Where can these managers receive the training they must have to succeed?

Information

1. Databases. A missing element in developing countries is a sound information base of the extent and diversity of the flora and fauna. It is hard to create a constituency for protection of wildlife among competing agendas when data on the status and even existence of that wildlife are sketchy. The creation of inventories is a priority activity.

2. Organizational expertise. A lack of coordination and networking among conservationists and conservation institutions means duplication of effort on the one hand and gaps on the other. Internal management of conservation institutions, from defining goals to raising funds, suffers from a lack of organizational and management expertise.

A Broadened Mandate. Conservation is seen now as just one more in a varied group of special-interest lobbies. The task before conservationists is a transformation from that status to one of a social force capable of bridging and uniting diverse interests by identifying joint solutions to common problems.

Conservationists should be able to play a key role in identifying political issues indirectly related to species protection, such as economic imbalances, whereas heretofore, they have concentrated too narrowly on direct threats to wildlife. Other, indirect effects that merit monitoring include population growth, market prices for wildlife, and equitable distribution of benefits of wildlife exploitation and protection.

1. The relationship between economic growth and conservation. To be recognized as a mainstream political force, conservationists should not let themselves be labeled as antigrowth. Currently, there is a dearth of growth-allowing solutions to conservation problems, solutions that satisfy development interests without sacrificing the quality of life. For example, the problem of disposal of toxic waste looms as an ever-growing issue (Bean, chap. 28). With some exceptions, we now lack technology to reduce the amount of such wastes through more efficient manufacturing (which in turn would increase industrial revenue), and we have lacked the ingenuity to create new markets for the utilization and breakdown of toxic waste products. In short, a goal for the next century is to find and promote solutions for wildlife conservation that serve the twin ends of environmental protection and economic advancement.

2. National conservation strategies. A conservation strategy is most meaningful when it is tied to other important national agendas, yet free of political partisanship. Nongovernmental, private organizations can play an especially useful role in the creation of their countries' national conservation strategies, following the pioneering effort of the International Union for the Conservation of Nature and Natural Resources. By their very nature, NGOs (nongovernmental organizations) can avoid the taint of being tied to one particular regime, should a government change. Yet even when prepared by nongovernmental organizations or a coalition of government agencies, universities, and NGOs, national conservation strategies have often been created by too elitist an authorship, causing the documents to be considered as foreign-imposed by those people most affected by their recommendations. The successful strategies of the future—that is, strategies that will become implemented—will pay more attention to changing social behavior and examining the effects of environmental events on human culture and will be the joint product of planning by all sectors of society. Tarak (chap. 26) and Olembo (chap. 27) have also identified other gaps in most national conservation strategies: lack of an education component, which fosters cooperation over the long term; lack of a coordination mechanism to ensure actual implementation of the plan; and lack of a realistic time frame. Overly optimistic schedules can discourage promoters of conservation plans and sabotage their chances for success.

National Laws and International Regimes to Protect Wildlife.

1. National Laws. As Bean pointed out (chap. 28) for the United States, legislation and legal developments follow, rather than anticipate, serious resource problems. We cannot expect legislators of the future to be any more knowledgeable than today's about conservation imperatives, and in fact, owing to the continuing explosion of information, they may well have less knowledge about isolated issues of any particular field. However, a legislator of the next century, like those of today, will respond to problem solvers who bring with them the promise of satisfying a large portion of that legislator's constituency.

2. International regimes. Environmental problems become political issues when there is a political constituency to label them as such. For nations mired in extreme poverty, there may be no constituency for what is considered on the international level to be a critical problem for the future of valuable wildlife. Thus one immediate task is to address international economic imbalances.

Nongovernmental bodies, expecially those in developing nations and/or with multinational roots, can comprise a constituency for international policymakers, who now often must wait years before being able to act on urgent international environmental problems (Olembo, chap. 27). The international support community for conservation can also act as watchdogs to ensure that conventions and treaties created to protect wildlife are followed by all signatories. Olembo cautions that international networking in this regard is useful only so long as patronizing advice that disregards the social and cultural context of other nations is avoided.

A final task for political planners into the next century is an ambitious one: to extend international cooperation in protection of global commons beyond the seas to other areas where national jurisdictions are ambiguous or ineffective (Olembo, chap. 27). Such areas include outer space, the atmosphere, irrigation water, fisheries, unique international ecosystems, and other living resources. There are major obstacles to achieving consideration of these areas as global commons, particularly where they clash with common law or traditional concepts of private ownership or national sovereignty. In addition, the international cooperation required can only occur in a much improved climate of peace and cooperation. This is a task for small and large nations alike. The superpowers can take the lead through nuclear disarmament and a vastly reduced international trade in weapons.

A Role for the Developed World

Aside from the very primary and urgently needed role of promoting world peace, there are many direct ways for developed nations to support conservation of the richest ecosystems, the tropical forests of the world. Two contrasting views of the developed world—one as crusader for the salvation of wildlife trapped in benighted third world countries, the other as gross usurper of natural resources against the will of poor nations—are unpromising premises for planning for the next century. In their place can come the realization that the economic and environmental goals of rich and poor country alike are converging: Self-interest on both sides dictates that the global economy cannot flourish with the increasingly inequitable distribution of wealth, and that the long-term success of any nation's economy rests on the careful management of its natural resource base (Lee, chap. 30). With the exponential growth and penetration of knowledge in developing countries of recent years, there is now the possibility of planning professionals from industry, governments, and NGOs of those countries working productively with those of the richer nations on an equal intellectual, if not economic, footing. Out of such dialogues can come methods to overcome the ways in which we currently fail to protect wildlife. Five agents of change warrant attention:

Multinational Corporations. Multinational corporations (MNC) have unrealized potential for promoting the related objective of environmental protection alongside that of sustainable economic growth (Pearl, chap. 29).

1. Environmental protection. A major current problem is that if a corporation even has an environmental protection policy, it is invariably remedial rather than preventative. The latter would be most economical and effective, and thus an intelligent goal for multinationals in the future is the production of long-term, proactive conservation plans. Corporations train their employees in technical, marketing, and management skills applicable to resource planning. Local governments can find incentives to cause these companies to extend training to interns from planning and wildlife ministries. Some corporations also have environmental testing and monitoring equipment that can be made available to government agencies and NGOs. Host countries can promote good environmental citizenship on the part of multinationals by promulgating and enforcing strict, fair, long-term regulations for all industry—domestic, governmental, and multinational alike.

2. Sustainable economic growth. Since economic development of a country leads to a reduction in heedless extraction of wildlife resources, it is in the interest of less developed nations to direct the multinationals in their countries to behave in ways that enhance development, such as transferring useful technology, managerial expertise and marketing skills, and building locally manufacturing plants that are normally located in the MNCs' home country.

Bilateral Aid Agencies.

1. Aid priorities. Aid is an instrument of a nation's foreign policy and reflects the donor's often shifting priorities. While the Nordic countries are notable for a continuing commitment to human needs in the poorest countries, the major donors often focus on security or commercial

objectives first, with relatively little attention being given to projects in forestry, natural resources, and the environment. Military assistance, for example, amounts to nearly three-quarters of all the U.S.'s budgeted foreign aid for 1987 (Wolf 1987), and Japan and West Germany, the next two largest donors, are known for tying aid closely to their economic and commercial interests. Despite an official mandate within USAID to promote biological diversity in 1987, the budgeted money to back up the mandate was cut by one-quarter, a result of the U.S. government's enormous debts compounded by the relatively low priority for conservation within the overall USAID framework of development assistance.

2.   Coordination. Aid assistance can fail in a recipient nation overwhelmed with projects from too many donor nations and institutions. It is the responsibility of both donors and recipients to ensure that the totality of aid amounts to a coordinated national strategy of sustainable development. Such coordination may require a separate government agency in countries already short on management expertise. In the absence of oversight within the recipient nation, elaboration of consultative groups among donors is necessary. Bilateral aid agencies must have more officials trained in resource conservation.

3.   Project design. Bilateral aid programs have been faulted for the overly large scale of projects, short timing, and financial waste. Scale is discussed later. Political will can be summoned to invest in some long-term environmental monitoring and restoration, and financial waste can be mitigated in part by reducing the scale of projects, using NGO intermediaries with lower overheads, and hiring local or regional field personnel.

Multilateral Aid. Multilateral development banks (MDB) are currently the world's largest lenders of money for public development. Their activities have enormous impact on the environment, through the scale of their projects and the degree to which they mitigate or ignore the impact of their plans on wildlife.

1.   Scale. As is also true of bilateral aid agencies, the banks' enormous budgets are divided into projects of a massive scale, often with bad consequences for the environment. Expensive, large-scale projects tend to emphasize high

technology dependent on developed-country products and expertise, relatively few employees, and vast expanses of land. Local people and traditional uses of land are ignored. A task for MDBs and aid agencies is to recognize the long-term sustainability of small-scale development projects and develop the administrative skills necessary to identify, monitor, and evaluate them.

2.   Mitigating the impact on wildlife. The largest multilateral development bank is the World Bank. It has recently adopted not only a dramatically new policy to protect wildlands, but a new administrative structure to ensure its success (Pearl, chap. 29). Other MDBs, including the Asian Development Bank, the Inter-American Development Bank, the Caribbean Development Bank, the African Development Bank and Fund, and the Arab Bank for Economic Development in Africa, have not yet followed the World Bank's lead. National and international nongovernmental conservation organizations, which will cooperate with the World Bank in the implementation of their wildlands policy in the role of watchdog, identifier of problem areas and land in need of protection, and source of basic biological and ecological data, can also urge the other development banks to adopt the World Bank wildlands policy and serve these banks in a similar vein.

Nongovernmental Organizations. For this discussion, NGO activities can be usefully divided into four major functions: They can act as watchdogs and advisors to governmental aid organizations, as innovators in new techniques for achieving conservation, as international lobbyists for global conservation regimes, and as educators of the public and professionals.

1.   Advice to aid organizations. International aid and development organizations are increasingly recognizing or being called to task for their difficulty in translating goals into action at the grass roots level. NGOs, because of long-term presence, lack of political taint, and the flexibility that comes with a small organization, are effective actors on the rural landscape. They not only can supply advice, but can provide services, such as village-scale reforestation or training of village women in less fuel-intensive cooking techniques, to cite two examples, which large-scale agents are unable to provide.

2.   Innovations. It was NGOs that saw the

environmental silver lining in the cloud of third world debt, with the innovative debt-swapping schemes currently taking place between U.S. conservation organizations and South American debtor nations. Other breakthroughs in such disparate fields of conservation as habitat restoration and methods whereby local villagers profit from the neighboring nature reserves through trekking schemes or carefully managed harvests, all come from the efforts of individuals acting through nongovernmental organizations.

3. Constituency for international regimes. Urgently needed conventions for the protection of global commons (see "International Regimes") will be created only in the wake of international public outcry, which can be supplied through the coordinated action of multinational NGOs.

Within industrialized nations, NGOs can lobby for their countries to join such international arrangements as the Law of the Sea Convention, the Bonn Convention on Migratory Species, and the World Charter for Nature (as yet, the United States has signed none of the three).

4. Education. The diffusion of conservation information to the public can be accomplished in as many different ways as there are conservation NGOs. For example, zoos, botanical gardens, and aquariums are changing from exclusively amusement parks to conservation education centers, using the wildlife in their collections as "ambassadors from the wild" to their urban visitors. Conservation organizations and private universities can play an increasing role in training current and potential leaders of conservation groups in tropical countries.

Media. The medium of television has the capacity to grip the viewer with compelling visual images. Recent leaps in broadcast technology make it possible to report at low cost from the remotest corners of the earth. Potentially, the tragic consequences of ecosystem decay to a family in Southeast Asia could enter the living rooms and touch the emotions of families on the other side of the globe. However, the problem we face in the case of media coverage of the environment is not technological, but theoretical and practical. Diffusion of information about the extinction crisis is stymied by the current definition of what is "news" and the division of labor in news gathering and reporting institutions (Crystal, chap. 31).

1. Definition of "news." The definition of news for a daily journalist is something concrete, tangible to the senses, and happening "now." The emphasis is on political individuals and governments. Wildlife problems are seen as events of "tomorrow" and uncertain. The test of newsworthiness is whether the topic concerns death or money. Thus toxic waste issues enter a broadcast the day some humans die of poisoning from their environment, and the shortage of oil is reported only when the cost of car fuel rises to an inconvenient level. A task for journalists is to find ways to portray causes as compellingly as consequences, and to tie intangible processes to the everyday lives of people.

2. Division of labor in news-gathering. Conservation issues are the responsibility of separate, less-than-equal science editors who must fight for space in the second half of a broadcast or the back pages of a newspaper. This state of affairs, and the current definition of news, is partly the result of poor scientific literacy on the part of most mainstream journalists, a remediable deficiency.

ACTING ON THE AGENDA

It is clear that global conservation requires a revolution in human behavior. Fortunately for the planet, the revolution has begun at many levels—economic development, scientific research, land-use planning, the rescue of endangered species, and the altering of public awareness—but it has only *just* begun.

We have listed here a broad array of possibilities for action by people concerned with the many threats to nature's integrity and survival. The fact that we do not have all the facts about any given crisis should not prevent us from joining the struggle on behalf of wild animals and wild lands. Biological complexity will always elude total human comprehension, and technological solutions for conditions of decay will never seem complete. More than anything, we need to reaffirm our reverence for incomprehensible and uncontrollable nature and to make it a condition of living in this world. Without such a reconciliation, the planet will neither support human needs nor satisfy human hearts in 2100 and beyond.

References

AAZPA (1983). *Species Survival Plan.* American Association of Zoological Parks and Aquaria, Wheeling, W.Va.

AAZPA (1986). *African Rhino Workshop.* Summary and Recommendations. Cincinnati, Oh.

Abelson, H. P. (1986). Future supplies of energy and minerals. *Science* 231:657.

Adams, L., and A. Geis (1981). Effects of highways on wildlife. Rept. #FHWA/RD-81/067. U.S. Dept. of Transportation, Washington, D.C.

Adamson, G. (1986). *My Pride and Joy: An Autobiography.* Collins Harvill, London.

Alexandratos, N., J. Bruinsma, and P. A. Yotopoulos (1983). Agriculture from the perspective of population growth. FAO, Rome.

Allen, G. M. (1911). Mammals of the West Indies. *Bull. Mus. Comp. Zool.* 54:175–263.

Allen, T. H. F., and T. B. Starr (1982). *Hierarchy: Perspectives for Ecological Complexity.* University of Chicago Press, Chicago, Ill.

Allendorf, F. W. (1983). Gene flow and genetic differentiation among populations. In: *Genetics and Conservation*, ed. C. M. Schonewald-Cox, S. M. Chambers, F. McBryde, and L. Thomas, pp. 241–261. Benjamin/Cummings, Menlo Park, Calif.

Allendorf, F. W., and R. F. Leary (1986). Heterozygosity and fitness in natural populations of animals. In: *Conservation Biology: The Science of Scarcity and Diversity*, ed. M. E. Soule, pp. 57–76. Sinauer, Sunderland, Mass.

Amerson, A. B. (1969). Ornithology of the Marshall and Gilbert Islands. *Atoll Res. Bull.* 127:1–348.

Andere, D. K., J. G. Stelfox, and S. W. Mbogua (1980). Distributions and densities of livestock and wild herbivores in the rangelands of Kenya. Kenya Rangeland Ecological Monitoring Unit, Technical Report. Nairobi.

Anderson, J. L. (1986). Restoring a wilderness: The reintroduction of wildlife to an African national park. *Intl. Zoo Yrbk.* 24/25:192–199.

Andrewartha, H. G., and L. C. Birch (1954). *The Distribution and Abundance of Animals.* University of Chicago Press, Chicago.

Andrews, J. (1986). The present status and future management of the Goeldi's monkey (Callimico goeldi) in captivity in the British Isles. Discussion Papers in Conservation No. 45. University College, London.

Andrews, M. (1986). Seeds of revolution. *BBC Wildlife*, July, 1986.

Angier, J. (1985). Acid rain: New bad news. "Nova," WNET-NY television, 1/1/85.

Angotti, J. (1979). Nuclear risk: Incident at Three Mile Island. "NBC News," 3/30/79.

Anon. (1984a). Notes and News. *Oryx* 16:299.

Anon. (1984b). The IUCN position statement on translocation of living organisms: Introductions, re-introductions and re-stocking. Final draft. Prepared jointly by SSC and COE. IUCN, Morges, Switzerland.

Anon. (1986a). How to grow a national park. *Threatened Plants Newsletter*, CMC/IUCN 16:14.

Anon. (1986b). Too much of a good thing. *Species*, Newsletter of the Species Survival Commission 7:32. IUCN, Gland, Switzerland.

Anthony, A. W. (1925). Expedition to Guadelupe Island, Mexico, in 1922. The birds and mammals. *Proc. Calif. Acad. Sci.* (14:)277–320.

Antonovics, J. (1988). Genetically based measures of uniqueness. In: *Conservation of Genetic Resources*, ed. G. H. Orians. University of Washington Press, Seattle.

Arp, A. J., and J. J. Childress (1981). Blood function in the hydrothermal vestimentiferan tube worm. *Science* 213:342–344.

Ascher, W. (1983). New development approaches and the adaptability of international agencies: The case of the World Bank. *Intl. Organiz.* 37(3):415–439.

Ashby, W. R. (1956). *An Introduction to Cybernetics*. Chapman and Hall, London.

Ashley, M. V., D. J. Melnick, and D. Western (In preparation). Conservation genetics of the black rhinoceros.

Atchley, W. R., and D. S. Woodruff, eds. (1981). *Evolution and Speciation*, p. 436. Cambridge University Press, Cambridge.

Atkinson, I. A. E. (1977). A reassessment of factors, particularly *Rattus rattus* L., that influenced the decline of endemic forest birds in the Hawaiian Islands. *Pacific Sci.* 31:109–133.

Atkinson, I. A. E. (1985). The spread of commensal species of *Rattus* to oceanic islands and their effects on island avifaunas. In: *Conservation of Island Birds*, ed. P. J. Moors, pp. 35–81. International Council of Bird Preservation Tech. Publ. 3.

Atkinson, I. A. E. (1988). The value of New Zealand islands as biological reservoirs. *Proceedings of the Concom Workshop on Island Management*. Barrow Island, Western Australia, Nov. 8–13, 1985.

Atkinson, I. A. E., and B. D. Bell (1973). Offshore and outlying islands. In: *The Natural History of New Zealand*, ed. G. R. Williams, pp. 372–292. A. H. and A. W. Reed, Wellington.

Aveling, R., and A. Mitchell (1980). Is rehabilitating orang utans worthwhile? *Oryx* 16:263–271.

Ayala, F. J., and T. Dobzhansky (1974). *Studies in the Philosophy of Biology: Reduction and Related Problems*. University of California Press, Berkeley.

Ayres, R. L. (1983). *Banking on the Poor:* The World Bank and World Poverty. MIT Press, Cambridge, Mass.

Baerl, C. D. N., R. Dorit, P. H. Greenwood, G. Freyer, N. Hughes, P. B. N. Jackson, H. Kawanabe, R. H. Lowe-McConnell, M. Nagoshi, A. J. Ribbink, E. Trewavas, F. Witte, and K. Yamaoka (1985). Destruction of fisheries in Africa's lakes. *Nature* 315:19–20.

Baker, R. H. (1946). A study of rodent populations on Guam, Mariana Islands. *Ecol. Monogr.* 16:393–408.

Bakus, G. J. (1981). Chemical defense mechanisms on the Great Barrier Reef, Australia. *Science* 211:497–498.

Balouet, J. C., and S. L. Olson (1988). Fossil birds from quaternary deposits in New Caledonia. *Smithsonian Contributions to Zoology* 469.

Bannerman, D. A. (1922). *The Canary Islands*. Gurney and Jackson, London.

Barclay, J. H. and T. J. Cade (1983). Restoration of the peregrine falcon in the eastern United States. *Bird Conserv.* 1:3–40.

Barbehenn, K. R. (1974). Recent invasions of Micronesia by small mammals. *Micronesica* 10:41–50.

Barigozzi, C., ed. (1982). *Mechanisms of Speciation*. Alan R. Liss, New York.

Barr, N. T. (1981). The world food situation and global grain prospects. *Science* 214:1087–1095.

Barth, R. (1958). Observações biologicas e meteorológicas feitas na Ilha de Trindade. *Memó. Inst. Oswaldo Cruz* 56:261–270.

Barton, N. H., and G. M. Hewitt (1985). Analysis of hybrid zones. *Annu. Rev. Ecol. Syst.* 16:113–148.

Battistini, R., and G. Cremers (1972). Geomorphology and vegetation of Iles Glorieuses. *Atoll Res. Bull.* 159:1–25.

Bayne, C. J., B. H. Cogan, A. W. Diamond, J. Frazier, P. Grubb, A. Hutson, M. E. D. Poore, D. R. Stoddart, and J. D. Taylor (1970). Geography and ecology of Cosmoledo Atoll. *Atoll Res. Bull.* 136:37–56.

Bean, M. J. (1986). The Endangered Species Program. In: *Audubon Wildlife Report 1986*, pp. 347–371. National Audubon Society, New York.

Beckmann, P. (1984). Solar energy and other "alternative" energy sources. In: *The Resourceful Earth*, ed. J. Simon and H. Kahn. Blackwell, New York.

Begley, S., and M. Hager (1987). An exemplary agreement: a treaty to safeguard the world's ozone cover. *Newsweek*, Sept. 28, 1987.

Belovsky, G. E. (1987). Extinction models and mammalian persistence. In: *Viable Populations for Conservation*, ed. M. Soulé. Cambridge University Press, New York.

Benirschke, K. (1983). The impact of research on the propagation of endangered species in zoos. In: *Genetics and Conservation. A Reference for Managing Wild Animal and Plant Populations*, ed. C. M. Schonewald-Cox, S. M. Chambers, B. MacBryde, and L. Thomas, pp. 402–413. Benjamin/Cummings, Menlo Park, Calif.

Bennett, D. (1986). Triage as a species preservation strategy. *Environ. Ethics* 8:47–58.

Berry, R. J., and J. L. Johnston (1980). *The Natural History of Shetland*. Collins, London.

Berry, W. (1977). *The Unsettling of America*. Sierra Club Books, San Francisco, Calif.

Bertram, B. C. R., and D. P. Moltu (1986). Reintroducing red squirrels into Regent's Park. *Mammal Rev.* 16(2):81–88.

Best, R. H. (1981). *Land Use and Living Space*. Methuen, London.

Bolin, B. (1986). *The Greenhouse Effect: Climatic Change and Ecosystems*. Wiley, New York.

Bonner, J. T. (1965). *Size and Cycle:* An essay on the structure of biology. Princeton University Press, Princeton, N.J.

Borner, M. (1985). The rehabilitated chimpanzees of Rubondo Island. *Oryx* 19:151–154.

Boynes, W. (1978). *U.S. Non-Profit Organizations in Development Assistance Abroad:* TAICH Directory 1978. Technical Assistance Information Clearing House, New York.

Bradbury, R. H., L. S. Hammond, P. J. Moran, and R. E. Reichelt (1985a). The stable points, stable cycles and chaos of the *Acanthaster* phenomenon: a fugue in three voices. *Proc. Fifth Intl. Coral Reef Congressm Tahiti* 5:303–308.

Bradbury, R. H., L. S. Hammond, P. J. Moran, and R. E. Reichelt (1985b). Coral reef communities and the crown-of-thorns starfish: Evidence for qualitatively stable cycles. *J. Theor. Biol.* 113:69–80.

Brady, J., and D. Maehr (1985). Distribution of black bears in Florida. *FL Field Nat. 13:*1–7.

Brewer, S. (1978). *The Forest Dwellers.* Collins Harvill, London.

Brink, R. A., J. W. Densmore, and G. A. Hill (1977). Soil deterioration and the growing world demand for food. *Science* 197:625–630.

Brion, C., J. Puntieri, D. Grigera, and S. Calvello (1987). *Flora de Puerto Blest y sus Alrededores.* Valle Graf, Gral Roca, Buenos Aires.

Brooks, J. E. (1986). Status of natural and introduced Sonoran topminnow (*Poeciliopsis o. occidentalis*) populations in Arizona through 1985. *Report to Offices of Endangered Species and Fishery Resources.* U.S. Fish and Wildlife Service, Albuquerque, N. Mex.

Brown, K. S. (1982). Paleoecology and regional patterns of evolution in neotropical forest butterflies. In: *Biological Diversification in the Tropics,* ed. G. T. Prance, pp. 255–308. Columbia University Press, New York.

Brown, K. S. (1984). Adult-obtained pyrrolizidine alkaloids defend ithomiine butterflies against a spider predator. *Nature* 309:707–709.

Brown, L. H. (1971). The biology of pastoralism as a factor in conservation. *Biol. Conserv.* 3(21):93–130.

Brown, P., R. Wilson, R. Loyn, and N. Murray (1985). The orange-bellied parrot—An RAOU conservation statement. RAOU Rpt. No. 14. Royal Australian Ornithology Union, Moonee Ponds, Victoria, Australia.

Brown, R. L., and L. J. Jacobsen (1986). Our demographically divided world. Paper 74, Worldwatch Institute, Washington, D.C.

Brown, R. L., and C. W. Wolf (1984). Soil erosion:

Quiet crisis in the world economy. Paper 60, Worldwatch Institute, Washington, D.C.

Browne, J. (1983). *The Secular Ark.* Yale University Press, New Haven, Conn.

Buden, D. W. (1986). Distribution of mammals of the Bahamas. *Fla. Field Naturalist* 14:53–84.

Budowski, G. (1986). Towards the shaping of a new code of ethics based on ecological principles. *Proceedings 3d. International Conference for Comparative Psychology.* San José, Costa Rica.

Bullock, D. J. (1986). The ecology and conservation of reptiles on Round Island and Gunner's Quoin, Mauritius. *Biol. Conserv.* 37:135–156.

Bullock, D. J., and S. G. North (1982). Round Island in 1982. *Oryx* 18:36–41.

Burbidge, A. A., and R. W. G. Jenkins (1984). *Endangered Vertebrates of Australia and its Island Territories.* Report of the Working Group on Endangered Fauna of the Standing Committee of the Council of Nature Conservation Ministers. Australian National Parks and Wildlife Service, Canberra.

Burgess, R. C., and D. M. Sharpe, eds. (1981). *Forest Island Dynamics in Man-Dominated Landscapes.* Springer-Verlag, New York.

Burgos, J. J. (1970). El clima de la region Noreste de la Republica Argentina en relación con la vegetación natural y el suelo. *Bol. Soc. Argentina Botan.* 9:37–102.

Burkart, A. (1979). *Flora Illustrada de Entre Rios.* INTA Colección Científica, Vol. 6, Parts 2,5,6. Buenos Aires.

Burrill, A., I. Douglas-Hamilton, and J. Mackinnon (1986). Protected areas as refuges for elephants. In: *Protected Areas Systems Review of the Afrotropical Realm,* ed. J. Mackinnon and K. Mackinnon. IUCN, Gland, Switzerland.

Butler, W. (1986). Interview with Bryan Norton, April 4, Audubon Society, N.Y.

Cabrera, A. L. (1976). Regiones fitogeográficas Argentinas. *Enciclopedia Argentina de Agricultura y Jardinería,* Fasciculo 1. Aime, Buenos Aires.

Cabrera, A. L. (1977). Threatened and endangered species in Argentina. In: *Extinction Is Forever,* ed. G. Prance and T. Elias. Proceedings of Symposium at N.Y. Botanical Garden, May 11–13.

Cabrera, A. L. (1983). *Flora de la Provincia de Jujuy.* INTA Colección Científica Vol. 13, Parts, 2,8,10. Buenos Aires.

Cade, T. (1984). Summary of peregrine falcon production and reintroduction by the Peregrine Fund in the United States, 1973–1984. *Avicultural Mag.* 91(1,2):72–92.

Cairns, J. (1986). Restoration, relcamation and regeneration of degraded or destroyed eco-systems. In: *Conservation Biology*, ed. M. Soulé. Sinauer, Sunderland, Mass.

Caldwell, L. K. (1984). *International Environmental Policy: Emergence and Dimensions.* Duke University Press, Durham, N.C.

California Nature Conservancy (1987). Sliding Toward Extinction: The State of California's Natural Heritage, 1987, 106 pp. + appendices. California Nature Conservancy, San Francisco.

Callicott, J. B. (1980). Animal liberation: A triangular affair. *Environ. Ethics* 2:311–338.

Callicott, J. B. (1986a). The intrinsic value of non-human species. In: *The Preservation of Species: The Value of Biological Diversity*, ed. B. G. Norton, pp. Princeton University Press, Princeton, N.J.

Callicott, J. B. (1986b). The metaphysical implications of ecology. *Environ. Ethics* 8(4):301–316.

Calvin, M. (1975). Chemical evolution. *Am. Scientist* 63:169–177.

Camp, S. L., and J. J. Speidel (1987). *The International Suffering Index.* Population Crisis Committee, Washington, D.C.

Campbell, D. G. (1978). *The Ephemeral Islands: A Natural History of the Bahamas.* Macmillan Press, New York.

Campbell, D. J., and M. R. Rudge (1984). Vegetation changes induced over ten years by goats and pigs at Port Ross, Aukland Islands (subantarctic). *N.Z. J. Ecol.* 7:103–118.

Campbell, H. S. (1987). Before we pilot the ark. In: *Primates. The Road to Self-Sustaining Populations*, ed. K. Benirschke, pp. 981–983. Springer, New York.

Campbell, K. E., Jr. (1979). The non-passerine Pleistocene avifauna of the Talara tar seeps, northwestern Peru. *Roy. Ont. Mus. Life Sci. Contr.* 118.

Campbell, K. E., Jr., and D. Frailey (1984). Holocene flooding and species diversity in southwestern Amazonia. *Quaternary Res.* 21:369–375.

Capstick, C. W. (1986). Future CAP price policies—What are the environmental implications? In: *Can the CAP Fit the Environment?* ed. D. Baldock and D. Conder. Institute for European Environmental Policy and the Council for the Protection of Rural England, London, U.K.

Carson, R. (1962). *Silent Spring.* Houghton-Mifflin, Boston, Mass.

Case, R. (1978). Interstate highway road-killed animals: A data source for biologists. *Wildl. Soc. Bull.* 6:8–12.

Case, T. J., and M. L. Cody, eds. (1983). *Island Biogeography in the Sea of Cortes.* University of California Press, Berkeley.

Cassels, R. (1984). The role of prehistoric man in the faunal extinctions of New Zealand and other Pacific islands. In: *Quaternary Extinctions: A Prehistoric Revolution*, ed. P. S. Martin and R. G. Klein, pp. 741–767. University of Arizona Press, Tucson.

Cassen, R., and Associates (1986). *Does Aid Work?* Report to an intergovernmental task force. Oxford University Press, New York.

Caughley, G., N. Shepherd, and J. Short, eds. (1987). *Kangaroos: Their Ecology and Management in the Sheep Rangelands of Australia.* Cambridge University Press, Cambridge.

Cavalli-Sforza, L. L., and W. F. Bodmer (1971). *The Genetics of Human Populations.* W. H. Freeman, San Francisco.

Cavanaugh, C. M., S. L. Gardiner, M. L. Jones, H. W. Jannasch, and J. B. Waterbury (1981). Prokaryotic cells in the hydrothermal vent tube worm *Riftia pachpyptila* Jones: Possible chemoautotrophic symbionts. *Science* 213:340–342.

Cei, J. M. (1980). Amphibians of Argenitina. *Monitore Zool. Ital.* (N.S.) Monogr. 2. Florence, Italy.

CELADE (1984). *Bol. Demográf.* 17(34).

Challies, C. N. (1975). Feral pigs (*Sus scrofa*) on Aukland Island: Status and effects on vegetation and nesting sea birds. *N.Z. J. Zool.* 2:479–490.

Chandler, U. W. (1984). Improving world health: A least cost strategy. Worldwatch Paper 59. Worldwatch Institute, Washington, D.C.

Channu, H., and P. Channu (1957). Seville et Atlantique (1504–1650). Ecole Pratique des Hautes Ecoles. SEVPEN, Paris.

Chapin, G. (1914). *Florida 1513–1913: Four Hundred Years of Wars and Peace and Industrial Development.* S. J. Clarke, Chicago.

Cheng, C. (1986). On the environmental ethics of the Tao and the Ch'I. *Environ. Ethics* 8(4):351–370.

Chesnais, J. (1979). L'effet multiplicatif de la transition demographique. *Population* 34:6.

Christensen, C. C., and P. V. Kirch (1986). Nonmarine mollusks and ecological change at Barbers Point, O'ahu, Hawai'i. *Occasional Papers B. P. Bishop Mus.* 26:52–80.

Christie, M. I. (1983). *Report of Wildlife Inventory Plan* No. 39. Administración de Parques Nacionales, Bariloche, Argentina.

Christophersen, E., and E. L. Caum (1931). Vascular plants of the Leeward Islands, Hawaii. *B. P. Bishop Mus. Bull.* 81:1–41.

CIDIE (1980). Declaration of Environmental Policies

and Procedures Relating to Economic Development of the Committee of International Development Institutions on the Environment, New York, Feb. 1, 1980.

CITES (1973). 27 U.S.T. 1087, T.I.A.S. No. 8249.

Clark, R. (1986). *Aves de Tierra del Fuego y Cabo de Hornos guía de Campo*. LOLA, Buenos Aires.

Clarke, B. C. (1979). The evolution of genetic diversity. *Proc. Roy. Soc. Lond. B.* 205:453–474.

Clarke, W., and R. Munn, eds. (1986). *Sustainable Development of the Biosphere*. Cambridge University Press, Cambridge, Eng.

Clutton-Brock, T. H., and P. H. Harvey (1980). The functional significance of variation in body size among animals. *Spec. Publ. Am. Soc. Mammals* 7:632–663.

Coale, J. A. (1983). Recent trends in fertility in less developed countries. *Science* 221:828–832.

Cobb, S. (1976). The distribution and abundance of the large herbivores of Tsavo National Park, Kenya. Ph.D. dissertation, Oxford University.

Cody, M. L. (1975). Towards a theory of continental species diversity. In: *Ecology and Evolution of Communities*, ed. M. L. Cody and J. M. Diamond. Belknap Press, Cambridge, Mass.

Cohic, F. (1959). Report on a visit to the Chesterfield Islands, September 1957. *Atoll Res. Bull.* 63:1–11.

Cole, L. C. (1954). The population consequences of life history phenomena. *Q. Rev. Biol.* 29:103–137.

Commoner, B. (1968). *The Closing Circle*. Lowe and Brydone, London.

Conable, Barber (1987). Speech to World Resources Institute, Washington, D.C. May 5, 1987.

CONICIT (1984). *Diagnóstico del Subsector Forestal*. Ministerio de Agricultura y Ganadería. Dirección General Forestal, San José, Costa Rica.

Connell, J. H., and W. P. Sousa (1983). On the evidence needed to judge ecological stability or persistence. *Am. Naturalist* 121(6):789–824.

Conservation 1970 (1970). Conference sponsored by the Conservation Society of the United Kingdom, London.

Conservation 2100: A Fairfield Osborn Symposium (1986). Conference sponsored by the New York Zoological Society and the Rockefeller University, New York.

Conservation Foundation (1984). *State of the Environment: An Assessment at Mid-decade*. Conservation Foundation, Washington, D.C.

Constantz, G. D. (1979). Life history patterns of a livebearing fish in contrasting environments. *Oecologia* 40:189–201.

Conway, W. (1978). A different kind of captivity. *Animal Kingdom* 81(2):4–9.

Conway, W. (1980a). Gene banks for higher animals. In: *Conservation Biology: An Evolutionary-Ecological Perspective*, ed. M. E. Soule and B. A. Wilcox, pp. 199–208. Sinauer, Sunderland, Mass.

Conway, W. (1980b). Where we go from here? *Intl. Zoo Yrbk.* 20:184–189.

Conway, W. (1982). The Species Survival Plan: Tailoring long-term propagation species by species. In: *1982 Annual Conference Proceedings*, pp. 6–11. AAZPA, Wheeling, W.V.

Conway, W. (1985a). The Species Survival Plan and the Conference on Reproductive Strategies for Endangered Wildlife. *Zoo Biol.* 4:219–223.

Conway, W. (1985b). The SSP Subspecies Dilemma; a report of an exploratory meeting of the AAZPA Species Survival Plan Subcommittee (SSPC) of the Wildlife Conservation and Management Committee. AAZPA, Oglebay Park, W.V.

Conway, W. (1986). The practical difficulties and financial implications of endangered species breeding programs. *Intl. Zoo Yrbk.* 24/25:210–219.

Conway, W. G., Foose, T., and R. Wagner (1984). *Species Survival Plan of the American Association of Zoological Parks and Aquariums*. AAZPA, Wheeling, W.Va.

Cook, B. R. (1984). Interacting with the elements: Man and the biochemical cycles. *Environment* 26(7):38–40.

Cooke, C. W. (1939). Scenery of Florida interpreted by a geologist. *Geol. Bull. 17*. Fla. Geol. Survey, Tallahassee.

Correa, M. (1977). *Flora Patagónica*, Vol. 8, Parts 2,3,4,7. INTA Colección Científica, Buenos Aires.

Countryside Commission (1986). *Monitoring Landscape Change*. Countryside Commission, Cheltenham.

Cowan, I. (1965). Conservation and man's environment. *Nature* 208:1145–1151.

Craton, M. (1962). *A History of the Bahamas*. Collins, London.

Cronk, Q. C. B. (1986). The decline of the St. Helena ebony *Trochetiopsis melanoxylon*. *Biol. Conserv.* 35:159–172.

Crosby, A. (1972). *The Columbian Exchange, Biological and Cultural Consequences of 1492*. Greenwood Press, Westport, Conn.

Crosson, P. (1986). Agricultural development: Looking to future. In: *Sustainable development of the Biosphere*, ed. W. C. Clark and R. E. Munn. Cambridge University Press, Cambridge.

Crow, J. F., and M. Kimura (1970). *An Introduction*

to Population Genetics Theory. Harper & Row, New York.

Crowell, K. L. (1968). Rates of competitive exclusion by the Argentine ants in Bermuda. *Ecology* 49:551–5551.

Cruikshank, H. (1986). *Bartram in Florida, 1774.* Fla. Fed. Garden Clubs, Tampa.

Cruz, C. J. (1986). *Population Pressure and Migration: Implications for Upland Development.* Center for Policy and Development Studies, University of the Philippines at Los Banos, Laguna, Philippines.

Daniel, M. J., and G. R. Williams (1984). A survey of the distribution, seasonal activity and roost sites of the New Zealand bats. *N.Z.J. Ecol.* 7:9–25.

Darling, F. (1960). *Wildlife in an African Territory.* Oxford University Press, London.

Darlington, P. J. (1957). *Zoogeography: The Geographical Distribution of Animals.* Wiley, New York.

Darwin, C. R. (1845). *Journal of Researches into the Geology and Natural History of Various Countries Visited by H.M.S. Beagle, under the Command of Captain FitzRoy, R.N. from 1832 to 1836.* John Murray, London.

Darwin, F., ed. (1958). *The Autobiography of Charles Darwin and Selected Letters.* Dover, New York.

Dasmann, R. F. (1964). *African Game Ranching.* Pergamon Press, Oxford.

Dasmann, R. F. (1973). A rationale for preserving natural areas. *J. Soil Water Conserv.* 28(3):114–117.

Dasmann, R. F. (1976). Life-styles and nature conservation. *Oryx* 13(3):281–286.

Dasmann, R. F. (1983). The relationship between protected areas and indigenous peoples. In: *Proceedings of the World Congress on National Parks,* ed. J. A. McNeely and K. R. Miller. IUCN, Gland, Switzerland.

Davies, S., ed. (1987). *Tree of Life.* Buddhist Perception of Nature, Hong Kong.

Davis, M. B. (1986). Climatic instability, time lags, and community disequilibrium. In: *Community Ecology,* ed. J. Diamond and T. J. Case, pp. 269–284. Harper & Row, New York.

Davis, S. D., (1986). *Plants in Danger. What Do We Know?* IUCN, Gland, Switzerland.

Davos, C. A. (1977). A priority-trade off-scanning approach to evaluation in environmental management. *J. Environ. Mgmt.* 5:259–273.

De Angelis, D. L., J. C. Waterhouse, W. M. Post, and R. V. O'Neill (1985). Ecological modelling and disturbance evaluation. *Ecol. Modelling* 29:399–419.

De la Sota, E. (1977a). The problems of threatened and endangered plant species and plant com-

munities in Argentina. In: *Extinction Is Forever,* eds. G. Prance and T. Elias. Proceedings of Symposium held at N.Y. Botanical Garden, May 11–13, 1977.

De la Sota, E. (1977b). Pteridophyta. In: *Flora de la Provincia de Jujuy,* ed. A. Cabrera. Colección Científica INTA, Vol. 13, Part 2. INTA, Buenos Aires.

De Vos, A., R. H. Manville, and R. G. Van Gelder, (1956). Introduced mammals and their influence on native biota. *Zoologica* 41:163–194.

Deagan, K. (1978). Cultures in transition: Assimilation and fusion among the eastern Timucuan. In: *Tacachole,* ed. J. Milanich and S. Proctor. University Presses of Florida, Gainesville.

Deagan, K. (1985). Spanish-Indian interaction in sixteenth century Florida and Hispaniola. In: *Cultures in Contact,* ed. W. Fitzhugh, pp. 281–320. Smithsonian Institution Press, Washington, D.C.

Deagan, K. (1987). Initial encounters: Arawak responses to European contact at the En Bas Saline site, Haiti. In: *Columbus and His World. Proceedings of First San Salvador Conference,* pp. 341–359. San Salvador Island, Bahamas.

Delcourt, P., H. Delcourt, R. Brister, and L. Lackey (1980). Quaternary vegetation history of the Mississippi Embayment. *Q. Res. 13:*11–132.

Dempster, J. P., and M. L. Hall (1980). An attempt at re-establishing the swallowtail butterfly at Wicken Fen. *Ecol. Entomol.* 5:327–334.

Deutsch, E. (1986). A metaphysical grounding for nature reverence: East-west. *Environ. Ethics* 8(4):293–299.

Dewar, R. E. (1984). Extinctions in Madagascar. In: *Quaternary Extinctions,* ed. P. S. Martin and R. G. Klein, pp. 574–593. University of Arizona Press, Tucson.

Diamond, J. (1972). Biogeophic kinetics: Estimation of relaxation times for avifaunas of southwest Pacific Islands. *Proc. Natl. Acad. Sci. USA* 69:3199–3203.

Diamond, J. (1973). Distributional ecology of New Guinea birds. *Science* 179:759–769.

Diamond, J. (1984a). "Normal" extinctions of isolated populations. In: *Extinctions,* ed. M. H. Nitecki, pp. 191–246. University of Chicago Press, Chicago.

Diamond, J. (1984b). Historic extinctions: A Rosetta Stone for understanding prehistoric extinctions. In: *Quaternary Extinctions,* ed. P. S. Martin and R. G. Klein, pp. 824–862. University of Arizona Press, Tucson.

Diamond, J. M. (1985a). How many unknown species are yet to be discovered? *Nature* 315:538.

Diamond, J. (1985b). Salvaging single-sex populations. *Nature* 316:104.

Diamond, J. (1986a). Carnivore dominance and herbivore coexistence in Africa. *Nature* 320:112.

Diamond, J. (1986b). The design of a nature reserve system for Indonesian New Guinea. In: *Conservation Biology: The Science of Scarcity and Diversity*, ed. M. Soulé. Sinauer, Sunderland, Mass.

Diamond, J. M. (1987). Extant unless proven extinct, or extinct unless proven extant? *Conserv. Biol.* 1:77–79.

Diamond, J. M., K. D. Bishop, and S. van Balen (1987). Bird survival in an isolated Javan woodland: Island or mirror? *Conserv. Biol.* 1:132–142.

Diamond, J. M., and T. J. Case (1986a). Introductions, extinctions, exterminations, and invasions. In: *Community Ecology*, ed. J. M. Diamond and T. J. Case, pp. 65–79. Harper & Row, New York.

Diamond, J., and T. J. Case, eds. (1986b). *Community Ecology*. Harper & Row, New York.

Diamond, J. M., and R. M. May (1976). Island biogeography and the design of natural reserves. In: *Theoretical Ecology*, ed. R. M. May. Blackwell Scientific Publications, Oxford.

Dickenson, R. E. (1982). Effects of tropical deforestation on climate. *Studies in Third World Societies* 14:411–441.

Dobson, A., and R. May (1986). Disease and conservation. In: *Conservation Biology: The Science of Scarcity and Diversity*, ed. M. E. Soulé and B. A. Wilcox, pp. 345–365. Sinauer, Sunderland, Mass.

Doherty, J. G. (1982). Satellite breeding programmes. *AAZPA 1982 Ann. Conf. Proc.* 44–51.

Dolman, A. J., ed. (1980). *Global Planning and Resource Management*. Pergamon Press, Oxford.

Dominguez, F., and J. J. Bacallado (1984). Mamíferos. In: *Fauna (marina y terrestre) del Archipelago Canario*, ed. J. J. B. Aránega, pp. 333–338. Imprime MAE/Spain.

Dorst, J., and R. de Naurois (1966). Presence de l'oreillard (*Plecotus*) dans l'archipel du Copvert et considerations biogeographiques sur le peuplement de ces iles. *Mammalia* 30:292–301.

Dressler, R. L. (1982). Biology of Orchid bees (*Euglossini*). *Annu. Rev. Ecol. Syst.* 13:373–394.

East, R. (1988). *Antelopes: Global Survey and Regional Action Plans*. Part 1: East and Northeast Africa. IUCN, Gland, Switzerland.

Ebenhard, T. (In press.) Introduced birds and mammals and their ecological effects. *Swed. Wild.*

Eckhardt, R. C. (1972). Introduced plants and animals in the Galápagos Islands. *Bio-Science* 22:585–590.

Eckholm, E. P. (1975). The deterioration of mountain environments. *Science* 189:764–770.

Edwards, A. (1986). An agricultural land budget for the United Kingdom. Working Paper No. 2. Wye College, Kent.

Edwards, S. R. (1987). The Species Survival Commission on a new path. *Species (Newsletter of the IUCN Species Survival Commission)* 8:9–10.

Ehrenfeld, D. (1976). The conservation of nonresources. *Am. Scientist* 64:648–656.

Ehrenfeld, D. (1981). *The Arrogance of Humanism*. Oxford University Press, New York.

Ehrenfeld, D. (1986a). The lesson of the tower. *Hudson Rev.* 39(3):367–381.

Ehrenfeld, D. (1986b). Thirty million cheers for diversity. *New Scientist* 110:38–43.

Ehrenfeld, D. (1988). Why put a value on biodiversity? In: *BioDiversity*, ed. E. O. Wilson, pp 212–216. National Academy Press, Washington, D.C.

Ehrlich, P. R. (1967). Paying the piper. *New Scientist* 36:652–655.

Ehrlich, P. R. (1986). *The Machinery of Nature*. Simon & Schuster, New York.

Ehrlich, P. R., and A. H. Ehrlich (1968). *Population Bomb*. Amereon, Maltituck, New York.

Ehrlich, P. R., and A. H. Ehrlich (1981). *Extinction: The Causes and Consequences of the Disappearance of Species*. Random House, New York.

Eigen, M. (1971). Selforganization of matter and the evolution of biological macromolecules. *Naturwissenschaften* 58:465–523.

Eisenberg, J. F. (1980). The density and biomass of tropical mammals. In: *Conservation Biology*, ed. M. Soulé and B. A. Wilcox. Sinauer, Sunderland, Mass.

Eisenberg, J. F. (1981). *The Mammalian Radiations: An Analysis of Trends in Evolution, Adaptation, and Behavior*. University of Chicago Press, Chicago.

Eisenberg, J. F. (1986). Unpublished remarks. Conservation 2100: A Fairfield Osborn Symposium. New York Zoological Society and The Rockefeller University, New York.

Eisenberg, J. F., and L. D. Harris (1987). Agriculture, forestry, and wildlife resources . . . Perspectives from the Western Hemisphere. In: *Agroforestry: Realities, Possibilities and Potentials*, ed. H. L. Gholz. Martinus Nijhoff Publishers in cooperation with ICRAF, Dordrecht, The Netherlands.

Eisenbud, M. (1983). The human environment—Past, present and future. NRCP Lauriston S. Taylor Lecture No. 7.

Eisner, T., and J. Meinwald (1966). Defensive secretions of arthropods. *Science* 153:1341–1350.

Eisner, T., S. Nowicki, M. Goetz, and J. Meinwald (1980). Red cochineal dye (carminic acid): Its role in nature. *Science* 208:1039–1042.

Elliott, D., ed. (1986). *Dynamics of Extinction*. John Wiley, New York.

Eltringham, S. (1984). *Wildlife Resources and Economic Development*. John Wiley, New York.

Emerson, R. W. (1836). Nature. In: *Selected Writings of Ralph Waldo Emerson*, ed. W. H. Gilman (1965), pp. 186–223. New American Library, New York.

Endangered Species Act (1973). Public Law No. 93-205, codified at 16 U.S.C. 1531 et seq.

Engel, J. R. (1983). *Sacred Sands*. Wesleyan University Press, Middletown, Conn.

Engelberg, J., and L. L. Boyarsky (1979). The noncybernetic nature of ecosystems. *Am. Naturalist* 114:317–324.

Erickson, R. (1980). Propagation studies of endangered wildlife at the Patuxent Center. *Intl. Zoo Yrbk.* 20:40–47.

Erwin, T. L. (1988). How many insects in tropical forest canopies? In: *BioDiversity*, ed. E. O. Wilson. National Academy Press, Washington, D.C.

Eudey, A. (1987). Action plan for Asian primate conservation. IUCN/SSC Primate Specialist Group, Gland, Switzerland.

European Economic Community (1985). *Perspectives for the Common Agricultural Policy*. COM(85)333, Luxembourg.

Everhard, W. C. (1972). *The National Park Service*. Praeger, London.

Falconer, D. S. (1981). *Introduction to Quantitative Genetics*, 2nd ed. Longman, London.

FAO (1981). *Agriculture: Toward 2000*. FAO, Rome.

FAO and UNEP (1982). *Tropical Forest Resources*. Food and Agriculture Organization of the United Nations, Rome, Italy, and United Nations Environment Programme, Nairobi, Kenya.

Fearnside, P. M. (1986). *Human Carrying Capacity of the Tropical Rain Forest*. Columbia University Press, New York.

Feiler, A. (1984). Über die Säugetiere der Insel Sao Tomé. *Zool. Abh. Mus. Tierk. Dresden* 40:75–78.

Felbeck, H. (1981). Chemoautotrophic potential of the hydrothermal vent tube worm, *Riftia pachyptila* Jones (Vestimentifera). *Science* 213:336–338.

Fernald, E. (1981). *Atlas of Florida*. Fla. St. Univ. Found., Tallahassee.

Fisher, J. (1951). *Watching Birds*. Penguin Books, Harmondsworth.

Fisher, J., N. Simon, and J. Vincent (1969). *The Red Book: Wildlife in Danger*. Collins, London.

Fitzgerald, J., and G. M. Meese (1986). Saving endangered species. Defenders of Wildlife, Washington, D.C.

Fitzgerald, S. (1986). World Bank pledges to protect wildlands. *Bioscience* 36(1):712–715.

Flesness, N. R. (1987). Captive status and genetic considerations. In: *Primates. The Road to Self-Sustaining Populations*, ed. K. Benirschke, pp. 845–856. Springer, New York.

Flier, J., M. W. Edwards, J. W. Daly, and C. W. Myers (1980). Widespread occurrence in frogs and toads of skin compounds interacting with the ouabain site of Na^+, K^+-ATPase. *Science* 208:503–505.

Flux, J. E. C., and P. J. Fullager (1983). World distribution of the rabbit (*Oryctolagus cuniculus*). *Acta Zool. Fenn.* 174:75–77.

Foose, T. J. (1983). The relevance of captive populations to the conservation of biotic diversity. In: *Genetics and Conservation*, ed. C. M. Schonewald-Cox, S. M. Chambers, F. McBryde, and L. Thomas, pp. 374–401. National Park Service, Washington, D.C.

Foose, T. J., R. Lande, N. R. Flesness, G. Rabb, and B. Read (1986). Propagation plans. *Zoo Biol.* 5(2):139–146.

Forbes, S. A. (1887). The lake as microcosm. *Bull. Peoria Sci. Assoc.*, pp. 77–87. Reprinted 1925 in *Ill. Nat. Hist. Surv. Bull.* 15:537–550.

Ford, J. (1971). *The Role of Trypanosomiasis in African Ecology. A Study of the Tsetse Fly Problem*. Clarendon Press, Oxford.

Forman, R. T., and M. Godron (1986). *Landscape Ecology*. John Wiley, New York.

Forsyth, A. (1982). Rain forest requiem. *Equinox* Nov./Dec.:64–67.

Fosberg, F. R. (1983). The human factor in the biogeography of oceanic islands. *C.R. Soc. Biogéogr.* 59(2):147–190.

Fowles, J. (1979). Seeing nature whole. *Harper's Mag.* November:49–68.

Frankel, O. H. (1982). The role of conservation genetics in the conservation of rare species. In: *Species at Risk. Research in Australia*, pp. 159–162. Springer, Berlin.

Frankel, O. H., and M. E. Soulé (1981). *Conservation and Evolution*. Cambridge University Press, New York.

Frankham, R., H. Hemmer, O. A. Ryder, E. G. Cothran, M. E. Soulé, M. Snyder, and N. D. Murray (1986). Selection in captive populations. *Zoo Biol.* 5(2):127–138.

Franklin, I. R. (1980). Evolutionary change in small populations. In: *Conservation Biology: An Evolutionary-Ecological Perspective*, ed. M. Soulé and B. Wilcox. Sinauer, Sunderland, Mass.

Freiberg, M. (1977). Reptilia: Testudines o Chelonia y Reptilia: Crocodilia. In: *Fauna de Agua dulce de la R. Argentina,* Vol. 42 (1,2). FECYC, Buenos Aires.

Fullager, P. J. (1978). *Report on the Rabbits on Phillip Island, Norfolk Island.* Division of Wildlife Research, CSIRO, Lyneham, A.C.T., 2602.

Fullager, P. J. (1985). The woodhens of Lord Howe Island. *Avicultural Mag.* 91(1,2):15–30.

Fullager, P. J., and H. J. de S. Disney (1974). The birds of Lord Howe Island: a report on the rare and endangered species. XVI World Conference of ICBP, Canberra, 1974.

Fuller, P. J., and A. A. Burbidge (1981). *The Birds of Pelsart Island, Western Australia.* Dept. Fisheries and Wildlife Report No. 44. Western Australian Wildlife Research Centre, Wanneroo, W.A.

Fung, V. (1984). Waste is welcome here. KCTS-Seattle (television), "The MacNeil/Lehrer Newshour," 12/19/85.

Furer-Haimendorf, Christoph von (1964). *The Sherpas of Nepal.* John Murray, London.

Gade, D. W. (1985). Man and nature on Rodrigues: Tragedy of an island common. *Environ. Conserv.* 12:207–216.

Garcia, Josi Rafael (1984). Waterfalls, hydro-power and water for industry: Contributions from Canaima National Park, Venezuela. In: *National Parks, Conservation, and Development: The Role of Protected Areas in Sustaining Society,* ed. J. A. McNeely and K. R. Miller, pp. 588–591. Smithsonian Institution Press, Washington, D.C.

Gardner, H. (1983). *Frames of the Mind: The Theory of Multiple Intelligences.* Heinemann, London.

Garratt, K. (1983). The relationship between adjacent lands and protected areas: Issues of concern for the protected area manager. In: *Proceedings of the World Congress on National Parks,* ed. J. McNeely and K. Miller. IUCN, Gland, Switzerland.

Geist, V. (1985). A brief in opposition to game ranching. *Wildl. Soc. Bull.* 13:594–598.

Gentry, A. H. (1986). Endemism in tropical versus temperate plant communities. In: *Conservation Biology: Science of Scarcity and Diversity,* ed. M. E. Soulé, pp. 153–181. Sinauer, Sunderland, Mass.

Gentry, A. H. (In press). Community diversity and floristic composition on environmental and geographical gradients. *Ann. Missouri Bot. Gard.*

Gerbi, A. (1975). *Nature in the New World from Christopher Columbus to Gonalazalo Fernandez do Oviedo,* transl. J. Moyle. University of Pittsburgh Press, Pittsburgh, Pa.

Gibson, R. W., and J. A. Pickett (1983). Wild potato repels aphids by release of aphid alarm pheromone. *Nature* 302:608–609.

Gibson-Hill, C. A. (1947). A note on the mammals of Christmas Island. *Bull. Raffles Mus.* 18:166–167.

Gilbert, L. E. (1980). Food web organization and the conservation of neotropical diversity. In: *Conservation Biology: An Evolutionary-Ecological Perspective,* ed. M. E. Soulé and B. A. Wilcox, pp. 11–33. Sinauer, Sunderland, Mass.

Gilbert, L. E., and P. H. Raven, eds. (1975). *Coevolution of Animals and Plants.* University of Texas Press, Austin.

Gilpin, M. E. (1987). Spatial structure and population vulnerability. In: *Viable Populations for Conservation.* ed. M. E. Soulé, pp. 125–139. Cambridge University Press, Cambridge.

Gilpin, M. E., and M. E. Soulé (1986). Minimum viable populations: Processes of species extinction. In: *Conservation Biology: The Science of Scarcity and Diversity,* ed. M. E. Soulé, pp. 19–34. Sinauer, Sunderland, Mass.

Gimingham, C. H., and J. T. De Smidt (1983). Heaths as natural and seminatural vegetation. In: *Man's Impact upon Vegetation,* ed. W. Holzner, M. J. A. Werger, and I. Ikusuria. Junk, The Hague.

Gladwin, T. N. (1987). Environment, development, and multinational enterprise. In: *Multinational Corporations, Environment, and the Third World: Business Matters,* ed. C. Pearson. Duke University Press, Durham, N.C.

Global 2000 (1980). *The Global 2000 Report to the President: Entering the Twenty-first Century.* Government Printing Office, Washington, D.C.

Goeller, H. E., and A. Zucker (1984). Infinite resources: The ultimate strategy. *Science* 223:456–462.

Goldsmith, E. (1987). Open letter to Mr. Conable, President of the World Bank. *Ecologist* 17(2):58–61.

Gomez-Pompa, A., C. Vazquez-Yanes, and S. Guevera (1972). The tropical rain forest: A nonrenewable resource. *Science* 177:762–765.

Goodman, D. (1975). The theory of diversity-stability relationships in ecology. *Q. Rev. Biol.* 50:237–266.

Goodman, D. (1987). The demography of chance extinction. In: *Viable Populations for Conservation,* ed. M. Soulé. Sinauer, Sunderland, Mass.

Goodpaster, K. (1978). On being morally consider-able. *J. Philos.* 75:308.

Goodwin, M. H., and G. Cambers (1983). *Artificial Reefs: A Handbook for the Eastern Caribbean.* Caribbean Conservation Association, Barbados.

Gould, S. J. (1980). Chance riches. *Nat. Hist.* 89(11):36–44.

Gould, S. J. (1983). Extemporaneous comments on evolutionary hope and realities. In: *Darwin's Legacy, Nobel Conference XVIII*, ed. C. L. Hamrum, pp. 95–103. Harper & Row, San Francisco.

Gould, S. J., and D. S. Woodruff (1986). Evolution and systematics of Cerion (Mollusca: Pulmonata) on New Providence Island: A radical revision. *Bull. Am. Mus. Nat. Hist.* 182:389–490.

Grant, V. (1981). *Plant Speciation*, 2nd ed., p. 563. Columbia University Press, New York.

Grassle, J. F. (1985). Hydrothermal vent animals: Distribution and biology. *Science* 229:713–717.

Green, B. H. (1972). The relevance of seral eutrophication and plant competition to the management of successful communities. *Biol. Conserv.* 4:378–384.

Green, B. H. (1979). *Wildlife Introductions to Great Britain: Some Policy Implications for Nature Conservation.* Nature Conservancy Council, London.

Green, B. H. (1981). *Countryside Conservation: The Protection and Management of Amenity Ecosystems*, 2nd ed. (1985). George Allen & Unwin, London.

Green, B. H. (1986). Controlling ecosystems for amenity. In: *Ecology and Design in Landscape*, ed. A. D. Bradshaw, E. Thorp, and D. A. Goode. 24th Symposium of the British Ecological Society. Blackwell Scientific Publications, Oxford.

Green, B. H. and I. Marshall (1987). An assessment of the role of golf courses in Kent, England in protecting wildlife and landscapes. *Landscape and Urban Planning* 14:143–154.

Green, B. H., and N. D. Townsend (1985). Tree colonization and the management of open heathland at Hothfield Common, Kent. *Trans. Kent Field Club.*

Greenway, J. C. (1958). *Extinct and Vanishing Birds of the World.* American Committee for International Wild Life Protection [Special Bulletin 13], New York.

Greeson, P. E., J. R. Clark, and J. E. Clark, eds. (1978). *Wetland Functions and Values: The State of Our Understanding.* American Water Resources Association, Minneapolis, Minn.

Gregg, W., and B. McGean (1985). Biosphere re-serves: Their history and their promise. *Orion* 4:40–51.

Grieg, J. (1979). Principles of genetic conservation in relation to wildlife management in South Africa. *S. Afr. J. Wildl. Res.* 9:57–78.

Grime, J. P. (1979). *Plant Strategies and Vegetation Processes.* John Wiley, Chichester.

Gulland, J. A. (1987). Seals and fisheries: A case for predator control? *Trends Ecol. Evol.* 2:102–104.

Gyllensten, U., D. Wharton, and A. Wilson (1985). Maternal inheritance of MtDNA during backcrosses of two species of mice. *J. Hered.* 76:321–324.

Hadley, M., and J-P. Lanly (1983). Tropical forest ecosystems: Identifying differences, seeing similarities. *Nature Resources* 19:2–19.

Haines, A. L. (1977). *The Yellowstone Story—A History of Our First National Park*, Vol. 1. Yellowstone Library and Museum Association and Colorado Associated Univ. Press.

Hales, D. (1983). The World Heritage Convention: Status and directions. In: *Proceedings of the World Congress on National Parks*, ed. J. McNeely and K. Miller. IUCN, Gland, Switzerland.

Halfon, E. (1979). *Theoretical Systems Ecology.* Academic Press, New York.

Hamann, O. (1981). Plant communities of the Galápagos Islands. *Dansk Botanisk Arkiv* 34(2):1–163.

Hamilton, J., and M. Coe (1982). Feeding, digestion and assimilation of a population of giant tortoises (*Geochelone gigantea*) on Aldabra Atoll. *J. Arid Environ.* 5:127–144.

Han. D. and Xu C. (1985). Pleistocene mammalian faunas of China. In: *Paleoanthropology and Palaeolithic Archaelogy in the People's Republic of China*, ed. R. Wu and J. W. Olsen. Academic Press, Orlando, Fla.

Hanks, J., W. D. Densham, G. L. Smutts, J. F. Jooste, S. C. J. Joubert, P. Le Roux, and P. Milstein (1981). Management of locally abundant mammals in the South African Experience. In: *Problems in Management of Locally Abundant Wild Mammals.* ed. P. A. Jewell and S. Holt. Academic Press, New York.

Hannah, H. C., and W. C. McGrew (In press). Rehabilitation of captive chimpanzees. In: *Primate Responses to Environmental Change*, ed. H. O. Box, Chapman and Hall, London.

Hardin, G. (1968). The tragedy of the commons. *Science* 162:1243–1248.

Hardoy, E. J., and E. D. Satherthwaite (1985). Third world cities and environment of poverty. In: *The Global Possible*, ed. R. Repetto. Yale University Press, New Haven, Conn.

Hargrove, E. C. (1979). The historical foundations of American environmental ethics. *Environ. Ethics* 1:209–240.

Hargrove, E. C., ed. (1986). *Religion and Environmental Crisis.* University of Georgia Press, Athens.

Hargrove, E. C. (1987). Foundations of wildlife protection attitudes. *Inquiry* 30(1):3–31.

Harlan, J. R. (1975). Our vanishing genetic resources. *Science* 188:618–621.

Harris, L. (1983). An island archipelago model for maintaining biotic diversity in old-growth forests. In: *New Forests for a Changing World. Proceedings of the Society for the American Forest, National Convention,* pp. 378–382.

Harris, L. (1984). *The Fragmented Forest, Island Biogeography Theory and the Preservation of Biotic Diversity.* University of Chicago Press, Chicago.

Harris, L. (1985). Conservation corridors, a highway system for life. ENFO 85-5. Florida Conservation Fund, Winter Park, Fla.

Harris, T. (1986). The selenium question. *Defenders* 61(2):10.

Harrison, P., and J. Rowley (1984). *Human Numbers, Human Needs.* International Planned Parenthood Federation, Washington, D.C.

Hassell, M. P., and R. M. May (1973). Stability in insect host-parasite models. *J. Animal Ecol.* 42:693–726.

Hauser, P. M., and R. W. Gardner (1970). Urban future: Trends and prospects. (cited in Brown, L. R. [1981]. *Sci. Am.* 213:995–1002.)

Haynes, C. V., Jr., P. J. Mehringer, Jr., D. L. Johnson, H. Haas, A. B. Muller, E. S. E. Zaghloul, A. Swedan, and T. A. Wyerman (1987). Evidence for the first Nuclear-age recharge of shallow groundwater, Arba'in Desert, Egypt. *Nat. Geogr. Res.* 3(4):431–438.

Hedrick, P. W. (1987). Genetic bottlenecks. *Science* 237:963.

Hedrick, P. W., P. R. Brussard, F. W. Allendorf, J. A. Beardmore, and S. Orzack (1986). Protein variation, fitness and captive propagation. *Zoo Biol.* 5(2):91–99.

Hedrick, P. W., M. E. Ginevan, and E. P. Ewing (1976). Genetic polymorphism in heterogenous environments. *Annu. Rev. Ecol. Syst.* 7:1–32.

Hemmings, E. T., and C. V. Haynes (1969). The Escapule mammoth and associated projectile points, San Pedro Valley, Arizona. *J. Arizona Acad. Sci.* 5:184–188.

Henderson-Sellers, A., and V. Gornitz (1984). Possible climatic impacts of land cover transformations, with particular emphasis on tropical deforestation. *Climatic Change* 6:231–257.

Hermes, N., ed. (1986). *A Revised Annotated Checklist of Vascular Plants and Vertebrate Animals of Norfolk Island,* revised ed. Flora and Fauna Society of Norfolk Island.

Hermes, N., D. Greenwood, and M. Hinchey (1986). Eradication of rabbits from Philip Island. *Aust. Ranger Bull.* 4(1):34–37.

Hattena, P. H., and G. N. Syer, eds. (1971). *Decade of Decision.* Conservation Society, London.

Hill, J. E. (1958). Some observations on the fauna of the Maldive Islands. II. Mammals. *J. Bombay Nat. Hist. Soc.* 55:3–10.

Hodgson, J. G. (1986). Commonness and rarity in plants with special reference to the Sheffield flora. Part I. The identity, distribution and habitat characteristics of the common and rare species. Part III. Taxanomic and evolutionary aspects. *Biol. Conserv.* 36:199–252, 275–296.

Hoffman, P. (1980). *The Spanish Crown and the Defense of the Caribbean. 1535–1585.* Louisiana State University Press, Baton Rouge.

Holden, C. (1987). World Bank launches new environment policy. *Science* 236:769.

Holdgate, M. W., M. Kassas, and G. F. White, eds. (1982). *The World Environment 1972–1982.* UNEP/Tycolly International Publishing, Dublin.

Holland, R. F. (1980). *Against Empiricism on Education Epistemology and Value.* Basil Blackwell, Oxford.

Holling, C. S. (1973). Resilience and stability of ecological systems. *Annu. Rev. Ecol. Syst.* 4:1–23.

Honegger, R. E. (1981). List of amphibians and reptiles either known or thought to have become extinct since 1600. *Biol. Conserv.* 19:141–158.

Hough, R. (1975). Islands beyond Cape Horn. *Geogr. Mag.* 47:561–566.

Houseal, B., C. MacFarland, G. Archibold, and A. Chiari (1985). Indigenous cultures and protected areas in Central America. *Cultural Survival* March:10–19.

Houston, D. B. (1982). *The Northern Yellowstone Elk. Ecology and Management.* Macmillan, New York.

Howe, H. F. (1982). Fruit production and animal activity in two tropical trees. In: *The Ecology of a Tropical Forest,* ed. E. G. Leigh, A. S. Rand, and D. M. Windsor, pp. 189–199. Smithsonian Institution Press, Washington, D.C.

Hrabovszky, P. J. (1985). Agriculture: The land base. In: *The Global Possible,* ed. R. Repetto. Yale University Press, New Haven, Conn.

Hubbell, S. P. (1979). Tree dispersion, abundance and diversity in a tropical deciduous forest. *Science* 203:1299–1309.

Hubbell, S. P., and R. B. Foster (1986). Commonness and rarity in a neotropical forest: Implications for tropical tree conservation. In: *Conservation Biology. The Science of Scarcity and Diversity*, ed. M. E. Soulé, pp. 205–231. Sinauer, Sunderland, Mass.

Hubbs, C. L., and R. R. Miller (1941). Studies of the order Cyprinodontes, XVII. Genera and species of the Colorado River system. *Occ. Pap. Mus. Zool. Univ. Mich.* 433:1–9.

Humphrey, S. R. (1985). How species become vulnerable to extinction, and how we can meet the crises. In: *Animal Extinctions*, ed. R. Hoage. Smithsonian Institution Press, Washington, D.C.

Hunziker, A. (1984). Los generos de fanerogamas de Argentina. *Bol. Soc. Arg. Bot.* 23(1–4):1–384.

Hutchinson, G. E. (1948). Circular causal systems in ecology. *Ann. NY Acad. Sci.* 50:221–246.

Huxley, J. (1961). *The Conservation of Wildlife and Natural Habitats in Central and East Africa.* United Nations Scientific and Cultural Organization, Paris.

IIED (1987). *Annual Report.* International Institute for Environment and Development, Washington, D.C.

Iltis, H. H. (1983a). From teosinte to maize: Catastrophic sexual transmutation. *Science* 22:886–894.

Iltis, H. H. (1983b). What will be their fate? Tropical forests. *Environment* 25(10):55–60.

Iltis, H. H., J. F. Doebley, R. Guzman, and B. Pazy (1979). *Zea diploperennis* (Gramineae): A new teosinte from Mexico. *Science* 203:186–188.

Imboden, C. (1987). Round Island rebounds after pests removed. *World Birdwatch* [Newsletter of the International Council for Bird Preservation]. 9(3).

INDEC (1984). *Annuario 1982/1983.* INDEC, Buenos Aires.

Ingham, R. E., and J. K. Detling (1984). Plant-herbivore interactions in a North American mixed-grass prairie. III. Soil nematode populations and root biomass on *Cynomys ludovicianus* colonies and adjacent uncolonized areas. *Oecologia (Berl.)* 63:307–313.

Ingham, R. E., J. A. Trofymow, E. R. Ingham, and D. C. Coleman (1985). Interactions of bacteria, fungi, and their nematode grazers: Effects on nutrient cycling and plant growth. *Ecol. Monogr.* 55:119–140.

IUCN (1974). *Proceedings of the World Congress on National Parks,* IUCN, Morges, Switzerland.

IUCN (1978). *Categories, Objectives and Criteria for Protected Areas.* IUCN, Morges, Switzerland.

IUCN (1980). *The World Conservation Strategy.* IUCN, Gland, Switzerland.

IUCN (1982). *World Conservation Strategy.* Taylor and Francis, London.

IUCN (1983). *Proceedings of the World Congress on National Parks,* IUCN, Gland, Switzerland.

IUCN (1984a). Categories, objectives and criteria for protected areas (Rev.). In: *National Parks, Conservation, and Development: The Role of Protected Areas in Sustaining Society,* ed. J. A. McNeely and K. R. Miller, pp. 47–53. Smithsonian Institution Press, Washington, D.C.

IUCN (1984b). *The National Conservation Strategies.* IUCN, Gland, Switzerland.

IUCN (1985). *United Nations List of National Parks and Protected Areas.* IUCN, Gland, Switzerland.

IUCN and UNEP (1980). *World Conservation Strategy.* IUCN, Morges, Switzerland.

Jablonski, D. (1986). Background and mass extinctions: The alternation of macroevolutionary regimes. *Science* 231:129–133.

Jablonski, D., and D. M. Raup, eds. (1986). *Patterns and Processes in the History of Life.* Springer-Verlag, New York.

Janzen, D. H. (1975). *Ecology of Plants in the Tropics.* Arnold Publishers, London.

Janzen, D. H. (1979). How to be a fig. *Ann. Rev. Ecol. Syst.* 10:13–51.

Janzen, D. H., ed. (1983). *Costa Rican Natural History.* University of Chicago Press, Chicago.

Janzen, D. (1986). The future of tropical ecology. *Annu. Rev. Ecol. Syst.* 17:305–324.

Janzen, D. H. (1986). The eternal external threat. In: *Conservation Biology. The Science of Scarcity and Diversity.* ed. M. E. Soulé, pp. 286–303. Sinauer, Sunderland, Mass.

Jarman, P. J. (1974). The social organization of antelope in relation to their ecology. *Behavior* 48:215–266.

Jefferies, D. J., P. Wayre, R. M. Jessop, and A. J. Mitchell-Jones (1986). Reinforcing the native otter *Lutra lutra* population in East Anglia: An analysis of the behaviour and range development of the first release group. *Mammal Rev.* 16(2):65–69.

Johns, A. D. (1985). Selective logging and wildlife conservation in tropical rain-forest: Problems and recommendations. *Biol. Conserv.* 31:355–375.

Jones, J. M. (1884). The mammals of Bermuda. *Bull. U.S. Nat. Mus.* 25:145–161.

Jones, R. D., and G. V. Byrd (1979). Interrelations between seabirds and introduced animals. In: *Conservation of Marine Birds of Northern North America.* ed. J. C. Bartonek and D. N. Nettleship, pp. 221–226. U.S.D.I. Fish and

Wildlife Service, Wildlife Research Report 11, Washington, D.C.

Joos-Vanderwalle, M. E., and N. Owen-Smith (In preparation). Migratory ungulates in the Savuti region of Chobe National Park, Botswana.

Jordan, W. R., J. P. Abert, and M. E. Gilpin (In press). *Restoration Ecology: Progress Toward a Science and Art of Ecological Healing.* Cambridge University Press, Cambridge.

Jouventin, P., and J-P. Roux (1983). Projet de réhabilitation écologique de l'île Amsterdam. Unpub. T.A.A.F. report, Montpellier.

Jung, C. G. (1984). *Arquetipos e Inconsciente Colectivo.* Paidos, Barcelona.

Jungius, H., and A. Loudon (1985). *Recommendations for the Re-introduction of the Père David's Deer to China.* IUCN and WWF, Gland, Switzerland.

Karr, J. R. (1982). Population variability and extinction in the avifauna of a tropical land bridge island. *Ecology* 63:1975–1978.

Kayanja, F., and I. Douglas-Hamilton (1984). The impact of the unexpected on the Uganda National Parks. In: *National Parks, Conservation, and Development: The Role of Protected Areas in Sustaining Society,* ed. J. A. McNeely and K. R. Miller, pp. 80–86. Smithsonian Institution Press, Washington, D.C.

Kear, J., and A. J. Berger (1980). *The Hawaiian Goose: An Experiment in Conservation.* T. and D. Poyser, Calton.

Kepler, C. B. (1978). Captive propagation of whooping cranes—a behavioral approach. In: *Endangered Birds: Management Techniques for Preserving Threatened Species.* pp. 231–241. Univ. Wisconsin Press, Madison.

Kepler, C. B., and J. M. Scott (1985). Conservation of island ecosystems. In: *Conservation of Island Birds,* ed. P. J. Moors, pp. 255–271. ICBP Tech. Publ. 3., Gland, Switzerland.

King, W. B. (1973). Conservation status of birds of central Pacific islands. *Wilson Bull.* 85:89–103.

King, W. B. (1981). *Endangered Birds of the World. The ICBP Bird Red Data Book.* Smithsonian Institution Press, Washington, D.C.

King, W. B. (1985). Island birds: Will the future repeat the past? In: *Conservation of Island Birds,* ed. P. J. Moors, pp. 3–15. ICBP Tech. Publ. 3, Gland, Switzerland.

Kirkpatrick, R. D. (1966). Mammals of Johnston Atoll. *J. Mammal* 47:728–729.

Kleiman, D. G. (1980). The sociobiology of captive propagation. In: *Conservation Biology: An Evolutionary-Ecological Perspective,* ed. M. E. Soulé and B. A. Wilcox, pp. 243–261. Sinauer, Sunderland, Mass.

Kleiman, D. G., B. B. Beck, J. M. Dietz, L. A. Dietz, J. D. Ballou, and A. F. Coimbra-Filho (1986). Conservation program for the golden lion tamarin: Captive research and management, ecological studies, educational strategies, and reintroduction. In: *Primates: The Road to Self-Sustaining Populations,* ed. K. Benirschke, pp. 959–979. Proceedings in Life Sciences, Springer-Verlag, New York.

Knoke, D., and J. H. Kuklinski (1982). *Network Analysis.* Sage Paper series on quantitative application in the social sciences 028. Sage, Beverly Hills, Calif.

Knoll, A. H. (1984). Patterns of extinction in the fossil record of vascular plants. In: *Extinctions,* ed. M. H. Nitecki, pp. 21–68. University of Chicago Press, Chicago.

Knoop, W. T., and B. H. Walker (1985). Interactions of woody and herbaceous vegetation in a southern African savanna. *J. Ecol.* 73:235–253.

Koch, A., and W. Peden, eds. (1944). *The Life and Selected Writings of Thomas Jefferson.* Random House, New York.

Koehn, R. K. (1969). Esterase heterogeneity: Dynamics of a polymorphism. *Science* 163:943–944.

Koestler, A. (1967). *The Ghost in the Machine.* Macmillan, New York.

Kohl, L. (1982). Père David's deer saved from extinction. *Nat. Geogr.* 161:478–485.

Kohlbert, L. (1981). *The Philosophy of Moral Development Moral Stages and the Idea of Justice.* Harper & Row, New York.

Kolata, G. (1987). Asking impossible questions and getting impossible answers. *Science* 234:545–546.

Krasner, S. D. (1985). *Structural Conflict.* University of California Press, Berkeley.

Krasner, S. D. (1988). Japanese-American relations: Prospects for stability. In: *Japan in the World Environment,* ed. D. Okimoto and T. Inoguchi. Stanford University Press, Stanford, Calif.

Krieber, M., and M. R. Rose (1986). Molecular aspects of the species barrier. *Annu. Rev. Ecol. Syst.* 17:465–485.

Kuenzler, E. J. (1961a). Phosphorus budget of a mussel population. *Limnol. Oceanogr.* 6:400–415.

Kuenzler, E. J. (1961b). Structure and energy flow of a mussel population in a Georgia salt marsh. *Limnol. Oceanogr.* 6:191–204.

Kunkel, G. (1968). Robinson Crusoe's island. *Pacific Discov.* 21:1–8.

Kuschel, G. (1971). Coleoptera: Curculionidae. In: *Entomology of the Auklands and Other Is-*

lands South of New Zealand, ed. J. L. Gressitt, pp. 225–259.

Kushlan, J. (1987). External threats and internal management: The hydrologic regulation of the Everglades, Florida, USA. *Environ. Mgmt.* 11:109–119.

Laca, E., and M. A. Demment (In review). A mechanistic model of a grazing ruminant: Harvesting limitations to food intake. *Agric. Sys.*

Lacy, R. C. (1987). Loss of genetic diversity from managed populations: Interacting effects of drift, mutation, immigration, selection, and population subdivision. *Conserv. Biol.* 1:143–158.

Ladd, W. N., and M. L. Riedman (1987). The southern sea otter. In: *Audubon Wildlife Report 1987,* pp. 457–477. National Audubon Society, New York.

Lande, R., and G. F. Barrowclough (1987). Effective population size, genetic variation, and their use in population management. In: *Viable Populations for Conservation,* ed. M. E. Soulé, pp. 87–123. Cambridge University Press, Cambridge.

Lando, B. (1985). Famine in Mali, 1975-1985-1995? "60 Minutes," Columbia Broadcasting System, 1/27/85.

Larson, L. (1980). *Aboriginal Subsistence Technology on the Southeastern Coastal Plain During the Late Prehistoric Period.* University Presses of Florida, Gainesville.

Lawren, B. (1987). Swine's way. *Omni* 9:18.

Laws, R. M. (1969). The Tsavo research project. *J. Reprod. Fertil.* Suppl. 6:495–531.

Laws, R. M. (1970). Elephants as agents of landscape change in East Africa. *Oikos* 21:1–15.

Laws, R. M. (1985). Animal conservation in the Antarctic. *Symp. Zool. Soc. Lond.* 54:3–23.

Leathwick, J. R., J. R. Hay, and A. E. Fitzgerald (1983). The influence of browsing by introduced mammals on the decline of North Island kokako. *N.Z. J. Ecol.* 6:55–70.

Ledig, F. T. (1986). Heterozygosity, heterosis, and fitness in outbreeding plants. In: *Conservation Biology. The Science of Scarcity and Diversity,* ed. M. E. Soulé, pp. 77–104. Sinauer, Sunderland, Mass.

Ledig, F. T., R. P. Guries, and B. A. Boenfield (1983). The relation of growth to heterozygosity in pitch pine. *Evolution* 37:1227–1238.

Leedy, D. (1975). *Highway-Wildlife Relationships. Vol. 1, A State-of-the-Art-Report.* Federal Highway Administration, Office of Research and Development, Report No. FHWA-RD-76-4, Washington, D.C.

Leedy, D., and L. Adams (1982). *Wildlife Considerations in Planning and Managing Highway Corridors.* U.S. Dept. of Transportation, Federal Highway Administration, Report No. FHWA-TS-82-212, Washington, D.C.

Leigh, E. G., Jr. (1981). The average lifetime of a population in a varying environment. *J. Theoret. Biol.* 90:213–239.

Leopold, A. (1923). Some fundamentals in conservation in the Southwest. *Environ. Ethics* (1979) 1:131–141.

Leopold, A. (1949). *Sand County Almanac.* Oxford University Press, New York.

Leopold, A. (1959). *Wildlife of Mexico, the Game Birds and Mammals.* University of California Press, Berkeley.

Leopold, A. (1966). *A Sand County Almanac—With Other Essays on Conservation from Round River.* Oxford University Press, New York.

Leslie, J. F., and R. C. Vrijenhoek (1977). Genetic analysis of natural populations of *Poeciliopsis monacha:* Allozyme inheritance and pattern of mating. *J. Hered.* 68:301–306.

Lever, C. (1985). *Naturalized Mammals of the World.* Longmans, London.

Lewin, R. (1984). Fragile forests implied by Pleistocene pollen. *Science* 226:36–37.

Lewin, R. (1986). In ecology, change brings stability. *Science* 243:1071–1073.

Lewis, D. M., and G. Kaweche (1985). The Luangwa Valley of Zambia: Preserving its future by integrated management. *Ambio* 14:362–365.

Lewis, J. C. (1986). The whooping crane. In: *Audubon Wildlife Report 1986,* pp. 659–676. National Audubon Society, New York.

Lewontin, R. C. (1974). *The Genetic Basis of Evolutionary Change.* Columbia University Press, New York.

Lloyd, A. T. (1987). Cats from history and history from cats. *Endeavour New Ser.* 11:112–115.

Lockley, R. M. (1964). *The Private Life of the Rabbit.* Andre Deutsch, London.

Long, J. L. (1981). *Introduced Birds of the World.* David and Charles, London.

Love, J. A. (1983). *The Return of the Sea Eagle.* Cambridge University Press, Cambridge, Eng.

Lovejoy, T. E. (1986). Species leave the ark one by one. In: *The Preservation of Species,* ed. B. G. Norton, pp. 13–27. Princeton University, Princeton, N.J.

Lovejoy, T. E., R. O. Bierregaard, A. B. Rylands, J. R. Malcolm, C. E. Quintela, L. H. Harper, K. S. Brown, Jr., A. H. Powell, G. V. N. Powell, H. O. R. Schubart, and M. B. Hays (1986). Edge and other effects of isolation on Amazon forest fragments. In: *Conservation Biology: The Science of Scarcity and Diversity,* ed. M. Soulé. Sinauer, Sunderland, Mass.

Lovejoy, T. E., J. M. Rankin, R. O. Bierregaard, K. S. Brown, L. H. Emmons, and M. E. Van der

Voort (1984). Ecosystem decay of Amazona forest fragments. In: *Extinctions*, ed. M. H. Nitecki, pp. 295–325. University of Chicago Press, Chicago.

Lowe, P., G. Cox, M. MacEwen, T. O'Riordan, and M. Winter (1986). *Countryside Conflicts*. Gower/Maurice Temple Smith, Aldershot.

Lubin, Y. D. (1984). Changes in the native fauna of the Galápagos Islands following invasion by the little red fire ant, *Wasmannia auropunctata. Biol J. Linn. Soc.* 21:229–242.

Lucero, M. M. (1983). *Lista y Distribución de Aves y Mamíferos de la Provincia de Tucumán*. Fundación Miguell Lillo Miscel., No. 75, Buenos Aires.

Lusigi, W. (1983). Future directions for the Afrotropical Realm. In: *Proceedings of the World Congress on National Parks*, ed. J. A. McNeely and K. R. Miller. IUCN, Gland, Switzerland.

Lydekker, R. (1908). *The Game Animals of Africa*. Rowland Ward, London.

Lyster, S. (1985). *International Wildlife Law*. Grotius, Cambridge.

MacArthur, E., and E. O. Wilson (1967). *The Theory of Island Biogeography*. Princeton University Press, Princeton, N.J.

MacArthur, R. H. (1955). Fluctuations of animal populations and a measure of community stability. *Ecology* 36:533–536.

Mace, G. M. (1986). Captive breeding and conservation. Primate Eye Supplement: Current issues in primate conservation. *Primate Eye* 29:53–57.

Mace, G. M., P. H. Harvey, and T. H. Clutton-Brock (1981). Brain size and ecology in small mammals. *J. Zool., Lond.* 193:333–354.

MacGillivray, W. (1928). Bird-life of the Bunker and Capricorn Islands. *Emu* 27:230–249.

Machlis, G. E., and D. L. Tichnell (1985). *The State of the World's Parks*. Westview Press, Boulder, Colo., and London.

Mack, R. N. (1986). Alien plant invasions into the intermountain west: A case history. In: *Ecology of Biological Invasions of North America and Hawaii*, ed. H. A. Mooney and J. A. Drake, Springer-Verlag, New York.

MacKinnon, J., K. MacKinnon, G. Child, and J. Thorsell (1986). *Managing Protected Areas in the Tropics*. IUCN, Gland, Switzerland.

Maguire, L. (1987). Decision analysis: A tool for tiger conservation and management. In: *Tigers of the World*, ed. B. Beck and C. Wemmer. Noyes Publications, Park Ridge, N.J.

Main, A. R. (1982). Rare species: Precious or dross? In: *Species at Risk. Research in Australia*, pp. 163–174. Springer, Berlin.

Malthus, T. R. (1798). *An Essay on the Principle of Population*. Reprinted 1970, Penguin Books, Harmondsworth, U.K.

Malzy, P. (1966). Oiseaux et mammiféres de l'île Europa. *Mém. Sér. A Zool.—Mus. Nati. Hist. Naturelle (Paris)* 41:23–27.

Mares, M. A. (1986). Conservation in South America: Problems, consequences, and solutions. *Science* 233:734–739.

Mares, M. A., R. Ojeda, and M. P. Kosco (1981). Observations on the distribution and ecology of the mammals of Salta Province. *Ann. Car. Mus.* 50(6):151–205.

Mares, M. A., and R. A. Ojeda (1984). Faunal commercialization and conservation in South America. *BioScience* 34:580–584.

Margalef, R. (1968). *Perspectives in Ecological Theory*. University of Chicago Press, Chicago.

Marks, S. (1984). *The Imperial Lion, Human Dimensions of Wildlife Management in Central Africa*. Westview Press, Boulder, Colo.

Marrs, R. H. (1985). Techniques for reducing soil fertility for nature conservation purposes: A review in relation to research at Roper's Heath, Suffolk, England. *Biol. Conserv.* 34:307–332.

Marsden, P. V., and N. Lin, eds. (1982). *Social Structure and Network Analysis*. Sage, Beverly Hills, Calif.

Marsh, G. P. (1864). *Man and Nature; Or Physical Geography as Modified by Human Action*, 1965 ed., ed. D. Lowenthal, Harvard University Press, Cambridge, Mass.

Marsh, J. (1986). Changes in U.K. farming. In: *Managing Change*. Farming and Wildlife Trust Limited, Sandy, England.

Marsh, R. E. (1981). Comments on the current status of European hare in Barbados. *Lagomorph Newslett.* 2:5–6.

Marshall, L., S. D. Webb, J. J. Sepkoski, Jr., and D. M. Raup (1982). Mammalian evolution and the great American interchange. *Science* 215:1351–1357.

Martin, E. B., C. B. Martin, and L. Vigne (1987). Conservation crisis—The rhinoceros in India. *Oryx* 21:212–218.

Martin, P. S. (1984). Prehistoric overkill. In: *Quaternary Extinctions*, ed. P. S. Martin and R. G. Klein, pp. 354–403. University of Arizona Press, Tucson.

Martin, P. S., and R. G. Klein, eds. (1984). *Quaternary Extinctions: A Prehistoric Revolution*. University of Arizona Press, Tucson.

Martinez, V. (1987). *Hacia la Creación del Sistema Interamericano de conservación de la Natualeza*. Cuadernos de la Fundación Ambiente y Recursos Naturales, Buenos Aires.

Maruyama, T., and M. Kimura (1980). Genetic variability and effective population size when local extinction and recolonization of subpopulations are frequent. *Proc. Natl. Acad. Sci. USA* 77:6710–6714.

Mathews, J. (1986). *World Resources, 1986*. World Resources Institute and International Institute for Environment and Development. Basic Books, New York.

Matthews, S. (1980). The Ogallala aquifer. "The MacNeil/Lehrer Newshour," KERA-TV, 11/27/80.

May, R. M. (1973). *Stability and Complexity in Model Ecosystems*. Princeton University Press, Princeton, N.J.

May, R. M. (1977). Thresholds and breakpoints in ecosystems with a multiplicity of stable states. *Nature* 269:471–477.

May, R. M. (1984). *Exploitation of Marine Communities*. Springer-Verlag, Berlin.

May, R. M. (1986). The cautionary tale of the black-footed ferret. *Nature* 320:13–14.

Maynard Smith, J. (1972). *On Evolution*. Edinburgh University Press, Edinburgh.

Mayr, E. (1942). *Systematics and the Origin of Species*. Columbia University Press, New York.

McDaniel, J. (1986). Christian spirituality as openness to fellow creatures. *Environ. Ethics* 8(1):33–46.

McIntosh, R. P. (1985). *The Background of Ecology: Concept and Theory*. Cambridge University Press, Cambridge.

McLellan, M. E. (1926). Expedition to the Revillagigedo Islands, Mexico, in 1925, VI. The birds and mammals. *Proc. Calif. Acad. Sci. (4th Ser.)* 15:279–322.

McNab, B. K. (1963). Bioenergetics and the determination of home range size. *Am. Naturalist* 97:133–140.

McNaughton, S. J. (1966). Ecotype function in the Typha community type. *Ecol. Monogr.* 36:297–325.

McNaughton, S. J. (1979). Grassland-herbivore dynamics. In: *Serengeti, Dynamics of an Ecosystem*, ed. A. R. E. Sinclair and M. Norton-Griffiths, pp. 46–81. University of Chicago Press, Chicago.

McNaughton, S. J. (1983). Serengeti grassland ecology: The role of composite environmental factors and contingency in community organization. *Ecol. Monogr.* 53:291–320.

McNaughton, S. J. (1984). Grazing lawns: animals in herds, plant form, and coevolution. *Am. Naturalist* 124:863–886.

McNaughton, S. J. (1985). Ecology of a grazing ecosystem: The Serengeti. *Ecol. Monogr.* 55:259–294.

McNaughton, S. J. (1988). The propagation of disturbance through grassland food webs. In: *The Role of Disturbance in Grasslands*, ed. W. K. Lauenroth and V. A. Deregibus. Springer-Verlag, New York.

McNaughton, S. J., and F. S. Chapin III (1985). Effects of phosphorus nutrition and defoliation on C_4 graminoids from the Serengeti Plains. *Ecology* 66:1617–1629.

McNaughton, S. J., and M. B. Coughenour (1981). The cybernetic nature of ecosystems. *Am. Naturalist* 117:985–990.

McNeely, J. A. (1986). Protected Areas and Human Ecology. Presentation at Conservation 2100: A Fairfield Osborn Symposium, The New York Zoological Society and Rockefeller University, New York (Abstract).

McNeely, J. A., and K. R. Miller, eds. (1984). *National Parks, Conservation, and Development: The Role of Protected Areas in Sustaining Society*. Smithsonian Institution Press, Washington, D.C.

McNeely, J. A., and D. Pitt, eds. (1984). *Culture and Conservation: The Human Dimension in Environmental Planning*. Croom Helm, London.

McNeely, J. A., and P. S. Wachtel (1988). *Soul of the Tiger: People and Wildlife in Southeast Asia*. Doubleday, Garden City, N.Y.

McNees, S. K., and J. Ries (1983). The tract record of macroeconomic forecast. *N. Engl. Econ. Rev.* Nov./Dec.:5–18.

McNeill, W. (1976). *Plagues and peoples*. Anchor Press, Garden City, N.Y.

McPherson, M. P. (1985). Preface, AID Congressional Presentation, Fiscal Year 1986.

Mead, J. I., P. S. Martin, R. C. Euler, A. Long, A. J. T. Jull, L. J. Toolin, D. J. Donahue, and T. W. Linick. (1986). Extinction of Harrington's mountain goat. *Proc. Natl. Acad. Sci. USA* 83:836–839.

Meadows, D. H. (1974). *The Limits to Growth: A Report for the Club of Rome's Project on the Predicament of Mankind*. Universe Books, New York.

Meads, M. J., K. J. Walker, and G. P. Elliott (1984). Status, conservation and management of the land snails of the genus *Powelliphanta (Mullusca:Pulmonata)*. *N.Z. J. Zool.* 11:277–306.

Meffe, G. K. (1985). Predation and species replacement in American Southwestern fishes: A case study. *Southwest. Naturalist* 30:173–187.

Meffe, G. K., D. A. Hendrickson, W. L. Minckley, and J. N. Rinne (1983). Factors resulting in decline of the endangered Sonoran topminnow *Poeciliopsis occidentalis* (Atheriniformes: Poeciliidae) in the United States. *Biol. Conserv.* 25:135–159.

Meffe, G. K., and R. C. Vrijenhoek (1988). Conservation genetics in the management of desert fishes. *Conserv. Biol.* 2:157–169.

Melillo, J. M., C. A. Palm, R. A. Houghton, G. M.

Woodwell, and N. Myers (1985). A comparison of recent estimates of disturbance in tropical forests. *Environ. Conserv.* 12:37–40.

Menni, R. C., R. A. Ringuelet, and R. H. Aramburu (1984). *Peces Marinos de Argentina y Uruguay.* Hemisferio Sur, Buenos Aires.

Merenlender, A. M. (1986). Studies of genetic variation and the differentiation of animal species: Asian schistosomes and African rhinoceroses. Ph.D. thesis, University of California, San Diego.

Merenlender, A. M., D. S. Woodruff, O. A. Ryder, et al. (In preparation). African and Indian rhinoceroses—Genetic variation and differentiation in endangered species.

Merton, D. V. (1978). Controlling introduced predators and competitors on islands. In: *Endangered Birds: Management Techniques for Preserving Threatened Species,* ed. S. A. Temple, pp. 121–128. University of Wisconsin Press, Madison.

Merton, D. V., R. B. Morris, and I. A. E. Atkinson (1984). Lek behavior in a parrot: The Kakapo *Strigops habroptilus* of New Zealand. *Ibis* 126:277–283.

Messiter, M. (1986). In the eye of the environmental storm. *Bank's World* [World Bank, Washington D.C.] 5(11):1.

Millener, P. R. (1981). *The Quaternary Avifauna of the North Island, New Zealand.* Ph.D. thesis, University of Auckland (unpublished).

Miller, K. R. (1980a). *Planificación de Parques Nacionales para el Ecodesarrollo en Latinoamerica.* FEPMA, Madrid, Spain.

Miller, K. R. (1980b). *Planning National Parks for Ecodevelopment.* University of Michigan Press, Ann Arbor.

Minckley, W. L. (1973). *Fishes of Arizona.* Arizona Fish and Game Department, Phoenix.

Minckley, W. L., and J. E. Deacon (1968). Southwestern fishes and the enigma of "endangered species." *Science* 159:1424–1432.

Mintzberg, H. (1971). The manager's job. In: *Organization Theory,* ed. D. S. Pugh, pp. 417–440. Penguin Books, Hamondsworth, England.

Miranda, M., G. Couturier, and J. Williams (1982). *Guía de los Ofidios Bonaerenses Asoc. Coop.* Jardin Zool. de la Plata. La Plata, Argentina.

Mishra, H. (1984). A delicate balance: Tigers, rhinoceros, tourists and park management vs. the needs of the local people in Royal Chitwan National Park, Nepal. In: *National Parks, Conservation, and Development: The Role of Protected Areas in Sustaining Society,* ed. J. A. McNeely and K. R. Miller, pp. 197–205. Smithsonian Institution Press, Washington, D.C.

Mitton, J. B., and M. C. Grant (1985). Associations among protein heterozygosity, growth rate

and developmental homeostasis. *Annu. Rev. Ecol. Syst.* 15:479–499.

Molofsky, J., C. A. S. Hall, and M. Myers (1986). *A Comparison of Tropical Forest Surveys.* U.S. Department of Energy, Washington, D.C.

Monod, J. (1972). *Chance and Necessity.* Random House, New York.

Mooney, H. A., and J. A. Drake, eds. (1986). *Ecology of Biological Invasions of North America and Hawaii.* Springer-Verlag, Berlin.

Moore, M. W., and M. D. Hooper (1975). On the number of bird species in British woods. *Biol. Conserv.* 8:239–250.

Moore, N. W. (1957). The past and present status of the buzzard in the British Isles. *Br. Birds* 50:173–197.

Moore, N. W. (1977). *Nature Conservation and Agriculture.* Nature Conservancy Council. London.

Moors, P. J. (1985). Eradication campaigns against *Rattus norvegicus* on the Noises Islands, New Zealand, using brodifacoum and 1080. In: *Conservation of Island Birds,* ed. P. J. Moors, pp. 143–155. ICBP Tech. Publ. 3, Gland, Switzerland.

Moors, P. J., and I. A. E. Atkinson (1984). Predation on seabirds by introduced animals, and factors affecting its severity. In: *Status and Conservation of the World's Seabirds,* ed. J. P. Croxall, P. G. H. Evans, and R. W. Schreiber, pp. 667–690. ICBP Tech. Publ. 2, Gland, Switzerland.

Moors, P. J., I. A. E. Atkinson, and G. H. Sherley (In press). *Prohibited Immigrants: The Rat Threat to Island Conservation.* IUCN Publication.

Moran, G. F., and S. D. Hopper (1983). Genetic diversity and the insular structure of the rare granite rock species, Eucalyptus caesia. *Aust. J. Bot.* 31:161–172.

Morgan, G. S., and C. A. Woods (1986). Extinctions and the zoogeography of West Indian land mammals. *Biol. J. Linn. Soc.* 28:167–203.

Mori, S. A., B. M. Bloom, and G. T. Prance (1981). Distribution patterns and conservation of eastern Brazilian coastal forest tree species. *Brittania* 33(2):233–245.

Moss, R. (1972). Effects of captivity on gut lengths in red grouse. *J. Wildl. Mgmt.* 36(1):99–104.

Moulton, M. P., and S. L. Pimm (1985). The extent of competition in shaping an experimental fauna. In: *Community Ecology,* ed. T. J. Case and J. M. Diamond. Harper & Row, New York.

Moutou, F. (1983). Introduction dans les îles: L'exemple de l'île de la Réunion. *C.R. Soc. Biogéogr.* 59(2):201–211.

Murie, O. J. (1959). *The Fauna of the Aleutian Islands and Alaska Peninsula.* U.S. Fish and

Wildlife Service, North American Fauna No. 61.

Murphy, R. C. (1936). *Oceanic Birds of South America* (2 vol.). American Museum of Natural History, New York.

Murray, G. (1987a). Land tenure and agroforestry in Haiti: A case study in anthropological project design. In: *Land, Trees and Tenure*. Proceedings of the International Workshop on Tenure Issues in Agroforestry. International Center for Research in Agroforestry and Land Tenure Center, Nairobi.

Murray, G. (1987b). The domestication of wood in Haiti: A case study in applied evolution. In: *Anthropological Praxis: Translating Knowledge into Action,* ed. R. Wulff and S. Fiske. Westview Press, Boulder, Colo.

Myers, J. P., R. I. G. Morrison, P. Z. Antas, B. Harrington, T. Lovejoy, M. Sallaberry, S. E. Senner, and A. Tarak (1987). Conservation strategy for migratory species. *Am. Scientist* 75(1):19–26.

Myers, N. (1972). National parks in savanna Africa. *Science* 178:1255–1263.

Myers, N. (1976). An expanded approach to the problem of disappearing species. *Science* 193:198–202.

Myers, N. (1979). *The Sinking Ark*. Pergamon Press, Oxford.

Myers, N. (1980). *Conservation of Tropical Moist Forests*. Report to National Academy of Sciences. National Research Council, Washington, D.C.

Myers, N. (1983a). *A Wealth of Wild Species*. Westview Press, Boulder, Colo.

Myers, N. (1983b). Eternal values of the parks movement and the Monday morning world. In: *Proceedings of the World Congress on National Parks,* ed. J. A. McNeely and K. R. Miller, IUCN, Gland, Switzerland.

Myers, N., ed. (1984a). *Gaia, an Atlas of Planet Management*. Anchor Press/Doubleday, Garden City, N.Y.

Myers, N. (1984b). *The Primary Source: Tropical Forests and Our Future*. W. W. Norton, New York.

Myers, N. (1985a). The global possible: What can be gained? In: *The Global Possible,* ed. R. Repetto. Yale University Press, New Haven, Conn.

Myers, N. (1985b). Endangered species and the North-South dialogue. In: *Economics of Ecosystem Management,* ed. D. Hall, N. Myers, and N. Margaris, Junk, Dordrecht, The Netherlands.

Myers, N. (1985c). The end of the lines. *Nat. Hist.* 94:2–12.

Myers, N. (1986). *Natural Resource Systems and Human Exploitation Systems: Physiobiotic and Ecological Linkages*. World Bank, Washington, D.C.

Myers, N. (1987a). *Not Far Afield: U.S. Interests and Global Environment*. Worldwatch Institute, Washington, D.C.

Myers, N. (1987b). Mass extinction of species: A sleeper issue awakening? Albright Lecture in Conservation, College of Natural Resources, University of California, Berkeley.

Myers, N. (1987c). The extinction spasm impending: Synergisms at work. *Conserv. Biol.* 1:14–21.

Myrberget, S. (1972). Introduction of hares to Spitzbergen in 1930 and 1931. *Fauna* 25:126.

Narosky, M., and D. Yzurieta (1978). *Aves Argentinas: Guía para el Reconocimiento de la Avifauna Bonaerense*. Associación Ornitológica de la Plata, Buenos Aires.

Nash, R. (1973). *Wilderness and the American Mind*. Yale University Press, New Haven, Conn.

Nash, R. (1986). The future of nature tourism. Unpublished remarks, Conservation 2100 Conference, New York Zoological Society and The Rockefeller University, New York.

National Audubon Society (1985). *Audubon Wildlife Report 1985*. National Audubon Society, New York.

National Audubon Society (1986a). *Audubon Wildlife Report 1986*. National Audubon Society, New York.

National Audubon Society (1986b). *Report of the Advisory Panel on the Spotted Owl*. National Audubon Society, New York.

National Audubon Society (1987). *Audubon Wildlife Report 1987*. National Audubon Society, New York.

National Research Council (1986). *Population Growth and Economic Development*. National Academy Press, Washington, D.C.

Nei, M. (1975). *Molecular Population Genetics and Evolution*. North Holland, Amsterdam.

Nei, M. (1987). *Molecular Evolutionary Genetics*. Columbia University Press, New York.

Nevard, T. D., and A. B. Penfold (1978). Wildlife conservation in Britain: the unsatisfied demand. *Biol. Conserv.* 14:25–44.

Newlands, W. A. (1975). St. Brandon: Fauna conservation and management. Unpub. report to the Ministry of Agriculture and the Environment, Mauritius.

Nicolson, M. H. (1963). *Mountain Gloom and Mountain Glory: The Development of the Aesthetics of the Infinite*. W. W. Norton, New York.

Nilsson, G. (1983). *The Endangered Species Handbook*. Animal Welfare Institute, Washington, D.C.

Nores, M., D. Yzurieta, and R. Miatello (1983). *Lista y Distribución de las Aves de Córdoba*

Argentina. Academia Nacional de Ciencias, Córdoba, Argentina.

North, S. G., and D. J. Bullock (1986). Changes in the vegetation and populations of introduced animals of Round Island and Gunner's Quoin, Mauritius. *Biol. Conserv.* 37:99–117.

Norton, B. G. (1982a). Environmental ethics and nonhuman rights. *Environ. Ethics* 4:17–36.

Norton, B. G. (1982b). Environmental ethics and the rights of future generations. *Environ. Ethics* 4:319–337.

Norton, B. G. (1984). Environmental ethics and weak anthropocentrism. *Environ. Ethics* 6:131–147.

Norton, B. G. (1986a). Conservation and preservation: A conceptual rehabilitation. *Environ. Ethics* 8:195–220.

Norton, B. G. (1986b). Epilogue. In: *The Preservation of Species,* ed. B. G. Norton, pp. 268–283. Princeton University, Princeton, N.J.

Norton, B. G. (1987). *Why Preserve Natural Variety?* Princeton University Press, Princeton, N.J.

Noss, R., and L. Harris (1986). Nodes, networks and MUM's: Preserving diversity at all scales. *Environ. Mgmt.* 10:299–309.

Nudler, O. (1984). *El Concepto de Desarrollo Humano y los Sistemas Ideológicos Conteporáneos.* Fundación Bariloche, Bariloche, Argentina.

Oates, J. F. (1986). Action plan for African primate conservation. IUCN/SSC Primate Specialist Group, Gland, Switzerland.

O'Brien, S. J., J. S. Martenson, C. Packer et al. (1987). Biochemical genetic variation in geographic isolates of African and Asian lions. *Nat. Geogr. Res.* 3:114–124.

O'Brien, S. J., M. E. Roelke, L. Marker, A. Newman, C. A. Winkler, D. Meltzer, L. Colly, J. F. Evermann, M. Bush, and D. E. Wildt (1985). Genetic basis for species vulnerability in the cheetah. *Science* 227:1428–1434.

O'Brien, S. J., D. E. Wildt, and M. Bush (1986). The cheetah in genetic peril. *Sci. Am.* 254:84–92.

O'Brien, S. J., D. E. Wildt, M. Bush, T. Caro, C. Fitzgibbon, I. Aggundey, and R. E. Leakey (1987). East African cheetahs: Evidence for two population bottlenecks? *Proc. Natl. Acad. Sci. USA* 84:508–511.

Odum, E. P. (1969). The strategy of ecosystem development. *Science* 1654:262–270.

Odum, E. P. (1977). The emergence of ecology as a new integrative discipline. *Science* 195:1289–1293.

Office of Technology Assessment, U.S. Congress (1986). Grassroots conservation of biological diversity in the United States. Background Paper #1, OTA-BP-F-38. U.S. Government Printing Office, Washington, D.C.

Oldfield, M. L. (1984). *The Value of Conserving Genetic Resources.* National Park Service, U.S. Dept. of Interior, Washington, D.C.

Olembo, R. (1983). UNEP and protected areas. In: *Proceedings of the World Congress on National Parks,* ed. J. A. McNeely and K. Miller. IUCN, Gland, Switzerland.

Oliver, W. L. R. (1985). The Jamaican hutia or Indian coney (*Geocapromys brownii*)—A model programme for captive breeding and re-introduction? In: *The Management of Rodents in Captivity,* pp. 35–52. Proceedings of Symposium 10 of Association of British Wild Animal Keepers.

Olmedo, E. V. de, and G. Carrizo (1984). *Ofidios-Provincia de Buenos Aires—Guías de la Naturaleza.* Museo Argentino de Ciencias Naturales, Buenos Aires.

Olney, P. J. S., ed. (1982). List of zoos and aquaria of the world. *Int. Zoo Yb.* 22:291–358.

Olrog, C. C. (1984). *Las Aves Argentinas: Una Guía de Campo.* Administración de Parques Nacionales, Buenos Aires.

Olrog, C. C., and M. M. Lucero (1980). *Guía de los Mamíferos Argentinos.* Fundación Miguel Lillo Tucumán, Buenos Aires.

Olson, S. L. (1975). *Paleornithology of St. Helena Island, South Atlantic Ocean.* Smithsonian Contributions to Paleobiology 23. Smithsonian Institution Press, Washington, D.C.

Olson, S. L. (1977). Additional notes on subfossil bird remains from Ascension Island. *Ibis* 119:37–43.

Olson, S. L., and H. F. James (1982). *Prodromus of the Fossil Avifauna of the Hawaiian Islands.* Smithsonian Contributions to Zoology 365. Smithsonian Institution Press, Washington, D.C.

Olson, S. L., and J. F. James (1984). The role of Polynesians in the extinction of the avifauna of the Hawaiian Islands. In: *Quaternary Extinctions: A Prehistoric Revolution,* ed. P. S. Martin and R. G. Klein, pp. 768–789. University of Arizona Press, Tucson.

Orians, G. H. (1974). Diversity, stability and maturity in natural ecosystems. In: *Unifying Concepts of Ecology,* ed. W. H. Van Dobben and R. H. Lowe-McConnell, pp. 139–150. Junk, The Hague.

O'Riordan, T. (1983). Putting trust in the countryside. In: *The Conservation and Development Programme for the UK.* Kogan Page, London.

Orians, G. H., ed. (1988). *The Conservation of Genetic Diversity.* University of Washington, Seattle.

Osborn, Fairfield (1948). *Our Plundered Planet*. Little, Brown, Boston.

Owen-Smith, N. (1987). Pleistocene extinctions: The pivotal role of megaherbivores. *Paleobiology* 13:351.

Oxford, G. S., and D. Rollinson (1983). *Protein Polymorphism. Adaptive and Taxonomic Significance*. Academic Press, New York.

Oxley, D., M. Fenton, and G. Carmody (1974). The effects of roads on populations of small mammals. *J. Appl. Ecol.* 11:51–59.

Paerl, H. W., and K. K. Gallucci (1985). Role of chemotaxis in establishing a specific nitrogen-fixing cyanobacterial-bacterial association. *Science* 227:647–649.

Paine, R. T. (1969). A note on trophic complexity and community stability. *Am. Naturalist* 103:91–93.

Paine, R. T. (1980). Food webs: Linkage, interaction strength and community infrastructure. The third Tansley lecture. *J. Animal Ecol.* 49:667–685.

Palmer, M., and E. Bisset (1985). *World of Difference*. World Wide Fund for Nature, Glasgow.

Parcells, S., and T. Stoel (1987). *The World Bank's New Wildlands Policy. Agenda* 3(2). IUCN, Gland, Switzerland.

Passmore, J. (1974). *Man's Responsibility for Nature: Ecological Problems and Western Traditions*. Charles Scribner's, New York.

Paterson, H. E. H. (1982). Perspective on speciation by reinforcement. *S. Afr. J. Sci.* 78:53–57.

Paterson, H. E. H. (1985). The recognition concept of species. In: *Species and Speciation*. Transvaal Museum Monograph, No. 4, pp. 21–29. Pretoria.

Patin, S. A. (1982). *Pollution and the Biological Resources of the Oceans*. Butterworth, London.

Payer, C. (1982). *The World Bank: A Critical Analysis*. Monthly Review Press, New York.

Payne, M. R., and P. A. Prince (1979). Identification and breeding biology of the diving petrels *Pelecanoides georgicus* and *P. urinatrix exsul* at South Georgia. *N.Z. J. Zool.* 6:299–318.

Pearsall, W. H. (1950). *Mountains and Moorlands*. Collins, London.

Pearson, C. S., ed. (1987). *Multinational Corporations, Environment, and the Third World: Business Matters*. Duke University Press, Durham, N.C.

Pearson, T. (1937). *Adventures in Bird Protection*. Appleton-Century, New York.

Penny, M. (1968). Endemic birds of the Seychelles. *Oryx* 9:267–275.

Penny, M. (1974). *Birds of the Seychelles*. Collins, London.

Perlas, N., and J. Rifkin (1986). Default at the gene banks. *Garden* 10(3):2–6.

Pernetta, J. C., and D. Watling (1978). The introduced and native terrestrial vertebrates of Fiji. *Pacific Sci.* 32:223–244.

Perry, R. (1980). Wildlife conservation in the Line Islands, Republic of Kiribati (formerly Gilbert Islands). *Environ. Conserv.* 7:311–318.

Peters, J., and R. Donoso-Barros (1970). *Catalogue of Neotropical Squamata. Part 2: Lizards and Amphisbaenians*. Smithsonian Institution Press, Washington, D.C.

Peters, J., and B. Orejas-Miranda (1970). *Catalogue of Neotropical Squamata. Part 1: Snakes*. Smithsonian Institution Press, Washington, D.C.

Peters, N. K., J. W. Frost, and S. R. Long (1986). A plant flavone, luteolin, induces expression of *Rhizobium meliloti* genes. *Science* 233:977–980.

Peters, R. L., and J. D. S. Darling (1984). The greenhouse effect and nature reserves. *BioScience* 35:707–717.

Peterson, M. (1965). *History Under the Sea: A Handbook for Underwater Exploration*. Smithsonian Institution Press, Washington, D.C.

Pettifer, H. L. (1980). The experimental release of captive-bred cheetah into the natural environment. *Proceedings of the First World Furbearer Conference*, ed. J. A. Chapman and D. Pursely, pp. 1001–1024. University of Maryland Press, Rockville.

Pielou, E. C. (1975). *Ecological Diversity*. John Wiley, New York.

Pimentel, D., E. C. Terhune, R. Dyson-Hudson, S. Rochereau, R. Samis, E. A. Smith, D. Denman, D. Reifschneider, and M. Shepard (1976). Land degradation: Effects on food and energy resources. *Science* 194:149–155.

Pimm, S. L. (1979). Complexity and stability: Another look at MacArthur's original hypothesis. *Oikos* 33:351–357.

Pimm, S. L. (1982). *Food Webs*. Chapman & Hall, London.

Pimm, S. L. (1984). The complexity and stability of ecosystems. *Nature* 307:321–326.

Pimm, S. L. (1987). Determining the effects of introduced species. *Trends Ecol. Evolution* 2:106–108.

Pinker, R. T., O. E. Thompson, and J. F. Eck (1980). The energy balance of a tropical evergreen forest. *J. Appl. Meteorol.* 19:1341–1350.

Plautus, T. M. *Rudens* (The Rope). Act. 4, Scene 3. Loeb Classical Library, 1928.

Pollock, J. I. (1986). Primates and conservation priorities in Madagascar. *Oryx* 20:209–216.

Porter, M. L., and R. F. Labisky (1985). Home range and foraging habitat of red-cockaded woodpeckers in northern Florida. *J. Wildl. Mgmt.* 50(2):239–247.

Postel, S. (1984). Air pollution, acid rain and the future of the forests. *Worldwatch Paper* 58:1–22, 44–49.

Potts, D. C. (1981). Crown-of-thorns starfish—Man-induced pest or natural phenomenon? In: *The Ecology of Pests. Some Australian Case Histories*, ed. R. L. Kitching and R. E. Jones, pp. 55–86. CSIRO, Melbourne.

Prance, G. T., ed. (1982). *Biological Diversification in the Tropics*. Columbia University Press, New York.

Prescott-Allen, R., and C. Prescott-Allen (1985). *What's Wildlife Worth?* Earthscan Publications, Washington, D.C.

Press, Robert M. (1987). U.S. takes aim at development plans that seem unsound. *Christian Science Monitor*, 1/15/87.

Pye, T., and W. N. Bonner (1980). Feral brown rats, *Rattus norvegicus*, in South Georgia (South Atlantic Ocean). *J. Zool. Lond.* 192:237–255.

Rabinowitz, D., S. Cairns, and T. Dillon (1986). Seven forms of rarity and their frequency in the flora of the British Isles. In: *Conservation Biology. The Science of Scarcity and Diversity*, ed. M. E. Soulé, pp. 182–204. Sinauer, Sunderland, Mass.

Racey, P. A., and M. E. Nicoll (1984). Mammals of the Seychelles. In: *Biogeography and Ecology of the Seychelles Islands*, ed. D. R. Stoddart, pp. 607–626. Monographiae Biologicae Vol. 55. Dr. W. Junk, Publ.

Rackham, O. (1980). *Ancient Woodland: Its History, Vegetation and Uses in England*. Edward Arnold, London.

Raiffa, H. (1968). *Decision Analysis*. Addison-Wesley, Reading, Mass.

Ralls, K., and J. Ballou (1983). Extinction: Lessons from zoos. In: *Genetics and Conservation*, ed. C. M. Schonewald-Cox, S. M. Chambers, F. McBryde, and L. Thomas, pp. 164–184. Benjamin/Cummings, Menlo Park, Calif.

Ralls, K., and J. Ballou (1986). Preface to the proceedings of the workshop on genetic management of captive populations. *Zoo Biol.* 5(2):81–86.

Ralls, K., and J. Ballou (1987) Captive breeding programs for populations with a small number of founders. *Trends Ecol. Evolution* 1:19–22.

Ralls, K., K. Brugger, and J. Ballou (1979). Inbreeding and juvenile mortality in small populations of ungulates. *Science* 206:1101–1103.

Ralls, K., P. H. Harvey, and A. M. Lyles (1986). Inbreeding in natural populations of birds and mammals. In: *Conservation Biology. The Science of Scarcity and Diversity*, ed. M. E. Soulé. Sinauer, Sunderland, Mass.

Randle, P. H. (1981). *Atlas del Desarrollo Territorial de la Argentina*. Vols. 1 and 2. Oikos, Buenos Aires.

Ratcliffe, D. A. (1984). *Nature Conservation in Great Britain*. Nature Conservancy Council, Shrewsbury.

Rauh, W. (1979). Problems of biological conservation in Madagascar. In: *Plants and Islands*, ed. D. Bramwell, pp. 405–421. Academic Press, London.

Raup, D. M. (1986). Biological extinction in earth history. *Science* 231:1528–1533.

Raup, D. M., and J. J. Sepkowski, Jr. (1982). Mass extinctions in the marine fossil record. *Science* 215:1501–1503.

Raven, P. H. (1985). Statement from meeting of IUCN/WWF Plant Advisory Group, Las Palmas, Canary Islands, Nov. 24–25, 1985. IUCN, Gland, Switzerland, and Missouri Botanical Garden, St. Louis, Missouri.

Regan, T. (1981). The nature and possibility of an environmental ethic. *Environ. Ethics* 3:19–34.

Renaud, J., and J. C. Renaud (1984). pp. 1–21. Centre d'introduction des cigognes en Alsace.

Rensberger, B. (1986). Scientists see signs of mass extinction. *Washington Post*, 9/29/86, p. A1.

Repetto, R., ed. (1985). *The Global Possible*. Yale University Press, New Haven, Conn.

Repetto, R. (1986). *World Enough and Time*. Yale University Press, New Haven, Conn.

Rich, B. (1985). The multilateral development banks, environmental policy and the United States. *Ecol. Law Q.* 12:681–745.

Robinson, J. G., and K. H. Redford (1986). Intrinsic rate of natural increase in Neotropical forest mammals: Relationship to phylogeny and diet. *Oecologia (Berl.)* 68:516–520.

Rodhe, H., and Rood, M. J. (1986). Temporal evolution of nitrogen compounds in Swedish precipitation since 1955. *Nature* 321:762–764.

Rohde, E. S. (1935). *Shakespeare's Wild Flowers*. The Medici Society, London.

Rolston, H. (1981). Values in nature. *Environ. Ethics* 3:113–128.

Rolston, H. (1986). *Values Gone Wild: Essays in Environmental Ethics*. Prometheus Books, Buffalo, N.Y.

Rudge, M. R. (1976). A note on the food of feral pigs (*Sus scrofa*) of Auckland Island. *Proc. N.Z. Ecol. Soc.* 23:83–84.

Ruess, R. W., and S. J. McNaughton (1984). Urea as

a promotive coupler of plant-herbivore interactions. *Oecologia (Berl.)* 63:331–337.

Ruess, R. W., and S. J. McNaughton (In review). Ammonia volatilization and the effects of large grazing mammals on nutrient loss from East African grasslands. *Science,* in review.

Ruess, R. W. and S. J. McNaughton (In press). Grazing and the dynamics of nutrient and energy regulated microbial processes in the Serengeti grasslands. *Oikos* 49.

Ruiz, M., and J. P. Ruiz (1986). Ecological history of transhumance in Spain. *Biol. Conserv.* 37:73–86.

Rundel, P. W. (1981). Fire as an ecological factor. In: *Encyclopedia of Plant Physiology New Series,* Vol. 12A, ed. O. L. Lange, P. S. Nobel, C. B. Osmond, and H. Ziegler, pp. 501–538. Springer-Verlag, New York.

Russell, B. (1974). *An Outline of Philosophy.* Meridian Books, New York.

Ryder, O. A., A. T. Kumamoto, B. S. Durrant, and K. Benirschke (In press). Chromosomal divergence and reproductive isolation in dik-diks (Madoqua, Mammalia, Bovidae). *Proc. Acad. Natl. Sci. Phila.*

Sachet, M. (1962). Geography and land ecology of Clipperton Island. *Atoll Res. Bull.* 86:1–115.

Saemundsson, B. (1939). Mammalia. *Zool. Iceland* 4(76):1–52.

Sagan, K. (1977). *The Dragons of Eden.* Random House, New York.

Sagoff, M. (1974). On preserving the natural environment. *Yale Law J.* 84:205–267.

Sagoff, M. (1985). Fact and value in ecological science. *Environ. Ethics* 7(2):99–116.

Sai, T. F. (1984). The population factor in Africa's development dilemma. *Science* 226:801–805.

Sailer, R. I. (1983). History of insect introductions. In: *Exotic Plant Pests and North American Agriculture,* ed. G. C. Wilson, pp. 15–38. Academic Press, New York.

Sakagami, S. F. (1961). An ecological perspective of Marcus Island, with special reference to land animals. *Pacific Sci.* 15:82–104.

Salati, E., and P. B. Vose (1984). Amazon basin: A system in equilibrium. *Science* 225:129–138.

Salt, G. W. (1979). A comment on the use of the term "emergent properties." *Am. Naturalist* 113:145–151.

Salvini-Plawen, L. v., and E. Mayr (1977). On the evolution of photoreceptors and eyes. In: *Evolutionary Biology,* Vol. 10, ed. M. K. Hecht, W. C. Steere, and B. Wallace, pp. 207–263. Plenum Press, New York.

Salwasser, H., S. P. Mealey, and K. Johnson (1984). Wildlife population viability: A question of risk. *Trans. N. Am. Wildl. Nat Resource Con.* 49(2).

Salwasser, H., C. M. Schonewald-Cox, and R. Baker (1987). The role of interagency cooperation in managing for viable populations. In: *Viable Populations for Conservation,* ed. M. E. Soulé, pp. 159–173. Cambridge University Press, Cambridge.

Sauer, C. (1966). *The Early Spanish Main.* University of California Press, Berkeley.

Sauer, C. (1971). *Sixteenth Century North America, the Land and People as Seen by the Europeans.* University of California Press, Berkeley.

Savidge, J. A. (1984). Guam: Paradise lost for wildlife. *Biol. Conserv.* 30:305–317.

Savidge, J. A. (1986). *The Role of Disease and Predation in the Decline of Guam's Avifauna.* Ph.D. dissertation, University of Illinois, Urbana.

Savidge, J. A. (1987). Extinction of an island forest avifauna by an introduced snake. *Ecology* 68:660–668.

Sax, J. L. (1980). *Mountains Without Handrails: Reflections on the National Parks.* University of Michigan Press, Ann Arbor.

Schaller, G. B. (1979). *Stones of Silence.* Viking Press, New York.

Schaller, G. B. (1986). Unpublished remarks. Conservation 2100: A Fairfield Osborn Symposium, The New York Zoological Society and The Rockefeller University, New York.

Schmidt, C. R. (1986). A review of zoo breeding programmes for primates. *Intl. Zoo Yrbk.* 24/25:107–123.

Schneider, S. H., and R. Londer (1984). *The Coevolution of Climate and Life.* Sierra Club Books, San Francisco.

Schoener, T. W. (1986). Mechanistic approaches to community ecology: A new reductionism? *Am. Zool.* 26:81–106.

Schoenherr, A. A. (1977). Density dependent and density independent regulation of reproduction in the Gila topminnow. *Ecology* 58:438–444.

Schonewald-Cox, C., S. M. Chambers, B. MacBryde, and L. Thomas, eds. (1983). *Genetics and Conservation. A Reference for Managing Wild Animal and Plant Populations.* Benjamin/Cummings, Menlo Park, Calif.

Schroth, M. N., and J. G. Hancock (1982). Disease-suppressive soil and root-colonizing bacteria. *Science* 216:1376–1381.

Seal, U. S. (1985). The realities of preserving species in captivity. In: *Animal Extinctions,* ed. R. J. Hoage, pp. 71–95. Smithsonian Institution Press, Washington, D.C.

Seal, U. S., P. Jackson, and R. L. Tilson (1987). A global tiger conservation plan. In: *Tigers of the World*, ed. R. L. Tilson and U. S. Seal, pp. 487–498. Noyes Publications, Park Ridge, New Jersey.

Sedjo, R. E., and M. Clawson (1984). Global forests. In: *The Resourceful Earth*, ed. J. Simon and H. Kahn. Blackwell, Oxford.

Segnestam, M. (1983). Future directions for the palaearctic realm. In: *Proceedings of the World Congress on National Parks*, ed. J. A. McNeely and K. Miller. IUCN, Gland, Switzerland.

Segonzac, M. (1972). Données recentes sur la faune des îles Saint-Paul et Nouvelle Amsterdam. *L'Oiseau et R.F.O. 42*, Special no.: 3–68.

Seidensticker, J., J. F. Eisenberg, and R. Simons (1984). The Tangjiahe, Wanglang, and Fengtongshai giant panda reserves and biological conservation in the People's Republic of China. *Biol. Conserv.* 28:217–251.

Senft, R. L., M. B. Coughenour, D. W. Bailey, L. R. Rittenhouse, O. E. Sala, and D. M. Swift (1987). Large herbivore foraging and ecological heirarchies. *BioScience* 37(11):789–795, 798–799.

Serventy, D. L. (1952). The bird islands of the Sahul Shelf. *Emu* 52:33–59.

Shabecoff, P. (1986). Ecologists press lending groups. *New York Times* 10/29/86:1.

Shaffer, M. L. (1981). Minimum population sizes for species conservation. *BioScience* 31:131–134.

Short, R. V. (1987). Primate ethics. In: *Primates. The Road to Self-Sustaining Populations*, ed. K. Benirschke, pp. 1–11. Springer, New York.

Sierra Club (1986). *Bankrolling Disasters: International Development Banks and the Global Environment*. Sierra Club Books, San Francisco.

Siljak, D. D. (1979). Structure and stability of model ecosystems. In: *Theoretical Systems Ecology*, ed. E. Halfon, pp. 151–181. Academic Press, New York.

Simberloff, D. (1986a). Are we on the verge of a mass extinction in tropical rain forests? In: *Dynamics of Extinction*, ed. D. K. Elliott, pp. 165–180. John Wiley, New York.

Simberloff, D. (1986b). Introduced insects: A biogeographic and systematic perspective. In: *Ecology of Biological Invasions of North America and Hawaii*, ed. H. A. Mooney and J. A. Drake, pp. 3–26. Springer-Verlag, New York.

Simon, J. L. (1980). Resource, population, environment: An oversupply of false bad news. *Science* 208:1431–1437.

Simon, J. L. (1984). Introduction. In: *The Resourceful Earth*, ed. J. L. Simon and H. Kahn. Blackwell, New York.

Simon, J. L., and H. Kahn, eds. (1984). *The Resourceful Earth*. Blackwell, New York

Simon, J. L., and A. Wildavsky (1984). On species loss, the absence of data, and the risk to humanity. In: *The Resourceful Earth*, ed. J. Simon and H. Kahn. Blackwell, New York.

Simons, P. (1985). A city fit for wildlife. *New Scientist* 1449:30–33.

Simpson, G. G. (1964). *The Meaning of Evolution*. Yale University Press, New Haven, Conn.

Singh, A. (1984). *Tiger! Tiger!* Jonathan Cape, London.

Slatkin, M. (1987). Gene flow and the geographic structure of natural populations. *Science* 236:787–792.

Snodgrass, R. E., and E. Heller (1902). The birds of Clipperton and Cocos Islands. Papers from the Hopkins-Stanford Galápagos Expedition. 1898–1899. XI. *Proc. Wash. Acad. Sci.* 4:501–520.

Soulé, M. E. (1980). Thresholds for survival: Maintaining fitness and evolutionary potential. In: *Conservation Biology: An Evolutionary-Ecological Perspective*, ed. M. E. Soulé and B. A. Wilcox, pp. 151–170. Sinauer, Sunderland, Mass.

Soulé, M. E. (1984a). Long-term conservation of habitats and populations: Realconserve or conservation-as-usual. In: *Conservation of Threatened Natural Habitats*, ed. R. W. Siegfried. CSIR, Capetown, South Africa.

Soulé, M. E. (1984b). Application of genetics and population biology: The what, where and how of nature reserves. In: *Conservation, Science and Society*, Vol. 2, UNESCO-UNEP. UNESCO, Paris.

Soulé, M. E. (1985). What is conservation biology? *BioScience* 35(11):727–734.

Soulé, M. E., ed. (1986). *Conservation Biology: Science of Scarcity and Diversity*. Sinauer, Sunderland, Mass.

Soulé, M. E., ed. (1987). *Viable Populations for Conservation*. Cambridge University Press, New York.

Soulé, M. E., M. Gilpin, W. G. Conway, and T. J. Foose (1986). The millenium ark: How long a voyage, how many staterooms, how many passengers? *Zoo Biol.* 5(2):101–113.

Soulé, M. E. and D. Simberloff (1986). What do genetics and ecology tell us about the design of nature reserves? *Biol. Conserv.* 35:19–40.

Soulé, M. E., and B. A. Wilcox, eds. (1980). *Conservation Biology: An Evolutionary-Ecological Perspective*. Sinauer, Sunderland, Mass.

Sousa, W. P. (1984). The role of disturbance in natural communities. *Annu. Rev. Ecol. Syst.* 15:353–91.

Southwick, C. H. (1976). Chapter 6. In: *Ecology and the Quality of Our Environment*. ed. C. H. Southwick, 2nd edition. Prindle, Weber, and Smidt, Boston.

Stanley Price, M. R. (1986). The reintroduction of the Arabian oryx *Oryx leucoryx* into Oman. *Intl. Zoo Yrbk.* 24/25:179–189.

Start, A. N., and A. G. Marshall (1976). Nectarivorous bats as pollinators of trees in West Malaysia. In: *Tropical Trees, Variation, Breeding and Conservation*. ed. J. Burley and B. T. Styles, pp. 141–150. Academic Press, London.

Staub, F. (1970). Geography and ecology of Tromelin Island. *Atoll Res. Bull.* 136:197–209.

Steadman, D. W. (1985). Fossil birds from Mangaia, Southern Cook Islands. *Bull. Bri. Ornithologists' Club* 105:58–86.

Steadman, D. W. (1986). *Holocene Fossil Vertebrates from Isla Floreana, Galápagos.* Smithsonian Contributions to Zoology 413. Smithsonian Institution Press, Washington, D.C.

Steadman, D. W. (In press). Fossil birds and biogeography in Polynesia. In: *Proceedings of the XIX International Ornithological Congress.* Ottawa.

Steadman, D. W., and S. L. Olson (1985). Bird remains from an archaeological site on Henderson Island, South Pacific: Man-caused extinctions on an "uninhabited" island. *Proc. Natl. Acad. Sci. USA* 82:6191–6195.

Steadman, D. W., G. K. Pregill, and S. L. Olson (1984). Fossil vertebrates from Antigua, Lesser Antilles: Evidence for late Holocene human-caused extinctions in the West Indies. *Proc. Natl. Acad. Sci. USA* 81(14):4448–4451.

Stenseth, N. C. (1984) The tropics: Cradle or museum? *Oikos* 43:417–420.

Stoddart, D. R., and M. E. D. Poore (1970). Geography and ecology of Desroches. *Atoll Res. Bull.* 136:155–165.

Stone, C. P. (1984). Alien animals in Hawaii's native ecosystems: Toward controlling the adverse effects of introduced vertebrates. In: *Hawaii's Terrestrial Ecosystem: Preservation and Management*, ed. C. P. Stone and J. M. Scott. University of Hawaii Press, Honolulu.

Stonehouse, B. (1962). Ascension Island and the British Ornithologists' Union Centenary Expedition 1857–1959. *Ibis* 103B:107–123.

Strahm, W. (1986). *Botanical Report, Round Island.* December, 1986, unpublished.

Strong, D. R. (1986). Density-vague population change. *TREE* 1:39–42.

Strong, D. R., D. Simberloff, L. G. Able, and A. B. Thistle (1984). *Ecological Communities: Conceptual Issues and the Evidence.* Princeton University Press, Princeton, N.J.

Strum, S. C., and C. H. Southwick (1986). Translocation of primates. In: *Primates: The Road to Self-Sustaining Populations*, ed. K. Benirschke, pp. 949–957. Proceeding in Life Sciences. Springer-Verlag, New York.

Stuart, A. (1986). Who (or what) killed the giant armadillo? *New Scientist* 1517:29–32.

Stuart, S. N. (1987). Why we need action plans. *Species* [Newsletter of the IUCN Species Survival Commission] 8:11–12.

Sun, M. (1986a). Fiscal neglect breeds problems for seed banks. *Science* 231:329–330.

Sun, M. (1986b). The global fight over plant genes. *Science* 231:445–447.

Swan, J. (1979). Uncovering Love Canal. *Columb. Journ. Rev.* Jan/Feb:46–51.

Szafer, W. (1968). The ure-ox, extinct in Europe since the seventeenth century: An attempt at conservation that failed. *Biol. Conserv.* 1:45–47.

Tachibana, K., M. Sakaitanai, and K. Nakanishi (1984). Pavoninins: Shark-repelling ichthyotoxins from the defense secretion of the Pacific sole. *Science* 197:885–886.

Tangley, L. (1984). Groundwater contamination: Local problems become a national issue. *Bioscience* 34(3):142–148.

Tansley, A. G. (1935). The use and abuse of vegetational concepts and terms. *Ecology* 16:284–307.

Tarak, A. (1978). *Proyecto de Parque Nacional Carahuasi—Jujuy.* INTALBID, Buenos Aires.

Tarak, A. (1979). *Niveles de Precepción de la Naturaleza.* Administración de Parques Nacionales, Buenos Aires.

Tarak, A., and P. Canevari (1983). *Politica de Investigacion Cientifica de los Recursos Naturales de Parques Nacionales.* Publicacion Tecnica 1. Administracion de Parques Nacionales, Buenos Aires.

Taylor, G. R. (1963). *The Science of Life.* McGraw-Hill, New York.

Taylor, P. (1986). *Respect for Nature.* Princeton University Press, Princeton, N.J.

Temple, S. A. (1977). Plant-animal mutualism: Coevolution with dodo leads to near extinction of plant. *Science* 197:885–886.

Templeton, A. R. (1986). Coadaptation and outbreeding depression. In: *Conservation Biology: the Science of Scarcity and Diversity*, ed. M. E. Soulé, pp. 19–34. Sinauer, Sunderland, Mass.

Templeton, A. R. (1987). Species and speciation. *Evolution* 41:233–235.

Templeton, A. R. (In press). The meaning of species and speciation—a genetic perspective. In: *Speciation and Adaptation*. National Academy of Sciences, Philadelphia.

Templeton, A. R., H. Hemmer, G. Mace, U. S. Seal, W. M. Shields, and D. S. Woodruff (1986). Local adaptation, coadaptation and population boundaries. *Zoo Biol.* 5:115–125.

Templeton, A. R., and B. Read (1983). The elimination of inbreeding depression in a captive herd of Speke's gazelle. In: *Genetics and Conservation*, ed. C. M. Schonewald-Cox, S. M. Chambers, F. McBryde, and L. Thomas, pp. 241–261. Benjamin/Cummings, Menlo Park, Calif.

Templeton, A. R., and B. Read (1984). Factors eliminating inbreeding depression in a captive herd of Speke's gazelle. *Zoo Biol* 3:177–199.

Terborgh, J. (1974). Preservation of natural diversity: The problem of extinction-prone species. *Bioscience* 24:715–722.

Terborgh, J. (1975). Faunal equilibria and the design of wildlife preserves. In: *Tropical Ecological Systems: Trends in Terrestrial and Aquatic Research*, ed. F. Golley and E. Medina. Springer-Verlag, New York.

Terborgh, J. (1986). Keystone plant resources in the tropical forest. In: *Conservation Biology: Science of Scarcity and Diversity*, ed. M. E. Soulé, pp. 330–344. Sinauer, Sunderland, Mass.

Terborgh, J., and B. Winter (1980). Some causes of extinction. In: *Conservation Biology*, ed. M. E. Soulé and B. A. Wilcox, pp. 119–134. Sinauer, Sunderland, Mass.

Terborgh, J., and B. Winter (1983). A method for siting parks and reserves with special reference to Colombia and Ecuador. *Biol. Conserv.* 27:45–58.

Thibodeau, F. R., and H. H. Field, eds. (1984). *Sustaining Tomorrow*, University Press of New England, Hanover, N.H.

Thomas, J. A. (1980). The extinction of the large blue and the conservation of the black hairstreak butterflies (a contrast of failure and success). In: *Annual Report*. Institute of Terrestrial Ecology.

Thomas, W. D., R. Barnes, M. Crotty, and M. Jones (1986). An historical overview of selected rare ruminants in captivity. *Intl. Zoo Yrbk.* 24/25:77–99.

Tilman, D. (1986). Nitrogen-limited growth in plants from different successional stages. *Ecology* 67:555–563.

Tinley, K. L. (1978). Framework of the Gorongosa ecosystem. D.Sc. thesis, University of Pretoria, South Africa.

Titus, J. G., T. R. Henderson, and J. M. Teal (1984). Sea level rise and wetlands loss in the United States. *Natl. Wetlands Newsl.* 6:3–6.

Tomich, P. Q. (1969). Mammals in Hawaii: A synopsis and notational bibliography. *Spec. Pub. Bernice P. Bishop Mus.* 57.

Torres, D., and A. Aguayo (1971). Algunas observaciones sobre la fauna del archipelago de Juan Fernandez. Mammals. *Bol. Univ. Chile* 112:34–35.

Toulmin, S. E. (1982). *The Return to Cosmology*. University of California Press, Berkeley.

Trollope, W. S. W. (1982). Ecological effects of fire in South African ecosystems. In: *Ecology of Tropical Savannas*, ed. B. J. Huntley and B. J. Walker, pp. 292–306. Springer-Verlag, New York.

Trotter, M. M., and B. McCulloch (1984). Moas, men, and middens. In: *Quaternary Extinctions: A Prehistoric Revolution*, ed. P. S. Martin and R. G. Klein, pp. 708–727. University of Arizona Press, Tucson.

Trow, G. W. S. (1984). The Harvard black rock forest. *New Yorker* June 11:44–99.

Tyndale-Biscoe, C. H. (1973). *Life of Marsupials*. Edward Arnold, London.

Tyson, W. (1956). History of the utilization of longleaf pine (*Pinus palustrus* Mill.) in Florida from 1513 until the twentieth century. M.A. thesis, University of Florida, Gainesville.

Ulanowicz, R. E. (1979). Prediction, chaos and ecological perspective. In: *Theoretical Systems Ecology*, ed. E. Halfon, pp. 107–117. Academic Press, New York.

U.N. (1981). *World Population Prospects as Assessed in 1980*. United Nations, New York.

UNEP (1982). *World Environment 1972–82*. United Nations, Nairobi.

U.S. Congress (1985). Hearings before the Subcommittee on Interior and Insular Affairs, March and May, 1985.

U.S. Congress (1987). *Technologies to Maintain Biological Diversity*, OTA-F-330. Office of Technology Assessment. U.S. Government Printing Office, Washington, D.C.

U.S. Department of Energy (1985). *Direct Effects of Increasing Carbon Dioxide on Vegetation*. U.S. Department of Energy, Washington, D.C.

U.S. Fish and Wildlife Service (1983). *Gila and Yaqui Topminnow Recovery Plan*. U.S. Fish and Wildlife Service, Albuquerque, N.Mex.

U.S. Fish and Wildlife Service (1986). *Whooping Crane Recovery Plan*. U.S. Fish and Wildlife Service, Albuquerque, N.Mex.

U.S. Fish and Wildlife Service (1987). *Florida pan-*

ther (Felis concolor coryi) Recovery Plan. Florida Panther Interagency Committee for the U.S. Fish and Wildlife Service, Atlanta, Ga.

USAID (1985). Congressional Presentation, Fiscal Year 1986. Main Volume, U.S. Government Printing Office, Washington, D.C.

USAID (1987). Summary of AID Biological Diversity Activities Under the FY 1987 Legislated Earmark. USAID Report 7/16/87.

Van Riper, C. III (1980). Observations on the breeding of the Palila in Hawaii. *Ibis* 122:462–475.

Van Riper, C., III, S. G. Van Riper, M. L. Goff, and M. Laird (1986). The epizootiology and ecological significance of malaria in Hawaiian land birds. *Ecol. Monogr.* 56:327–344.

VanTighem, K. V. (1986). Have our national parks failed us? *Park News* 31–33.

Van Valkenburgh, B. (1985). Locomotor diversity within past and present guilds of large predatory mammals. *Paleobiology* 11(4):406–428.

Varner, J., and J. Varner (1983). *Dogs of the Conquest*. University of Oklahoma Press, Norman, Okla.

Varvio, S-L., R. Chakraborty, and M. Nei (1986). Genetic variation in subdivided populations and conservation genetics. *Heredity* 57:189–198.

Vedant, O. S. (1986). Afforestation in India. *Ambio* 15(4):254–255.

Veitch, C. R. (1985). Methods of eradicating feral cats from offshore islands in New Zealand. In: *Conservation of Island Birds*, ed. P. J. Moors, pp. 125–141. Tech. Publ. 3. ICBP. Gland, Switzerland.

Vietmeyer, N. (1986). Lesser-known plants of potential use in agriculture and forestry. *Science* 232:1379–1384.

Vrba, E. S. (1985b). Introductory comments on species and speciation. In: *Species and Speciation*, pp. ix–viii. Monograph No. 4. Transvaal Museum, Pretoria.

Vrijenhoek, R. C., M. E. Douglas, and G. K. Meffe (1985). Conservation genetics of endangered fish populations in Arizona. *Science* 229:400–402.

Vrijenhoek, R. C., and S. Lerman (1982). Heterozygosity and developmental stability under sexual and asexual breeding systems. *Evolution* 36:768–776.

Wace, N. (1986). The arrival, establishment and control of alien plants on Gough Island. *S. Afr. J. Antarctic Res.* 16:95–101.

Wace, N. M., and M. W. Holdgate (1976). *Man and Nature in the Tristan da Cunha Islands*. IUCN Monograph No. 6. International Union for Conservation of Nature and Natural Resources, Morges, Switzerland.

Wagner, R. O. (1982). State of the association address. *Proceedings AAZPA Annual Conference.* 1982:1–5.

Wald, G. (1974). Fitness in the universe: Choices and necessities. In: *Cosmochemical Evolution and the Origins of Life,* eds. J. Oro et al., pp. 7–27. D. Reidel, Dordrecht, The Netherlands.

Walker, B. H., R. Emslie, N. Owen-Smith, and R. J. Scholes (In preparation). To cull or not to cull: Lessons from a southern African drought.

Walker, B. H., and M. E. Joos-Vanderwalle (In preparation). Vegetation of the Savuti region of Chobe National Park, Botswana.

Walker, B. H., D. Ludwig, C. S. Holling, and R. M. Peterman (1981). Stability of semi-arid savanna grazing systems. *J. Ecol.* 69:473–498.

Wallace, L. L. (1981). Growth, morphology and gas exchange of mycorrhizal and nonmycorrhizal *Panicum coloratum* L., a C_4 grass species, under different clipping and fertilization regimes. *Oecologia (Berl.)* 49:272–278.

Warner, R. E. (1963). Recent history and ecology of the Laysan duck. *Condor* 65:2–23.

Warner, R. E. (1968). The role of introduced diseases in the extinction of the endemic Hawaiian avifauna. *Condor* 70:101–120.

Warner, W. (1948). The present status of the Kagu, *Rhynochetos jubatus*, on New Caledonia. *Auk* 65:287–288.

Warren, M. A. (1983). The rights of the non-human world. In: *Environmental Philosophy: A Collection of Readings*, ed. R. Elliot and A. Gare. Pennsylvania State University Press, University Park.

Washington Post (1985). California's liquid asset. *Washington Post,* Nov. 3, 1985:A1.

Waterbury, J. B., C. B. Calloway, and R. D. Turner (1983). A cellulolytic nitrogen-fixing bacterium cultured from the gland of Deshayes in shipworms (Bivala: Teredinidae). *Science* 221:1401–1403.

Watkins, B. P., and J. Cooper (1986). Introduction, present status and control of alien species at the Prince Edward islands, sub-Antarctic. *S. Afr. J. Antarctic Res.* 16:86–94.

Watson, R. A. (1979). Self-consciousness and the rights of non-human animals and nature. *Environ. Ethics* 1:99–129.

Watts, W., and B. Hansen (1988). Environments of Florida in the late Wisconsin and Holocene. In: *Wet Site Archaeology*, ed. B. Purdy. Telford Press, Telford N.J.

Watts, W., and M. Stuiver (1980). Late Wisconsin climate of northern Florida and the origin of species-rich deciduous forest. *Science* 210:325–327.

Wayne, R. K., L. Forman, A. K. Newman, J. M. Simonson, and S. J. O'Brien (1986). Genetic monitors of zoo populations: Morphological and electrophoretic assays. *Zoo Biol.* 5:215–232.

Webb, G., S. Manolis, and P. Whitehead (1987). *Wildlife Management: Crocodiles and Alligators.* Surrey Beatly, Chipping Norton, N.S.W.

Webb, N. R., and L. E. Haskins (1980). An ecological survey of heathlands in the Poole Basin, Dorset, England. *Biol. Conserv.* 17:281–296.

Webb, S. D., ed. (1974). *Pleistocene Mammals of Florida.* The University Presses of Florida, Gainesville.

Webb, S. D. (1984). Ten million years of mammal extinctions in North America. In: *Quaternary Extinctions: A Prehistoric Revolution,* ed. P. S. Martin and R. G. Klein. University of Arizona Press, Tucson.

Webb, S. D., and K. T. Wilkins (1984). Historical biogeography of Florida Pleistocene mammals. In: *Contributions in Quaternary Vertebrate Paleontology,* ed. H. Genoways and M. Dawsen, pp. 370–383. Special Publications of the Carnegie Museum, Vol. 8. Carnegie Museum, Pittsburgh.

Wecker, S. C. (1970). The role of early experience in habitat selection by the prairie deer mouse (*Peromyscus maniculatus bairdi*). In: *Behavioral Ecology,* ed. P. H. Klopfer, pp. 2–41. Dickenson, Belmont, Calif.

Weins, J. A. (1984). On understanding a non-equilibrium world: Myth and reality in community patterns and processes. In: *Ecological Communities: Conceptual Issues and the Evidence,* ed. D. R. Strong, D. Simberloff, L. Abele, and A. Thistle, pp. 439–457. Princeton University Press, Princeton, N.J.

Wemmer, C. (1983). Sociology and management. In: *The Biology and Management of an Extinct Species, Père David's Deer,* ed. B. B. Beck and C. Wemmer, pp. 126–132. Noyes Publications, Park Ridge, N.J.

Wemmer, C., J. L. D. Smith, and H. R. Mishra (1987). Tigers in the wild: The bio-political challenges. In: *Tigers of the World,* ed. R. L. Tilson and U. S. Seal. Noyes Publications, Park Ridge, N.J.

West Churchmann, C. (1979). *The Systems Approach and Its Enemies.* Basic Books, New York.

Westermann, J. H. (1953). *Nature preservation in the Caribbean.* Foundation for Scientific Research in Surinam and the Netherlands Antilles, No. 9, Utrecht.

Western, D. (1973). The structure, dynamics and changes of the Amboseli ecosystem. Ph.D. dissertation, University of Nairobi.

Western, D. (1976). A new approach to Amboseli. *Parks* 1:1–4.

Western, D. (1979a). Size, life history and ecology and mammals. *Afr. J. Ecol.* 17:185–204.

Western, D. (1979b). The environment and ecology of pastoralists in arid savannahs. In: *The Future of Hunter-Gatherers in Africa,* ed. J. Swift. International African Institute, London.

Western, D. (1983a). Production, reproduction and size in mammals. *Oecologia* 59:269–271.

Western, D. (1983b). Enlisting landowners to conserve migratory wildlife. *Ambio* 11(5):302–308.

Western, D. (1985). Conservation-based rural development. In: *Sustaining Tomorrow,* F. R. Thibodeau and H. Field, eds. University of New England Press, Hanover, N.H.

Western, D. (1986). The role of captive populations in global conservation. In: *Primates: The Road to Self-Sustaining Populations,* ed. K. Benirschke, pp. 13–20. Proceedings in Life Sciences. Springer-Verlag, New York.

Western, D. (1987). Africa's elephants and rhinos: Flagships in crisis. *TREE* 2:343–346.

Western, D., and W. Henry (1979). Economics and conservation in third world national parks. *BioScience* 29:414–418.

Western, D., and J. Ssemakula (1980). *The Present and the Future Patterns of Consumption and Production of Wood Energy in Kenya.* Energy Report Series. UNEP, Nairobi.

Westman, W. E. (1977). How much are nature's services worth? *Science* 197:960–964.

White, G. (1977). In: *The Natural History of Selborne,* ed. R. Mabey. Penguin Books, Harmondsworth, Eng.

White, M. J. D. (1978). *Modes of Speciation,* p. 455. Freeman, San Francisco.

Whittaker, R. H. (1972). Evolution and measurement of species diversity. *Taxon* 21:213–251.

Whitten, A. J., K. D. Bishop, S. Nash, and L. Clayton (1987). One or more extinctions from Sulawesi, Indonesia? *Conserv. Biol.* 1:42–48.

Wiener, N. (1948). *Cybernetics.* John Wiley, New York.

Wijewardene, R. (1978). Appropriate technology in tropical farming systems. *World Crops* May/June.

Wilcox, B. (1983). In-situ conservation of genetic resources: Determinants of maximum area requirements. In: *Proceedings of the World Congress on National Parks,* ed. J. A. McNeely and K. Miller. IUCN, Gland, Switzerland.

Wiley, E. O. (1981). *Phylogenetics.* John Wiley, New York.

Wiley, J. W. (1985). The Puerto Rican parrot and competition for its nest sites. In: *Conservation of Island Birds,* ed. P. J. Moors, pp. 213–223. Tech. Publ. 3. ICBP. Gland, Switzerland.

Wilkins, K., and D. Schmidly (1980). Highway mortality of vertebrates in Texas. *TX J. Sci.* 22:343–350.

Willey, Z. (1985). Salinity and toxic chemical build-up in the San Joaquin Valley's West Side—Economic and environmental issue. Presented to the National Planning Association's Food and Agricultural Committee, April 1985.

Williams, A. J., W. R. Siegfried, A. E. Burger, and A. Berruti (1979). The Prince Edward Islands: A sanctuary for seabirds in the southern ocean. *Biol. Conserv.* 15:59–71.

Wilson, D. S. (1980). *The Natural Selection of Populations and Communities.* Benjamin/Cummings, Menlo Park, Calif.

Wilson, E. O. (1985a). Time to revive systematics. *Science* 230:4731.

Wilson, E. O. (1985b). The biological diversity crisis. *BioScience* 35:700–706.

Wilson, E. O. (In press). Biological diversity as a scientific and ethical issue. *Proc. Am. Philos. Soc.*

Wilson, E. O., ed. (1988). *Biodiversity.* National Academy Press, Washington, D.C.

Wilson, E. O., and W. L. Brown (1953). The subspecies concept and its taxonomic application. *Syst. Zool.* 2:97–111.

Wilson, E. O., and E. O. Willis (1975). Applied biogeography. In: *Ecology and Evolution of Communities,* ed. M. L. Cody and J. M. Diamond. Belknap Press, Cambridge, Mass.

Wing, E. (1965). Early history. In: *The White-tailed Deer in Florida,* ed. R. Harlow and F. Jones, Jr., pp. 5–12. Tech. Bull. No. 9. Florida Game and Freshwater Fish Commission. Tampa.

Wingate, D. B. (1985). The restoration of Nonsuch Island as a living museum of Bermuda's precolonial terrestrial biome. In: *Conservation of Island Birds,* ed. P. J. Moors, pp. 225–238. Tech. Publ. 3. ICBP. Gland, Switzerland.

Witkamp, M. (1966). Decomposition of leaf litter in relation to environment, microflora, and microbial respiration. *Ecology* 47:194–207.

Wodzicki, K. A. (1950). Introduced mammals of New Zealand. *Dept. Sci. Indust. Res. Bull.* 98.

Wodzicki, K. A. (1969a). *A Preliminary Survey of Rats and Other Land Vertebrates of Niue Island, South Pacific, Wellington.* Ecology Division, Dept. of Scientific and Industrial Research, New Zealand.

Wodzicki, K. A. (1969b). Preliminary report on damage to coconuts and on the ecology of the Polynesian rat (*Rattus exulans*) in the Tokelau Islands. *Proc. N. Z. Ecol. Soc.* 16:7–12.

Wolf, A., ed. (1979). *Agricultural Production: Research and Development Strategies for the 1980s.* Rockefeller Foundation, New York.

Wolf, E. C. (1987). *On the Brink of Extinction: Conserving the Diversity of Life.* Worldwatch Paper 78. Worldwatch Institute, Washington, D.C.

Wood, J., ed. (1984). *Proceedings of a Workshop on Biosphere Reserves and Other Protected Areas for Sustainable Development of Small Caribbean Islands.* USDI National Park Service S.E. Reg. Office. Atlanta, Ga.

Wood-Jones, F. (1912). *Corals and Atolls.* Levell Reeve, London.

Woodmansee, R. G. (1978). Additions and losses of nitrogen in grassland ecosystems. *BioScience* 28:448–453.

Woodruff, D. S. (1979). Postmating reproductive isolation in Pseudophryne and the evolutionary significance of hybrid zones. *Science* 203:561–563.

Woodruff, D. S. (1988). Genetic aspects of conservation biology—An emerging applied science. In: *Conservation of Genetic Resources,* ed. G. H. Orians. University of Washington, Seattle.

Woodruff, D. S. (In press). Genetic anomalies associated with Cerion hybrid zones: The origin and maintenance of new electromorphic variants called hybrizymes. *Biol. J. Linn. Soc.*

Woodruff, D. S., and S. J. Gould (1980). Geographic differentiation and speciation in Cerion—A preliminary discussion of patterns and processes. *Biol. J. Linn. Soc.* 14:389–416.

Woodruff, D. S., and S. J. Gould (1987). Fifty years of interspecific hybridization: Genetics and morphometrics of a controlled experiment on the land snail Cerion in the Florida Keys. *Evolution* 41:1022–1045.

Woodruff, D. S., and O. A. Ryder (1986). Genetic characterization and conservation of endangered species: Arabian oryx and Père David's deer. *Isozyme Bull.* 19:35.

Woods, C., and L. Harris (1986). *Stewardship Plan for the National Parks of Haiti.* Florida State Museum, Gainesville.

World Bank (1986). Wildlands: Their protection and management in economic development. Operational policy paper issued 6/21/86. World Bank, Washington, D.C.

World Resources Institute (1984). *Improving Environmental Cooperation: The Roles of Multinational Corporations and Developing Countries.* Report of a panel of business leaders and other experts. World Resources Institute, Washington, D.C.

World Resources Institute (1985). *Tropical Forests:*

A Call for Action. World Resources Institute, Washington, D.C.

Wright, S. (1977). *Evolution and the Genetics of Populations.* Vol III. *Experimental Results and Evolutionary Deductions.* University of Chicago Press, Chicago.

Wyatt, R. (1984). The evolution of self-pollination in granite outcrop species of Arenaria (Caryophyllaceae). I. Morphological correlates. *Evolution* 38:804–816.

Yalden, D. W. (1986). Opportunities for reintroducing British mammals. *Mammal Rev.* 16(2):53–63.

Zimmerman, E. C. (1970). Adaptive radiation in Hawaii with special reference to insects. *Biotropica* 2:32–38.

Zouros, E., and D. W. Foltz (1987). The use of allelic isozyme variation for the study of heterosis. *Isozymes: Curr. Topics Biol. Med. Res.* 13:1–59.

Index